KU-548-592

Hospitality World!
An Introduction

En Värld av gästfíihet

Il Mondo D'Ospitalita φιλόξενος κόσμος

LUMEA HOSPITALITĂTII

Le Monde de L'Acceuil

كرم العالم *EL MUNDO DE LA HOSPITALIDAD*

Mundo da Hospitalidade

Die Welt der Gastfreundschaft

Frendlikite Velt עולם האירוח

Gostinitza Myr

Giới Giữ Lại Người

Hospitality World!
An Introduction

Harold E. Lane
Professor Emeritus, Boston University

Denise Dupré
C.E.O., Dupré LTD.

VAN NOSTRAND REINHOLD
I(T)P® A Division of International Thomson Publishing Inc.

New York • Albany • Bonn • Boston • Detroit • London • Madrid • Melbourne
Mexico City • Paris • San Francisco • Singapore • Tokyo • Toronto

Copyright © 1997 by Van Nostrand Reinhold

I⟨T⟩P® A division of International Thomson Publishing, Inc.
The ITP Logo is a registered trademark under license

Printed in the United States of America

For more information, contact:

Van Nostrand Reinhold
115 Fifth Avenue
New York, NY 10003

Chapman & Hall GmbH
Pappelallee 3
69469 Weinheim
Germany

Chapman & Hall
2-6 Boundary Row
London
SE1 8HN
United Kingdom

International Thomson Publishing Asia
221 Henderson Road #05–10
Henderson Building
Singapore 0315

Thomas Nelson Australia
102 Dodds Street
South Melbourne 3205
Victoria, Australia

International Thomson Publishing Japan
Hirakawacho Kyowa Building, 3F
2–2–1 Hirakawacho
Chiyada-ku, 102 Tokyo
Japan

Nelson Canada
1120 Birchmount Road
Scarborough, Ontario
Canada, M1K 5G4

International Thomson Editores
Seneca 53
Col. Polanco
11560 Mexico D.F. Mexico

All rights reserved. No part of this work covered by the copyright hereon may be repro-
duced or used in any form or by any means—graphic, electronic, or mechanical,
including photocopying, recording, taping, or information storage and retrieval systems—
without the written permission of the publisher.

1 2 3 4 5 6 7 8 9 10   QEB-FF   01 00 99 98 97 96

Library of Congress Cataloging-in-Publication Data
Lane, Harold E.
    Hospitality world: an introduction / Harold Lane and Denise Dupré
        p.   cm.
    ISBN 0-442-00118-5
        1. Hospitality industry--Management.   I. Dupré, Denise.
    II. Title
    TX911.3.M27L363   1996
    647.94'068--dc20

96-8345
CIP

Dedication

To M.E.N., for agreeing one day to intensely
encourage me to reach my full potential.

D.M.D.

To Connie (Mason) Lane, who not only read the manuscript with
discriminating and unerring eye but endured and sustained her lifelong partner
through the throes of writing—and to our children, Steve, Hank, and Nancy, for
putting up with it all.

H.E.L.

Contents

Part Three: Places to Eat 205

Part Four: Management Tools 253

Part Six: Issues and Trends 403

Part Seven: For Students Only 443

About the Authors

Denise Dupré has spent her hospitality career both in the field and in the classroom. In addition to various operations assignments with both public and private hotel companies including Marriott and Seven Springs, she has worked in hospitality marketing for Leo Burnett in Chicago and as a consultant for Laventhol and Horwath in New York. She was a teaching fellow at Cornell's School of Hotel Administration, and after a decade as a professor and six years as the director of Boston University's School of Hospitality Administration, she has returned to full-time entrepreneurship as CEO of Dupré LTD. She serves on numerous boards, including those of Seven Springs Resort, Inc., the Mercersburg Academy, and the Hanover Inn.

Harold E. Lane is professor emeritus at Boston University's School of Hospitality Administration. Previously he was professor of Hotel, Restaurant, and Institutional Management at Michigan State University. He was originally appointed by Dean Meek as summer school instructor at Cornell University's School of Hotel Administration, where he served for twenty years. He also served as vice president of Sheraton Corporation of America, retiring in 1968 at the time of its merger with ITT.

Acknowledgments

It was our students, really, who first suggested this book. Why isn't there an upbeat introductory text to challenge—not bore—us? Something current? Something invigorating? A text that would make us want to learn more and work harder? (A task no text would likely achieve alone ... but in the hands of a gifted teacher, perhaps.) We offer thanks to some twelve sections of students who shared honest feedback as we "classroom tested" the book. In addition to Professor Dupré's students, several colleagues, Professors Beals, Hudson, and Oshins's students put various versions of the book to the test. Professor Oshins also lent creative insight, good humor, and true camaraderie in team teaching the text. Several students became invaluable research assistants, in particular, Iolanda Mastre and Michael Klein. Former students Kira Rukin-Forer and Gil Forer made a major contribution. They found no task insurmountable and came back with first-rate sources and ideas in response to assigned topics.

Faculty at our past universities—Boston University, Cornell University, and Michigan State University—have significantly shaped the contents of this book. We are especially grateful to our many colleagues who over the years have contributed excellent ideas about teaching materials—which we have generously drawn upon in developing this book. We were fortunate to have our manuscript reviewed by the following talented professors from hospitality management schools across the country. We incorporated their critical feedback and were encouraged by their enthusiasm:

Deborah Breiter, New Mexico State University; Edward Coon, University of South Carolina; Taylor Ellis, University of Central Florida; Marie Green, Bay State College; Susan Gregory, Colorado State University; J. Michael Hayes, Belleville Area College; Chuck Hamburg, Roosevelt University; Barbara Luck, Jackson Community College; Ruth Ann Myers, Arkansas Tech University; David Pavesic, Georgia State University; Jayne Pearson, Manchester Community Technical College; William Petersen, La Salle College; Peg Shaw, University of Guelph, Canada; Susan Sheridan, University of Houston; Fred Smith, University of Massachusetts–Amherst; Don St. Hilaire, California State Polytechnic University–Pomona.

In addition, we are deeply indebted to many helpful suggestions from:

Hugh A. Andrews, president and founder, Williams Hospitality Management Corporation, San Juan, PR

Paul Beals, professor and director, the Statler Hotel Management Program, Canisius College, Buffalo, NY

Richard Brooks, vice president, Stouffer Hotels and Resorts, Solon, OH

Robin Brown, general manager, The Four Seasons Hotel, Boston, MA

Daniel Daniele, Ernst & Young, Consultants, Chicago, IL

Gregory Delin, human resources director, Mandarin Oriental Hotel Group, Hong Kong

Gregory R. Dillon, vice chairman, Hilton Hotels Corporation, Beverly Hills, CA

Tom R. Engel, executive vice president, Hospitality Asset Management Group, Equitable Real Estate, Investment Management, Inc., Atlanta, GA

Ron Erdman, United States Department of Commerce, United States Travel and Tourism Administration, Washington, DC

Carl F. Frost, professor emeritus, Industrial Psychology, Michigan State University, East Lansing, MI

Edwin D. Fuller, senior vice president and managing director, Marriott Lodging-International, Washington, DC

Bradford Hudson, assistant professor, School of Hospitality Administration, Boston University, Boston, MA

Ann Hales, associate professor, School of Hotel Administration, Cornell University, Ithaca, NY

Mark Van Hartesvelt, senior vice president, Guest Quarters Suite Hotels, Boston, MA

Louis Kane, cochairman, Au Bon Pain, Boston, MA

Michael L. Kasavana, professor, Hotel, Restaurant and Institutional Management, Michigan State University, East Lansing, MI

Hon. Edward M. Kennedy, chairman, U.S. Senate Committee on Labor and Human Resources, Washington, DC

Michaela Larson, owner, Rialto Restaurant, Boston, MA

Saul F. Leonard, Saul F. Leonard Company, Inc., Los Angeles, CA

David A. Ley, professor, James Madison University, Harrisonburg, VA

Matt Marshall, general manager, The Hanover Inn, Hanover, NH

Robert Maxey, president and CEO, MGM Grand Inc., Las Vegas, NV

Joseph A. McInerney, president and CEO, Forte Hotels, Inc., El Cajon, CA

Lee M. Ozley, management consultant, Hilton Head Island, SC

Michael Oshins, assistant professor, School of Hospitality Administration, Boston University, Boston, MA

Allen J. Ostroff, senior vice president, The Prudential Property Co., Newark, NJ

Leo Renaghan, associate professor of marketing, Cornell University, Ithaca, NY

W. Earl Sasser, Jr., professor, Harvard Business School, Boston, MA

Robert Sage, president, Sage Hotel Corporation, Boston, MA

Bernard Seiler, Seiler Hotel–Neues Schloss, Zurich, Switzerland

Leonard Schlesinger, professor, Harvard Business School, Boston, MA

Raymond S. Schmidgall, associate professor, Hotel, Restaurant and Institutional Management, Michigan State University, East Lansing, MI

Horst Schulze, president and chief operating officer, The Ritz-Carlton Hotel Company, Atlanta, GA

Marc Shapiro, vice president, Facilities, Loew's Corporation, New York, NY

Gary Vallen, Northern Arizona University, Flagstaff

George J. Wimberly, Wimberly, Allison, Tong & Goo, Architects, Newport Beach, CA

We are especially grateful for profound expertise lent from the profession by Herman Dupré, chief architect of Seven Springs Resort and Engineer for Snow Economics. He represents rarely found entrepreneurial genius and has shared exuberantly his expertise, his rules of thumb and his passion for business. Mary McSwigan has shared her expertise as a great teacher and has lent compassion, a sense of humor, and Irish luck!

A special vote of thanks is also due to Lori Schwartz and Jennifer Weissman, former staff members at Boston University, whose dedication, energy, and enthusiasm kept the process moving as we "classroom tested" and revised the book. We are grateful to Jo Grandstaff, of East Lansing, Michigan , who exercised the magic of word processing in the early stages.

All the people at Van Nostrand Reinhold—Pam Chirls, Stephen McNabb, Julie Markoff, Jackie Martin, Mimi Melek, Melissa Rosati, and Amy Shipper—who have worked with us so assiduously, warrant special recognition. Each has shared our commitment to excellence and brought their own expertise to the project. We are especially grateful to Melissa for her encouragement as we entered the homestretch. Maxine Chuck, our Boston-based editor, left no comma unturned as she carefully reviewed each word of the manuscript and constantly encouraged us to achieve consistency and clarity. Andrea Mulligan and Lissa Smith at Benchmark Productions made our book real. They conceived and produced the design and shared genuine enthusiasm for the project.

We are profoundly indebted to Eileen Grabowski, without whom this book simply would not have become a reality. She lent a critical editorial eye, offered creative insight, and masterfully demonstrated research skills from the library to the Internet. Her legendary fortitude and patience in deciphering our garbled prose have benefited every page. Moreover, with uncommon dedication and engaging good humor, she kept us on track, and kept in order the numerous editions of the manuscript, charts, tables, boxes, exhibits, footnotes, permissions, idea lists, student feedback, reviewers' comments, classroom notes, and every other element that contributed to the book.

Our spouses have been patient and consistent supporters. The quality of their input has been matched only by their encouragement and enthusiasm—however many successive drafts of the manuscript required their time and effort. Our children, and children and grandchildren, respectively, were constant sources of inspiration—gentle reminders that young minds are why one goes about this effort to teach in the first place. Special thanks to Cameron, whose five-year-old mind set about to xerox hundreds of copies of a paper heart glued to a popsicle stick, that all of his Mom's readers might have a copy of her original bookmark. Special thanks, as well, to Casey, a six pound thirteen ounce miracle, for being.

As indicated in the chapter endnotes, we are deeply grateful to the many publishers who graciously granted permission to use their materials. Responsibility for any errors or omissions, however, is ours alone.

Denise Dupré
Harold E. Lane

Preface

Welcome to *Hospitality World!* We are honored to share this book with students and teachers of hospitality management, for they have been instrumental in its development. Every page of the book has been "classroom tested." Our customers —students and teachers who used earlier editions-- helped us to think critically about the book and to make it more useful.

Around the world, the coming of age of hospitality has been marked by rapid movement in the closing decades of the twentieth century. The information highway, new ways of shaping service experiences and a changing technological, political and social landscape have resulted in many challenges. Though much has changed, much of hospitality has also remained exactly the same. Across centuries, some tried and true elements of a warm welcome, comfortable accommodations and good food have remained the keystones of successful hospitality management. Whether a guest is handed an old-fashioned brass skeleton key or a computer generated key card, the principles of a friendly and efficient check-in are the same. It is this picture of the old and the new, the cherished and the innovative, that the authors endeavor to bring together in this book.

The book has been designed as an introductory text. With a readable style as well as a sophisticated grasp of world-wide hospitality management, *Hospitality World!* offers an exciting approach to the study of the hospitality business. In short, this book has two primary objectives: (1) to meet students' desire for a hospitality management text with real challenge and (2) to view the world of hospitality, quite literally, from the perspective of various nations around the globe.

Overview of the Contents

Part I, "An Overview," the first five chapters, sets the stage for later discussion of managerial and operational approaches to the industry. Chapter One points out how the historical development of hospitality correlates with the development of modern society and business. Chapter Two focuses on the "big picture," setting the framework of understanding for how the industry is structured and how it has developed. Chapter Three analyzes what is meant by the hospitality business as a service business and underscores the meaning of each "moment of truth" when a customer encounters a hospitality provider. Chapter Four examines the global dimensions of the world of lodging and foodservice, and of the world of travelers. Chapter Five offers perspectives on tourism and uses the Olympic Games as an example of the component pieces of tourism in action.

"Places to Stay," discussed in Part II, and "Places to Eat," discussed in Part III, are mirror images of one another as they apply to lodging and to foodservice. Thinking beyond hotels to the many different kinds of lodging operations is the subject of Chapter Six. The multitude of foodservice operations beyond restaurants is the domain of Chapter Eight. Chapter Seven covers the basic ingredients of how things work in lodging operations, while similar ground is covered for foodservice operations in Chapter Nine. Together these two sections outline the what and how of lodging and foodservice.

Part IV, "Management Tools" embraces Chapters Ten, Eleven, and Twelve and Thirteen, which collectively focus upon four management disciplines: human resources, marketing, management information systems and accounting. Each describes the distinguishing features of the discipline as it relates to hospitality management and then sorts out the sharpest tools in the respective manager's tool kit. Chapter Ten deals with the idea of giving individuals in organizations greater information, knowledge, power, and rewards. Chapter Eleven discloses the importance of identifying customer needs and provides vision and marketing tools to best to meet those needs. Chapter Twelve provides valuable insights on the ways in which a company's management information system operates and the rapid evolution of technology. Chapter Thirteen aims to clarify such important accounting concepts as the Uniform System of Accounts, balance sheet, income statement, and cash flow - all of which are essential to understanding how accountants keep score of business performance in the hospitality industry.

Part V defines the "Structural Elements of the Industry." Chapter Fourteen puts you square in the shoes of the owner of a hotel. Chapter Fifteen does the same, but for the owner of a restaurant. Decisions involving development, ownership, management, franchising, and affiliation are presented as they would be to a real owner. Similarly, an entrepreneur who dreams of opening a restaurant, is faced with decisions involving development, ownership, management, franchising and strategic alliances. In the course of the discussion of these decisions, the evolution of franchising, its advantages and disadvantages, the origin and development of management contracts and the important provisions they contain, how ownership and financing arrangements are made, and the costs and benefits associated with developing a property, are revealed.

"Issues and Trends" are the broad subjects of Part VI. Chapter Sixteen explores ethics and those activities that require "tough choices" in several areas of managerial decision making: choices about whether or not to obey the law; choices about "people values" such as promise-keeping, honesty, fairness, and the avoidance of injury to others; and choices about one's own self-interest versus the interest of the company. Chapter Seventeen, Strategic Thinking, places emphasis upon scanning the environment to find clues and patterns which could potentially lead to a winning strategy. Like the strategic-thinking Cheshire Cat in Lewis Carroll's *Alice In Wonderland* demonstrates, good strategic planning means knowing where you are now and where you want to go, and most importantly, finding the best way to get there.

The last part of the book, VII, is reserved "For Students Only." Chapter Eighteen offers a comprehensive set of steps to developing and excelling along a hospitality career path. The chapter takes a hands on approach offering tactics and resources. The second element of the section is a master case which explores the world of Disney. The case offers a series of questions associated with each section of the book as well as capstone questions which challenge students to integrate Yearnings from the entire text.

Learning Tools

Each chapter contains a number of elements designed to encourage an enthusiasm for learning. The tools are integrated throughout the text in a package designed to enliven discussion, organize thinking, test understanding and encourage exploration.

Opening Quotations

The opening quotations, from a variety of sources, ancient to modern, give an unusual perspective on the chapter contents. They can be used to launch a general discussion of the subject matter. These contributions from the literary world are intended to provoke discussion from a different slant. A corresponding question or assignment directly related to the quotation can be found at the end of each chapter.

Chapter Objectives

The chapter objectives, which precede each chapter, capture the key learnings which will follow. They serve to guide students through the major points.

Hospitality Vignettes and Cartoons

In the spirit that a sense of humor can enliven a discussion, included are a series of vignettes and cartoons with a humorous side and a lesson. These stories and picture stories package complex learnings in a simply illustrated fashion and can be identified by the pineapple icon.

International Boxes

An increasing focus on the globalization of hospitality are refected in the international boxes, identified by an international stamp icon. Events related to each chapter's subject are drawn from around the globe and explored in a way which lends focus to a particular country or region. These boxes are current in thinking and shed light on just how international the hospitality business is.

Chapter Summaries

The chapter summaries reinforce the learning objectives and synopsize the main topics covered in the chapter.

Discussion Questions

To test learning and to encourage critical thinking a series of questions follow each chapter.

Assignments

The assignments require investigation beyond the contents of the book, though the chapter will serve as a springboard for the additional research. Often the assignments involve interacting directly with some facet of the hospitality business.

Mini Cases

The mini cases draw from numerous kinds of situations that can be found in hospitality operations. Through the analysis of a specific problem students are encouraged to take a closer look at managerial decision-making. The mini cases vary in length and complexity.

Part One

Overview

Section I introduces the concept of the Hospitality World as an industry of global dimensions and provides a profile of its historical and present developments. Each of the five chapters in this section is intended to give a broad overview of the hospitality business. Chapter 1 sets the stage for today's world of hospitality by reviewing the important milestones of the past. The structure of the industry today has much to do with how it has evolved over time.

Chapter 2 identifies the principal components of this large industry as lodging services, foodservices, entertainment, travel distribution channels, and transportation. The key attributes of the hospitality business, as well as the important players involved in the business, are highlighted.

Chapter 3 underscores the importance of the service component to hospitality. The emphasis here is on creating outstanding service experiences for customers and on successfully managing service encounters.

The international scope of our industry is the key message of chapter 4. Being an international player in the Hospitality World is not an easy job. The kinds of hurdles encountered by lodging and foodservice establishments in a global marketplace are revealed. An international player is obligated to understand guests' different cultures, religions, and languages as well as the host country's customs, climate, levels of technology, and extent of government.

Chapter 5 explores the component pieces of hospitality as they relate to tourism. In the course of their travels, tourists use a variety of transportation options, travel services, and activities and recreational outlets, providing a ready demand for lodging and foodservice. The interaction of these pieces is explored in the context of the 1996 Olympic Games.

Chapter One

*"There is nothing which has yet
been contrived by man by which
so much happiness is produced as
by a good tavern or inn."*

Samuel Johnson March 21, 1776

Hospitality's History: Then and Now ✍

When you finish this chapter, you should:

1. Be able to explain what gave rise to innkeeping and the laws governing it in the pre-Christian era.

2. Be able to link modes of transportation with the growth and development of the hospitality industry.

3. Explain why and how advertising emerged during the Middle Ages.

4. Know what spurred the design of Renaissance inns with amphitheater-style courtyards.

5. Know what societal developments set the stage for the emergence of public restaurants in America.

6. Explain the historical roots of the concept of a resort and identify important resorts in the nineteenth century.

7. Explain what significant forces in modern society have helped to shape today's hotel chains, restaurant chains, and franchising operations.

8. Identify the important "firsts" in the evolution of the hospitality industry and understand why they were important.

9. Identify patterns that repeat in the history of hospitality.

Where or when the first inns and eating places actually originated is unknown. Even so, clues to their antiquity and evolution are clearly visible from a stream of diverse global sources. Ever since the discovery of the Babylonian Code of Hammurabi, a 2067 B.C. law code containing the first recorded reference to innkeeping and its legal responsibilities, historians have been on the lookout for additional signs of hospitality enterprise as it has unfolded through the centuries.

Looking "fast-forward" through the kaleidoscope of history, therefore, one stumbles upon just such signs in the discovery of notable "firsts" in the annals of the hospitality business. In a sense, these events are milestones marking the evolution of innkeeping. Thus, they are seen here initially in Exhibit 1.1 as snapshots of historic "firsts," and secondly in the ensuing text, as the product of the forces of transportation, tourism, and entertainment.

▬▬▬ ***Exhibit 1.1*** Snapshots of "Firsts" in the Hospitality Industry

Babylonia (Iraq)
2067–405 B.C.

- First innkeeping laws appear in the Code of Hammurabi, in Babylon, capital of Babylonia.

Ancient Rome and Greece
405 B.C.–A.D. 200

- Aristophanes' play *The Frogs*, first written document since the Code of Hammurabi, mentions inns.
- Origin of the first theater-festival concept of entertainment (i.e., plays, athletic games, parades, musical extravaganzas).
- First "snack bars" (thermopoliums), forerunners of today's "fast food" establishments, emerge along new military and commercial highways of the expanding Roman Empire.
- Beginning of inn segmentation into two types:
  A. *Posting Houses*, located on all main roads, functioning as governmental postal service and providing overnight accommodation only for Roman officials.
  B. *Inns (tabernae or cauponae)* providing accommodations only for the general public.

The Middle Ages
600–700

- Inns of Rome, and later those in Britain make first use of trademarks, such as vine leaves, local foliage, family coats of arms, red lions, and green dragons to publicize their offering of food and shelter. A harbinger of today's brand name recognition in the hotel business.

- By royal decree, the king's glassware was the first to be made with round bottoms, hence named "tumbler," in order to guarantee that the king's cup—continuously replenished—would always remain within the royal grasp.

The Renaissance
1400–1800

- First use of inn courtyards by strolling entertainers (actors, musicians, gymnasts) who created their own stage by resting boards on barrels.

■ *Exhibit 1.1* (Continued)

The Renaissance
1400–1800 (Continued)

- First appearance of the stagecoach during the 1480s (the period of Tudor reign in Britain), inaugurates proliferation of inns (6,000 British inns by the late sixteenth century).
- First design and construction of amphitheater-style inn, a three-sided structure facing a courtyard (so guests could watch arriving stagecoaches from their respective balconies).

Evolution of Modern Restaurants and Hotels
1500s

- Emergence of the public dining room, a forerunner of the restaurant.

1576

- First theater ever constructed in Britain replicates an enlargement of the standard design of an inn courtyard.
- Restoration of fork and dinner plate, missing since the days of the Roman Empire.

1610

- First inn in the colonies, at Jamestown, Virginia. Settlement failed to survive; hence, no other information available.

1634

- First tavern of record, Coles Tavern, opens with table d'hôte or set menu in Boston.

1765

- First establishment ever to be identified as a restaurant is opened in Paris by a Monsieur Boulanger. He names his menu items "restorants," reportedly intended either for pregnant women patrons, or for patrons suffering from hangovers.

1768

- First attempt to build a tunnel connecting the island of England to the continent of Europe. Idea later abandoned due to fears of invasions by both countries, and not resurrected until the twentieth century.

1794

- City Hotel, New York City, is built; the first structure specifically designed as a hotel and funded by a company with shares of stock.

1815

- Industrial catering gets its beginning with in-plant foodservice offered to employees of a mill in Scotland. About five years later, the cotton mills in Massachusetts will offer the same.

1825

- First steam passenger railroad opens in England, ultimately displacing nearly two centuries of stagecoach mode of travel.

(Continued)

████████ *Exhibit 1.1* Snapshots of "Firsts" in the Hospitality Industry *(Continued)*

Evolution of Modern Restaurants and Hotels *(Continued)*

1826

- Union Oyster House opens in Boston; claimed to be the first American restaurant.

1827

- Delmonico's, in New York City, opens; traditionally regarded as the first American restaurant.

1829

- First modern hotel, The Tremont, designed by the world's first hotel architect, Isaiah Rogers, opens in Boston. Other Tremont firsts include such innovations as bellboys, gaslighted chandeliers, inside bathing rooms, French cuisine, washbowl and pitcher in each room, inside toilets (basement location), and push button in each guest room to facilitate front-desk communication.

1829–1860

- More hotels open in the USA than at any other time in history until the 1920s.
- Hotels elevated to being showcases for technological developments, such as central heating, elevators, electric lights, telephones.

1832

- First golf course introduced at a resort in the USA at the Homestead in Hot Springs, Virginia.

1834

- First industrial foodservice opens at Bowery Savings Bank, New York City.

1836

- Astor House, New York, the first hotel in the USA fully illuminated with gas.

1841

- Thomas Cook establishes himself as a steamship excursion booking agent in England. The company he founded became known as Thomas Cook Travel, one of the world's largest travel agencies in the twentieth century.

1855

- Parker House, Boston, the first American hotel to operate on the European Plan.

1876

- First restaurant chain inaugurated by Fred Harvey at Atchison, Topeka, and Santa Fe railroad stations. First Harvey unit opens in Topeka, Kansas.

██████████ **Exhibit 1.1** *(Continued)*

Evolution of Modern Restaurants and Hotels *(Continued)*

1882

- First U.S. country club, The Country Club, opens in Brookline, Massachusetts.

1891

- First cafeteria opens in a YWCA in Chicago.

The Twentieth Century

1903

- Historic first flight by the Wilbur brothers at Kitty Hawk, South Carolina.

1908

- First modern commercial hotel in the USA, the Buffalo Statler, is opened by Ellsworth Statler. Amenities and facilities include: private bath, telephone in every room, light switch in every room, mail chutes on every floor, lighted closets, and free newspapers.

1916

- First annual National Hotel Exposition held at New York's Grand Central Palace in November, and attracted over 150 firms doing business with the hospitality industry. Show is now known as the International Hotel, Motel and Restaurant Show.

1919

- First crossing of the Atlantic Ocean by air. Advances in air travel continue through the 1920s and 1930s, with Charles Lindbergh's solo flight across the Atlantic, and the German Graf Zeppelin circling the globe in 1929. In 1926, the first American airline was formed, Varney Airlines, later to evolve into United Airlines.

1920

- Conrad Hilton, founder of Hilton Hotels, purchases his first property in Cisco, Texas.

1920s

- First use of franchising in the restaurant industry. Initiated by Roy Allen and Frank Wright, A&W root beer chain operators whose first root beer stand in 1919 had opened in Lodi, California.
- Era of automobile travel emerges, enhancing the role of transportation in the development of hotels and restaurants. Dramatic increase in travel by salesman and middle class Americans.

1921

- First drive-in restaurant chain named the Pig Stand opens in Dallas, Texas.
- First hamburger restaurant chain, The White Castle, opens in Wichita, Kansas.

(Continued)

■■■■■■■ *Exhibit 1.1* Snapshots of "Firsts" in the Hospitality Industry *(Continued)*

The Twentieth Century *(Continued)*

1922

- First four-year-level U.S. hotel school founded at Cornell University by Howard B. Meek, a 1917 graduate of Boston University.

1924

- First motel founded by James Vail on Highway 101 at San Luis Obispo, California.

1926

- First entry of Marriott enterprise in the hospitality industry. J. Willard Marriott and Hugh Colton purchased an A&W franchise for Washington, D.C. In 1927, Marriott dropped the A&W logo and adopted the name Hot Shoppe for his restaurant chain.

1927

- First 3,000-room hotel, Stevens Hotel, opens in Chicago as "The World's Largest Hotel." It is now known as the Chicago Hilton and Towers.

1930s

- U.S. economic depression spawns widespread business failures. Prohibition amendment (Eighteenth), in effect from 1920 to 1933, gives rise to "speakeasy" establishments, many of which, like the "21" Club in New York City, became well-known restaurants following the 1933 repeal of the Eighteenth amendment.

1937

- Marriott serves the first in-flight meal, a box lunch from their Washington, D.C.-based operation.

1939

- Regular air travel established, when the *Dixie Clipper* flew from New York to Europe. Technological advances in air travel, such as speed and fuel efficiency, developed to assist the war effort, applied to passenger service in the following decades.

1941

- First casino hotel, El Rancho (later renamed The New Frontier), opens in Las Vegas, Nevada.

Post–World War II Era

1946

- First airline-owned hotel chain, Inter-Continental Hotels, established as a subsidiary of Pan American World Airways to operate in the beginning in Latin America and later, worldwide.

■■■■■■■■ **Exhibit 1.1** *(Continued)*

Post–World War II Era *(Continued)*

1948

- First McDonald hamburger drive-in opened in San Bernardino, California. Owned and operated by two brothers, Tom and Maurice McDonald.

1950s

- Growth of airline travel and auto rental agencies driven by tourist quest for entertainment and recreation, evolution of business seminars and meetings at airport hotels/motels. Emergence of international hotel chains.

1952

- First Holiday Inn opened in Memphis by Kemmons Wilson, founder of the chain with a worldwide, middle-class market objective.

1955

- McDonald's concept purchased by milkshake salesman Ray Kroc. Before the end of 1955, Kroc had opened a McDonald's in Des Plaines, Illinois, thus marking a significant milestone in the history of the fast food industry.
- First theme park, Disneyland, opens in Anaheim, California.

1960s

- The American Hotel Association decides to admit motels as members, thus changing its name to the American Hotel and Motel Association (AH&MA).
- Frozen foods attain popularity.

1963

- First budget motel chain, Motel 6, opens in Santa Barbara, California. Such chains are now identified as economy/limited service hotels/motels.

1967

- TWA purchases Hilton International Hotels, the first airline investment in the hotel business since Pan American Airways launched its Inter-Continental Hotels in 1946.

1970

- United Airlines merges with Western International Hotels. Edward E. Carlson, president of Western, becomes Chairman and CEO of the merged organizations. This company later merges with Hertz Rent a Car to form Allegis. Allegis has a short-lived life, and the three companies are broken up again.

1970s

- With the spectacular growth of companies like McDonald's leading the way, fast food restaurant sales now exceeding $100 billion per year.

(Continued)

■■■■■■■ *Exhibit 1.1* Snapshots of "Firsts" in the Hospitality Industry *(Continued)*

Post–World War II Era *(Continued)*

1970s

- Time sharing—a new concept of time ownership of houseboats, yachts, cruise ships, condominium vacation homes, apartments, hotels, and motels—enjoys sudden upsurge of popularity coincident with a sharp decline in resort real estate values.

- Revival of cruise ship industry, as Caribbean cruises attract increasing vacationers.

1977

- As concern for the environment grows, George J. "Pete" Wimberly, president of Wimberly, Whisenand, Allison, Tong and Goo, a Honolulu-based architectural firm renowned for its innovative designs of Pacific-area resort hotels, discloses in the *Cornell Quarterly,* for the first time the Wimberly design philosophy. Hotel design, in his view, must make a positive contribution not only to the economy, but also to the culture and environment of the local community as well. This will be an early indicator of hotels and restaurants "going green" in the 1990s.
- Emergence of all-suite hotel chains. Guest Quarters and Granada Royale Hometels generally considered to be the first chains.

1980s

- Introduction of supersonic commercial air transport.
- Health and fitness clubs become increasingly attractive.
- Trend toward healthier foods.
- Cruise ship itineraries downsized to attract middle-class market, desiring shorter and less expensive cruises.

1990s

- Concept of virtual reality, defined as the human experience of perceiving and interacting through sensors and effectors with a computer-modeled environment. Sega Enterprises of Japan announces in July 1993 its intent to build small theme parks that will provide the same thrills as Disney roller coasters except that the thrills will be produced by computer simulation. This process is called virtual reality, or in other words, Disneyland in a box. The plan is to build dozens of such parks in the USA and Japan.
- Increased "nicheing" and segmentation, such as boutique hotels, in the marketplace.
- Proliferation of hotel chains and restaurant chains.
- The capacity to make reservations on the Internet grows dramatically as more hospitality companies launch web sites.

1992

- Foxwoods, the largest, most profitable casino in the world, opens on land of the Native American Mashantucket Pequot tribe in Connecticut.

███████ **Exhibit 1.1** *(Continued)*

Post–World War II Era *(Continued)*

1993

- Beginning of the Las Vegas Megaresort War as headlined by *The Wall Street Journal*, October 15, 1993, in describing Luxor, a $390 million glass-skinned pyramid-shaped resort grand opening that day; the opening of Treasure Island's $475 million casino two weeks later; and in December, the opening of the $1 billion MGM Grand hotel-casino and 33-acre theme park.

- Rise of gaming facilities in the United States through efforts of Native American groups. Riverboat gaming also flourishes.

1994

- Completion of the Chunnel, linking Great Britain to France, a project begun but not completed in the Eighteenth century.

1994

- Boeing's latest and largest passenger aircraft, the 777, goes into service by United Airlines.

1995

- Universal Studios announces a new theme park celebrating Dr. Seuss, Popeye, and Marvel Comics, scheduled to open in 1999.

1996

- International hotel companies and fast-food restaurant companies increase development efforts in Asia, Africa, and Eastern Europe.

Babylonia

Although the sites where the first inns actually surfaced in the world remain shrouded in ancient history, clues to their antiquity have come to light in two significant documents of the pre-Christian era:

- The Code of Hammurabi, enacted between 2067–2025 B.C.

- *The Frogs*, a Greek comedy written by Aristophanes in 405 B.C.

The earliest reference is found in the Code of Hammurabi, a collection of 282 amendments to the Babylonian common law enacted during the reign of King Hammurabi, which lasted from 2067 to 2025 B.C.[1]

Babylon, a metropolis of lavish splendor, was situated in the Valley of the Two Rivers, an area whose rich fields occupied the land between the Tigris and Euphrates rivers and is now known as Iraq. While the king, as head of state, concerned himself with all matters of trade and commerce, the priesthood also figured prominently in the life of the business community, renting out land, bartering and exchanging the wool, cattle, birds, fruits, grain, oil, and perfumes.[2]

Oddly enough, as the historian Daniel Boorstin has noted, we know more about some aspects of daily life in the ancient Babylon of 2000 B.C. than we do about daily life in some parts of Europe or America a hundred years ago. "By happy coincidence," writes Boorstin, "ancient Babylonians wrote not on paper or on wood, but on the clay they found underfoot. . . . Our grand dividend is thousands of clay tablets recording everything from codes of laws and religious texts to teachers' copybooks, the notes of schoolchildren, the records of war booty, recipes, scientific works, diaries, and receipts for the sale of slaves and cattle."[3]

When it came to innkeepers and their profession, King Hammurabi was a firm believer in capital punishment, as the following excerpts from the Code suggest: [4]

1. If an alewife does not accept grain for the price of liquor but accepts silver by the heavy weight or if she reduces the value of beer given against the value of corn received, they shall convict that alewife and cast her into the water.[5]

An **alewife** was a woman engaged in the preparation and sale of intoxicating liquors and who invariably kept an inn. Although the exact circumstances that prompted the enactment of this particular statute have been lost to history, scholars account for the severity of the punishment by the "bad character borne by innkeepers."[6]

2. If felons are banded together in an alewife's house and she does not seize those felons and she has not hauled them to the palace, that alewife shall be put to death.[7]

Allowing criminals to congregate in an inn was such a risk to public safety and security that the innkeeper, on penalty of death, was legally obligated to have them arrested and escorted to the palace. Even in England today, the harboring of thieves by an innkeeper, or allowing them to deposit goods, if known to be stolen, is a summary offense, punishable by fine or, in default, by imprisonment and by the forfeiture of the innkeeper's license.[8]

In the only other reference to innkeeping in the Code of Hammurabi, mention is made of the fate befalling any priestess who opens or enters an alehouse:

3. If a priestess or high priestess who is not dwelling in a cloister opens an alehouse or enters an alehouse for liquor, they shall burn that woman.[9]

Although it is not clear whether opening an alehouse meant starting a business or simply opening the doors of such a place to customers, there is no doubt that under Babylonian law a priestess, even though no longer dwelling within a cloister, must live respectably. The severity of the punishment—execution by burning—suggests that the offense was a serious one. And indeed it was. The punishment of burning, as prescribed in Babylonian law, also applied to a mother and son guilty of incest and, in the Hebrew law, to the priestess guilty of "playing the harlot." Because burning was originally a form of religious sacrifice, scholars speculate that fire served to remove pollution from the land while at the same time avoiding the shedding of sacred tribal blood.

As trade and travel developed during the post-Babylonian era, it was apparent from inscriptions found in chapels along the way that travelers inevitably faced grave perils from such misfortunes as "storms, robbers, plagues, drunken soldiers, soothsayers, devils in hermits' disguises, murderous innkeepers, avalanche, floods, and earthquakes."[10] Ultimately, the center of cultural gravity found its way in succeeding centuries to the ancient city of Athens.

Ancient Greece and Rome

For the Athenian theatergoer, the year 405 B.C. began in celebration. It was festival time. No fewer than 60 festivals took place, bringing people from all over the Greek world to pay homage to the gods. Athletic games, chariot races, musical extravaganzas, processions, and the production of great dramas all provided color, excitement, and keen competition. The winning playwright that year was Aristophanes, who took first prize for his comedy *The Frogs*.

In that play, the first written document to make reference to an inn since the Hammurabi statutes, the central character is the god Dionysos. As one who presides over the Greek theater, Dionysos resolves to go down into Hades, rescue Euripides (the fifth-century B.C. Greek dramatist), and bring him back to Athens, thus inspiring hope that the future of great drama will continue undiminished. In preparation for his descent into Hell, Dionysos asks Herakles (god of the Olympic games) the best route to take:

"I'm on my way to Hell in your uniform,
and of course I turn to you for information.
What was it like down there when you made the Dog?
The natives? The hospitality? The general tone of the place? The sights? The shops?
Whorehouses, taverns, restaurants, and hotels with the fewest bedbugs?"[11]

The historian Arthur White wryly observes that it is not just chance that this reference to hotels mentions bedbugs. "Right down through the centuries until our own period any history of inns could be a history of lice, fleas and bugs."[12] Some idea of the indignities sustained by a traveler in nineteenth-century America may easily be surmised from this account of an Englishman's visit to Fredericktown, Missouri. There, at a local inn, he fought a losing battle with bedbugs all night long, "but was entertained in the midst of his sufferings by his roommate in the next bed who was constantly doubling himself up on his hams, to scratch away as energetically as if he were paid for it— at the same time uttering deep blasphemies which were unequaled."[13]

The era of Greek festivals also marked the glorious age of Athens's greatest splendor. It was a time when an abundance of artisans, foreign traders and craftsmen, artists, poets, philosophers, teachers, naval experts, scientists, physicians, historians, and religious teachers characterized the rapidly growing population. Moreover, ships from all over the world were sailing into Athens where facilities to accommodate foreign sailors were so inadequate that the government intervened to encourage additional inns to be created to meet the needs of a burgeoning travelers' market. With Athenian attention thus fixed on inns, government became involved in order to assure that innkeepers obeyed the various laws regulating liquor sales and taxes. However, the quality of hotel service as such was of little concern to the bureaucracy.

The philosopher Plato took issue with the way inns were being run. He complained that all aspects of life connected with innkeeping had become "utterly disreputable." All in all, though, Plato and his learned contemporaries did little to elevate the standards of Greek innkeeping. Instead, they had their own dream of a highway across Greece, modeled on the Persian Royal Road—stretching 1,800 miles from Sardis to the Persian Gulf. This dream, however, went unrealized. Presumably, such a system failed to attract attention for several reasons: (1) population was concentrated in the cities, not spread out over the countryside; (2) the cities were too close together to make an expensive highway system work; and (3) sea travel was such an easy and accessible method of communication that there was no need for other modes of transportation.

The Romans, however, were quick to see that highways of land and sea were essential lifelines of their expanding Empire. Thus, they considered the Mediterranean their sea. Roman food ships followed all sea lanes from Italy to ports of the Mediterranean, Aegean, Adriatic, and even into the Atlantic along the coast of Africa. Moreover, realizing the necessity of land highways for military and commercial purposes, the Romans built and maintained good roads into every area as the Empire expanded. By the time they had conquered nearly all the then civilized world, Roman inns, taverns, and even "snack shops" had been well established for the convenience of travelers.

Despite the superb quality of their roads, bridges, and tunnels (these that were chopped out of solid rock at the rate of a foot or two a month), a Roman foot-traveler averaged no more than 16 miles per day. A journey from Rome to Alexandria, therefore, would have required five months. By pack animal or carriage, the travel time would have been cut at least in half.

Why Alexandria? Because as early as 340 B.C., it had become a famous center of intellectual life and international trade. A museum had been established for study in the arts and sciences, with privileged resident scholars and an ambitious program for the acquisition of manuscripts. Trade was flourishing with the Greeks and Romans, whose caravans populated the commercial-military road between Rome and Alexandria. For their part, Egyptian merchants likewise traveled far and wide, on foot or with slow-moving animal caravans, in search of new markets for their products. For accommodations along the way, these merchant travelers brought with them live animals and birds for food, and tents for shelter.

Together with the growth of the Roman Empire, wine shops or "snack bars" (called thermopoliums) and inns (called posting houses and tabernae or cauponae) began to emerge along major trade routes. A glimpse of what some of these establishments were like is afforded by the archeological discoveries at Herculaneum in southern Italy. The eruption of Mt. Vesuvius in A.D. 79 had smothered the town in lava and ashes, thus preserving its antiquities for scholarly excavation in modern times.

The snack bars (**thermopoliums**) typically had a standard counter faced with irregular pieces of polychrome marble and large jugs inserted into the counter. **Posting houses** were located on all the main roads, usually in towns or villages. Their function was to provide a postal service for the government as well as overnight accommodations for a select few, generally officials and couriers of the Roman government, but not for the general public.

The other variety of inns lining some 51,000 miles of imperial highways were the **cauponae** or **tabernae**.[14] The cauponae provided lodging accommodations, and in some cases included a basic menu of wine, bread, and meat. Tabernae (from which the English word *tavern* is derived) were bars and pubs in Rome that provided patrons with food, beverages, and entertainment.

Middle Ages

In due time, however, the Roman Empire ended (A.D. 476), bringing to a standstill whatever benefits innkeepers had enjoyed from a flourishing period of Roman trade and travel. Nearly a thousand years were to elapse, a period historically known as the Middle Ages, before the innkeeping business revived. Even so, the period was not without its unique character. For the most part, the Middle Ages was a time of serfs and kings.

The serfs, living in mud or thatched huts, existed on a diet of black bread, salt pork, beans, turnips, and cabbage. Royalty, on the other hand, managed to exist on a minimum of 30 menu items at every meal. Wild game such as venison, rabbit, and badger, were frequently available along with poultry, swans, pheasants, cranes, and herons. Occasionally such seafood items as seal, porpoise, and whale appeared on the menu. Seldom did fruit or vegetables emerge as menu items, it being royalty's firm belief that such food was fit only for pigs. Food was eaten from a round slice of bread called a "trencher." There were no plates or utensils. Royalty preferred to eat with their fingers the bite-size portions that were stuck together with a thick sauce or gravy.

Once, in the great hall of the castle where the king of Saxony dined, the servant in charge of the royal goblet incurred the royal wrath. His job was to hold the goblet, keep it filled, and whenever the king wished to drink to hand it to him. He had no other task.

> *On one occasion he put the goblet down and was not there the instant the king called for him. This fellow's fate is not recorded, but the king was so angry over this failure that he immediately ordered all goblets to be made with round bottoms so they would tip when set down. Ever since that time drinking glasses have been known as "tumblers."*[15]

Innkeeping Laws and Rules in the Middle Ages

Sleeping accommodations in the Middle Ages usually meant not occupying a bedroom alone, or even a bed alone. It was customarily taken for granted that an establishment of 10 or 12 rooms could accommodate 200 visitors, sleeping on the floor or wherever they could. When beds were provided, guests slept in "spoon fashion" with no suggestion of any segregation of the sexes.[16] Furthermore, in what must have been a boon to the innkeeping industry, in 1425, Scotland passed a law that is unique to the annals of hospitality industry. The statute provided that travelers were liable to be fined 40 shillings (a huge sum of money at that time) if they elected to stay with friends when there was an inn available.

Innkeeping in the medieval world took place under circumstances of no small peril either to guests or to innkeepers. In ancient Greece and Rome, inns and taverns were generally regarded with contempt. In Fourteenth- and Fifteenth-century England, where innkeeping law originated, road conditions were so primitive that travelers were forced to travel on foot or horseback, frequently along roadways infested with outlaws and robbers.[17] A wayfarer's only recourse was to find some house devoted to the business of furnishing food, drink, and safe lodging to hungry and weary travelers. Thus emerged the English inn, which, in the long run, gave rise to the principle in common law of the innkeeper's duty to serve the public without discrimination. Traditionally, under this common law principle, no guest desiring to stay in a hotel or inn can be refused accommodation, except for lawfully established reasons.[18]

Publicity in the Middle Ages

Publicity made its debut in medieval society when innkeepers decided that some form of identification was needed to attract customers. Thus, first in Rome and then in Britain, inns became identified by some foliage—such as vine leaves around a pole, or a bush or some leaves to indicate the presence within of a fresh vintage. More sophisticated identification signs appeared later as the houses of nobility frequently functioned in the role of hostelries for travelers. Family coats of arms served the purpose admirably, resulting before long in their widespread adoption by innkeepers, who hung out red lions and green dragons to inform the public that they offered food and shelter. Accommodations were another matter. Hospitality dispensed by monastic institutions not infrequently reflected discriminatory policies with respect to accepting travelers as guests. "The nobility were received amiably because it was through their bounty and protection that monasteries existed; the poor were also received, out of charity. But the middle classes—merchants, small landowners, and others having no special claim to favor—were directed to the local inn." [19]

The Renaissance and Beyond

As the Middle Ages drew to a close, probably nothing was more important to the future development of the hospitality industry than the **stagecoach**. The stagecoach had made its debut a century earlier in England, where long journeys, such as a trip from London to Edinburgh, frequently took a week or more, necessitating overnight stops at inns along the way. Not only were the roads unspeakably bad, but there was no way in which a coach could be heated. In fact, it was not uncommon in winter for some coach passengers to arrive at their destinations literally frozen to death. Hence, it was not surprising that when a citizen of consequence announced his intention to travel any distance, his church held a day of prayer as a matter of course and saw to it that he did not set off on his journey without first making a will.[20] Considering the life-threatening risks of travel, it is a wonder that stagecoach service managed to survive for nearly 200 years until the railways came.

Nonetheless, the surge in coach travel spurred the development of inns, which numbered about 6,000 in Great Britain by the late sixteenth century. By the early 1800s, there were some 4,000 mail and stagecoaches on the road, with 10,000 people a day using the mail coaches alone. In London's more than 3,000 inns, accommodations were needed not only for travelers, but also for the stabling of as many as 150,000 horses. However, as the lyrics to the boisterous song *Master of the House,* (from the 20th-century musical *Lés Miserables,* based upon Victor Hugo's novel of the same name) not so subtly intimate, innkeepers of the time were more than equal to the challenge. See Exhibit 1.2.

▬▬▬ *Exhibit 1.2* Master of the House

Thernadier

Welcome M'sieur	Seldom do you see
Sit yourself down	Honest men like me
And meet the best	A gent of good intent
Innkeeper in town.	Who's content to be
As for the rest,	Master of House
All of them crooks	Doling out the charm
Rooking the guests	Ready with a handshake
And cooking the books.	And an open palm

Exhibit 1.2 Master of the House *(Continued)*

Thernadier (Continued)

Tells a saucy tale

Makes a little stir

Customers appreciate a bon-viveur!

Glad to do my friends a favour

Doesn't cost me to be nice

But nothing gets you nothing

Everything has got a little price!

Master of the house

Keeper of the zoo

Ready to relieve 'em

Of a sou, or two

Watering a wine

Making up the weight

Pickin' up their knick-knacks

When they can't see straight

Everybody loves a landlord

Everybody's bosom friend

I do whatever pleases

Jesus! Don't I bleed 'em in the end!

Thenardier and Chorus

Master of the house

Quick to catch yer eye

Never wants a passer-by

To pass him by

Servant to the poor

Butler to the great

Comforter, philosopher

And lifelong mate!

Everybody's boon companion

Everybody's chaperone.

Thenardier

But lock up your valises

Jesus! won't I skin yer to the bone!

Enter M'sieur

Lay down yer load

Unlace yer boots

And rest from the road

This weighs a ton

Travel's a curse

But here we strive

To lighten your purse.

Here the goose is cooked

Here the fat is fried

And nothing's overlooked

Till I'm satisfied . . .

Food beyond compare

Food beyond belief

Mix it in a mincer

And pretend it's beef.

Kidney of horse

Liver of a cat

Filling up the sausages

With this and that!

Residents are more than welcome

Bridal suite is occupied!

Reasonable charges

Plus some little extras on the side!

Charge 'em for the lice

Extra for the mice

Two percent for sleeping with the window shut!

Source: "Master of the House," from the musical *Les Misérables* by Alain Boublil and Claude-Michel Schönberg. Music by Claude-Michel Schonberg. Lyrics by Alain Boublil, Jean-Marc Natel, and Herbert Kreztmer. Copyright Alain Boublil Music Ltd. Reprinted by permission of the publisher.

Inns were built in a somewhat standard design, usually around three sides of the inn yard, so that each floor would have a balcony overlooking the yard. Guest rooms opened onto the balconies so all could look out and enjoy the coming and going of the stagecoaches. The amphitheater-like arrangement of inn courtyards provided ideal settings for bullfighting, strolling musicians, and other theatrical entertainment. In fact, in 1576 James Burbage built the first theater in Great Britain. When theaters did proliferate, they took the shape of enlarged courtyards—the pit, balconies, and boxes simply replicating the original yards where itinerant actors had first performed.[21]

During the Renaissance, the public dining room, which ultimately became known as the restaurant, emerged as another aspect of the hospitality industry. Food had become the popular conversational topic of sixteenth-century travelers, many of whom had begun to carry recipes with them as they journeyed from place to place. It was a time when an overabundance of cattle made it possible for Europeans to discover the joy of eating good beefsteak.

The seventeenth century saw the reintroduction of the table fork and dinner plate, missing since the days of the Roman Empire.[22] It remained for the eighteenth century, however, to produce in France what *The Wall Street Journal* has called "almost certainly the world's first restaurant—or at least the first real restaurant in the Western world."[23] It was originally established in 1765 by Monsieur Boulanger at a site on the then rue des Poulies in Paris, a location investigative reporters identify today as the rue Baileul.

Monsieur Boulanger was a specialist in the preparation of fortifying bouillons made of finely minced chicken and other meat, broth, and ground barley, Boulanger called his dishes **"restorants,"** or, in an alternative spelling, **"restaurants,"** because they were intended for pregnant women or as cures for hangovers. Above the entrance to his establishment he carved a motto in Latin: *Venite ad me omnes qui stomacho laboris et ego vos restaurabo* (Come to me all those whose stomachs labor and I shall restore you). As a person, Boulanger (we are told by *The Wall Street Journal*) was dressed like a man of quality, strutting up and down outside his shop, his sword clinking on the pavement and the grand cordon of some order on his breast; yet this blatant charlatanry did not close any fashionable doors to him, for he mixed with all the best people of the time, guiding them to their pleasures and diversions and inevitably leading them to his restaurant with its daintily set-out tables.

The Nineteenth Century: Restaurants, Hotels, and Resorts

Though "eating out" has a long history stretching back to the days of ancient Rome, when snack bars (thermopoliums) were popular, the stage for eating out in America did not occur until colonial times. It was then, in the 1600s and early 1700s, that taverns and inns were emerging in response to population growth and to stagecoach travelers whose hearty appetites for food and drink were unmistakably evident at roadside inns. The advent of the American Revolution, however, saw the gradual decline of such roadside inns and taverns in favor of a more elaborate establishment, the restaurant. This was modeled on Monsieur Boulanger's creation.

A Perspective on Nineteenth-Century Restaurants

Despite historians' disagreement as to which one of a rapidly growing number of early restaurants merits the designation of the *first* American restaurant, tradition favors the famous establishment known as Delmonico's in New York City. (This claim is disputed by the Union Oyster House of Boston, founded in 1826 and still in operation.) The first Delmonico's, a cake and wine shop on William Street, New York City, was founded by John Delmonico, a retired Swiss sea captain, and by his brother, Peter, in 1827. Their menu consisted of wines, little chocolate cakes (petits gâteaux), and fancy ices. Success in this venture induced their 19-year-old nephew, Lorenzo, to come from Switzerland in 1832 to launch their second enterprise, a second-story restaurant on Broad Street in New York.

During the ensuing fifty years, Lorenzo demonstrated uncanny skills as a creator and marketer of grande cuisine. Banquets at Delmonico's were famous—and expensive. A yachtsman in 1870 paid $400 per person for a banquet that featured, for each guest, a personal yacht basin, 20 inches in diameter, containing a floating model of the host's yacht. On another occasion, Lorenzo created a 30-foot lake in which four swans were swimming and golden cages of songbirds decorated the banquet room.

Delmonico's menus, the first to be printed in both English and French, contained 371 separate dishes to order, such as the following: 12 soups, 32 hors d'oeuvres, 46 varieties of veal, 27 of mutton, 47 of poultry, 22 of game, 46 of fish, shellfish, turtle, and eels, 51 vegetable and egg dishes, 19 pastries and cakes, 28 additional desserts, 24 liqueurs, and 64 wines. The highest-priced menu item: Canvasback duck fed on sherry.[24] (It is perhaps worth noting that lobster newberg originated at Delmonico's as a creation of one Mr. Wenberg who, alas, quarreled with one member of the Delmonico family and as a consequence suffered the indignity of having his lobster dish spitefully spelled newberg instead of Wenberg!)

When Lorenzo died in 1881, Delmonico's—then operating in four locations, each operated by a different family member—began to lose momentum. The last of the Delmonico family died in 1910, and by 1923, with the Eighteenth amendment to the U.S. Constitution having taken its toll of the country's wine and liquor business, Delmonico's closed forever.

With rare exception—such as Antoine's renowned restaurant, which has been operating continuously in New Orleans since 1840—few cities in nineteenth-century America were capable of supporting restaurants in the grand style of Delmonico's. Nonetheless, the rapid expansion of the population that accompanied the industrial revolution of the post–Civil War era not only spawned lunchrooms, coffee shops, and cafeterias for office and industrial workers, but yielded attractive dining opportunities at convenient railroad station locations along routes traveled by the Atchison, Topeka & Santa Fe Railroad. Thus, under the aegis of an enterprising British immigrant, Fred Harvey, America experienced its first **chain restaurant** organization.

With the opening of the first Harvey House in 1876, at the railroad station in Topeka, Kansas, Harvey's reputation for clean, dependable, quick-service facilities inspired the growth in 12 states of more than 45 Harvey Houses by the turn of the century. Good food and flawless service by the "Harvey Girls" (about whom a popular Hollywood film was made in the mid-1930s) became the hallmarks of Harvey excellence and consistency. Later, as rail travel gave way to airplane and automobile travel, the luster of railroad restaurants began to fade. Thus, with revenues beginning to decline rapidly, Fred Harvey made a vigorous effort to branch out into superhighway and airport terminal restaurants while, at the same time, trying to break in to the hotel business. But by the late 1960s, all such endeavors had proved unavailing. As a result, the company was sold in the early 1970s and is today known as Amfac Resorts, operator of six hotels with headquarters in Flagstaff, Arizona.

A Perspective on Nineteenth-Century Hotels

In nineteenth-century Europe and America, the unprecedented growth of cities, fueled by a rapidly increasing population, resulted in such an enormous demand for improved transportation that when the railway age was inaugurated at Darlington, England, in 1825, it was clear that steam had pushed the stagecoach into history. Five years later, the Liverpool to Manchester line was carrying half a million passengers. By 1840, the United States had built 178 railroads covering 3,000 miles, causing some foreign visitors to marvel at how American railroads stretched "from Nowhere-in-Particular to Nowhere-at-All."[25] At the same time, the wedge of urbanism being driven into America's nineteenth-century wilderness was being powered by something recognizably new, an American-style hotel.[26] In Memphis, the Gayoso House, completed three years before the city had been incorporated and 10 years before it had a railroad, was being advertised in 1846 as a "spacious and elegant hotel" even though it then stood in the heart of a dense forest.

Above all, nineteenth-century America was not only an age of upstart towns and cities but also an age rich in the traditions of the Greek Revival movement—a development that reflected the "enthusiasm which the whole Western world, and particularly the new republic, showed for the struggles of Greece during the wars of independence."[27] Such names as Athens, Troy, Ithaca, and Ypsilanti were given to newly developed towns.

In keeping with the Greek Revival movement, young Isaiah Rogers, a self-educated architectural prodigy, created an epoch-making design of the Tremont House in Boston. When it opened on October 15, 1829, critics agreed that Rogers—at the age of 26—had scored an architectural breakthrough by his design of the world's first modern hotel. Moreover, the Tremont House's advanced mechanical equipment so aroused the envy and admiration of designers and engineers the world over that Rogers was soon widely acclaimed as the world's premier hotel architect. Remarkable as it was to his contemporaries, Rogers's inclusion of inside plumbing on the ground floor and basement levels (plumbing above the ground floor was still unknown) turned out to be but a rudimentary forerunner of what was in store for hotels of the future.

Nothing accelerated the growth of American hotels as much as their readiness to become laboratories and showcases of technological progress. In one hotel after another, inventions were first tried out and then widely adopted by the rest of the lodging industry. Thus, by the turn of the century, hotels had ushered into American life such conveniences as central heating, private bathrooms, passenger elevators, electric lights, and telephones.

Between the time that the Tremont House opened in Boston (1829) and the start of the Civil War 30 years later (1860), more hotels were opened than at any time in U.S. history until the 1920s. The decades immediately preceding the war had witnessed the rapid development of railroad networks. Burgeoning American cities and towns were quick to see that locations near their railroad stations were ideal sites for hotels. Thus, after long train rides, tired travelers would quickly be able to find a hotel in which they would find food and shelter. As historians have noted, the excitement and competition of hotel building was contagious. No city could amount to very much unless it had at least one first-class hotel to show the world the greatness and hospitality of its people.

Innovative "Grand Hotels" of the Nineteenth Century

Eagerly competing to build bigger, better, and more luxurious hotels, architects and developers of nineteenth-century America sought not only to match the opulence of Boston's Tremont House, but, more important, to surpass it. Thus, nineteenth-century America witnessed the rise of "grand hotels" unique for their innovations as well as for their splendor. Several notable examples follow:

1836—The Astor House, New York This 300-room, five-storied structure was designed by Isaiah Rogers. This was the first American hotel fully illuminated by gaslight powered by its own gas-producing plant.

1855—Parker House, Boston This was the first hotel in America to operate on the **European Plan**, which meant that lunch and dinner meals were not included in the room rate.

1870—Palmer House, Chicago Prior to its opening, this 227-room hotel was widely advertised as "the only fireproof hotel in the world." One year later, 1871, it burned to the ground in the great Chicago fire. Its owner, Potter Palmer, a wealthy textile merchant, replaced it with a new 650-room hotel, which in turn was torn down and replaced in 1924 by a majestic 2,250-room hotel, now owned and operated by Hilton Hotels.

1892—The Brown Palace, Denver This was an ornate 440-room hotel with a spectacular atrium, which was said to be America's first. The atrium was eight stories high and featured a stained-glass interior roof, onyx walls, and elaborately designed tiled floors.

1893—The Waldorf Astoria, New York In the closing decade of the nineteenth century, feuding factions of the aristocratic Astor family built two New York hotels. One of them, the Waldorf, was built on the site of William Waldorf Astor's mansion at Fifth Avenue and 33rd Street. The other, the Astoria, was built in 1897 on the site of the mansion owned by Colonel John Joseph Astor at Fifth Avenue and 34th Street. The two hotels were later joined by an underground passageway, giving rise to the hyphenated name, Waldorf-Astoria, as a symbol of a world-class luxury hotel. The present 47-story, 1,800-room Waldorf-Astoria at Park Avenue and 50th Street, opened in 1931 and is operated by Hilton Hotels under an agreement that reportedly requires the hotel to be identified only as The Waldorf-Astoria, never as a Hilton Hotel.

Resort Hotels of the Nineteenth Century

The concept of **resort hotels** had its origins in second-century Rome, whose citizens and legionnaires were seeking rest and relaxation at renowned Roman spas. In seventeenth-century America, fashion-conscious Pilgrims patronized the colonies' first resort at Stafford Springs, Connecticut, a favorite watering hole of a Native American tribe known as the Nipmucks. In nineteenth-century America, several classic resorts were founded. Here are three examples:

1832—The Homestead, Hot Springs, Virginia This luxurious mountain resort of 600 rooms, with three golf courses, claims to possess the oldest tee in the United States. In the mid-

1900s, this family-owned property was inherited by the then chairman of the Sanskrit language department at Harvard University.

1857—The Greenbriar Hotel, White Sulfur Springs, West Virginia A 700-room luxurious resort hotel, formerly owned and operated by the Chesapeake & Ohio Railroad, is now operated by the Greenbriar Resort Management Company, operator of three resort hotels at Grand Teton National Park, Wyoming.

1887—The Grand Hotel, Mackinac Island, Michigan Located on one of the Great Lakes, Lake Huron, this 275-room hotel opened as "the largest summer resort in the world." The island, three miles long and two miles wide, allows transportation only by horse and carriage or bicycle. Today no automobiles are permitted.

▊ Nazareth: Planning for 2000

The ancient and the contemporary in the hospitality industry meet in the eternal city of Nazareth, a city today of over 60,000. Its citizens are eagerly awaiting the year 2000. That year will see the culmination of years of development as the city celebrates the anniversary of the start of the Christian faith and the birth of the modern calendar. Nazareth, located in northern Israel near Haifa, is the country's largest Arab city, and is perhaps only second to Jerusalem as a tourist destination in Israel. Already under way are a $20 million road repair and expansion project, and a $2.5 million development program for the city's main bazaar or market. This market will include food vendors and shops, just as it has for thousands of years. But now it will include lights and modern public facilities.

The city faces a number of challenges as the world prepares to enter the next millennium. One of the most basic concerns? Hotel rooms. The Nazareth Hotel, the only large hotel in the city, has 87 rooms, not nearly enough to accommodate the thousands of anticipated visitors. Some local businesspeople have already begun to address this need. One developer has converted an old monastery on top of a nearby mountain into the St. Gabriel Hotel (another abandoned monastery has become a restaurant). Several international hotel companies, such as the French-based Accor, and the U.S.-based Hospitality Franchise Systems, have submitted requests to the government to construct new hotels in the area. Potential developers, and local and state governing bodies, will need to work together to ease the transition to the next century.

Dawn of the Twentieth Century Gives Rise to New Concepts

Early on, it became clear to Ellsworth Milton Statler, an enterprising former bellboy of the McClure House in Wheeling, West Virginia, that the hotel industry could ill afford to neglect America's burgeoning population of traveling salesmen. Accordingly, he conceived the first **commercial hotel**, the Buffalo Statler, which opened January 18, 1908, and was the forerunner of the country's first commercial hotel chain and the first to advertise "A Room and a Bath for a Dollar and a Half."

In a provocative *Harvard Business Review* article, "Risking the Present for a Powerful Future," the authors assert that reacting to changes in the business world cannot be done incrementally, or in stages. Rather, to stay competitive, companies need to create change, and create opportunities by thinking like entrepreneurs: "Incremental change isn't enough for many companies today. They don't need to change what is; they need to create what isn't."[28] Ostensibly, innovative entrepreneurs of the early twentieth century, such as Ellsworth Statler, were hard at work trying to create "what isn't" in the hospitality industry.

We have already seen Statler's creation in Buffalo of the nation's first commercial hotel, forerunner of the Statler hotel chain—a twentieth-century "first." Ultimately, Statler hotel chain properties appeared in Cleveland, Detroit, New York, Boston, St. Louis, and Los Angeles.

Transportation Accelerates Chain Growth During the "Roaring Twenties"

The advent of the automobile during the post–World War I era of the 1920s prompted the invention of the first motel. In 1924, when roadside cabins were in vogue, James Vail's cabins on Route 101 in San Luis Obispo, California, were called "Motel Inn." He erected an electric sign with the word _OTEL, with the sign being programmed to flash the letters *H* and *M* alternately, thus introducing the hotel industry's first use of the word *motel*.

The decade of the 1920s, often called "the golden age of hotels," was an age that saw the opening of the 2,200-room Hotel Pennsylvania in New York, across the street from the main entrance to the Pennsylvania Railroad terminal. It also witnessed the openings of many other hotels such as the Ritz Carlton and the Statler, Boston, in 1927; the Roosevelt, 1924, and the New Yorker, 1927, in New York City; the Biltmore, 1927, in Santa Barbara; the Mayflower, 1925, in Washington, D.C.; the Palmer House, 1924, and the Stevens, 1927, in Chicago.

Moreover, the "roaring twenties" enjoyed guest occupancy averaging 80 percent or more, an accomplishment hitherto unknown in the hotel industry. Such success was due to advances in transportation. Faster railroads, better highways, and automobile improvements paved the way for a booming hotel industry. But the Great Depression interrupted the building boom, and just as the international economy began to make a comeback, the world was thrown into the Second World War.

Development in the hospitality industry was put on hold during World War II. All industries around the world were dedicated to the war effort, and raw materials were at a premium. Additionally, a number of hotels in the United States had either failed or been converted to other uses during the Depression. As the war progressed, however, the need for lodging grew substantially. The U.S. government moved over 12 million servicemen and -women between 1941 and 1945, and families traveled more and more. By the end of the war, with gas rationing lifted, hotels were turning guests away. Nationally, occupancy averaged almost 90 percent.

One industry made tremendous strides during the war, and that was air transportation. The incredible advances in fighter, transport, and bomber airplane design and production were easily transferred to commercial air travel. Airlines such as Pan Am, Northwest, KLM, and others, although formed before World War II, grew at a revolutionary pace in the late 1940s and early 1950s. Consumer demand to see far-off and exotic places was growing.

By the end of World War II, major hotel chains, such as the Statler, Hilton, and Sheraton, were in the ascendancy, with Holiday Inns looming on the horizon of the 1950s. In the ensuing decade, hotel chains literally "took off," with their total numbers increasing to more than 900 by the 1990s. In a sense, ancient history repeated itself. **Market segmentation**, or directing marketing efforts to appeal to a certain classification of customer, resurfaced in the hotel industry in new contemporary garbs, such as the emergence of economy/limited-service lodging chains and suite hotels.

The jet age, which began in 1958 and subsequently offered the luxury of supersonic air travel via the *Concorde*, not only has vastly increased the volume of air travelers, but also has focused on international hotel development. As a consequence, airlines stepped up their entry into the hotel business. By the mid-1980s, airline hotel linkage had increased from 30 hotels in 1972 to more than 1,200 hotels worldwide, prompting the expectation that airline diversification into the hotel business would embrace 2,000 hotels by the year 2000.

Transition to the Twenty-First Century

The hospitality industry's success at the forefront of the global economy is solidly rooted in its historic ability to anticipate customer needs. Now that the industry is in the final stages of its countdown to the year 2000, this history dictates a future of growth. This growth is evident in a number of areas, outlined below.

Resort hotels, comprising more than 500 properties with over 350,000 rooms in the mid-1990s were showing solid occupancy rates of 69.5 percent.[29] With the growth of air travel, resort guests have been quick to seek new destinations. For some seasonal resorts, drastic business losses have occurred. As a result, many resort hotels today have become year-round operations. Some are associated with successful theme parks, such as Disney World. Others, such as Marriott's Camelback Inn, have moved successfully into the year-round conference center market.

Fast food restaurant chains, led by McDonald's, enjoyed spectacular development in the twentieth century. McDonald's, with 14,000 restaurants already operating in 68 countries, raised its expansion sights in 1993 by announcing that it expected to open as many as 1,200 restaurants each year for several years, beginning in 1994.[30] Answering the question "What's next in the hot chain growth area," a well-known foodservice industry consultant suggested the following as "multiple hot new areas" of the future: Adult Fast Food, Entertainment, Family Style Restaurants, "Fresh Mex" (Mexican), "Healthy" Chicken, Specialty coffee/bakery, Steakhouses.[31] Chains such as Taco Bell, Boston Market, and Au Bon Pain, all of which have grown rapidly in the 1990s, are credible evidence of this trend.

As lavish theme parks have been surfacing in the late 1990s, costs have been skyrocketing. MGM Grand Adventures Theme Park, on 33 acres in Las Vegas, opened its $1 billion entertainment megaplex with Barbra Streisand's multimillion-dollar two-night engagement on New Year's Eve in 1994. In November 1993, EuroDisney theme park in Paris announced a $900 million loss for 1993, its first year of operation. Meanwhile, Disney's future plans include such projects as a new $3 billion theme park and resort complex to adjoin Disneyland in Anaheim, California. Another major player in the theme park business, Universal Studios, is planning to bring Dr. Seuss's characters to life in a new park scheduled to open in the summer of 1999.

In late November 1993, the Lego Group, a Danish toy manufacturer, announced its plan to build a Lego Family Park in Carlsbad, California, 30 miles north of San Diego. It will start construction in 1995 and expects to open in the spring of 1999. Sega's high-tech theme parks, featuring virtual reality, are serious challengers to the Disney market as the hospitality industry heads into the 21st century, awash with unprecedented entertainment costs. The gaming industry is also experiencing unprecedented growth. Once found only in Atlantic City and Las Vegas, casinos are being built on Native American reservations at a rapid pace. Riverboat gambling is another popular development, as the hospitality industry strives to expand into new ventures. By all accounts, gaming will be a segment to watch in the coming decades. The scope of the future potential is vast.

With all the increased focus on entertainment concepts, the good news for hospitality companies as they prepare for the twentieth century is the surge of "show biz" training in the employee selection process. At the Paramount Hotel in New York, applicants for the job of desk clerk, bartender, and reservationist audition in response to a "casting call." Prior experience as a hotel employee is usually discounted in favor of acting ability and "star quality." The rationale, as explained by the hotel's owner, is: "I consider myself in the entertainment business. It's magic we are selling. It's the show. There are the players. We cast them."[32]

If Clinton Orders Double Cheese and All the Toppings, It's a Crisis

How's this for a slice of life? Domino's Pizza Inc. says orders rose 11 percent when Amy Fisher or either of the Buttafuocos was on the tabloid TV show *A Current Affair*. When basketball's Michael Jordan retired at a daytime press conference, lunchtime pizza orders set a national record.

Such are the results of the pizza meter for 1993, the fourth edition of Domino's attempt to link pizza sales, delivery person sociology, and actual events. The logic is that dialing Domino's is a sign that people are really engrossed in a TV show and aren't willing to sweat over a hot microwave.

"We get to see Americans as they really are," says Tim McIntrye, Domino's national director of communications, who runs the survey. His staff interviews more than 200 drivers and correlates their observations with actual sales data for particular periods. He concedes that "we take great pride in how unscientific our survey is," but he notes that some observations make sense.

Domino's became interested in pizza sociology during the Reagan administration, when a Washington franchisee observed that he could tell when a crisis was brewing by soaring nighttime orders at the White House and the Central Intelligence Agency. "After we publicized that, CIA orders dried up," says Mr. McIntrye.

Pizza orders from the Clintons and their workaholic staffers are up 31 percent from the best Bush year. And when Hillary is out of town, pizza orders rise 18 percent above normal.

Nationally, the biggest pizza day of the year was when the House voted on the Clinton budget, the first time the biggest day wasn't a sports event.

But the Clinton budget has been bad for delivery people. Since it passed, tipping has declined by 4 percent nationally, 8 percent in the House and 13 percent among House Republicans, Domino's delivery people say. Other tipping news: The best tippers are advertising firms, nonprofit organizations, and military bases. The worst: TV studios, investment bankers, and lawyers.

And then there are regional factors. Since the fat content of Chinese food was publicized this fall, Sunday evening pizza orders are up 7 percent nationally and 34 percent in New York. Los Angelenos mostly order veggie toppings, except after disasters; following riots or earthquakes, they order meat toppings 64 percent of the time. And delivery people say New Jerseyites are 12 percent more likely to ask for extra napkins.

Reprinted with permission of *The Wall Street Journal*, © 1993 Dow Jones & Company, Inc. All rights reserved worldwide.

Summary

In these introductory pages, you share our adventures in briefly tracing the significant highlights of mankind's efforts at hospitality spanning some four thousand years. This is a period covering such historic eras as the Roman Empire, the Middle Ages, and the Renaissance. Beginning with the death penalties imposed under the Hammurabi Code for certain violations of innkeeping laws, this chapter focuses on the impact of the stagecoach and other modes of transportation on the evolution of inns and taverns. Advancements in transportation also contributed to the explosive growth in later centuries, with the advent of the modern restaurant and chain hotels.

Exhibit 1.1 shows chronologically snapshots of important "firsts" in the hospitality industry, foreshadowing an exciting transition from the twentieth to the twenty-first century, as the industry copes with such innovations as supersonic air travel, mega-resort hotels and casinos, theme parks, virtual reality entertainment, and worldwide growth of chain restaurants. In chapter 2, we will direct our attention to the big picture, in the belief that with a clear image will come a better understanding of the world of hospitality.

Discussion Questions

1. What do the laws pertaining to innkeeping during the pre-Christian era have in common? What clues do they provide about the nature of the hospitality business?

2. Discuss the significance of Athens in spurring early development of the hospitality industry.

3. What food establishments of the Roman Empire foreshadowed the development of today's fast food chains? Describe them. Can you note any other patterns where history repeated itself, that is, where modern concepts had ancient roots?

4. What would you consider to be the most important "firsts" in the history of the hospitality industry? Why?

5. How has the evolution of transportation influenced the development of the hospitality industry? Discuss your answer by "type" of transportation innovation.

6. When was the first evidence of market segmentation in the lodging business?

7. Why is a Greek comedy, *The Frogs*, important in the history of the hospitality industry? Explain.

8. What did the Roman Empire have that caused so many inns, taverns, and snack shops to flourish? Discuss.

9. What makes the stagecoach play such a significant role in the history of inns? Explain in detail. How were hotels reflective of the advances of the industrial revolution?

10. Isaiah Rogers has been described as a prodigy in the field of hotel architecture. Why so? Discuss.

11. The decade of the 1920s has been called the "golden age of hotels." Explain.

12. What are some the more important forces said to be shaping the transition of the hospitality industry from the twentieth to the twenty-first century? Explain why you think so.

13. Why were bathrooms so prominently mentioned in the Buffalo Statler's turn-of-the-century marketing materials?

14. What do second century Roman spas and the Homestead and Greenbriar resorts have in common? (Note location of resorts.)

15. Across historic times, why did people travel? Why do people travel in modern times? What are the similarities and differences?

16. The opening quotation refers to the benefit of a good tavern or inn. Do you think this quotation is relevant across all time periods? Why or why not?

Assignment

Research the evolution of a hospitality company. What external influences or events in history shaped the company's history? What legal, political, or technological changes were important to that company's growth or decline? Create a time line of major events in the company.

End Notes

Portions of this chapter are adapted and abridged from two sources: Harold E. Lane, "Innkeeping: A New Role for the Airlines," *Columbia Journal of World Business* (July-August 1972) and Harold E. Lane and Mark Van Hartesvelt, "Behavioral Architecture," *Essentials of Hospitality Administration* (Reston, Virginia: Reston Publishing Co., 1983), chapter 5.

1. G. R. Driver and John C. Miles, *The Babylonian Laws* (Oxford: The Clarendon Press, 1952), Legal Commentary, 41.

2. Helen Gardner, *Art Through the Ages* (New York: Harcourt, Brace & Co., 1926), 56.

3. Daniel J. Boorstin, *Hidden History* (New York: Vintage Books, A Division of Random House, 1987), 14.

4. Arthur White, *Palaces of the People: A Social History of Commercial Hospitality* (New York: Taplinger Publishing Co., 1970), 1. White characterizes it as "Almost the Oldest Profession."

5. Driver and Miles, vol. 2, 45.

6. Ibid, 205.

7. Ibid.

8. Ibid.

9. Ibid. vol. 2, 320. The Priestly Code, it should be noted, forbade a priest to marry a harlot, a slave girl, a woman separated from her husband, or an innkeeper. There were no penalties for violation, however.

10. Louis Gaulis and René Creux, *Swiss Hotel Pioneers* (Switzerland: Editions de Fontainemore, National Tourist Office, 1976), 11.

11. Aristophanes, *The Frogs*. An English version by Dudley Fitts (New York: Harcourt, Brace and Co., 1955), 12.

12. White, 5.

13. Paton Yoder, *Taverns & Travelers* (Bloomington: Indiana University Press, 1969), 153–54.

14. White, 22. Note that the English word *tavern* derives from the Latin *taberna* and originally meant a shop.

15. Henry W. Anderson, *The Modern Food Service Industry* (Dubuque, Iowa: Wm. C. Brown Company, Publishers, 1976), 24–25.

16. White, 54.

17. John H. Sherry, *The Laws of Innkeepers* (Ithaca, N.Y.: Cornell University Press, 1972), 2–7.

18. Sherry, 8.

19. I. S. Medlik, *Profile of the Hotel and Catering Industry* (London: William Heineman Ltd., 1972), 23.

20. White, 75-76.

21. White, 65.

22. Anderson, 27.

23. Paul Levey, "The First Restaurant," *The Wall Street Journal,* July 21, 1989, B1. It is important to note here that Samuel Coles, a founder of Harvard College, opened the Ships Tavern in Boston in 1634. Though classified as an "inn," it took almost no overnight guests, and specialized in meals. For this reason, Coles is generally regarded as America's first restaurant.

24. Donald A. Lundberg, *The Hotel and Restaurant Business* (New York: Van Nostrand Reinhold, 1984), 224.

25. Boorstin, 250.

26. Harold E. Lane and Mark Van Hartesvelt, *Essentials of Hospitality Administration* (Reston, Virginia: Reston Publishing Co., 1983), 134.

27. Talbot Hamlin, *Greek Revival Architecture in America: Being an Account of Important Trends in American Architecture and American Life Prior to the War Between the States* (New York: Oxford University Press, 1944), xi–xvii.

28. Tracy Goss, Richard Pascale, and Anthony Athos, "The Reinvention Roller Coaster: Risking the Present for a Powerful Future," *Harvard Business Review,* (November–December, 1993), 98.

29. Smith Travel Research, Gallatin, Tennessee, November 1993.

30. *The Wall Street Journal,* November 23, 1993, A4.

31. Ron Paul, President Technomic, Inc., *TRA Foodservice Digest,* October 1993.

32. New York Times, November 7, 1993, 8v.

Chapter Two

" God is in the details. "

Ludwig Mies van der Rohe [1]

The
Big Picture ↵

When you finish this chapter you should:

1. Understand the different kinds of establishments that comprise hospitality.

2. Understand how a traveler interacts with the various components of the hospitality business.

3. Understand the key features that distinguish hospitality from other businesses.

4. Understand the simple economics of supply and demand in the hotel and restaurant business.

5. Understand key terminology used by hospitality industry professionals, and know how to calculate occupancy rate, average daily rate, turnover, and average check.

6. Understand the size and scope of the hospitality business.

7. Know the difference between a chain and an independent operation and understand the importance of chain operations in the hospitality business.

8. Know what a management company is and does.

9. Know what a consortium or referral or voluntary group is in the hotel business.

10. Know what a rating service is and why customers care about ratings.

11. Understand what role travel agents play in the hospitality business.

12. Know how the industry has evolved in recent years and what trends are likely to emerge.

13. Know who the major players are in the world of hospitality.

After comprehending the history of the hospitality industry, the next challenge emerges: keeping up with the present changes. This task is no small feat considering the number of hospitality companies that have recently changed names or changed hands. There has been an increasing complexity of players involved in a hotel or restaurant's development and operation, a proliferation of segments within the hospitality business, and the emergence of a number of new concepts. This chapter and those that follow paint the hospitality landscape. Many questions emerge in detailing that panorama:

- How can hospitality providers effectively manage the service experience?
- From an international perspective, how do hospitality operations differ from country to country?
- How are components of tourism interrelated?
- How do things really work in hotels and other lodging operations?
- How do things really work in restaurants and other foodservice operations?
- How has a diversification toward entertainment reshaped the hospitality business?
- What are successful strategies for reacting to a changing workforce, and why is human resource productivity so important in the hospitality business?
- What features of hospitality services dictate marketing strategies?
- How do hospitality companies use technology to manage information?
- What principles of accounting are used in hospitality establishments?
- What features of hospitality services shape the tools in the toolbox of an effective hospitality manager?
- What role do chains and franchising play in the hospitality business?
- How do management contracts, franchises, and affiliations fit into the hospitality business?
- What's the difference between developing, owning, managing, leasing, franchising, and creating an affiliation or a strategic alliance for a hotel? For a restaurant?
- What ingredients contribute to the success of restaurant operations that survive?
- What factors influence ethical choices of hospitality professionals?
- What trends will influence how the hospitality industry will evolve?
- What strategies make a hospitality operation succeed?
- How can one successfully enter and flourish in a hospitality career?

Before detailing the answers to each of these questions in subsequent chapters, we will first step back and survey the big picture.

Under the Hospitality Umbrella

Let's start at the very beginning. What exactly is the hospitality business? What categories of businesses make up hospitality? A common answer is "hotels and restaurants," or more broadly, "lodging and foodservice." A third, fourth, and fifth component are frequently added: "entertainment," "travel distribution channels," and "transportation." Exhibit 2.1 describes these components.

Exhibit 2.1 Components of the Hospitality Industry

I. Lodging	II. Foodservice	III. Entertainment: Attractions, Recreation, and Special Events	IV. Travel Distribution Channels	V. Transportation
1. Defined by Price 　Luxury/Upscale 　Boutique 　Upscale Commercial 　Midscale Commercial 　Budget/Economy	1. Stand Alone Restaurants 　Quick Service 　Cafeteria 　Buffet/Smorgasbord 　Theme 　Ethnic (Various) 　Luxury 　Family 　Diner 　Specialty 　Deli 　Specialty Coffee 　Ice Cream Parlor 　Chain	1. Attractions 　Amusement Parks 　Outdoor/Indoor 　Sightseeing 　Shopping	1. Travel Agencies 　Full-Service 　Group and Incentive 　Corporate	1. Air Transportation 2. Ground Transportation 　Car Rental 　Rail Companies 　Motor Coaches 　Taxi Service 3. Water Transportation
2. Location Specific 　Airport 　Motor Hotel/Motel 　Downtown 　Suburban 　Boatels	2. Within a Lodging Property 　Dining Room(s) 　Room Service 　Lounge/Bar 　Banquet and Catering 　Minibar 　Carts & Convenience Stores 　Vending Machines 　Stand-alone that lease space 　Employee Cafeteria	2. Recreation 　Public Parks/Playgrounds 　State & National Parks 　Outdoor Activities	2. Tour Wholesalers/Tour Operator 3. Convention and Meeting Planners 4. Credit Card Companies 5. Consumer Direct Access 　Reservations by Phone 　Reservations by Internet	
3. Defined by Room Configuration 　All-Suites 　Extended Stay/Residential 　Capsule Hotels 　Bed & Breakfast 　Youth/Elder Hostel 　Private Clubs		3. Festivals & Special Events 　Local Events 　Festivals 　Fairs 　Sporting Events 　International Events 　World's Fair 　Olympics	6. Tourism Offices 　National 　State 　Local 　Convention and Visitors Bureau	
4. Convention Related 　Conference Centers 　Convention Hotels		4. Gaming 　Native American Casinos 　Riverboat/Dockside Casinos 　Gaming on Cruise Ships 　Gaming on Airlines		

(Continued)

33

Exhibit 2.1 Components of the Hospitality Industry (*Continued*)

I. Lodging	II. Foodservice	III. Entertainment: Attractions, Recreation, and Special Events	IV. Travel Distribution Channels	V. Transportation
5. Lodging with Entertainment Components Casino Hotels Destination Resorts Mega Resorts Urban Resorts Condominium/Timeshare Resorts Theme Parks Spas Cruise Ships River Boats 6. Parks and Recreation Camping Recreational Vehicle Parks 7. Health Care Assisted Living Centers Patient and Visitor Inns	3. Catering Special Occasion On-Premise/Off-Premise Airline Mobile Wholesale Accommodation Concession 4. Clubs Country Club Fraternal 5. Within Other Establishments Food Courts in Malls Department/Retail Stores Travel Plazas/Truck Stops Convenience Stores 6. Special Entertainment Concepts Dinner Theater Visible Kitchen 7. Institutional School/College Military Correctional Hospital/Lifecare Corporate/Executive Dining Employee Cafeteria			

What are the elements of each of these components, and how do they fit together? Fundamentally, what creates the business of hospitality is that a traveler away from home has need for certain services. The hospitality industry provides these services to the traveler.

A traveler's motivation for going varies. Two commonly cited purposes of travel are "for pleasure" and "for business," but in fact a person usually travels for more than one reason. These reasons can include a need to rest and relax, by choice or on doctor's orders, wanting to learn about other cultures, wanting to meet new people or visit old friends or family, or to expand personal development, whether through business seminars or pursuit of a new hobby. [2]

Before travelers leave home, they may plan ahead for the trip. In so doing, they may access a **travel service** for the hospitality industry. Travel services, which are **channels of distribution** for the business, consist of organizations that facilitate arrangements between the producers and consumers. A simple example is the use of a travel agency for making airline and hotel reservations.

Next the traveler has to move physically, and thus will access some type of **transportation service**: airplanes, rental cars, trains, and so on. Once travelers arrive at the away–from–home destination, they will have need for other services like **lodging and foodservice**. In addition to needing lodging and foodservice, travelers will often interact with various kinds of **entertainment**, such as attractions, recreation, and special events. When the traveler returns home, the process is repeated in the opposite direction. Figure 2.1, "Tourism: How the Hospitality Components Fit Together," illustrates how a traveler interacts with various components of the hospitality business.

Considered collectively, all of the components found under the hospitality umbrella define **tourism**. In an economic sense, tourism is measured by the total expenditures that the business of hospitality brings to a particular nation or political subdivision of the nation. Tourism as a field also considers the sociological, political, and cultural impact of travel on a particular area. We will explore tourism further in chapter 5, "Tourism Visited."

Lodging Subdivisions

Each of the key categories discussed above can be further subdivided according to distinguishing criteria. Perhaps the most important characteristic that separates one type of lodging from another is price. For example, the range of prices would include inexpensive, indicating a budget or economy hotel, to expensive, indicating a luxury hotel. Location is another important characteristic. Where a hotel is located, anywhere from near an airport to downtown, will lend clues as to the type of hotel it is. The hotel's target audience is also critical. A convention or conference hotel has a specific type of group business in mind. A hotel could have more than one descriptor, such as a "downtown, luxury hotel." As lodging establishments often provide different forms of entertainment, categories such as casinos are also ways to describe types of lodging. We will look at lodging in depth in chapters 6 and 7.

Foodservice Subdivisions

Foodservice includes stand-alone restaurants of many different kinds, restaurants within hotels and institutions, catering operations, and foodservice associated with transportation, retail, and leisure

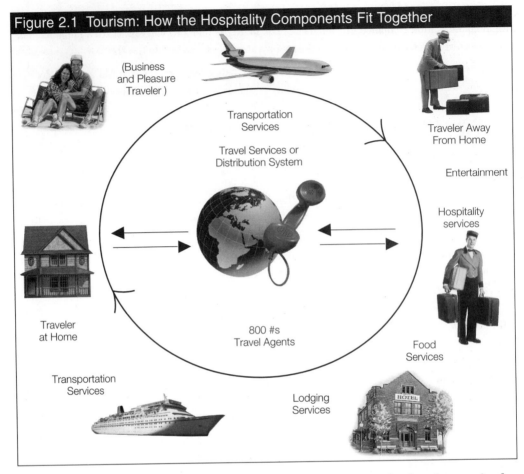

Figure 2.1 Tourism: How the Hospitality Components Fit Together

businesses. Foodservices can also be distinguished based on price, ranging from inexpensive fast food to expensive gourmet, or based on location. Foodservice that is not stand-alone is, by definition, located in conjunction with something else, such as a hotel, an institution, or a club. The quantity in which food is prepared and served offers insight into the type of foodservice. For example, a banquet generally means that many people are served the same thing at the same time, whereas a hot dog vendor serves one person at a time. The way the food is served, ranging from take-out, to self-service in a cafeteria line, to table service, is another way restaurants can be typed. Finally, foodservice can be described by the type of food served, be it ethnic, like Chinese or Greek, or be it a specialty like barbecue or pizza. Just like hotels, foodservice establishments can also have more than one description, for example, an Italian take-out restaurant. The array of foodservice options and the complexities of operations are discussed in chapters 8 and 9.

Entertainment Subdivisions

Entertainment may be part of a lodging or foodservice establishment, or may be found separately. Various kinds of attractions, such as sightseeing, and recreation, such as hiking in a national park, or special events such as the Super Bowl or the Iowa State Fair, are also part of the hospitality business.

Transportation Subdivisions

The transportation component of the hospitality business includes various modes of physically getting from here to there: airplanes, boats, rental cars, trains, bus service, and taxis. Since by definition hospitality is extended to someone away from home, "getting there" is a necessary component of hospitality. This point is underscored by the historical linkage that transportation has had with hospitality establishments.

Travel Distribution Channels Subdivisions

The remaining component of the hospitality business, travel services, is the piece of the business that facilitates arrangements for travelers. Travel distribution channels can be either retail travel agents, tour wholesalers, convention and meeting planners, credit card companies, state or local tourism offices, or just the customer. Wholesale travel agents put together various **travel packages**, or a variety of services sold together, which are then sold to retail travel agencies. They, in turn, sell directly to customers. Different retail travel agencies can be distinguished by the kinds of services they offer. For example, some agencies may only service corporate clients. Tourism offices can function on a national, state, or local level. These offices generally serve as a source of information for travelers.

Industry Structure

In studying the hospitality industry, it is important to understand the structure of the business. What features of the hospitality business are the same as, and different from, other businesses? What are some of the problems and operational issues that distinguish the hospitality industry from others? How could you analyze hospitality as a business in terms of simple economics? We will answer each of these questions in this chapter.

Distinguishing Features of the Hotel Business

In an attempt to understand what distinguishes the hospitality business from others, consider the following:

- Hotels are in operation 24 hours a day, 365 days per year. This creates some unusual operational issues. For example, closing for repairs is not possible as it is in other businesses. There is no official end to the day; it is generally sometime in the wee hours of the morning. Also, because of the unlimited hours and the public access of a hotel, hoteliers must play a difficult dual role, that of hospitable innkeeper and that of security officer, to insure that invited guests feel welcome and that uninvited guests do not present security problems. In the hubbub of a large hotel lobby, it's not always easy to distinguish between the two types of guests!

- There are many peaks and valleys in operating a hotel. Not only are there seasonal fluctuations (e.g., high, low, and **shoulder season,** which is a time of moderate business between the high and low periods at a resort) but there are also weekly fluctuations (e.g., weekday versus weekend business at a center city hotel), but daily ones as well (e.g., extensive business during meal periods in restaurants or many guests showering at the same time in the morning).

- The hospitality business is primarily a service business that serves guests who are away from home. Considering all the operational costs that the manager of a hotel or restaurant must watch, the largest is labor. Even when compared to other kinds of service business, hospitality employs a higher than average number of employees relative to sales.

- Getting into the hotel business is capital intensive (which means that a substantial amount of money is required to get into the business) and therefore there exist high barriers to entry. While restaurants are less capital intensive, they still usually require the purchase or lease of major pieces of equipment.

Connecting Continents

The English Channel Tunnel, or the Chunnel, had its first passenger train service from England to France on May 6, 1994. Inaugural guests included Queen Elizabeth II of England and France's President François Mitterand. The trip concluded over 200 years of proposals and planning. There are now three ways to travel from England to the continent of Europe: by air, by ferry, and by train.

In 1753, a French engineer first suggested the idea that a tunnel be built connecting England and France. By 1802, the idea had Napoleon's support. By 1880, a mile of the tunnel had actually been dug, but fears of invasion in England and political pressure canceled further progress. It was not until 1975 that the project was back on the table. Construction on this massive civil engineering project did not begin again until 1987, when the two countries agreed on the layout and timetable.

In late fall 1994, Le Shuttle trains began to offer scheduled passenger service between London, Paris, and Brussels. Le Shuttle is designed to accommodate tourists traveling by car. Passengers pass through security devices, and passports are checked. Cars are then driven by the passengers onto the loading dock, and then onto the double-decker shuttle train. Once the trip begins, passengers can remain in their cars, or walk around inside the train. Premium service provides attendants serving food and beverage, and is designed to attract a business clientele. Upon arrival, approximately 35 minutes and 31 miles later, cars are driven off directly onto a highway.

While cost is a factor for Chunnel use (it is currently twice as expensive to cross under the English Channel than it is to cross it via ferry service), demand for tickets has been high. The ease of taking an automobile, the speed, and the novelty of the service all contribute to the Chunnel's initial popularity. Technology once again brings the international community a little bit closer.

Features Shared with Many Other Businesses Though it does have some distinguishing features, the hospitality business is much like other businesses. For example, repeat business is critical to success. Many hotel companies have followed the airline and other industry's example by creating **frequent guest** programs, recognizing that keeping current guests happy is more cost effective than generating new ones. In fact, a study done for Raddisson Hotels revealed that it costs $2.50 to keep a repeat guest and $15 to generate a new guest.[3] A frequent guest program tracks each time a guest stays in every Hyatt Hotel for example, and after a predetermined number of stays, a guest may receive a free room night, complimentary dinner, or other reward.

As with many other businesses, the customer cares about the relationship between the price paid and the value received. An analysis that compared customer satisfaction and price is presented in Figure 2.2. It is interesting to note that many of those companies that performed the worst—Ramada, Days Inn, Holiday Inn, Rodeway, and Howard Johnson—found themselves in fiscal trouble and on the auction block in the late eighties. In interpreting the chart, note that the companies above the line registered the highest customer satisfaction for price point.

Supply and Demand To understand the simple economics of the business, let's start with the concept of supply and demand. The unit for sale in a hotel is a **room night**, and for a restaurant a **cover** or a meal. The supply of rooms or restaurant seats is fixed. Demand fluctuates. Filling up all of your hotel rooms or restaurant seats, at the highest rate possible without turning anyone away would mean you have a perfect match between supply and demand.

The measure of how much of a hotel's supply is sold is the **occupancy percentage**. The number of rooms available for sale in a hotel may be less than the total in the hotel. If a room is under repair, for example, it is "not available" and thus would not be included when calculating occupancy percentage.

A simple example illustrates the calculation. A hotel with 60 rooms sold of its 100 rooms available for sales on a given night is 60 percent occupied. The measure of what price the supply is sold

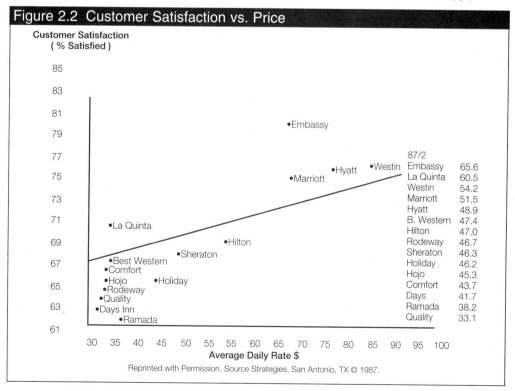

Figure 2.2 Customer Satisfaction vs. Price

	87/2	
	Embassy	65.6
	La Quinta	60.5
	Westin	54.2
	Marriott	51.5
	Hyatt	48.9
	B. Western	47.4
	Hilton	47.0
	Rodeway	46.7
	Sheraton	46.3
	Holiday	46.2
	Hojo	45.3
	Comfort	43.7
	Days	41.7
	Ramada	38.2
	Quality	33.1

Reprinted with Permission. Source Strategies, San Antonio, TX © 1987.

for is the **average daily rate per room sold**. Since not every customer pays the same rate, an average is used. If 30 of the 60 rooms in the above example were sold for $100.00 and the other 30 were sold for $120.00, the total revenue for the evening would be $6,600.00. The average daily rate would be $6,600/60 or $110. A variation of this statistic is to consider the **average rate per available room**. This statistic comprehends an average of all rooms in the hotel, whether they were sold or not. A room that was not sold contributes zero dollars. In the above example, 30 rooms were sold for $100.00, 30 rooms were sold for $120.00, and forty were not sold. Thus the average rate per available room is $\{(30 \times 120) + (30 \times 100) + (0 \times 40)\}/100 = \$66.00$.

Typically, the **breakeven occupancy** for a hotel, or the occupancy needed for revenues to match expenses, will be in the mid-sixties, or approximately 65 percent. The typical average daily rate has a wide variance depending on the type and location of a given hotel. For example, the average daily rate for center city hotels in Montreal, Quebec, in 1995 approximated $89. Occupancy and average daily rate are probably the two statistics used most frequently by hotel managers.

The comparable measures of occupancy rate and average daily rate for a restaurant are **number of turns or turnover** and **average check**. The number of turns is the number of sittings in a given meal period (breakfast, lunch, or dinner) that a restaurant seat provides. The average number depends very much on the type of restaurant service. A quick service family-style restaurant might have four turns per meal period, where a gourmet restaurant would likely not have more than two turns. The average check, or price per cover served, is also dependent on the style of restaurant and the location. In Table 2.6, "The Top 20 Independent Restaurants," the Four Seasons, an exclusive restaurant in New York City, had an average check of $70.00. Spenger's Fish Grotto, a more informal family run seafood restaurant, had an average check of $14.00. These two restaurants had an average 1.2 and 5.5 turns per day, respectively. The turnover was calculated by dividing the number of people served per year by 365 days (e.g., 175,000/365 = 480 persons served per day), then by dividing that daily figure of persons served by the number of seats in the restaurant (e.g., 480/400 = 1.2 turns).

In summary, the calculations for these important hospitality measures are:

- Occupancy Percentage = Total # of Rooms Sold / Total # of Rooms Available for Sale
- Average Daily Rate per Room Sold = Total Revenue / Total Number of Rooms Sold
- Average Rate per Available Room = Total Revenue / Number of Rooms Available for Sale
- Number of Turns or Turnover = Number of Persons or Covers Served / Number of Seats in the Restaurant
- Average Check = Total Revenue / Number of Persons or Covers Served

All of these statistics can be calculated for different time frames. They can be calculated on a daily, weekly, monthly, or yearly basis. Even the "average daily rate," despite its name, can be considered annually, for example.

Big Picture Snapshots

The components, the structure, and the economics of hospitality give us a sense of the scope the business, so we now turn our attention to the size of the industry. A look at some important statistics reveals a growing and consolidating business. The system of interrelated parts that make up the hospitality industry or tourism is big business. Worldwide tourism spending in 1994 was in excess of three trillion dollars. This represents 12 percent of the world's consumer spending.[4] This growth should continue, particularly in certain parts of the world. As citizens in Eastern Europe, former Soviet Union countries, and parts of Asia become more free to travel abroad, as they build a tourism infrastructure in their respective countries, and as international flight restrictions are lessened, expansion is likely.

The growth in hotel rooms is following the same pattern. Worldwide there are approximately 12 million hotel rooms. (A breakdown of all the world's hotel rooms is presented in chapter 4, Table 4.1.) In the United States, although hotel room construction slowed dramatically in the early 1990s, the hotel industry has grown steadily over the last two decades.[5]

There is similarly good news for restaurants as the foodservice industry continues to capture an increasing proportion of America's food budget. According to the U.S. Department of Agriculture, the percentage of America's food budget spent on food away from home has grown steadily, from approximately 15 percent in 1955 to 34 percent in 1970, to 40 percent in 1980, to 46 percent, nearly half of all meals, by 1993.

In addition to growing, the hotel industry is also consolidating. This means that the percentage of the market, or market share, of the largest chain operations is increasing. Table 2.1 illustrates the changes. The consolidation has taken place through an extensive number of mergers and acquisitions. Table 2.13, "Twelve Years of Acquisitions Activity," details some of the industry's major hotel acquisitions in recent years.

The market share of the 100 largest restaurant chains grew dramatically in the 1970s and consolidation continued into the 1980s. In 1972, market share of the 100 largest restaurant chains was approximately 30.2 percent; by 1983, it was 44.7 percent; and by 1989, it was over 46 percent.

Table 2.1 Growth of Hotel Rooms Controlled by the 25 Largest Hotel Companies

	1980	1994
TOTAL number hotel rooms in U.S.A.	2.4 million	3.1 million
TOTAL number hotel rooms controlled by the 25 largest companies	1.2 million	2.0 million
Market share of 25 largest companies	50%	65%

Source: World Tourism Organization, *Lodging's Chain Reports* 1980, 1995. Calculations are the authors'.

Major Players

Now that you see the big picture of the hospitality business, we turn to the major players and their respective roles. Some of these important players include hotel and restaurant chains, independent restaurants, management companies, referral groups, rating services, and travel agencies.

Largest Service Companies First, for a frame of reference consider the largest hospitality companies relative to all service companies. *Fortune Magazine* does a survey that ranks all service companies in terms of total sales. They also note the ranking of the top companies in terms of number of employees.

In terms of total sales, relative to other service businesses, hospitality companies rank 13th, 42nd, 45th, 64th, 86th, 92nd, and 96th in *Fortune Magazine* 100 Largest Diversified Service Companies. These six companies are highlighted in Table 2.2. The largest of the six, French-based Cie International Des Wagon-Lits, had annual sales of approximately $18 billion. (For comparison, Sumitomo, a Japanese trading company, led the world's diversified service companies with $158 billion in sales.) Fortune conducted this survey on an international basis last in 1991.

The number of employees employed by the hospitality companies rank even higher. Marriott ranks second in the world, with 209,000 employees! The other companies finished 6th, 10th, 12th, 24th, 26th, and 31st (see Table 2.2). Importantly, each hospitality company employs well above the average number of people employed in the largest service companies. This has important implications for human resource management, which is discussed in chapter 10.

For the United States only, *Fortune* ranks the top 1,000 corporations each year. Under the categories of Foodservices, Hotels, Casinos and Resorts, the top 20 companies for 1995, along with their rank in the top 1,000, are detailed in Table 2.3. The largest U.S. corporation overall, General Motors, had revenues of $154,951.2 million.

Largest Worldwide Hotel Chains Since the largest chains, as opposed to independent operations, control a substantial and growing portion of the hotel and restaurant business, those companies represent important players in the hospitality business.

A **chain**, quite simply, is two or more operations open under the same name. A chain is distinguished from an **independent**, which is a stand–alone property. Some chains are structured such that all of the units are owned by one parent company. This would be a **corporate-owned chain**. Others are **franchised**. This means that a parent company, or **franchisor**, gives an individual, or franchisee, the right to open a unit for a set of fees described in a **franchise agreement**.

Worldwide, the largest hotel chains are dominated by the American chains (see Table 2.4). The top three chains, and 15 of the top 25, are headquartered in the United States. Note however, that Holiday Inn Worldwide, though headquartered in Atlanta, is a subsidiary of Bass Plc, a British parent. The largest European chains are Accor, a French company that ranks fourth; Forte, Plc, a British company that ranks ninth; Club Meditérraneé, also a French company, that ranks 13th; and Hilton International, a British company that ranks 15th. The largest Eastern European company is Poland's Orbis, ranked 52nd. The largest Asian companies are New World/Renaissance, based in Hong Kong, ranked 16th; and Prince Hotels, 22nd, which is Japanese. The largest Australian company, Southern Pacific Hotels Corp., ranks 40th; the largest African company, Sun International, is 78th.

Largest U.S. Restaurant Chains The largest U.S. restaurant chains, presented in Table 2.5, are clearly dominated by the fast food industry. McDonald's, an American institution under golden arches, leads the list by a considerable margin. As with the hotel companies, it is not uncommon for more than one brand name chain to be owned by the same parent company. For

Table 2.2 Hospitality Companies Listed in Fortune's 100 Largest Diversified Service Companies ($ in Millions)

Rank by Sales 1990	Company (Major Industry)	Sales $	Profits $	Rank	Assets $	Rank	Stockholder's Equity $	Rank	Employees	Rank
13	Cie Int'l Des Wagons-Lits (leisure), France (parent of Wagon–Lit Travel)	18172.1	1004	59	14866.3	15	2,495.60	25	54,000	24
42	Marriott (hotels), USA	7693	47	77	6928	42	407	83	208957	2
45	Bass (leisure), England (parent of Holiday Inn Worldwide)	7583.8	769.9	4	10848	26	5498.7	6	98957	10
64	Walt Disney (theme parks), USA	5924.50	824	3	8022.3	36	3488.60	17	52000	26
86	ARA Group (foodservice), USA	4595.5	51.8	76	1917.2	86	68.9	98	134000	6
92	ACCOR (hotels), France	4194.1	146	47	5309.2	56	1793.3	40	41976	31
96	Trusthouse (hotels), England	4024.2	330.7	15	7142.5	40	4534.5	8	92900	12

Source: (C) 1991 Time Inc. All Rights Reserved.

Table 2.3 Fortune's Top 20 U.S. Hospitality Corporations
Foodservices, Hotels, Casinos, and Resorts

Company	Rank in Top 1000	Revenues 1994 (in millions)	Profits 1994 (in millions)	Number of Employees
Pepsico	20	$28,472	$1,752	471,000
Marriott International	138	8,415	200	163,440
McDonald's	140	8,321	1,224	183,000
Aramark	223	5,162	86	133,000
Flagstar	324	3,526	364	90,000
Bally Entertainment	624	1,604	(68)	12,900
Promus	630	1,582	78	28,500
Hilton Hotels	649	1,506	122	44,000
Host Marriott	651	1,501	(25)	22,000
Wendy's International	682	1,398	97	44,000
Mirage Resorts	696	1,371	113	16,800
Circus Circus Enterprises	769	1,170	136	19,800
Morrison Restaurants	745	1,213	45	33,000
Shoney's	770	1,166	66	30,000
Family Restaurants	794	1,113	384	51,700
Foodmaker	825	1,053	(40)	26,170
Caesars World	847	1,016	78	10,100
Brinker International	925	878	62	38,000
MGM Grand	972	813	75	7,120
Gillett Holdings	997	785	30	800

Source: Fortune, April 1995 © 1995 Time, Inc. All Rights Reserved.

Table 2.4 The World's Largest Corporate Hotel Chains

Rank 1994	Corporate Chain Headquarters	Rooms 1994	Rooms 1993	Hotels 1994	Hotels 1993
1	Hospitality Franchise Systems, Parsippany, NJ	424,352	384,452	4,291	3,790
2	Holiday Inn Worldwide, Atlanta, GA	356,000	340,881	1,930	1,795
3	Best Western International, Phoenix, AZ	280,144	272,743	3,409	3,308
4	Accor, Evry, France	256,607	250,319	2,265	2,181
5	Choice Hotels International, Silver Spring, MD	247,069	229,784	2,827	2,607
6	Marriott International, Washington, DC	180,500	173,048	851	782
7	ITT Sheraton Corp., Boston, MA	132,477	129,714	425	407
8	Hilton Hotels Corp., Beverly Hills, CA	92,452	94,952	226	237
9	Forte Plc, London, England	88,153	78,691	888	855
10	Carlson/Radisson/SAS, Minneapolis, MN	79,482	75,986	349	341
11	Promus Cos., Memphis, TN	78,690	78,309	570	509
12	Hyatt Hotels/Hyatt International, Chicago, IL	77,882	76,057	170	165
13	Club Méditerranée SA, Paris, France	65,128	65,128	262	262
14	Inter-Continental Hotels, London, England	53,092	48,510	141	121
15	Hilton International, Watford Herts, England	53,052	52,930	141	159
16	New World/Renaissance Hotels, Central, Hong Kong	47,139	48,657	140	136
17	Sol Group, Palma de Mallorca, Spain	46,500	43,178	175	165
18	Westin Hotels & Resorts, Seattle, WA	39,470	38,021	76	76
19	La Quinta Inns, San Antonio, TX	29,276	27,960	227	218
20	Société de Louvre, Paris, France	29,120	27,906	468	437
21	Red Roof Inns, Hilliard, OH	24,543	23,432	219	210
22	Prince Hotels, Tokyo, Japan	24,087	22,243	58	77
23	Doubletree Hotels, Phoenix, AZ	23,918	21,415	91	84
24	Tokyu Hotel Group, Tokyo, Japan	23,836	23,500	107	106
25	Hospitality International, Tucker, GA	19,886	23,000	347	368
26	Hôtels & Compagnie, Les Ulis, France	18,939	18,939	362	362
27	Knights Lodging Systems, Cleveland, OH	19,000	21,500	72	9828
28	Walt Disney Co., Burbank, CA	16,386	10,642	15	13

(Continued)

Table 2.4 The World's Largest Corporate Hotel Chains (*Continued*)

Rank 1994	Corporate Chain Headquarters	Rooms 1994	Rooms 1993	Hotels 1994	Hotels 1993
29	Fujita Kanko, Tokyo, Japan	15,941	15,412	71	69
30	Queens Moat House Hotels, Rumford, Essex, England	15,821	17,096	140	162
31	Nikko Hotels International, Rumford, Essex, England	15,369	14,388	38	34
32	Scandic Hotels AB, Stockholm, Sweden	15,000	17,190	94	122
33	Omni Hotels, Hampton, NH	14,631	16,246	41	45
34	Red Lion Hotels & Inn, Vancouver, WA	14,442	14,442	53	53
35	Dusit Thani/Kempinski, Bangkok, Thailand	14,361	4,008	61	20
36	Circus Circus, Las Vegas, NV	13,660	13,627	6	27
37	Shangri-La International, Hong Kong	13,627	12,640	27	25
38	Wyndham Hotels & Resorts, Dallas, TX	13,552	10,530	59	43
39	Thistle & Mount Charlotte Hotels, Leeds, England	13,215	14,500	93	112
40	Southern Pacific Hotels Corp., Sydney, NSW, Australia	12,939	12,026	76	72
41	Four Seasons/Regent, Toronto, Canada	12,909	12,449	38	37
42	Husa Hotels Group, Barcelona, Spain	12,500	10,000	131	72
43	Maritim Hotels, Bad Salzuflen, Germany	11,700	11,465	43	42
44	Park Plaza International Hotels, Larkspur, CA	11,698	8,980	82	51
45	Budgetel Inns, Milwaukee, WI	11,162	10,429	105	98
46	Rui Hotels, Playa Palma Mallorca, Spain	11,036	—	48	—
47	Canadian Pacific Hotels, Toronto, Canada	10,961	11,048	26	26
48	National 9 Inns, Salt Lake City, UT	10,821	9,360	177	174
49	Occidental Hotels, Madrid, Spain	10,674	10,623	49	50
50	ANA Hotels, Tucker, GA	10,440	23,000	34	368
51	Delta Hotels & Resorts, Toronto, Canada	10,434	8,352	37	25
52	Orbis Co., Warsaw, Poland	9,946	10,677	47	55
53	Ritz–Carlton Hotel Co., Atlanta, GA	9,909	9,454	30	29
54	Sunroute Hotel System, Tokyo, Japan	9,865	8,252	76	72

Rank	Company / Location	Rooms	Hotels
55	Barcelo Hotels	9,424	36
	Palma de Mallorca, Spain	—	—
56	Steigenberger Hotels AG	9,254	56
	Frankfurt/Main, Germany	8,879	53
57	Outrigger Hotels & Resorts	8,765	28
	Honolulu, HI	8,600	24
58	Mirage Resorts	8,156	4
	Las Vegas, NV	8,156	4
59	Dai-ichi Hotels Ltd.	8,142	43
	Tokyo, Japan	8,309	42
60	Taj Group of Hotels	8,045	50
	Bombay, India	6,336	40
61	ShoLodge	7,776	76
	Gallatin, TX	7,190	73
62	Grupo Posadas de Mexico SA	7,772	29
	Mexico City, Mexico	8,207	26
63	Treff Hotels	7,698	46
	Arolefen, Germany	6,230	42
64	Fiesta Hotels	7,600	26
	Ibiza, Spain	7,450	26
65	Lonrho Plc	7,459	26
	London, England	7,190	23
66	Budget Host International	7,442	176
	Arlington, TX	7,200	172
67	Grupo Situr	7,368	26
	Guadalajara, Mexico	4,493	18
68	Sokos Hotels	7,139	44
	Helsinki, Finland	7,132	43
69	New Otani Co. Ltd.	7,078	23
	Tokyo, Japan	8,177	34
70	Loews Hotels	6,938	14
	New York, NY	6,938	14
71	Shanghai Jin Jiang Group	6,857	17
	Shanghai, China	6,653	17
72	Dorint Hotels & Resorts	6,686	45
	Monchengladbach, Germany	5,617	43
73	Reso Hotels	6,622	28
	Stockholm, Sweden	9,398	42
74	Jolly Hotels	6,453	38
	Valdagno, Italy	6,346	36
75	Okura Hotels	6,319	21
	Tokyo, Japan	5,402	17
76	Movenpick Hotels International	6,231	29
	Toronto, Canada	8,352	25
77	Drury Inns	6,184	61
	St. Ann, MO	6,122	54
78	Sun International	6,140	34
	Sandton, South Africa	4,808	31
79	NH Hotels SA	6,080	61
	Barcelona, Spain	5,400	54
80	Protea Hospitality Corp.	6,000	81
	Cape Town, South Africa	7,100	19
81	Rihga Royal Hotels	5,964	20
	Osaka, Japan	5,675	19
82	Miyako Hotels	5,860	20
	Kyoto, Japan	5,860	20
83	LTI International Hotels	5,831	36
	Dusseldorf, Germany	4,622	23
84	Euro Disney	5,682	6
	Marne–la Vallée, France	5,777	6
85	Paradiana International	5,660	27
	Oberursel, Germany	—	—
86	Swissotel Ltd.	5,535	14
	Zurich, Switzerland	5,085	14

(Continued)

Table 2.4 The World's Largest Corporate Hotel Chains (*Continued*)

Rank 1994	Corporate Chain Headquarters	Rooms 1994	Rooms 1993	Hotels 1994	Hotels 1993
87	Adam's Mark Hotels St. Louis, MO	5,446	5,155	12	11
88	Regal Hotels International Hong Kong	5,432	4,662	10	9
89	Country Club Hotel Group Luton, England	5,430	4,000	101	76
90	Tryp Hotels Madrid, Spain	5,370	5,000	37	25
91	Jarvis Hotels High Wycombe, England	5,100	3,500	68	45
92	Paradores Madrid, Spain	5,000	6,214	84	83
93	Helmsley/Harley Hotels New York, NY	4,941	4,815	19	19
94	Crown Sterling Suites San Fransisco, CA	4,909	5,775	19	22
95	Oberoi Hotels Delhi, India	4,888	5,404	23	27
96	Aston Hotels & Resorts Honolulu, HI	4,680	4,345	44	27
97	Shilo Inns Portland, OR	4,653	4,716	44	46
98	Grecotel SA Stockholm, Sweden	4,580	9,398	18	42
99	Restel Helsinki, Finland	4,580	4,580	28	28
100	Allegro Resorts Corp. Santo Dominican	4,557	3,555	17	15

Reprinted with permission from *DATAMATION Magazine*, July, 1995 © by Cahners Publishing Company.

Table 2.5 Largest U.S. Restaurant Chains

1995 Rank	Company	1994 Sales in Millions	1994 Units
1	McDonalds	$25,987.0	15,205
2	Burger King	7,500.0	7,547
3	KFC	7,100.0	9,407
4	Pizza Hut	4,797.4	10,648
5	Taco Bell	4,500.0	5,950
6	Wendy's	4,200.0	4,406
7	Hardee's	3,670.0	3,456
8	Subway Sandwiches and Salads	2,700.0	9,893
9	Domino's Pizza	2,500.0	5,079
10	Dairy Queen	2,450.0	5,540
11	Little Caesars	2,000.0	4,700
12	Red Lobster	1,915.8	715
13	Arby's	1,800.0	2,792
14	Dunkin' Donuts	1,610.0	3,958
15	Denny's	1,550.0	1,548
16	Shoney's	1,317.2	922
17	The Olive Garden	1,250.0	478
18	Baskin-Robbins	1,100.0	4,044
19	Jack in the Box	1,049.9	1,224
20	Chili's Bar and Grill	1,000.0	426
21	Big Boy	970.0	850
22	Long John Silver's Seafood Shoppes	939.2	1,456
23	T.G.I. Friday's	913.4	315
24	Applebee's Neighborhood Grill & Bar	888.9	505
25	Sizzler	870.4	604

Source: Restaurants and Institutions, July 1995. Reprinted with Permission.

example, Pepsico Inc. owns Kentucky Fried Chicken, Taco Bell, and Pizza Hut, all three of which are large chains in their own right.

Largest U.S. Independent Restaurants Though they are just single units without chain affiliation, the largest independent restaurants are big business. Each of the largest 100 independent restaurants outperforms the average unit of the top 100 chains. Tavern on the Green in Central Park in New York City is the largest grossing single restaurant, with annual sales of more than $30 million. A list of the largest 20 independent restaurants is included in Table 2.6.

Largest Institutional Catering Companies Some restaurant companies are aimed specifically at institutions such as universities or military bases. According to the National Restaurant Association, approximately 11 percent of all foodservice sales are **institutional**. The remaining 89 percent are classified as **commercial**. (We discuss the differences at greater length in chapter 8, "Foodservice: More Than Restaurants.")

The contract or institutional foodservice industry can be broken down into six segments: contract, institutional, recreation, health care, education, and transportation. Commercial outfits service, among other customers, U.S. military bases, sports arenas, theme parks, hospitals, and correctional facilities. All caterers are led by Aramark, formerly ARA, and Marriott Management Services. Ranked by revenue generated, the top military caterer is U.S. Army. Airline caterers are led by Caterair International, and the Walt Disney Company tops the recreation segment. The largest health care provider, HCA/Columbia Healthcare enters the top 50 at number 14. Note that the New York City Board of Education is only five spots away from Disney! A list of the top 50 is found in Table 2.7.

Largest Hotel Management Companies Other important players include the largest hotel **management companies**, which play an increasingly important role as the real estate and management functions of hotels divide. By this we mean that increasingly ownership and operation of hotels involve two players, the **owner** and the **operator**–not just one company playing both roles. A management company is concerned with the operation of a hotel. While they usually do not own, or own only a small percentage of, the hotel they are managing, they enter into an agreement called a **management contract**, with the owner of a hotel. This contract sets the terms for the management company to receive a management fee for operating the hotel for the owner.

The largest management companies are noted in Table 2.8. These management companies, led by Richfield Hotel Management, Interstate Hotels Corp., and Doubletree Hotels Corp., are not recognizable names to hotel guests. That is because these companies manage hotels that are franchisees of the various hotel chains. It is typical for a management company to manage several or many different **brands** or **flags**. A brand or flag is a name that customers recognize. Some companies have one brand, such as Red Roof Inns. Some companies have several brands such as Hilton Garden Inns, Hilton Hotels, Hilton Inns, Hilton Suites, and Conrad Hotels, which are all Hilton Hotels Corporation flags. Interstate Hotels Corp., a management company, for example, manages Marriott, Sheraton, Hilton, and Radisson hotels. Collectively, the top 50 companies manage nearly half a million rooms. The largest management company manages over 33,000 rooms. Seventy–five percent of these management companies have between 3,000 and 11,000 rooms in their portfolios.

Table 2.6 Top 20 Independent Restaurants

1995 Rank	Restaurant/City/Year Opened/Owner	1994 Sales ($ millions)	Seats Including Banquet	Average Dinner Check w/Beverage	Dayparts	People Served per Year
1	Tavern on the Green, New York, NY 1976 Warner LeRoy	$30.080	1,000	$45.00	L,D	567,000
2	Rainbow Room, New York, NY 1934 Joseph Baum & Associates	25.300	1,600	110.00	B,L,D	350,000
3	Smith & Wollensky, New York, NY 1977 New York Restaurant Group	21.060	450	57.50	L, D	398,000
4	Bob Chinn's Crabhouse, Wheeling, IL 1982 Robert Chinn, Marilyn Chinn	20.496	650	26.10	L, D	870,261
5	Sparks Steakhouse, New York, NY 1964 Pat Cetta, Mike Cetta	15.300	300	70.00	L,D	289,000
6	The Manor, West Orange, NJ 1957 Harry Knowles & Family	14.000	1,200	49.00	L,D	275,000
7	Anthony's Pier 4, Boston, MA 1963 Anthony Athanas & Family	13.400	625	33.00	L,D	NA
8	Scoma's Restaurant, San Francisco, CA 1965 A.J. Scoma	12.626	320	31.81	L,D	470,600
9	The "21" Club, New York, NY 1923 21 International Holdings	12.500	525	75.00	L,D	158,000
10	Spenger's Fish Grotto, Berkeley, CA 1890 Frank Spenger, Jr., Frank L. Spenger	12.300	450	14.00	B,L,D	907,500
11	Joe's Stone Crab, Miami Beach, FL 1913 JoAnn Bass, Grace Weiss	12.000	380	35.00	L,D	405,000

(Continued)

Table 2.6 Top 20 Independent Restaurants (*Continued*)

1995 Rank	Restaurant/City/Year Opened/Owner	1994 Sales ($ millions)	Seats Including Banquet	Average Dinner Check w/Beverage	Dayparts	People Served per Year
12	Four Seasons, New York, NY 1959 Tom Margittai, Paul Kovi	11.400	400	70.00	L,D	175,000
13	Gladstone's 4 Fish, Pacific Palisades, CA 1973 Seaview Restaurants	11.315	785	21.00	B,L,D	530,230
14	Montgomery Inn at the Boathouse, Cincinnati, OH 1989 The Ted Gregory Family	11.078	550	18.50	L,D	820,000
15	Trattoria Dell' Arte, New York, NY 1988 Sheldon Fireman	10.800	300	36.00	L,D	350,000
16	Sequoia, Washington 1990 Ark Restaurants	10.512	1,000	22.25	L,D	288,288
17	Del Frisco's Double Eagle Steak House, Dallas, TX 1985 Del Frisco	10.462	360	55.00	D	190,224
18	Space Needle Restaurant, Seattle, WA 1962 The Howard S. Wright Family	10.426	244	34.00	B,L,D	416,000
19	Dock's Oyster Bar and Seafood Grill, New York, NY 1988 Arthur Cutler, Barry Corwin, Howard Levine	10.274	275	32.00	L,D	309,400
20	Commander's Palace, New Orleans, LA 1883 Ella, Dick, John & Dottie Brennan	10.200	350	45.00	L,D	250,000

Source: Restaurants and Institutions, March 15, 1995. Reprinted with Permission.

Table 2.7 Top 50 U.S.A. Institutional Foodservice Companies

1995 Rank	Company	1994 Sales in Millions	1994 Units	Segment
1	Aramark, Philadelphia, PA	$3,200.0	2,566	Contractor
2	Marriott Management Services, Washington, DC	2,663.9	2,670	Contractor
3	Gardner Merchant, Trumbull, CT	1,900.0	6,500	Contractor
4	Sodexho, Waltham, MA	1,800.0	5,145	Contractor
5	Canteen Corporation, Charlotte, NC	1,103.7	1,612	Contractor
6	U.S. Army Center of Excellence, Fort Lee, VA	1,028.2	471	Military
7	Caterair International, Bethesda, MD	1,000.0	118	Transportation
8	Naval Supply Systems, Arlington, VA	792.4	485	Military
9	Service America, Stamford, CT	725.0	1,090	Contractor
10	Walt Disney Co., Burbank, CA	700.0	350	Recreation
11	Dobbs International Services, Memphis, TN	671.0	68	Transportation
12	Army & Air Force Exchange, Dallas, TX	592.9	1,765	Military
13	Sky Chefs, Arlington, TX	469.0	31	Transportation
14	Columbia/HCA Healthcare, Nashville, TN	463.2	200	Health Care
15	New York City Board of Education, NY	385.5	1,386	Education
16	Restaura Dining Service, Phoenix, AZ	380.0	409	Contractor
17	California Dept. of Corrections, Sacramento, CA	366.8	285	Institutions
18	Daka Restaurants, Danvers, MA	350.0	770	Contractor
19	The Wood Company, Allentown, PA	310.0	301	Contractor
20	U.S.A.F Clubs Branch, San Antonio, TX	308.0	171	Military
21	Quorum Health Resources, Brentwood, TN	306.7	255	Health Care
22	U.S.A.F. Restaurants and Snack Bars, San Antonio TX	302.0	1,500	Military
23	U.S. Marine Corp., Washington, DC	289.5	78	Military
24	Beverly Enterprises, Fort Smith, AK	273.9	770	Health Care
25	Dept. of Veteran's Affairs, Washington, DC	264.4	170	Military
26	Service Master, Downer's Grove, IL	254.2	310	Contractor

(Continued)

Table 2.7 Top 50 U.S.A. Institutional Foodservice Companies *(Continued)*

1995 Rank	Company	1994 Sales in Millions	1994 Units	Segment
27	U.S.A.F. APF Food Operations, San Antonio, TX	250.5	360	Military
28	Ogden Entertainment Services, NY	236.0	110	Contractor
29	Royal Caribbean Cruise Line, Miami, FL	229.6	86	Recreation
30	Ogden Aviation Services, NY	220.0	18	Transportation
31	Federal Bureau of Prisons, Washington, DC	218.7	75	Institutions
32	Morrison Health Care, Atlanta, GA	216.1	276	Contractor
33	National Medical Enterprises, Santa Monica, CA	210.0	430	Health Care
34	Club Corp. of America, Dallas, TX	200.0	250	Contractor
35	Los Angeles Unified School District, CA	194.6	700	Education
36	U.S. Navy Club System, Washington, DC	194.0	257	Military
37	U.S. Army Community & Family Centers, Alexandria, VA	184.8	539	Military
38	United Airlines, Elk Grove Village, IL	179.1	2	Transportation
39	Florida Dept. of Corrections, Tallahassee, FL	169.6	149	Institutions
40	Daughters of Charity Health Systems, St. Louis, MO	168.0	152	Institutions
41	Sportservice, Buffalo, NY	156.0	66	Recreation
42	Chicago Public Schools, IL	154.0	600	Education
43	Texas Department of Criminal Justice, Hunstville, TX	152.9	148	Institutions
44	CA One Services, Buffalo, NY	144.0	34	Contractor
45	Cineplex Odeon, Toronto, Canada	142.0	354	Recreation
46	Universal Ogden, Seattle, WA	138.0	445	Contractor
47	Harry M. Stevens, Cranbury, NJ	138.0	20	Contractor
48	Universal Studios, FL	138.0	69	Recreation
49	U.S. Marine Corp., Quantico, VA	137.5	271	Military
50	Six Flags, Parsippany, NJ	132.5	358	Recreation

Source: Restaurants and Institutions, July 1995. Reprinted with Permission.

Table 2.8 Top 50 Management Firms

Rank 1993	Management Company Headquarters	Rooms 1994	Rooms 1993	Hotels 1994	Hotels 1993
1	Richfield Hotel Management, Denver, CO	33,500	33,217	141	141
2	Interstate Hotels Corp., Pittsburgh, PA	29,569	22,879	130	80
3	Doubletree Hotels Corp., Phoenix, AZ	21,569	24,480	81	97
4	Queens Moat Houses Plc, Romford, Essex, England	21,238	22,100	172	191
5	American General Hospitality, Dallas, TX	16,907	14,331	96	76
6	Carnival Hotels & Casinos, Miami, FL	16,000	15,000	57	56
7	Hostmark Management Group, Rolling Meadows, IL	13,636	10,800	71	51
8	Grupo Situr, Guadalajara, Mexico	13,266	13,639	50	49
9	Prime Hospitality Corp., Fairfield, NJ	12,743	13,358	87	87
10	Remington Hotel Corp., Dallas, TX	12,266	10,056	75	63
11	Winegardner & Hammons, Cincinnati, OH	12,242	12,150	58	59
12	Lane Hospitality, Northbrook, IL	11,928	6,519	60	30
13	Sage Hospitality Resources, Denver, CO	11,898	8,000	85	66
14	Columbia Sussex Corp., Fort Mitchell, KY	11,072	11,559	46	51
15	Journey's End Corp., Belleville, Canada	10,993	11,168	120	120
16	Grupo Posadas Management, Mexico City, Mexico	10,265	10,716	41	38
17	Southern Sun Hotels, Johannesburg, South Africa	10,218	9,864	60	55
18	Motels of America, Des Plaines, IL	9,967	5,679	121	82
19	H.I. Development Corp., Tampa, FL	9,912	10,898	101	105
20	Harvey Hotel Mgmt. Corp., Dallas, TX	9,616	—	35	—
21	John Q. Hammons Corp., Springfield, MO	9,398	9,304	37	39
22	Ocean Hospitalities, Boynton Beach, FL	9,382	9,275	54	53
23	CDL Hotels, Singapore	9,282	7,141	34	28
24	Servico, W. Palm Beach, FL	8,600	8,000	44	39
25	Beck Summit Hotel Mgmt. Group, Boca Raton, FL	8,550	11,900	60	75
26	Tharaldson Enterprises, Fargo, ND	8,185	6,304	135	106

(Continued)

Table 2.8 Top 50 Management Firms (*Continued*)

Rank 1993	Management Company Headquarters	Rooms 1994	Rooms 1993	Hotels 1994	Hotels 1993	Rank 1993	Management Company Headquarters	Rooms 1994	Rooms 1993	Hotels 1994	Hotels 1993
27	Tollman-Hundley Hotels, Vaalhalla, TX	8,085	8,309	39	39	39	Boyd Gaming Corp. Las Vegas, NV	5,241	4,666	10	5
28	Gencom American Hospitality, Houston, TX	7,170	—	31	—	40	Kahler Corp. Rochester, MN	4,830	4,100	21	18
29	Larken Hotels, Cedar Rapids, IA	7,075	15,000	32	65	41	Outrigger Lodging Services Encino, CA	4,789	3,500	28	19
30	CapStar Hotels, Washington, DC	6,948	6,936	46	43	42	McNeill Hospitality Corp. Memphis, TN	4,737	—	41	—
31	RFS Management Co., Memphis, TN	6,891	3,248	50	22	43	Starwood Lodging Los Angeles, CA	4,700	2,381	25	15
32	Horizon Hotels Ltd., Eatontown, NJ	6,764	3,850	36	14	44	Vista Host Inc. Houston, TX	4,693	6,474	32	44
33	Capitol Hotel Group, Rockville, MD	6,760	6,940	23	23	45	Shaner Hotel Group State College, PA	4,600	—	37	—
34	Commonwelath Hospitality Ltd., Etobicoke, Canada	6,115	7,706	30	36	46	Aztar Corp. Phoenix, AZ	4,400	4,427	3	3
35	Hotel Group, Edmonds, WA	5,808	4,997	30	31	47	Dimensions Development Natchioches, LA	4,354	—	26	—
36	Westmont Hospitality Group, Houston, TX	5,617	4,107	39	38	48	Cooper/CSS Hotel Group Memphis, TN	4,347	4,167	21	20
37	Amerihost Properties, Des Plaines, IL	5,604	5,913	53	54	49	WestCoast Hotels Seattle, WA	4,315	3,600	20	22
38	DePalma Hotel Corp., Irving, TX	5,301	4,231	30	21	50	Regency Inns Management Sioux Falls, SD	4,228	3,847	32	27

Source: Hotels, July 1995. Reprinted with permission from *DATAMATION Magazine*, July 1995 © by Cahners Publishing Company.

56

Management companies have shown the same trend for consolidation as the major chains. For comparison, a handful of years ago, the top 100 companies managed the same number of rooms as the top 50 do today.

Largest Global Consortia or Referral Groups Hotel companies search for ways to promote their properties, and can do so by working with certain competitors. **Referral groups**, which are also sometimes called **consortia**, **affiliations**, or **voluntary chains**, are a group of independent hotels that have joined together in an association, each member having satisfied a specific set of criteria. For example, Leading Hotels of the World is a group of luxury city and resort hotels. This elite group requires a very high level of service and facilities. Best Western, though it sometimes appears on chain listings instead of with referral groupings, would be considered by many to be a referral group. Referral groups are created to establish marketing advantages, like a toll-free reservations number, referral of business from one property to another, and other kinds of economies for its members, such as discounts on credit card fees and purchasing economies. Referral groups provide some of the advantages of chains but in general are much less expensive to join than chains. Referral groups tend to operate on a not-for-profit or breakeven basis. Membership in a referral group is common, and a hotel could belong to more than one group. Table 2.9 lists the top 25 referral groups worldwide, representing over two million hotel rooms.

Rating Services Rating services are sometimes confused with referral groups, but they are not the same. Hotels do not join rating services. A rating service is an independent organization that rates the quality of the hotel or restaurant. Well known rating services are Michelin, which is used extensively in Europe, Mobil, the American Automobile Association (AAA), and Zagat's. Mobil is known for its awarding of stars—the most coveted prize is a five-star rating, which is held by approximately 15 properties. AAA awards diamonds. Their top award, five diamonds, is also given to relatively few properties. Michelin uses a star system. Its highest award, three stars, is a well-respected prize among European restaurateurs. A restaurant critic's newspaper column is another widely read form of a rating service. Hospitality establishments will often advertise the awards they receive, as customers value the credibility of an independent evaluation.

Largest Travel Agencies Travel agencies, we learned earlier, serve as an important intermediary in the hospitality business, linking the customer or traveler to many different kinds of hospitality services from hotel rooms, to airline seats, to resort vacation packages. About 25 percent of all hotel business in the U.S. is booked through a travel agency, and the number is expected to grow.[6] The largest travel agency in the United States is American Express, which is double the size of the next largest competitor, Carlson Travel Network. The top U.S. travel agencies are presented in Table 2.10.

Then and Now: How the Industry is Evolving

Finally, to fill in the big picture, we look for patterns that describe how the industry is changing and trends that suggest how the industry will evolve. Much of the story is told by placing side by side the top 25 largest U.S. hotel chains in 1980 versus 1992. Five important patterns emerge that reveal the way the hospitality industry is evolving. The comparison of Tables 2.11 and 2.12 illustrates these changes.

Table 2.9 Top 25 Referral Groups Worldwide

Rank 1994	Referral Group / Headquarters	Rooms 1994	Rooms 1993	Hotels 1994	Hotels 1993
1	Utell International, London, England	1,360,000	1,360,000	6,800	6,800
2	JAL World Hotels, Tokyo, Japan	168,875	173,271	410	419
3	Lexington Services Corp., Irving, TX	102,435	74,414	758	475
4	Supranational Hotels, London, England	93,000	9,500	565	600
5	Leading Hotels of the World, New York, NY	82,000	76,000	295	277
6	Keytel SA, Barcelona, Spain	80,000	70,000	800	883
7	LRI/Grande Collection of Hotels, New York, NY	82,000	90,000	295	425
8	SRS Hotels Steigenberger, Frankfurt/Main, Germany	75,000	75,000	350	323
9	Logis de France, Paris, France	71,960	72,758	4,050	4,122
10	Golden Tulip Worldwide Hotels, Hilversum, The Netherlands	49,315	44,000	247	240
11	Hotusa-Eurostars, Barcelona, Spain	45,500	59,459	650	676
12	Travel Resources–Sterling, Irving, TX	42,914	47,234	160	178
13	Transeurope Hotels, Paris, France	35,467	60,951	578	675
14	Minotel International, Lanne, Switzerland	30,000	3,100	670	700
15	Flag International Hotels, Melbourne, Australia	29,590	27,992	495	474
16	Prima Hotels, New York, NY	29,000	30,794	495	253
17	Associated Luxury Hotels, Washington, DC	28,873	26,167	44	38
18	Robert F. Warner, New York, NY	27,886	26,752	168	152
19	Preferred Hotels Worldwide, Oakbrook Terrace, IL	24,750	28,000	105	107
20	TOP International Hotels, Dusseldorf, Germany	24,000	225,000	225	210
21	Historic Hotels of America, Washington, DC	22,140	—	115	—
22	ILA Châteaux & Hotels, Brussels, Belgium	18,495	16,902	468	392
23	Concorde Hotels Group, Paris, France	14,000	14,760	70	73
24	Summit International Hotels, Secaucus, NJ	13,699	11,554	59	46
25	Relais & Châteaux, Paris, France	13,000	13,000	406	410

Source: Hotels, July 1995. Reprinted with permission from *DATAMATION Magazine*, July 1995 © by Cahners Publishing Company.

◼ *Table 2.10* Top U.S. Travel Agencies

Sales Rank	Agency	Headquarters	Gross Sales ($ in Millions)	Gross Sales 1992	Air Sales 1991	Air Sales 1992
1	American Express	New York, NY	$6,900.0	$6,5000.0	$4,500.0	$4,200.0
2	Carlson Travel Network	Minneapolis, MN	3,400.0	3,200.0	2,200.0	2,100.0
3	Thomas Cook Travel US	Cambridge, MA	1,692.0	2,000.0	1,100.0	1,300.0
4	Rosenbluth International	Philadelphia, PA	1,538.0	1,800.0	1,000.0	1,200.0
5	US Travel	Rockville, MD	1,500.0	1,400.0	975.0	915.0
6	Liberty Travel	Ramsey, NJ	900.0	920.0	300.0	330.0
7	IVI Business Travel Int.	Northbrook, IL	884.0	911.0	575.0	660.0
8	Maritz Travel	Fenton, MO	846.0	800.0	550.0	704.0
9	Japan Travel USA	New York, NY	620.5	700.0	91.3	96.0
10	Omega World Travel	Fairfax, VA	303.0	341.0	285.0	326.6
11	Wagons-Lits Travel USA	Dublin, OH	303.5	319.0	293.5	290.0
12	Total Travel Management	Troy, MI	240.0	268.0	149.5	145.0
13	World Travel Partners	Atlanta, GA	220.0	262.0	190.0	250.0
14	Travel & Transport	Omaha, NE	230.0	258.0	207.0	232.0
15	Northwestern Travel Service	Minneapolis, MN	152.0	239.0	139.0	232.0

Source: Travel Industry Word Yearbook, Somerset R. Waters, ed. (New York: Child and Waters, 1992). Reprinted with Permission.

Note: Thomas Cook Travel U.S. was purchased by American Express subsequent to this ranking.

Segmentation of Brands

The most striking change that emerged in the decade of the eighties is a proliferation of different brands within the same chain. For example, in addition to its standard hotels, Marriott also has all-suites and resorts. Under separate brands, but still under the Marriott chain, it also has Residence Inns for longer-term stays, Courtyard Inns for the midpriced market, and Fairfield Inns, its economy lodging product. Many other companies have similarly created separate brands to capture different pieces of the market. Holiday Inns Worldwide, a familiar name to many, has four brand segments. Choice Hotels International has 7 brands. This tiering of products at different prices to capture different pieces of the market is known as **market segmentation.**

Table 2.11 The Top Lodging Chains in the USA 1980

Name of Chain	U.S. Properties		Status of Properties				Average Rate	Total Properties U.S. and Foreign		
	Number	Rooms	Company Owned	Franchise or Member	Management Contract	Other		Average % Occupancy	Number	Rooms
Holiday Inns	1,544	256,186	184	1,344	12	4*	$32.65	73.8	1,752	299,584
Best Western International	1,814	152,503	0	1,814	0	0	31.50	73.0	2,604	197,939
Ramada Inns	606	87,012	108	498	0	0	31.00	(NA)	648	95,167
Sheraton Hotels	319	74,584	17**	272	30	0	37.90	72.0	400	103,961
Hilton Hotels	200	70,845	17	152	31	0	50.27	73.3	200	70,845
Friendship Inns International	932	68,300	0	932	0	0	34.00	78.0	1,502	93,450
Howard Johnson	513	58,801	130	394	0	0	(NA)	(NA)	524	60,045
Days Inns of America	312	41,988	58	254	0	0	18.87	86.0	313	42,180
Trusthouse Forte	505	37,830	33	208	2	262*	(NA)	(NA)	548	41,592
Quality Inns International	324	37,453	23	300	1	0	(NA)	(NA)	340	39,783
Best Value Inns (BMHA)	547	31,300	0	547	0	0	18.00#	(NA)	547	31,300
Motel 6	291	30,639	291	0	0	0	11.95#	81.6	291	30,639
Hyatt Hotels	53	27,100	3	0	36	14*	(NA)	(NA)	53	27,100
Marriott Hotels	64	26,785	19	19	26	0	(NA)	80.0	70	28,600
Rodeway Inns International	143	17,294	0	143	0	0	26.23	67.0	151	18,163

Western International Hotels	23	15,300	6	0	17	0	(NA)	81.3	55	27,000
La Quinta Motor Inns	92	10,847	76	14	2	0	23.25	84.0	92	10,847
Red Carpet/Master Host Inns	89	10,749	0	89	0	0	31.00	73.0	94	11,575
Amfac Hotels and Resorts	24	10,500	24	0	0	0	(NA)	(NA)	24	10,500
Hotel Systems of America	63	8,545	1	62	2	0	26.18	68.0	64	8,895
Pick Americana Hotels	28	8,299	31	4	0	0	40.00+	72.5	35	10,866
Econo–Travel Motor Hotels	135	8,007	20	115	0	0	20.00##	68.0	135	8,007
Dunfey Hotels	20	7,780	14	0	6	0	37.90	76.0	22	8,790
Radisson Hotels	22	7,192	14	0	8	0	(NA)	(NA)	22	7,192
Stouffer Hotels	20	7,018	10	7	3	0	(NA)	(NA)	20	7,018

* Joint Ventures
# One person in room
** Includes leased properties
Two persons, one bed; excluding resort locations
+ Approximate

Source: Lodging Hospitality, August 1980. Reprinted with Permission.

Table 2.12 Top Lodging Chains in the USA 1992

Rank	U.S. Lodging Chain	U.S. Properties		Status of Properties				Foreign Properties	
		Rooms	Number of Properties	Company Owned	Franchised or Licensed	Management Contract	Other	Rooms	Number of Properties
1	**Hospitality Franchise Systems**								
	Parsippany, NJ								
	Days Inns of America	131,816	1,217	0	1,217	0	0	4,162	41
	HoJo Inns	8,934	114	0	114	0	0	332	3
	Howard Johnson	48,126	358	0	385	0	0	3,828	32
	Ramada Inns/Hotels	94,409	568	0	568	0	0	0	0
	Ramada Limited	412	7	0	7	0	0	0	0
	Total	283,697	2,291	0	2,291	0	0	8,322	76
2	**Holiday Inn Worldwide**								
	Atlanta, GA								
	Holiday Inn	255,435	1,333	0	1,230	0	*103	48,132	217
	Holiday Inn Crowne Plaza	9,346	24	0	12	0	*12	10,322	34
	Holiday Inn Express	4,708	41	0	38	0	*3	138	1
	Holiday Inn Garden Court	0	0	0	0	0	0	1,969	18
	Total	269,489	1,398	0	1,280	0	*118	60,571	270
3	**Choice Hotels International**								
	Silver Spring, MD								
	Clarion Hotels/Suites/Resorts	9,403	51	1	51	0	0	4,501	28
	Comfort Inns/Suites	67,331	764	3	764	0	0	3,712	45
	Econo Lodges	50,603	695	0	695	0	0	241	4
	Friendship Inns	6,417	134	0	134	0	0	139	3
	Quality Inns/Hotels/Suites	49,996	390	7	390	0	0	12,096	106
	Rodeway Inns	10,838	107	1	107	0	0	195	1
	Sleep Inns	1,365	17	0	17	0	0	372	4
	Total	195,953	2,158	12	2,158	0	0	21,256	191

	Company / Property								
4	**Best Western International**								
	Phoenix, AZ								
	Best Western	1,800	165,000	0	0	0	1,800	101,000	1,500
	Total	1,800	165,000	0	0	0	1,800	101,000	1,500
5	**Marriott Corporation**								
	Washington, DC								
	Courtyard by Marriott	29,000	200	53	7	140	0	0	0
	Fairfield Inn	10,000	99	30	19	50	0	0	0
	Marriott Hotels/Resorts/Suites	90,000	212	25	60	127	0	10,000	24
	Residence Inns	21,000	179	29	67	83	0	0	0
	Total	150,000	690	137	153	400	0	10,000	24
6	**Hilton Hotels Corporation**								
	Beverly Hills, CA								
	Conrad Hotels	0	0	0	0	0	0	2,920	8
	Hilton Garden Inns	658	4	0	2	2	0	0	0
	Hilton Hotels	46,097	60	35	0	25	0	0	0
	Hilton Inns	48,171	195	0	195	0	0	0	0
	Hilton Suites	1,246	6	5	1	0	0	0	0
	Total	96,172	265	40	198	27	0	2,920	8
7	**ITT Sheraton**								
	Boston, MA								
	Sheraton Hotels & Resorts	59,466	151	7	105	*39	0	45,179	132
	Sheraton Inns	23,277	126	0	125	*1	0	1,836	10
	Sheraton Suites	994	4	1	2	*1	0	0	0
	Total	83,737	281	8	232	41	0	47,015	142
8	**Motel 6**								
	Dallas, TX								
	Motel 6	76,145	671	665	0	6	0	0	0
	Total	76,145	671	665	0	6	0	0	0

(Continued)

Table 2.12 Top Lodging Chains in the USA 1992 (*Continued*)

Rank	U.S. Lodging Chain	U.S. Properties		Status of Properties				Foreign Properties	
		Rooms	Number of Properties	Company Owned	Franchised or Licensed	Management Contract	Other	Rooms	Number of Properties
9	**The Promus Companies, Inc.**								
	Memphis, TN								
	Embassy Suites	25.149	102	15	45	19	**23	322	1
	Harrah's	4.542	5	0	0	0	5	0	0
	Hampton Inn	39.042	314	15	277	3	**19	0	0
	Homewood Suites	2.520	23	8	15	0	0	0	0
	Total	71,253	444	38	337	22	47	322	1
10	**Super 8 Enterprises, Inc.**								
	Aberdeen, SD								
	Super 8 Motels	57,806	887	48	839	0	0	605	11
	Total	57,806	887	48	839	0	0	605	11
11	**Hyatt Hotels Corporation**								
	Chicago, IL								
	Hyatt Hotels	55,557	103	***0	0	103	0	20286	56
	Total	55,557	103	0	0	103	0	20286	56
12	**Carlson Hospitality Group, Inc**								
	Minneapolis, MN								
	Colony Hotels & Resorts	6,901	40	0	0	23	****17	614	3
	Country Lodging by Carlson	2,677	31	0	30	0	****1	0	0
	Radisson Hotels International	42,541	171	0	148	23	0	17,118	73
	Total	52,119	242	0	178	48	18	17,732	76

	C1	C2	C3	C4	C5	C6	C7	C8
13 Forte Hotels, Inc. *El Cajon, CA*								
Travelodge	39,050	500	50	500	75	**125	0	0
Forte Hotels	0	0	0	0	0	0	40,190	353
Total	39,050	500	50	500	75	125	40,190	353
14 La Quinta Motor Inns, Inc. *San Antonio, TX*								
La Quinta Inns	27,057	213	210	3	0	0	0	0
Total	27,057	213	210	3	0	0	0	0
15 Red Roof Inns *Columbus, OH*								
Red Roof Inns	23,261	290	290	0	0	0	0	0
Total	23,261	290	290	0	0	0	0	0
16 R&B Realty Group *Los Angeles, CA*								
Oakwood Corporate Apartments	23,000	40	28	0	12	0	0	0
Total	23,000	40	28	0	12	0	0	0
17 Hospitality International *Atlanta, GA*								
Downtowner	191	2	0	2	0	0	0	0
Master Hosts Inns/Resorts	2,643	21	0	21	0	0	170	2
Passport Inns	1,266	22	0	22	0	0	0	0
Red Carpet Inn	8,097	112	0	112	0	0	123	2
Scottish Inns	8,309	148	0	148	0	0	37	1
Total	20,506	305	0	305	0	0	330	5
18 Aoki Corporation *Seattle, WA*								
Westin Hotels and Resorts	20,439	37	14	0	23	0	0	0
Caesar Park Hotels	0	0	0	0	0	0	417	3
Camino Real	0	0	0	0	0	0	3,448	10
Total	20,439	37	14	0	23	0	3,865	13

(Continued)

Table 2.12 Top Lodging Chains in the USA 1992 (Continued)

Rank	U.S. Lodging Chain	U.S. Properties		Status of Properties				Foreign Properties	
		Rooms	Number of Properties	Company Owned	Franchised or Licensed	Management Contract	Other	Rooms	Number of Properties
19	**Economy Lodging Systems**								
	Cleveland, OH								
	Arborgate Inn	810	9	0	6	3	0	0	0
	Knights Court	1,400	11	0	11	11	0	0	0
	Knights Inn	17,140	156	1	156	53	0	0	0
	Knights Stop	150	3	0	3	0	0	0	0
	Total	19,500	179	1	176	67	0	0	0
20	**Preferred Hotels**								
	Oakbrook Terrace, IL								
	Preferred Hotels	10,019	66	0	0	0	66	11,726	41
	Total	10,019	66	0	0	0	66	11,726	41
21	**Doubletree Hotels Corporation**								
	Phoenix, AZ								
	Doubletree Club Hotel	2,939	16	0	7	9	0	0	0
	Doubletree Hotel	12,784	40	0	2	38	0	0	0
	Total	15,723	56	0	9	47	0	0	0
22	**Wharf Holdings Ltd.**								
	Hampton, NH								
	Omni Hotels	14,352	38	6	13	25	0	3,042	7
	Total	14,352	38	6	13	25	0	3,042	7

23	**Stouffer Hotels & Resorts**							
	Solon, OH							
	Stouffer Hotels & Resorts	13,685	33	24	0	9	0	0
	Stouffer Presidente Hotels/Resorts	0	0	0	0	0	2061	7
	Total	13,685	33	24	0	9	2061	7
24	**Red Lion Hotels & Inns**							
	Vancouver, WA							
	Red Lion Hotels & Inns	13,632	52	*40	0	12	0	0
	Total	13,632	52	*40	0	12	0	0
25	**Ramada International Hotels & Resorts**							
	Coral Gables, FL							
	Ramada Int. Hotels & Resorts	9,703	26	0	7	19	0	24,863	95
	Total	9,703	26	0	7	19	0	24,863	95

* Managed or leased properties
** Joint Ventures
*** Partial Ownership in some hotels
**** Affiliates of Colony Hotels & Resorts and Country Lodging by Carlson

Source: Lodging Hospitality, July 1992. Reprinted with Permission.

Consolidation Through Merger and Acquisition

Many hotel chains that appeared on the list in 1980 were merged with or acquired by other hotel companies. Friendship Inns International, Quality Inns, and Econo-Travel Motor Hotels, later Econo Lodge, the sixth, 10th, and 22nd largest companies in 1980, along with several other brands, are now part of Choice Hotels International, the third largest company in 1992. Rodeway Inns changed hands several times before also becoming part of Choice. Ramada and Howard Johnson, the third and seventh largest companies in 1980, are now part of a company formed in the early 1990s, Hospitality Franchise Systems (HFS). Days Inn, which appeared on the 1980 list as the eighth largest company, was also purchased by Hospitality Franchise Systems in 1992, effectively making the trio of companies the largest number of hotel rooms controlled by one parent. Super 8 was acquired in March of 1993, further assuring the first place slot for HFS. RedCarpet/Master Host Inns are now part of Hospitality International, Inc., which also includes Passport and Scottish Inns. These changes are only part of the story. International investors tell the rest. Figure 2.3 graphically illustrates how two large parent companies acquired several hotel brands. Tables 2.13 and 2.14, which follow the chapter summary, chronicle merger and acquisition activity.

Foreign Investment in the United States

In the late 1980s and early 1990s many hotel companies were purchased by foreign investors. Some specific examples illustrate the point. Motel 6 was acquired by Accor, a French hotel company. Stouffer Hotels was purchased by Nestle, a Swiss-based company; Nestle then sold Stouffers in 1993 to the Cheng family in Hong Kong. Travelodge was purchased by Trusthouse Forte, a British parent. Doubletree became part of the Canadian Pacific chain. The Aoki Corporation of Japan purchased Westin, which was known as Western International in 1980. This chain was sold again in 1995 to a group funded by Starwood Capital, Goldman, Sachs & Co., and Nomura Asset Capital Corporation. The selling price? $537 million. Holiday Inn was sold in 1987 to Bass PLC. Omni Hotels, once owned by Aer Lingus, Ireland, was purchased by World International Holdings, Hong Kong Ramada Renaissance, renamed simply Renaissance in 1993, is now owned by NewWorld Hotels, Hong Kong. These are just some of the important foreign investments.

Growth Overseas

The aggregate number of hotel rooms in foreign countries in 1980 versus 1992 for the top 25 U.S. hotel chains increased almost fivefold. In 1980, there were approximately 80,000 rooms abroad versus approximately 376,000 rooms in 1992. Though some of this growth should be attributed to a merger with a foreign partner, as in the case of Forte Hotels, several other companies such as Best Western (which is a consortium where properties are independently owned), Marriott, Sheraton, Choice's Quality Inns, Hyatt, and Stouffer, showed dramatic growth in foreign hotel rooms from 1980 to 1992.

Restructuring of Ownership: Less Owned, More Managed

A major shift in the ownership structure of hotels occurred in the 1980s and early 1990s. Though some companies, like Motel 6, Red Roof, and La Quinta, continue to own and operate all or nearly all of their hotel properties, others like Holiday Inns, Ramada, Sheraton, and Howard Johnson, which had a number of company-owned properties in 1980, no longer own any! Instead, they have retained only management contracts and/or a franchising relationship with a third party. (A more

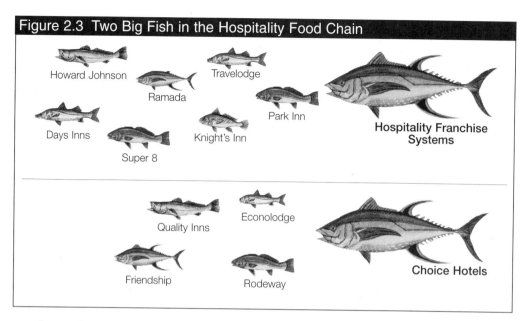

Figure 2.3 Two Big Fish in the Hospitality Food Chain

Howard Johnson

Travelodge

Ramada

Park Inn

Days Inns

Knight's Inn

Super 8

Hospitality Franchise Systems

Quality Inns

Econolodge

Friendship

Rodeway

Choice Hotels

complete explanation of the nature of franchising, management contracts, and hotel ownership and development is presented in later chapters.)

Other Trends

In addition to continued growth and consolidation, the future is likely to reveal other trends. For example, improved transportation alternatives, the continued deregulation of the airlines, and the opening of new tourist destinations overseas, particularly in Eastern Europe, the former Soviet Union countries, Southeast Asia, and, in the longer term, South America, will mean that more people will likely travel to more places. Growth in some specific types of travelers, new travelers from the countries just noted, the mobile elderly, two-career couples, and two-career families will be particularly strong.

There will be ongoing applications of computer technologies—for such tasks as yield management (a technique that tries to allocate the right type of room to the right customer at the right price to maximize hotel room revenue), for shrinking transaction time when making reservations, and for expediting check-in and check-out; but hoteliers will continue to stress not losing sight of the **high-touch** as opposed to **high-tech** needs of the customer.

Some would argue that the middle price range of hotels is being squeezed out and that the two ends of the price spectrum, luxury and economy, will eat away at the middle. Certain areas of hospitality, like fast food with a health-conscious slant, new kinds of leisure alternatives (for example, adventure trips), institutional feeding, lifecare, casinos, and retirement facilities will show particular promise as growth sectors.

Hotel companies will be faced increasingly with an employee base with diverse cultural origins, especially in entry-level positions. Managers therefore increasingly will need the human relations skills to manage diversity, and will need the ability to speak several languages. Managers who themselves are minorities will be increasingly in demand.

After the Big Picture, It's On to the Details

A Hotel Is a Place that Gives Free Soap, by Shelly Berman

Dear Maid,

Please do not leave any more of those little bars of soap in my bathroom since I have brought my own bath-size Dial. Please remove the 6 unopened little bars from the shelf under the medicine chest and another three in the shower soap dish. They are in my way. Thank you.

S. Berman

Dear Room 635,

I am not your regular maid she will be back tomorrow (Thurs) from her day off. I took the 3 hotel soaps out of the shower soap dish as you requested. The 6 bars on your shelf I took out of your way and put on top of your Kleenex dispenser in case you should change your mind. This leaves only the 3 bars I left today which my instructions from the management is to leave 3 soaps daily I hope this is satisfactory. If anything else comes up please call Mrs. Corum in the linen room.

Kathy (relief maid)

Dear Maid (I hope you are my regular maid),

Apparently Kathy did not tell you about my note to her concerning the little bars of soap. When I got back to my room this evening I found you had added 3 little Camays to the shelf under my medicine cabinet. I am going to be here in the hotel for two weeks and have brought my own bath-size Dial so I won't need those 6 little Camays which are now on the shelf. They are in my way when shaving, brushing teeth, etc. Please remove them.

S. Berman

Dear Mr. Berman,

My day off was last Wed so the relief maid left 3 hotel soaps which we are instructed by management. I took the 6 soaps which were in your way on the shelf and put them in the soap dish where your Dial was. I put the Dial in the medicine cabinet for your convenience. I didn't remove the 3 complimentary soaps which are always placed inside the medicine cabinet for all new check-ins and which you did not object to when you checked in last Monday. Also I did place 3 hotel soaps on your shelf per my instructions from the management since you left no instructions to the contrary. Please let me know if I can be of further assistance or call the linen room her name is Mrs. Korm. Have a pleasant stay.

Your regular maid, Dotty

Dear Mr. Berman,

The assistant manager, Mr. Kensedder, informed me this a.m. that you called him last evening and said you were unhappy with your maid service. I have assigned a new girl to your room. I hope you will accept my apologies for any past inconvenience. If you have any future complaints please contact me so I

can give it my personal attention. Call extension 1108 between 8:00 a.m. and
5:00 p.m. Thank you.

Elaine Carmen, Housekeeper

Dear Miss Carmen,

It is impossible to contact you by phone since I leave the hotel for business at 7:45 a.m. and don't get back before 5:30 or 6:00 p.m. That's the reason I called Mr. Kensedder last night. You were already off duty. I only asked Mr. Kensedder if he could do anything about those little bars of soap. I did not want a new maid. The new maid you assigned me must have thought I was a new check-in today, since she left me another 3 bars of hotel soap in my medicine cabinet along with her regular delivery of 3 bars on the bathroom shelf. In just 5 days I have accumulated 24 little bars of soap. I'm beginning to dread the next 9 days. Why are you doing this to me?

S. Berman

Dear Mr Berman,
Your maid, Kathy, has been instructed to stop delivering soap to your room
and remove the extra soaps. If I can be of further assistance, please call
extension 1108 between 8:00 a.m. and 5:00 p.m. Thank you.

Elaine Carmen, Housekeeper

Dear Mr. Kensedder,

My bath-size Dial is missing. Every bar of soap was taken from my room including my own bath-size Dial. I came in late last night and had to call the bellhop to bring me a bar of soap so I could take a shower. He brought me 4 little Cashmere Bouquets.

S. Berman

Dear Mr. Berman

I have informed our Housekeeper, Elaine Carmen, of your soap problem. I cannot understand why there was no soap in your room since our maids are instructed to leave 3 bars of soap each time they service a room. The situation will be rectified immediately. Please accept my apologies for the inconvenience. If you prefer Cashmere Bouquet to Camay, please contact Mrs. Karmin on extension 1108. Thank you.

Martin L. Kensedder, Assistant Manager

Dear Mrs. Carmen,

Who the hell left 54 little bars of Camay in my room? I came in last night and found 54 little bars of soap. I don't want 54 little bars of Camay. I want my 1 damn bar of bath-size Dial. Do you realize I have 58 bars of soap in here? All I want is my bath-size Dial. Give me back my bath-size Dial.

S. Berman

Dear Mr. Berman,
You complained of too much soap in your room so I had them removed. Then
you complained to Mr. Kensedder that all your soap was missing so I person-
ally returned them: the 24 Camays which had been taken and the 3 Camays
you are supposed to receive daily. I don't know anything about the 4

Cashmere Bouquets. Obviously your maid Kathy did not know I had returned your soaps so she also brought 24 Camays plus the 3 daily Camays. I don't know where you got the idea that this hotel issues bath-size Dial. I was able to locate some hotel-size bath-size Ivory which I left in your room. We are doing our best here to satisfy you.

Elaine Carmen, Housekeeper

Dear Mrs. Carmen,

Just a short note to bring you up-to-date on my latest soap inventory. As of today I possess:

- On shelf under medicine cabinet: 18 Camays in 4 stacks of 4 and 1 stack of 2.
- On Kleenex dispenser: 11 Camays in 2 stacks of 4 and 1 stack of 3.
- On bedroom dresser: 1 stack of 3 Cashmere Bouquet, 1 stack of 4 hotel-size bath-size Ivory, 8 Camays in 2 stacks of 4.
- Inside medicine cabinet: 14 Camay in 3 stacks of 4 and 1 stack of 2.
- In shower soap dish: 6 Camay (very moist).
- On northeast corner of tub: 1 Cashmere Bouquet (slightly used).
- On northwest corner of tub: 6 Camay in 2 stacks of 3.

Please ask Kathy when she services my room to make sure the stacks are neatly piled and dusted. Also, please advise her that stacks of more than 4 have a tendency to tip. May I suggest the bedroom window sill is not in use and will make an excellent spot for future soap deliveries. One more item. I have purchased another bar of bath-size Dial which I am keeping in the hotel vault in order to avoid future misunderstandings.

S. Berman

Summary

The hospitality industry is a vast one. The five key components of hospitality lodging, foodservice, entertainment, travel distribution channels, and transportation all have various subcategories. These various businesses all revolve around the need of a traveler away from home. The structure of the industry includes chain and independent organizations, management companies, and franchise companies. Referral groups, rating services, and travel agents also play an important role in the hospitality business. The dynamics of the hotel industry have changed dramatically in the last decades. Mergers and acquisitions, foreign investment, segmentation of brands, growth overseas, and a shift in ownership have all emerged.

Looking at the big picture of the hospitality industry also includes understanding supply and demand, and how the industry is different from and the same as other businesses. This familiarity will help establish a keen grasp of how the industry has and will evolve. A true connoisseur of the art of hospitality management, however, must study the details. Details follow.

Discussion Questions

1. Outline the key categories of businesses that make up the hospitality industry. Offer as many specific examples for each category as you can.

2. How is the hospitality industry distinguishable from other businesses? Why is it the same?

Table 2.13 Twelve Years of Acquisition Acitvity of Hotel Companies (1984–1995)

Year	Company	$	Seller	Buyer	Comments
1984	American Motor Inns	$242.5 million	American Motor Inns, USA	Prime Motor Inns, USA	
1994	Caesars World, Inc.	$1.7 billion	Caesars World, Inc., USA	ITT Corp., USA	Sale pending; 1,500-room Caesar's Palace in Las Vegas, 641-room Caesar's Atlantic City casino & hotel, 440-room resort casino in Lake Tahoe and a joint agreement with Hilton Hotels and Circus Circus to operate casino in Windsor, Ontario
1988	Canadian National Hotels	$203.7 million	Canadian government, Canada	Canadian Pacific Hotels Corp, Canada	9 hotels
1985	Ciga Hotels S.p.A	$83 million	Orazio Bagnasco, Italy	Fimpar SpA, holding company for Aga Khan, Italy	Aga Khan completed his acquisition of control of Ciga Hotels by buying control of Fimpar S.p.A, a holding company that owned 50.03% stake in Ciga.
1994	Ciga Hotels S.p.A	N/A	Fimpar SpA, holding company for Aga Khan, Italy	ITT Sheraton, USA	21 luxury hotels and 8 resorts; ITT Sheraton owns 70.32% of Ciga as of March 1995
1987	Copthorne	$30 million	British Caledonian Airways, England	Air Lingus, Ireland	11 hotels
1994	Country Hearth Inns	N/A	Lodge Keeper Group, USA	Buckhead America Corp., USA	Franchise rights of six properties. The two companies will create a joint venture to develop new properties of Country Hearth.

Continued

Table 2.13 Twelve Years of Acquisition Acitvity of Hotel Companies (1984–1995) (*Continued*)

Year	Company	$	Seller	Buyer	Comments
1990	Crest Hotels	$300 million	Bass PLC, England	Trusthouse Forte, England	43 hotels, 4,753 rooms
1994	Colony Hotels & Resorts	$1–3 million (estimate)	Carlson Hospitality Group, USA	Interstate Hotels Corp., USA	Acquisition of business operation only; Interstate Hotels is one of the largest hospitality management companies.
1984	Days Inns	$615 million	Day Family, USA	Reliance Capital Group, USA	285 hotels
1989	Days Inns	$765 million	Reliance Capital Group, USA	Tollman-Hundley Hotels, USA	900+ hotels, 117,000 rooms
1992	Days Inns	$250 million	Tollman-Hundley Hotels, USA	Blackstone Capital Partners LP (Hospitality Franchise Systems), USA	Blackstone formed Hospitality Franchised Systems; The acquisition consisted of franchise system of 1,352 hotels.
1994	Fairmont Hotels	N/A	Fairmont Hotels, USA	Prince Al-Walid Bin Talal Bin Abdulaziz Al Saud, Saudi Arabia	The prince became a 50% partner in Fairmont Hotel Management Corp. and in the Dallas, New Orleans, and San Francisco Fairmont properties. Eventually the prince will have also 50% ownership at the other two Fairmont hotels in San Jose, CA, and Chicago, IL.
1989	Friendship Inns International	N/A	Friendship Inns / Al Olshan, USA	Econo Lodges of America, USA	Franchise rights of 129 properties in North America
1994	Four Seasons • Regent Hotels & Resorts	$122.4 million	Four Seasons Regent Hotels & Resorts, Canada	Prince Al-Walid Bin Talal Bin Abdulaziz Al	25% interest in the company (and 25% of the personal holdings of chairman Isadore Sharp for

Year	Company	Price			
				Saud, Saudi Arabia	$16.28 a share); Isadore Sharp continues to control the company with 65% shares. The prince is also the owner of 50% of Fairmont Hotels and 24% of Euro Disney.
1990	Econo Lodges of America/Friendship Inns	$60 million	New Image Realty Inc. (Econo Lodge), USA	Manor Care Inc. (Choice Hotels International), USA	52,000 rooms (Quality International changes name to Choice Hotels in 1990); 615 Econo Lodges franchise hotels in North America and 85 Friendship Inns franchises
1990	Embassy Hotels	$331 million	Allied Lyons PLC, England	Jarvis Hotels Ltd., England	3,150 rooms
1992	Guest Quarters	N/A	Beacon Company, USA	General Electric Capital Corp., USA	38 hotels
1986	Hilton International	$980 million	Transworld Corp. (TWA), USA	UAL Inc.(United Airlines), USA	
1987	Hilton International	$1.07 billion	Allegis (United Airlines), USA	Ladbroke, England	142 hotels (including the Vista International brand name)
1987	Holiday Inn International (International Division)	$475 million	Holiday Corp., USA	Bass PLC, England	Assets in 200 Holiday Inn International and 13 USA Holiday Inn
1989	Holiday Inn Hotels Worldwide	$2.23 billion (including the assumption of $2.1 billion in debt)	Holiday Corp., USA	Bass PLC, England	Ownership of 55 hotels owned by Holiday and the control of another 1,400 hotels that Holiday Inn operates in North America through franchise agreements, management contracts and joint ventures
1985	Howard Johnson	$314 million (including the assumption of $138 million in debt)	Imperial Group, England	Marriott Corp., USA	Lodging and restaurants assets

(Continued)

Table 2.13 Twelve Years of Acquisition Acitvity of Hotel Companies (1984–1995) *(Continued)*

Year	Company	$	Seller	Buyer	Comments
1985	Howard Johnson	$235 million	Marriott Corp., USA	Prime Motor Inns, USA	125 hotels and motor lodges and franchise system
1990	Howard Johnson & Ramada Inc.	$170 million	Prime Motor Inns, USA	Blackstone Capital Partners (Hospitality Franchise Systems), USA	604 Ramada franchises; 557 HJ franchises
1988	Inter-Continental Hotels	$2.15 billion	Grand Metropolitan PLC, England	Seibu / Saison Group, Japan	100 hotels with 37,000 rooms
1989	Inter-Continental Hotels	$500 million	Seibu / Saison Group, Japan	Scandinavian Airlines System (SAS), Sweden	SAS bought 40% equity stake; SAS & Saiso will jointly manage Iter-Continental; SAS owns also 22 SAS International hotels.
1992	Inter-Continental Hotels	N/A	Scandinavian Airlines System (SAS), Sweden	Seibu / Saison Group, Japan	Saison bought back the 40% stakethat SAS had in Inter-Continental.
1995	Knights Inn	$15 million	Knights Lodging Inc., USA	Hospitality Franchise Systems, USA	180 properties (about 16,000 guest rooms) in 29 states and Canada. HFS acquired the rights to the franchise name as well as the existing Knights Inn franchise contracts.
1987	Melia Hotels	9.5 billion ptas.	Melia, Spain	Sol, Spain	5,340 rooms
1994	Meridien Hotels	$360 million	Air France, France	Forte PLC, England	Acquisition of Air France's 57 controlling stake; 54 hotels in 34 countries

Year	Hotel	Price			
1990	Met Hotels (Doubletree & Compri)	$62.6 million	Metropolitan Life, USA	Canadian Pacific, Canada	28,000 rooms; Canadian Pacific acquired 80% of Met Hotels from Met Life
1993	Metro Hotels	N/A	Metro Hotels, USA	The Continental Cos. (TCC), USA	15 properties
1984	Motel 6	$565 million	City Investing Co., USA	Kohlberg, Kravis, Roberts & Co., USA	
1990	Motel 6	$1.3 billion	Kohlberg, Kravis, Roberts & Co, USA	Accor, France	63,765 rooms
1988	Omni Hotels	$135 million	Aer Lingus, Ireland	World International Holdings and Wharf Holdings (both controlled by family of Sir Y.K. Pao, Hong Kong)	39 hotels total (12 franchised), Omni Hotels became a division of Wharf Hotel Investment, a subsidiary of Wharf Holdings.
1993	Pannonia	$57 million	Hungarian government, Hungary	Accor, France	Accor bought 51% of Pannonia; 25 hotels with 4,000 rooms.
1993	Park Inns	N/A	Park Inn International Hotel Group, USA	Blackstone Capital Partners (Hospitality Franchise Systems), USA	Franchise rights in the USA and Canada; 61 properties; Brands include Park Inn, Park Inn Limited, Park Inn Club & Breakfast, Park Plaza and Park Inn Suites; Park Inn International retained the rights to the Park Inn name in the rest of the world.
1993	Penta Hotels	N/A	Lufthansa Airlines, Germany	Ramada International (New World Development—Cheng Family), Hong Kong	49% purchased; Lufthansa retained 51% control but Ramada International took over management and operation of all Penta properties.

(Continued)

Table 2.13 Twelve Years of Acquisition Acitvity of Hotel Companies (1984–1995) (Continued)

Year	Company	$	Seller	Buyer	Comments
1988	Ramada Inc.	$91 million	Ramada, Inc., USA	BAA PLC, England	Ramada International & Ramada Renaissance Worldwide
1989	Ramada Inc.	$540 million	BAA PLC, England	New World Development (Cheng Family), Hong Kong	825 hotels; Prime Motor participated in the acquisition with a $180 million investment for U.S.A. operation & franchised system; New World retained Ramada's Renaissance & International properties; New firm formed (Aztar) to own & operate the gaming hotels
1989	Ramada Inc.	$180 million	New World Hotels Holdings, Hong Kong	Prime Motor Inns, USA	Prime bought the franchise rights for Ramada USA and Rodeway Inns; this acquisition was part of the above deal.
1990	Ramada Inc. & Howard Johnson	$170 million	Prime Motor Inns, USA (filed bankruptcy)	Blackstone Group (Hospitality Franchise Systems), USA	604 Ramada franchises; 557 Howard Johnson franchises
1984	Red Lions Inns Inc.	$600 million	Red Lions Inns Inc., USA	Kohlberg, Kravis, Roberts & Co. (and three other investment concerns), USA	52 motels
1993	Red Roof Inns	$620 million	Red Roof Inns, Barbara Trueman, Ohio, USA	Morgan Stanley Group Inc., USA	No franchises. All properties owned; 210 motels

Year	Name	Amount	Seller	Buyer	Notes
1991	Regal Inns and Affordable Inns	$100 million (estimate)	Tollman-Hundley Co., USA	Accor, France	5513 rooms; will become Motel 6es
1992	Regent Hotels International	$122 million	Hotel Investment Corp.	Four Seasons Hotels, Canada	15 hotels (some under construction at deal time)
1987	Residence Inn	$51.4 million	Holiday Corp., USA	Marriott, USA	Marriott purchases Holiday's 50% share; name was changed to Residence Inn By Marriott.
1988	Resorts International	$231.6 million	Resorts International. (major shareholder was Donald Trump), USA	Merv Griffin Group, USA	
1993	Resthotel Primevere & Resthotel Saphir	$10 million	Inovest, France	Manor Care Inc. (Choice Hotels International), USA	110 two- and three-star hotels in France; Choice expects to rebrand the hotels as Comfort and Quality Inns.
1995	Ritz–Carlton Hotel Co.	$200 million	Ritz–Carlton Hotel Co., USA	Marriott International, Crescent Real Estate Trust and Fred Malek, USA	49% of the company; the investors have the option to buy the balance of the luxury hotel company over the next few years; the Ritz-Carlton, of which 31 hotels would retain its name and be operated as a separate company; sale pending.
1985	Rodeway Inns	$13 million	Rodeway Inns International, USA	Ladbroke PLC, England	139 franchises
1987	Rodeway Inns	N/A	Ladbroke PLC, England	Ramada, USA	161 economy hotels
1990	Rodeway Inns	$14.9 million	Prime Motor Inns, USA	Manor Care (Choice Hotels International), USA	Franchise system purchased: 16,662 rooms

(Continued)

Table 2.13 Twelve Years of Acquisition Acitvity of Hotel Companies (1984–1995) *(Continued)*

Year	Company	$	Seller	Buyer	Comments
1989	Sixpence Inns	$200 million	Sixpence Inns of America, USA	Motel 6 LP, USA	46 motels
1993	Super 8	$125 million	Super 8 Enterprises Inc., USA	Blackstone Capital Partners (Hospitality Franchise Systems), USA	954 properties
1993	Stouffer Hotels & Resorts	$1.5 billion (estimate)	Nestle S.A., Switzerland	New World Development (Cheng Family), Hong Kong	40 hotels; New World Development named Renaissance Hotels International Inc. the hotel group of Renaissance, Stouffer and Ramada International hotels. Nestle S.A. bought Stouffer Hotels as part of a total acquisition of the Stouffer company in 1973.
1990	Tourist Hotel Group	$43 million	New Zealand Government, New Zealand	Southern Pacific Hotel Corp., Ausatralia	1,400 rooms
1994	Villager Lodge Franchise System	N/A	Villager Franchise Systems, USA	Blackstone Capital Partners (Hospitality Franchise Systems), USA	21 franchise agreements with 2,400 extended–stay economy rooms.
1988	Wellesley Inns and other hotels	$87 million	Wellesley Group, USA	Prime Motor Inns, USA	9 Budget Inns, 9 Wellesley Inns, and one Days Inn
1987	Westin Hotels and Resorts	$1.35 billion	Allegis (United Airlines), USA	Aoki Corp., Japan & Bass Group, USA	61 properties with 33,000 rooms in 10 countries; Eventually Aoki bought all of Westin.

Year	Asset	Price	Seller	Buyer	Description
1994	Westin Hotels & Resorts	$537 million in cash and the assumption of debt	Aoki Corp., Japan	Starwood Capital Group L.P., Goldman, Sachs & Co. and Edward Thomas Cos., USA	Aoki will retain interests in 9 U.S. and Canadian hotels. Westin will manage those properties, will license the Westin trademark in Asia and will own the trademark in the rest of world. The Westin chain consists of 80 hotels with 40,000 rooms.
1994	Winthrop Hotel & Resorts – Management contracts	N/A	Winthrop Hotels & Resorts (subsidiary of Winthrop Financial Associates), USA	Interstate Hotels Corp., USA	Seven management contracts for upscale properties in New England; Winthrop Financial Associates decided to dispose their hotel management operations.

■■■■■■ *Table 2.14* Merger and Joint Venture Activity of Hotel Companies

Year	Companies Involved	New Company	Comments
1991	Hostmark International, USA and The Management Group, USA	Hostmark Management Group	Merger of two management companies; 65 management contracts of budget and full service hotels
1992	Forte PLC, England and Agip, Italy		50-50 joint venture; Forte run 18 Agips in Italy under Forte brands
1992	Fisher Hotels Group, USA, and Paramount Hotels Corp., USA	Allied Hospitality Group	Merger
1992	Beck Hospitality Inc., USA, and Summit Hotel Management, USA	Beck Summit Hotel Management Group	Merger
1993	Journey's End Corp., Canada, and Choice Hotels International, USA	Choice Hotels Canada Inc. (a newly formed company)	50-50 joint venture; 175 properties (121 managed by Journey's End and 54 Choice locations); all Journey's End properties reflagged under one of choice brands; the new company is the largest lodging chain in Canada
1993/4	Doubletree Hotels (owners are Canadian Pacific & Met Life), USA, and Guest Quarters Suite Hotels (owned by General Electric), USA	Doubletree Hotels (former Guest Quarters hotels named Guest Quarters by Doubletree Hotels)	Merger; the merger involves 29 Guest quarters properties, 11 properties owned by Guest quarters under other brand names, and 57 Doubletree properties.
1993	Riu Hotel, Spain, and Iberotel (part of TUI travel group), Germany	Riu Hotel	Merger; the two companies are considered Spain's largest vacation hotel specialists; total of 44 properties with 21,000 beds.

3. Explain the components of supply and demand in the hotel and in the restaurant business.

4. What "big picture" snapshots describe the size and scope of the hospitality business? For example, how important are the largest hotel chains?

5. What is an independent? A chain? A management company? A consortium or affiliation? A rating service? Give specific examples of each.

6. How is the industry evolving? What patterns can you note by comparing the largest chain hotels in 1980 and in the 1990s?

7. When you consider the historic link between transportation and lodging and restaurants, why do your think a tire company, Michelin, and a oil company, Mobil, and a road service company, AAA, became important "raters" of hospitality?

8. What organizations, private and public, do you think were involved in the design and construction of the Chunnel? What segments of the hospitality industry benefit from this new way to cross the English Channel? Why?

9. What is average daily rate? Turnover? Occupancy rate? Average check? Why are these calculations important to hospitality providers?

10. What is market segmentation? Provide examples.

11. Ludwig Mies van der Rohe, a famous architect, said of design, "God is in the details." As you review the vignette box "Free Soap," why is the quotation applicable to the story presented here?

Assignment

Find an advertisement from a hospitality company that includes mention of an independent rating service's award or comment. Why do hospitality companies make this mention? Why is this mention particularly valuable in a word–of–mouth business? Do all rating services carry the same clout? Why or why not? Are *you* influenced by the rating?

End Notes

[1] Ludwig Mies van der Rohe, from *And I Quote*, edited by Ashton Applewhite, William Evans III, and Andrew Frothingham (New York: St. Martin Press, 1992), 221.

[2] Robert W. McIntosh, Charles R. Goeldner, *Tourism: Principles, Practices, Philosophies* (New York: John Wiley & Sons, 1984), pp. 171–172.

[3] Pannell Kerr Forster, *Trends in the Hotel Industry* U.S. edition. (Houston, Texas: 1991).

[4] Somerset R. Waters, ed. *Travel Industry World Yearbook* (New York: Child and Waters, 1994–95). Data also from the World Travel and Tourism Council.

[5] Timothy N. Troy, "Franchisors Face Hot Race," *Hotel and Motel Management* (August 1992), 1.

[6] Toni Giovanetti, *Hotel Business*, 2 (12) (21 June–6 July 1993).

Chapter Three

"People don't care how much you know until they know how much you care."

Leonard Schlesinger [1]

The Hospitality Business is a Service Business ❧

When you finish this chapter, you should:

1. Understand what "service" is.

2. Be able to explain why service is a process, not a series of independent functions.

3. Be able to identify and sequence the links of the service-profit chain.

4. Understand why loyal, lifelong customers are valuable, and why they are more profitable over time.

5. Know what is meant by "managing the customer's moments of truth."

6. Be able to identify each of the three points of the service triangle and explain their respective relationships with each other and with the customer or guest.

7. Know the criteria for successful operation of unconditional service guarantees.

8. Be able to explain how information can be used to improve service.

9. Know the significance of the phrase *high tech/high touch* as it applies to the hospitality industry.

10. Recognize the importance of Benihana's unique concept of restaurant operation as "show business."

11. Be familiar with the five principles of Total Quality Management that enabled The Ritz-Carlton Hotel Company to be the first hotel group to win the Malcolm Baldrige National Quality Award.

12. Be able to explain what recovery means and why it is important.

13. Be able to explain the elements needed to empower an employee.

With 70 percent of the U.S. economy already engaged in services, now more than ever the hospitality industry cannot ignore what customers want, and thereby unloose the same forces that led to the decline of manufacturing. Early on, one news weekly described the situation this way:

> *Personal service has become a maddeningly rare commodity in the American marketplace. Flight attendants, sales clerks and bank tellers all seem to have become too busy to give consumers much attention. Many other service workers are underpaid, untrained, and unmotivated for their jobs, to the chagrin of customers who look to them for help. ...Customers know service when they miss it, and now they want it back. Says Thomas Peters, a management consultant and co-author of In Search of Excellence: "In general, service in America stinks."* [2]

In a way, this sorry state of customer services could be seen as a result of the post-baby-boom shortage of workers available to take minimum wage jobs, or even as a result of what Cornell Hotel School professor Tom Kelly believes to be a shift in cultural values, under which service jobs are no longer regarded as worthwhile occupations. On the other hand, there have been efforts to invigorate customer service that have met with great success. Here, after describing a bit about what service is in hospitality, we will share with you some lessons from the service sector and the companies that are winning because of them.

What Is Service?

Service, as defined in the dictionary, is "the act or means of serving"; to serve is "to provide goods and services for" and "to be of assistance to."[3] Service is a complex and critical component in the hospitality industry, and can be looked at from many perspectives. In their book *Service America*, Albrecht and Zemke begin by defining two basic kinds of service: "help me" and "fix it."[4]

1. "Help Me." This mode of service caters to an individual's special needs, such as "help me find a taxi," "help me find a restaurant with the best French pastry," "help me make a hotel reservation for next summer in Lausanne, Switzerland," "help me find a hotel porter to carry my display cases to the exhibits in the main ballroom," "help me to obtain a pair of tickets for tonight at Broadway's sold-out musical show."

2. "Fix It" Service. This refers to services such as "fix my hotel room television set which is out of order," "transfer me to another room with a TV that does work," "fix the coin-operated Xerox machine now so I can run off copies for the press of my Rotary Club speech to be given at luncheon within the hour," or "can you repair a torn suit coat for my 9:00 a.m. meeting?"

These categories of service provide the bare minimum to the customer. Customers are increasingly demanding that service providers add value to the service and that the service be a managed endeavor. This, according to Albrecht and Zemke, means "the ability to effectively and efficiently manage the design, development, and delivery of service." In other words, the service-driven economy of the 1990s will not stand for restaurant tables that are awkward or uncomfortable, airline seats that jam people in like sardines, or confusing hotel check-out procedures that unreasonably delay a guest's departure. Simply stated, we have already entered the age of service management, an age in which each interaction is being perceived by each and every customer to be the company. Thus, *every* person in a hospitality company, regardless of his or her job title, is responsible for providing good service. For, as Donald Porter, director of quality assurance for British Airways, puts it:

> *If you get it wrong at your point in the customer's chain of experience, you are very likely erasing from the customer's mind all the memories of the good treatment he or she may have had up until you. But if you get it right, you have a chance to undo all the wrongs that may have happened before the customer got to you. You really are the moment of truth.*[5]

Eating In, in Hong Kong

Gone are the days of soggy toast and cold coffee. In Hong Kong, the luxury hotels are in a competition over ... roomservice. Yes, roomservice. Traditionally, roomservice does not generate significant income, and can actually negatively influence profit margins. But to the five-star hotels in Hong Kong, in-room dining is an opportunity to shine. And to keep business growing.

At the Peninsula, the roomservice staff keeps extensive guest files. By having a detailed history of guest orders, a staff member can offer an enhanced level of service, by noting that a guest prefers milk and not cream in his or her coffee, or is on a specific diet. They can even congratulate guests on a birthday or anniversary! At the Mandarin Oriental, an orchid accompanies each order, to match the orchids already in the rooms. At the Ritz-Carlton, cross training of employees is put to the test. Should a guest request breakfast in a hurry, the order taker is encouraged to ask if the guest would like a taxi waiting at a certain time.

Technology plays a big role in expanded customer service. Without computer files that can be readily updated and accessed, it would be difficult for roomservice personnel to offer such personalized service. And training plays a big role. Encouraging employees to act upon service opportunities, and training roomservice staff to act as restaurant waiters and not just delivery personnel, send strong messages to the guest. These hotels are dedicated to retaining their guests, and offering superb service. They have set high expectations for their roomservice divisions, knowing the impact these staff members can have on each guest.

Treat Service as a Process—It Is

In a well-run service company, the distinction between the goals of the "**front-of-the-house**" and those of the "**back-of-the-house**" virtually disappears. Every employee works toward customer satisfaction, even if some of those employees never meet the customer. Good service is best described as a process, not a series of functions. Just as a chain is only as strong as its weakest link, every step, every moment matters. How a service is designed, how it is bundled (for example, a travel package), how it is delivered, how it is billed, *all* influence how it is remembered. The insight for service companies whose departments are still working as separate functions is to realign their organization to generate profit, insure quality, and make every moment count. As described in a lead article in a 1994 issue of *Fortune* magazine, "bold, fast, imaginative and customized" service is the ultimate strategic imperative.[6]

Eliminate Weak Links in Your Service-Profit Chain

One way to think about how to deliver good service is to understand the relationship between service and profit. A group of professors at the Harvard Business School's service management group describes a series of links that are part of this relationship: Profit and growth are stimulated by customer loyalty. Loyalty comes from customer satisfaction. Satisfaction results from value provided to customers. Value is created by loyal, productive, and satisfied employees. Satisfied employees come from high-quality support services and policies that enable employees to deliver results to customers.[7]

Successful service managers must pay attention to *all* the links in the service–profit relationship, a radical shift from management's traditional emphasis on profit goals and market share. Indeed, the most arresting aspect of this shift is the revelation that *customer* loyalty and satisfaction are on a par with *employee* satisfaction, loyalty, and productivity.[8] It is not just important to give your employees a sense of how valuable they are to you and the business. It's also critical to make clear how valuable the customers are to the employees and the business. Figure 3.1 graphically shows the relationship between service and profit.

Create Customer Loyalty

Consider the power of retaining current customers and the costs of losing them. It costs five times more to generate a new customer than it does to retain a current one.[9] Companies can boost profits 25 percent to 85 percent, depending on the industry, by retaining just 5 percent more customers.[10] Losing a customer isn't one lost sale—it can be a lifetime of them. As Fromm and Schlesinger, two experts who have written extensively on service, point out, "when you are rude or dismissive or inattentive to a $2.50 take-out customer, you're not blowing off $2.50; you're blowing off $312.50 a year from loyal customers—and $3,125.00 from every customer you've kept for ten years."[11]

Why is a loyal customer so valuable? The longer a company keeps a customer, the more profit it stands to make. The one-time costs of generating the customer are spread over more and more returns, reducing operating costs. Thus a longtime customer is more profitable in percentage terms. Research also shows that a loyal customer will tend to consume more over time. Service providers with longtime customers can also charge a price premium. Loyal customers will pay more for services that they trust. Loyal customers are also a source of new business, as they are the most likely to generate referrals.[12] Figure 3.2 illustrates why customers are more valuable over time, based on experience in many industries.

Figure 3.1 The Links in the Service-Profit Chain

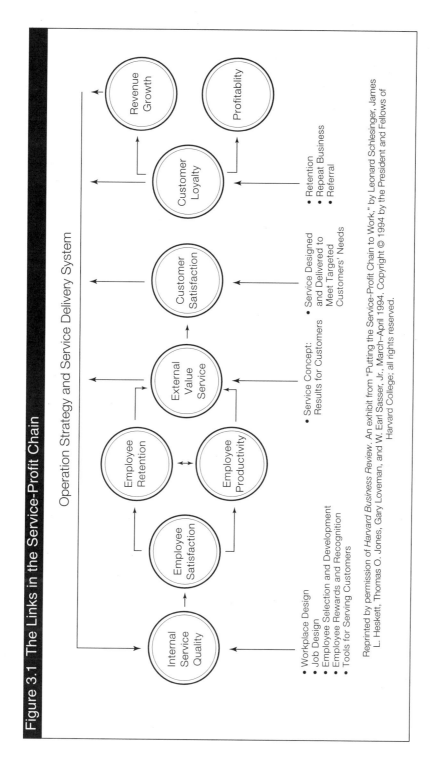

Operation Strategy and Service Delivery System

- Workplace Design
- Job Design
- Employee Selection and Development
- Employee Rewards and Recognition
- Tools for Serving Customers

- Service Concept:
  Results for Customers

- Service Designed
  and Delivered to
  Meet Targeted
  Customers' Needs

- Retention
- Repeat Business
- Referral

Reprinted by permission of *Harvard Business Review*. An exhibit from "Putting the Service-Profit Chain to Work," by Leonard Schlesinger, James L. Heskett, Thomas O. Jones, Gary Loveman, and W. Earl Sasser, Jr., March–April 1994. Copyright © 1994 by the President and Fellows of Harvard College; all rights reserved.

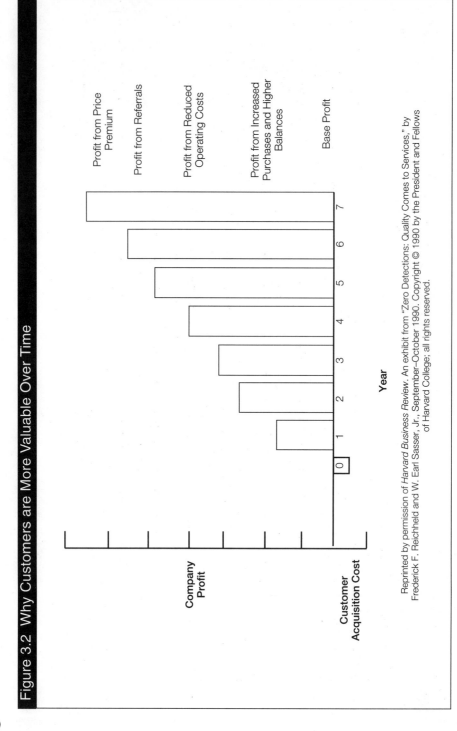

Figure 3.2 Why Customers are More Valuable Over Time

Reprinted by permission of *Harvard Business Review*. An exhibit from "Zero Detections: Quality Comes to Services," by Frederick F. Reichheld and W. Earl Sasser, Jr., September–October 1990. Copyright © 1990 by the President and Fellows of Harvard College; all rights reserved.

The lesson to be learned is to keep customers out of the "customer scrap heap." And if you do lose customers, ask them why. The reasons why customers leave are not hypothetical, but real and concrete.

Empower and Keep Employees

Just as customers are an important link in the service-profit chain, so too are employees. It is important that employees not only understand the value of a loyal, lifelong customer, but also that they be given the support and the tools to create them!

To be empowered, employees must have authority, responsibility, and incentives.[13] Authority encompasses the resources an employee can access and the decisions an employee is allowed to make. Responsibility takes the next step. Not only can an employee help a customer, the employee is *supposed* to help. Incentives are tools that management uses to align the needs of the customer with the behavior of the employee. We talk about other ways to effectively manage employees in chapter 10, "A Human Resources Tool Box." For example, one theme park gave each customer that entered the park a handful of what they called "warm fuzzies." Customers were asked to give them away to employees who were particularly attentive. The theme park in turn offered cash and prizes to its employees in exchange for the "warm fuzzies."

The hospitality business is known for its **high turnover**. Turnover describes how often employees vacate their position and need to be replaced. An annual turnover rate of 100 percent, for instance, means on average, that every employee is replaced once a year. The American Hotel and Motel Association estimates an average turnover rate of 89 percent in hotels, and the rate in restaurants is thought to be even higher.[14] Turnover in fast food restaurants can reach 200 to 300 percent! The costs associated with turnover, including recruiting, training, and lost customer costs, can be staggering. Marriott, in a study of two of its divisions, concluded that reducing turnover by just 10 percent would create savings much greater than the current profits of those divisions.[15] Thus, the economics of keeping employees is compelling.

Southwest Airlines is an excellent example of a company that takes the economics to heart and has done much to enhance its employee productivity. Because of systems like open seating and reusable boarding cards, Southwest deplanes and reloads faster than do its competitors. The company has approximately 40 percent more pilot and aircraft utilization than its competitors have. Because of the higher utilization, it can offer more frequent service and can charge fares that are 60 percent to 70 percent lower than the existing ones when it enters a new market. Because of lower fares, and more frequent, on-time, and friendly service, customers think Southwest is a great value. By objective measures, like the Federal Aviation Administration performance measures, Southwest regularly achieves the highest on-time arrivals, lowest numbers of complaints, and fewest pieces of lost baggage.[16]

Make Every Moment Count

When Jan Carlzon became president and CEO of Scandinavian Airlines System (SAS) a little over a decade ago, he asserted that SAS business is not flying airplanes. Rather, he said, it is serving the needs of the public. And in Carlzon's view, a satisfied customer is really the company's only valuable asset. Accordingly, to stress the overriding importance of customer service, he came up with the concept of managing the customer's "moments of truth" …in other words, those transactions a customer has with SAS. He pointed to the fact that in a given year, each of the 10 million customers came in contact with five SAS employees, and that his contact lasted an average of 15 seconds each time.

> *Thus, the company is created in the minds of our customers 50 million times a year, 15 seconds at a time. These 50 million "moments of truth" are the moments that ultimately determine whether the company will succeed or fail … If we are truly dedicated to orienting our company toward each customer's individual needs, then we cannot rely on rule books and instructions from distant corporate offices. We have to place responsibility for ideas, decisions, and actions with the people who are SAS during those 15 seconds… If they have to go up the organizational chain of command of a decision on an individual problem, then those 15 golden seconds will elapse without a response, and we will have lost an opportunity to earn a loyal customer.[17]*

In their book *Service America*, Albrecht and Zemke recorded their observations of some shining moments and as well as dull moments as shown in the following excerpts:

Dull Moment

> *A customer looked over the menu in a restaurant and saw very few choices that seemed appealing. Suddenly, she spotted an interesting option: a peanut butter and jelly sandwich. "Now that sounds like just the thing," she beamed. "I haven't had a good peanut butter and jelly sandwich in ages. That and a glass of milk will hit the spot." When she asked the waitress for the sandwich, she received the chilly reply: "Sorry—that's the children's section on the menu. You can't order that."*

> *The customer asked, "I don't understand. Why does a person have to be a child to order that particular sandwich? That's really what I would like to have." When the waitress firmly refused to place the order, the customer asked to speak to the restaurant manager. He offered the same story. "I'm sorry, ma'am. We don't serve children's orders to adults." Angry and incredulous, she decided to have lunch somewhere else.[18]*

Shining Moment

> *A man wrote a letter to a small hotel in a Midwestern town he planned to visit on his vacation. "I would like very much to bring my dog with me," he wrote. "The dog is well-groomed and very well behaved. Would you be willing to permit me to keep him in my room overnight?"*

> *An immediate reply came from the hotel owner, who said, "I've been operating this hotel for many years. In all that time, I've never had a dog steal towels, bed clothes, silverware, or pictures off the walls. I've never had to evict a dog in the middle of the night for being*

drunk and disorderly. And I've never had a dog run out on a hotel bill. Yes, indeed, your dog is welcome at my hotel. And if your dog will vouch for you, you're welcome to stay here, too."[19]

Managing the Moments of Truth

As the preceding discussion suggests, when the moments of truth go unmanaged, the quality of service seldom meets customer expectations. Accordingly, getting a high grade on the customer's report card pretty much depends on treating him or her as a person who expects to be dealt with promptly and with dignity. "Most of us will forgive 'system' screw-ups, even to a preposterous degree, if there is someone there who acknowledges our personal needs and makes an effort to set things right."[20]

Take Marriott Hotels, for example. Its 140,000 employees are estimated to make six million customer contacts each day—compared, say, to the 50,000 contacts per day being made by employees of the Scandinavian Airlines System. A Marriott model for maximizing the quality of the customer's daily experience at millions of moments of truth is shown in Figure 3.3, "The Service

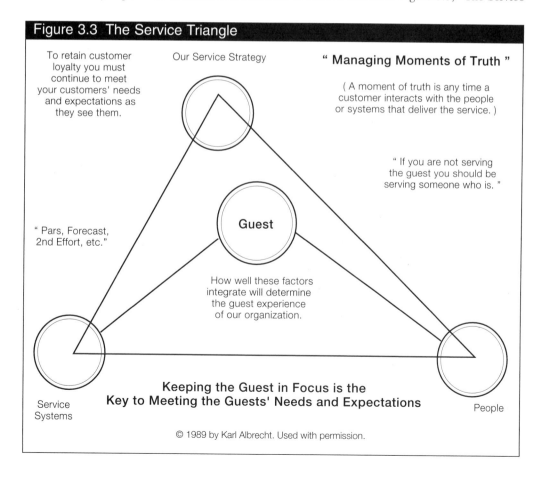

Figure 3.3 The Service Triangle

To retain customer loyalty you must continue to meet your customers' needs and expectations as they see them.

Our Service Strategy

" **Managing Moments of Truth** "

(A moment of truth is any time a customer interacts with the people or systems that deliver the service.)

" If you are not serving the guest you should be serving someone who is. "

" Pars, Forecast, 2nd Effort, etc."

Guest

How well these factors integrate will determine the guest experience of our organization.

Service Systems

Keeping the Guest in Focus is the Key to Meeting the Guests' Needs and Expectations

People

© 1989 by Karl Albrecht. Used with permission.

Triangle" as prepared by Karl Albrecht. This triangle model portrays a *process* rather than a structure, reflecting the interplay of three critical elements that must perform smoothly if Marriott is to sustain its high level of service quality. Conspicuously focused on the *guest* at the center of the triangle, these elements are:

1. **Service Strategy**—To retain customer loyalty, you must continue to meet your customers' needs and expectations as they see them.

2. **People**—If you (as a customer-oriented person) are not serving the guest, you should be serving someone who is. That is, even if you don't come in contact with guests, you should be helping those who do.

3. **Service Systems**—the words "pars, Forecast, 2nd Effort, etc." are methods that Marriott uses to help employees deliver customer friendly service.

To the leaders of the Marriott organization, this triangular framework is one of the most effective ways of keeping the guest in focus—and thus the key to meeting the guest's needs and expectations.

Use Service Guarantees to Your Advantage— If It Makes Sense to Use Them!

Timothy W. Firnstahl, founder and chief executive officer of Satisfaction Guaranteed Eateries, Inc., a Seattle restaurant chain, is certain that "hassle-free" service transactions produce customer satisfaction, increased employee motivation, and bigger profit margins. How has this been accomplished? Simply by unwavering adherence to three operating principles:

1. Make your guarantee simple, easy to understand, unconditional—and memorable. Each of Firnstahl's four restaurants uses the acronym WAGS (We Always Guarantee Satisfaction), a promise not unlike that of Avis ("We Try Harder") and Federal Express ("Absolutely Positively Overnight").

2. Give employees themselves the power to make good on the promise of the guarantee—*at once and on the spot*. Employees can and should "do anything to keep the customer happy," including providing complimentary wine or desserts or, if necessary, picking up the entire check. There are no ifs, ands, or buts about this process. To Firnstahl, no guarantee can be any good if it makes complaining an ordeal for the customer—no matter how much in error the customer may be.

3. Reward employees monthly with generous bonuses based on their having reduced telephone-survey complaint rates as well as their having reduced system-failure costs. As a consequence, over a two-year period sales have risen by 25 percent at Satisfaction Guaranteed Eateries, profits have doubled, cash in the bank has grown two and one half times—and employees of each restaurant in the chain have divided monthly bonuses as high as $10,000.[21]

For fear that waiters wearing buttons that proclaim "We Always Guarantee Satisfaction" may be overdoing what is rapidly becoming a popular cliché, Firnstahl now wants to switch to something more specific, like "Enjoyment Guaranteed," to make his promise unmistakably compelling.[22]

Slogans aside, Christopher Hart, a former Harvard Business School professor who has authored several articles on service guarantees, points to the fact that while service guarantees are powerful marketing tools, they are usually successful only when the following criteria are met:

1. They are unconditional

2. They are easy to understand and to communicate

3. They are meaningful

4. They are easy and painless to invoke

5. They are easy for the customer to collect on.[23]

Not by a long shot, argues the chairman and president of Four Seasons Hotels in rebuttal to Professor Hart:

> *I don't want my money back. I want the service I am buying to be right the first time and every time. He insists, "At Four Seasons Hotels we have built our reputation by providing a service level we are able to deliver consistently. ...Our clientele is not interested in roller-coaster service levels. No company should promise more than its ability to deliver day after day after day. I don't believe that you need a guarantee to force you to focus on customer satisfaction.*[24]

Hampton Inn takes another approach. Advertising "HAMPTON INN PUTS GUARANTEED SATISFACTION 100% ON THE MAP," that company claims that 2 percent of its guests choose its hotels because of its "100% satisfaction guarantee," originally established in late 1989. If you're unhappy with your hotel room at Hampton, just say so, and your money will be cheerfully refunded. According to *The Wall Street Journal*, the chain calculates that it receives $8 in revenue for every dollar it pays out to disgruntled guests.[25]

What About Cheats?

Inevitably the question of cheating arises whenever ironclad guarantees are discussed. In Professor Hart's view, there are indeed a handful of customers who will take advantage of a service guarantee to get something for nothing. But whatever such cheats may cost the company "amounts to very little compared to the benefits derived from a strong guarantee." According to Michael Leven, former president of Days Inns, now heading up US Franchise Systems, management too often "spends its time worrying about the 1% of people who might cheat the company instead of the 99% who don't." Nonetheless, Hart admits that:

> *where the potential for false claims is high, a no-questions-asked guarantee may appear to be foolhardy. When Domino's first offered its delivery within 30 minutes or the pizza is free guarantee, some college students telephoned orders from hard-to-find locations. The result was free pizza for the students and lost revenue for Domino's. In this environment, the guarantee was problematic, because some students perceived it as a game against Domino's. But Bressler (owner of 18 Domino's Pizza franchises in the Baltimore, Maryland, area) takes the view that the review thus lost was an investment in the future. "They'll be Domino's customers for life, those kids."*[26]

Manage Quality Totally

Much has been said and written about a concept called total quality management, or TQM, as a way of doing business. TQM is rooted in a series of scientific measurement tools that enable a company to measure things like productivity and customer satisfaction. The Ritz-Carlton company, for example, which adopted TQM with a vengeance in 1988, measures its employee turnover rate, 30 percent, versus an industry average three or more times greater; customer satisfaction, 97 percent of all customers surveyed are satisfied; and its defect rate, for every one million transactions with customers, fewer than 60,000 could be counted as defects.[27] What is a defect? A **defect** is any interaction with a customer that goes wrong, from cold scrambled eggs to relocating a customer with a guaranteed reservation.

TQM has an unrelenting focus on quality, and at its heart it shares the same fundamental principles as other techniques for improving service. It essentially involves "attention to process, commitment to the customer, involvement of employees, and bench marking of best practices."[28] TQM is aimed at increasing productivity by rethinking processes.

An essential part of TQM is collecting and evaluating data. Customer comment cards provide a hospitality manager with a tremendous amount of information about different departments. To evaluate the comments on phone calls to the hotel reception, for instance, the manager plots, over a 30-day period, each complaint. A sample is found in Figure 3.4.

Clearly, being treated rudely was the chief customer complaint, followed by the line ringing busy, clearly indicating need for training and additional staff. By graphing the data, the manager has a visual representation of the problem, and can share it with the employees.

But say the managers want to know more about what's happening. Is there a pattern to the complaints? Maybe they occur mainly on weekends, or during busy check-in times. The manager chooses to plot the complaints against the number of hours worked by the front desk staff. The results are shown in a scatter diagram, Figure 3.5.

The manager finds that when the employees at that front desk have worked longer, complaints go up! This would make sense, because as the workers become tired, the enthusiasm and energy they need to do a good job wanes. Now, in addition to using the initial graph to show the employees what the customers are most upset about, the manager perhaps can also use the scatter diagram to rearrange the schedule. Or it could be used to encourage human resources to step up the recruiting efforts for additional employees. The manager can also solicit ideas from the front desk staff on scheduling, shifts, phone duty, and other issues, to help address the number of complaints and improve service overall.

The application of measurement tools is not without costs. The efforts put forth to create and use management tools can be time consuming and may not provide benefits. A company that collects data but doesn't do anything with it because "there's no time" is caught in the worst-case scenario!

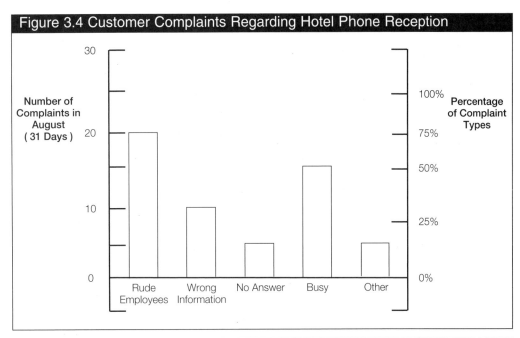

Figure 3.4 Customer Complaints Regarding Hotel Phone Reception

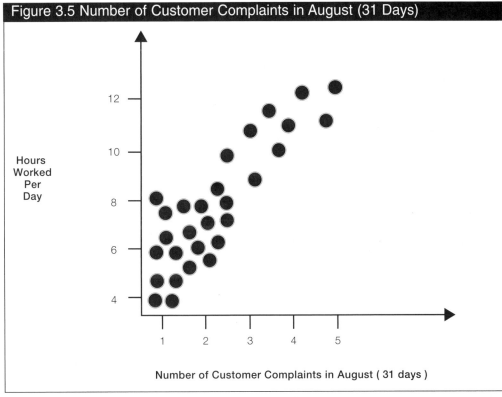

Figure 3.5 Number of Customer Complaints in August (31 Days)

The Malcolm Baldrige National Quality Award

To round out our consideration of ways in which quality improvement may take place, we turn our attention to the Malcolm Baldrige National Quality Award.[29]

In response to growing concerns about the quality of goods and services being produced in the United States, Congress in 1987 passed Public Law 100-107, a groundbreaking piece of legislation representing the government's endorsement of quality as an essential part of successful business strategy. Named for a former Secretary of Commerce, this award is administered by the Commerce Department's National Institute of Standards and Technology. The purpose of the law is "to provide for the establishment and conduct of a national quality improvement program under which (1) awards are given to selected companies and other organizations in the United States that practice effective quality management and as a result make significant improvements in the quality of their goods and services, and (2) information is disseminated about the successful strategies and programs."

Applications for the Baldrige Award are graded on a point scale. (See Exhibit 3.1, "The Categories of Evaluation for Baldridge Award.") Those companies with the highest scores are visited by a team of examiners. Their findings go to a board of nine judges, who provide feedback reports to applicants and select award recipients. The awards offer promise of recognition for excellence to not more than two manufacturing, two service, and two small business firms each year. Since 1987, only 22 companies in total have won the Baldrige Award, among them AT&T, Texas Instruments, and Motorola. Only four of them were in the service sector; of those four, there was only one winner in the hospitality industry. Quality service in the hospitality industry can be very difficult to measure.

Baldrige Award Winner: The Ritz-Carlton Hotel Company It wasn't until October 14, 1992, that the Ritz–Carlton Hotel Company received the Baldrige Award, making it the first hotel group ever to win this honor. Considering the fact that only about 10 percent of award applicants receive scores high enough to warrant visits from teams of Baldrige examiners, the question arises as to what the Ritz-Carlton did to satisfy the rigorous quality standards demanded of award winners. The process involved undeviating focus on total quality management (TQM). In short, the key elements of success from the Ritz-Carlton experience are:[30]

1. The unwavering commitment of Horst Schulze, president, and all other senior executives to the TQM program.

Exhibit 3.1 Categories of Evaluation for Baldrige Award

Category	Maximum Points
Leadership	120
Information and Analysis	60
Planning for Quality	80
Human Resource Utilization	150
Quality Assurance of Products and Services	140
Quality Results	150
Customer Satisfaction	300
TOTAL POINTS	1000

2. The appointment of a corporate director of TQM.

3. The Ritz-Carlton Gold Standards, which include a credo, a motto, three steps of service, and 20 Ritz-Carlton "Basics."

4. Five Principles of TQM:

   A. Commit to Quality
      - From the president on down, all employees are committed to quality through communication, education and training, teamwork and recognition. (See Exhibit 3.2, "The Ritz-Carlton Credo.")

   B. Focus on Customer Satisfaction
      - Defining the customer and his/her needs is critical. There is great value over time in a loyal customer.

   C. Assess Organizational Culture
      - Organization culture is the style of the company. Providing a good work environment for employees is an important component of quality customer service.

   D. Empower Employee Participation in Strategic Management Teams
      - Provide employees with the knowledge and information they need to do their jobs, and to do them well. Employees with information will take responsibility for ideas and decisions that impact the customer.

   E. Measure Quality Efforts
      - Collect and analyze data to measure success and shortcomings. Use tools, such as scatter diagrams to represent results visually so employees can recognize areas for growth.

5. Above all, the Baldrige Award criteria serve as a rigorous guide for establishing and monitoring a TQM program.[31]

Exhibit 3.2 The Ritz-Carlton Credo

The Ritz-Carlton Credo

The Ritz-Carlton is a place where the genuine care and comfort of our guests is our highest mission. We pledge to provide the best service and facilities for our guests who will always enjoy a warm, relaxed, yet refined ambiance. The Ritz-Carlton experience enlivens the senses, instills well-being, and fulfills even the unexpressed wishes and needs of our guests.

Build a Quality Service Information System

Having service come out well takes on added significance as we reflect upon each technological development in the hospitality industry. Why? Partly because of what John Naisbitt's book *Megatrends* calls **high tech/high touch**. In other words, whenever a technological advancement occurs in the hotel/restaurant industry, it often must be counterbalanced by a human response. We want the greater service which the new systems deliver—but not at the expense of "old-fashioned hospitality," which guests value in terms of personal contacts with employees. Technology and customized service do not necessarily have to be at odds with one another, however. In fact, technology can actually assist companies in offering more customized service. This can only happen if information is gathered and used effectively. What kind of information should be gathered, and what should it be used for? We address this more extensively in chapter 12, "A Management Information Tool Box." The following is a list of possible answers:

- As noted above in the discussion of customer loyalty, track and interview customers that defect. Discover why they left and what you can do to improve the quality of the service experience.

- Gather customer complaint information. Make it easy for customers to complain. What can it tell you about dissatisfied customers? Where does service failure occur?

- Gather immediate reaction to service. Obtain customer feedback while the experience is still fresh.

- Interview customers in focus groups. This format helps to identify new service improvement ideas.

- Use incognito customers. This allows the service system to behave as it normally would, yet gives the company a way to assess service directly through the eyes of the customer.

- Survey employees. Discover the obstacles that employees face in providing good service.

A concrete example of management's action in today's fast food industry involves Taco Bell, a subsidiary of Pepsico. Top management there tracks profits daily by unit, market manager, zone, and country. The resulting information is then correlated with the results of exit interviews that Taco Bell conducts with its 800,000 customers annually. As a consequence, the company has found that "stores in the top quadrant of customer satisfaction ratings outperform all others by all measures," thus enabling the company to link no less than 20 percent of all operations managers' compensation in company-owned stores to customer satisfaction ratings.[32]

Remember That Customer Service is a Performing Art

There are many analogies that can be drawn between hospitality businesses and the theater. Many people are involved in the production. There are both onstage and backstage participants. Casting is critical to success. Without the right people in the right roles, failure results. Even if one person of the many involved doesn't perform well, the entire production can be a flop. This analogy as applied to service companies underscores the need for hiring the right people, not just filling jobs, but casting performers in roles and then assuring that they have the stage props needed to perform well.

Disney World Onstage

Perhaps no company is better known for setting up service onstage than the Walt Disney Company. In what has been characterized as one of the most imaginative business seminars today, Disney teaches business executives its distinctive approach to developing good customer service.[33] Every year, some 1,600 business leaders come to Orlando to get a glimpse into the practices used by Disney to create what it calls its "corporate culture." In a business where a single rude encounter can leave a family vacation in ruins, Disney aims "to make its 36,000 employees think and act as one." To achieve this aim, "Disney language" becomes an essential element of the corporate culture. For example, employees are called "cast members," and customers are called "guests." Working cast members are said to be "on stage," while all recruits are taught popular slogans like "Don't take yourself seriously, take your job seriously," and "What does Disney make? It makes people happy." Signs are everywhere—on bulletin boards and in parking lots. One parking lot sign reads: "If you're happy, tell your face."

In short, the three-day Disney seminar leaves no stone unturned as it drives home a single concept: the care and feeding of its corporate culture in a multi-billion-dollar operation. As one company vice president remarked upon completing the seminar: "There's no way we can control those moments of truth in the field unless we have a corporate culture that does for our employees what Disney World does for its 'cast members.'"

Food as Theater

At the Wegman's store in Greece, New York, shoppers are not greeted at the door by a row of check-out counters and aisle upon aisle of packaged goods. Instead, their first impression is of a farmers' market, with enormous displays of fresh fruits and vegetables. To the right is the Wokery, a Chinese restaurant and takeout, plus 88 feet of cases of fresh meats and salads, breads and doughnuts, and other fresh foods—most of them prepared in Wegman's store. The check-out area is to the left of the entrance, and behind it is the pizza shop where bakers select five offerings each day from among fourteen possible varieties. This 100,000–square-foot supermarket is described by one industry consultant as "incredible perishable theater."[34]

Also included in this account of mainstream trends in supermarket services is a photograph of a troubleshooter shown rollerskating through the aisles of the Grand Union market in Middletown, New Jersey. The slogan prominently displayed in large letters on the back of her uniform reads: ASK ME, I'M HERE TO HELP.[35]

Just as customers want more than food when they go out to shop at supermarkets, they also want more than food when they go out to a restaurant to eat. What they expect is friendliness and sociability—at times, with a theatrical flourish.[36] Note, for example, the relaxed, fun atmosphere created by Benihana's unique Theater of the Stomach advertising, which makes no mention of the word *restaurant*. Instead, it emphasizes show-business: "samurai warrior," "whirling dervish," "the show goes on," "he [i.e., the chef] performs choreography," "he walks off," and receives "a standing ovation." Such creative, offbeat advertising has not only improved bottom-line performance for Benihana but also has continued to build its repeat customer market.

In view of the Benihana paradigm, it may be no exaggeration to say that restaurants aren't *like* show business. They *are* show business—for at least three basic reasons:[37]

1. As customers decide what to order, sometimes in full view of the chef's production, "the result is audience-participation theater of the most demanding kind."

2. To produce an experience which involves customer participation requires a "structured framework for action to guide those who own and work in restaurants." Accordingly,

"the owner is like the producer ... who brings together talent, capital and a script... Scripting the restaurant entails creating a story" which will not only attract customers but also yield staff behavior aimed at making the script work ... *"Management must recognize the actor-like nature of the server's work... It is no accident that restaurants and out-of-work actors so often find each other."*

3. Moreover, the model of a restaurant as theater is also valuable for another reason, namely: "It provides methodologies for shaping and supporting the emotional expenditures of the contact staff." This means:

Developing a sophisticated restaurant repertory company ... carefully trained in reading the customer ... and in performing with such authenticity *that the audience believes that what is being said is spontaneous and original—night after night, again and again.*[38]

Recover Well

Inevitably, even if all the lessons from the service sector are applied, mistakes will happen. As hard as a company tries, the room may not be ready for check-in, the plane may not leave the gate on time, and the eggs may be cold. Thus service companies need to know how to recover well. How? Service companies need to "measure the cost of effective service recovery, break customer silence and listen closely for complaints, anticipate the needs for recovery, act fast, train employees, empower the front line and close the customer feedback loop."[39]

We have already described the costs associated with losing a loyal customer. There are also additional costs associated with fixing errors, be they money-back guarantees, free replacements, or others. If the true costs of losing a customer are not measured and understood, then a company will not go to great lengths to recover from a mistake when it should go to great lengths. Breaking customer silence means encouraging customers to complain—especially the ones that normally wouldn't, and in all cases listening for ways to solve the customer's problem. These include problems that may not even be the company's fault. Anticipating problems means planning ahead, such as staffing up at the airport when weather is likely to cause delays or having jackets available for dinner guests who show up unaware of the dress code. In order for employees to respond quickly, or act fast, they must not only be empowered to make amends but must be encouraged to do so. Training to develop recovery skills is often accomplished through role play of real life situations. Finally, closing the customer feedback loop means letting the customer know what correction was made as a result of the complaint. Taken together, these measures allow a service company to make memorable recoveries.

■■■■■■■ **A Different Kind of Recovery—Is There a Doctor in the Hotel?**

Ron French

The Detroit News
_____

You're on a business trip out of town to give an important speech when suddenly you become nauseous.

Help for this stomach-churning problem now is as close as a hotel phone. Business travelers and other guests can call HotelDocs and ask a physician to visit their room.

To treat toothaches in Tuscaloosa or allergies in Allegheny, HotelDocs promises to have a doctor at bedside within 35 minutes.

The service is the brainchild of San Diego entrepreneur Ian Becker, who realizes there's money to be made from sick salespeople. HotelDocs now covers 54 cities in the United States, including Detroit. Advance sign-up isn't needed.

Travelers call (800) HOTELDR (468-3537) and a dispatcher sends a physician, dentist, or specialist. Doctors generally can provide medications, saving a drugstore trip.

Charges start at $150 for an exam and basic care, and an insurance form is provided for patients to seek at least partial reimbursment from their carrier or Medicare.

"We have many doctors standing by around the clock," Becker said. "Some of them even speak more than one language."

The roster includes Dr. Jeffrey McErlean, a West Bloomfield surgeon who enjoys the change of pace of hotel assignments.

He recently examined a Japanese auto executive visiting Detroit on business. "Between his English and my Japanese, we were able to figure out he probably had food poisoning from ill-prepared fish," said the Oakland County doctor.
_____

Copyright © 1995, *The Detroit News.*
_____

Summary _____

This chapter's emphasis is on the continually emerging age of *service management*, underscoring the finding that "it's hard to get big productivity gains by substituting capital and technology for labor, since high-touch customer service by definition means lots of flexible, warm, human contact."[40] Our high-tech, high-touch society does indeed want its hospitality unblemished. "Great service providers inform customers what to expect and then *exceed* the promise."[41]

In the end, the pieces we have assembled here show us, among other things, the sources of the "moments of truth" in customer encounters, and the profound significance of treating customer service as a process. It highlights the importance of every link in the service-profit chain in developing a framework for managing customer interactions. It shows the power of information and the power of the sense of great theater so evident in such service-minded organizations as Disney and Benihana of Tokyo. It provides the prospect that quality can be measured and that the Baldrige Award criteria have the capacity to become a global standard by which total service quality is judged.

In summary, benchmarking from, or comparing standards to, the best practices used by companies that are faring well is a good start to understanding what makes a service company successful:

- Treat service as a process. It is.
- Eliminate weak links in the service-profit chain.
- Develop customer loyalty.
- Empower employees.
- Make every moment count.
- Use service guarantees to your advantage.
- Manage quality totally.
- Build a quality information system.
- Remember that customer service is a performing art, and
- Recover well.

Discussion Questions

1. Why is a loyal customer valuable? Why is a loyal customer more valuable over time?

2. What are the important links of the service-profit chain? How are they related?

3. What are the three points of the service triangle? Why is the guest the center of the triangle?

4. How can a hospitality company build a quality information system? How can information be used to improve service?

5. How are authority, responsibility, and incentives related to employee empowerment?

6. What is a service guarantee? What must be true about a service guarantee in order for it be useful?

7. Explain how service guarantees serve as devices for achieving total customer satisfaction. Give examples. What about customers who cheat?

8. How does the expression *theater of the stomach* explain what takes place at Benihana of Tokyo? How is the same idea applied at Disney World?

9. What is the Malcolm Baldrige National Quality Award? What criteria are used to determine the winners? How are those criteria related to quality service?

10. It has been said that all hotel employees should bear responsibility for responding instantly to customer needs in those "moments of truth" that determine a company's success or failure. Discuss the advantages and disadvantages of placing responsibility for ideas, decisions, and actions upon the shoulders of the employees who serve the customer directly.

11. Discuss what the following means to you:

    "We have 50,000 moments of truth out there every day." (Jan Carlzon, former president of Scandinavian Airlines)

    "When the moments of truth go unmanaged, the quality of service regresses to mediocrity." (Albrecht and Zemke)

12. The opening quotation suggests that attitude is more important than aptitude at the onset of a service experience. Do you agree?

Assignments

1. Recall an encounter with a service provider that you found to be poor. Recall one that you found to be excellent. Write two letters, one offering critique, the other praise, and address them to the appropriate service provider. Why did you critique the first experience? Praise the second? (Mail the letters if the encounters were recent!)

2. How would you evaluate the responses you received from the service providers? Did you receive a response at all? Was the response fairly timely? Did it come from the appropriate person? Did you feel like you were treated as an individual or do you feel you received a form letter? In your unsatisfactory situation, did the service provider recover?

End Notes

1. From remarks by Leonard Schlesinger of Harvard Business School, at a lecture at the School of Hospitality at Boston University.

2. Thomas Peters, "Why is Service So Bad ... Pul-eeze! Will Somebody Help Me? ... Frustrated American Consumers Wonder Where the Service Went," *Time*, 2 February, 1987: 48–55.

3. Webster's New Word Dictionary, David B. Guralnik, Editor in Chief (New York: William Collins Publishers, Inc.) 1979, p. 544.

4. Karl Albrecht and Ron Zemke, *Service America!* (Homewood, Illinois: Dow Jones-Irwin, 1985), 2–18.

5. Albrecht and Zemke, 32.

6. Ronald Henkoff, "Service Is Everybody's Business," *Fortune* (27 June, 1994): 26.

7. James L. Heskett, et al. "Putting the Service Profit Chain to Word," *Harvard Business Review* (March–April 1994): 164–165.

8. Ibid., 164–165.

9. Christopher W.L. Hart, James L. Heskett, and W. Earl Sasser, "The Profitable Art of Service Recovery," *Harvard Business Review* (July–August 1990): 149.

10. Reichheld and W. Earl Sasser, "Zero Defections: Quality Comes to Services," *Harvard Business Review* (September–October, 1990): 105.

11. Bill Fromm and Leonard Schlesinger, *The Real Heros of Business: And Not a CEO Among Them* (New York: Doubleday, 1994), 1:0–1:1.

12. Reichheld and W. Earl Sasser, "Zero Defections: Quality Comes to Services," *Harvard Business Review* (September–October 1990): 105.

13. Hart, Heskett, and Sasser, "The Profitable Art of Service Recovery," 154.

14. John J. Weaver, "Want Customer Satisfaction? Satisfy Your Employees First," *HR Magazine* (February 1994): 110.

15. Leonard A. Schlesinger, and James L. Heskett, "Breaking the Cycle of Failure in Services," *Sloan Management Review* (Spring 1991): 23.

16. James L. Heskett, et al. "Putting the Service Profit Chain to Work," *Harvard Business Review* (March–April 1994): 164–165.

17. Christopher H. Lovelock, *Service Marketing*, 2nd ed. (Englewood Cliffs, New Jersey: Prentice Hall, 1991): 425.

18. Albrecht and Zemke, 120. Reprinted with permission.

19. Ibid., 128.

20. Ibid., 32.

21. Timothy W Albrecht. Firnstahl, "My Employees Are My Service Guarantee," *Harvard Business Review* (July–August 1989): 28–34.

22. Daniel Pearl, "More Firms Pledge Guaranteed Service," *The Wall Street Journal*, 17 July 1991, B1.

23. Christopher W. L. Hart, "The Power of Unconditional Service Guarantees," *Harvard Business Review* (July–August 1988), 55.

24. Letter from Isador Sharp to the Editor, *Harvard Business Review* (September–October 1988), 169.

25. Pearl.

26. Hart, 61.

27. Galagan, "Putting on the Ritz," *Training and Development* (December 1993): 41.

28. Rahul Jacob, "TQM More Than a Dying Fad," *Fortune* (18 October 1993): 66.

29. The following constitute excellent sources of information about the Malcolm Baldridge National Quality Award:

   Charles G. Partlow, "How Ritz-Carlton Applies TQM", *The Cornell H.R.A. Quarterly* (August 1993): 16–24.

W. Earl Sasser, Jr., Christopher W. L. Hart, and James L. Heskett, *The Service Management Course: Cases and Readings* (New York: The Free Press, 1991), 445–460. See also *Instructor's Manual for The Service Management Course: Cases and Readings* (New York: The Free Press, 1991), 363–376, especially the summaries of key Baldridge concepts shown in Exhibits TN–3, TN–4, and TN–5.

James L. Heskett, W. Earl Sasser, Jr., and Christopher W. L. Hart, *Service Breakthroughs: Changing the Rules of the Game* (New York: The Free Press, 1990), 46 112–143.

30. Key product and service requirements of TQM at Ritz-Carlton's 27 hotels and resorts are extensively documented in the August 1992 *Cornell Quarterly*.

31. Ibid., 16–24.

32. Heskett, et al., 169.

33. "A Mickey Mouse–for Real," *New York Times*, 27 August 1989, 24.

34. "Supermarket as Theater, Service as Star," *New York Times*, 8 November 1989, C1.

35. "Supermarket as Theater, Service as Star," *New York Times*, 8 November 1989, C1.

36. David Romm, "'Restauration' Theater: Giving Direction to Service," *Cornell Hotel and Restaurant Quarterly* (February 1989): 38.

37. Ibid.

38. Ibid., 37–39.

39. *Hart, Heskett, Sasser, "The Profitable Art of Service Recovery," *Havard Business Review* (July–August 1990): 150.

40. William H. Davidow and Bro Uttal, "Service Companies: Focus or Falter," *Harvard Business Review* (July–August 1989): 80.

41. Ibid., 85.

Chapter Four

❝ *Why, then the world's mine*

oyster... ❞

William Shakespeare [1]

An International Perspective ✍

When you finish this chapter you should:

1. Know how the world's hotel rooms are distributed across the globe.

2. Be able to compare international and intranational travel for a given country.

3. Compare the differences in hotel operations, development, physical plant, and customer mix for hotels around the world.

4. Understand the nature of the hurdles that an international hotelier faces.

5. Understand how historical influences have shaped some of the physical plants of hotels throughout the world.

6. Compare the finances, both in terms of how money is made and spent, in the United States versus abroad.

7. Compare occupancy percentages and average daily rates for various countries and world parts.

8. Comprehend the key elements necessary to operate a multinational hotel operation successfully.

9. Explain how international restaurant chains must adapt to local customs and culture.

10. Identify the key development and operations hurdles faced by international restaurant chains.

11. Explain how changing economic conditions can affect the profitability of a foreign company.

An International Perspective —————

Being an international player in the hospitality business is not an easy job. Though the business principles of providing first–class accommodations and food to a traveler is fundamentally the same in any major city, added dimensions of foreign language, food, customs, and culture present a more complex set of challenges than occur in a domestic operation. A hospitality company operating in Boston, Budapest, Berlin, and Bangkok should take a global perspective, one that comprehends the scope of the world of hospitality and the similarities and differences in lodging, foodservice, travel, and entertainment management around the world.

The World of Hotels

There are approximately 12 million hotel rooms around the world. By continent, Europe has the largest number, with just under half of all hotel rooms; just more than a third are in the Americas. The remaining continents are have far fewer rooms. Asia has approximately 13 percent, Africa 3 percent, and Australia/Oceania about 1 percent. Figure 4.1 shows the distribution of hotel rooms across the global map.

Growth in Hotel Rooms

Ranked according to the number of hotels rooms that they have, most of the top 40 countries in the world have seen growth over the last decade. The world's hotel rooms in total grew nearly 3 percent annually between 1985 and 1993. Austria, Switzerland, Romania, and South Africa are the exceptions. These countries have seen slight declines since 1983; as a result, all of these countries have slipped in the rankings. South Africa, for example, moved from the 22nd to the 36th largest country in terms of hotel rooms.

Table 4.1 compares the top 40 countries' hotel rooms in 1985 and 1993. The growth in the majority is supported by the ever increasing number of dollars spent on tourism worldwide. As we view tourism toward the year 2000, several countries merit special mention.

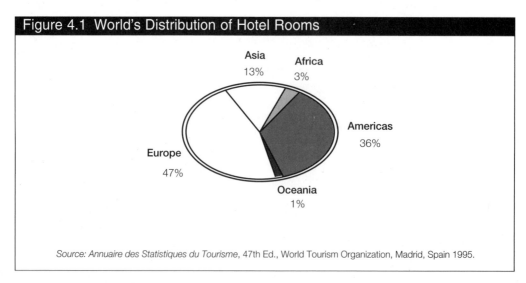

Figure 4.1 World's Distribution of Hotel Rooms

Asia 13%

Africa 3%

Americas 36%

Europe 47%

Oceania 1%

Source: Annuaire des Statistiques du Tourisme, 47th Ed., World Tourism Organization, Madrid, Spain 1995.

Table 4.1 World's Hotel Room Distribution by Country

Top 40 Countries *Rank Order 1993*

	Country	Number of Rooms 1993	Number of Rooms 1985	Rank 1985	Average Annual Growth Rate (%) 1985/1993	% Share of Rooms World-Wide 1993	% Share of Rooms World-Wide 1985
	World	11,767,573	9,499,507		2.71	100.00	100.00
1.	United States	3,080,000	2,416,678	1	3.08	26.17	25.44
2.	Italy	942,350	895,921	2	0.63	8.01	9.43
3.	France	589,216	487,664	4	2.39	5.01	5.13
4.	Spain	437,754	330,661	5	3.57	3.72	3.48
5.	Germany	387,128	256,355	8	5.29	3.29	2.70
6.	China	386,401	107,513	14	17.34	3.28	1.13
7.	Mexico	366,423	300,500	7	2.51	3.11	3.16
8.	United Kingdom	363,602	500,000	3	-3.90	3.09	5.26
9.	Austria	319,565	323,394	6	-0.15	2.72	3.40
10.	Greece	257,383	163,830	9	5.81	2.19	1.72
11.	Thailand	212,389	110,003	13	8.57	1.80	1.16
12.	Indonesia	167,592	97,136	16	7.06	1.42	1.02
13.	Australia	166,743	111,458	12	5.16	1.42	1.17
14.	Japan	140,302	97,166	15	4.70	1.19	1.02
15.	Brazil	139,098	116,702	11	2.22	1.18	1.23
16.	Switzerland	128,265	131,161	10	-0.28	1.09	1.38
17.	Croatia	118,096	N/A	N/A	N/A	1.00	N/A
18.	Argentina	89,841	63,250	18	4.48	0.76	0.67
19.	Turkey	87,713	26,703	35	16.03	0.75	0.28
20.	Romania	84,525	85,037	17	-0.08	0.72	0.90

(Continued)

Table 4.1 World's Hotel Room Distribution by Country (*Continued*)

Top 40 Countries *Rank Order 1993*

	Country	Number of Rooms 1993	Number of Rooms 1985	Rank 1985	Average Annual Growth Rate (%) 1985/1993	% Share of Rooms World-Wide 1993	% Share of Rooms World-Wide 1985
21.	Tunisia	72,004	46,637	24	5.58	0.61	0.49
22.	Netherlands	70,150	51,859	21	3.85	0.60	0.55
23.	Czech Republic	66,429	N/A	N/A	N/A	0.56	N/A
24.	Peru	63,817	43,021	26	5.05	0.54	0.45
25.	Malaysia	61,005	35,720	29	6.92	0.52	0.38
26.	Sweden	60,523	55,434	19	1.10	0.51	0.58
27.	Bulgaria	59,181	53,610	20	1.24	0.50	0.56
28.	Norway	57,248	48,425	23	2.11	0.49	0.51
29.	Belgium	54,102	43,439	25	2.78	0.46	0.46
30.	Morocco	52,734	38,581	27	3.98	0.45	0.41
31.	Venezuela	52,690	36,940	28	4.54	0.45	0.39
32.	India	49,068	32,609	31	5.24	0.42	0.34
33.	Finland	46,705	31,617	33	5.00	0.40	0.33
34.	Republic of Korea	44,285	23,091	38	8.48	0.38	0.24
35.	Colombia	44,004	27,455	34	6.07	0.37	0.29
36.	South Africa	43,368	49,296	22	-1.59	0.37	0.52
37.	Egypt	39,441	25,665	37	5.52	0.34	0.27
38.	New Zealand	39,330	32,917	30	2.25	0.33	0.35
39.	Denmark	38,433	32,038	32	2.30	0.33	0.34
40.	Portugal	37,302	26,507	36	4.36	0.32	0.28

Data from *Annuaire des Statistiques du Tourisme*, 47th ed., Madrid, Spain: World Tourism Organization 1995.

Growth has been particularly strong in several Asian countries, notably China, which showed more than 17 percent annual growth since 1985. This means that for every 100 rooms that existed in China in 1985, 17 new rooms have been built every year through 1993. In all, China has nearly quadrupled the number of rooms in the country during this time period. Indicators are for solid growth to continue. Korea, Malaysia, Indonesia, and Thailand are also countries to watch, based on growth in the late 1980s and early 1990s.

In Indonesia, well known for destinations like Bali and Borneo, the government took an active role in promoting tourism. It dramatically reduced the paperwork needed to apply for a license to build a hotel. Bali opened its airport to foreign carriers, and visa requirements from more than 20 countries were abolished. Malaysia, similarly, received strong government support for the growth of tourism.

Thailand saw such rapid growth that cities like Bangkok experienced an overabundance of hotel rooms. In the industry, this market condition is termed **overbuilt** As a result, room rates dropped dramatically in the mid 1990s. South Korea has had rapid economic growth as well as changes in its foreign relations, including gaining a seat in the United Nations, which strengthened tourism. Restrictions lifted at the end of the 1980s on outbound travel have meant rapid growth in South Koreans traveling abroad.

Of the European countries, Turkey showed the largest growth by far through 1993. In 1994, however, political upheaval, terrorism, and a large devaluation of the currency reversed the fortune of this country, which is heavily dependent on tourism. The lesson learned is that the political, legal, social, and economic landscape of a country have strong influence on the direction of tourism.

The World of Travelers

The world's 12 million hotel rooms are filled by a mix of both **domestic** and **international** guests. Domestic travelers are citizens traveling within the boundaries of their own country, in **intranational** travel. International travelers cross foreign boundaries. Relative to the number of guest rooms, some countries host many more international travelers than others do, and therefore must place greater emphasis and importance on understanding the needs of international travelers. It turns out that the United States, for example, has few international travelers relative to other countries. In the operation of lodging and foodservice businesses, it should come as no surprise, then, that multilingual staff is much less common in the United States than it would be in European or Asian countries. Hungary is an example of a country that has extensive international travelers but very few domestic or intranational ones. Hungary must be very sensitive to accommodating the needs of international travelers and to the economic importance of tourism.

The International Hospitality Market Table 4.2 lists in rank order the top 20 international tourist destinations in the world. As with many things, the **"80/20 rule,"** which suggests that as few as 20 percent of all causes are responsible for 80 percent of all outcomes, applies to international travel! These top 20 international travel destinations (about 11 percent of all countries in the world),[2] led by France, represent nearly 75 percent of the world's total international travel. The table notes how many hotel rooms there are in each of these countries. It then compares the number of annual international arrivals in any given country relative to the number of hotel rooms available in that country, or **ratio of arrivals to rooms**. For example, in Switzerland, there are 85 international arrivals for every hotel room.

Table 4.2 World's Top Twenty Tourist Destinations

Rank	Country	Arrivals (in thousands) 1993	% Share of Arrivals Worldwide	# of Hotel Rooms	Ratio of Arrivals to Rooms	Population (in thousands)	Ratio of Population to Rooms
1.	France	60,100	11.73	589,216	101	58,000	98
2.	USA	45,779	8.93	3,080,000	14	260,800	84
3.	Spain	40,085	7.82	437,754	91	39,200	89
4.	Italy	26,379	5.15	942,350	28	57,200	60
5.	Hungary	22,804	4.45	22,261	1024	10,300	462
6.	England	19,488	3.80	363,602	54	58,400	160
7.	China	18,982	3.70	386,401	49	1,192,000	3084
8.	Austria	18,257	3.56	319,565	57	8,000	25
9.	Poland	17,000	3.32	20,000	850	38,600	1930
10.	Mexico	16,534	3.23	366,423	45	94,800	258
11.	Canada	15,105	2.95	285,415	53	29,100	101
12.	Germany	14,348	2.80	387,128	37	81,200	209
13.	Switzerland	12,400	2.42	128,265	97	7,000	54
14.	Czech Republic	11,500	2.24	66,429	173	10,300	155
15.	Greece	9,413	1.84	257,383	37	10,400	40
16.	Hong Kong	8,938	1.74	27,031	330	5,800	103
17.	Portugal	8,434	1.65	37,302	226	9,900	265
18.	Malaysia	6,504	1.27	61,005	106	19,500	319
19.	Turkey	5,904	1.15	87,713	67	61,800	704
20.	Singapore	5,804	1.13	27,100	214	2,900	107
	Total	383,761	74.88%	7,922,343			
	World Total	512,523	100.00%	11,767,573			

Data from *Annuaire des Statistiques du Tourisme*, 47th ed., Madrid, Spain: World Tourism Organization, 1995; and *Information Please Almanac*, 48th ed. New York: Houghton Mifflin, 1995. Calculations are the authors'.

Note that each of the top 20 tourist destinations has a multiple of international arrivals more than the United States! Hungary has 1,024 international arrivals for every guest room in the country; Hong Kong has 330. In terms of the customers it serves, the hospitality industry is significantly more "international" in these countries than in the United States. The comparison becomes even more dramatic if Canadian arrivals, who are about 40 percent of the United States' total international arrivals, are removed from the tally.

It is important to note that these comparisons are done on a countrywide basis. The number of international travelers would be significantly more concentrated in major cities. For example, the Imperial Hotel in Tokyo would have a much greater concentration of international guests than a traditional bed and breakfast (**ryoken**) in a smaller Japanese city.

The Intranational Hospitality Market Table 4.2 also provides information on the relative size of each country's domestic hospitality industry by comparing its population to the number of hotel rooms, or **ratio of population to rooms**. Some countries have an underdeveloped hotel industry relative to the population. For example, China has only one room for every 3,084 people in the country. To put this in perspective, if every person in China wanted to spend just one night in a hotel, it would take more than 80 years to accommodate them! By contrast, Austria, which has one room for every 25 people in the country, could provide a more than two-week vacation for each citizen every year. The United States falls in between, but much closer to Austria, with one room for every 84 people in the country. This could provide a four-day vacation per citizen every year.

An Inter/Intra Country Travel Matrix What can we learn if we look at both a country's international and intranational travel? Consider the ratio of arrivals to rooms as a proxy for intenational travel. For example, Poland has a very large number of arrivals relative to rooms, and thus likely has a large percentage of international travelers in its mix. Consider the ratio of population to rooms as a proxy for intranational or domestic travel. Poland has a high ratio (1930 people per room) or very few rooms relative to its population, and thus would have a small percentage of domestic travelers. Plotting both sets of ratios results in the following "intra-inter" national matrix results, which describes the nature of travel to that country (see Figure 4.2).

The countries in or closest to the corners of the matrix provide the sharpest contrasts. Switzerland, for example, has a very large domestic travel market and a large international travel market, unlike China, which has a small domestic market and a medium-sized international market. (One should remember, however, that *all* countries in the matrix are among the top 20 tourist destinations.) The United States has a large domestic market, but a small international market. Hungary has the reverse: a very large international market, but a small domestic one. One need only spend an afternoon in the lobbies of the Budapest Hilton and the New York Hilton to draw a contrast in how "international" the guest lists are.

Hotel Management and Operations Around the World

Comparing one hotel to another in an international arena yields a number of differences. These differences can be found in:

- the many facets of operations,
- the physical plant,

Figure 4.2 Relative Comparison of Intra- and Intercountry Travel

| | | INTRACOUNTRY TRAVEL | | |
	Very Large	**Large**	**Medium**	**Small**
Very Large				Poland Hungary
Large	Switzerland	Czech Republic Spain Singapore FRANCE Hungary Hong Kong	Portugal Malasia	
Medium	Austria Greece Italy	Canada England	Germany Mexico	Turkey China
Small		USA		

(Row labels at left, under the heading **INTERCOUNTRY TRAVEL**)

Figure compiled by Authors. Data from *Annuaire des Statistiques du Tourisme*, World Tourism Organization, Madrid Spain, 1991.

- the development of hotels,
- the customer mix in hotels, and
- the economics of running the hotels.

An international hotel must comprehend and cater to guests' different cultures, religions, and languages, and recognize that the host country's customs, climate, levels of technology, or degree of government regulation may seem unusual to the guest.

Operations

A multicultural, multilingual environment is the key difference between a hotel that caters to an international clientele and a hotel that caters to a domestic clientele. The multiplicity of language and culture and the complexities that this causes means clearing more hurdles in the operations of hotels.

Language Hurdles The more nationalities that a particular hotel caters to, the more languages must be spoken by staff, the more languages room service menus must offer, and the more newspapers the newsstand must stock. Based on the relative comparison of international travel, hotel staff working in the front of the house in Asia and Europe more commonly speak at least two languages, versus the United States, where English only is more the norm.

International hotel companies have responded to the need for foreign language skills in a variety of ways. For example:

- One major international company places national flags on employee name badges, a visual representation of the languages spoken by each employee.
- The Peninsula Hotel in New York has introduced a telephone that speaks six languages and voice mail with multilingual prompts. This feature eliminates translation and allows

a message to be taken directly from the caller.[3] This substitution of technology for staff is a logical solution for American hotels where staff is less likely to be multilingual.

- The Kowloon Hotel in Hong Kong has a computerized address directory that prints in both Chinese and English so that a guest can hand a printout to a taxi driver.

Language translation is not always easily accomplished and can present an interesting set of guest instructions. The following messages illustrate how instructions, though well-intended, change meaning in translation.

Language Translations

When there is something missing in language translation, interesting directions result.

The sign in a Norwegian cocktail lounge reads:
"Ladies are requested not to have children in the bar."

Tacked on the door of a Moscow hotel room:
"If this is your first visit to the USSR, you are welcome to it."

An airline ticket office in Copenhagen reminds you:
"We take your bags and send them in all directions."

A bar in Tokyo informs clients:
"Special cocktails for ladies with nuts."

In a certain African hotel you may choose between:
"A room with a view on the sea or the backside of the country."

This notice was posted on a Romanian hotel elevator:
"The lift is being fixed for the next days. During that time we regret that you will be unbearable."

The room service in a Lisbon hotel tells you:
"If you wish for breakfast, lift the telephone and ask for room service. This will be enough for you to bring your food up."

A Polish hotel informs prospective visitors in a flyer:
"As for the trout served you at the Hotel Monopol, you will be singing its praise to your grandchildren as you lie on your deathbed."

The concierge in a Sorrento hotel lets guests know he's on the job:
"Contact the concierge immediately for informations. Please don't wait last minutes than it will be too late to arrange any inconveniences."

One hotel in Zurich displays a sign reading:
"Because of the impropriety of entertaining guests of the opposite sex in the bedroom, it is suggested that the lobby be used for this purpose."

A Berlin café serves:
"Five o'clock tea at all hours."

A notice in a Vienna hotel urges:
"In case of fire do your utmost to alarm the hall porter."

Source: Bello Nino Lo, *English Well Speeched Here and Other Fractured Phrases from Around the World*, Los Angeles: Price Stern Sloan, 1986

Scheduling Hurdles Since guests arrive from many different time zones, it is important to comprehend the different needs of a guest with respect to "what time it is." Time zone differences mean the hotel's restaurants need to have lengthened operating hours and offer meals at times outside the host country's appointed hours. Similarly, the reception desk needs to accommodate unusual arrival and departure schedules.

Customs and Culture Hurdles Understanding the differences between local customs and cultures and those of foreign guests can give a hotel an advantage. For example, such considerations are important for long-term decisions like staffing a hotel.

When Marriott opened its Hong Kong property in 1989, it decided to offer a five–day work week (as is customary for other Marriott hotels around the world) despite the fact that it defied the Hong Kong custom of a six-day work week. Though it angered members of the Hong Kong Hotels Association, it proved to be a drawing card for attracting employees in a tight labor market.[4] The critical point here is that understanding the culture of a country can help a hospitality company plan rather than react.

Understanding various customs is also important in the face of immediate decisions, like appropriate guest interaction. A European traveler, for example, does not expect to shop for room rates, and doesn't expect a discount or a negotiation. They expect to pay at the appropriate tier: rack rate, corporate rate, group rate, or airline rates.[5] For a reservationist or a front desk clerk, understanding this would be important in booking a sale. For a Japanese guest, the number four is considered unlucky. In Japanese, four is *shi* and "to die" is *shinu*. This would be good to know when assigning a room number; it would be better not to put a Japanese guest in room 444.[6] Similarly, in the United States many hotels do not have a thirteenth floor. It's a superstitiously unlucky number to Americans.

Staffing Hurdles A frontline position in a Western European hotel could be viewed as a profession; in Asia, it may be viewed as a ticket to a lifelong career; and in the United States, it is more likely viewed as a way station, a place to earn a living while aspiring to another career. These descriptions are presented as generalizations to emphasize some broad-based differences in the attitudes of hotel staff across continents. There are many exceptions. For example, the United States can boast of talented, professional waiters and waitresses who treat their profession as a career.

Europeans, in general, have a very serious attitude toward the skills required to be a waiter. Extensive formal food and beverage training is the norm, and being a waiter is a very respectable career. By contrast, there is little formal hotel management education in Japan, where "hospitality" is not recognized by the Ministry of Education as an official field of education, but schooling abroad or extensive, detail-oriented on-the-job training is a must.[7] For example, at the Hotel Okura in Tokyo, bellmen practice smiling and bowing in front of a mirror. They also are trained to grasp a baggage claim check with two hands, never just one, and deliver it with a bow. The young bellmen at the hotel pay attention; they consider their jobs with the company to be lifetime employment. Though flipping a claim check to a guest may seem a small infraction, it's high stakes when your career, not just a job, is on the line.[8] By contrast, the bellman and waiters at the Helmsley Hotel in New York have different and "higher" aspirations; some want to be actors.

One general manager, working in New York for a Hong Kong–based luxury hotel chain, compared hotel management in Asia versus the United States this way: "The principle is the same. You deal with people. In Asia, you have a more natural situation of people wanting to serve, and they don't see it as something negative. People there are self-motivated to give the service, to give the natural smile."[9]

He also commented on how labor rates shape differences in staffing and a hotel's ability to deliver attentive service. "The real difference between Asia and the West (including Europe) is that you have to work more strategically here. Labor is cheaper in Asia. In the West, you can't afford to hire as many people. In the Far East it is easy to add on an additional employee."[10] The proof is in the ratio of staff to guest rooms, as Table 4.3 illustrates. Two to three employees per guest room is not uncommon in Asia—in fact, the Hong Kong Marriott's and the Tokyo Okura's ratio is two to one. The Hong Kong Peninsula's is three to one. In the United States a ratio of one to one, or less, like the New York Helmsley's, is closer to the average.

For developing countries, a different kind of staffing hurdle arises: finding or importing sufficient talent to operate hotels. To staff the first Western hotel in Tbilisi, the capital of Soviet Georgia, the Austrian operators found they had plenty of job applicants, but none with hotel experience. The job pool included a pig farmer, a violinist, and a veterinarian, creating quite a training challenge for the small team of Western managers.[11] The Tanzanian government, which owns most of its country's

Table 4.3 Staff-to-Guest–Room Ratios in Select First–Class Hotels Worldwide

City/Hotel	Number of Staff Members	Number of Guest Rooms	Ratio of Staff to Guests
Hong Kong			
Marriott	1,100	607	1.8:1
Hong Kong Peninsula	630	210	3:1
Tokyo			
Okura	1,600	880	1.8:1
New York			
Helmsley	1,000	1,008	1:1
Boston			
Hyatt Regency	390	469	.8:1
Bangkok			
Shangri La	1,523	871	1.8:1
Boston			
Royal Sonesta	275	400	.7:1
Shanghai			
Novotel	350	220	1.6:1

Table compiled by authors.

hotels and game lodges, found it difficult to provide guests with soap, toilet paper, and light bulbs, let along manage its hotels. In an effort to modernize and improve service, the government courted foreign management, signing its first management contract with Sheraton in 1987.[12]

Security Hurdles It is no wonder, with the shifting of global boundaries and threats of terrorism, that maintaining tight security has become an increasing important operational issue in international hotels. When the International Hotel Association asked its members to rank the influences most likely to affect their business in the twenty-first century, the number one response was "the safety and security of hotels," outranking even "the use of computers by management" and "effective marketing techniques." The places where security is of greatest concern are in Africa, South Asia, and North America.[13]

In more than one part of the world, hotels have suffered the dramatic impact of disaster striking. When terrorists opened fire in the Rome airport in 1985, U.S. tourism to Italy dropped nearly 60 percent the following year. Many five-star hotels, which were the hardest hit, were forced to drop rates and reposition to attract European and Asian markets.[14] The aftermath of the crackdown in Tiananmen Square, China, in 1989, when the Chinese Army shot thousands of prodemocracy demonstrators, had a catastrophic effect on tourism. Three years later, in Shanghai, all 14 foreign-managed hotels continued to lose money.[15] The impact of the Persian Gulf invasion in 1992, when Iraq invaded Kuwait, went well beyond Kuwaiti City and Baghdad, stalling air travel and hotel reservations in the United States and abroad for months after the fighting stopped.

Government Regulation Hurdles China provides some of the best examples to illustrate how government regulation can cause havoc to hotel operations. In early 1992, for example, the government issued an instruction that all hotels should change their signs so that they would be identical, causing a sharp reaction from the International Hotels Association. Additionally, Western hotel managers in China complained that they did not have the *guanxi*, or local contacts, to fend off the Chinese authorities who control things like the health inspection of hotels and the awarding of stars.[16] Thus the star system was not necessarily reflective of the merit of the hotels themselves.

Physical Plant

The physical plant of hotels, the buildings, grounds, furnishings and decor, are usually reflective of a host country's culture. Though many modern international hotels may look somewhat alike, most will still reflect their surroundings in ways ranging from the architecture to small amenities; the architecture of the hotel speaks to its location. The Budapest Hilton incorporates ruins from the old city. The Oriental Bangkok delivers laundry wrapped and tied with ribbons and its native orchids.[17]

History has played a role in creating some differences in the physical structures of the world's hotels. Concepts like the **parador, château, hacienda**, or **ryokan** are unique to their respective parts of the world. The Spanish paradors are "inns" (the translation from classic Spanish literature) that have been converted from architecturally significant sites such as castles, convents, and palaces. They tend to be in less traveled locations and try to capture links with the history and geography of their locations. The French concept of a château is the same principle, capturing historical architecture in a unique hotel offering. The haciendas of Mexico, formerly great estates of land granted to the conquistadors by Spain during the colonization of America, are today accommodations that boast extensive woodlands and gardens, often replanted to mirror the original grounds. The original ryokans, the traditional accommodations of Japan, were probably built some 1,200 years ago. The inns provide traditional landscaped gardens, use of natural building materials, and asymmetrical, nature-inspired architecture.[18]

Customer Mix

One can look at customer mix at various levels. Every hotel, country, and continent hosts a different mix of international arrivals. The native countries of the guests will shape the services needed by a host country or host hotel. The mix of customers can be considered by various sample sizes: by continent, by country, or by hotel. An example of each follows. In Asia, about half of the international arrivals come from other countries in Asia, about a quarter come from Europe, 10 percent each from the Middle East and the Americas, and a small percentage from Africa (see Figure 4.3). This describes where Asia's customers come from by continent. From the perspective of tourism and generating foreign visitors to a host country or group of countries, this information could be very useful for strategic planning.

A glimpse at a single country's international mix, the United States, shows that Canada leads the top 20 source countries (see Table 4.4). This information helps the United States to understand where its current tourism dollars are coming from. Canada and Mexico provide the lion's share of arrivals, with Japan, the United Kingdom, and Germany ranking third, fourth, and fifth.

An individual hotel may break down its customer mix by type, such as business, leisure travelers, or group, and may also track the international mix of its guests. The more specifically a hotel can identify who visits, the more apt it is to be able to provide the kinds of services and facilities

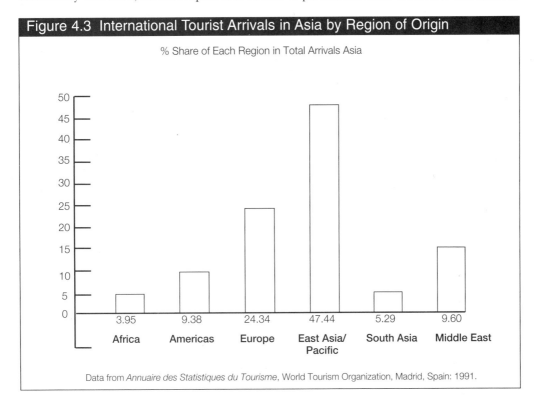

Figure 4.3 International Tourist Arrivals in Asia by Region of Origin

% Share of Each Region in Total Arrivals Asia

Africa	Americas	Europe	East Asia/Pacific	South Asia	Middle East
3.95	9.38	24.34	47.44	5.29	9.60

Data from *Annuaire des Statistiques du Tourisme*, World Tourism Organization, Madrid, Spain: 1991.

■■■■■■ *Table 4.4* Top 15 Arrivals for the USA for 1994

Country	Arrivals YTD 1994 (in thousands)
1. Canada	15,000
2. Mexico	11,300
3. Japan	4,065
4. England	2,921
5. Germany	1,705
6. France	863
7. Brazil	661
8. Italy	551
9. South Korea	504
10. Taiwan	379
11. Venezuela	424
12. Australia	411
13. Netherlands	393
14. Argentina	390
15. Switzerland	367

Data from U.S. Travel and Tourism Administration, July 1995

that are needed in its operations. For example, it is no mystery that the Marriott Copley in Boston, which attracts a sizable market from Japan, has Japanese-speaking staff and a sushi bar in the lobby. These facilities and amenities will bring Japanese guests back to the hotel.

Development

Developing hotels in foreign countries is not a vacation—every country, every project, presents a different, and often difficult set of development challenges. The economic and political climate, varying ownership structures, cultural differences, and cost variances mean a different game plan is needed from one country to the next. In Eastern Europe, for example, an area which has potential for explosive growth from the 1990s forward, it is difficult just to establish who has title to land; much land was confiscated after World War II by governments that have since fallen.[19] Hungary, which initially launched major construction to host the World's Fair in 1996, canceled its plans. It simply couldn't overcome all of the obstacles quickly enough. Political stability is also of concern in this part of the world, and could put more than one project on ice.

The structure of hotel development on foreign lands is generally not outright ownership by one player, but often involves franchising, joint ventures, or a licensing arrangement between an international and a local partner. For example, in India, there are many restrictions on foreign business operations. When Days Inns launched a plan to expand its chain throughout India, it teamed up with an Indian partner, best known not for its expertise in hotels, but for producing jeeps and tractors.[20]

Cultural differences can cause difficulties in development. Club Meditérranée (Club Med), a French resort company, tried to develop a resort on China's southern coast, with the Chinese government. The resort was eventually built, after two years of negotiations, but Club Med was not in the picture when it opened. A manager from Hong Kong working in China summed up the conflict: "Club Med had a lot of big ideas, but China is in a completely different world. They've never even seen a bikini on the Xiaomeisha Beach."[21]

Budgeting the development of a project can have huge variations from one country to the next. In Tokyo, land costs are estimated at 80 percent of the cost of a new hotel.[22] Compare this with the land costs for developing a U.S. hotel, which are generally 10 to 15 percent of the total.

Financial Comparison

Fundamentally, the way one makes money in a hotel is not the same in all parts of the world. Comparing the sources and uses of the industry dollar in the United States and abroad yields some important differences. These differences in the profitability of various international hotels are linked to those operational and development issues discussed above. Consider the implications of the following sources and uses of the industry dollar, as illustrated in Figures 4.4A and 4.4B: The first illustration breaks down sources and uses of the industry dollar for the United States; the second illustration shows sources and uses for an aggregate of international hotels.

Two important conclusions result from this comparison, one each from sources and uses:

- Hotels outside the United States, on average, are more dependent on food and beverage as a source of revenue and are less dependent on rooms than hotels in the United States. Of the world's revenue, 36.9 percent comes from food and beverage, versus 26.6 percent in the United States. It follows, then, that food and beverage training receive higher priority in Europe and in Asia. Hotel restaurants abroad are also generally held in higher esteem than are their counterparts in U.S. hotels.

- The United States spends more on payroll and related expenses than do the rest of the world's hotels: 32.4 percent versus 26.9 percent. This is reflected in the staffing of operations. Lower labor rates abroad generally translate to an ability to hire more staff. The one exception is Europe, where labor costs approximate costs in the United States. Thus, as we noted earlier, since more employees can be hired for less cost, the ratio of staff to guests is generally higher abroad.

As labor is such a large component of the cost structure for any hotel or restaurant operation, it is useful to take a closer look at labor expenses by world part and by country. Table 4.5 presents labor expenses as a percentage of revenue for different parts of the world. This comparison yields the following conclusions:

1. Africa, as a continent, has by far the lowest labor rates in the world; Europe and the United States have the highest.

2. Relatively cheaper labor rates in the Asian countries help fuel a reputation for better service.

3. Costs in Europe and the United States are very similar.

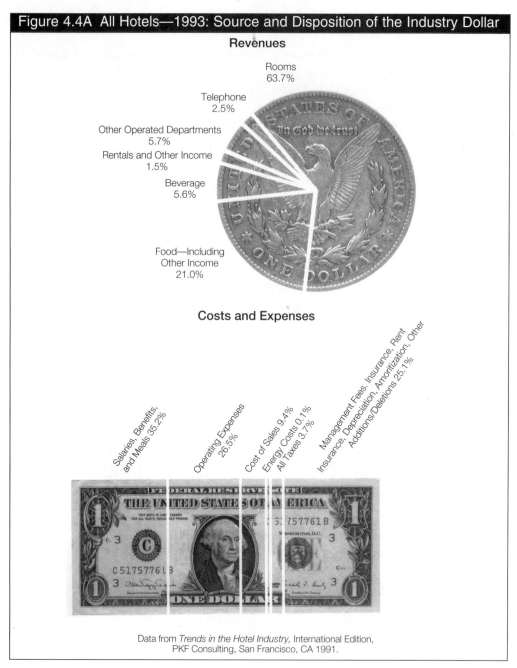

Figure 4.4A All Hotels—1993: Source and Disposition of the Industry Dollar

Revenues

Rooms
63.7%

Telephone
2.5%

Other Operated Departments
5.7%

Rentals and Other Income
1.5%

Beverage
5.6%

Food—Including
Other Income
21.0%

Costs and Expenses

Salaries, Benefits,
and Meals 35.2%

Operating Expenses
26.5%

Cost of Sales 9.4%

Energy Costs 0.1%

All Taxes 3.7%

Management Fees, Insurance, Rent
Insurance, Depreciation, Amortization, Other
Additions/Deletions 25.1%

Data from *Trends in the Hotel Industry,* International Edition,
PKF Consulting, San Francisco, CA 1991.

Occupancy and Average Daily Rate Finally, there are two key statistics that concern every hotelier in evaluating the operation of a hotel, wherever it is–occupancy and average daily rate. The average occupancy rate in the United States in 1993 was 67.5 percent and internationally was 62.4 percent.[23] These occupancy rates are near the breakeven point, around 65 percent, or above. The range of occupancy rates is within a band, between 60 and 85 percent. When occupancy

Figure 4.4B Source and Distribution of the Industry Dollar International, 1990

Revenues   **Total Revenue 100%**

Rooms 53.7%

Food—Including Other Income 26.3 %

Beverages 10.6 %

Other Operated Department 4.0%

Rentals and Other Income 2.3 %

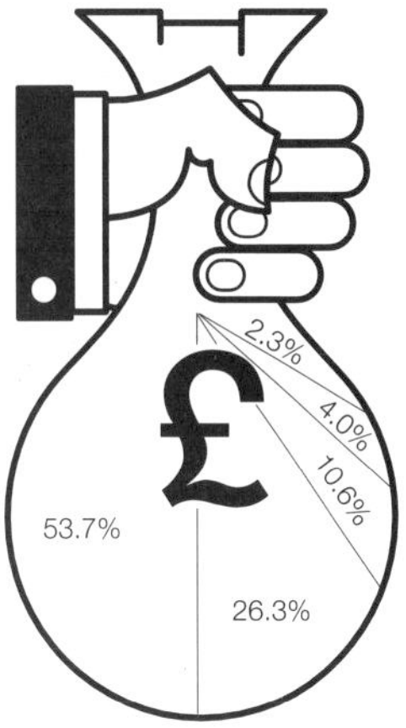

Total Costs and Expenses 100 %

26.9%

Operating Expenses 19.3%

Costs of Sales 12.4 %

Energy Costs 2.5 %

All Taxes 2.8 %

Management Fees, Insurance, Rent, Interest, Depreciation, Amortization, Other Additions/Deletions 36.1%

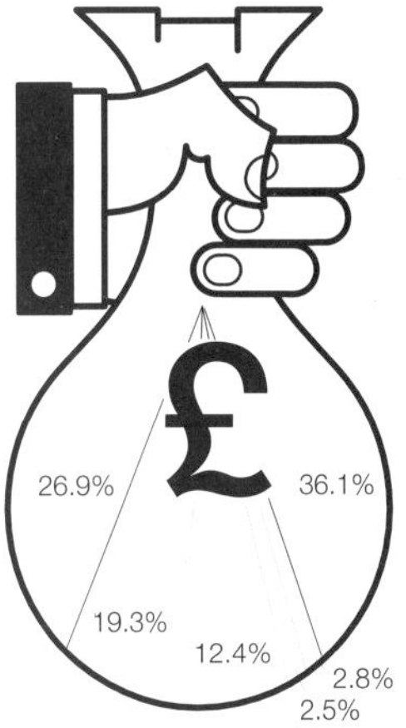

Data from *Trend in the Hotel Industry*, International Edition, PKF Consulting, San Francisco, CA, 1991.

in an area is well above breakeven for a period of time, then new hotels will be built. For example, Hong Kong is a likely candidate for new hotel rooms. The opposite is also true; weak occupancy will cause supply to shrink.

The variance in room rate can be considerably wider than occupancy rate, with the highest average daily rate being more than twice the lowest in the countries presented. Table 4.6 shows that the average daily rate is somewhat higher in international hotels, $87.38 versus $77.47 in the United States, making them greater revenue generators in absolute cents. Europe, as a continent, shows the highest average daily rate.

Restaurant Operations and Management Around the World

Many restaurants around the world are hosts to international clientele. Most of these restaurants are local owners whose location services international travelers. Any restaurant with an interna-

███████ *Table 4.5* Payroll and Related Costs in Rooms and Food and Beverage by World
Part, 1990

Country/World Part	Rooms Payroll Cost as a % of Rooms Revenue	Food and Beverage Payroll Costs as a % of Food and Beverage Revenue
World	**17.2**	**39.47**
USA	18.1	44.0
Asia/Pacific	12.8	27.7
Africa	6.3	22.6
Middle East	10.4	27.2
Europe	18.8	43.0

Table compiled by authors. Data from PKF Consulting International Hotel Trends, San Francisco, CA, 1994.

███████ *Table 4.6* Occupancy and Average Daily Rate by Country and World Part

Country/World Part	Occupancy % 1990	Occupancy % 1993	Average Daily Rate 1990	Average Daily Rate 1993
World	**67.2%**	**62.4%**	**$94.45**	**$87.38**
USA	66.2	67.5	78.76	77.47
Pacific Basin (Asia & Australia)	71.4	77.6	97.02	95.27
Africa	66.6	58.6	65.05	81.7
Middle East	60.6	63.4	83.02	99.97
Europe	68.7	62.9	116.79	101.21
Canada	66.3	61.2	77.95	65.2
Mexico	61.7	50.2	64.78	85.01
France	74.8	59.2	148.48	169.34
Germany	69.2	62.5	110.55	109.05
England	69.8	64.8	115.41	82.19
Italy	77.7	65.7	118.44	100.46
Spain	69.9	55.4	126.62	130.74
Austria	69.3	55.9	142.5	1224.74
Portugal	65.9	53.4	111.98	104.77
Switzerland	65.4	61.9	122.45	126.94
Thailand	85.9	62.2	114.57	75.47
Hong Kong	79.4	87.4	112.82	102.23

Adapted from *Trends in the Hotel Industry*, International and U.S. editions. (PKF Consulting) San Francisco, CA, 1991 and 1994. Latest data available.

tional clientele, not unlike hotels, is faced with customs and culture hurdles. "Restaurante Trente," a small trattoria in the heart of Tuscany, illustrates the point. This restaurant, though it has less than 50 seats, may find itself, on any given evening in August, trying to respond to the needs of the following customers: a German family on holiday; four British senior citizens celebrating a 70th birthday; a local, boisterous Italian table of eight; and an American couple out for a romantic evening. Not only are the needs of each table different, but so are the cultural expectations about what the restaurant experience should be. Adapting to the expectations of a wide range of international guests is a challenging task for a restaurateur.

Management and Operations of Foreign Restaurant Chains

The complexitites faced by a local restauranteur in serving a mixed international market are just one of the challenging sets of hurdles faced by foreign restaurant chains. The rapidly growing phenomenom of large chains opening on foreign soil has been dominated by American-based chains. Most of the growth has been in Western Europe and the Asia-Pacific region, with expansion potential noted in the Middle East, Canada, Australia, China, and Eastern Europe, and Central and South America.

The foreign expansion odyssey began a quarter century ago, when McDonald's opened its first foreign unit in Canada and its first European unit in the Netherlands. This was the beginning of what is now a corporation with units in 73 countries. At about the same time, Peter Morton, an American entrepreneur, launched the first Hard Rock Cafe in London, beginning an internationally known chain. Many companies followed suit, attempting to capitalize on a rapidly emerging middle class in some countries, and an increased desire for the Western quick-service concept. In addition, foreign expansion has been an important hedge against a mature domestic market. Pizza Hut, TGI Friday's, Dairy Queen, Burger King, Kentucky Fried Chicken, and Baskin-Robbins are just some of the examples of chains that have set their sights overseas. Table 4.7 gives a comparison of the geographic distribution of the top chain's international development.

In the course of opening restaurants, these chains face a number of obstacles, some more difficult than others. Each individual country presents its own set of hurdles. These obstacles are typically found in the following areas:

- responding to customs and culture
- the development of restaurants
- the economic conditions of the country of operation
- the many facets of operations.

Customs and Culture

In addition to language barriers, which can be a key impediment for any company doing business in a foreign country, restaurant companies are faced with customs and cultural hurdles as they relate to food, the way it is prepared, and the way it tastes to a local palate.

■■■■■■ *Table 4.7* Every year the periodical *Restaurants and Institutions* ranks the top food-service operations by various criteria. They rank the top international growth companies by number of outlets. The top 10 for 1995 follow.

Chain	Total	Canada	Europe	Asia	Latin America	Middle East
McDonald's	5,513	720	2,130	2,187	445	39
KFC	4,207	835	433	2,173	357	409
Pizza Hut	2,989	531	940	913	451	154
Baskin–Robbins	1,428	211	707	97	274	139
Burger King	1,375	207	625	254	272	17
Subway	1,037	823	17	118	66	13
Dunkin' Donuts	964	232	527	165	34	6
Domino's	722	165	125	206	196	30
Wendy's	432	187	18	142	60	25
Arby's	168	113	3	7	36	9
Taco Bell	139	76	7	7	40	9
Hardee's	69	0	0	38	4	27
Sbarro	53	8	16	6	15	8
TGI Friday's	44	0	21	18	5	0

Source: Restaurants and Institutions, July 1995. Reprinted with permission.

A restaurant company opening in a foreign location may find that the local market does not yet have an acquired taste for the kind of food that it serves. Sometimes, after some exposure, the menu items gain popularity. At other times, the restaurant concept simply doesn't make it. For example, nachos and fajitas, which are trendy novelties in Germany, have caught on. In fact, this ethnic trend has become so popular that German companies, which traditionally leave ethnic options to foreigners, are opening their own chains of Mexican units. Two such chains are Sal Doloris and Hacienda.

Even if there is a generally positive response to a particular cuisine, restaurants must also be willing to adapt certain menu items to suit local palates. Burger King, in its menu offerings in the Pacific Rim, includes a durian milkshake. This Southeast Asian fruit has been likened to an onion, and though it would not sell well in Miami, Burger King's corporate headquarters, it sells very well in the Asian market. In Germany, many fast food restaurants, such as McDonald's and Burger King, which traditionally do not serve alcohol, have added beer to the menu in response to local tradition. In China, Pizza Hut, learning of the Chinese distaste for cheese, printed special tent cards explaining the nutritional benefits of cheese and how it is made. Restaurant chains must be sensitive to important, religious customs associated with food. Though the foundation of their business, the McDonald's menu offerings in the country of India does not include beef. (Including beef would be a blatant violation of religious custom.) Also in response to religous custom, McDonald's opened its first kosher outlet near Tel Aviv, Israel, in July 1995. In Mecca, Saudi Arabia, all meat is slaughtered according to Islamic rules. All of these specific adaptations require an understanding of the local region.

Development

The developer of a new restaurant in a foreign country can face formidable financial challenges. Expensive real estate costs and other-start up costs can make it difficult to get into business in the first place. Some countries are particularly expensive, such as Japan, where land is at a premium. Strict historic preservation laws can make renovation expensive. Often, the oldest sections of cities provide the best locations, but also the most stringent architectural constraints.

In some countries, it may not necessarily be clear who owns what you are trying to buy. A restaurant chain must be sure that it is dealing with a legitimate owner. As an investment is being contemplated, fluctuating exchange rates and economic conditions can make the equation all the more uncertain.

The first set of developers in a particular country can confront particular hardships. The idea of foreign companies' setting up shop may not meet with universal approval. Kentucky Fried Chicken's launch into India, for example, met with mixed reviews in the city of Bangalore. Though the Indian government has been encouraging foreign investment, city officials closed down the brand-new KFC, citing alleged violations of the health code. A court order swiftly reopened the restaurant, but Pepsico, the parent company of KFC, must continue to face protests from local residents who have lobbied against foreign investors.[24]

The first developers in a country may also find that the costs associated with purchasing its food may be prohibitive to local buyers. In Vietnam, where the first American quick-service chain opened in 1995, a single scoop of Baskin-Robbins ice cream cost $1.60. For the average Vietnamese factory worker, that's the equivalent of a day's wages. These developers are clearly betting on a long-term expected improvement in economic conditions.

Navigating bureaucracy is another time- and resource-consuming step in the development process. To help in this regard, as is the case with hotel development, it is not unusual for international restaurant chains to be working with native partners. Because they are more adept at dealing with local regulations, franchises are likely to be from the host country, or that part of the world. For example, Deutsche Inter-Hotels/American Bistro is a Berlin-based franchisee of T.G.I. Friday's. The Tong Yang Group of Seoul, Korea, is the Korean franchisor of Bennigan's Restaurants. Taco Cabana, a Mexican chain, has teamed up with Kuwait-based AlMazaya International, to open units in Kuwait, Saudi Arabia, the United Arab Emirates, Bahrain, Egypt, and Lebanon. It may also happen that the local franchisee is the government itself! In China or Russia, for example, growth in restaurant franchising has been with a strong government presence.

Economics

As is true in the development process, uncertain or changing economic conditions can make success in the operation of a foreign restaurant chain risky business. The structure and governance of the business community may be very different from that of the home country. In Russia, for example, the strong hold of organized crime in the business community creates obstacles to doing business.

In some countries it can also be difficult to repatriate, or get the money that you earn out of the country. The vice president of operations for Dairy Queen, Ed Watson, in speaking of business in China, notes that some companies have to settle for lower black market exchange rates to get their revenues out of the country.[25]

When the broad economic conditions of a particular country suffer, so too do restaurant sales. The Australian Kentucky Fried Chicken operations faced a large dip in sales in 1992, when unemployment soared to 15 percent. Similarly, when the value of the Mexican peso dropped sharply in 1995, restaurant chains such as Domino's suffered.

Operations

In the day-to-day operations of its restaurants, foreign chains meet with some of the same hurdles that a domestic operation would, such as hiring and training a qualified workforce and creating efficient preparation and distribution methods. (We will consider restaurant operations in detail in chapter 9.) In addition, foreign operations have particular problems in sourcing goods, staffing, and responding to local conditions.

Sourcing of Goods In a chain operation, replicating specific standards for food items worldwide is important. Consistent quality, in every unit, in every country, is part of customers' expectations. However, the local economy does not always offer the correct specifications of the raw ingredients needed for menu items. In England, McDonald's helped to build a hamburger bun factory, as traditional hamburger buns were simply unavailable in Britain. Similarly, in Thailand, potato farmers were shown how to grow the Idaho potatoes used for McDonald's french fries, as locally grown potatoes did not meet McDonald's specifications.

Some countries have restrictive import regulations. When Dairy Queen was preparing to open stores in Korea, it found a problem importing its sundae toppings. Though Korean law permitted them to import these items, they could not do so if the products contained preservatives. The company had to set up special batch processing in the United States to make the toppings without preservatives, so that they would be suitable for shipping.[26]

Staffing Though staffing a restaurant can be thought of as a universal problem, some countries have particularly difficult conditions that must be met. Tough labor laws and strong labor unions in certain countries are a good examples. Some countries impose high social taxes on employers. Some labor markets are just plain expensive and so present a vigorous competitive challenge. For example, Robert Martin, the vice president of development and international operations for The Old Spagetti Factory International, notes that the social taxes and required vacation pay imposed on its Hamburg, Germany, unit drives costs sky high.[27]

Adapting to Local Conditions Finally, being aware of and able to quickly respond to local conditions is an ingredient for success. For example, if you were an American ice cream chain set up to do business in Canada, you would do well to mind your P's and Q's, or pints and quarts.[28] Canada restricts "to go" packaging to full or half liters. This presented a challenge to Baskin-Robbins, which traditionally sells by the pint, quart, and half gallon.

The very infrastructure of a country can also be important to note. For pizza delivery chains like Domino's, the countries like Slovokia and Hungary have promise, but only 30 to 40 percent of all households have phone service.[29] This fact speaks to the current and future potential of the business.

A final example involves the legal environment. In South Africa, trademark laws have not stopped a McDonald's lookalike from setting up shop, complete with burger offerings and golden arches. Though McDonald's has sued the competitor, the business can continue to operate until the court system makes a ruling. The traditional methods of doing business at times just don't apply in the international market.

Developing restaurants operations internationally can be considered to be even more complex than opening a hotel. Customs, culture, expensive start-up costs, government bureaucracies, the difficulty of finding adequate suppliers, and the uncertainty of political situations are formidable challenges for an international restaurateur. These challenges must be faced clearly and objectively when deciding to go global.

In a practical sense, that may mean that an international company might find its development arm forming a strategic alliance with a global partner from the host country who can access and understand the local economic structure; locating hotels in major gateway cities, such as New York or London if it is trying to establish presence in the United States or Europe; or purchasing a local company that already has an established identity so it can grow abroad quickly. The company might find its marketing arm opening international sales offices or promising today's exchange rate for an international traveler planning to visit in the future, or it might join the tourism efforts of its host countries to encourage travel.

South America Looks Northward

While international hotels have long been in business in South America, it is only within the latter part of the 1990s that the midpriced chain has discovered this continent. With rising standards of living in South America, newly democratically elected governments, and a move toward open markets, more U.S. business travelers than ever are heading south of the border. Not to be discounted, too, is the lure of the natural beauty of South America, the home of exotic animals, dangerous beasts, birds of paradise, friendly natives, and wilderness sunsets.

With this new found attention comes the need for value-priced but comfortable accomodations, for both intra- and international travelers. In countries like Chile, Argentina, Brazil, and Peru, more and more hotels are being developed by North American companies. Chains like Holiday Inn and Comfort Inn are beginning to expand into smaller cities and away from traditional downtown areas. Aimed at local business travelers, these hotels provide a clean, yet economical, place to stay. In March of 1996, Days Inns of America signed a licensing pact with a South American developer, Compania Topasia SA. The agreement reportedly called for the construction of at least 500 rooms in Argentina, Paraguay, and Uruguay by the year 2001.

Summary

The worldwide tour of hotel operations presented in this chapter lays the groundwork for becoming a successful international hotel company. It is clear that a successful international hotelier, must, at a minimum:

- understand the supply of and demand for hotel rooms
- master the different operational issues, including language, scheduling, customs and culture, staffing, security, and government regulations
- understand the development issues in each host country, and
- understand the economics of generating profit.

In the restaurant sector, nearly all international expansion is with large chain restaurant companies. Not unlike hotel operations, restaurateurs must be responsive to local conditions. This includes:

- responding to customs and culture
- understanding the dynamics of development
- preparing for fluctuating economic conditions, and
- responding to local conditions.

A restaurant company may find itself changing menu items to adapt to local tastes, changing preparation techniques to respond to local customs or religion, or importing raw materials to achieve consistent quality. It may also attempt to create manufacturing plants in the local area for unavailable items such as hamburger buns. Most important, a restaurant chain operation, like a hotel chain, must be relentlessly attentive to local conditions and must respond within the context of the social, political, and economic climate of the host country.

If an international hotel or restaurant company can truly understand where the world's hotel rooms are, and who stays in them, both in terms of international and domestic travelers, and can hurdle the many obstacles faced in operations, development, and making a profit, it might just find the world as its oyster!

Discussion Questions

1. In which parts of the world are the largest concentrations of hotel rooms? Why?

2. How does the 80/20 rule apply to international travel?

3. How can we compare the amount of international and intranational travel from one country to the next?

4. Why is security an important consideration in an international hotel? What historical events illustrate the point?

5. How, in general, would you compare the front–line employees in a hotel in the United States, in Europe, and in Asia?

6. Why would an international company team up with a local player in the development of a hotel or restaurant?

7. Explain the following hotel concepts and note their country of origin: ryoken, hacienda, parador, château. What do they have in common?

8. Is the food and beverage department of a hotel more important in the United States or abroad?

9. Why are occupancy rates very similar around the world?

10. What makes for a successful international hotel company? Restaurant company?

11. What kinds of local conditions influence menu items for a restaurant chain?

12. To what lengths must a restaurant chain sometimes go to achieve consistent quality worldwide?

13. The spirit of the opening quotation offers up the world as the relevant way to think about the potential of a hospitality company. Why?

Assignment

Research a hotel or restaurant company that operates in more than one country. How do the hotels or restaurants differ from country to country? What obstacles did the company encounter in developing new establishments?

End Notes

1. William Shakespeare, *The Merry Wives of Windsor*, act II, scene 2.

2. The 11 percent is based on 185 countries officially recognized by the United Nations as of 1995.

3. "Strategies for Winning Guests in Competitive Times," *Hotels* 26 (3 March 1992): 50.

4. Barbara Basler, "Marriott Defies a Hong Kong Custom," *New York Times* (6 February, 1989): 27.

5. "Strategies for Winning," 52.

6. Somerset R. Waters, "World Intelligencer," *Travel Industry World Yearbook 1991* (New York: Child and Waters, Inc., 1991), 13.

7. William H. Kaven, "Japan's Hotel Industry: An Overview," *Cornell Quarterly* 33 (2): 26–32.

8. Brent Bowers and Damon Darlin, "How Hotels in Japan and the U.S. Compare in the Services Game," *The Wall Street Journal*, 21 September 1988, 1.

9. Manfred Timmel, general manager of the Peninsula, New York, quoted in "Strategies for Winning Guests in Competitive Times," *Hotels* 26 (3 March 1992): 52.

10. Ibid.

11. Frederick Kempe, "Fancy New Hotel is Reluctant Godfather to Soviet Georgians," *New York Times*, 21 March 1991, A–1.

12. Sheila Rule, Tanzania Courting Foreigners to Manage Its Hotels," *New York Times*, 23 April 1987, C1.

13. "Safety, Cost of Travel Will Be Major Concerns in 21st Century," *Hotels and Restaurants International* (September 1992): 29.

14. John A. Hurley, "The Hotels of Rome: Meeting the Marketing Challenge of Terrorism," *Cornell Quarterly* (May 1988): 71–79.

15. Nicolas D. Kristof, "Hotels with 5 Stars, Huge Staffs (and Few Guests)," *New York Times*, 2 March, 1992, A4.

16. Ibid, A4.

17. Mary Williams Walsh, "Bangkok's Hotels Pile on the Pampering," *The Wall Street Journal*, 27 April 1989, p. B1.

18. Hana Ayala, "International Hotel Ventures: Back to the Future," *The Cornell H.R.A. Quarterly* (February 1991): 38–45.

19. Kate Trollope, "Wanted: Imagination, Courage in East Europe," *Hotels* (January 1992): 21.

20. "Days Inns Plan in India," *New York Times*, 23 April, 1990, D8.

21. Maria Shao, "Club Med in China: It's No Vacation," *Business Week* (1 September 1986): 54.

22. Charles Smith, "A Taste for Exotica," *Far Eastern Economic Review* (16 February 1989): 55.

23. Adapted from *Trends in the Hotel Industry*, International Edition. (Houston, Texas: Pannel Kerr Foster, 1991).

24. John F. Burns, "India Effort vs. Foreign Business Upsets American Chain," *New York Times,* 14 September 1995, D6.

25. Bill McDowell, "The Global Market Challenge," *Restaurants and Institutions* (1 November 1994): 59.

26. Ibid, 52.

27. Richard Martin, "US Chains Brave Tough Obstacles," *Nation's Restaurant News* (1995): 50.

28. As a point of interest, the term P's and Q's originated in British pubs. Hanging chalk boards kept track of a patron's beer tab. Chalk lines were drawn under the catagories P's and Q's, as a customer consumed Pints and Quarts of ale.

29. McDowell, 54.

Chapter Five

"*The gladdest moment in human
life, methinks, is the departure
upon a distant journey.*"

Sir Richard Burton

Tourism Visited ✍

When you finish this chapter you should:

1. Be able to define tourism.

2. Understand the universal truths about tourism.

3. Understand the impact of tourism on international development.

4. Explain how the elements of hospitality are intertwined in tourism.

5. Be able to name the variety of activities that can comprise tourism.

6. Be able to name the major travel distribution channels and understand how they operate.

7. Understand the components of transportation, and its effects on tourism.

What is Tourism?
Establishing a Definition

If we tried to define tourism in short form, here's some of what we'd be up against. Tourism has been defined in many ways, involves many different businesses, and can be considered from many perspectives. As we learned in chapter 1, a person needs to be away from home for the businesses that comprise tourism to have a purpose. But for how long do people need to be away, and how far do they have to go, and for what purposes, before we call them tourists? The League of Nations—which established its definition of a tourist in 1937—thought 24 hours away was enough, unless the tourists were on a sea cruise, in which case fewer than 24 hours were acceptable! They didn't comment on distance, but traveling for pleasure, to meetings, or for business were acceptable purposes to classify someone as a tourist. Today, the National Tourism Resources Review Commission considers a tourist someone who travels at least 50 miles for business, pleasure, or any other purpose except to commute to work, whether the traveler stays overnight or not. In Canada, to be a traveler, you only have to travel 25 miles. According to the United States Census Bureau, a person must go at least 100 miles, whether or not the trip involves a stay overnight out of town.[1]

Multiple Pieces

The moving about of tourists, who are travelers away from home and require the services the hospitality industry provides, is what defines the tourism industry. The person still must travel to get there, and thus all the different types of transportation are a part of tourism. The traveler may use some kind of **travel distribution channel** to gather data before departure. A travel distribution channel is the method the traveler chooses to get from point A to point B. Thus travel agencies and tourism offices are also a part of tourism. Once away from home, the traveler must be serviced by a variety of businesses. Among these businesses, which are included as a part of tourism, are lodging and foodservice establishments. Upon arrival to a destination, a traveler may also be entertained by various types of attractions, recreational activities, and special events.

Multiple Perspectives

Tourism can be viewed from various perspectives, each with a special concern about tourism. From an economic perspective, tourism involves all the receipts from these businesses, including foreign exchange and tax receipts, capital expenditures, the employment payrolls of everyone who works in these businesses, and the **multiplier effect** of these monies. For example, The multiplier effect means that when a taxi driver drives a traveler from the airport, the payment for that service is spent by the driver in the community; the effect of the payment for one taxi ride has a multiplied effect on the economy. From a sociological perspective, tourism involves the study of leisure activities and the habits and customs of hosts and guests. From an environmental perspective, tourism involves land use and ecological impact. Other disciplines offer other perspectives: anthropological, psychological, cultural, historical, and legal. The complexities are vast.

Universal Truths About Tourism

There are some universal truths about tourism: It is an important part of the economy for nearly every developed nation in the world, and of potential importance to undeveloped nations. It is also big business. Companies that constitute tourism are the world's largest generators of jobs.

Arrivals and Receipts South Asia, Africa, the Americas, East Asia and the Pacific, the Middle East, and Europe each express their international **arrivals** in thousands and their **receipts** in millions (of dollars, currency exchange adjusted). Arrivals are simply the people who enter the country as travelers, with the intent to leave within a specified time frame. Receipts are defined as the funds spent by the traveler in the country of destination. As illustrated in Table 5.1, in 1993, the total arrivals in the world were nearly half a billion. The world's tourism receipts were over $300 billion dollars in 1993.

World's Top Employer According to the World Travel and Tourism Council, tourism is the world's number one employer, employing more than 200 million people worldwide. By the year 2005, the number may reach 350 million. Worldwide, one job in every nine is a part of travel and tourism. In some parts of the world, the ratio is even more staggering. In the Caribbean, Belgium, Luxembourg, and Portugal, for example, the ratio is one out of every six jobs.[2]

Tourism is Growing

Tourism, as measured by international arrivals, has grown and continues to grow at remarkable rates. In 1950, there were 25 million international tourist arrivals; by 1960, the number more than doubled, jumping to 69 million. By 1970, the number more than doubled again, to 160 million arrivals; by 1980, there were 285 million and 1990 scored 443 million. Projections indicate that the number will continue to grow to the close of the decade in the year 2000.[3]

Table 5.1 Arrivals and Receipts

Region	1993 Arrivals (in thousands)	1993 % Share of World Total	1993 Receipts (in million U.S. $)	1993 % Share of World Total
Africa	14,000	4	$4,200	1
Americas	100,000	21	$83,552	28
Asia/Pacific	74,000	9	$56,005	18
Europe	288,000	63	$156,955	51
Middle East	6,000	3	$6,659	2

Source: Annuaire des Statistiques du Tourisme, World Tourism Organization, Madrid, Spain, 1995.

Review of Component Parts As we saw in chapter 1, the entire world of tourism can be thought of in five major categories:

1. Lodging
2. Foodservice
3. Entertainment
4. Travel Distribution Channels
5. Transportation

In sections 2 and 3 of the book, "Places to Stay" and "Places to Eat," we will cover lodging and foodservice in detail. In the remainder of this chapter, we will explore the last three components.

Entertainment: Attractions, Recreation, and Special Events

In addition to lodging and eating, pleasure travelers who are away from home will seek various kinds of entertainment. Sometimes that entertainment is directly associated with lodging, such as a theme park or a casino, that also accommodate overnight guests. There may also be entertainment directly associated with eating establishments, such as visible kitchens that are designed for patrons to view, or murder mystery dinner theaters where waiters and waitresses double as an acting team. Still other kinds of entertainment may be stand-alone entities. Many activities fit in to the entertainment category. Travelers will often be lured to a destination because of the attractions, recreation, or special events. These various kinds of entertainment will typically be found in proximity to lodging and foodservice. Overseas travelers to the United States, for example, are attracted by a wide range of activities. In descending order of priority, these activities included shopping, sightseeing in cities, and participating in water sports or sunbathing. A more complete list of activities is included in Table 5.2.

Table 5.2 Activities Participated in by Overseas Travelers, 1993

Overseas Travelers* (in thousands)	18,662	Art Gallery/Museum	25%
		Guided Tours	21
Shopping	83%	Nightclub Dancing	16
Dining in Restaurants	69	Concert/Play/Musical	15
Sightseeing in Cities	65	Golf/Tennis	10
Water Sports/Sunbathing	34	Attend Sports Event	9
Touring Countryside	24	Camping/Hiking	6
Visit Historical Places	33	Cruise, 1 Night plus	4
Amusement/Theme Park	29	Hunting/Fishing	4
Visit National Parks	27	Snow Skiing	3

*Includes travelers from Europe, Far East, South America, Caribbean, Oceania, Central America, Middle East, Africa. Mexico and Canada not included.

Source: U.S. Travel and Tourism Administration.

Attractions

A varied number of complexes offer family entertainment, sometimes on a grand scale. Nashville, Tennessee, for example, offers an entertainment complex whose theme involves the music of the area in the form of Opryland, USA. EuroDisney, in Paris, brings Mickey and Minnie Mouse to Europe in one of several Disney theme parks around the world. Because these attractions are end point destinations for visitors who likely have traveled far, these theme parks offer overnight lodging and food-service. We will discuss theme parks more extensively in the lodging chapters. Other attractions that do not have a lodging component include amusement parks, sightseeing, and shopping.

Amusement Parks Amusement parks generally conjure up images of carousels, Ferris wheels, and family entertainment. In fact, amusement parks include traditional amusement parks, water parks, miniature golf, and family entertainment centers. Presently, many of the amusement facilities being built are associated with the casino industry. One need look no further than Las Vegas to find New York, New York, a hotel and casino complex that will mimic the architecture of the New York City skyline in its physical facility and house everything "New York" inside. The International Association of Amusement Parks and Attractions measures the annual revenue of amusement parks to be over $6 billion dollars in the United States alone.[4]

Outdoors Indoors Other examples of unusual attractions were recently introduced in Japan. An indoor beach, complete with waves, sand, and a leeward breeze, was created in a completely enclosed environment. This beach is probably the only one in world that people can enjoy 365 days a year without any weather interruptions. Similarly, an indoor ski resort was also created. The attraction boasts artificial snow, varying terrain, and ski lessons. One main advantage of the creation of these attractions is the ability to operate predictably year-round. These attractions were also located near a large population base and far from the alternative, the real thing.

Sightseeing Sightseeing is generally associated with some form of transportation and always involves a tour of some set of attractions. Major cities offer sightseeing by bus, double-decker bus, trolley, or boat. One can see London by guided tour from the top of a double-decker bus, or walk the Freedom Trail's historic sites in Boston, or see the banks of Buda and Pest by boat in Budapest. Sightseeing tours can also be customized for particular groups and can be offered in multiple languages. In Prague, for example, evening boat tours allow passengers to select an audio program in several languages. Aerial tours are also offered by helicopter in at least 200 locations by member companies of the Helicopter Association International.

Shopping According to the International Council of Shopping Centers (ICSC), shopping malls, factory outlet centers, and large discount malls continue to grow in popularity as entertainment centers. Theme parks, virtual reality games, and kids' playgrounds are more and more frequently appearing in shopping complexes. Retail outlets are also commonly associated with other kinds of entertainment, ranging from gift shops in theme parks, ball parks, and national parks to shops in restaurants selling trademark items like T-shirts with company logos. Shopping streets, in major cities where clusters of retail stores exist, are a form of entertainment worldwide. For overseas travelers in the United States, shopping was a popular activity, with some 83 percent of all visitors in 1993 having shopped, as is recorded in Table 5.2.

Recreation

Recreation generally refers to activities associated with the great outdoors and often involves physical activity. As society's emphasis on physical fitness increases, especially in the United States, so too does the demand for recreational activities. These activities are supported by public parks and playgrounds, state and national parks, and facilities for outdoor sports.

Public Parks/Playgrounds Public parks and playgrounds serve as the great outdoors of cities and communities. They vary in size, location, and the recreational facilities that they offer. Services can range from playgrounds for children to cafés and carousels. Public parks do not have any entrance fees or accommodations. A new trend is to open children's playgrounds in malls. The Mall of America in Minnesota boasts the world's largest indoor mall playground.

State and National Parks The national park system in the United States includes some 367 sites, including recreation areas, preserves, battlefields, historic sites, and monuments. There are also 156 national forests and 20 national grasslands. Many parks serve as major tourist attractions and sometimes offer a variety of lodging and foodservice in addition to guided tours and information centers. Lodging facilities can range from camping grounds and cabins to midscale and upscale hotels. **Ecotourism,** or culturally and environmentally responsible tourism, has become increasingly important as more and more visitors use the system.

Outdoor Activities A wide variety of outdoor activities attract visitors. These include white water rafting, cycling, hiking, water sports, skiing and snowboarding, snowmobiling, and rock climbing. Natural attractions, such as rivers, lakes, or mountains are the anchors for these activities. In the rural locations where they exist, they can form a substantial part of the local economy. A relatively new type of travel has emerged in conjunction with outdoor sports known as **adventure travel**. The typical adventure traveler has interest in both physical fitness and the environment. Camping and hiking are the most popular adventure trips, followed by skiing and water sports such as snorkeling, scuba diving, and sailing.

Festivals and Special Events

Many communities in various parts of the world celebrate a particular piece of heritage, an event in history, the commerce of the area, or special talents in the area. These events may offer entertainment from the arts, such as handicrafts, dance, painting, storytelling, puppet shows, music, or drama. Food and beverage offerings, typically in keeping with the festival's theme and varied shopping choices, are also found. Two such events are the International Festival of Contemporary Music in Zagreb, Croatia, and the Edinburgh International Festival in Scotland. Special events may also involve a competition of wit or sport. These events can range from the sporting events such as the Running of the Bulls in Pamploma, Spain; to the Palio horse race in Siena, Italy; to the International Camel Race in the northern Sinai. Other events celebrate the food and entertainment of a particular place such as the Oktoberfest in Munich, Germany, or Mardi Gras in New Orleans. The International Festivals Association (IFA) estimates that there are more than 50,000 annual festivals and special events worldwide.

■■■■■■■ *Oktoberfest!*

Oktoberfest, the annual festival in Munich, Germany, is the largest festival in the world. Some six million visitors from around the world will travel to Munich for the festival of music, parades, and the 14 famous beer tents.

Oktoberfest can trace its history to 1810. In that year, in honor of the wedding of Crown Prince Ludwig and Princess Therese of Saxony-Hildburghausen on October 12, the citizens of Munich were invited to attend the festivities, and have celebrated ever since.

Want more information on Oktoberfest? Looking for reservations for the beer tents? Need a current map of Munich? Want train schedules from Paris to Munich?

Go no further than the Internet, for Oktoberfest has a Web page. The City of Munich Tourist Office has hooked up with a company called Siemens Nixdorf Informationssyteme AG. Siemens is one of the largest European suppliers of information technology in Europe. The company concentrates on developing new technologies that enhance the distribution channel to the customer.

Together, Siemans and the Munich Tourist Board have put together a lengthy, full-color, interactive on-line brochure on Oktoberfest. It even includes a video! Along with photos of all the important spots to visit, it provides the customer with dates, and phone numbers—and all for free! The Web page provides the Munich Tourist Board with an inexpensive way to deliver information to customers all over the world.

Some events are held periodically, or only once. They may be events that are repeated periodically in different geographic locations such as the Olympics, the World's Fair, or World Cup Soccer Playoffs, all of which are widely recognized events. It is a major commitment for a city or country to host such an event. Having the world at your doorstep entails major capital expenditure. The Eiffel Tower is a monumental example of construction for a World's Fair, held in Paris in 1885. It has had tourism impact on Paris and France for more than a century. Planning for events can take years and involves massive coordination to arrange feeding, housing, transportation, and entertainment for thousands of visitors in a short period of time.

A good example of a one-time event was the historic gathering of the Tall Ships in New Haven, Connecticut, in 1995. Sailing vessels from around the world gathered in the New Haven harbor for a historic boat party. Another was the series of 50th-anniversary celebrations throughout Europe in 1995, commemorating the end of World War II.

Gaming

Gaming, or gambling, is the act of playing various games, and betting on the outcome. Gaming usually includes card games, slot machines, and such other games as roulette and craps. Participants place bets, and win or lose depending on the outcome. Hotel casinos were for a long time permitted in only two states, Nevada and New Jersey. By 1993, a gaming industry study had shown that by

1993, some form of gaming was legal in every state except Hawaii and Utah. In point of fact, that year gaming activity had driven U.S. gross gaming revenue from $10 billion in 1982 to approximately $30 billion in 1992. Government operated lotteries were fixtures in most states, while video lotteries were operating in six states. Riverboat gambling was highly visible in five states. Casino gaming was commonplace aboard oceangoing cruise ships. And in 12 states, gaming was open to the public on 55 Native American reservations.

Native American Casinos On October 17, 1988, the landmark Indian Gaming Regulatory Act (GRA) became law, giving Native American tribes the right to offer games that were permitted by a state in any form to all comers—untaxed by the state unless the Native Americans agree to it. The law classifies gaming in three categories:

Class I—Indian games and other social games

Class II—Bingo, pulltabs, punchtabs, etc.

Class III—All other commercial forms of gaming

Tribes are required to negotiate **compacts**, or legal agreements, with their host states before specific games are allowed. If a state fails to negotiate in good faith, a tribe may sue the state in federal court to arbitration. As of early 1993, according to the Indian Gaming Association, there were a total of 55 Class III casinos, in various states operating a variety of games, such as: video games, slot machines, table games, roulette, blackjack, and poker. The gambling facilities on reservations range from gaming areas, with games noted above, to extensive gaming, lodging, and food and beverage facilities. In the "Places to Stay" section of the book, we review casinos with overnight accommodations.

The gaming facilities are either managed and owned by the local tribe, or leased by major corporations in exchange for percentage of revenues. The gaming business has become the main source of revenues and profits for many Native American tribes. The highest grossing casino in the world is Foxwoods in Connecticut, run by the Mashantucket Peqout tribe. It currently grosses more than $800 million annually.

Riverboat Casinos Riverboat casinos commenced operations in April 1981, and have thus far have surpassed all expectations. As of January 1, 1994, five states had approved riverboat casinos. They are Iowa, Illinois, Mississippi, Louisiana, and Missouri. As of 1994, at least a dozen other states either have legislative initiatives under way for riverboat gaming, or have undertaken studies of such enterprises. Some 50 boats have gone into action since 1990, and that number again is under construction.[5] The expectation is that by 1995 riverboat gaming revenue will exceed $2 billion.

Dockside Casinos The state of Mississippi legalized dockside gambling in 1990. The dockside option was chosen, as opposed to land-based gaming, because the legislators believed that casinos on the water limit impact on the local communities and are more accessible from land than riverboats. The dockside casino industry has grown significantly since the beginning of the 1990s. There are more than 24 dockside casinos on the Mississippi River and the Gulf Coast. Neither dockside casinos nor riverboat casinos provide lodging facilities. They offer gaming and food and beverage outlets.

Gaming on Cruise Ships and Airlines Once a ship is 12 miles from American shores, it is in international waters, and gaming is permitted. Thus, most cruise ships have casinos. Casinos operate sometimes for day trips only, and sometimes for overnight guests. Overnight trips offer casino gaming as part of their extensive attractions and amenities services. Some day trip cruises are marketed as gambling cruises and are sometimes called "no-where cruises." The gamblers are allowed to play in the ship's casino after the ship has entered international waters. Elaborate meals and other attractions are usually offered on board. Gambling cruises, like the cruise industry itself, is appealing to wider and wider audiences.

Several non-U.S. carriers, such as Transbrazil Airlines and Virgin Atlantic Airways, are currently offering in-flight gambling activities. Virgin Airways offers video poker and blackjack at every seat. A customer inserts a credit card to play video games of chance. Winnings or losses are applied to the credit card. Some American airlines have tried to persuade the U.S. government to change the law that prohibits American carriers from providing gaming in any flight.

See Exhibit 5.1 for a summary of entertainment components.

Exhibit 5.1 Summary of Entertainment Components

Category	Examples
Attractions	
Amusement Parks	1. Vienna Fairgrounds, Vienna, Austria
	2. Warner Brothers Movie World, Bottrop, Germany
	3. Canada's Wonderland, Toronto, Ontario, Canada
	4. Port Aventura, Barcelona, Spain
Outdoors Indoors	1. Somerville Rock Climbing Gym, Somerville, MA
	2. Indoor Ski Area, near Tokyo, Japan
Sightseeing	1. Circle Line Tour, Manhattan, New York, NY
	2. Helicopter Tours of the Grand Canyon, AZ
Shopping	1. The Mall of the Americas, Bloomington, MN
	2. Kittery Outlet Shopping Center, Kittery, ME
	3. Bon Marché, Paris, France
Recreation	
Public Parks	1. Central Park, New York, NY
	2. Hyde Park, London, England
State and National Parks	1. Old Faithful Inn, Yellowstone National Park, WY
	2. The Ahwahnee Hotel, Yosemite National Park, CA
Outdoor Activities	1. Boston Pops Esplanade Concerts, Boston, MA
	2. Cheyenne Frontier Days, Cheyenne, WY
Festivals and Special Events	1. The 1995 Special Olympics, New Haven, CT
	2. 1995 All-Star Baseball Game, Arlington, TX
	3. Chicago Jazz Festival, Chicago, IL

(Continued)

■■■■■ **Exhibit 5.1** *(Continued)*

Category	Examples
	4. V-E Celebrations throughout Europe, May 1995
	5. Carnival, Rio de Janeiro, Brazil
Gaming	
Native American Casinos	1. Foxwoods, Ledyard (Mashantucket Pequot Indian reservation), CT
	2. The Shakopee Mdewakanton Sioux Casino, MN
River Boats/Dockside	1. Sheraton Casino, Northern Tunica County, MI
	2. Dockside, St. Louis, MO
Cruise Ships	1. Crystal Harmony, Caesar's Palace at Sea Casino, Crystal Cruises, Los Angeles, CA
	2. Discovery Cruises, Fort Lauderdale, FL (Discovery I—a no-where cruise)
	3. Regal Cruises, St. Petersburg, FL (Regal Empress—a no-where cruise)
Airlines	1. Transbrazil Airlines
	2. Virgin Airways

Travel Distribution Channels

Consumers gather information about their destinations and make reservations for their trips using different approaches. Some customers book directly with the service they are reserving. For example, a customer can call the airlines to book an airline seat. In the same phone call, the airline passenger may reserve a rental car. In this case, the airline serves as a booking agent for the rental car company. A representative of the passenger, such as an administrative assistant, may book the car rental, even though the assistant is not the enduser! In this simple scenario, two agents are involved, one for the customer and one for the rental car company. Thus, agents are commonly found in the travel and tourism business.

Customers may also access information directly, via toll-free numbers, **on-line services**, such as those available on the Internet, or contacting a tourism office. All of these links to information and reservations, or the travel distribution channels, connect the customer to the tourism industry. They are crucial to the customers' ability to understand and consume the available services. Because of the perishability of services, that is, because they cannot be stored like products, an efficient information and reservations system is crucial to success.

Retail Travel Agencies

Retail travel agencies are perhaps the best known of travel distribution channels. Unlike wholesalers, retail outlets deal directly with customers. Retail agencies may focus on full-service, group and incentive, or corporate bookings.

Full-Service A **full-service travel agency** is a company that serves as a middleman between the end user, the customer, and hospitality suppliers such as airlines, tour operators, and hotels. The customer can either buy individual products, such as an airline ticket or hotel weekend, or a combination of products in a travel package. The package will usually include accommodations, transportation, attractions, and some food and beverage. Travel agents receive **commissions**, or payments based on sales, from the travel vendors. Travel agents in a full-service retail travel agency are specialists who can provide and arrange travel information such as regulations, routing, prices, accommodations, and so on. Some travel agencies specialize in specific destinations or vacations. Others may specialize in last-minute travel at discounted rates.

Group and Incentive Some travel agencies specialize in incentive or group packages. Incentive tours are usually marketed to companies that wish to reward their agents, special clients, or employees. For example, a company may choose to reward its salespeople for exceptional performance. Those who exceed target goals would receive an all-inclusive tour package as a reward. A group of salespeople will likely be winners, and thus this type of agency typically deals in blocks of space from hospitality providers. For example, if Smith's Travel Agency specializes in group packages, it has agreements with certain hotels in specific destinations. Those hotels may block off sets of rooms, or even entire floors, in anticipation of the travel agency's group. When agents are rewarded with trips, they are most often trips to these hotels, as the rooms are already reserved for the agency.

Corporate Some travel agencies or agents specialize in **corporate travel**. Corporate travel includes the arrangement of airline tickets, accommodations, transportation, and other travel needs for business travelers. Corporate agencies or agents can be either independent entities that specialize in corporate travel, or internal departments within big corporations. The main objectives of these professionals are to receive better prices due to high travel volume, to provide better control of companies' travel expenses, and to provide better service for corporate executives and salespersons.

Tour Wholesaler/Tour Operator

A **tour wholesaler** is a company that plans, markets, and operates travel tours. The marketing is done through the retail travel agents, clubs, associations, businesses, and other organizations. The main advantage of the wholesalers is the ability to sell tours at reduced prices due to large volumes. The **tour operator** is a company that plans and operates prepaid and preplanned vacations. These vacations are usually available to the public through a retail travel agent. Some companies act as both a wholesaler and an operator.

Convention and Meeting Planners

Convention planners and **meeting planners** can be either independent entities that provide convention and meeting planning services, or internal employees of big corporations, associations, trade shows, and government agencies. The main objective of convention and meeting planners is to plan and execute conventions or business meetings. Responsibilities of meeting and convention planners include: negotiation of hotel contracts regarding accommodations and food and beverages, negotiation with airlines, planning meetings and seminars, planning incentive programs and leisure tours, providing promotion, public relations, and all other organizational aspects of a convention. Conventions and meetings vary in size, theme, and objective.

Credit Card Companies

Credit card companies, most notably American Express, can be an important distributor of tourism-related information. Credit card companies may team up with hospitality providers in promoting travel. For example, a credit card company and a hotel might offer a special rate if the cost is charged to that particular card. Credit card companies may feature a particular restaurant in their advertising, noting it as an establishment that accepts the card.

Many companies, particularly airlines, have also set up what are known as affinity cards. These are credit cards with a relationship to a hospitality provider. American Airlines, for example, offers a Citibank Visa card whereby every purchase that is made is credited with frequent flyer miles. The miles can be redeemed for free travel and class upgrades on American Airlines. Most airlines have set up similar agreements with Mastercard or Visa.

Consumer Direct Access

Increasingly, because of technological advances, most notably the information superhighway, customers are able to search for information and make reservations themselves, bypassing the retail travel agency. For example, a consumer can now access all European train schedules through the Internet, find information on over 15,000 hotel properties via Travel Web, the Internet's first interactive hotel catalog, and book air travel anywhere in the world.

Reservations by Telephone/Facsimile Though telephone reservations from a customer to a service provider (such as calling a toll-free number to book and purchase an airline ticket) have been relatively common, the increased availability and use of facsimile machines has allowed customers to conveniently confirm bookings in different time zones. This approach is increasingly being used by international travelers. A company in the international hospitality business almost always lists a fax number along with its phone number.

Reservations by the Information Highway The changes and capabilities of on-line communication are rapidly evolving. More and more companies and services are accessible via the internet, and more and more people have access to on-line communications. The future potential of this form of communication with customers is vast. We explore this topic further in chapter 17, a discussion of trends.

Tourism Offices

Tourism offices offer another way for a consumer to gather information about a particular destination. Tourism offices exist on the world, national, state/province (or equivalent), regional, and local levels. The World Tourism Organization, which is headquartered in Madrid, Spain, collects information on international travel and tourism. The kinds of information this organization collects were explored in chapter 4. Offices found at other levels, from national to local, also serve to promote tourism in their respective areas of jurisdiction.

National National offices are those government agencies in each country that focus on the tourism industry. The range of responsibilities for these offices includes: tourism promotion and regulations, planning of national tourism objectives, providing assistance for tourism investors and professionals, and determining national tourism standards.

Three of the important national agencies in the United States are: the Travel Industry Association of America (TIA), the United States Travel and Tourism Administration (USTTA), and the Tourism Works for America Council. The first agency, TIA, was established in 1941. It attempts to benefit all businesses that are part of the tourism industry by promoting travel to and within the United States. Its members include travel-related businesses such as hotels and restaurants, and local, regional, and state travel promotion agencies. The USTTA, established in 1961 through the International Travel Act, is an agency of the U.S. Department of Commerce. It serves as the nation's government tourism agency and is concerned with developing tourism as a stimulus to economic growth. The newest of the agencies, the Tourism Works for America Council, was established in 1986. The Council concerns itself with enhancing public awareness of the importance of tourism to the country's social, economic, and cultural well-being.

State Every state in the United States has a travel and tourism agency. The main objective of each agency is to promote tourism within the state. Their activities include: promotion and advertising programs in the mainland and overseas, travel market research, and travel and tourism information programs. The state agencies usually report to the state governor and legislators, and are responsible for allocating budgets to local agencies.

Local Local tourism offices are not-for-profit organizations designed to promote trade export to and from their countries, states, regions, and cities. Their main responsibilities include: tourism promotion, assistance for prospective investors, assistance for local businesses and trade organizations, promotion of local goods and products, and promotion of trade relations between local businesses and out-of-country or -region businesses. A local chamber of commerce, a typical local tourism office, serves as a liaison between the local trade and business community, and the outside prospective partners.

Convention and Visitors Bureau Most major cities and regional counties have Convention and Visitors' Bureaus as the local travel and tourism agencies. Their main objectives are to provide assistance and service for travelers in their areas and to promote travel and tourism for their areas. These organizations are not-for-profit entities that serve as liaisons between the local tourism providers, such as hotels and attractions, and the prospective visitors. Small communities use the local chambers of commerce as their travel promoters.

See Exhibit 5.2 for a summary of travel distribution channels.

Exhibit 5.2 Summary of Travel Distribution Channels

Category	Examples
Travel Agencies	
Full-Services	1. American Express Travel Services, New York, NY
	2. Carlson Travel Network, Minneapolis, MN
Group & Incentive	1. Francorosso Incentive, Milano, Italy
	2. Metaphor Incentive Design, Toronto, Canada
	3. Creative Group Inc., Appleton, WI
Corporate	1. Bain Travel, division of Bain & Co., Boston, MA
Tour Wholesalers/ Tour Operator	1. Isram, New York, NY (Wholesaler)
	2. GWV Travel, Needham, MA (Wholesaler)
	3. Peter Pan, Boston, MA (Tour Operator)
Convention & Meeting Planners	1. Nancy B. Holder & Associates, Inc., Winston-Salem, NC
	2. Meeting Solutions, Middleton, WI
	3. International Conference Services, Hellerup, Denmark
Credit Card Companies	1. American Express Membership Miles
	2. USAIR Mastercard
	3. Hilton/American Express Card
Consumer Direct Access	
Telephone	1. Hilton Reservations 800 #
	2. USAir 800 #
Internet	1. World Wide Web page for Hyatt Hotels
	2. Web sites of various state travel promotions
	3. American Airlines SABRE reservation system

(Continued)

![] **Exhibit 5.2** *(Continued)*	
Category	**Examples**
Tourism Offices	
National	1. Comércio e Turism de Portugal (Portuguese National Tourist Office)
	2. Tourism Canada, Canada
	3. Ministry of Tourism, Jerusalem, Israel
	4. Netherland Convention Bureau, Amsterdam, The Netherlands
State	1. Massachusetts Travel & Tourism Office, Boston, MA
	2. Hawaii Visitors Bureau, HI
Local/Chamber of Commerce	1. Vermont Chamber of Commerce, Montpelier, VT
	2. Nantucket Island Chamber of Commerce, Nantucket, MA
	3. Tourist Information Office, Florence, Italy
Convention & Visitors Bureau	1. The Greater Boston Convention & Visitors Bureau, Boston, MA
	2. Cobb County Convention & Visitors Bureau, Marietta, GA
	3. Vancouver Convention Bureau, Vancouver, BC, Canada

Means of Transportation

Transportation has always been linked to tourism. History shows that, repeatedly, when there is a change in transportation, there is a change in the hospitality services that surround the means of travel. With the evolution of the vast network of ancient Roman roads came the need for snack bars at periodic intervals. With the evolution of the automobile and the network of interstate highways came a proliferation of fast food at highway exits. Other examples abound. Transportation can be thought of as the physical means that links the traveler to the destination. It is a component necessary to the entire tourism industry.

Air Transportation

Airlines around the world provide an extensive network of domestic and international flights. The main advantage of using airline services is the time it saves, when compared to ground transportation. The airline industry is composed of international carriers, national carriers, commuters, and private airplanes and jets. In some parts of the world, the airline industry is regulated by governmental bodies, and in some parts it is not. The United States deregulated its airline industry in the late 1970s, removing laws determining ticket prices, and Europe is moving now to deregulate its airline industry as well. The competition in the airline industry is fierce, and carriers compete for every percentage of market share that they can capture. Competition is based on prices and service. The major costs for an airline company are fuel, labor, and equipment. As a marketing effort, many airlines offer frequent flyer programs. Frequent passengers can redeem flight points for discounted, upgraded, and free flight tickets, hotel rooms, and car rentals.

The airlines were the first companies to develop and offer **central computerized reservation systems.** These systems allow an agent to check for flight times and prices instantly, and therefore to be able to give that information directly to the customer. Today the new generation of reservation systems is being developed by airlines and hotel companies in a joint venture. The world airline industry is supported by two major organizations: International Air Transport Association (IATA) and International Civil Aviation Organization (ICAO).

In major cities, helicopters are used by a small number of passengers to travel to specific destinations. As a form of transportation, helicopters are almost exclusively used for business travel. Landing requires an area much smaller than an airport runway that can be in a downtown location. Although not a usual means of sightseeing, helicopters are occasionally used as a form of recreation, as are hot air balloons.

Ground Transportation

Ground transportation includes automobiles, trains, buses, taxis, and private cars such as limousines. It is the method of transportation used most frequently, usually the most economical, and available to the greatest number of travelers.

Car Rental The car rental industry provides services for both business and leisure travelers who need to rent a car away from home. The largest car rental companies are international in scope. They provide an extensive network of locations around the world and operate through a central reservation system. Travelers can find car rental offices in major cities and communities, near airports, tourist destinations, attractions, and seaports. In addition to the rental service, rental car agencies also provide long-term leasing services.

Car rental companies offer frequent user programs and clubs. Travelers can accumulate points and redeem them for car rentals, airline tickets, or hotel accommodations. Car rental agencies compete in price and service. Many of them offer VIP service, cellular phones, and other amenities.

Rail Companies Rail companies provide train services for passengers and goods (freight trains). Most of the modern economies in the world enjoy a wide network of railroads that connect domestic and international destinations. With the growth of the airline industry, the rail industry has faced tough challenges. The main challenge has been to convince air travel passengers to use trains as an alternate means of transportation. In addition to quality service, many rail companies have developed and introduced high-speed trains that can compete more closely with the overall time of air travel (flight, transportation to the airport, check-in time, and so on). For example, the flight time between New York City and Washington, D.C. is approximately 70 minutes. Adding in 45 to 60 minutes to reach the airport from Manhattan, 30 minutes between check-in and departure, and 45 minutes for the ride to downtown Washington, the trip comes closer to three hours. Train stations are usually located downtown, eliminating travel time to the airport. In this case, the train ride between midtown Manhattan and Washington, D.C. is approximately three hours. In some parts of the world, train travel is even faster. The French TGV, the Swedish X-2000, and the Japanese high-speed Bullet Train are all examples of high-speed trains that are direct competitors to air travel.

Motor Coaches Motor coaches or bus services offer inexpensive transportation between cities, states, and countries. Bus services are more popular in areas that do not enjoy airline or train services. The customer mix includes students, senior citizens, military personnel, tourists, and people who cannot afford to buy an airline ticket. Due to tough competition from the airline and rail industries and the increased use of private or rental cars, many bus companies were forced to drop prices significantly. In addition to intercity bus services, every city provides local bus transportation for intracity services. Motor coaches are also used for sightseeing in many locations.

Taxi Service, Private Car Service, and Limousines Taxi companies provide an important means of local transportation. Taxis serve every place in their local area, including attractions, airports, hotels, restaurants, train stations, and so on. Local or state regulations may specify boundaries, such as within a certain radius or within a specific set of towns in which taxis may operate. Prices are usually regulated and published. Sometimes taxi drivers are an informed resource for local information and can be considered a distribution channel for a restaurant, for example. Taxi services in many cities have become a famous identification mark of the city. For example, London is well known for its black cabs, and New York City is known for its yellow ones.

Growing in popularity are private car services. These car services provide transportation between two locations, and prices are set in advance, as opposed to taxis, which clock payment on a meter. Private car services are more expensive than taxis, but provide a more comfortable ride, and often include cellular phones and fax machines. Corporations often own a fleet of cars, or contract with a provider, to transport employees to and from the airport or meetings. At the luxury end of ground transportation are limousines, shuttling passengers in total luxury between destinations. One important reason to have a private car service or limousine at your disposal is convenience; the traveler does not have to wait (sometimes a long time) for a taxi.

Water Transportation

Most major cities in the world can be found on water; therefore, it is no surprise that water transportation is part of the public transportation network. Water shuttles are particularly helpful at peak commuting times, when roadways are overtaxed. Good examples of frequently used water shuttles can be found in New York City and Bangkok, Thailand. Water shuttles often provide intermediary transportation to another service. In Boston, the downtown water shuttle provides a means for travelers to get to and from and the airport from a downtown location.

For pleasure travelers, luxury liners such as the *QE II* might be considered a means of transportation. The *QE II* makes transatlantic crossings, between New York and Great Britain; many travelers sail on one crossing and then fly on their return. While not a time-efficient method of travel, it does provide a means of getting from the United States to Europe, or the reverse. For those on a budget, some freight liners will allow passengers on the voyages. Accommodations are bare, at best, and freighters are selected by the unusually adventurous traveler.

See Exhibit 5.3 for a summary of transportation components.

███████ *Exhibit 5.3* Summary of Transportation Components

Transportation Services	Examples
Airlines	1. KLM Royal Dutch Airlines, The Netherlands
	2. American Airlines, USA
	3. JAL, Japan Airlines, Japan
	4. Air Tanzania, Africa
Rental Cars	1. Avis, various locations around the world. USA based.
	2. Hertz Corporation, various locations around the world. USA based.
	3. Eurocar, various locations throughout Europe. Europe based.
Rail	1. Amtrak, USA
	2 The Chunnel—Train services between London, England; Paris, France; and Brussels, Belgium
	3. The Bullet Train, Japan
Motor Coach	1. Greyhound Lines, various locations around the United States
	2. Bonanza Bus Lines, Boston, MA
Taxis/Private Car Service	1. Checker Cab, New York, NY
	2. Boston Coach, Boston, MA
	3. The Livery Service, Chicago, IL
Water Transportation	1. The Water Shuttle, Boston, MA
	2. The Water Shuttle, Bankok, Thailand

Perspectives on Tourism

Tourism is a business that is of interest to many of the world's professions, ranging from anthropologists and economists to environmentalists and sociologists. As travel to a particular area increases, so too does the potential impact on the area. The effects can be both positive and negative. The goal of much of the study of tourism, from whatever perspective, is to create tourism policies that maximize the benefits of human traffic to an area.

An Economic Perspective

Tourism, we have already learned, is an important part of the world's economy and an important employer of the world's people. Tourism is also major component of the balance of payments for many countries. The balance of payments weighs a country's imports against its exports. If a country hosts an international visitor, it is providing a **tourism export**. The visitor pays foreign money in exchange for a travel experience, which is considered an export. Though the travel experience is an intangible, as we will explore further in the chapter on marketing, it is nonetheless an exported good.

Consider a British traveler who tours San Francisco, spending 1,000 British pounds during her stay. The money that she spends is income, which helps the American economy. The British traveler also pays taxes, just as a resident would. Sometimes certain taxes are refunded, such as the **value added tax (VAT)** found in Europe, in an effort to stimulate foreign spending. Taxes in Europe are much higher than they are in other parts of the world. When a traveler leaves Europe, certain taxes assessed to the traveler for such services as hotel rooms, meals, and even souvenirs purchased, are recorded on a form at the airport. The traveler then is reimbursed for a portion of the taxes paid.

The economic impact of tourism goes beyond the 1,000 pounds spent by the British traveler in San Francisco, because of the **multiplier effect.** The multiplier, a number calculated by economists, is used in the attempt to comprehend how the visitor's spending circulates and recirculates within the local economy. The hospitality providers that received the pounds may use the money to pay wages. Those wages may in turn be spent, perhaps to buy software at the local computer store, and so on. The money continues to circulate until it is either saved or spent outside the local economy. The spending also has an important effect on employment. Not only are jobs generated in the hospitality sector, but there is also a ripple effect on employment in other areas as well, such as gas station attendants who service taxis.

The British traveler's pounds can also have negative economic impact, in the form of inflationary pressure on local prices. Tourists typically have higher spending capabilities than do residents, particularly if they consider the trip a special event. Demand for certain goods or services goes up when the numbers of tourists is high, and thus the price of goods can be bid up, to the disfavor of local residents.

A Social and Cultural Perspective

An influx of tourism dollars may create new jobs. This may mean greater competition for the local labor force or an influx of additional people. New entrants don't always assimilate well into the local culture, and thus, they add social complexities.

As tourism first develops, the local community may begin by embracing the benefits of increased income and improvements in infrastructure that result. Particularly where growth comes too quickly, further development can turn the initial embrace into conflict and hostility toward tourists. Competition over resources such as energy, land, water, and use of recreational facilities may cause resentment in the community.

In its simplest form, a tourist in a strange land is a contrast of cultures. It may happen that interest in and support for local art forms such as dance, theater, crafts, art, and music provide a means for the arts to thrive. It may also happen that traditional ceremony or approach is eroded in favor of economic gain, and that the true art is lost.

An Environmental Perspective

Crowds, noise, air pollution, water treatment, land use, security, and public safety are all issues that affect the environment of a community. Worldwide, increasing attention is being paid to these environmental issues, in both developed and underdeveloped countries. The attempt to enhance or preserve the human and the natural environments of communities is being met by increasing

■■■ **A Travel Distribution Channel in Action**

"We're interested in the ad you sent us about 'Club Mud'."

restrictions. Such restrictions can range from limiting the number of visitors at any given time, to restrictions on real estate development.

Seeing the Components in Action: An Example

One way to understand all of the component parts of tourism and how they interact is to focus on a real life example of tourism in action. International events that bring visitors from around the world on a large scale provide an opportunity to study tourism. Such events can be held just once or periodically. An international event brings together people from many cultures and places enormous demands on the host community.

Atlanta: The 1996 Olympics

An internationally important event such as the Summer Olympic Games lends itself to a discussion of how tourism works. All of the components of tourism are affected by such an event: lodging, foodservice, entertainment, the travel distribution channels, and modes of transportation. Further, the city of Atlanta, Georgia, will feel the economic, environmental, social, and cultural impact.

The Games at a Glance Consider the games at a glance. More than 10,000 athletes representing nearly 200 nations will participate in the games. By the time the 16 days of competition are completed, approximately two million visitors will have come to Atlanta. Staging the games will cost an estimated $1.58 billion dollars. A total of 1,933 gold, silver, and bronze medals will be awarded for 271 events. Some 11 million tickets to the events will be available for sale. It is estimated that 3.5 billion people, two thirds of the world's population, will watch the television coverage of the Games.

The sheer size and complexity of the event means an extensive amount of planning and coordination. Consider some of the logistics of tourism that Atlanta must manage. Where will everyone stay? Where will they eat? How will 10,000 athletes, 5,000 coaches and officials, and two million visitors get from one place to another?

The Transportation System Atlanta will have established an Olympic Transportation System, an interconnecting network that will add 2,000 buses to its existing bus and rail system. Though most events will be held in Atlanta, the system must also service Athens, Columbus, and Savannah, Georgia; and the Ocoee River in Tennessee. For the preliminary rounds of soccer contests, stadiums will be used in Alabama, Florida, and Washington, D.C. Unable to hold all contests in Atlanta in a reasonable time frame, the Olympic Committee is using the facilities of nearby cities. Coordinating use of stadiums and transportation to and from them is just one component of one sport that must be managed.

Providing Accommodations Most of the athletes and coaches will be housed in Atlanta Olympic Village on the campus of Georgia Institute of Technology. There will also be seven satellite Olympic Villages outside Atlanta. Because of the large concentration of rooms in a single setting, the downtown location, the suitability of the accommodations for the athletes, and their availability in the summertime, the use of university housing makes a lot of sense. This strategy was employed in previous games, such as the Los Angeles Summer Games in 1984, during which athletes were housed on the UCLA campus. Spectators to the events will fill the city's more than 55,000 hotel rooms as well as those of surrounding cities and towns, up to several hours' drive away. Savannah, Georgia, alone will provide more than 15,000 rooms. A network of private homes and apartments in Atlanta will rent rooms, and sometimes entire homes will be sublet. As we learned earlier, the lodging business is capital intensive, so to build additional accommodations for this 16-day time period in 1996 would be completely impractical. Thus, rooms with other uses will be converted into lodging for the games.

Providing Foodservice Contract foodservice companies will play an important role in feeding all of the athletes and the spectators. Temporary satellite kitchens and foodservice outlets will be set up throughout the city at the various game locations. It's important to note that feeding the athletes presents a special challenge. Providing for special dietary restrictions, as well as satisfying the palates of people from 200 countries, will be no small challenge. Thousands of temporary staff will be hired and trained to host the food outlets. The volume of food that must be produced presents extraordinary production challenges. All of the components of purchasing, receiving, issuing to various outlets, preparation, and service on a large scale are present. Those kinds of service setups that allow for the maximum number served in the shortest time frame will be frequently employed. This includes buffet lines in the Villages and fast foodservice for take-away items at the various game sites. Local restaurants will also gear up for maximum production. Any venue resembling take-out will be one way that restaurants will increase their capacity to serve the crowds.

For the games themselves, some 40,000 people will be recruited as volunteers to help staff the games. Because of the vast number needed, recruiting began in January of 1995. All volunteers went through an interview and a series of training programs that were completed well before the commencement of the games.

Getting to the Games As the spectators for the Olympic Games will come from around the world, the travel distribution channels will truly be global in nature. An event such as this is commonly sold as a bundled package, including airfare, lodging, some meals, and tickets to the events. Travel agents throughout the world will handle such bookings. Two unusual "agents" will serve as distribution channels for tickets to the events. Brochures and mail order forms will be available at retail locations where Coca-Cola (an Atlanta-based company and worldwide sponsor of the games) is served and in Home Depot stores throughout the United States. Because tickets to the popular events can be precious commodities, it is not uncommon for tickets to be purchased by brokers and then sold again at a premium.

Economic Impact

Ticket sales are just one way that the Atlanta Committee for the Olympic Games hopes to recoup the $1.58 billion in costs. To pay for the Games, it also expects revenues from television rights fees, corporate sponsorships, and merchandise sales. Shopping as an attraction will be provided as part of the Olympic entertainment package. Retail stores, T-shirt and souvenir vendors, and the like will see a significant increase in business.

An important portion of the costs, some $500 million, will be spent on infrastructure, which will leave behind a legacy of capital improvements for the citizens of Georgia. The facilities built include an 85,000-seat Olympic Stadium. After the Games, it will become a 45,000-seat baseball stadium and the new home of the Atlanta Braves. Maximizing the capacity of the stadium in the short run is one way that has allowed Atlanta to increase the number of tickets sold to traditionally sold-out events. Because this large structure has an "afterlife," its economic value to Atlanta is great. Without a future use, the likelihood of such construction would be nil.

The economic impact to Atlanta is expected to be $5.1 billion dollars over the course of the period 1991 through 1997. This number reflects the value of the investments made, as well as hoped-for increased tourism, both leading up to and after the Games. To help with increasing tourism, several other events are planned in conjunction with the Olympics. A multiyear, multidisciplinary program presenting a series of arts performances and exhibitions, as well as an eight-week Olympic Arts Festival, will accompany the games. This series of events, called the Cultural Olympiad of the Centennial Olympic Games, is an attempt to broaden the tourism appeal from sport to art. Atlanta will also sponsor the Paralympic Games, a 17-medal event that will happen after the Olympic Games are concluded.

Environmental, Social, and Cultural Impact

On a local level, citizens will face issues ranging from the environmental impact of construction and security issues associated with hosting a multitude of visitors at one time, to traffic congestion and pollution. In response to such issues, the Olympic Committee has created advisory groups and task forces. Their mission is to receive input from a wide range of constituencies, which range from neighborhood groups to environmental, transportation, and security specialists. As part of its operations, the Olympics will spend millions of dollars to increase its security forces and medical care availability dramatically. It also completed an environmental impact statement, which was a requirement of the city's bid package.

As with any new development, the responsiveness and awareness of organizers, their ability to plan ahead, to anticipate and to correct problems, and to nurture support in the local community will determine the event's success on dimensions beyond economics.

Summary

Tourism is the way that people come to the world and the world comes to people. A traveler in another part of the world brings his or her own culture to a new one. Such travel has economic, social, cultural, and environmental impact on the host community. In order to travel, a tourist may use a variety of methods to gather information and to make travel arrangements. All of the choices, ranging from using a toll-free number to contacting the local chamber of commerce, comprise the travel distribution system. As the age of technological improvements in communication reshapes the ways that people around the world can be in touch with one another, the travel distribution channels will experience substantial changes.

A tourist may use a variety of transportation options in the course of traveling. This transportation network is a fundamental component of the tourism system and provides the means to the end for hospitality services. Such services consist of foodservice, lodging, and entertainment. The nature of the entertainment available is diverse, including recreation, attractions, and special events. Tourism continues to be a profound component of the economy of many countries in the world. Understanding the size and shape of this important conglomeration of businesses yields a respect for the world's number one employer.

Discussion Questions

1. What impact (positive and negative) could tourism have on a developing country?

2. What government agencies are involved in tourism? What are their goals?

3. How can a special cultural event be promoted as a tourist attraction? What government agencies might be involved?

4. What are the most popular activities for overseas travelers? Why do you think they are popular?

5. What are the ways a business traveler could make flight, hotel, transportation, and activity reservations? A pleasure traveler? Are they different? If so, how and why?

6. Explain the multiplier effect, and give an example.

7. What impact does gaming have on the economy? Do you think gaming will continue to grow in the United States? Internationally?

8. Explain how the components of hospitality are intertwined.

9. Write your definition of tourism.

10. List the components of tourism that you would experience if you went to the Olympics in Atlanta, Georgia.

Assignments

1. Research a special event or festival in your local community. How are the components of tourism influenced by such an event? What are the economic, social, cultural, and environmental impacts of such an event? How do you think income might be "multiplied"?

2. Trace the evolution of some form of transportation. How has it influenced other components of hospitality?

3. Choose a foreign destination of interest to you. Gather information about that destination from as many travel distribution channels as possible. Which do you prefer as a consumer? Why?

4. Consider the opening quotation from Sir Richard Burton, a British author and translator of *Arabian Nights*. Why is travel an adventure? Why do so many people choose to travel? Research different motivations for travel over time.

End Notes

1. Robert W. McIntosh and Charles R. Goeldner. *Tourism: Principles, Practices, and Philosophies*, 4th ed. (New York: John Wiley and Sons, Inc.), 3-13.

2. Bob Gatty, "World's No. 1 Employer," *Hotel and Motel Management*, 208 (19) (1 November 1993): 1.

3. John Latham, *Progress in Tourism, Recreation and Hospitality Management*, vol. 4. In book review in *Economic Geography*, vol. 70, no. 1, 95, reviewed by Rudi Hartmann (January 1994).

4. *Tourism Works for America Report*, 1994 Annual Edition, 23. The Tourism Works for America Council, Washington, D.C.

5. Travel Industry World Yearbook 1994-1995, Somerset R. Waters, 13. (Rye, New York: Child & Waters Inc.)

Part Two

Places to Stay

Historically, travelers have always found places to stay, even though they were not all known by the same name. Thus from time immemorial, travelers have found accommodations at inns, taverns, posting houses, hotels, motels, resorts, lodges, clubs, conference centers, and other places. Chapter 6 outlines the various classifications of accommodations that can be found in the lodging industry: defined by price, location, room configuration, by whether they are convention related or whether they are lodging with entertainment, and by the health care they provide. These various classifications result from asking a series of questions about the property, such as its size and service level. A complete set of questions for classifying properties and descriptions of the many different kinds of properties serve as a framework for understanding the lodging industry.

The lodging industry operates 24 hours a day, 365 days a year. The transactions that take place in hotels are spread throughout various points of sale. The functions of the front office—housekeeping, security, human resources, sales and marketing, accounting, food and beverage, and maintenance and engineering—appear in all large lodging operations in some form. In smaller or less expensive lodging operations, traditional functions may be performed by the same person or may not be performed at all. The way these key functions work together in both the front and the back of the house are presented in chapter 7.

Chapter Six

The ancient, true and proper use of Inns, Ale Houses and Victualling Houses is for the Receipt, Relief and Lodging of Wayfaring People, traveling from place to place and not meant for the entertainment and harbouring of Lewd and Idle People to spend and consume their Money and Time in Lewd and Drunken Manner.

Act of 1604 Britain

Lodging: More Than Hotels

When you finish this chapter you should be able to:

1. Classify a hotel by type, size, price, location, room configuration, facilities and service levels, customer, or affiliation.

2. Describe the various kinds of lodging establishments, and give examples of each.

3. Explain why a hotel can fit into more than one category.

4. Understand the major segments of the lodging industry, including conventions, entertainment components, parks and recreation, and health care.

5. Understand the history of the casino hotel in the United States and its impact on lodging.

6. Understand the development of mega resorts.

7. Discuss the background of the cruise industry and its potential for growth.

8. Explain what comprises the lodging health care segment, and why it is a growing area.

Introduction

Say the word *hotel* and what comes to mind? The places you've stayed? The places you've worked? What you've seen in brochures or in travel magazines? For some, the image of the Waldorf-Astoria might represent the image of a hotel—large, dark, formal, old. For others, it could be a Holiday Inn, near the amusement park they visited every summer, complete with a pool and family-style restaurant. What about other kinds of places to stay, like a cruise ship that tours the Caribbean or a lodge in a national park?

If you really stop to consider all of your options, you will realize that there's a lot more to the lodging industry than just hotels. There are many different kinds of lodging properties. With business and pleasure travel having become such an important component of our hospitality world, this chapter highlights the developments and diversity in the ever growing lodging sector.

Classifying Lodging Properties

To begin to understand the differences in lodging operations, take a seat in the lobby. There are many clues about a particular property that can be found there. The **lobby** is the gateway for the arrival of a guest and it very much shapes a guest's first impression. Consider the following descriptions of the Algonquin Hotel in New York City:

> Some people just sit in the lobby and let New York go by; it is a New Yorker magazine cartoon come to life. The lobby which looks as if it was decorated by Brooks Brothers, was also [recently] refurbished.... It still has that Victorian loathing of sunlight. The velvet chairs and tapestry settees still look dusty (the good kind of dust). The little side tables all still seem to be varnished with maple syrup.... The lobby's well-starched waiters are a breed distinct.... Like much of the staff, they are an older, loyal bunch.... Buck Buckholz [is] at the piano, as he is Tuesday through Saturday from 5 p.m. to 8 p.m. The Algonquin's bookish crowd [is] dressed like Paul Newman and JoAnn Woodward in Mr. and Mrs. Bridge. The women seem to like plaid kilts. For a man, a corduroy suit and a Harris tweed jacket (elbow patches optional) does quite nicely. There [is] also a young, apres-ski contingent in bright layered sweaters.[1]

Gathering Key Information

How do you classify the Algonquin Hotel? The following set of criteria, which address the customer, the size of the property, the price tag, the location, the facilities and amenities, the room configuration, and affiliations should help in determining the type of lodging property that it is. These are the criteria that are critical to understanding the makeup of a property. The breadth of information will demonstrate why there are so many segments of lodging properties within the industry.

The Customer—Ultimately the Most Important Category Who stays at the lodging property? The **customer** is the first priority in any lodging category, whether business or pleasure, short stay or long-term visit, individual or family. Each customer has different needs, to which the hospitality property responds by servicing those needs. Looking at the customers in the lobby of a hotel provides clues. If a group of men and women carrying garment bags and briefcases are checking in, chances are the hotel is close to the business or financial district of a city. If a group of sunburned kids lugging towels, pails, and shovels is being ushered through the lobby by a parent with groceries, the property could very well be a condominium timeshare on the beach. Business travelers would not find their needs met in the timeshare, nor would the family have chosen an urban, commercial hotel for their vacation. The customer's preference determines every detail.

Often, lodging properties will be accommodating more than one type of guest at the same time. For example, a budget hotel in a suburban area may be hosting traveling salespersons doing business in the area, relatives in town for a family reunion, and a family on vacation at an interim stop during a long drive. Guests may also have more than one reason for staying during the same visit. A businesswoman attending a conference on Wednesday and Thursday may be joined by her family for a mini-vacation on the subsequent Friday and Saturday.

Size How big is the property? **Property size** is classified in terms of the number of rooms. A small hotel would usually have fewer than 100 rooms; a convention hotel could have upward of 3,000 rooms. A bed and breakfast could have just one or more rooms with one bed, while a youth hostel could have one big room with 20 beds. The range of size can be from one room to thousands of rooms.

Price How much does it cost to stay there, or what is the property's average room rate? Again, this is the average price charged per night per room over a given time period. (You can review this calculation in chapter 2, "The Big Picture.") Price is often dependent on the location of the property. For instance, it is more expensive to stay in the Marriott Marquis, a convention hotel in the heart of New York City, than to stay at the downtown Marriott in Kansas City. Price is a good reflection of the kinds of facilities and amenities that are offered. Naturally, more expensive properties have more extensive services.

Location Where is the property? For example, is it downtown, in a suburb, off a highway, at an airport, in a resort area, in a small town? **Location** affects price, as well as who stays there, affiliation, room configuration, size, and facilities and amenities.

Service Levels/Amenities and Facilities What kinds of **facilities** does the property have? For example, does it have a swimming pool, health club, or meeting rooms? Does it offer entertainment components such as casinos or amusement rides? What kind of amenities does the hotel have? For example, does it have fancy soaps, bathrobes, or faxing service available? It is in this category that luxury hotels, which are expensive properties with extensive services, are markedly different from other lodging operations.

Configuration The **configuration** of a hotel speaks to its purpose. How is the property physically laid out? Is it a motel with exterior corridors? Does it have an atrium or courtyard configuration? Is it situated on a huge lot of acreage or a small amount? For example, a resort property would have much more extensive grounds than would an economy lodging property.

Affiliation Does the property have any kind of **affiliations**? Here we refer to affiliation in its broadest sense, as a part of any kind of larger group. Is the hotel part of a chain organization? Is the hotel a member of a referral group? Being a part of a chain or referral group means that the customer may have been attracted by the brand name of the property.

Applying the Questions

In summary, the above questions ask: Who stays there? How big is it? How much does it cost? Where is it? What does it have? How is it configured? With whom is it affiliated? After gathering information on the lodging property by asking these questions, we are ready to determine what *type* of property it is. For example, is it an all-suite, luxury, commercial, economy, convention, mid-priced, resort, bed-and-breakfast, or motel? We will learn more about what each of these categories mean later in the chapter. It is important to remember that any given property could fit into more than one category.

The Algonquin Going back to the Algonquin lobby, we might conclude from the lobby view that it is a relatively small (perhaps 200 rooms), luxury hotel in a center city location. It probably has extensive services. Given its size, it probably does not have extensive facilities, like a health club, or extensive grounds. It would appear to be expensive and to cater to the high-income pleasure traveler. Though the lobby itself does not help in determining the affiliation of the hotel, the name of the hotel would suggest that it is not part of a chain. We would guess the hotel to have several floors, given its city location.

The Westin Bonaventure The Bonaventure Hotel lobby, in Los Angeles, California, yields a different set of clues. The following Westin Bonaventure description is of a very different kind of property, on the opposite coast from the Algonquin. The same set of criteria can be applied, however.

> *[It] looks like the set of a James Bond movie. The walls are of naked cement, and there are almost always hundreds of people scurrying around.... Designed by architect John Portman, the Bonaventure has a six-layer wedding cake of a lobby—pods (the hotel's signature oval balconies), walkways, waterfalls, marquee lighting and hanging plants below a clear glass ceiling.... There are a dozen elevators in glass tubes around a central atrium.... The elevators are continually popping up by surprise, firing like rockets just a few feet away from the pods, as if Portman didn't want anyone to relax.*[2]

This hotel lobby also suggests a center city location, but one would expect it to be much larger than the Algonquin, having perhaps more than a thousand rooms. The hotel appears to cater to large business groups, and may also attract pleasure travelers. The hotel probably has a reasonably high level of services, and most likely extensive facilities such as meeting rooms and a health club. This hotel is part of a chain, as the name indicates, and is probably expensive. It has an atrium configuration to help bring a sense of space in to a confined urban location.

The descriptions of the Algonquin and the Westin Bonaventure are just two of the many types of lodging operations in the world today. From large, chain-affiliated convention hotels in Atlanta, to small, family-run bed-and-breakfasts in the south of France, to roadside motels at the end of the interstate exit ramp, the hotel business is varied. Guests' needs differ—and the hotel industry responds by building and operating all kinds of facilities. It is, after all, a business that relies on satisfied customers.

Types of Lodging: An Overview

There are many ways to define lodging properties, and the definitions can and often do overlap. By using the key questions, though, we can develop specific categories to help outline the major divisions, and to give some structure to the industry. Exhibit 6.1 offers a summary of the many different kinds of lodging and provides examples of actual properties around the world that fit into each of the categories. The main categories are:

- Hotels
- Conference Centers and Convention Properties
- Lodging with Entertainment Components
- Lodging Affiliated with Parks and Recreation
- Lodging Affiliated with Health Care

Exhibit 6.1 Lodging Components

Category	Examples
Defined by Price	
Luxury	1. The Imperial Hotel, Tokyo, Japan
	2. The Ritz-Carlton, Cancun, Mexico
	3. St. Regis, New York, NY (ITT Sheraton Luxury Properties)
	4. The Kowloon Shangri-La Hotel, Hong Kong
Boutique	1. Morgans, New York, NY (Morgans Hotel Group)
	2. Triton Hotel, San Francisco, CA (Kimco Hotel & Restaurant Management Company)
	3. Beverly Prescott, Los Angeles, CA (Kimco Hotel & Restaurant Management Company)
	4. Banyan Tree Phuket, Phuket, Thailand
Upscale—Commercial	1. The Hyatt Regency, Chicago, IL
	2. The Tel Aviv Sheraton, Israel
	3. Kempinski Hotel, Beijing, China
	4. SAS Royal Hotel, Brussels, Belgium
	5. Istanbul Hilton, Turkey (Hilton International)
Mid-scale—Commercial	1. Quality Inn Hotel, Vancouver, Canada
	2. Holiday Inn Hotel, Boston, MA
	3. Howard Johnson Hotel, San Diego, CA
	4. Radisson Inn Oslo, Oslo, Norway
Budget/Economy	1. Holiday Inn Express, Clearwater, FL
	2. Fairfield Inn, Atlanta, GA

(Continued)

◼◼◼◼◼ *Exhibit 6.1* Lodging Components *(Continued)*

Category	Examples
	3. Rodeway Inn, Tempe, AZ
	4. Sleep Inn, San Jose, Costa Rica
	5. Travelodge, Surabay, Indonesia
Location Specific	
Airport	1. Ramada Inn, Augusta Airport, GA
	2. Wyndham Garden Hotel Phoenix Airport, AZ
	3. O'Hare Marriott, Chicago, IL
	4. Sofitel Marseilles Aeroport, Marseilles, France
Motor Hotel/Motel	1. Tidewater Motor Lodge, Cape Cod, MA
	2. El Pueblo Lodge, Taos, NM
	3. Tatum's Radisson Slavjanskaya Motel, Moscow, Russia
Downtown	1. Holiday Inn (Downtown), Nashville, TN
	2. Movenpick Hotel, Zurich, Switzerland
	3. Parker Meridien, New York, NY
Suburban	1. Courtyard by Marriott, Norwood, MA
	2. Sheraton Design Center Hotel, Fort Lauderdale, FL
	3. Paris Penta Hotel, northern suburb of Paris, France
	4. Renaissance Palm Garden, Kuala Lumpur, Malaysia
Boatels	1. Saigon Floating Hotel, Saigon, Vietman
	2. Barken Viking, Gothenburg, Sweden
Defined by Room Configuration	
All-Suites	1. Embassy Suites (Promus), Toronto, Canada
	2. Doubletree/Guest Quarters Suite Hotels, Waltham, MA
	3. Sheraton Suites, Dallas, TX
	4. Westin Suites, Bangkok, Thailand
Extended Stay/Residential	1. Residence Inn by Marriott, East Lansing, MI
	2. Summerfield Suites, Lake Buena Vista, FL
	3. Hawthorn Suites Hotels, Atlanta, GA
	4. Inn Side, Frankfurt, Germany

▬▬▬ *Exhibit 6.1* *(Continued)*

Category	Examples
Capsule Hotels	1. Green Plaza Shinguku (Train Station), Tokyo, Japan
	2. Ueno Capsule Room Hotel (Train Station), Tokyo, Japan
	3. Capsule Inn Akasaka, Tokyo, Japan
Bed & Breakfasts	1. Birch Hill Inn, Manchester, VT
	2. Grange Country House, Keswick, England
	3. The Guadeloupe Inn, Santa Fe, NM
Youth Hostel	1. YMCA, New York, NY
	2. YMCA, Jerusalem, Israel
Private Club	1. The Harvard Club, New York, NY
	2. The Cornell Club, New York, NY
	3. Hilton Beach Club, Dubai, United Arab Emirates
Convention Related	
Conference Centers	1. Radisson Hotel & Conference Center, Cromwell, CT
	2. Sheraton New Orleans Hotels, New Orleans, LA
	3. Brocket Hall Conference Center, England
Convention Hotels	1. Marriott Marquis, New York, NY
	2. San Francisco Hilton Hotel & Towers
	3. Sheraton Boston Hotel & Towers
Lodging with Entertainment Components	
Casino Hotels	1. MGM Grand hotel (5,005 rooms), Las Vegas, NV
	2. Sheraton Casino Halifax, Nova Scotia
	3. Trump Taj Mahal Casino & Resort, Atlantic City, NJ
	4. Hotel Mirabeau, Monte Carlo
Destination Resorts	1. Four Seasons, Bali, Indonesia
	2. Westin Regina Resort, Los Cabos, Mexico
	3. Club Med, Eilat, Israel

(Continued)

■■■■■■■■ *Exhibit 6.1* Lodging Components *(Continued)*

Category	Examples
	4. Hyatt Regency, Maui, HI
	5. Reoma Nikko Resort Hotel, Ayauta, Japan
Mega Resorts	1. The Luxor, Las Vegas, NV
	2. Silver Legacy Resort, Reno, NV
Urban Resorts	1. Swissôtel Chicago, Chicago, IL (offers an extensive fitness room and a golf course in the heart of Chicago)
	2. Caribbean Village, Santo Domingo, Dominican Republic
Condominium/Timeshare Resorts	1. Disney Vacation Club, Orlando, FL
	2. Marriott Ownership Resorts Inc. (various locations— the biggest chain in the timeshare segment)
	3. Hilton Grand Vacation Club (various locations)
	4. Hyatt Vacation Ownership Inc.
Theme Park Hotels	1. Walt Disney World Grand Floridian Hotel, Orlando, FL
	2. Universal Studios, Orlando, FL
	3. Canada's Wonderland, Toronto, Ontario, Canada
Spas	1. Canyon Ranch, AZ
	2. Saturnia International Spa Resort, Miami, FL
	3. Givenchy Spa, Versailles, France
	4. Chewton Glen, New Milton, England
	5. PGA National Resort & Spa, Palm Beach Gardens, FL
	6. The Homestead, Hot Springs, VA
Cruise Ships	1. Carnival Cruises, Miami, FL
	2. Princess Cruises, Miami, FL, and Alaska
	3. Queen Elizabeth II, Cunard Line, New York City & South Hampton, England
Riverboats	1. The Mississippi Queen, New Orleans, LA
	2. Bally's Riverboat Casinos, New Orleans, LA

████████ *Exhibit 6.1* (*Continued*)

Category	Examples

Lodging Affiliated with Parks and Recreation

Camping
1. Annisquam Campgrounds, Gloucester, MA
2. Sawmill Campgrounds, CA

RV Campgrounds
1. Barcadia Tent and Trailer Grounds, Bar Harbor, ME

Ranches
1. The Cirle K Ranch, WY

Lodging Affiliated with Health Care

Assisted Living Centers
1. Maccabi Living Center, Ramat Ha'Sharon, Israel
2. Eskaton Village, Carmichael, CA
3. The Ledges, Laconia, NH

Patient & Visitor Inns
1. Ronald McDonald House, New Haven, CT
2. The Inn at Children's, Children's Hospital, Boston, MA

Hotels

Though there are many types of lodging properties that are not **hotels** per se, the category of hotels is still the largest, the most familiar, and has the most subcategories. There is no one right way to list all the different kinds of hotels. Here we attempt, however, to draw the greatest distinction between hotel properties by classifying them according to price, location, and room configuration. Again, it is important to emphasize that some hotels will fit into many categories.

Defined by Price

One way to classify hotels is by **price**—from the inexpensive to the exorbitant. Price, from the guest's perspective, is how much is paid for a night's stay. A hotelier would consider price the average room rate. Other charges are associated with restaurant meals, charges for services, or charges associated with a conference or event. What determines price? Well, all of the key classification questions affect price.

Luxury **Luxury** properties pride themselves on the opulent service, extensive facilities, and amenities that they provide. Health clubs, gourmet restaurants, salons, limousine services, and more can all be found in a luxury property. These hotels have a high **staff-to-guest ratio**, meaning that for every guest, there can be upward of two to three staff members dedicated to the needs of that guest. The guest at such an establishment can be traveling for pleasure or for business. Luxury hotels generally range from 100 to 400 rooms each, and most are located in major cities and resort destinations. Prices in the luxury category range from expensive to very expensive. What is very expensive? A penthouse suite, with multiple room and rooftop views, in a luxury hotel in a city like Los Angeles could go for $10,000 a night!

Boutique **Boutique hotels** distinguish themselves by their design. Each hotel has a different style and flair. The distinguishing architectural and design styles are continued in each guest room. Styles range from classic European atmosphere, to Victorian, to a clean, modern decor. Boutique hotels often have gourmet restaurants and are located in what might be termed "trendy," urban areas. These hotels tend to have a narrow customer **target market**, and cater to a specific client. Because the clientele is limited, the staff works hard to cultivate a high rate of repeat business. They tend to be relatively expensive, but less so than a luxury hotel. Most of the boutique hotels are relatively small, averaging less than 150 rooms. The Paramount Hotel in New York City, which has an art deco theme, is a good example of a boutique hotel.

Upscale-Commercial The **upscale-commercial** property is geared toward the business traveler, convention guest, or tourist. These hotels provide upscale, full-service amenities and facilities and feature a variety of food and beverage options, business centers with computers and fax machines, meeting facilities, and, in some cases, health clubs. Most of these properties are located in urban areas, usually within easy access to downtown areas and financial districts. The number of rooms can range widely, from 400 to 2,000. Room rates are generally considered expensive.

Midscale-Commercial These properties are moderately to expensively priced hotels, and are generally located in downtown areas. **Midscale-commercial** properties offer accommodations for the traveler who is more price sensitive than those who can stay in full service commercial properties. Target markets are business travelers during the weekdays and families during the weekends. These properties offer meeting space, a variety of food and beverage facilities, and limited amenities. Property size can range from 400 to 2,000 rooms.

Budget/Economy These are inexpensive, limited service properties with 50 to 150 rooms. The primary target customer market is the short-stay, automobile traveler. Some brand names focus on special niches, such as senior citizens and economy-minded corporate travelers. The **budget/economy properties** are usually located in suburban areas or near major highways. Although there are no restaurants on the premises, some properties provide a complimentary continental breakfast buffet, and most are located near one or more chain restaurants. Most budget/economy hotels are franchised. This is a relatively new segment of lodging, compared to luxury hotels. Costs are kept low by having a low staff-to-guest ratio, limited facilities and amenities, and limited construction costs. There are a number of economy chains, especially in the United States. Older economy properties that are independently owned are more often referred to as **motels**. Those with chain affiliation would tend to be newer and more often would be referred to as an **economy property**.

Worldwide, the budget/economy segment is the fastest growing segment of the hotel industry, especially in Europe and Asia, where the budget label doesn't always mean an inexpensive room. Overseas, hotels are typically more expensive to operate, and the weak dollar in the 1990s means high prices for American visitors. In many underdeveloped countries, there just aren't enough hotel rooms to accommodate travelers, meaning that the Best Western in New Delhi can charge up to $135 a night. The Holiday Inn in Beijing runs upward of $160 a night, while the Quality Inn advertises rates of $160 a night in Rome. As companies reduce budgets for business travel, the demand for budget accommodations means a rise in room rates.[3]

Location Specific Hotels

Where a hotel is located can often provide all the clues you would need to determine what kind of property it is, without even seeing it! Think about the difference between The Inn at Telluride, located at a Western ski area, and The Manhattan Midtown Hotel, in the heart of New York City, New York. What images of each property come to mind? Location is a significant indicator of what a hotel may offer.

Airport **Airport hotels** are located right in the airport area, or near airports with an easy access and transportation to the terminals, and cater primarily to the business traveler. The services and facilities of these hotels can range from economy and midscale to full service. Usually these hotels schedule their services, such as restaurants and transportation, according to the operational hours of the airport. Some hotels offer business centers and limited meeting space. Prices range from inexpensive to very expensive, according to the level of service provided.

Motor Hotel/Motel As people became increasingly mobile, particularly in the 1950s and 1960s, the **motor hotel/motel** lodging segment started responding to middle-class travel needs. These properties tend to be older, and offer limited service and inexpensive to moderate nightly rates. The range of facilities and level of service vary from one property to another. Some of these properties are **independent**, that is, they are independently owned and not associated with a national brand name. Location is a vital factor in the operation of the independent **motor hotels**. They tend to be located off highway interchanges, near tourist attractions, or in suburban areas. Usually, their marketing and reservations rely on membership in a referral group.

Downtown By definition, **downtown hotels** are located in a center city, urban area, often near major attractions, financial and business centers, and in the heart of the city. Customer mix consists of tourists and corporate travelers. The properties can range from luxury and full service to economy and youth hostels. Price varies accordingly, depending on size, service, and type of customer.

Suburban **Suburban** properties are located in city suburbs and offer limited service and moderate prices. Some properties offer limited food and beverage services and small meeting spaces. They are often located near suburban business and industrial parks. The primary target market is the corporate traveler. Prices vary, but are usually considered to be moderate.

Boatels **Boatels** are floating hotels that are docked permanently and serve as regular hotels. Boatels can be found in harbors of major cities in Europe, where land is unavailable or very expensive. In other cases, boatels can serve as extra accommodation facilities in cities that host international events. For example, Boston's Olympic Games in 2000 Proposal suggests that additional rooms can be offered on boatels that can dock in the Boston harbor. Boatels provide the same services as do their land colleagues. Services and facilities differ, based on the level of service provided.

Defined by Room Configuration

As we know, people travel and book hotel rooms for many reasons. When prominent people such as heads of state or famous musicians travel, their lodging needs can be very different from those of the college student driving from New York to Los Angeles for the summer. Likewise, the needs of a family are very different than the needs of a single business traveler. As a result, the kind of room each person wants can be very different.

All-Suites In the **all-suite hotel**, every room is a suite, which includes living area and separate bedroom, and perhaps limited kitchen facilities. All-suites cover a variety of price ranges, from economy to luxury. This segment experienced rapid growth in the 1980s and 1990s, due to increased customer demand. Customer mix consists of corporate travelers during the work week, and families over the weekends. The average stay is around three to six days.

Extended Stay/Residential **Extended stay/residential** lodging accommodations are aimed at the long-term customer, mainly the corporate business traveler. The average stay is between eight and 14 days. Residential hotels have full kitchen facilities, in addition to living and dining areas. Most properties provide special amenities, such as an on-site convenience store and an evening social hour. Most residential type hotels are located in the suburban areas. Prices tend to be moderate.

Capsule Hotels This unusual concept of a **capsule hotel** is very popular in Japan. The concept consists of regular-size rooms that contain multiple capsules, minibars, and common showers. The number of capsules in each hotel can range from less than a hundred to over 600. Each capsule is roughly the size of a twin bed, and the guest can either sit or lie down. Each capsule has its own door and lighting fixtures. Capsule hotels are usually located in train stations and business areas. Capsule hotels were developed in response to the need to offer inexpensive overnight accommodations in Tokyo, one of the most expensive cities around the world (real estate and land are very expensive in Tokyo).

Bed-and-Breakfasts **Bed-and-breakfasts** are small properties that are very popular in Europe and in some places in the United States. B&Bs provide a warm ambiance and a great opportunity to meet people from around the world in an open atmosphere. They are usually family-owned properties with five to 25 rooms, and often are located in converted homes. Guest rooms may or may not have a private bath. Amenities include personal service, breakfast, and sometimes evening appetizers or dinner. Some larger B&Bs have upscale restaurants on the premises. Bed-and-breakfasts may have an affiliation, but generally are not franchised. The location can vary, but they are usually near tourist attractions.

Youth/Elder Hostel **Youth hostels** are inexpensive accommodations that usually house multiple unrelated guests in the same room. They provide very basic services, such as clean sheets and towels and showers. Most youth hostels are located in downtown areas with easy access to public transportation, and are very popular in Europe. The customer mix is almost exclusively the college-age traveler. A similar concept gaining popularity is the **elder hostel**, which targets senior citizens. Elder hostels, like youth hostels, provide basic services and most often have central locations.

Private Clubs Most of the **private clubs** with lodging facilities are city clubs. They offer various facilities and services for the exclusive use of their members. Facilities and services include overnight rooms, dining rooms, meeting space, and access to a health club. Prices vary based on location, and the number of rooms is generally less than 100. In addition to city clubs, other clubs, such as yacht clubs and military clubs, can offer accommodations.

Conference Centers
and Convention Hotels

The conference center and convention hotel grew out of the ease of travel that developed in the latter half of the twentieth century. Less expensive airfares, more frequent flight schedules, and the customers' desire to travel all helped to build the convention business. A nation or worldwide organization can now gather all its members together in one location to conduct business, exchange information, allow employees to meet face-to-face, make announcements to the media, or just reward employees for a job well done. And it is a big business. According to the Convention Liaison Council, over $76.5 billion per year is directly generated from the convention business.

Meetings have many purposes and many names. A meeting can be called a convention, a technical or medical conference, a congress (a term commonly used in Europe), a forum, symposium, lecture, seminar, workshop, clinic, retreat, or trade show. Whether the meetings are large or small, they all have similar needs. Meeting rooms, large meeting halls, well-organized registration areas, transportation services, food and beverage options throughout the day, audiovisual services, and access to evening entertainment are the basic needs of a convention.

Conference Centers

Conference centers are a relatively new concept, and provide service to the group travel market. Services and facilities include meeting rooms, banquet facilities, business centers, recreation options (such as a golf course), and audiovisual services. Conference centers can be in close proximity to a city, or to a resort area. They may or may not provide lodging accommodations, but when they do, the number of rooms can range from 100 to 1,000, and the price can range from moderate to expensive, depending upon the facilities and the level of service. Price can be a distinguishing feature for conference centers; many conference centers are much more flexible in pricing policies than are convention hotels. The flexibility in pricing comes from location (development costs are generally lower outside city centers) and the volume of business. A conference center concentrates its sales efforts on groups, and therefore hopes to greatly reduce unsold space and rooms.

Convention Hotels

Convention hotels are usually located in urban areas as part of a convention complex or near a convention center. Convention hotels have 1,000 to 2,000 or more rooms, in order to accommodate large groups of people. Facilities and services include a variety of restaurants, a health club, large banquet facilities, meeting spaces, a business center (for access to the Internet, faxing services, copying machines, and typing services), audiovisual services, and full-service lodging accommodations. Some resorts would be considered convention hotels as well, offering the above as well as extensive recreation and entertainment.

Lodging with Entertainment Components

The quote that began our chapter comes from a seventeenth-century statute that said that British inns were meant for *lodging*, not for *entertainment*. In America, on the other hand, especially during the eighteenth and nineteenth centuries, inns came to offer both lodging *and* entertainment. To the historian of inns and taverns of the early Midwest, it seemed that everything took place there. "For some villagers and townspeople.... the inn was well-nigh indispensable as a social center. It was the theater, the ballroom, the youth center, the restaurant, the bowling alley, the billiard parlor, the saloon, and the sports arena, all in one."[4] More than that, it was the quintessential entertainment hub where "fiddling, dancing, drinking, banqueting, and gambling—and even spectacular brawling—were to be found at all hours of the day and night."[5]

By the turn of the century, however, such rambunctious attractions were giving way to the charm of faraway places. Apart from the easing of long-distance transportation occasioned by the early development of railroads, oceangoing steamers, and automobiles, the twentieth-century traveler could scarcely resist the allure of entertainment being offered by casino hotels, theme parks, ski resorts, or cruises to the Caribbean.

In our time, the advent of supersonic air transport together with a rapidly developing coast-to-coast network of interstate super highways, virtually assured everyone of easy access to the renowned entertainment and recreational centers of the world. With business and pleasure travel having become such an important component of our hospitality world, this section accordingly highlights lodging concepts in resorts, casinos, theme parks, cruise ships, and other forms of diversified entertainment which hold the greatest opportunities for growth as we approach the threshold of the third millennium.

Casino Hotels

In the United States, **hotel casinos** were for a long time permitted in only two states, Nevada and New Jersey. By 1993, a gaming industry study had shown that some form of gaming was legal in every state except Hawaii and Utah. At that point, Foxwoods Resort and Casino in Connecticut was just one of the many casino complexes developing new hotels. Tommy Hull, a developer, is credited with pioneering the hotel business in Las Vegas in 1941. One day, while driving on the outskirts of Las Vegas, he had a flat tire. While his companion went for help, Hull began counting cars. He became so fascinated with the volume of traffic that he continued his counting for two days. Then, returning to Hollywood, he persuaded the Hollywood Roosevelt Hotel owners to construct a hotel in Las Vegas. It was the 80-room El Rancho, later renamed The New Frontier.[6]

Soon thereafter, the so-called Golden Age of Las Vegas was ushered in by Bugsy Siegal, a Los Angeles gangster with deep pockets.[7] Accompanied by several suitcases full of cash, Siegal arrived in Las Vegas in 1946. To celebrate the occasion, he awarded a contract to the Del E. Webb Construction Company of Phoenix to build the 97-room Flamingo Hotel on what is now known as the Las Vegas Strip. Originally estimated to cost $1.5 million, its final cost had exceeded $6 million by the time of its grand opening on December 26, 1946.[8] (Alas, excessive construction costs, together with enormous losses incurred in the casino operation, so infuriated his underworld backers that Bugsy paid the ultimate price for his indiscretions. He was murdered in June 1947 by an unidentified assailant at Virginia Hill's pink Moorish mansion in Beverly Hills.)

In the decades following the births of the El Rancho and Flamingo hotels, the casino hotel industry skyrocketed to new heights. In downtown Las Vegas in 1993, there were 36 major casino hotels enjoying revenues totaling in excess of $9 billion.[9]

The casino expansion has continued in other states, including Atlantic City, New Jersey, and Native American lands across the United States. The main attractions in these hotels are the gaming facilities. Room rates and food and beverage charges are usually inexpensive to moderate, in order to attract guests to spend money in the casinos. These are full-service hotels with luxurious amenities, attractions, and services. In addition to Las Vegas and Atlantic City, most casino hotels are found in Monte Carlo in Europe, and Sun City in South Africa. Other growing gaming industries can be found in Louisiana, China, the Caribbean, Eastern Europe, and Greece and Turkey.

Destination Resorts

Destination resorts are the answer for a pampered vacation, providing full amenities, guided activities for children and adults, attractions, and several food and beverage outlets. Destination resorts offer full service, four- or five-star hotels, and are located in exotic vacation sites and near tourist attractions. Activities can include sport activities, lectures, guided tours, and **eco-tourism** activities. Prices tend to be expensive, and various package deals covering airfare, transportation, food, activities, and lodging are popular. The main target markets are families and affluent vacationers. Some of these resorts have extensive meeting space in order to attract convention business.

Mega Resorts

The current trend of casino hotels is the **mega resort hotel**, which offer unique theme design, extensive food and beverage outlets, and attractions for children and adults. Beginning in November 1989, in Las Vegas, the first of a new generation of mega resorts gave a compelling promise of becoming the wave of the future. It was $600 million, 3,000-room Mirage casino hotel that occasioned much excitement, with its traffic-halting fantasy world. It was a structure 29 stories high with a 108,000-square-foot casino, housing 2,300 slot machines and 115 table games, 12 food and beverage outlets, over 1.1 million square feet of public space, and a 20,000-gallon saltwater tank with four-foot-long sharks swimming behind the front desk to keep waiting guests fascinated.

Hotel occupancy averaged over 90 percent during its first year of operation, while its revenues from both gaming and nongaming sources exceeded $650 million. This heralded the prelude to a new "entertainment economy" of the 1990s. With consumers willing to "spend big bucks on fun, companies were plowing billions into theme parks, casino-hotels, sports and interactive TV."[10] As a result of Mirage's success, three additional mega hotel-casinos opened in the mid-1990s.

Circus Circus Enterprise's spectacular enterprise, the Luxor, consists of a 350-foot pyramid (30 stories high) on a indoor Nile. Mirage Resorts has the fanciful Caribbean pirate Treasure Island. Outside the main entrance to the 2,900-room, $439 million casino hotel sits a full-size "pirate" ship afloat on Buccaneer Bay; nearby is another ship of the "rival" British navy. Every hour during the evening, a sea battle rages as these two full-size ships set in a manmade desert lagoon visible from inside the gaming rooms shoot it out. Then there is the MGM Grand, which, together with the Luxor and Treasure Island, raised the total number of hotels rooms in Las Vegas to 86,645. The MGM stresses extravagant entertainment as well as architecture worthy of a Walt Disney enterprise. Such mega resorts have attempted to widen their target audience to compete in the family vacation market, as opposed to attracting an adult-only audience.

Urban Resorts

An **urban resort** is usually a full-service commercial or luxury hotel that offers amenities, services, and facilities of a destination resort hotel. Some midscale and suburban properties also provide resort facilities and services. These facilities and services can range from extensive spa and fitness facilities to tennis courts and golf courses. The target market is transient travelers and vacationers from relatively close locations, perhaps residents of the same city, who seek an urban alternative to remote resorts. Prices vary based on the level of property and service.

Condominium/Timeshare Resorts

Timeshare refers to the purchase of equity interest in future vacations, for the guests who know they want to go away every year, but aren't sure just where they want to go. Many timeshare properties allow "swapping" weeks with other timeshare owners around the world. Timeshare properties are condo-type buildings with resort amenities, such as tennis courts, daily activities for all members, spa facilities, or golf courses. Most timeshare properties are located in resort destinations, but some of them are in urban sites. Some timeshare properties are converted hotels, or specific floors of an existing urban hotel.

The concept is relatively simple. The customer or the buyer purchases future time, perhaps a week per year, for decades or for forever. The purchase price depends on the site and the desired season of travel. The key factor in the timeshare segment is a flexible point-based system, meaning that the customer purchases a number of points to be redeemed at a later date. Each option of the timeshare, which provides flex time, split weeks, weekends, and opportunities to swap with other locations, is worth a certain number of points. The average purchase price for timeshares is about $10,000, and average annual condo fees are approximately $350 per year. The customer mix consists of upscale families and young couples. Management companies provide books of available properties for members to choose from.

Lodging at Theme Parks

The 1990s ushered in the concept of family entertainment. It did not envision the typical amusement park of roller coasters and merry-go-rounds. Instead, the streamlined amusement parks had become **theme parks**, which were more about show business and technology than they were about Ferris wheels and carousels. And, after a long day of attractions, shows, events, parties, tours, and sporting activities, visitors are tired. Lodging at theme parks has grown in response to increased customer demand. Accommodations range from luxury to economy, with every other kind in between, including camping and RV facilities. An important component of the lodging facilities is a theme—and the industry benchmark is Disney.

The Disney Success Story Disneyland opened in 1958 in Anaheim, California, and the land of Mickey Mouse became America's first modern theme park. Later, when Walt Disney World, a 27,000-acre theme park in Orlando, Florida, was opened, it instantly became the prime tourist destination of the world. In 1982, a new concept in theme parks was added to Disney World with the opening of EPCOT, an Experimental Prototype Community of Tomorrow, designed to exhibit working models of the future.

Disneyland does not own or operate any hotels within the California theme park, an error the Disney executives sought to correct in both Orlando and Paris. Theme parks want to capitalize on the customer base that flows through their gates every day. The lodging options within the Disney World complex are staggering. The Grand Floridian is a beautiful rendition of an old Victorian resort, while the Swan Hotel is structurally built to resemble a swan.

Other theme parks and entertainment complexes around the world seek to copy the success of Disney. In Windsor, England, the Lego Family Theme Park is under construction, due for completion in 1996. The Opryland Hotel is the centerpiece of the Opryland theme park, in Nashville, Tennessee. And while it is not a theme park, the Skydome Hotel in Toronto, Ontario, is attached to the Toronto Bluejays ball park; many rooms allow guests to watch the game right from their own windows.

Virtual Reality Invades and Transforms Theme Parks Sensing that entertainment centers and/or theme parks offered creative opportunities for computer-simulated forms of entertainment, in the late 1980s and early 1990s, scientists sharpened their focus on the field of interactive entertainment. It promises to shape the future of theme parks. Instead of roller coasters or Bavarian castles, visitors will be placed inside windowless, truck-size capsules and feel as though they are driving a race car or piloting a space ship. The Luxor Hotel in Las Vegas today has SEGA Virtualand, which gives a sense of what is to come. Sega's virtual reality helmet, for example, allows players to feel as if they are actually inside the game they are playing. In planning for the future, Sega intends to build many small regional parks, one to five acres each. Unlike Disney attractions, which stay fixed for years, Sega's virtual reality package can be changed just by changing the software. Sega plans to build 50 amusement parks in Japan and another 50 parks in the United States at an estimated cost of $10 million to $50 million each.

Spas as Lodging Options

The **spa resort** offers special packages that include overnight accommodations, various activities, and special cuisines. Guests who want to become physically fit represent a significant target market of spa resorts. Other spas concentrate on providing a relaxing holiday, and to that end remove all televisions, phones, fax machines, and any other high-tech devices that would encourage guests to work.

Spas can provide a special healthy cuisine, fitness classes, and spa amenities and services such as massages, mud baths, and educational lectures. As resort properties, spas are located in resort destinations around the world. Overall, prices tend to be more expensive than regular upscale hotels, due to the lodging, food, activities, and level of services provided.

Cruise Ships

A **cruise ship** is a floating hotel and resort, and is becoming a more popular vacation activity in North America. Cruise ships are designed to provide full-service accommodations with extensive food and beverage and entertainment facilities. Traditionally, cruise ships pamper their guests with a wide array of services and amenities. In addition to exotic cocktail lounges and deluxe dining ranging from gourmet buffets to seven-course theme dinners, cruise lines may provide casino gambling, night clubs, entertainment, discos, and courses in such topics as self-improvement, flower arranging, common stocks for prospective investors, bird-watching for amateur ornithologists, and learning how to speak foreign languages. Also, there are first-run movies, one or more dance bands, special programs for toddlers and teenagers, as well as health spas, tennis and handball courts, aerobics, jogging tracks, swimming pools, and golf pros for those who want to improve their game.

Cruises are usually package deals that include three, four, or seven days with full room and board. Room sizes range from luxury suites to small, economy staterooms, depending on ship location. Prices tend to be expensive, but vary based on the length of the cruise, the cruise plan and the ship category.

In the 1990s the cruise ship industry is on the move in the United States and elsewhere. With the demise of overseas passenger ship travel in the late 1960s, an incipient cruise ship market grew from 500,000 Americans who went on vacation cruises in 1970 to an estimated 12 million cruisers by the 1990s.[11]

In Asia, tour operators in Singapore, Thailand, Malaysia, Indonesia, Singapore, and Hong Kong are offering imaginative fly-cruise packages aimed not only at North American and European markets but also at the newly affluent markets of Taiwan and South Korea. Customer interest is growing, albeit slowly. As one Hong Kong travel agent remarked, Asian stereotypes about cruising are deep-rooted. "A lot of people have this misconception that when you travel on a cruise, you must be very old or very rich.... We need to do a bit more publicity."[12] This is not unlike the perception that most Americans would have had in 1960s.

Riverboats as Lodging

Riverboats are very popular in Europe as a unique way to travel and see the country. An extensive and developed river and canal system in Europe facilitated the use of riverboats. Riverboats can range from small river barges with 11 cabins, to large river vessels of over 70 cabins. Tour packages of four, seven, or more days include full room and board and guided tours. The larger boats offer lounges, bars, dance floors, sun decks and entertainment. Prices tend to be moderate to expensive, and are based on the services offered and the length of the cruise.

In the United States, riverboats do not usually have overnight accommodations, although they are gaining popularity, especially on the Mississippi River. Fall foliage tours, or historic sites of the antebellum South, are just some of the themes associated with these riverboats. Russia has recently opened up to riverboat tourism. On the Volga River, boats offering meals and accommodations are doing a booming business, sailing between Moscow and St. Petersburg. International visitors have kept this operation fully booked since its inception.

▉▉▉▉▉ The Palace of the Lost City

In the midst of a volcanic crater hundreds of miles from civilization sits the Palace of the Lost City, in the Republic of Botwsana, in southern Africa. The hotel is a renovated palace, surrounded by natural vegetation and wildlife. A nomadic tribe settled in this region and built a magnificent city, which was destroyed by an earthquake. Only recently was the site rediscovered. One look, and guests believe they have traveled back in time, to a true lost city.

While this may look old and mystical, this resort complex was built in 1992, and was completed in under three years. With 350 guest rooms on 68 acres, the intention of the owner and the architectural firm was to create a myth—a myth of lost city and all its glory. The palace/hotel is surrounded by water, which plays a central role in the design. Small reflecting pools and waterfalls lend the impression that the palace is rising out of a lake. A dramatic bridge leads over the water to the main entrance to the hotel, heightening the drama. Nothing was left to chance; every detail, from the smallest ornament on a pillar to the material used for the roof, conveys opulence and mystique. Deep in the African jungle, the hospitality industry restored a lost city and its palace.

Lodging Affiliated with Parks and Recreation

Throughout the United States there are numerous local, state, and national parks open to visitors. Some of the more famous are Yellowstone National Park, the Grand Canyon, and Yosemite. There are various government agencies assigned to the many parks, who oversee the use of public lands.

Camping

One of the ways to spend time exploring the national park service is to camp. Campgrounds are located in nearly every park in the United States. Some are nothing more than a clearing in the woods, while others provide water and shower facilities. At Hamonasset State Park in Madison, Connecticut, for example, campers are assigned sites through a reservation process. Many sites may be rented by the week, month or season, allowing the camper access to the beach, playing fields, and sanitary facilities. This park and others are monitored by park service employees, who help maintain a clean and safe environment.

Along hiking trails, such as the Appalachian Trail, which stretches from Georgia to Maine, mountain huts are available. Simply constructed, they provide some shelter from the elements for hikers. Hut to hut hiking is also popular in Europe in the Alps region.

Recreational Vehicle/Mobile Home and Campgrounds

Recreational vehicle (RV) parks and campgrounds are located near tourist attractions, in rural sites, and in major city suburbs. The park management provides electricity and sewer hookups, public showers and restrooms, and convenience shops. Entrance fee is per vehicle. These parks are very popular in North America. **Campgrounds** offer places to pitch tents, public showers, and restrooms and occasionally convenience shops.

Ranches

There are two kinds of ranches providing lodging options to travelers. The commonly known **dude ranch**, designed for the city dweller, offers simple to luxurious accommodations for the vacationer searching for the great outdoors. **Bunk houses**, with or without private baths, are common setups. Carefully crafted weeks of horseback riding, learning the cowboy ropes, and perhaps enjoying a gourmet dinner or cookout are all a part of the dude ranch experience.

In response to the eager traveler's desire to experience the great outdoors, many working ranches are now offering a "bed and work" option. Guests come and stay in an extra room in the main house, and are put to work, learning how to herd cattle or bring in a crop. The ranchers benefit from the extra help and the income generated by renting out rooms, while the guest leaves with a true appreciation for ranch life.

Lodging Affiliated with Health Care

Parallels have been drawn between the services that are provided by hotels and by hospitals. Both provide beds for overnight "guests" and both serve meals, especially "room service" for patients. Both have check-in and check-out and housekeeping services. Given the parallels, it is no wonder that several hotel companies have crossed over into the health care market. As the world's population ages, there has been an increasing need for living facilities that provide both hospitality and health care. This is an exploding segment in hospitality, and as the industry realizes benefits of operating the care facilities with the same approach as a more traditional lodging property.

Assisted Living Centers

The elderly population in the United States is estimated at 8.5 million, and growing. The vast majority are not yet in need of the facilities of nursing or convalescent home, but do need help with various daily activities. As this population has special needs, retirement communities and **assisted-living centers** with health care services have been developed to assist the elderly.

There is a broad range of assisted living centers, from ones that provide minimal services to those that can offer care for the elderly 24 hours a day. These communities can offer full room and board facilities for senior citizens, or allow senior citizens to rent studios or one or two bedroom units and prepare some or all of their own meals. Although most of the units have kitchen facilities, the residents can enjoy meals in the center's snack bar or dining room if they so desire.

Assisted living centers offer various services such as social activities, educational courses, dining rooms with nutritional services, and 24-hour on-premise medical care. Rental or purchase prices differ based on location and level of service, and most are independently owned and operated. There are some centers that allow residents to purchase individual homes, with the provision that they will be admitted to the adjoining assisted living center when they are no longer able to care for themselves. The idea of varying levels of care is built into many facilities.

Entrance into the health care market by the large hotel chains is relatively new. Major hotel companies such as Marriott and Hyatt have recently developed properties in this category. Senior Living Services is the Marriott division dedicated to assisted living. With about 150 centers, it is the fastest growing health care division in the industry. Fifty or more centers are planned for the next five years.

Patient and Visitor Inns

Located close to medical centers and hospitals, **patient and visitor inns** are designed for the medium- to long-stay customer who is related to a patient hospitalized for an extended period of time. These kinds of inns are common near children's hospitals, so parents can remain close by.

The configuration of a patient inn ranges from a bed-and-breakfast type property, to an extended stay or all-suite hotel. The amenities and facilities are generally limited and simple, to keep the average room rate moderate. Some provide kitchens and kitchenettes, for families to use at any time of day. They might provide meals and boxed lunches, but overall the food and beverage offerings are basic. The emphasis here is on providing primary, thoughtful service to guests facing medical situations.

Nicety of the House

"The Candy on the pillow is the nicety of the house."

Summary

In this chapter we examined just how many kinds of lodging properties there are in the world today—and realistically, we could come up with more. The lodging segment of hospitality is one that is so broad and complex that some accommodations can often fit into more than one category.

We can, however, make certain observations that can help classify a lodging property. We can look at type, size, price, location, room configuration, facilities, and service levels, the type of customer, or affiliation. Beyond those classifications, a lodging property may be associated with entertainment concepts, such as a theme park, resort, casino, or cruise ship, or it may be associated with the parks and recreation service. The fastest growing segment is lodging associated with health care, as the rise in assisted living centers can attest to. Just as each guest can have different needs, the hospitality industry can respond with the appropriate type of lodging property to meet that guest's expectations.

Discussion Questions

1. What clues can you obtain from observing a hotel lobby that can help you classify the hotel?

2. What key questions are used to identify a lodging property? Why are they important? Would you choose any others?

3. If you were told to build a hotel in downtown Chicago, how would you decide what to build? What about on the lonely interstate highway between Nebraska and Wyoming? What factors would influence your decision?

4. Look in a travel or hospitality magazine for lodging advertisements. Do any properties overlap categories? Why? Give some examples.

5. What are the newest categories of lodging? Why have they evolved?

6. What argument could you make to categorize a boutique hotel according to room configuration?

7. Why do you think lodging affiliated with health care is a growing segment? What particular concerns do these operators face?

8. Why have hotels in Las Vegas added entertainment themes?

9. Why did Disney want to develop and operate the hotels at the Disney World complex in Orlando, Florida? Do they operate the hotels nearby Disneyland?

10. Why do you think the Palace of the Lost City is a success?

11. Referencing the opening quotation, how has the perspective of entertainment associated with lodging changed over time?

Assignments

1. Spend one hour in a hotel lobby. Note your observations. Observe only. Do not interact with the employees, guests, etc. You may wish to structure your observations as follows: "Because I saw … I believe this hotel is … " In this assignment you should try to define everything you can about the hotel. (Review the various ways a hotel can be classified.) You should make educated guesses about the hotel and why you have drawn the conclusions you have drawn.

2. The opening quotation comments on how a seventeenth-century law governed the operations of hotels. Research other laws, ancient and modern, that also affect hotel operations.

End Notes

1. Stephen Drucker, "Ever a Hotel Whose Heart Is in Its Lobby," *New York Times*, 18 January 1991, C-1.

2. Tom Johnson, "Real-Life Hotel," *Los Angeles Magazine* 32 (8) (August 1987): 85. Authors' note: John Portman is a very well-known hotel architect, credited by many for developing the atrium hotel.

3. "Budget Hotels Aren't Bargains Abroad," *The Wall Street Journal*, 17 November 1995, B1.

4. Paton Yoder, *Taverns and Travelers: Inns of the Early Midwest* (Bloomington: Indiana University Press, 1969), 121.

5. Ibid., 106.

6. Donald E. Lundberg, *The Hotel and Restaurant Business*, 4th ed. (New York: Van Nostrand Reinhold, 1984), 201.

7. Ed Reid and Ovid Demaris, *The Green Felt Jungle* (New York: Trident Press, 1963), 23.

8. Ibid., 14.

9. *Thirteenth Annual Study of the U.S. Gaming Industry and Its Financial Results* (Los Angeles: Saul F. Leonard Company, Inc.), 25, 1994.

10. "The Entertainment Economy," *Business Week* (14 March 1994): 58-66.

11. Chuck Y. Gee, James C. Makens, and Dexter J. L. Choy, *The Travel Industry*, 2nd ed. (New York: Van Nostrand Reinhold, 1989), 225.

12. Susan Carey, "Cruise Industry Turns to Southeast Asia," *The Wall Street Journal*, 1 December 1991, B-6B.

Chapter Seven

In a few days I had grasped the main principles on which the hotel was run. The thing that would astonish anyone coming for the first time into the service quarters of a hotel would be the fearful noise and disorder during the rush hours. It is something so different from the steady work in a shop or a factory that it looks at first sight like mere bad management. But it is really quite unavoidable.

George Orwell[1]

How Things Work: Lodging Operations ✍

When you finish this chapter you should:

1. Understand the key functions of the rooms division of a lodging property, including front office, reservations, telephone, uniformed services, and housekeeping.

2. Understand the functions of the marketing department in a lodging property, and the roles played by advertising and public relations.

3. Understand the functions of the human resources department in a lodging property.

4. Understand the functions of food and beverage operations within a lodging property.

5. Know the roles the accounting, security, and maintenance and engineering departments play within a lodging property.

6. Know the key positions on a hotel's organizational chart.

7. Understand industry terms commonly associated with a hotel's operations.

8. Know the difference between front-of-the-house and back-of-the-house.

Introduction _____

There are two common divisions to a lodging property, the **front-of-the-house** and the **back-of-the-house**. The back-of-the-house is also sometimes referred to as the heart of the hotel. What the customer experiences, the front-of-the-house, includes the lobby and related services, the dining areas, and sometimes a health club or recreational facilities. The back-of-the-house includes support services, such as the kitchens, reservations and office support for the front desk, housekeeping, human resources, sales and marketing, accounting, security, and maintenance and engineering. All of the physical systems that literally tie the property together—heating, ventilation, air-conditioning, water, electricity—come together to form the heart of the hotel.

Departmental Function within a Hotel _____

As you learned in the previous chapter, the hotel lobby provides many clues about a hotel. There is much more, however, that lies beyond the lobby. In this chapter, we will discuss the various departments within a hotel that are responsible for the day-to-day operations of a lodging facility. Not every establishment will be structured in the same way. For example, a bed-and-breakfast would likely have many departmental functions performed by the same person. The person who checked you in may carry your baggage, serve tea, take reservations, and balance the books at the end of the evening. On the other hand, a mega resort may have many departments responsible for the many aspects of running the resort. Regardless of size, there is a series of key functions performed in all lodging operations.

Some departments generate revenue for the hotel, and are referred to as **revenue centers**. Others incur expenses, and are known as **cost centers**. Revenue centers include the front office, telephone (if surcharges are added to guests' bills), restaurant outlets, and laundry (if that service is available). Health clubs, golf courses, retail stores, and parking are also places in an hotel where revenues can be generated. Other departments, such as marketing, accounting, and maintenance and engineering typically do not contribute income. Rather, these departments, which are cost centers, provide support services to enhance the overall operation and to ensure guest satisfaction within the hotel.

The Rooms Division

The **rooms division** of a hotel usually consists of the front office, reservations, telephone, uniformed services, and housekeeping.

The Front Office The **front office** is the first department with which the guest has contact. **Front desk clerks** perform three critical functions at **check-in**: they offer a warm **reception**, by greeting guests and making them feel welcome; they **register** the guests, having the guests sign in and present a form of payment, usually by leaving an imprint of a credit card; and they **assign** rooms to guests, giving them a room key or key card.[2] If all goes smoothly, the process can take minutes, or even less if the guest checks in electronically. However, the hotel business is a service business and has elements that cannot be controlled. For example, any of the following could happen at the front desk: the guest could arrive distressed and be difficult; the reservation could be lost; or the room status could be "not ready." Three minutes may turn into many minutes, and for this reason, a front desk clerk must be prepared to perform a vital fourth function: troubleshooting, or thinking quickly to make the guest happy!

Another situation that a front desk clerk may encounter is a **skip**, a person who leaves the hotel without paying his bill. Or the clerk might face a situation in which a guest must be **walked**. This means putting a guest with a **guaranteed reservation**, that is, a guest who has either paid in advance or provided a credit card number as a deposit to hold the room, in another hotel, at the same rate, because of **overbooking**. If a reservation is **confirmed**, that is, it has been made but not guaranteed by a credit card, it will likely have a time of expiration, typically 6:00 P.M. Thus, it is treated not unlike a guaranteed reservation before the time of expiration. Because of the uncertainty associated with confirmed reservations, many hotels insist on a guarantee. Overbooking occurs when a hotel has more reservations than available rooms. A hotel does not have to secure a room for a **walk-in**, a guest who arrives without a reservation, as the hotel has no contractual obligation to a walk-in. If there is a room available, then the walk-in guest has found accommodations for the night.

At **check-out** time, the customer traditionally settles the bill at the front desk. A bill, itemizing room, food, phone, and miscellaneous charges, is generally prepared the night before, and often is slipped under the door so the guest may review it in advance. Many establishments today have installed computer programs that allow the guest to review the bill on the television screen in the room. If guests feel the bill is correct, they can authorize the hotel to charge the total to the credit card used at registration, simply by following the directions on the screen. Guests can then leave the key or key card in the room, and depart from the hotel without making a stop at the front desk. The latest technological advancement, already in use, is in-room printers. The guest can review the bill on the television screen, print a receipt with the in-room printer, and depart. This process can also be found near the front desk, if the in-room option isn't available. This is commonly known as **express check-out**. Where this option is unavailable, or the guest would like to change the method of payment or question part of the bill, a trip to the front desk can settle these issues. The front desk staff then serves a **cashiering** function. The reception part of the front desk and the check-out or cashiering functions are generally in two separate places. In small hotels, both functions would be performed by the same person.

Because a front office services guests 24 hours a day, there are typically three shifts of staff involved, and at least two managers, a **day manager** and a **night manager**. During the course of a guest's stay, it is the front office that is the front line in terms of handling guest complaints or requests, providing information about the hotel and the surrounding community, and sending and receiving guest mail.

Reservations The **reservations** department, though often considered to be back-of-the-house, has a very important front-of-the-house function. It is often the first contact that a guest has with a hotel, and therefore serves an important public relations and sales function. The reservations agents are the sales force for individual reservations, and their interaction with a guest can influence whether that guest chooses the hotel again. Many major hotel companies have a toll-free number to call for reservations. This kind of reservations service is not physically located in the hotel at all, but in a separate **reservations center**, which functions as an independent office.

Telephone Service The **telephone** system in a hotel operation is commonly referred to as the **PBX**, which is a derivative of *public board of exchange*. The telephone staff connects calls coming into the hotel to different departments and guest rooms, as well as assisting the guests with interhotel phone calls. Although PBX is not really a department within a hotel, it is a revenue-generating center. Though it generally contributes much smaller amounts to profits, relative to rooms or to food and beverage, it nonetheless is important.

The telephone system did not contribute as a source of revenue for a hotel prior to the early 1980s. Before 1981, hotels were paid a flat 15 percent commission by the nationwide Bell system for the handling of telephone service. With this commission, a hotel could break even on the costs to provide phone service in each guest room, or perhaps even incur a loss, if the commission did not cover all expenses associated with the phone service. In 1981, the Bell system decided to eliminate commissions to hotels. The American Hotel and Motel Association (AH&MA) negotiated an extension of the commission agreement until the end of 1982. At the same time, the FCC (Federal Communications Commission) gave hotels the right to add surcharges to interstate calls. Hotels could also begin to shop for new telephone service providers, such as MCI or Sprint, as the industry moved toward **telephone deregulation**.[3] Deregulation brought the breakup of the Bell company into smaller telephone companies such as Nynex and Bell South, and allowed customers to pick a long distance provider, such as MCI. By the mid-1980s, hotels could choose a phone service provider and set prices for local and long distance calls from guest rooms. Some hotels have passed on more savings to their customers than others have, but telephone sales now generally contribute to a hotel's profits.

Other services related to the phone system, which offer potential for additional revenues, are increasingly being added to the list of guest amenities. Many rooms now have facsimile machines, voice mail, and modem connections for computers. Cellular phones are also being made available for the use of guests staying in the hotel. Some convention hotels even offer conference call service with video connections, **teleconferencing**, which allows guests to see and hear, over video screens, their business associates in other parts of the world.

Uniformed Services There is no mistaking a **doorperson**, traditionally called a **doorman**, at an upscale hotel. He usually has a distinguishing hat and uniform, a whistle, and an air of ownership of the hotel entrance. He helps coordinate some of the other members of a hotel's uniformed service: the shuttle bus driver or other transportation services; the valet parking attendants who park guests' cars; and bellpersons, led by a **bell captain**, who transport luggage to and from guest rooms and provide other assistance as needed while guests check in and out. Members of the bell staff can also function as salespersons by explaining the features of the property and by answering guests' questions.

The **concierge desk**, usually located in the main lobby, is also part of uniformed services and provides information ranging from restaurant options to theater tickets. The concierge may also assist guests with more unusual predicaments. A collection of New York City hotel concierges, for example, noted these as some of the most unusual requests that they had encountered: an art dealer from Italy who wanted to rent gallery space for a few days; a financier who bought a sailboat and needed to ship it home; and a pet lover who was in search of a tarantula.[4]

Not all hotels have **uniformed service**. In fact, this service is unique to the more expensive hotels, where the guest expects to find a doorman and a concierge. Some upscale hotels even have what is called a **concierge floor**, which is a floor of the hotel with its own concierge staff, dedicated to the comfort of the guests on that floor. Concierge floors charge a premium price. For frequent travelers, an upgrade to this floor is sometimes offered as a perk.

Housekeeping The **housekeeping department** performs the cleaning function for the hotel, for guest rooms, for public spaces, and behind the scenes. Housekeepers are also responsible for stocking rooms with additional items such as an ironing board, cribs, extra towels, and so on. They also attend to dry cleaning and guest laundry, if that service is offered by the hotel. Laundry from the hotel such as sheets, towels, and uniforms may be done in on-site laundry facilities or sent to an outside contractor.

The function of a housekeeper on any given day is driven by room status. A **check-out** means the room needs to be remade completely. A **stay-over** means the room will be scheduled for a **makeup**, a quick clean of the room. Beds are made, but linens are not changed. Housekeepers are generally assigned a quota of rooms for a given shift. Public spaces are cleaned by a separate crew late at night, when the hotel is quieter and least trafficked.

Housekeepers must pay close attention to detail with respect to cleaning, and at the same time respect the guests' privacy. For example, a housekeeper must be careful to omit ashtrays in non-smoking rooms while remembering to be discreet when cleaning around guests' personal items (like toupees and false teeth!).

A Week at Forest Mere

Spas are gaining popularity around the world, and one that is attracting attention is Forest Mere, in Hampshire, England. Just an hour outside of London, the spa is located in the county that Jane Austen's literature made famous. The spa experience involves a lot of intangibles; how the guest feels is critical to generating repeat customers and good word-of-mouth advertising. Guests pay a flat rate for a weekend or a week, and generally, all meals and activities are included in that price. It's up to the management and staff to carry through on all promises. At Forest Mere, beyond the expected plush guest room and gourmet yet healthy meals, the spa provides beauty treatments, massages, and exercise classes. Facilities include gyms for aerobics and weight training, and a 250-acre ground for hiking, walking, and golfing. There's even a lake for boating.

Operating a spa has particular concerns, not the least of which is the high expectations of the guest. Everything has to run perfectly—that's part of the purchase price. Guest interactions with the front-of-the-house must be flawless. Those high expectations put a great deal of pressure on the management and staff to pay attention to each and every detail, and those expectations drive every decision. The back-of-the-house at a spa has an especially critical role. Forest Mere is located in a former manor house, and while the old-fashioned charm is part of the appeal, an old building requires daily upkeep.

Engineering and maintenance personnel must be on site, staff must be exceptionally well trained to respect the privacy of the guests, and the food and beverage operation must be flawless. After a long day of hiking, a hot shower and dinner will, without doubt, be critically evaluated.

Forest Mere, seizing on its location in a well-loved section of England, has positioned itself as a world-class spa. Operationally, it takes the coordination of all departments and staff members to fulfill its promises.

Sales and Marketing

A hotel's **sales and marketing department** must perform a series of functions that maximize customer satisfaction and simultaneously maximize revenues. This department attempts to achieve these two goals through a combination of tools described at length in chapter 11, "A Hospitality Marketer's Tool Box."

Most marketing departments have a **sales force**. Each member of the sales team is usually assigned a special type of market, for example, **corporate**, **international**, or **association sales**. These **market segments** are dictated by the type of customer the hotel attracts. It is important that the marketing department has a keen understanding of the profile of its customer base and the corresponding needs and wants of each category of customers.

A hotel may choose to use **advertising** as a means of marketing, either through mass media (such as a television spot, an ad in the travel section of a newspaper, or a radio campaign), or **direct mail**. Using direct mail means that the hotel isolates a specific audience and sends out a customized mailing. A hotel may send an invitation for a complimentary visit to travel agents in the geographic areas most likely to send them business. For example, a Florida hotel might target Canadian travel agents, to promote a warm and sunny February vacation for those who live in the snow belt. Direct mail pieces, such as color brochures and rate cards, are usually the primary marketing pieces to attract individual (as opposed to group) guests' bookings.

Public relations is another facet of the marketing department. Unlike advertising, media attention generated by public relations is not paid for directly. Advertising, by contrast, is paid for, and what is printed is completely controlled by the hotel. Public relations news articles are the words of an independent writer who may be assisted by a press release from the hotel. Public relations efforts are intended to generate good will. Some efforts are managed and well planned by the marketing department. For example, one major hotel company invited hundreds of fifth graders from across the country to work in its hotels for a day, to promote the chain's appeal to parents with kids. Kids sported white chef hats and helped in the kitchen or tackled basic computer instructions for a guest check-in. Other public relations events happen by chance. For example, a local magazine, unprompted, decided to do a story on the best hotel brunches in the city. The resulting increase in business from a great review is credited to public relations.

Human Resources

The **human resource department** provides support for all employees of the hotel—as recruiter, ombudsperson, record keeper, trainer, benefits provider, manager, coach, and sounding board. In these capacities, the human resources department is responsible for a diverse set of functions. These include the following:

- The hiring and firing process—recruiting, selecting, orienting, and training new employees, and terminating employees who are not meeting expectations.

- Record keeping—keeping track of employees' personal information, payroll records, compensation structure, and benefits.

- Relocation—assisting in the geographic relocation of employees. In the hotel business, particularly in chain organizations, promotion is often tied to relocation.

- Employee relations—assuring a comfortable work environment, responding to the needs of employees as if they were internal customers, also called internal marketing.

- Serving as a sounding board—playing a mediating role if an employee has a conflict with a fellow employee or a supervisor.

- Discipline—assuring the notification and correction of inappropriate behavior in a methodical way. This function is particularly important if the hotel is unionized.

The issues that confront the human resources department are discussed at greater length in chapter 10, "A Human Resources Tool Box."

Food and Beverage

The function of the **food and beverage department** can be described best by following the pathway that food and drink travels within the hotel. Foodservice planning starts with a menu, either for a restaurant operation, room service, the employee cafeteria, or a catered function. Once the raw food and beverage ingredients are determined, based on the menu, the food and beverage is then purchased, received, stored, issued, produced, and served. After the food is ordered by a purchasing agent, it is received by a receiving clerk, who stores it appropriately. In larger kitchens that require a more formal account of inventories, the food is then issued to the chefs in the kitchen. This procedure is less formal in smaller hotels.

The next steps, production and service, vary greatly, depending on the size and complexity of the meal offerings at a particular hotel. An economy lodging property, for example, would likely have no food and beverage offerings at all, but might be located near a stand-alone restaurant, often a fast food or family restaurant chain. The number of possible restaurants, banquet facilities, room-service, and employee cafeterias are tied to the size and type of hotel. A luxury hotel might have an informal restaurant, a fine dining choice, twenty-four-hour roomservice, and afternoon tea service. A large convention property might have several restaurant choices, including a fast food or take-out option, a specialty restaurant, and a 24-hour coffee shop, in addition to banquet facilities.

Restaurants in hotels are not always managed by the hotel. They are sometimes leased by the hotel. A good example would be Legal Sea Foods, Inc., a restaurant chain in Boston that has a restaurant on the first floor of the Park Plaza Hotel, a large upscale downtown property. More information on foodservice operations can be found in chapter 9.

In addition to restaurants, most hotels also provide beverage service through some type of cocktail lounge or public bar. These areas are generally under the jurisdiction of a beverage manager and are operated separately from the restaurants. Drink service for restaurant guests is provided by a service bar, for servers only and not open to the public. Finally, minibars with a selection of alcoholic and nonalcoholic beverages and snacks, are sometimes offered in guest rooms.

Accounting

The **accounting department** is overseen by the hotel's **controller**, who manages the hotel's finances. The department's functions include recording, classifying, summarizing, and reporting financial information.[5] Recording information involves accounting for the day-to-day operational events such as issuing payroll checks or receiving guests' payments. Since the hotel business operates on a 24-hour basis, the end of the accounting day is generally some time in the wee hours of the morning. It is then that the **night auditor**, the person who balances the books for the hotel, accounts for every nickel from the previous day's transactions. Among the night auditor's duties are reviewing posting charges to **guests' folios** (the statements of the guest's account) from various points of sale within the hotel, such as a restaurant or health club. The auditor also reconciles the cash register tapes with actual cash deposits. A night auditor may also serve a dual role as a front desk clerk for the overnight shift.

Classifying information means placing the recorded information into useful categories. For example, sales revenue could be divided into rooms, food and beverage, telephone, and **minor operating departments** (such as a health club operation, dry cleaning services, or a gift shop—all smaller sources of revenue for the hotel). Revenue could also be categorized by type of payment: cash or check, credit card, or charge to **city ledger**, which is an in-house charge account. A **Uniform System of Accounts for Hotels** is commonly used. This provides a standard classification framework and follows generally accepted accounting principles to which all businesses adhere.

Once the information is classified, it is then summarized in the form of reports. These reports have a variety of uses: a tax return for the government, a quarterly or annual report for shareholders, an income or cash flow statement for lenders, a departmental sales journal for all income-generating departments, or a daily accounting of occupancy and average room rate year-to-date for the general manager. Analyzing reports, or interpreting the financial information, is the function of not only the accounting department, but all managers in the hotel. This final step in the accounting process shapes the operational decision-making of the business. Accounting practices and principles are further reviewed in chapter 13, "An Accounting Tool Box."

Security

The **security division** of the hotel is responsible for the physical safety of guests and employees, as well as for the hotel's property, including both the outside—grounds, gates, and parking lots, and inside—public spaces, stairwells, corridors, elevators, and guest rooms. This division is responsible for taking preventive measures with respect to fire, accidents, pilferage, break-ins, and so on. When things go wrong, such as an emergency medical situation or theft of guest property, the security department is available to assist. The security staff of the department usually has police and emergency medical training.

Throughout the world, the most common incidents affecting hotels include: fires; accidents involving guests, staff, or others; equipment breakdown or failure resulting from sabotage; and criminal acts, ranging from theft, assault, arson, sabotage to property, and to terrorist acts.[6] In order to avoid the above incidents, the security department must be mindful on a day-to-day basis about a wide range of items. A sampling of the work that might be included on the department's checklist are: watching for unauthorized loitering in public spaces; patrolling the various areas of the hotel regularly, checking that doors to the back-of-the-house are secured against entry from outside; checking fire extinguishers; reminding employees not to give out room numbers; and removing cash daily from the premises.

The success of the security department rests on prevention, and when things go wrong, it is up to this department to ensure that an orderly set of procedures is in place. For example, if the hotel receives a bomb threat, does the hotel operator have a detailed set of instructions to follow? (These might include instructions to note characteristics of the caller's voice, accent, manner, any information about where the bomb is, when it will go off, and a set of action steps to follow immediately after the call.) The task of the security department in a hotel is made particularly complicated because of rapid turnover of personnel, which is common to the hotel industry, and because of a constant flow of guests in and out of the property.[7] Imagine the work and expense that go into setting up security procedures in a casino hotel. Installation of surveillance cameras, use of chips instead of money, and adequate screening of employees are just some of the security concerns in a casino.

Quick! Somebody Call Security!

Say the word *amenity* to a hotel guest, and what usually comes to mind are those little extra perks a lodging property provides, from in-room modems, coffee makers, and hair dryers, to 24-hour room service, free airport transportation, and a free continental breakfast. But the amenities that have proven to be most popular over time are those little bottles of shampoo and those tiny soaps. In some hotels, they are more valuable than gold.

A check of the major hotel chains reveals something disturbing about today's traveler—they're collectors! No matter how expensive the room, no matter how wealthy or successful the guest, the soaps, shower caps, shoeshine kits, sewing kits, and mouthwash bottles, the laundry sacks and the lint brushes, are valuable commodities. Every day, housekeeping staffs around the country and world have to replace all those little bottles that find their way, unused, into guests' suitcases. The hotel amenities business is estimated at almost $300 million per year! That's a lot of soap.

Holiday Inn was the first hotel chain to promise a shower cap and a bar of soap in every room, back in 1952. Shampoo came a little later, and an industry was born. Today, Choice Hotels International buys an estimated 30 million shampoo bottles for 2,500 U.S. hotels. The Hyatt Regency in Chicago goes through over 250 million shampoo bottles annually, while ITT Sheraton has been known to spend $4.5 million on its bathroom amenities per year. And all for the guests to add to their home collection!

Some hotels, responding to the rising costs of those little shampoo bottles along with the environmental concerns associated with the use of plastic, have installed refillable shampoo containers that are permanently mounted in the shower. And others are providing amenities on demand; that is, if the guest calls housekeeping and makes a request for the shoeshine kit, it will be provided, but no longer will it be found on the bathroom vanity. A good move? Perhaps a wise move for the hotel bottom line, but in a world of fierce competition, it could be amenities, and the ease of taking them home, that create a repeat customer.

Source: The Wall Street Journal, November 1, 1993

Maintenance and Engineering

Finally, we come to the inside of the hotel, where all the physical systems of the hotel literally converge: elements related to heating, plumbing, ventilation, air-conditioning, and electric, water, and steam distribution. All of these systems are the responsibility of the **maintenance and engineering** department. In addition to the systems, the balance of the **physical plant**, both the building and **FF&E** (an industry term that stands for Furniture, Fixtures, and Equipment) also come under the jurisdiction of this department.

On a daily basis, the engineers and maintenance persons respond to **work orders** to fix what is broken and to undertake routine inspections to keep everything functioning properly. A sampling of work orders could range from repairing a leaky faucet to tacking down a loose piece of carpet. The skills of carpenters, plumbers, painters, electricians, or engineers might be needed. On an ongoing basis, the department must do preventive maintenance on the capital equipment of the hotel. Such work might involve, for example, changing the expendable parts of machinery. Driven by soaring costs, the department must also increasingly undergo a constant analysis of ways to save energy.

Organizational Charts

Much can be learned about how hotels work from **organizational charts**, as well as from a physical walk-through. A series of charts from large hotels in four major hotel companies—Hyatt, Marriott, Ritz-Carlton, and Sheraton—are shown in Figures 7.1, 7.2, 7.3, and 7.4. These charts reflect the top-level managers of the hotel, often known as the executive committee, and the assistant managers who report to them. All four have a general manager, with additional managers overseeing the functions discussed throughout this chapter.

There are some notable differences, however, in the organizational charts of the specific companies. The Ritz-Carlton has added a senior person in charge of total quality management, a topic we discussed in chapter 3. It also has a hotel manager, as second in command on a separate tier. Sheraton segments human resources, sales and marketing, and the controller from all other duties

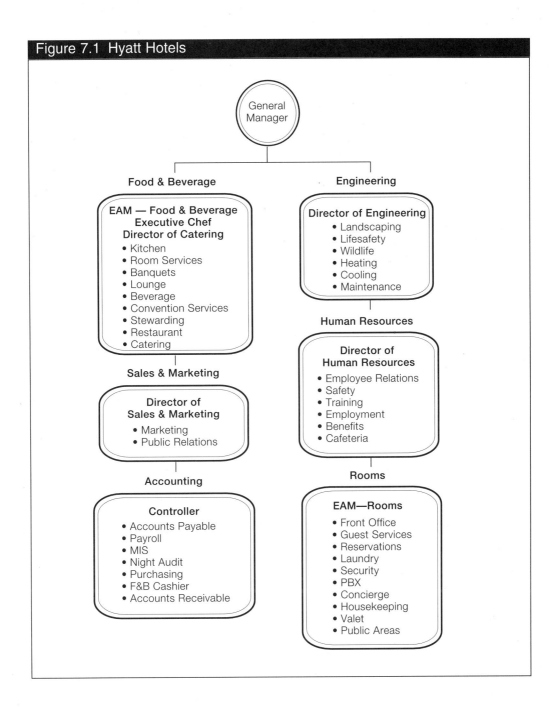

Figure 7.1 Hyatt Hotels

General Manager

Food & Beverage

EAM — Food & Beverage
Executive Chef
Director of Catering
- Kitchen
- Room Services
- Banquets
- Lounge
- Beverage
- Convention Services
- Stewarding
- Restaurant
- Catering

Sales & Marketing

Director of
Sales & Marketing
- Marketing
- Public Relations

Accounting

Controller
- Accounts Payable
- Payroll
- MIS
- Night Audit
- Purchasing
- F&B Cashier
- Accounts Receivable

Engineering

Director of Engineering
- Landscaping
- Lifesafety
- Wildlife
- Heating
- Cooling
- Maintenance

Human Resources

Director of
Human Resources
- Employee Relations
- Safety
- Training
- Employment
- Benefits
- Cafeteria

Rooms

EAM—Rooms
- Front Office
- Guest Services
- Reservations
- Laundry
- Security
- PBX
- Concierge
- Housekeeping
- Valet
- Public Areas

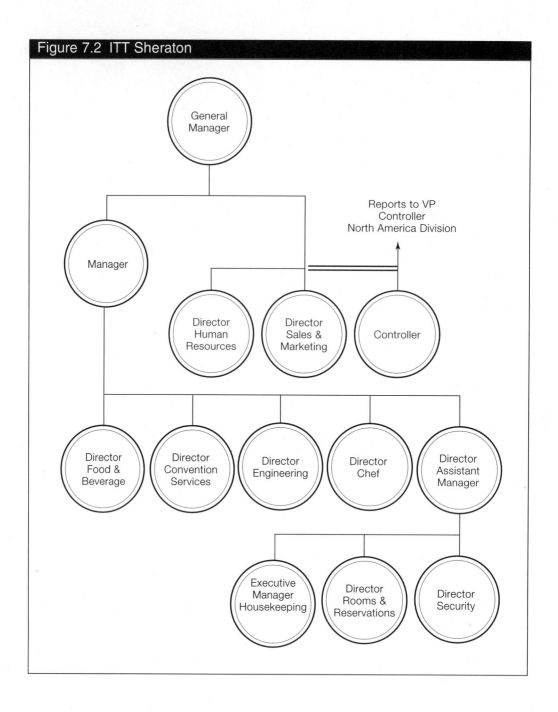

Figure 7.2 ITT Sheraton

Figure 7.3 Ritz-Carlton Hotels

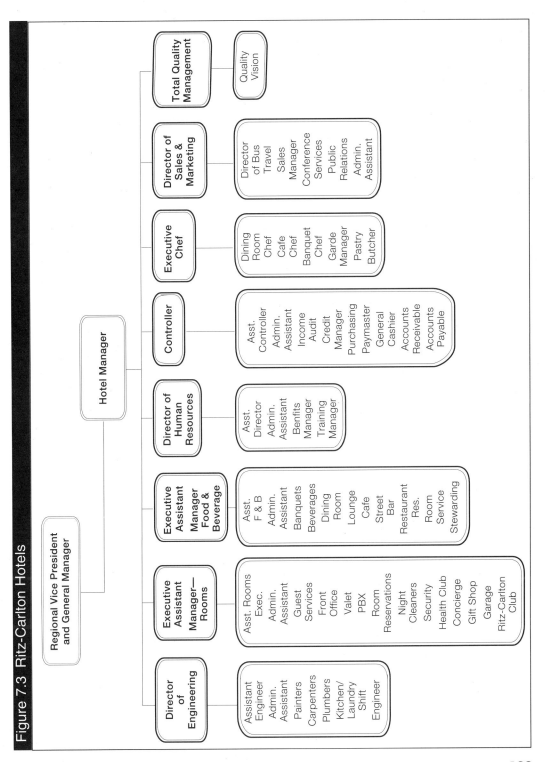

Figure 7.4 | Marriott Hotels

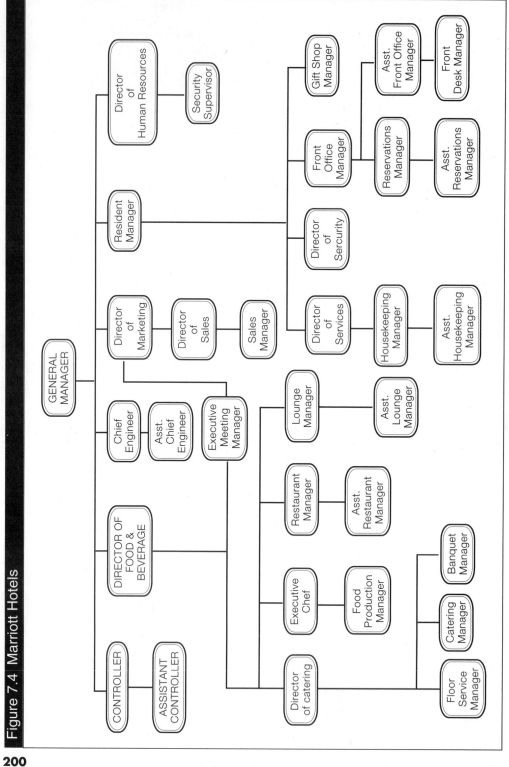

of the hotel, which are supervised by a manager. Sheraton also groups some functions of the hotel together: housekeeping, rooms, and security all report to an **executive assistant manager**. Marriott groups together the front office, housekeeping, security, and the gift shop under the direction of a **resident manager**. (Historically, a resident manager lived in the hotel. This is not always the case today, although the title remains.) Hyatt's organizational chart speaks to a series of functions and handles them using six executive committee members.

Summary

When considered collectively, the tour of the front-of-the-house and the back-of-the-house offer some key information about the way hotels work. To start, a hotel operates 24 hours a day, 365 days a year. Hotels are basically in the business of providing overnight accommodations to guests who are away from home. In providing this service, most hotels are structured similarly: the functions of a front office, housekeeping, human resources, marketing, accounting, security, maintenance and engineering, and food and beverage appear in most large hotels in some form. In smaller or less expensive hotels, more than one function may be performed by the same person, or not performed at all. At large hotels, there are many managers, one or more assigned to each department, including specialized areas such as customer service.

The transactions that constitute the hotel's business are physically spread throughout the hotel at various points of sale, such as the front desk or roomservice. Thus, you can divide a hotel into revenue centers—those areas where the hotel brings in funds, and cost centers—those areas where the hotel spends money to operate.

The main task of a hotel's general manager are: keeping customers satisfied, employees motivated, and revenue maximized. If he or she succeeds, the service in the front-of-the-house creates a repeat guest, and the back-of-the-house is, we hope, a more orderly encounter than George Orwell described in the opening quotation!

Discussion Questions

1. What three basic functions are performed at the front desk of a hotel? What other functions are part of the rooms division of a hotel?

2. Why has the telephone system of a hotel become a revenue center?

3. Explain the sales, advertising, and public relations functions of a hotel's marketing department.

4. What are the key roles performed by the human resources department of a hotel?

5. Trace the pathway of food and beverage through a hotel restaurant operation. What functions are involved?

6. When is the end of the business day for a hotel operation?

7. What are financial reports, and how are they used in a hotel?

8. What are the most common incidents that a hotel security department faces?

9. What kinds of physical systems converge in a hotel?

10. Define the following hotel-related terms: PBX, skip, walk, walk-in, FF&E, uniformed services, check-out, stay-over, night auditor, concierge, post charges, guest folios, city ledger, minor operating department, resident manager, Uniform System of Accounts for Hotels. What department(s) would likely encounter each of these terms? Explain the connection.

11. Does the opening quotation by George Orwell refer to the front-of-the-house or the back-of-the-house? When you consider peak demand times within hotels, do you think the quotation mirrors the truth?

Assignments

1. Collect information about both a small and a large lodging property. Set up organizational charts for each. You may wish to consider visiting the establishments, interviewing members of the management teams, reviewing current periodicals about the companies, and assembling samples of advertisements or brochures available. Remember to include the following information:

   - number of rooms
   - location
   - facilities and amenities
   - estimate the average room rate
   - type of guest (short-term, business, vacationer)
   - how do the properties compare? why are the organizational charts different?

2. Gather rate information on a hotel. Select a date, two weeks ahead of today's date. Choose the type of room (single, double, suite) you'll be gathering information about. Obtain the room rate through the following sources:

   - the hotel's 800 number
   - the hotel's local number
   - a travel agent
   - a referral organization
   - on-line (the Internet)

   Record your results. Repeat the process 48 hours later, and record your results. Are the rates different? How? What conclusions can you draw?

3. George Orwell, in the opening quotation, found that the back-of-the-house operation, when in full swing, appeared to be disorderly. Visit a back-of-the-house operation within a hotel during a peak time. For example, view the banquet kitchen about to serve a large convention or the back of a front office during a busy check-in. Did you find that the operation ran smoothly? If there were difficulties, what would you suggest for improvement?

End Notes

[1] George Orwell, *Down and Out in Paris and London* (London: Penguin Books, 1933), 67.

[2] Albert L. Wrisley, "Hotel and Motel Management: The Rooms Division," *Introduction to Hotel and Restaurant Management*, 4th ed., ed. Robert A. Brymer (Dubuque, Iowa: Kendall/Hunt Publishing Co., 1984), 101–103.

[3] Jerome J. Vallen and Gary K. Vallen, *Check-In Check-Out* (Dubuque, Iowa: Wm. C. Brown, 1991), 381–382.

[4] Ron Alexander, "A Concierge Means Never Having to Find It Yourself," *New York Times*, 11 February 1990, 56.

[5] Michael M. Coltman, "Introduction to Hospitality Accounting," *Introduction to Hotel and Restaurant Management*, 5th ed., ed. Robert A. Brymer (Dubuque, Iowa: Kendall/Hunt Publishing Co., 1984), 209.

[6] Bruno Dammert, "The Hotel Industry as Terrorist Target," *Hotel Security Worldwide Magazine* (January 1987): 21.

[7] Ibid.

Part Three

Places to Eat

Much of the enjoyment in travel comes from dining out. In many parts of the world, food consumed away from home is not only a convenience, but a pleasurable leisure time activity. Foodservice operations range in scope from street corner hot dog vendors to sumptuous full-service restaurants.

In chapter 8 you will learn about the different ways to classify foodservice operations. In brief, such differences break down into stand-alone concepts, catering, foodservice within lodging establishments, clubs, special entertainment concepts, foodservice within other establishments such as malls and travel plazas, and institutional offerings such as school and hospital dining.

In addition to classifying foodservice operations, this section focuses on how they work, both in setting them up and in maintaining them. Factors such as engineering a menu that works, knowing where costs and profits are, and understanding what criteria a customer uses to evaluate a restaurant experience, emerge in the understanding of commercial operations. Knowing both the client and the customer, setting up solid proposals, and being ready for quantity food preparation come into play in institutional settings.

Chapter Eight

Wherever we have been in the world, from Australia to Europe to Japan, we can't help but be impressed by the high standard of cleanliness and consistency we find in every McDonald's hamburger outlet.

Thomas J. Peters and Robert H. Waterman Jr. [1]

Foodservice: More Than Restaurants ✍

When you finish this chapter you should:

1. Know the key classification questions that will help you identify the different types of foodservice in operation today.

2. Understand the difference between commercial and institutional foodservice operations.

3. Know the main categories of commercial foodservice, and understand the many subsegments.

5. Know the characteristics of stand-alone restaurants, or those restaurants that function independently from other hospitality segments.

6. Know the characteristics of foodservice found within lodging operations, and its importance to those operations.

7. Understand why foodservice is found within other establishments, such as shopping malls.

8. Know the main categories of institutional foodservice, and be familiar with their subsegments.

9. Understand how foodservice and special entertainment concepts can work together.

10. Know what distinguishes the different types of catering operations.

Introduction

Imagine this: You entered a space via a vertical hatch door. In front of you is the nose cone of a life-size submarine. You are crashing through a wall of water. Lights are flashing. You see bubbles outside your porthole and an ever turning periscope offers perspective on the world above. Sights, sounds, and a 210-foot projection screen and a myriad of monitors broadcast underwater sea life. On board a submarine? No, actually this scene is from DIVE!, the first of what may become a chain of new-wave restaurants. Though surrounded by good fun, this restaurant takes seriously the kind of profit that can be found in satisfying customers with what has been dubbed *eatertainment*.

This is just one of many examples in a widely varied business that generates billions of dollars of revenue around the world. The range of **foodservice operations** is expansive and extends well beyond "eatertainment" restaurants, and well beyond restaurants. In this chapter, we look at the range of foodservice operations; we begin by collecting information about them.

Classifying Foodservice

Many clues offered in the above description help to determine the kind of foodservice operation that it is. A picture of the dining space comes to mind with just a little imagination, but what other information would be important to get a complete picture of the entire foodservice operation? Gathering such information involves asking the right questions. The answers to the questions form the framework for classifying foodservice operations, which are detailed later in the chapter.

Gathering Key Information

Just as in lodging operations, it's helpful to analyze the foodservice industry by breaking it down into subsegments. Asking key questions uncovers information which can be used to categorize the various kinds of foodservice. These criteria involve an understanding of the kind of customer, food, configuration, and service delivery system, as well as the size, price, and affiliations that the restaurant may have. As with lodging, it is important to remember that a foodservice operation can be classified in more than one way.

The Customer—Ultimately the Most Important Category Who eats at the foodservice operation? It is common for a potential customer to look in the window of a restaurant to evaluate whether to eat there or not. Based on their observations about the customers inside, they form an impression of the space (similar to our example of sitting in a hotel lobby). A brightly lit restaurant filled with large parties of noisy college students conveys a very different image from that of a dimly lit restaurant with quiet tables for two. Some foodservice operations have a very specific audience, such as residents of a lifecare community, or members of a private club.

The Menu What kind of food does the operation serve? Is it a deli with traditional sandwiches? An ethnic restaurant that specializes in a specific country's cuisine? The kind of food served is often the single way that a restaurant is defined. It may be called "Italian," "Continental," "German," or "fast food." It would be very difficult to understand a foodservice operation without knowing about its food.

Service Delivery How is the food served or delivered? There is a wide range of answers to this question, which speaks to the number of market niches that foodservice covers. A foodservice operation can have **table service**, meaning that wait staff take orders and then deliver food directly to the customer. Food can be **self-serve** from a buffet or a cafeteria line, served **family style**, which means the food is brought to tables in serving bowls and passed from person to person, or delivered to your door. In a lodging operation, delivery service to the door is known as **roomservice**. Food can also be picked up at the counter of a **take-out** window, which is counter service, or picked up by car, which is known as **drive-through** service. The service delivery system dictates the physical configuration of the restaurant.

Configuration How is the foodservice operation physically configured? Is it configured to imitate a diner from the 1950s, or an hotel restaurant dining room? Physical **configurations** vary widely and offer clues to the style and ambiance of an operation. Where the kitchen is physically located depends on the menu, and the kind of service delivery. An employee cafeteria will have a very different kitchen and seating area from a truck stop. A take-out only restaurant will have no dining room at all. In some catering operations, food is physically prepared in one place and served in another.

Size How big is the foodservice operation? For restaurants with table seating, the size of a foodservice operation is defined in terms of the number of seats in the establishment. Again, the menu and the service delivery system come into play. An upscale, dimly lit, fine dining establishment would lose its ambiance quickly if it could accommodate 500 people comfortably. On the other hand, a college cafeteria that wasn't large enough to seat all its patrons at lunchtime would encounter numerous problems. For some operations such as airline catering, take-out, or drive-through, the size can be quantified in terms of the number of persons or **covers** served, or the total sales.

Price How much does the food cost from the foodservice establishment? The answer for many kinds of restaurants is the average meal costs per person, or what is known as the **average check**. When foodservice is provided to institutions such as military bases, or catered to special events such as weddings, the payment will not come from each individual, but there is nonetheless a cost per person for the foodservice. The prices on the menu tell a patron a lot about the foodservice establishment. For example, two restaurants might have identical pasta dishes on their menus. One restaurant might be charging $6.50 for the linguine with clam sauce, while the other charges $12.00. Right away, the patron can make an observation about the two restaurants based solely on the price.

Affiliation with Another Operation Is the foodservice operation **affiliated** with any other kind of operation? Food is often provided in conjunction with other operations ranging from shopping malls, sports stadiums, and hospitals to retail stores, hotels, and airplanes. In many of these cases, the attraction for the customer is not the foodservice operation, but shopping or perhaps a ball game. However, for both the customer and the affiliate, the foodservice is an important amenity. Baseball games across the United States would not be the same without hot dogs; movies would not be the same without popcorn; in London, theatergoers would miss their bitter lemon and other refreshments at intermission!

Brand Affiliation Does the foodservice operation have a **brand affiliation**? Well-known brands are common in restaurants, particularly at the medium and lower price end of the marketplace. Because different units of the same brand name tend to be relatively consistent, the fact that a restaurant is a Hard Rock Cafe or a Burger King conveys important information to a customer who has been to another unit in the same chain. Operations that do not have any brand affiliation are known as **independents**, and those that do are known as **chain restaurants**.

In institutional foodservice operations, the foodservice provider is typically not known to the customer. For example, Marriott and Aramark serve thousands of meals in institutional settings, but consumers are unaware of who is providing the service. Increasingly, however, institutional providers are entering into **franchise agreements**, agreements with well-known foodservice operators, to offer their menus in places like airports. For example, Aramark, which is a frequent provider of foodservice to colleges, has Burger King and Pizza Hut operations in student dining halls. We will discuss franchise agreements in detail in chapter 15.

Would You Like Some Memory with That?

The theme and specialty foodservice segment just becomes more and more specialized. The lastest trend is termed the "cyber café." At these (mostly) coffee shops, patrons can log into the Internet, and with the assistance of the wait staff (if needed) can spend the morning, afternoon, or evening surfing the 'net. Ordering is done directly from your table, via e-mail, or, if you're craving a little human interaction, you can order through a member of the wait staff. Menu options are usually limited to gourmet coffees, pastries, and sandwiches, but most customers are there for the thrill of online services. There's a catch, though; for every hour you're logged in, you'll have to pay a fee, generally averaging $10 an hour. Interested in finding a cyber café near you? There's a web site listing all the online cafés—http://www.easynet.co.uk/pages/cafe/ccafe_us.htm.

Applying the Questions

In summary, the criteria cover: Who eats at the foodservice operation? What kind of food does the operation serve? What kind of service delivery system is used? How is it configured? How big is the operation? How much does it cost? Is it affiliated with another kind of operation? Does it have a brand name affiliation? By answering these questions, we are well equipped to determine different types of foodservice operations.

Types of Foodservice: An Overview

Traditionally, foodservice operations have been divided into two major categories, **commercial** and **institutional** or **noncommercial**. Commercial operations are those that compete in a free market and are open to all customers. Restaurants, food courts in malls, outlets in convenience stores, and street vendors would all be classified as commercial foodservices. Institutional or noncommercial foodservices are those operations set up within a specific kind of institution to serve a specific audience. These establishments may be found in hospitals, on military bases, or in lifecare centers, for example. These two major categories are not separated as distinctly as they once were. Some institutions now have foodservice provided by commercial operations, such as the examples mentioned earlier of college cafeterias' increasingly including units of chains like Pizza Hut and Burger King. The same is true of military bases and hospitals, where brand name quick-service restaurants, like McDonald's, are found on site. Table 8.1 illustrates the relative size of institutional versus commercial foodservice.

▇▇▇▇ *Table 8.1* Foodservice Expenditures

1993

Commercial	$234,462,377,000	88.6%
Institutional	$30,224,379,000	11.4%
Total	$264,686,756,000	

1994 Projections

Commercial	$244,142,222,000	88.7%
Institutional	$30,996,609,000	11.3%
Total	$275,138,831,000	

Source: NRA 1994 Food Service Industry Forecast

These two categories of foodservice can be broken down further, and can be organized into seven major categories, the first four of which are commercial operations. The categories include: stand-alone restaurants, foodservice within a lodging property, clubs, catering, restaurants within other establishments, and "eatertainment." The last category is institutional establishments.

Stand-Alone Restaurants

Stand-alone restaurants are perhaps the most common and perhaps the best-known category, and include a large variety. The category derives its name from the physical configuration; it literally stands alone, apart from other hospitality establishments. Examples would include the local pizza place, a famous restaurant in a downtown location, or the seafood restaurant by an ocean pier. Eating at the restaurant is the primary reason that customers have come to the location. Stand-alone restaurants come in different sizes and price ranges, offer different cuisines, and have different service systems and configurations. All restaurants, however, share one thing in common. They must all be attentive to customers to stay in business.

Quick Service

Quick service restaurants are also known as **fast food restaurants**. There is really nothing fast about the food; it is the timing of the service that defines the segment. The common denominator among these restaurants is instant production for the customer. Because the growth in this category over the last two decades has been so explosive, subsegments have emerged within it.

Traditional Quick service and high traffic locations are the hallmarks of traditional fast food outlets. They tend to be located near highways, malls, and downtown areas, and offer a standard menu with limited choices that attempt to satisfy a broad audience. Menu items might include hamburgers, french fries, and pizza, but increasingly menus offer salads and low-fat sandwiches. Many fast food outlets offer breakfast items in addition to the lunch and dinner menu. Most outlets are either chain operated or franchised, and the average check is inexpensive. Many outlets offer both counter and drive-through service, and many companies have expanded internationally. The most famous names in this segment? McDonald's and Burger King.

Quick Comfort To meet the increased demand for traditional family meals in a fast-service fashion, fast food chains have developed the quick comfort segment. The main characteristics of this relatively new segment are quality and traditional family meals, but quicker service than cafeterias or midscale food outlets. Customers are time conscious, yet they want nutritious "home-cooked" meals quickly and inexpensively. As a customer, one might find roasted chicken, mashed potatoes, baked ham, a selection of vegetables, breads, salads, and desserts. This segment tends to be a chain of multiple outlets, predominantly in the United States. Limited seating may be available, but most customers take their orders home.

Double Drive-Through This segment has no indoor seating. The customer wants inexpensive, basic fast food items such as hamburgers and fries. The double drive-through concept is based on limited menu and service, reduced development and operational costs, and cheaper products. This segment represents approximately 10 percent of the fast food market.

Cafeteria

Yes, **cafeterias**. And yes, they work on the same concept as the one you had in high school, and perhaps the one you have at college. Cafeterias are characterized by customer self-service. Customers move along a line where a wide variety of hot food is plated by a server, cold food is already prepackaged, and drinks are self-serve. Cafeterias are inexpensive to moderately priced food outlets and are usually located near or in malls. They are very popular in the southern United States. Seating capacity can range from 100 to 400 seats, and the typical customer mix is families, senior citizens, and price-conscious customers. As with buffets, cafeterias allow for a large number of persons to be served in a short period of time. Seating, therefore, is adjusted accordingly.

Buffet and Smorgasbord

A **buffet** or **smorgasbord** is characterized by "all you can eat" for a fixed price. A wide variety of food is displayed, and the customer can select items individually. Prices vary based on location, service, and quality, but tend to be moderate to expensive. Buffet meals are very popular as Sunday brunch in many hotels and restaurants, and can range from hot and cold entrees to desserts, buffets, or combinations of the three. The Meridien Hotel in Boston has a Sunday afternoon chocolate buffet! Many restaurants offer salad buffets—salad bars—as a menu item.

The smorgasbord is a traditional buffet meal in the Scandinavian and Germanic countries, and features traditional food items. These restaurants are also known for family-style seating—large tables that seat six to 20 guests.

Theme

Theme restaurants are characterized by a special theme that incorporates the design, menu, and service of the restaurant. Themes might revolve around a time period in history, a famous movie, or a character. Often the restaurant is part of a chain. Diners can enjoy a meal in an atmosphere of the

Middle Ages or the Roman Empire. Service, dining habits, and food fit the historical theme and kitchen. Some restaurants offer live entertainment, such as jousting tournaments, during dinner. Many of the historical theme restaurants require their guests to dress in period clothes, to fit the historical theme. Other special themes can involve sports and science.

Many theme restaurants are located in theme parks as part of the food and beverage system of the park. As Disney's Epcot Center, for example, the host of foreign countries within offer cuisine and costume appropriate to each native land. Prices of theme restaurants vary, but they tend to be moderately priced. The customer mix consists mainly of families and young adults.

Ethnic

Food and design in **ethnic restaurants** reflect a specific international cuisine such as Chinese, Italian, Middle Eastern, Greek, Indian, Mexican, or Japanese. Many ethnic restaurants are owned and managed by families of a specific cultural heritage who prepare their own ethnic cuisine. Some ethnic restaurants are chain operated or franchised. Prices tend to range from inexpensive to moderate, though outstanding food and service commands a premium price.

Bars and Taverns

Bars offer a light food menu, ranging from prepackaged snacks and sandwiches to limited hot snack items, and an extensive alcoholic and nonalcoholic beverage menu. Bars can have an ethnic theme, such as a British pub, or other common themes, such as sports. Hours of operation are usually from midafternoon to after midnight. Prices vary from inexpensive to expensive, based on location, design, and service. One recent trend in bars is the **micro-brewery**, which offers extensive local and international beer listings along with lunch and dinner menus. The production plant of the beer is often in full view of the customer, making it part of the dining experience. **Taverns** tend to offer a more extensive food menu, along with traditional drinks and family dishes.

Luxury or Upscale

Price is the distinguishing criteria of the **luxury** or **upscale restaurant**, and these are mostly independent food establishments. Each often profiles the notoriety of the owner, chef, or owner/chef. Food selection can be eclectic or ethnic. Prices are expensive to very expensive, and these restaurants are usually located in business and cultural centers. Luxury restaurants offer impeccable service, gourmet food, and an extensive wine list. Some are open only for dinner and require reservations made far in advance. A dress code is often required of customers.

Family

By definition, the prevailing customer base of the **family restaurant** is families. Most offer moderately priced meals for breakfast, lunch, and dinner. Family restaurants are located in small towns, suburbs, near tourist attractions, and at major highway intersections. Family restaurants usually offer table service, but some provide buffets. Most family restaurants are either chain operated or franchises. The numbers of seats in family restaurants range from 100 to over 300.

Diner

There are a number of **diners** across in the United States; some are refurbished originals, and others are authentic reproductions. A traditionally American restaurant, the diner is reflective of the 1950s in decor and menu. Diners offer traditional American food dishes for breakfast, served generally all day, as well as lunch and dinner. Prices tend to be inexpensive to moderate. Customers can enjoy either counter, table, or booth service. Diners can be found in cities, suburbs, near major highway exits, and near tourist attractions.

Specialty

The **specialty restaurant** concept revolves around a particular category of menu items or specialty, such as steak or seafood. They can be either independent restaurants or a chain. Prices tend to be moderate. Some quick-service chains could be considered specialty restaurants, such as Kentucky Fried Chicken.

Delicatessen

Over the counter, made to order sandwiches with a wide selection of meats and cheeses are the anchor of the **delicatessen** menu. Most delis offer traditional Eastern European Jewish food, hot and cold deli sandwiches, and famous pickles. Delis can be found in major cities in the United States with large populations as well as in smaller towns. Prices tend to be moderate to expensive and are based on location and prestige.

Specialty Coffee

The **specialty coffee** segment has shown significant growth in the last couple of years. The coffee/espresso bars are either chain operated facilities or independent establishments. They offer a variety of coffee beans, sold whole or ground, and well as an extensive menu of coffee drinks. In addition to coffees, customers can enjoy a variety of pastries, and in some coffee bars even sandwiches are available. The service concept is based on counter service and some coffee tables. The bars are usually small, and located in highly trafficked areas. Specialty coffee has an emerging subsegment, the drive-through. These facilities are mainly franchised, offering a limited variety of coffees and pastries, which are generally less expensive than coffee bar prices.

Ice Cream Parlor

Specialty ice cream outlets offer multiple varieties of ice cream, frozen yogurt, special cakes, frozen shakes, and so on. Prices tend to be inexpensive to moderate, and offer counter and table service. The customer mix consists of all ages and income levels. Ice cream parlors can be either franchised or independent operations. Some outlets, traditionally known for their ice cream, have expanded to full family-style menus.

Chain

Many familiar names in the restaurant business are either owned and operated by, or franchised by, international chains. **Chain** operations range from fast food and family-style dining to coffee bars and pizza places, and thus can be frequently found in all of the categories discussed, with the exception of the gourmet category. Prices and clientele are based on location, service, and food. Revenues of foodservice chains can vary widely, from a two-unit, less than one million in revenue chain, to a midsize chain such as Applebee's, with $15 million in revenues per year, to significant corporate giants. These large companies may even have multiple brand names, such as Pepsico's Pizza Hut, Taco Bell, and Kentucky Fried Chicken, generating over $8 billion per year.

Foodservice within a Lodging Property

The kinds of foodservice offered by a lodging property can range from vending machines to multiple choices of restaurants. The choices could include a selection of restaurants at different prices and service speeds, minibars, roomservice, and banquet service. In general, the more upscale the property, the more complex the offerings. Variety is also shaped by what alternatives the customer has. A guest at a center city hotel can choose from nearby restaurants, unlike a guest at a destination resort, who often will eat all meals within the resort itself.

Dining Rooms

Hotel dining rooms can range from upscale gourmet restaurants to casual and family dining rooms, and tend to be correlated with the size and level of service that the lodging property provides. Service, food, prices, and design vary according to the establishment and the target markets of the hotel itself. Luxury and full-service hotels have at least one fine dining room on the premises for lunch and dinner and one quicker service outlet for all meals. Midscale hotels usually offer one dining room for all meals. Budget properties tend to have no foodservice at all.

Roomservice

Most of the luxury and full-service hotels offer a 18- to 24-hour **roomservice**, and menus are provided in guest rooms. Roomservice menus offer breakfast, lunch, and dinner selections along with appetizers and beverages. Prices tend to be expensive due to special roomservice charges. Due to high labor needs of roomservice operations and the uncertainty of orders, many lower-priced hotels either have eliminated the roomservice option or offer it only during limited hours. Recently, hotel chains such as Marriott have signed agreements with fast food chains, like Pizza Hut, to offer fast food products as part of roomservice.

Lounge/Bar

Lounges and bars can be found in most luxury, commercial, and midscale hotels. Guests can enjoy light food, coffee and tea, an assortment of desserts, and an extensive drink list appropriate to the hour. Usually located near the lobby and the restaurant, some bars and lounges have separate street entrances in order to attract more customers from outside the hotel. Live music can often be heard during the evenings. Prices tend to be moderate to expensive.

Banquet and Catering

The banquet or **catering department** is responsible for executing catering events that range from a fancy white-glove, sit-down dinner, to coffee breaks during business meetings. Events can range from weddings in the hotel ballroom to private small lunches and business dinners. The catering sales managers are responsible for promoting and selling the hotel's catering abilities. In addition, the catering sales managers are responsible for coordinating event schedules, staff, flower orders, music, and any other customer request. On-premise catered events are common, particularly in convention and resort hotels. Many catering departments also offer off-premise catering services, in order to generate more business.

Minibar

Most full-service and luxury hotels provide **minibars** in guest rooms. Minibars offer a variety of beverages and an assortment of snacks. Minibars' products are usually very expensive compared to prices of the same products in the grocery store. Today, most of the minibars are part of a computerized system. This system provides actual and accurate data about each minibar in each room, and the service attendants can know the stock level of each minibar at any given time. If a computerized system is in place, minibar charges are automatically added to the guest's room bill when a product is removed from the minibar by the guest.

Carts and Convenience Store

Based on surveys of hotels and business travelers, various properties have developed **breakfast carts** and **convenience stores**. Business travelers indicated that they disliked sitting alone in restaurants and wasting precious time waiting for service during breakfast. In response, breakfast carts are often located in the lobby of the hotel, and include coffee, juice, and pastry items.

Though they are within the hotel, convenience stores are set up to look like they could be on a street corner. They offer breakfast items, such as cereals, pastries, and coffee; and lunch items, such as pizza, soups, and salads, and a variety of prepackaged snack foods. The store may also provide dining counters. Prices in the store are more expensive than a regular retail convenience store. The Hyatt O'Hare, located at O'Hare International Airport in Chicago, is one of the first properties to introduce the convenience store concept. Early success from hotel chain operations has launched in-house branding of the stores, such as Sarah's Pantry in Hyatt Hotels, which appear to the guest like stand-alone operations.

Vending Machines

Vending machines provide convenient prepackaged food and drink items. Money is placed directly into the machine that dispenses the item. Vending machines offer cold and hot drinks, platters, frozen desserts, baked goods, sandwiches, and fresh prepared foods. Advances in technology allow vending machines to have a variety of heating and cooling systems that provide more food items accessible to vending. Recent developments include french fry and pizza vending machines. In addition to being in hotels, vending machines are located in workplaces, universities, schools, and other public places.

Stand-Alone Restaurants That Lease Space

Due to the high costs and low profit margins of food and beverage operations, some hotels lease their food and beverage outlets to national chains or independent operators with a following in the local community. Some hotels are even leasing their roomservice and banquet services to outside contractors. Besides the savings in food and beverage costs, a recognized name restaurant can serve as an important marketing tool. In the United States, customers tend to believe that restaurants independent of the hotel provide better value than traditional hotel dining rooms. Food prices in chain or stand-alone restaurants in hotels vary based on the food establishment. In addition to hotel guests, these restaurants target customers who are not guests.

Employee Cafeterias

Nearly every large hotel has an **employee cafeteria**. In most hotels, the food is free for employees; some hotels charge just enough to cover the cost of providing the meals. The employee cafeteria provides a variety of food and beverage items for breakfast, lunch, and dinner.

Catering

Catering, by definition, involves preparing food for a special event. The size of a catered event can vary from a quiet dinner party for four to a premarathon spaghetti feast for thousands. Different catering segments are defined by their service delivery system.

Special Occasion

Special occasions can range from an anniversary celebration to the Olympic Games or World's Fair. The size, location, foodservice needs, and length of the event can vary greatly. Only major foodservice companies can successfully handle foodservice for events such as the Olympic Games. Such an event requires strategic planning, a comprehensive delivery system, a trained and professional staff of food managers and dietary experts, international operational ability, and the ability to provide a wide range of food types and menus.

On-Premise

On-premise caterers own and manage their own facilities. The customer rents or leases the caterer's facilities and services, and the caterer provides a wide range of services in order to meet customers' requests. Usually the facilities include a large dining hall, several small meeting or dining rooms, and a kitchen. The main advantage for the caterer and the client is that all the facilities and services are under the same roof. The on-premise caterer, however, has the burden of overhead and operational costs of a large facility. On-premise catering facilities can range from medium-size private dining halls to conference and convention centers. The on-premise caterer can be either a local catering company or a national foodservice contract company.

Off-Premise

Off-premise caterers own and manage kitchen facilities, but do not serve food on their premises. The off-premise caterer's food is served at a location chosen by the customer. This location can be either indoors or out. Although the off-premise caterer does not have all the costs of owning dining facilities, there is a need for good delivery and setup systems. Off-premise caterers include private local caterers, gourmet food shops, hotels, department stores, supermarkets, and foodservice contractors.

Airline

The key factor for the **airline catering** business is timing, or the delivery system. Caterers to major airlines around the world have to provide thousands of airline meals daily. The delivery schedule is tied strictly to airlines' arrival and departure schedules. Any delay in food delivery can be costly, as it can delay flights for the airlines. Other key characteristics of the in-flight service are creativity and cost consciousness. Preparing meals that have visual appeal after a long holding period is a challenge.

The three main categories of airline meals are first class, business class, and economy class. The meals served also depend on the time of day and the length of the flight. In addition, airline caterers provide a wide range of special meals such as kosher, low fat, low sodium, and vegetarian. Because of competitive pressures to keep costs down, airlines increasingly are reducing the complexity of offerings and are reducing the number of flights that even serve meals.

Every major airport has at least one in-flight catering kitchen. Each kitchen carries supplies and menus for different airlines, because, for example, a first-class meal on Delta Airlines is different from a first-class meal on British Airways. Some in-flight caterers are owned by the airlines, and some are owned by foodservice companies. Charges are based on each menu's quality, variety, and volume of business. For example, major U.S. airlines spent between $4.10 and $7.85 on each in-flight meal in the mid-1990s.

Mobile

Have you ever seen a white sandwich truck next to construction site or in front of an office building? Steaming hot coffee next to doughnuts and muffins sitting out on the gleaming aluminum counter that is formed when the side wall of the truck is opened? That's a **mobile caterer**. The main markets for mobile catering are construction sites, movie production sites, and other outdoor events. The mobile caterer delivers semiprepared food to the site, and finishes preparation on the spot. Mobile caterers can be divisions in major foodservice contract companies or independent, individual operators.

Wholesale

A **wholesale caterer** is a food preparation company that provides cooked and prepared food for catering companies and other organizations. It does not sell food directly to consumers. The strategy for the wholesale caterer is to sell large quantities of prepared food without having the responsibility of serving the food. For caterers that do serve food, wholesale purchases effectively increase kitchen capacity. Examples would include bread and pastry products and sauces.

Accommodation

An accommodator is a small caterer who prepares and cooks food at the client's premises. People use **accommodation caterers** for parties and special dinners. In this instance, the caterer is responsible for preparing the food, serving the guests, and cleaning up at the end of the event. This operation is usually a one-person business or a small company that serves primarily in people's homes. A current trend is for customers to hire a well-known chef to prepare a meal in the home, in a way creating a tiny restaurant right where they live.

Concession

Most of the leading stadiums, arenas, race tracks, and airports provide foodservices from contract food companies. The key factor in **concession** management is logistical planning. A food provider for a sports event needs to have accurate ticket sales forecasts to decide how many hot dogs to prepare. A major airport concession must provide food 24 hours a day in order to meet customer demand. The concession operation is based on simple menus, a huge number of customers, and a short period of time. Hence, the focus is to maximize utilization of labor and delivery and preparation systems. In addition to regular concession operations, the contract foodservice companies often offer upscale dining facilities and lounges in airports or new sports stadiums. Customer mix varies based on the event and the location.

Clubs

Clubs offer food to members of the organization and their guests. There are various kinds of clubs that serve food, including country clubs, city clubs, and fraternal clubs. Foodservice is also provided to officers' clubs on military bases as part of the institutional foodservice provider's offerings.

Country Clubs

Some **country clubs** own and operate their own food establishments. Other country clubs lease their foodservice from contract foodservice companies. Usually, the foodservice setting in a country club is upscale, with elegant bars and gourmet restaurants. The food establishment is used by club members and their guests; the guest pays a yearly membership fee to join the club, as well as for the meals themselves. Country clubs are often rented for special functions such as wedding receptions, so the foodservice operation must be able to provide banquet-style service.

City Clubs

City clubs offer a wide variety of facilities, including guest rooms and recreational facilities, but almost all have a foodservice component. City clubs revolve around a particular membership such as a business or college association. These clubs, which tend to be in city centers or business districts, might be restricted to graduates of Yale, such as the Yale Club in New York City, or a particular profession, such as a lawyer's club.

Fraternal

Many association and **fraternal clubs** offer on-premise dining for their members. Dining can range from snack bars to family dining. Fraternal clubs usually have a banquet facility available for rent by their members. Better-known fraternal clubs include organizations like the Shriners, the Lions Club, or the Elks. These clubs can be found in cities or small towns.

Within Other Establishments

Foodservice that is associated with other establishments is offered as an amenity. The primary purpose of the customer's trip is not for the foodservice but for the establishment itself. Foodservice can be found in shopping malls, department stores, truck stops, and convenience stores.

Food Courts in Malls

The **food court** area in a mall is an integral and important part of the shopping complex. To help eliminate the possibility that families or individuals would stop shopping and leave the mall for a dining experience, malls offer a wide variety of food outlets. Usually, the food court has a main seating area surrounded by many fast food and sandwich outlets. Mall food court outlets can include brand names such as McDonald's, Sbarro, Pizza Hut, Panda Express, Au Bon Pain, Nathan's, and TCBY. Some malls offer also family restaurants in other locations at the mall.

Department and Retail Stores

Thirty or more years ago, every major department store had foodservice, from an elegant dining room in Lord & Taylor to counter service at Woolworth's. Costs of operation to the retailer became prohibitive, however, and most of these outlets closed. Now, once again in the search for value added services, retail stores have begun to offer food and beverages on the premises, but with consideration for costs. Some retail and wholesale stores now offer limited menu snack bars. Bookstores offer espresso and dessert bars and more on premise. Barnes and Noble, a major bookstore chain, is adding coffee and pastry bars to its stores. Other bookstores are offering a complete menu, as well as an assortment of beverages. Patrons are encouraged to browse, read, and sip.

Some department stores sign foodservice contracts with national food contractors to provide snack bars and more upscale restaurants on premise. Many retail operators have found that by offering food, they can attract more families and can change the traditional shopping trip back to one of shopping and dining.

Travel Plazas and Truck Stops

It's nearly noon, you've been driving since dawn, the gas tank is nearly empty, and so is your stomach. Time to stop at the **travel plaza** and fill up. At travel plazas, highway drivers can stop, fuel their cars, and buy food and drinks in familiar brand name stores such as Burger King, Sbarro, Subway, Baskin-Robbins, and Howard Johnson. In many plazas, state travel agencies also provide a rest area, maps, and visitor assistance. In some areas of the country, there are also a number of independently owned restaurants catering to the highway driver. Joint ventures between international gasoline companies and foodservice companies are very common today in travel plazas. A more traditional name for such foodservice is truck stop.

Convenience Stores

Though convenience stores themselves offer food choices, they are generally prepackaged items. Increasingly, there has been a marriage between fast food restaurants and convenience stores. Limited menu selection from the fast food restaurant, such as sandwiches, are offered within the convenience store. Limited or no kitchen facilities is typical. Dunkin' Donuts, for example, has numerous doughnut cases in convenience stores, but no preparation facilities within the stores.

Special "Eatertainment" Concepts

There is seemingly no limit to the variety of entertainment concepts that have been associated with restaurants. As the opening "underwater" dining experience suggests, sound, lights, and action all come together to create special effects. Well-established companies like Lettuce Entertain You and Hard Rock Cafe are two of many organizations that have taking dining well beyond food and service. That's not to say that food and service don't matter. Far from it—all the special effects in the world can't save a customer who is treated rudely or served mediocre food. Here we offer a small sampling of restaurant concepts that offer entertainment:

Dinner Theater

Picture yourself at a wedding reception, except that you don't know the bride. Or the groom. Or anyone, except the friends you arrived with. The food's not bad, the band is pretty good—and then a fight breaks out between the bride and the maid of honor. Sound strange? Not if you are a participant in *Tony and Maria's Wedding*, a long-running dinner theater concept. The **dinner theater** concept combines the enjoyment of a restaurant with a play or a musical. Patrons can enjoy dinner while watching a play, or even participate in the night's activities. In some locations, patrons can have dinner while being entertained by a musical cabaret, a popular concept in casino hotels.

Visible Kitchen

Rather than having the kitchen separated from the customer, some restaurants incorporate the two. The kitchen itself becomes entertainment. The design can range from a view of the tandoor ovens in a Indian restaurant, watching the chef toss pizza dough in a trattoria, or tableside preparation of interesting dishes. Some restaurants allow patrons to sit in the kitchen, meet the chef, and ask questions about the food preparation process.

Customers who are anxious about the quality of the food or the cleanliness of the kitchen would find relief in this approach. For the operator, a **visible kitchen** may be a way to utilize precious square footage to its maximum advantage; and for kitchen staff, seeing customers enjoying themselves imparts satisfaction.

Institutional Foodservice

Noncommercial or institutional foodservice operations are distinguished by the audience they serve. Institutional operations, unlike commercial operations, have a more captive audience. Revenue may be earned by institutional providers in lump sums, such as a contract with a hospital, or through contracts with individuals, such as college meal plans.

School/College

While some schools own and operate their own foodservice operations, most schools and colleges around the world contract out their foodservice operations. These operations include students kiosks, cafeterias, and dining rooms; faculty dining rooms; special catering events; and sports facilities' food counters. Many foodservice companies and colleges redesign their traditional cafeterias to fit updated consumer behavior and market trends. Thus, many student cafeterias have adopted the design of mall food courts, offering national brands such as Burger King and Pizza Hut. Other foodservice innovations in the campus dining sector are in-dorm pizza delivery and mobile snack carts.

High-Tech Ordering in the Czech Republic

Remember finally finding yourself, after a long wait, at the front of the cafeteria line, only to discover that the only option left was a bologna sandwich? For an institutional foodservice provider, accurately predicting and preparing the right number of the meals for a school lunch period is perhaps the most difficult task. With unpredictable customers, too much of one entree could mean waste; too little of a popular item means unhappy customers.

The international foodservice provider Sodexho has a contract to provide school meals in the Czech Republic. To combat the forecasting problem, Sodexho has installed computer card readers in schools, and has given each student a food card. This computer system allows the students to preselect their meals. On Monday, for instance, a student inserts a personalized card into the reader, and can then choose from a selection of entrees and side dishes from Tuesday's lunch menu. This system allows students to exercise control over food choices, while limiting waste in the food preparation process.

Military

Many military facilities use contract foodservice companies to operate and manage dining facilities. The facilities can range from large dining halls to officers' clubs. **Military foodservice** can present special challenges, such as providing for forces deployed to action or on board a submarine (which does not have the luxury of DIVE!'s kitchen preparation space!).

Correctional

Correctional facilities can feed anywhere from 100 to 5,000 persons. The main challenge of providing foodservices in correctional facilities is the setting. Food contract companies need to train their staff to deal with the correctional facilities' population, and teach them how to provide the needed service in such institutions.

Hospital/Lifecare

Contract foodservice companies provide dining services to hospitals, nursing homes, and retirement and lifecare centers. Although more than 60 percent of hospitals in the United States still manage their own foodservices, many self-managed hospitals are concentrating on medical care, and have realized that it is more economical to contract out the foodservice operations. Teams of culinary professionals, dietary experts, and foodservice managers and staff are the core of each health care foodservice provider. The foodservice companies provide a wide range of services, such as nutrition counseling, wellness programs, nutrition education programs, a variety of dietary meals, public and staff cafeterias, and retail convenience stores. Some foodservice companies have expanded their services to include housekeeping, laundry, engineering, and security services.

Corporate Dining

Executive dining entails usually more upscale service and food than do employee cafeterias. The main purpose of having executive dining rooms is to provide an elegant facility for hosting corporate clients. Some companies that do not have employee cafeterias, provide corporate or executive dining for the service of their executives. Corporate dining rooms can differ in service and decor. Usually, the foodservice contractor who provides the employee cafeteria foodservice also provides the executive dining services.

Employee Cafeteria

In order to attract employees to dine at the employee cafeterias, the foodservice contractors, which operate employee cafeterias within the office building, try to focus on upscale, more innovative and up-to-date products, cooking techniques, and inviting displays. Employee cafeterias accounts can range in size and location. Often the company subsidizes the meal costs, as a benefit to the employees.

Exhibit 8.1 gives examples of the various components of the foodservice industry.

Exhibit 8.1 Components of the Foodservice Industry

Category	Examples
Stand-Alone Restaurants	
Quick Service/Fast Food	
Traditional	1. McDonald's, Paris, France
	2. Burger King, Miami, FL
	3. Kentucky Fried Chicken, Louisville, KY
Quick Comfort Food Segment	1. Boston Chicken, Golden, CO
	2. Hearth Express (McDonald's), Oak Brook, IL
	3. Roy's Double-R Grill (Roy Rogers), Linthicum, MD
Double-Drive-Through Segment	1. Rally's Hamburgers Inc. Louisville, KY
	2. Checkers Drive-In Restaurants, Clearwater, FL
	3. Hot 'n Now, Irvine, CA
Cafeteria	1. Morrison's Cafeterias, Mobile, AL
	2. Luby's Cafeteria, San Antonio, TX
	3. Piccadilly Cafeterias, Baton Rouge, LA
Buffet and Smorgasbord	1. Smörgasboard, Stockholm, Sweden
	2. Miller's Smorgasbord, Lancaster, PA

(Continued)

■■■■■■ *Exhibit 8.1* Components of the Foodservice Industry *(Continued)*

Category	Examples
	3. Hometown Buffet, San Diego, CA
Theme	1. Hard Rock Cafe, Tokyo, Japan
	2. 50's Prime Time Cafe, Disney-MGM Studios, Orlando, FL
	3. Nos Ancetres Les Gaulois, Paris, France
	4. Medieval Times (Dinner & Tournament), Lyndhurst, NJ
	5. The Roman Restaurant, Jerusalem, Israel
	6. Dive! Los Angeles and Los Vegas (submarine theme)
Ethnic (Various)	1. The Border Cafe, Cambridge, MA (Mexican)
	2. Yunis, Tel Aviv, Israel (Middle Eastern)
	3. Moti, Tokyo, Japan (Indian)
	4. Sabatinis, London, England (Italian)
Bars and Taverns	1. Au Général La Fayette, Paris, France
	2. The Oak Bar, Hotel Plaza, New York, NY
	3. Boston Beer Works, Boston, MA
	4. Warren Tavern, Charlestown, MA
	5. Brass Rail Tavern, Toronto, Canada
Luxury/Upscale	1. La Tour d'Argent, Paris, France
	2. Le Lion D'or, Geneva, Switzerland
	3. The Pump Room, Chicago, IL
Family	1. Denny's, Spartanburg, SC
	2. Perkins, Memphis, TN
	3. Cracker Barrel Old Country Store, Lebanon, TN
	4. Auberge du Père Bise, Talloires, France
Diner	1. Broadway Diner, NYC
	2. Blue Diner, Boston, MA
	3. Glory Jeans Diner, Plymouth, NH
Specialty	1. Legal Sea Foods, Boston, MA
	2. Outback Steakhouse, Tampa, FL
	3. Red Lobster, Orlando, FL
	4. International House of Pancakes, Brighton, MA
	5. Ponderosa Steak House, North Haven, CT
	6. Berghoff's Beers, Chicago, IL
Deli	1. Carnegie Deli, New York, NY
	2. Schlotzsky's Deli, Austin, TX

▬▬▬▬▬ **Exhibit 8.1** *(Continued)*

Category	Examples
	3. Zingerman's Deli, Ann Arbor, MI
	4. Ben's Deli, Quebec, Canada
Specialty Coffee	1. Starbucks Coffee, Seattle, WA
	2. Quikàva, Chicago, IL
	3. Tirana Coffee House, Tirana, Albania
Ice Cream Parlor	1. Ben & Jerry's, Waterbury, VT
	2. Baskin-Robbins, Glendale, CA
	3. Dr. Lek, Tel Aviv, Israel
Chain	1. Wendy's, Dublin, OH
	2. Dunkin' Donuts, Randolph, MA
	3. Hippopotamus, Paris, France

Within Lodging Operations

Category	Examples
Dining Room(s)	1. The Jockey Club, Ritz-Carlton Hotel, New York, NY
	2. The Polo Lounge, The Beverly Hills Hilton, LA
	3. Le Restaurant, The Regent Hotel, Melbourne, Australia
	4. Relais de Parc, Le Parc Victor Hugo Hotel, Paris, France
	5. The Blue Room, The Peninsula Hotel, Hong Kong
Roomservice	1. The Four Seasons Hotel, Toronto, Canada
	2. The Oriental Hotel, Bangkok, Thailand
	3. Ville d'Este, Lake Como, Italy
Lounge / Bar	1. Le Patio, Hotel Méridien, Paris, France
	2. La Noblesse Bar, Renaissance Hotel, Istanbul, Turkey
Banquets/Catering	1. Stouffer Grand Beach Resort, St. Thomas, VI
	2. Hotel New Otani, Tokyo, Japan
Minibar	1. The Grand Floridian, Walt Disney World, Orlando, FL
	2. The Four Seasons, Washington, DC
	3. Hyatt Regency Tel Aviv, Tel Aviv, Israel
Carts and Convenience Stores	1. Sarah's Pantry, Hyatt O'Hare, Rosemont, IL
	2. The Deli, Hyatt Beaver Creek, Beaver Creek, CO
	3. Hôtel du Rhone, Geneva, Switzerland
Vending Machines	1. Canteen Corporation, Charlotte, SC
	2. Marriott Management Services, Washington, DC

(Continued)

■■■■■■ *Exhibit 8.1* Components of the Foodservice Industry *(Continued)*

Category	Examples
Stand-Alone Restaurants That Lease Space	1. TGI Friday's in Raddison Hotels
	2. Rialto, The Charles Hotel, Cambridge, MA
	3. Red River Steaks & BBQ (Azar Inc.), Fort Wayne Marriott Hotel, Fort Wayne, TX
	4. Spago, MGM Grand Hotel & Casino, Las Vegas, Nevada
Employee Cafeterias	1. The Greenbriar, White Sulfur Springs, WV
	2. The Peninsula Hotel, Hong Kong
	3. Televisa, Mexico City, Mexico
Catering	
Special Occasion	1. Special Events Services (1988 Olympics in Seoul), ARA Services, Philadelphia, PA
	2. Special Events Services, (1996 Olympics in Atlanta, GA) Aramark, Philadelphia, PA
On-Premise	1. World Trade Center, Boston, MA
	2. Convention Center Services, Aramark Services, Philadelphia, PA
	3. Service America Corp.(Javits Center, NYC), Stamford, CT
Off-Premise	1. East Meets West, Boston, MA
	2. Danabeth's Kitchen, Somerville, MA
Airline (in-flight catering service)	1. Gate Gourmet (Swissair), Zurich, Switzerland
	2. Caterair International, Bethesda, MD
	3. Dobbs International Services, Memphis, TN
Mobile	1. Canteen Truck Unlimited, Boston, MA
	2. Global Canteen, nationwide locations
Wholesale	1. Christie Food Products, Boston, MA (desserts, salad dressings, etc.)
	2. Mexican Food Distributors, Inc., Somerville, MA
	3. Tsukiji Central Wholesale Market, Tokyo, Japan
Accommodation	1. New England Clambakes, Boston, MA, and Los Angeles, CA
Concession	1. Host Marriott Operating Group, Washington, DC
	2. Leisure Services, Aramark Services, Philadelphia, PA
	3. CA One Services, Buffalo, NY

Exhibit 8.1 *(Continued)*

Category	Examples
Clubs	
Country Clubs	1. The Country Club, Brookline, MA
	2. Franklin Hills Country Club, Birmingham, MI
	3. Old Orchard Golf Club, Ibaraki, Japan
	4. Cherry Hill Country Club, Denver, CO
City Clubs	1. The Harvard Club, Boston, MA
	2. The Yale Club, New York, NY
Fraternal Clubs	1. The Lions Club (various locations)
	2. Elks (various locations)
Within Other Establishments	
Food Courts in Malls	1. The Cambridgeside Galleria Food Court, Cambridge, MA
	2. Food Court, Mall of America, Bloomington, MN
Department Stores and Other Retail Stores	1. Depot Diner at Home Depot Stores
	2. Espresso and dessert bars in Barnes & Noble bookstores
	3. Restaurant Plus by Aramark in Bon Marché's department store (Seattle)
Travel Plaza	1. Host Marriott operates travel plazas in Massachusetts. Among the food outlets in these travel plazas are Burger King and TCBY.
	2. Roy Rodgers, various locations along highways.
Convenience Stores	1. 7-11 (various locations)
	2. Wawa (various locations)
	3. Turkey Hill Mini-Mart (various locations)
Special "Eatertainment" Concepts	
Dinner Theater	1. Wizardz, Universal City (Universal Studios), Los Angeles, CA
	2. Le Lido, Paris, France
	3. Marie-Paule Pellé Dinner Theater, Paris, France
Visible Kitchen	1. Hammersley's Bistro, Boston, MA
	2. Chef Allen, Miami, FL
	3. The Tuscan Grill, Waltham, MA

(Continued)

■■■■■■ *Exhibit 8.1* Components of the Foodservice Industry *(Continued)*

Category	Examples
Institutional	
School/College	1. Daka Inc., Danvers, MA (various campuses)
	2. Aramark, Philadelphia, PA (various campuses)
Military	1. U.S. Army, Dallas, TX
	2. U.S.A.F. Restaurants and Snack Bars, San Antonio, TX
Correctional	1. Szabo Correctional Services (Aramark Services), Philadelphia, PA
	2. California Department of Corrections, Sacramento, CA
Hospital/Lifecare	1. The Wood Co., Allentown, PA
	2. Marriott Health Care Services, Avon, CT
	3. Morrison Health Care Group, Mobile, AL
Corporate/Executive Dining	1. Business Dining Services, Aramark Services, Philadelphia, PA
	2. Marriott Corporate Services, Washington, DC
	3. Sodexho, Marseilles, France
Employee Cafeteria	1. Gardner Merchant Food Services, Trumbull, CT
	2. Canteen Corp. Charlotte, SC
	3. Service America Corp., Stamford, CT

Summary

Just as we saw in the lodging industry, the foodservice business is as varied as the customers it serves. From luxury, full-service restaurants to clambakes in your backyard, to everything in between, nearly every kind of meal and type of service is available in the world today. When you are trying to classify a foodservice operation, it is important to analyze the customer, the menu, the configuration of the physical space in which the food is prepared and/or served, the size or the number of customers served in a given period, the average meal price, the location, and the brand affiliation. The two main segments of foodservice are commercial and institutional. The foodservice business can then be broken down into subsegments, including stand-alone concepts; catering; foodservice associated with lodging properties, clubs, and other establishments such as department stores and travel plazas; special entertainment concepts; and institutional offerings such as school and hospital dining. In the next chapter, we will take a closer look at how a foodservice operation actually works.

Discussion Questions

1. Who is the customer in institutional foodservice? The institution? The consumer? Why?

2. Why is a micro-brewery like a restaurant with a visible kitchen?

3. Why has the quick-service business evolved into different subsegments?

4. What distinguishes different kinds of catering operations? Which kind is the most dependent on volume sales? Which kind requires the least amount of capital equipment to start?

5. Why do retail establishments offer foodservice? Is it advantageous? Why or why not?

6. What determines what kind of foodservice would be offered in a lodging property?

7. What two classifications of restaurants are the most different? Why?

8. Can a customer always tell the difference between a chain and an independent restaurant?

9. Why would a hotel lease space to an independent restaurateur?

10. What are the key criteria to use when analyzing foodservice types?

Assignments

1. Research an unusual restaurant entertainment concept. Will the concept have broad appeal? What customer base do you think the restaurant is appealing to? Do you think it has a good chance of surviving?

2. Visit a series of restaurants from the outside only. What can you learn before you ever enter the door? What do customers that you can see through the window tell you about the restaurant? Review the questions presented at the beginning of the chapter. Based on your observations, answer as many of them as possible. Now classify each restaurant that you observed.

3. The authors of the quotation that began this chapter evaluated many businesses in their famous book, *In Search of Excellence*. They were clearly impressed with the consistency of product and cleanliness at McDonald's outlets throughout the world. What kinds of problems do you think a McDonald's outlet in Eastern Europe faces? One in Asia? Give thought to the ease or difficulty of procuring raw materials, pricing, cultural or religious concerns, and traditional food offerings.

End Note

1. Thomas J. Peters and Robert H. Waterman, *In Search of Excellence* (New York: Harper & Row 1982), xix.

Chapter Nine

" *You know, it's not like running a restaurant.* "

Daniel Wachspress, rocket scientist[1]

How Things Work: Foodservice Operations ✌

When you finish this chapter you should:

1. Understand some of the key elements that create success in a restaurant operation, both in the opening and in the ongoing operations.

2. Know how to quantify the potential revenue that a restaurant can produce.

3. Know how to engineer a menu that works with respect to profitability and popularity.

4. Know the major costs of running a restaurant and understand the difference between fixed and variable costs.

5. Understand the importance of customer feedback, and how to collect it so it is useful.

6. Be able to identify the things that are on a restaurant patron's scorecard, and how it is used to evaluate a restaurant experience.

7. Know what happens to restaurants that lose focus.

8. Understand the similarities and differences between commercial and institutional foodservice.

9. Be able to identify the unique challenges facing institutional and commercial operations.

Introduction

The reasons that people open restaurants are probably as numerous as the people themselves: an entrepreneurial instinct, a desire to play host to many, a love for food, a love for entertaining. The reasons that people succeed in restaurants are not so numerous. Many don't. Optimists estimate that after one year of operation, about a third of all restaurants fail. After three years, one half have failed.[2] Pessimists say three fourths fail in the first year.[3] It's no wonder that one rocket scientist, in describing his profession, noted that perhaps rocket science is *easier* than running a restaurant.

Establishing a successful restaurant operation is hard work and requires a keen understanding of what matters and what doesn't matter to success. Frank Zagat, editor of the popular *Zagat Restaurant Surveys*, comments on restaurant operations: "Unfortunately, there's no simple formula to create....success. You just know it when you see it."[4] Though the formula may not be simple, in this chapter we will try to demystify what creates success. Though it's true that many successful restaurants have a certain magic, here we get down to basics. In two parts, opening feats and ongoing operations, we will uncover some basic principles of running a restaurant, take a close look at several restaurateurs, and then see how things work in their operations.

Developing Commercial Foodservice

In addition to capturing the spirit of an independent restaurant **entrepreneur**, this chapter will also offer examples from successful chain operations. Many of the largest chains began as entrepreneurships, like that of the McDonald brothers, whose first shop had humble beginnings in San Bernadino, California. That one restaurant evolved under the leadership of another entrepreneur, Ray Kroc, into millions and millions served. Even today the most successful of the chains still want an entrepreneurial approach at the individual units. McDonald's, for example, has a corporate "Vice President for Individuality." This corporate-level position looks to individual units for good ideas and menu items that can be implemented systemwide. Another example are Michael and Marian Ilitch, respectively the chairman and secretary-treasurer of Little Caesars, a 4,400-store pizza chain. They have been described as still acting like "the proprietors of a fledgling mom-and-pop business."[5]

The number of entrepreneurs that translate their restaurant concept to a multiunit chain must succeed twice: first as a "one" and then as "many." They must find, as Rosabeth Moss Kanter writes in her popular book, *When Giants Learn to Dance*, "something that marries the entrepreneurial spirit to discipline and teamwork, something that helps loosely managed companies get a little tighter and tightly controlled companies to loosen up—a post-entrepreneurial response."[6] This evolution is increasingly important. As we uncovered in chapter 2, restaurant chains are controlling more and more of the market.

Developing Institutional Foodservice

The entrepreneurial spirit can also be found at the beginnings of institutional foodservice companies. Aramark, one of the world's largest food servers, was started by two entrepreneurs in 1959. Thus the learnings from the entrepreneurial restaurant experience can not only be applied to chains, but to foodservice in institutional settings as well. Though much of the learning applies, there are some differences. This chapter uncovers some of the unique complexities of achieving success in the institutional foodservice segment. Though institutional foodservice represents only about 10 percent of all foodservice expenditures, it is a very important part of the business. It also has excellent prospects for growth. Less than half of all institutional foodservice is currently under contract.[7] The balance is called **self-operated**, operated by the institution itself. The New York City Board of Education, one of the largest providers of meals in the country, is a good example. For historical perspective, about ten years ago, only a quarter of institutional foodservice was contracted to companies like Aramark or Marriott. The optimism for growth lies in continued conversion of self-operated locations.

Unlike many restaurants, a **contract provider** must do more than prepare and serve one meal at a time; it must prepare and serve a multitude. Because of volume feeding, this segment faces some particular challenges. In just one institutional setting—a large military base, for example—the same thousands of people must be served three meals a day, every day. This segment not only faces the challenges of quantity food production, but it typically services a captive audience. Thus, this segment is also called **contract feeding**, because institutions typically have a contract with the foodservice provider to service a particular audience or institution for a set length of time. Contract providers must be concerned with offering variety and interest to their customers, as it will see them over and over again.

Though they do have some distinguishing characteristics, institutional operations do face many of the issues that restaurants face, and much of the same learning applies. In fact, one could argue that in some institutional settings, particularly those that adapt well to stand-alone retail concepts, such as colleges and offices, there is an increasingly blurred line between what is institutional and what is commercial. One major contract provider, DAKA International, declares in fact that as more and more affordable restaurant choices become available, captive audiences no longer exist. They warn that customers are demanding more than the traditional production line service approach that has dominated the industry for decades.[8] In response, more than one contract feeder has introduced retail concepts in institutional settings, each with its own identity and menu. Participants include Burger King, Pizza Hut, and D'Angelo sandwich shops. These concepts are virtually indistinguishable from traditional chain restaurant units.

Restaurant Operations

A restaurant can be thought to begin on the back of an envelope—or a napkin, as the case may be. Ideas start with a conceptual design, and then evolve through the logistics of choosing a location, developing a menu, formulating an efficient kitchen and dining room layout, and testing for financial viability. Deep regard for target customers' wants will combine with careful planning, hard work, passion, and vision, in pursuit of a successful opening night.

Opening Feats

What follow are some key decisions that pave the road to success in the restaurant design and development process. Herein lie some of the signs to point the way to the successful one fourth at the end of the first year of operation. We begin with restaurant openings—what to do, and what not to do.

Engineer a Menu That Works Most restaurants begin with the planning of a **menu concept**. Several examples illustrate the point. Boston-based Au Bon Pain, a restaurant chain that offers "good food served quickly—not fast food," at the onset planned its restaurants around one thing: a better-baked croissant. As new items were added, the restaurant chain took care that each was consistent with the original objective.

Odette Bery, owner of Another Season restaurant, on Beacon Hill in Boston, wanted her menu to reflect fresh ingredients that change with the seasons. She planned to have her menu change often and to follow the harvest. Richard Melman, creator of the Chicago-based Lettuce Entertain You chain, emphasized fun and entertainment in his menu concepts. He planned that each restaurant would be a one-of-a-kind creation, like Hat Dance, a highbrow Mexican restaurant he describes as "romantic, avant-garde, existential, ancient Mexican, and 5 percent Japanese."[9]

Once the menu concept has been established, it must then evolve to individual menu items. In its final form, a menu may be only one or two pages, but the amount of thought and research that goes into planning and executing a menu is extensive. A number of considerations emerge in menu planning.

The menu must meet its customers' needs. This includes satisfying nutritional requirements, which are becoming increasingly important to customers. The menu must comprehend the service style that will best suit the customer and the concept. For example, quick-service restaurants usually have counter service or self-service, so that the customer has a very short wait.

The kitchen must suit the menu. The culinary skills of the kitchen crew must be capable of producing the menu items. A menu that suits the ego of the owner but is too ambitious for the chefs to prepare will inevitably lead to an unhappy kitchen crew and disappointed customers. The preparation of menu items must match the physical equipment available in the kitchen. An overabundance of steamed items might create a backlog at the steamer, while other underutilized pieces of equipment function only as stainless steel artwork.

The ingredients on the menu must be available, and available consistently. Some restaurants keep the same basic menu for long periods of time. For this kind of restaurant, much thought must revolve around how ingredients will be sourced. Dependable suppliers of goods become very important. This is why companies like McDonald's create **value managed relationships (VMRs)**, or strong, actively managed, formal ties with its suppliers. Such relationships ensure, for example, a consistent quality of potato for its french fries. This is not necessarily an easy process and can be especially difficult in the international arena. More than once McDonald's has had to train potato farmers in foreign countries.

Other restaurants will change menus seasonally or even daily to take advantage of fresh ingredients. These restaurants still focus on obtaining quality products, but have the luxury of substitutions if necessary.

Finally, the menu items must be successful. Success of each item depends on two things: profitability and popularity. The first criterion, profitability, must be met with a sharp pencil before the restaurant even opens. This involves calculations associated with determining profitability, like determining how much profit an item contributes, or how a restaurant calculates food costs. These calculations are reviewed extensively in chapter 13, "An Accounting Tool Box."

The second criterion, popularity, will ultimately be determined on opening day and the days thereafter. Those restaurant concepts which have restricted flexibility to change menu items, or which plan to roll out a new item in multiple units at once, should gather feedback in consumer taste tests or in test markets prior to the launch. A matrix, which considers the outcome of menu items evaluated on the dimensions of profitability and popularity, is presented in Exhibit 9.1.

In summary, a well-planned menu should:

- Meet customer needs.
- Be attentive to nutritional values.
- Comprehend service style.
- Match the culinary skill set of the kitchen staff.
- Match the capabilities of the kitchen equipment.
- Reflect consistently available ingredients.
- Offer items that are both profitable and popular.

After the menu is carefully planned, it must be equally carefully executed. This means, for starters, that items should be what the menu says they are. This involves a strict adherence to **truth-in-menu** laws. These are statutes that govern how foodservice establishments represent themselves. For example, fresh means fresh, not frozen and freshly thawed. The combination of ingredients that are noted by a menu item should be those that appear in the finished dish. Cream should be cream, not half and half, or half milk and half cream. In particular, the laws governing low fat and other nutritional claims have very specific guidelines. Customers are increasingly sensitive to truthfulness with respect to nutritional claims. Even when yogurt is substituted for sour cream in a particular dish, it is not necessarily low fat and should not be advertised as such on that account alone.

Exhibit 9.1 Menu Popularity/Profitability Matrix

	Popular	Not Popular
Profitable	A winning recipe	Nice idea from an operations perspective, but if people won't order it ... this menu item requires a little sweetener: different preparation? larger portions? a zippier ingredient? a name they can pronounce ?
Not Profitable	Perhaps a drawing card to get people into the restaurant, but demands that profit be made up elsewhere. Not a good long-term strategy.	A sure loser. The problem here is that many restaurateurs don't know they are in this box until it's too late.

A menu should also reflect the spirit of the restaurant concept. The menu itself is an important part of the restaurant's marketing package. The size of the menu, typeface, choice of paper or other medium like chalkboards, shape, layout, tone and length of item descriptions, the addition of rules, such as "no smoking" or "no substitutions," the names and description, if any, of the proprietors and the establishment, all can shape the customer's perception of the restaurant. These choices should be made deliberately. A customer should be able to get a solid understanding of what the restaurant experience will be like, just from the menu. Remember that customers may make a decision to stay and eat or look elsewhere simply based on a cursory glance of a menu posted outside the front door.

Finally, the menu should be accurate and well proofread. All good planning can be greatly compromised if a service provider is forced to say "I'm sorry, we only have that selection on Fridays, even though it is on the menu. We don't have that special today."

In summary, a well-executed menu should:

- Be truthful.
- Reflect the spirit of the establishment.
- Be accurate.

Open Smartly, and Not Too Soon The restaurant business depends heavily on word of mouth. There's no second chance to make a good first impression, so don't open until you are ready. Opening smartly requires addressing the following considerations:

- Having enough money to complete the restaurant as it was designed.
- Allocating sufficient capital to the first year's working budget.
- Containing and controlling non-revenue-generating expenses.
- Sizing the restaurant correctly, for all days the restaurant is open during the week.
- Weighing correctly the tradeoffs between renting or buying space.

First, part of opening smartly requires having enough money to complete the restaurant as it was designed. Opening a restaurant is **capital intensive**, meaning that the developer needs a lot of cash up front. Too often, owners are forced to cut corners at the end of the building phase. Sometimes no funds or not enough funds were allocated as a contingency for unforeseen problems, and sometimes deliberate design changes along the way add to the building cost. As the project evolves, it is important to keep accurate track of **incremental costs**, those unplanned costs that always come along. Restaurateurs who don't allocate funds strategically find themselves in a financial pinch, and desperate to open, even if they aren't quite ready. One need only remember the importance of first impressions and word of mouth to see the shortsightedness of rushing to open.

Some items can be easily overlooked by an inexperienced restaurateur, and therefore are not included in the planning. One item that is overlooked is the first year's **working capital**, which is the money a restaurant needs just to complete its transactions, such as electricity and phone bills. Another item that can be neglected is **preopening expenses**, which include the costs to advertise that the restaurant is open, training costs for staff, or perhaps a grand opening celebration. Sufficient funds for inventory and insurance are also on the most missed list.

Ideas that satisfy the owner's ego and don't contribute to the bottom line can get in the way in this phase of a restaurant's development. For example, exotic marble trim, an original mural and hand-fired terra-cotta floor tiles may look just as the owner wanted, a dream fulfilled, but may also turn out to be unnecessarily extravagant expenses. In the thrill of the development phase, it can be easy to lose sight of whether a design decision will help contribute to sales or not.

In terms of size, it's easy to start out with too many seats. It is important to peg a restaurant operation to be profitable on Monday and Tuesday night (traditionally the slowest nights of the week), and then Friday and Saturday will take care of themselves! A restaurateur should have realistic expectations and not build the equivalent of a stadium for the Super Bowl crowd.

Another part of opening smartly is weighing the costs and benefits of buying or leasing space. Buying space requires much more **up-front capital**, the money actually provided by the restaurateur, than leasing requires. Buying is a longer-term decision. Should the restaurant fail, the ongoing costs of a purchased property, as opposed to a leased one, are longer in term. It is easier to transfer a lease than to sell a property. After an extended period of time, a purchase does allow an owner to build **equity**, the value of ownership, in the property, which a lease does not. A critical comparison in this decision is weighing the monthly lease rate against the monthly mortgage payment. Regardless of the decision, you should negotiate hard on the cost of renting or buying space. This cost is forever, or for as long as you stay in business, whichever is shorter.

Testing the Numbers Before you open a restaurant, you need to project the estimated revenues and costs associated with the operation. This is sometimes called a **pro forma analysis**. Essentially, you are trying to determine if the restaurant will operate **in the black**—make a profit, or **in the red**—operate at a loss. The projection of revenues and expenses hinges on the assumptions that you make about the restaurant.

To help quantify the potential revenue that a restaurant could make, one should ask three key questions: "How many?" "How fast?" and "How much?" It is important to answer each of these three questions carefully early on, as so much of the design execution depends on the answers. The answer to "How many?" is simply a matter of determining how many seats will be in the restaurant. The seats can be allocated to counter space, tables of two, (**two-top**), four or more (**four-top**), booths, or other configurations. (For restaurants that only have take-out or drive-through service, this question relating to numbers of seats does not apply.) "How much?" is the question that relates to how much money you expect to receive on the average check. In other words, on average, how much will each person who eats in the restaurant spend? "How fast?" translates to the time it takes people to eat. As mealtimes have a fixed number of hours, the faster a customer eats, the faster the restaurant can turn over the seat to a new customer. From chapter 2 you will recall that this is the **number of turns**. Again, a take-out restaurant without seats is not concerned about turnover of seats. These restaurants are instead concerned with how quickly a meal can be prepared and packaged.

For a restaurant with seating capacity, by multiplying the answers to these three questions together, you can project a restaurant's potential revenue. To determine the answers, you must make the key assumptions about the restaurant. For example, assume you are interested in opening a 50-seat coffee house. You assume that each person will spend, on average, $6.00. You also assume that, on average, people will stay for 45 minutes. You plan to be open for lunch from 11:00 A.M. until 2:00 P.M. Therefore, in this time frame, the restaurant will do four turns each lunch period. (There are four blocks of 45 minutes in three hours.)

If it is filled to capacity the entire lunchtime, how much revenue can the restaurant possibly make? The answer is:

50 people multiplied by 4 turns multiplied by a $6.00 average check, or

$50 \times 4 \times 6.00 = \$1,200.00$.

Changing any of the assumptions can make a big difference. What if you decided to have 75 seats? Or if your average check estimate is too aggressive, and more conservatively should be $4.50? What if customers linger for an hour and fifteen minutes? The answers to these questions shape how the restaurant should be designed and how much money the restaurant will generate.

The other half of the numbers equation focuses on the cost side. Costs are often estimated as a percentage of revenues. In other words, for every dollar of revenue generated, some portion of that dollar will be spent in a particular cost category. In general, the largest costs of running a restaurant fit into three buckets: labor costs, food and beverage costs, and operating expenses (administration, advertising, utilities, repairs, and, for a chain, royalties). In a typical restaurant, these three items would represent roughly 30 cents, 30 cents, and 20 cents for every dollar the restaurant earns. Note that these numbers are only general estimates. Restaurants located in large cities where labor rates are high would have higher labor costs, perhaps as much as 40 to 45 cents per dollar. Restaurants with a higher percentage of beverage sales would have a lower food and beverage cost percentage, as the margin of profit tends to be higher on beverage than food. Nonetheless, for the sake of example, this leaves roughly 20 cents of **net operating income**, or the amount the owner has made before rent or mortgage payments. About six cents would typically go to pay the rent. For some operators, that leaves 14 cents, per dollar collected, to take home. For others, these precious pennies can disappear quickly. For example, in locations where real estate costs are high, the percentage of every dollar that goes toward rent rises dramatically. In the food and beverage category, lack of controls can result in waste, theft, spoilage, or not getting what was purchased. In the labor bucket, not having staff that is informed and enthusiastic about the menu, not staffing correctly to meet demand, or not inspiring employees to do the right thing also can eat away at profits.

If we use as a starting point the $1,200 revenue from our coffee house lunch hour, we can then estimate the restaurant's costs based on the above percentages. Labor costs would be $360 (30 percent of $1,200); food and beverage costs would be $360 (30 percent of $1,200); operating expenses would be $240 (20 percent of $1,200); and rent would be $72 (6 percent of $1,200). Though it could happen easily, if other cost increases didn't occur, $168 would be left over. It is important to remember that these estimates are general ones, and that each individual establishment will have its own particular cost structure. More extensive information on the accounting of restaurant profits is offered later, in chapter 13, "An Accounting Tool Box."

Be Thoughtful in Choosing a Location An old saying in the hospitality business is that there are only three things that matter to success: location, location, and location! Though there obviously are many other considerations, the importance of choosing the right location should be taken to heart. It is a crucial decision. A true story of a relocation decision made by a well-established restaurant chain illustrates the point. The chain had a booming business established on the second floor of a highly trafficked shopping and office complex. It served excellent coffee and baked goods as well as fresh sandwiches. Many businessmen stopped in for a quick lunch, and shoppers found it a convenient stop for a coffee break. Then another, much larger space opened up on the first floor. The new space would allow for much more seating, an outdoor seating area that the chain thought would be a real plus, and easier access for delivery of ingredients and garbage pickup. The space was also cheaper per square foot to lease. The shopping/office complex was happy to assist in the relocation, as they already had a retail store interested in the second-floor space. Immediately after the move, the restaurant saw a drop in sales. At first, they thought it was because its regular customers didn't know they had moved. As time passed, they came to realize that the location was not in the thick of the high-traffic shopping area and that the regular office crowd found the extra flight of stairs and walk to the restaurant bothersome. The relocated restaurant found itself in financial trouble. Though its costs had dropped, its revenue dropped even further.

Not every restaurant needs to be in a high-traffic area, but it is important to distinguish between a restaurant concept that requires lots of traffic to succeed, and one that is a destination for the diner. If the restaurant is in the first category, it should be clear that location can be everything. If it is in the latter category, you must feel confident that your customers will go out of their way to come to you, or that the location creates other advantages, such as offering free parking or lower rents, but not at the expense of losses in revenue.

Avoid Physical Design Pitfalls There is a certain hum to a well-run restaurant in full swing. A well-designed kitchen and dining room are able to accommodate many different moving pieces simultaneously with fluidity. A restaurant with design pitfalls reveals clatter and inefficiency. A cacophony of events competing for the same space results. One such event is a waiter with a full tray negotiating his way around an overflow of customers waiting to sit down. Another is a cart full of dirty dishes en route to the kitchen, temporarily parked on the pathway to the restrooms. For a smooth operation, the flow of food; wares, which include dishes, silverware, glasses and the like; service staff; and customers—all need to be coordinated. These flows involve both the **front-of-the-house**, where customers meet service providers, and the **back-of-the-house**, where food is prepared.

Design pitfalls can occur in a restaurant operation if one or more of the following items are not taken into consideration:

- compatibility among all parts of the restaurant,
- attention to special design features,
- ongoing maintenance of the restaurant,
- sizing of the kitchen versus the dining area, and
- efficiency of the overall design and layout.

Above all, a restaurant, especially the kitchen, must be efficient. Having more than enough space for every kitchen function would be ideal; however, for about every 12 to 18 square feet you add to the kitchen, you lose a revenue-producing seat in the dining room! Therefore, in allocating square footage to the front- and to the back-of-the-house, a restaurateur must strike a careful balance.

Why does a restaurant need to be efficient? There are many things moving at once in a busy restaurant operation. Customers are arriving, being greeted, and if the restaurant is busy, waiting; then being seated, and at the completion of the meal, exiting. Food moves through purchasing, receiving, storing, issuing, advance preparation, holding, finishing, plating, serving, eating, clearing, and disposing. Tableware is removed from storage, plated or set, if plated then transported out, used, cleared, stacked, transported back, washed, dried, sorted, and restored. Staff is orchestrating the movements of all of the above happenings. The trick is to allocate enough space to the kitchen for a smooth operation, but not one square foot more.

Consideration for ongoing maintenance early in the design is important. Designer dishes that have nooks and crannies may offer a striking table setting but come out of the dishwasher full of pockets of water, which then need to be dried by hand before storing. The terra-cotta floor may be the perfect color for the restaurant's motif, but may be impossible to keep looking clean. What at first seem to be dream-come-true materials could turn out to be maintenance nightmares.

Restaurants have some other unusual but necessary design features that need to be taken into account. These include exhaust systems, fire prevention systems, electrical requirements for various kinds of equipment, garbage disposals, kitchen noise control, and ventilation. Cutting corners on any of these items at the beginning often results in a more expensive fix down the line. Finally, it all has to work together; the table top, lighting, spacing—even the customers (who they are, what they are wearing), all need to be compatible.

Ongoing Operations

Once a restaurant is up and running, it must face the day-to-day challenges of the ongoing operations. There are some basics of daily operations that every restaurant must get right: acting responsibly, focusing on what the restaurant does well, continually training and empowering employees, choosing the right raw ingredients, preparing for constant revision, monitoring costs and profits, listening to customers, and remembering that there is no guarantee in the restaurant business.

Act Responsibly One need not look further than the news pages to see the debilitating effects of irresponsible behavior. For example, not maintaining appropriate food handling measures can result in sickness and even death. In recent times, one Philadelphia hotel was closed because of an outbreak of a food-borne illness. In this case, Legionnaire's Disease, which infected hundreds of people at a banquet, received such widespread publicity that the hotel never recovered. Though all cases don't have such dramatic outcomes, appropriate attention should be paid to food protection and sanitation. Following important guidelines, such as the temperature at which wares should be washed or that hamburger should be cooked, can literally be lifesaving.

Responsible behavior is also important with respect to the serving of alcoholic beverages. The restaurant as well as wait staff can be prosecuted for violations of the **Alcoholic Beverage Commission (ABC)**, the governmental agency that oversees the sale of alcoholic beverages. This includes not serving alcohol before or after the legal appointed hour, not serving alcohol to persons under the minimum drinking age, and not serving alcohol to an obviously intoxicated person. Responsible beverage service includes training employees to prevent violations. Some restaurants with a significant bar business go a step beyond and offer free soft drinks to the designated driver of a particular party.

In addition to those laws relating to alcoholic beverages, restaurants are also subject to other governing requirements. As with any service business, a restaurant must not discriminate in its hiring practices. A review of laws relating to human resources is discussed in chapter 10, "A Human Resources Tool Box." One additional law that applies to restaurants and that has been under much scrutiny requires wait staff to report tips as income to the Internal Revenue Service. Though the law requires tipped employees to keep accurate track of income, tips are difficult to verify and thus are susceptible to underreporting, or misrepresentation on tax filings.

Focus: Find It and Keep It A restaurant must not lose sight of its customer niche. If a restaurant *is* succeeding, it is important for the restaurateur to understand why. And if the restaurant is *not* succeeding, it is even more important to understand why not, and quickly. A true example of a restaurant entrepreneur illustrates the importance of sticking to your knitting. Mrs. M's Muffins opened a coffee and muffin shop on a busy city street corner, just adjacent to a subway stop. The restaurant was well situated, for it had a constant stream of people passing by. The establishment offered counter service with a limited amount of seating.

In the opening weeks, business was brisk, and it looked like Mrs. M was off to a good start. Business was strongest during the breakfast hours. There was also an increase in traffic in the late afternoon, presumably coinciding with the evening commute. To try to fill in the weak times of the day, the muffin shop began to experiment with other menu items. They gave up one display case to make room for a frozen yogurt machine. That helped some during midday, but the restaurant still hoped to capture more consumer dollars over the lunch and dinner hours. Within months, the windows of the restaurant become completely cluttered with signs, one advertising that it was "THE BEST LUNCH IN TOWN." Other signs offered descriptions of its newest menu items, hot pastrami sandwiches, homemade chili, and calzones. The ending to the story is easy to predict. A well-known coffee chain took over the space within a year.

The cluttered window is a good reflection of the clarity of management's thinking. A muffin shop that sells hot pastrami sandwiches because it is trying to expand its profit is doing just the opposite. The lesson: Stay focused on what you do well.

Continually Train, Inspire, and Empower Employees Many restaurateurs would delight in an evening table turnover as high as the average annual employee turnover—an estimated 240 percent.[10] This means that on average, a restaurant replaces each employee 2.4 times per year. Turnover is a fact of restaurant operations, and those that succeed must take seriously the costs associated with losing employees. Chapter 3, "The Hospitality Business Is a Service Business," and chapter 10, "A Human Resources Tool Box," both underscore the importance of training, inspiring, and empowering employees. The Au Bon Pain restaurant chain, which uses a partner/manager program, offers an excellent illustration of how to inspire employees to align their goals with the company's. All unit managers are part owners of the restaurant units they manage. Their compensation packages are heavily dependent on the profits of their stores. The kinds of behavior that Au Bon Pain noted when this program was put in place included: more efficient staffing schedules, new ideas for menu items, cleaner stores, and managers happily working extra hours.

Remember that Raw Ingredients Matter The food items you start with are the biggest determinant of the menu items you end up with. If the raw ingredients are not of appropriate quality, all the culinary skill in the world cannot change that fact. The owner of La Sapotillier, a very successful French restaurant in the Caribbean, notes that the most important part of his contribution to his restaurant is over at 8:00 A.M. He goes to the fish dock himself to select the fish for the day. In the off-season, he spends weeks interviewing food purveyors in France and the United States to set up contracts for food shipments during the balance of the year. Another well-known restaurateur, Wolfgang Puck, uses a similar approach. He too goes to the fish market in downtown Los Angeles four times a week. He also works with local farms in selecting produce. The food you start with is the biggest determinant of the menu you end up with.

Be Prepared for Constant Revision By definition a restaurant can't be "hot" forever. Recent times have seen a heyday for Cajun, Tex-Mex, ribs, gourmet pizza, and a host of other concepts that have come and gone, repeatedly. Some restaurant companies go into business prepared to reposition the same space completely in five to seven years. Others constantly make incremental changes to adapt to the changing times. Adding healthier menu items, offering a "great buy" price-fixed selection on an otherwise à la carte menu to communicate value, sponsoring a "hunger brunch" after which part of the profits go to a community cause, are all examples of tactics that respond to a change in a short time frame. Some changes may be riskier than others. One example is Burger King. Feeling pressure from family-oriented sit-down restaurant chains, after decades of offering only counter service, they announced table service during the dinner hour in some outlets. This change may win business from the competition; however, it runs the risk of disorienting the customer base.

Know Where Your Costs Are; Know Where Your Profits Are The restaurant business has both **fixed costs** and **variable costs**. Fixed costs stay the same no matter how much business the restaurant does. If a restaurant is owned, there are certain fixed costs associated with the land and building such as depreciation, property taxes, insurance, and, most likely, debt service or mortgage payments. If the restaurant space is leased, the monthly lease payments are fixed. Variable costs are those that rise or fall in proportion to sales volume. Variable costs include food costs, labor costs, utilities, and other supply costs such as cleaning supplies.

One way of thinking about the profitability of a restaurant is called **breakeven analysis**. This analysis tries to determine the breakeven point, or that sales volume at which the establishment neither makes a profit nor incurs a loss. Consider again the $1,200.00 revenue from the coffee house lunch hour. The restaurant incurred a series of costs because it was open for business. If the volume of sales doubled the next day, call it Tuesday, to $2,400, then the variable costs would double as well. If the restaurant was closed on Wednesday, it would have no variable costs. However, the fixed costs remain the same on Monday, Tuesday, and Wednesday. For example, the charge for lease rental is the same on all days. Keeping a keen eye on costs, every day of the week, as well as understanding which costs are variable and which are fixed, allows a restaurant manager to understand the profit potential of the establishment more accurately.

There are other parts of the equation that affect profits. It's no secret in the restaurant business that the profit margins on beverage items are significantly greater than they are in food. Therefore, where possible, encouraging additional drink sales can help the bottom line. We talked earlier about correctly sizing a restaurant. Selling as close to the restaurant's capacity as possible is critical. The goal is: no empty seats. Only seats that are sold can make a contribution to fixed costs.

Once a restaurant chooses to spend money on advertising or some other form of marketing, that too becomes a fixed cost. The marketing may or may not be effective. One type of advertising that has no cost is entirely in the hands of the customer: word of mouth. Research shows that if people have a good experience at a restaurant, they will share their reaction with their friends; if they have a bad experience, they will share their reaction with roughly twice as many friends.

Listen to Your Customers in a Setting Where They Feel Like Talking This is a classic piece of advice, with an important added dimension. Most restaurant patrons have experienced a member of the wait staff inquiring about the meal. "How was everything?" is a common question. Consider if and how you have answered that question. It is typical, if the meal is over and you are on your way out the door, to answer "Just fine." A host collecting a series of "Just fines" as customers leave a restaurant in response to "How was everything?" is not useful. They may be saying "Just fine" to make an unobtrusive exit, but they may actually be planning never to return. The customer is not necessarily motivated to answer more completely or candidly.

Some restaurants offer comment cards with the promise of a response or some type of reward. Others offer a toll-free number for customers to call. One restaurant chain, Boston Market, has recently introduced touch screen technology at their store exits, to collect feedback. The screens ask a few simple questions about the food and service. Patrons hold their hands on a thermometer until it reads the selected level of satisfaction. The important learning is to be sure to collect feedback from the customers when they feel like talking. Allow or encourage them to take the first step.

Apply Technology There are numerous examples of ways in which technology can be applied to the restaurant business to increase profits and decrease costs. Whether it be handheld order pads that automatically transmit customer choices to the kitchen, saving the wait staff precious steps, or cash registers that automatically keep track of food and beverage inventory, making reordering a snap, even the smallest of operations should consider ways that computer technology can be helpful. Multiunit chains can use technology to link restaurants together, making comparison from operation to operation possible. Technology also allows a central means of communication and a way for units to learn from one another. We devote all of chapter 12, "A Management Information Tool Box," to various computer systems and their applications. As many sophisticated programs can be run on a single personal computer, the cost of integrating technology into a restaurant operation can be a deal too good to pass up.

There's No Annuity in the Restaurant Business. Act Accordingly—Every Day Once some businesses set up an infrastructure, with appropriate maintenance, an income stream follows; in the restaurant business, there's no such thing. Restaurants are not unlike theaters, and restaurateurs sing for their supper at every meal. Repeat customers are only as dependable as their last dining experience. La Coupole, a once fashionable restaurant in New York City, illustrates the point. It opened to rave reviews; the critics couldn't say enough good things. The onslaught of eager customers was literally too much to handle. It closed 14 months later, slammed by the same critics who had launched its success.[11]

Consistency from meal to meal and day to day matters. In an automated environment, such as a fast food chain, consistency may be easier to control than in a gourmet restaurant serving one-of-a-kind dining experiences at each meal. Nonetheless, in both instances delivering a meal that consistently meets customers expectations is critical. (We talk more about the importance of consistently meeting customers' expectations in chapter 11, "A Hospitality Marketer's Tool Box.") Though it might not seem apparent, customers are constantly reviewing a scorecard. Some of the items that they see are reviewed in Exhibit 9.2, "A Restaurant Critic's Checklist: From the Eyes of the Customer." Restaurateurs would do well to carry the same checklist.

Exhibit 9.2 A Restaurant Critic's Checklist: From the Eyes of a Customer

Though customers don't arrive with a formal checklist, they are likely to react and evaluate many elements in a restaurant. Their internal scorecards are likely to notice:

FOOD: quality, portions, garnish, presentation, temperature
SERVICE: timing, friendliness, professional, appropriateness
MENU: physical piece, layout, readability, ease of use, variety, appropriateness
BEVERAGE SERVICE: wine list, presentation of wine
AMBIANCE: decor, lighting, sound, visuals, comfortable temperature, well ventilated
TABLE SETTING: dishes, tabletop, silverware, spacing, presentation
CHAIRS: comfortable, appropriately sized
LINEN/PAPER: clean, appropriate
CHECKROOMS: available, secure, organized
BATHROOMS: clean, supplied, appropriate decor
WAITING AREAS: comfortable, bar service/snacks available
WAITING LINES: fair, managed, informed
FLOWS: people, dishware, service persons, food
EXTERIOR: neighborhood, window, advertisements, endorsements, other customers eating, entrance
BEFORE THE VISIT: advertising, word of mouth, reservations handled well
PARKING: available, secure, other kinds of cars, valet
SMOKING/NONSMOKING SECTIONS: well separated
PARKING: available, secure, other kinds of cars, valet
SMOKING/NONSMOKING SECTIONS: well separated
HANDICAP FACILITIES: available, accessible

Institutional Foodservice Operations _____

We now turn our attention to institutional or contract foodservice. Though a great deal of the learning from the earlier section on restaurants applies quite nicely, we will first focus on the differences that emerge because of the unique characteristics of volume production and feeding.

Most institutional food providers serve food in a variety of settings such as: a teaching hospital, a state university campus, the banquet hall of a convention center, a federal government building, a fine dining facility within a corporate headquarters, special events such as the Super Bowl or World Series, a national park, or on board an airline, to name a few. Within each category, just as within the different kinds of restaurant categories, there are different requirements for service styles, such as: vending, catering and banquet services, fine dining services, concessions, fast food, and dietary and nutrition management–focused delivery. Often, a variety of service styles is used in one location. For example, Aramark catered the 1992 Olympics in Barcelona, Spain, through its special events division. There they served 2.5 million meals in a combination of 400 different service points, including locations at all sporting events, box lunches, and four specialty restaurants within the Olympic Games Village, one of which was a VIP fine dining facility.[12]

Opening Feats

In general, getting into the institutional foodservice business requires significantly more capital than opening a restaurant. Because of the large volume of customers who are typically fed, extensive equipment and staff are needed to service the operation. Take an extreme example: At the Barcelona Olympics, for example, the contract services included coordinating with manufacturers to ensure delivery and installation of food preparation and storage equipment. (The same kinds of setup issues are faced by any caterers who service off-premise locations.) Food also had to be purchased from an assortment of suppliers and delivered to appropriate locations. This was no small feat considering the ingredient tallies: some 275 tons of fresh fruit, 110,000 loaves of bread, 50,000 gallons of milk, and half a billion pounds of meat and poultry. In the context of preparation, some 20 concession contractors and 12 foodservice subcontractors were supervised. All of this had to happen in compliance with the health standards of the city and the province.

No matter what the foodservice operation, because of sheer size, the opening of a contract foodservice facility is likely to span a lengthy time period. Openings begin with an analysis of need, which leads to a proposal. Successful openings also require engineering a menu that works for many.

Be Thorough in Setting Up a Proposal Contract food servers typically have a salesforce within their organization who sell their services to the various client organizations. In order to be successful, the salespersons must meet extensively with the prospective clients in order to understand their needs. They must also do on-site analysis to determine the operational requirements, including, size, service style, and physical requirements. A detailed proposal that outlines how the foodservice will be arranged, and the resulting financial terms then are presented. It is important to judge the right amount of detail. The proposal must be enough to be thorough and convincing to the client, but not so detailed that the cost of preparing it is prohibitive.

Engineer a Menu that Works for Many So much of the rule book for generating an effective menu for a restaurant applies to institutional foodservice. The profitability/popularity matrix is still applicable, especially in situations in which the customers are experiencing table service. The profitability equation changes somewhat with a contract arrangement. Typically, the negotiation revolves around a fixed sum to be paid, per person/per meal. For example, in a high school cafeteria or food court lunch service, the contractor is paid a set amount for each student in the school. In a college setting, profit is collected based on the number and kinds of meal plans sold.

Customer needs, nutritional values, and service style are also critical, just as they are in restaurants. The culinary skill and kitchen equipment must match the menu, and ingredients must be available. Because the audience in institutional foodservice settings may be captive in varying degrees, the foodservice operation must have sufficient variety to please everyone, but not so much variation and complexity that the operation becomes difficult to manage. This is why popular stations such as salad bars or frozen yogurt bars are offered at every meal in school settings.

With respect to the menu itself, there often is no paper menu at all, as one would expect in a restaurant. In food court settings, menus are posted above the various stations. Hospitals may not have menus at all, but may respond individually to the dietary needs of their various patients. On airlines, menus are used more as marketing tools rather than for passengers to select from various choices. In coach class, typically for overseas travel, choices are usually limited, if any choice is involved. The main use of the menu is to communicate, with a tangible element, the quality of the airline's service. In first or business class, the menus often become more descriptive and do offer choices. This becomes a way to distinguish the different classes of service.

Location: Definitely Different from Restaurants Probably the most dramatic difference between restaurants and institutional foodservice is location. For restaurateurs the decision is critical; for institutional food servers there is no decision to make. The setting is predetermined by the location of the institution itself. Further, the decision between leasing or buying space is already made. In permanent settings, the space is effectively leased. When the foodservice facility is temporary, such as at a special event, the operation is in place for such a short period of time, that neither leasing nor buying applies.

As the institutional foodservice operation prepares to open, it may be replacing another contractor. In this case, a smooth transition is important. It may be that the contractor is opening a brand-new facility, in which some of the restaurant rules apply, such as having enough funds to complete the project and allocating sufficient capital for the first year's operation. For large operators, this tends to be less of a problem than it is with restaurants. Typically, formal financing arrangements are in place and the same kind of service facility may already have been opened in other locations. Sizing the facility may be easier for institutions, as the variables in an institutional setting may be less variable than in a restaurant. Estimating the volume of meals served for a given meal period, for example, can be fairly straightforward. If a hospital runs at a consistent 60 percent occupancy rate, the anticipated number of patients served can be quickly determined. In other arenas, such as special events, the unpredictability may be greater.

Making the numbers work and testing the profitability of a potential setting is an equally important exercise for both restaurants and institutions. Estimating potential revenue and a thorough analysis of the cost components associated with the operation are still key exercises that should be performed early on in the development process. One important distinction is that making the numbers work in institutional settings revolves heavily around the negotiation of a contract. The contract terms may take some of the risk out of the revenue side when fixed numbers are established, but costs can be just as hard to control as they are in a restaurant operation.

With respect to physical design pitfalls the same principles apply; all pieces of the operation should be compatible, attention should be paid to maintenance and efficiency, and the kitchen should be sized appropriately for the outlets. Getting the kitchen size right is often more complex. One kitchen may serve a number of outlets, and those outlets may be in distant locations. In the design and execution of an institutional foodservice facility, any problems that might arise because of poor design are greatly magnified. Any mistake is typically a big mistake.

Around the World in Foodservice

There's an industry publication called the *Technomic Foodservice Digest*, which outlines major happenings in food trends, developments in the hotel and recreation industries as related to foodservice, and changes in independent restaurants. It also tracks up-to-the minute developments on the international scene. In just a few months in 1995, here is some of what happened internationally in foodservice:

- After KFC suffered substantial losses for three years in Chile, they sold out to local investors, who were able to revise the menu, relocate some outlets, and watch sales jump 60 percent. (January 1995)
- McDonald's opened in Mecca, Saudi Arabia, using meat that is in accord with Muslim standard. This outlet is part of McDonald's goal to have 38 units in the Middle East by the end of 1995. (January 1995)
- More chains are heading into China: TGI Friday's launched a joint venture with China National Aero Technology Import and Export Co. of Beijing. They plan on 45 outlets in Taiwan, Beijing, and Tianjin by 2005. (February 1995)
- Domino's Pizza International signed an agreement with Enpro India Ltd. of New Delhi to develop 150–200 franchised and company-owned stores in India. (February 1995)
- Baskin-Robbins is the first American quick-service chain to open in Vietnam, and is located in downtown Ho Chi Minh City. A single scoop is $1.50, more than a day's wages for the average worker. (March 1995)
- Burger King is focusing on international expansion. It has 254 units in the Asia-Pacific region, 272 in Latin America, and hopes to expand its 17 units in the Middle East. They are also considering entering Russia and China. (June 1995)

Ongoing Operations

We again underscore that much of the complexity in ongoing operations for contract providers occurs because of the volume of production.

Focus on the Customer** and **the Client In a very real way, contract providers have two important relationships. One is with the customer who consumes food on a daily basis; the second is with the client. The way companies must interact with customers is not unlike the relationship that a restaurant has with its patrons. All of the learnings about listening and paying attention to the customer's scorecard apply. In addition, contractors must pay equal attention to their **clients**, those individuals from the institution, executives, administrators or managers, who are the liaisons to the contract foodservice company. Keeping both groups happy is key to a successful foodservice operation.

In situations where the patrons have a vested interest in the foodservice operation, such as in a private club, the foodservice contractor may feel as if all of the customers are clients. Input from members on the quality of the foodservice may happen frequently. Satisfying all parties in such situations can be particularly tricky.

Serve Beyond the Dining Room Successful institutional foodservice companies should look for innovative points of delivery. For example, not only have traditional cafeteria lines in colleges been replaced by modern food courts, some providers deliver pizza to student rooms and allow charges to meal plans, in the equivalent of a 24-hour convenience store. In office buildings, one might find sandwich carts indoors and out, and vending machines providing much fresher choices than expected. Bakeries, ice cream shops, coffee counters, and gift shops on the clients' premises are additional points of distribution that look well beyond the traditional. Opportunities for catering can exist in many venues, such as for office birthday parties or graduation celebrations for departments within universities.

Some large foodservice companies have even expanded the range of services offered to include nonfood services. These opportunities include maintenance services, or laundry and uniform services.

Special Features of Special Audiences Just as various restaurant classifications must be attentive to the customers' needs, so too, must a contract feeder note the special features of the audience that it serves. The menu items, timing of service, kinds of service, and special features are dictated in part by the purpose of the institutional setting itself. In a baseball stadium, for example, food needs to be served on multiple floors and in multiple sections. The audience, in this case baseball fans, swamps the foodservice operations between innings and during the seventh inning stretch. Therefore, food must be served very quickly during those intervals, to meet the peaks in demand. The food offerings must also be easily transportable, as most people in the audience will eat at their seats.

A correctional facility market poses unique operational problems. Security is a key issue. Kitchen design and mirrors eliminate any blind spots. Supplies cannot be packed in glass. Certain spices that can be smoked are eliminated from the menu and imitation extracts are always used in place of real extracts that contain alcohol. Service time must be met precisely. In a few correctional facilities, state-of-the-art technology is used as an additional security measure. A programmed vehicle is used to deliver and pick up food trays.

Staff Special Needs Accordingly The special needs of various institutions also demand specific staffing. For health-related facilities, such as lifecare centers and hospitals, nutrition specialists are an important addition to the formal part of organization. With an increased concern for nutrition nationwide, these specialists also play a role in many other kinds of foodservice. In campus dining facilities, vegetarian, low-fat, and well-balanced meals are most certainly incorporated into the menu offerings. In office buildings, weight watchers are leading the charge for health-conscious selections.

Because contract foodservice companies are often in the position of designing the foodservice operation, facilities planners are full-time members of the team. Salespersons who call on new accounts are also full-time, and integral to institutional foodservice.

A Captive Customer is Not So Captive It may seem that an institutional foodservice company does not have to sing for its supper every day. Contracts are typically in place for several years and have a fixed date for renewal. One could argue that the audience is therefore fixed for a period of time. This may be true to a degree, and small declines in quality may not cause the client to protest today. However, when the contract renewal time is up, the lack of quality service over time may result in the loss of the contract. Because there are enormous fixed costs in the start-up phase of a foodservice facility, losing a contract can be a painful financial burden. Thus, treating the contract as if there were no guarantee is a good posture for a foodservice provider to take.

In some cases, a decline in quality may translate to a decline in customers in shorter order than the contract renewal date. In corporate buildings, people often don't have far to go to find an alternative. Take the Standard Oil Building in Chicago, affectionately known as "Big Stan," which is serviced by a contract feeder. People who work in the office have a choice of 110 other restaurants within a three-block radius.[13] Management must stay keenly aware that the competition is literally just around the corner.

Act Responsibly and Stay Focused Acting responsibly is something every business should do; thus contract foodservice is no different than restaurants on this count. One example of a corporation showing leadership in this area is Aramark's launch of a designated driver program in all of its athletic stadium accounts. It dispenses free soft drinks to those volunteering for the program. It also encourages its clients to stop alcoholic beverage sales three quarters of the way through events. Though it actually has had a negative impact on stadium sales, it is a good example of an operator and a client working together for the benefit of its fans.

The focus of institutional foodservice companies cuts across many different kinds of institutions, but always involves the same core service of food production and distribution to a large audience. An institution may find, though, that it must offer a package of services in order to land a contract. One such example is a foodservice contract for a national park that includes marina management and the operation of white-water rafting excursions! Whether or not diversifying to such a degree is good business (it didn't work for Mrs. M's Muffins), it is a conversation worth having.

All the rules of effective human resource management apply to institutions. Because of the vastness of their operations, institutions are faced with the special challenge of training many people at a time. For special events, training needs are especially demanding. As the workforce is only temporary, they must be trained and motivated in a cost effective yet productive way.

Technological applications are very much in use and worthwhile. In a large convention facility for example, food supply routing to the far-flung corners of the center are controlled by personal computers. This helps in delivering food to what can be hundreds of hospitality suites, which are corporations hosting small affairs at their exhibitor space throughout the day. Computer databases can also be used to access the event histories of previous trade shows and conventions that have been serviced. Thus the information from an individual client can be accessed to deliver ever improving service.

■■■■■■■■ **Listen to Your Customers**

"Fish, without complications"

Finally, continual and relentless focus on understanding the needs of the customer base is of paramount importance for both restaurants and institutions. Though marketing and merchandising to a fixed audience is different from the challenge of always trying to capture new customers, generating repeat and loyal customers is consequential for any kind of foodservice operation, however big or small.

Summary

There is no one recipe card that yields success. Some restaurants are noisy and boisterous; others are quiet and romantic. Some use Waterford Crystal, others paper cups. Some have just one location; others are everywhere. There are some basic ingredients that matter to the success of all foodservice operations, however, whether they be independent restaurants or huge institutional caterers. The basic ingredients to successful foodservice operations start with plenty of strategic thought. That includes selecting the appropriate menu and hiring the right chef and kitchen staff. Working out an adequate budget with enough left over for emergencies, thoughtfully selecting a location, and maintaining perspective in design follow. Once you're up and running, acting responsibly, keeping an eye on inventory, remaining flexible, and controlling costs will contribute to success. Always listening to your customers and clients is a critical ingredient, as is utilizing appropriate technology. Finally, remember that in any foodservice operation, there are no guarantees. What is working today may not work tomorrow, so no restaurateur, no matter how large or small, can afford to rest.

Identifying these basic ingredients of success is what this chapter is all about, and that's not rocket science; successfully applying all of the learnings just might be harder.

Discussion Questions

1. What does it mean to open smartly and not too soon? What common pitfalls does a restaurateur encounter? What are the odds that a restaurant will succeed beyond the first year?

2. Explain the four boxes of the profitability/popularity matrix. What are the action implications for menu items that fall into each of the four categories?

3. What are the key elements of successful operation once a restaurant is up and running?

4. Why do some restaurateurs deliberately limit the lifetime of a restaurant concept?

5. Why is there no annuity in the restaurant business? As an owner, how important is the last meal that a customer had in your restaurant?

6. How is contract foodservice different from commercial foodservice? How is it the same?

7. What is a captive audience? How does it affect the ongoing operations of the foodservice provider?

8. Define: variable costs; fixed costs; preopening expenses; net operating income; value managed relationships; equity; breakeven analysis; pro forma analysis.

9. Why are truth-in-menu laws important to foodservice operations?

Assignments

1. The International Box discusses some of the chain restaurants operating around the world today. Select a chain that operates internationally, and research its growth over the past two years. Construct a time line of activities. What are the company's plans for the next two years? How long does it take the chain to open a new outlet? Is the chain concentrating on a particular part of the world? If so, why? Have outlets closed, and if so, why? If you were to open outlets abroad, what country or countries would you select? Support your claims.

2. What is on a restaurant critic's checklist from the eyes of a customer? Eat out and evaluate an actual restaurant experience, using the checklist.

3. The opening quotation (from a real rocket scientist!) describes his views on foodservice operation; that, in fact, it is easier to travel to the moon than to run a restaurant. Research the success and failure rates for restaurants in your area or state (a good place to start is your state restaurant association). Are these statistics surprising? In your opinion, what are the critical elements to a successful foodservice operation? Rank them in order, from most important to least important. What factors influenced your decisions?

End Notes

1. As quoted to Professor Michael Oshins, Boston University School of Hospitality Administration.

2. David Farkas, "Failure Rates Better than Expected," *Restaurant Hospitality* (March, 1992): 60.

3. Martin. E. Dort, *Restaurants that Work* (New York: Whitney Library of Design, 1992), 11.

4. Jacob Grierson, "Trendy Restaurants Work Hard Shooting from the Hip," *The Wall Street Journal*, 28 August 1990, B1.

5. Adam Bryant, "He Marketing, She's Finance: A $2 Billion Mom-and-Pop Shop," *New York Times*, 6 December 1992, 8F.

6. Nancy Jackson, "Authors," *Harvard Business School Bulletin*, April 1989, vii.

7. Data from National Restaurant Association, 1994.

8. Information from DAKA International's Annual Report, 1994.

9. Erik Larson, "The Man with the Golden Touch," *Inc. Magazine* (October 1988): 67.

10. Joshua Hyatt, "The Odyssey of an Excellent Man," *Inc. Magazine* (February 1989): 69.

11. Grierson, B1.

12. Aramark brochure entitled "The Games of the XXV Olympiad of Barcelona, Facts and Figures, 1992."

13. Carolyn Walkup, "Feeding the Office in the Office at Amoco," *Nations Restaurant News* 24 (50).

Part Four

Management
✎Tools

Part IV embraces four disciplinary toolboxes of management: chapter 10, human resources; chapter 11, marketing; chapter 12, management information systems; and chapter 13, accounting.

Each of these chapters begins with an understanding of the features of the management discipline as it relates to the field of hospitality. These features reveal a set of characteristics that a manager in the field would encounter. Each chapter then offers a set of tools that can be used in response to a particular feature. For example, because hospitality services are predominantly intangible, a marketer would do well to be able to apply clue management, a way to make tangible the intangible as a success tool. A management information systems manager would discover that timely information is critical as a feature of hospitality MIS. In response, a manager could apply seamless integration, a success tool that keeps all of the elements of a system working together. This features-linked-to-tools approach provides a theoretical understanding of the discipline as well as practical applications that can be applied to management decisions in the hospitality business.

Each chapter closes by placing the reader directly in the shoes of managers around the world: a human resources manager for a 1,200-room convention hotel in Hong Kong, the director of marketing for a Native American casino, an MIS manager of the European division of a restaurant chain, and a controller for an Italian cruise line. The issues presented in each manager's in box offer a way to tackle real problems through the application of the success tools presented earlier.

Chapter Ten

" *People will behave the way they have always behaved until you can measure the difference and reward them accordingly.* "

Mark E. Nunnelly [1]

A Human Resources Tool Box ✍

When you finish this chapter, you should:

1. Understand the features of hospitality human resources and the success tools that can be employed in response to those features.

2. Understand the scope of legal and social policy that shape the role of a human resources manager.

3. Know the elements of successful recruiting and why the recruiting function is important.

4. Know what it means to treat employees as internal customers.

5. Understand what elements make an employee feel empowered.

6. Be familiar with the scope of such recruiting tools as child care and flextime.

7. Understand the functions performed by a human resources manager and be able to give examples of them.

8. Be familiar with the kinds of performance measures human resources managers use.

9. Be able to identify the kinds of issues that might be found in the in box of a hospitality human resources manager.

Introduction

The **human resource** department of hospitality organizations used to be referred to as **personnel**. As the name has changed to comprehend the importance of human input into the hospitality equation, so too has the sophistication of the human resources function. Human resources today has come to mean creating a dynamic environment that produces the best possible work and the best possible service. Human resources express the hope of forward-looking organizations intending to remain viable and adaptive in a rapidly changing world. The field has come to embrace with high visibility and importance many of the functions formerly performed by a personnel department. Like a Polaroid picture that slowly emerges on paper, the vision of a human resources concept has evolved in full color, revealing numerous critical issues.

Critical Issues Facing Human Resources Managers

Any service industry is a labor-intensive one. Human beings are responsible for the production and delivery of the services. Thus, the attitude and competence of human interaction determines the success or failure of every service establishment.

Because of the high concentration of human capital in hospitality operations, there is a need for a department that can orchestrate all the human relations and issues. Such a department, however small, can be found in every lodging, foodservice, or travel company.

The human resources department and staff deal with numerous issues and tasks that include: planning, recruiting, orientation, development, employee discipline, employee rights, communications, morale, diversity, ADA regulations, AIDS, promotion, service quality, discrimination, sexual harassment, and many others. How these issues are handled determines the success or failure of a service delivery process, and thus the success or failure of the entire service establishment. It is important that the human resources manager be familiar with these issues and educate and train employees accordingly. In addition, the human resources manager must be an active listener and sensitive to the company's employees' needs, requests, and rights. The manager must also recognize the goals of the company and serve, simultaneously, management and front-line employees.

Distinguishing Features of Hospitality Human Resources Management

Hospitality human resources has a set of special features or characteristics that make it the business that it is. Knowing how to respond to each of these features with the right action steps is what makes a manager successful. As with any profession, assessing the situation, knowing which tools to use, and knowing how to use them correctly yields competitive advantage.

Feature: Hospitality Organizations are Labor Intensive

Hospitality is a **labor-intensive** industry, characterized by large numbers of employees all dedicated to service as a performing art. Upward of 25 percent to 45 percent of every dollar earned by a hospitality service organization is spent on labor. Furthermore, because of the nature of the performance component, and because a service experience is a series of interactions with many people, any *one* of which can alter the customer's perception for the worse, having and keeping the right employees is of paramount importance.

Success Tool: Effective Recruiting Employee **recruitment**, the process by which qualified applicants are sought and screened, requires superior assessment skills. It goes beyond choosing just the right person—that is, a person having the "right stuff"—to function effectively in a service industry job. To assure the right numbers of employees with a mix of skills required to implement the company's policies and practices, a number of key questions must be addressed: How can employees be recruited that will fit the company's needs? Will such recruiting take into account contemporary recruiting issues like flextime, child care, minorities, and persons with disabilities? How will employee effectiveness be defined and evaluated? In the event that the company operates within the context of a participative management program, what training mechanisms exist, or are planned, that enable employees to learn right from the start exactly what the company expects of them? These questions, as well as others, need to be addressed, because in the eyes of the hospitality world, such recruits collect the customers' money, and if they don't have the "right stuff," they can easily cause customers to go elsewhere.

There is no simple formula for effective recruiting, but in addition to asking the questions above, one perspective offers these two elements for recruiting world-class service workers:

1. Interview recruits *in person* in order to gauge their energy, attitude, presentation skills, and charm. Typically, application form questions simply yield *data* but precious little *information*.
2. Ask open-ended questions that allow people to reveal how they think about their work, their customers, their employers, and themselves.[2]

Traditionally, before a recruiter begins interviewing prospective employees, he or she must know the requirements of the job to be performed. This entails preparing a **job description**, listing the general responsibilities as well as the specific standards of job performance required. Nonetheless, contemporary service organizations are now replacing straitjacket job definitions with what some have termed **boundaryless service**. For example, Ruby Tuesday, a restaurant chain based in Greenville, South Carolina, practices this type of service. When a customer's food is ready, the first available server delivers it, even if that particular server is not assigned to that table.

Success Tool: Training and Development Not long ago, while seated at the dining room table of a Midwestern hotel, four guests experienced a problem that was obviously training related. The server, a young man who had distributed the menus, noticed that the tablecloth had not been properly crumbed following the departure of previous diners. He grabbed a linen napkin, brushed the crumbs onto the floor, and then proceeded to take the guests' meal orders. Asked by one of the guests how soon someone would sweep the crumbs off the floor, the waiter replied, "Oh, that just gives the houseman something to do whenever he comes on duty."[3]

The impact of this anecdote is that three critical elements to success are missing in the server's training. First is to train the employee by example, that is, to pair him or her with a world-class service worker so the new server will seat customers only at tables that are properly set up. A second important element is to give new employees specific guidelines so that they don't have to worry about making a mistake; and last, if the employee thought of the houseman as a member of *his* team, he might have behaved differently.

A four-step **training program** widely used and featured in training courses by both the National Restaurant Association and the American Hotel and Motel Educational Institutes embraces the following points:

- Tell—Explain the task to the worker, explain why it is necessary to be done and explain the reasons why it must be done in this particular way.

- Show—Demonstrate how the job is to be performed, explaining along the way each of the tasks to be performed. Continue to demonstrate patiently until the worker is ready to try it.

- Do—Allow the worker to perform each aspect of the job slowly, asking questions of the trainee in order to determine his ability to perform the job unassisted by the trainer.

- Follow-up—Once the trainee performs independently to the satisfaction of the trainer, then frequent follow-ups will be required until the trainer is satisfied that the new employee has indeed developed in to a world-class performer.

Retraining, with a Twist

Think that cops only like doughnuts? Feel that lawyers would rather scoop up their opponents instead of chocolate mousse? Fear that astronauts equate Tang with a fine French champagne?

Not at the New York Restaurant School. This culinary school has a whole new breed of student, and you'd be surprised who's learning to sauté. Job retraining in the culinary arts is more popular than ever, and hundreds of aspiring Julia Childs are slicing, dicing, and chopping their way into new careers.

Bus drivers, insurance agents, and accountants are just some of the school's new patrons. These nontraditional students are enrolling in an intensive four-month training program, followed by a two-month internship. And the students are discovering that turning out well-prepared and tasty meals isn't as easy as Julia makes it look. Hectic kitchens, long hours, and temperamental ovens can be harder to handle than walking the beat. Sloping soufflés, overcooked omelets, and mangled minestrone can all lead to disaster in a restaurant.

But the rewards are worth it, the students say. Realizing life-long desires to become chefs keeps them in the kitchen, learning to master mouthwatering mousse along with the perplexities of pâté.

Success Tool: Encouraging Diversity Statistics indicate that by the year 2000, nearly a third of all new entrants into the labor force will be minorities, twice as many as in the 1980s. Discovering that a major impediment to minority applicants' being able to take full advantage of available job opportunities is the lack of basic skills, hotel and restaurant companies have inaugurated a variety of educational programs. Bakers who had trouble reading instructional manuals on how to make doughnuts are being taught how to read. English as a second language is being taught in a restaurant chain where 80 percent of the employees are Spanish speaking. Hotel chains are offering nationwide college scholarship plans aimed at attracting minority college students to the profession of hotel and restaurant management. Nonetheless, a JOBS survey by the magazine *Restaurants and Institutions* reported job discrimination to be the major complaint among minorities.[4] The highest percentage of discrimination was for race.

A U.S. Department of Labor report, *Opportunity 2000*, indicates plainly that companies need to do much more to promote minorities and the economically disadvantaged into higher-level positions. The maximum potential for each individual, and therefore for each company, will not be reached until every employee is viewed as a candidate for advancement.[5]

Feature: Turnover is Common and Expensive

Besides wage rates generally, one of the major reasons for the high cost of labor is high **turnover**. Turnover is expensive for several reasons. There are definite costs involved with recruiting and training replacements. There is also the cost to the remaining employees. Turnover can hurt morale and require others to put in extra effort while a replacement is found. In "revolving-door" organizations, service can suffer too. A seasoned, well-trained employee is equipped to handle problems more efficiently than a new employee who is just starting up the learning curve.

Success Tool: Treating Employees as Internal Customers A service establishment needs to focus on its customers in order to generate quality service, success, and profits. Likewise, every manager or owner in the service sector needs to focus on employees as internal customers. This is also a critical and fundamental practice. Keeping employees satisfied is just as important as keeping customers satisfied. Hence the goal is **employee retention** just as much as it is customer retention, and one is linked to the other: a happy employee equals a happy customer.

Success Tool: Constantly Addressing Motivation and Morale Creating an environment where employees are productive and satisfied means paying attention to what motivates them. Research makes clear that people derive much of their satisfaction at work, provided it possesses at least five basic characteristics:

1. Skill variety—different skills and talents are used in carrying out the work.

2. Task identity—the task requires doing a whole job from beginning to end with a visible outcome.

3. Task significance—the job has a substantial impact on the lives of other people.

4. Autonomy—the job provides employee empowerment opportunities.

5. Job feedback—the job performance itself is a source of direct and clear information about how well the employee did the work.[6]

Success Tool: Empowering Employees Job **empowerment** is a key ingredient to reducing turnover. If employees are empowered to make a difference, they can, and then they can feel good about having done so. In the book *On Great Service*, Leonard Berry, a scholar who has written extensively on service, defines empowerment as a state of mind. Employees with this state of mind should feel the following:

- First, control over the job performance process.
- Second, the knowledge and the familiarity with the overall situation, the "big picture."
- Third, accountability for his or her work output.
- Fourth, an understanding and shared responsibility for the team's performance.
- Last, equity in the appraisals and rewards based on the performance.[7]

Empowerment can be translated into giving employees the authority and responsibility to apply their skills, education, knowledge, creativity, and incentives in serving their customers effectively. A service organization that is able to ensure empowerment is one more step closer to employee satisfaction and improved productivity.

Portuguese, French, German, Spanish, Chinese, and English Spoken Here

Research on cultural diversity in the workplace has exploded in the 1990s. Changing demographics continue to influence the makeup of the workforce. In North America, especially, immigrants from Asia, South America, and now even Eastern European countries, are comprising a greater percentage of the hospitality workforce.

Toronto, in the province of Ontario, Canada, is one North American city facing this human resource challenge. How does a hotel company incorporate personnel from all over the world and put out a quality product, when cultural differences among employees can be overwhelming? A study by Julia Christen-Hughes, of the University of Guelph, in Canada, addressed just these issues. She interviewed human resource directors at hotels in Toronto, and came to a number of interesting conclusions.

Language differences can have great impact on hotel operations, often greatly hindering communication between employees, and between employees and guests. Cultural differences, often intertwined with language barriers, seemed to be at the root of many employee–management problems. While some employees were accustomed to treating management deferentially, others were uncomfortable with autocratic rule.

How did human resources managers in Toronto deal with these issues? Successful companies recognized, and rewarded, employees' commitment to learning English, and employees were encouraged to attend multicultural training classes, to learn more about their coworkers. This helped establish the common ground for all employees. Second, a climate of mutual respect for ethnic backgrounds had to be encouraged. It had to be clear that all employees were valued as individuals, regardless of the position he or she held, or the country of origin.

Diversity in the workplace poses a great challenge to hospitality companies. How a hotel approaches the issue impacts the eventual success or failure of the hotel. From the experiences in Toronto, it is clear that valuing diversity at all levels of management helps provide a supportive work environment. In this environment, employees can strive to provide quality service to guests, the goal of any hotel company.

Source: Julia Christensen Hughes, "Cultural Diversity: The Lesson of Toronto Hotels" *Cornell HRA Quarterly*, April 1992. pp. 78-87.

Feature: Hospitality is Time Intensive, with Peaks and Valleys

Many hospitality organizations are open lengthy hours. Year-round lodging properties are open 24 hours a day, 365 days a year. Foodservice organizations serving three meals begin production early in the morning and end cleanup from the last meal late in the evening. These organizations also experience peaks and valleys in the business cycle. A ski lodge cafeteria, for example, must feed lunch to all of its hungry skiers in a relatively short time window. A downtown restaurant will also see a surge of business at the lunch hours.

Success Tool: Supplementing with Part-Time Help Many hospitality organizations use part-time help to cover the business peaks. In chapter 11, "A Hospitality Marketer's Tool Box," you will learn about other ways, besides using additional human capital, that hospitality organizations can address the peaks and valleys of the business operation. An extra set of challenges surfaces in an effort to keep part-time help motivated and fully informed. Expanding the population of potential employees for part-time (as well as full-time) help involves the implementation of the next two success tools, implementing flextime and providing child care.

Success Tool: Implementing Flextime Where Useful With today's workforce being younger, more mobile, more educated, and with more female employees than ever before, the evidence is overwhelming that alternative work schedules are one key way to recruit and retain working parents. Thus, new tools such as **flextime**, or flexible working hours, have appeared. If the hours can be established to coincide with the peak times of operation, so much the better. The Radisson Hotel chain provides a good example. Housekeepers are encouraged to establish a work schedule whereby young mothers come into work between 7:00 and 9:00 A.M. and go home at 3:00 P.M. Given that check-in time for most hotels is in the midafternoon, this scheduling is flexible and effective.

Interestingly enough, the concept of flextime had its beginnings in Munich, Germany, in 1967. At that time, an aerospace firm's access road for the establishment to the autobahn had become so obstructed with traffic that a system of flexible work hours was installed, thus solving a major traffic gridlock problem, as well as making life more comfortable for its people.

Success Tool: Implementing Child Care Where Useful One hospitality research study found that child care problems are highly significant predictors of employee absenteeism and unproductive work time. This study suggests that hospitality companies that offer some form of employee assistance in child care stand to benefit in the recruitment and retention of quality employees.[8] Radisson Hotels began reaching out to potential female employees, a group making up nearly half of the hotel industry's labor force, by inaugurating an advertising campaign, as follows:

- EXCELLENT BENEFITS for employees working 20+ hours per week. We recognize your need for a *part-time* position with flexible hours. Apply in person to …

- YOU WORK … WE PAY! Our hotel is a "family" and we offer child care subsidies for employees working 20+ hours per week …

- OUR SCHEDULE FITS YOURS! Flexible hours, part-time positions and excellent benefits create a great working environment …

- CHILD CARE??? WE CARE!!! Besides having a great place to work, we provide child care subsidies to employees averaging 20+ hours per week …[9]

Asked if she thought such novel recruitment advertising would pay off, Sue Gordon, Radisson's vice president of human resources responded; "IYAD,WYAD,YAG,WAG … **I**f **Y**ou **A**lways **D**o **W**hat **Y**ou **A**lways **D**id, **Y**ou'll **A**lways **G**et **W**hat **Y**ou **A**lways **G**ot."[10]

The foodservice segment of hospitality also found success in implementing child care as a worker benefit. Burger King billboards heralded: "I'm getting free day-care from Burger King" as part of its advertising campaign. Burger King involved local communities in its efforts. In Grand Rapids, Michigan, for example, its program for employees with dependent children involved subsidizing referral services and child care fees in collaboration with the local Community Coordinated Childcare Corporation (known locally as the 4C service). The 4C service maintains a network of information and referrals covering licensed and registered child care providers prepared to furnish competent care within Burger King's subsidy range. Once an employee selected a care provider, Grand Rapids Burger King paid $1.50 per hour per family, up to 32 hours per week.[11]

Meanwhile, Taco Bell's plan, their Choice Pay Reserve Account, providing employee reimbursement for dependent day care expenses, was being hailed by management as a breakeven solution to day care costs: "People are always asking 'Who's paying for this?' But the bottom line—we're coming out even because these women's work habits are so much better than [those of] the average employee that we've actually been able to reduce the number of workers needed."[12]

Feature: Effective Communication is Critical

No organization can function well without effective channels of communication. Using tools that foster employee participation, encourage employees to give quality service to one another, create quality teams, and manage a flow of information in all directions, enables a company to create an environment where human resources flourish.

Success Tool: Encouraging Participation Having employees be an integral and important part of the decision-making process of a company is not a new idea. The implementation of participation has taken several forms over time, having been presented under such rubrics as the Scanlon Plan, quality of work life, quality circles, and participative management. Though each approach is different in title and execution, the guiding philosophy behind all of these approaches is the same: People give more to their work when they have more say in how the company is run.

Early on, elements of participative management had become visible in the development of the **Scanlon Plan** of the 1930s. By the 1990s, the advantages of that plan were being featured by such companies as United Airlines, which, after its employees became its owners, proudly included in its advertising campaigns, "Come fly *our* friendly skies." In a nutshell, the Scanlon Plan created an organizational atmosphere in which:

a. Employees feel free to make suggestions without fear of ridicule. They can criticize and ask questions about company operations that used to be considered none of their business.

b. Managers come to see the value in sharing *all* of the company operating information and in benefiting from suggestions that reveal managerial weaknesses.

The early 1970s saw the emergence of joint union-management **quality of work life (QWL)** experiments. By 1977, these QWL experiments were being defined by the American Center for the Quality of Work Life in the following way:

Any activity at every level of an organization which seeks greater organizational effectiveness through the enhancement of human dignity and growth...a process or approach through which the stakeholders in the organization (management, employees, and the union, if any) learn how to work together more effectively in order to determine for themselves what actions, changes, and improvements are desirable and workable in order to achieve the twin and simultaneous goals of improved quality of life at work for all employees of the organization and greater effectiveness of the organization itself.

During the 1980s, **quality circles** emerged as one of the more popular forms of employee participation. Essentially, the "circles" tended to take the form of work teams engaged in problem-solving. Several hotel and restaurant companies established some form of quality circles. Days Inns, for example, ran a full-page advertisement in the December 1987 issue of *Lodging Hospitality* magazine. It headlined "People Circles" a winner at Days Inns, and described "People Circles as our way of bringing employees into the decision-making process for work rules and incentive plans that affect them directly."[13]

The idea of quality circles was not going unnoticed in European hotels. For Accor, a French hotel company, quality circles had achieved positive results. By 1988, the chain had 130 quality circles in operation, with more than 10 percent of its hotel employees in France having participated in at least one circle. Accor had discovered that the opportunity to participate in management increased employees' commitment to their jobs so dramatically that participative management had become an integral part of the entire Accor hotel management system.[14]

However, although several hospitality companies and 70 percent of the Fortune 1000 companies were reported to be using quality circles in 1987, one scholar, Edward E. Lawler III, found that such arrangements in general were bureaucratic, top down, and deficient in those characteristics usually associated with participative approaches to management.[15] An important lesson is that implementation does not necessarily mean success.

These historical examples of engendering participation continue to be applied today in new forms. The restaurant chain, Au Bon Pain, for example, has done much in the structuring of its compensation package to have its managers behave like owners. Sheraton is restructuring its hotels to create individual profit centers within the hotel. This restructuring, it is hoped, will create greater participation and accountability from each manager. Thus an individual restaurant's managers are responsible for and empowered to change that particular outlet's profit and loss.

Success Tool: Employing Internal Guarantees As we learned in chapter 3, "The Hospitality Business Is a Service Business," companies should be aware of the advantages of service guarantees and use them when it makes sense. The same kinds of guarantees can also be applied with great advantages when used internally. Internal guarantees are applied when employees commit to providing breakthrough service for one another. For example, interviewers of prospective employees might assure the human resources manager that feedback will be returned the same day, allowing the manager to deliver quick response to candidates. Managers might also guarantee a same day response for messages left for one another if the messages are labeled urgent.

The guarantees, which are provided by and for internal customers, have guidelines similar to those of service guarantees. Not only do internal guarantees help employees work well with one another; research suggests that when implemented, they can also achieve greater customer satisfaction.[16]

Success Tool: Investing in Quality Teams By nature, the hospitality business requires a team-oriented approach to operations. A front desk clerk is unable to deliver complete and high-quality check-in service without the cooperation of the bellstaff. The server at the restaurant can't deliver the best service if the kitchen staff doesn't cooperate. The success of every service delivery depends on team cooperation in the front and the back of the house. In addition, management can create more effective service delivery by listening to and involving employees from all departments in a cross-functional team effort. In smaller operations, cross functionality happens automatically, when often one person serves more than one role. In larger organizations, exposure to other departments and other levels of the organization must be built in. Several large companies such as McDonald's and Hyatt make a point of having senior managers do nonmanagerial work as part of their training. Such training serves as a vivid reminder of what happens at the french fryer or the front desk and means that managers don't have to ask or imagine what it's like to do the work; they experience it.

Success Tool: Managing Top Down and Bottom Up Free-flowing communication in a service establishment is vital for motivation, morale, teamwork, and productivity. Free-flowing communication means flexible bottom-up and top-down communication. Employees should not feel any hesitation to voice their opinions and comments about their work, managers, company, and peers. On the other hand, management should share information with its employees. In return, employees will appreciate the free-flowing communication, and consequently their satisfaction and loyalty will increase.[17]

The bottom-up and top-down communication can be achieved via regular staff meetings, a company newsletter, flyers, voice mail, e-mail, training and development workshops, regular performance appraisal procedures, and one-on-one interaction between all employees and managers.

Feature: Legal and Social Policies Have Influence

As is true for all American employers, a whole series of legislation governs the hiring and employment practices of hospitality companies. These laws range from the Family and Medical Leave Act of 1993, which grants leave of 12 weeks per year in companies of 50 or more persons, to the Americans with Disabilities Act (ADA) of 1990, which dictates that an employer cannot discriminate based on a worker's disabilities. Other laws, in effect for some time, are also in place to assure fair and equitable treatment in employment. Title VII of the Civil Rights Act of 1964 prohibits discrimination based on an individual's race, sex, color, religion, or national origin. The Equal Pay Act of 1963 prohibits discrimination in pay rates on the basis of gender. Legislation and individual contracts also govern the rights of labor unions in the country.

In addition to legislation, the actions of human resources managers are governed by social conditions, and in particular health issues related to AIDS, substance abuse, and alcoholism.

Success Tool: Understanding the Impact of Labor Unions Collaboration between management and labor unions is one mode through which the participative process of involving employees may function effectively. It was not always so.

The power of employees to bargain collectively with employers to protect themselves from unfair treatment has haunted both industry and government since ancient times. As far back as the fourteenth century, concerted employee strikes and/or slowdowns were being prosecuted in the English courts for violation of the criminal conspiracy laws. Not until the middle of the nineteenth century did the British Parliament decide that the doctrine of criminal conspiracy did not apply to labor unions.

In the United States, this doctrine of criminal conspiracy served to restrain the right of workers to organize until 1842. It was then that the Massachusetts Supreme Court ruled in *Commonwealth vs. Hunt* that the act of union formation could scarcely be considered unlawful, especially since its aim was simply to get all the workers employed in a craft to join.

Even so, the U.S. labor movement has had a long and turbulent history, from the Philadelphia shoemakers' strike in 1794, to the founding of the Chicago Bartenders and Waiters Union in 1866, the American Federation of Labor in 1886, the Waiters and Bartenders National Union in 1891 (known today as the **Hotel Employees & Restaurant Employees International Union**, AFL-CIO), the CIO in 1935, and the merger of the AFL-CIO in 1955. Even today, unions struggle for survival.

While more than 30 percent of the workforce belonged to unions in the 1950s, data from the U.S. Bureau of Labor Statistics show that union membership generally had fallen to 17 percent of the workforce by the early 1990s. In the case of the Hotel Employees & Restaurant Employees International Union (HEREIU), membership had dropped to 12 percent of the workforce in the hotel and restaurant industry. While efforts to excite hotel unions in the United States about quality of work life (participative management) have thus far been unavailing, momentum for such ideas has been building in other corporate sectors for over two decades.

With respect to the Hotel Employees & Restaurant Employees Union, despite the implication that organized crime may be gaining a foothold in big-city hospitality organizations, seasoned observers believe it to be most unlikely. In fact, with nearly 90 percent of the workforce being nonunion in the hospitality industry, it is probable that this industry remains untainted by the threat of organized crime.

Though only a small percentage of hotels is unionized, in one that is, comprehending the rights and policies and maintaining a good relationship with the union is critical to success. A case in point from a unionized New York City hotel in which a small detail became a big headache illustrates the point.

The food and beverage department of the hotel decided to implement a fresh orange juice promotion. The promotion was to include placing a fresh orange with a sign attached by a toothpick on the breakfast tables each morning. The management was not on particularly good terms with the union at the time, and union members refused to put the oranges on the table. They cited the paragraph from the union contract that listed the salt and pepper shakers, napkins, and so on, that were to be put on the table as part of the job description. An orange was not among the list. Until relations improved, management found itself carrying trays of oranges in the morning.

Success Tool: Addressing Workplace Health Concerns: AIDS, Drugs, Alcoholism Among the myriad of problems facing the hospitality industry today, perhaps none is more devastating or complex than that posed by the worldwide epidemic of AIDS (Acquired Immune Deficiency Syndrome). Within the next two decades, according to the U.S. Secretary of Health and Human Services, some 50 to 100 million people in the world may contract this disease. In 1992, the National Center for Disease Control (CDC) announced that 210,000 people in the United States had either been diagnosed as having AIDS or had already died from AIDS complications. At the same time, the CDC pointed out that approximately one million Americans had contracted the HIV virus, the forerunner to AIDS.[18]

Issues concerning AIDS in the workplace generally arise when one or more of the following situations occur:

1. Employees who test seropositive for AIDS are hired.

2. Fellow employees express concern about exposure to a worker with AIDS.

3. Customers/guests come in contact with employees who have AIDS.

4. Applicants and incumbent employees are tested for the HIV virus (indicative of a likelihood of developing AIDS).

5. Employers exercise their duties with respect to a worker with AIDS.[19]

When the **Americans with Disabilities Act** (ADA) took effect in 1992 (the Act was signed in 1990, but took effect in 1992) AIDS, along with drug and alcohol addiction, was included in the wide-ranging list of disabilities protected by that act. The hospitality industry fought a losing battle in support of the **Chandler Amendment**, which would have allowed operators to assign employees with communicable diseases to non-food-handling jobs. The amendment suffered defeat because no evidence could be adduced to show that AIDS is transmitted by food or by casual contact. Accordingly, hospitality operators must make all positions open to all disabled individuals, including those with a disabling disease, such as AIDS.[20]

Drug abuse, and what to do about it, is also a critical health issue faced by hospitality operations. There is some evidence that treating the problem head-on is a viable option. An in-depth study of the costs and benefits of substance abuse treatment programs was undertaken at two casino hotels, the Mirage in Las Vegas and Resorts International in Atlantic City. The study indicated positive results from the implementation of **Employee Assistance Programs (EAPS)** in these casino hotels.[21] Neither hotel screens applicants or employees for substance abuse unless there is persuasive evidence of erratic work behavior. If a medical examination discloses substance abuse, the employee may be dismissed, or, at the company's option, be given a one-time chance to participate in an EAP. A treated employee who is still "clean" after a six-month period of EAP participation is counted as a success. In the case of Resorts International, 85 percent of the 137 treated employees were still employed one year after their EAP enrollment. Eighty percent of Mirage employees were clean after six months of treatment. The cost-benefit conclusion of the study was that the employers' investment in substance abuse EAPs can be paid for in part by the savings due to reduced absenteeism and turnover, as well as savings generated through increased employee productivity.

Employee Assistance Programs have also been cited as a potential solution to problems caused by alcoholism. In support of this conclusion are two hotel companies that regarded their EAP investments to be most worthwhile:

1. Ramada's John Rock said, "Two dollars are gained for every dollar you spend on the program."

2. At the Nugget Hotel and Casino in Sparks, Nevada, the turnover rate among supervisors and middle- and upper-level management decreased about 10 percent, while the turnover rate of hourly workers dropped about 3.5 percent.[22]

The Role of the Hospitality Human Resources Manager

Having reviewed the characteristics that shape hospitality human resources management and their corresponding success tools, we now take the understanding of the role of a human resources manager one step further. In this section we look on the desk top and in the in box of a hospitality professional, and place you squarely in the shoes of a human resources manager.

Responsibilities of a Human Resources Manager

The short answer is "Hiring and firing." The question is "What do most people perceive as the key responsibilities of a human resources manager?" It is no surprise, given the constant turnover in hotels and restaurants, especially at the entry-level positions, that people see the HR department as the circular driveway of employment. A new employee comes on board as another one leaves. Contrary to popular belief, human resources managers spend less of their time on managing entry and exit of personnel than on the many other aspects involved. Actually, a majority of their time is focused on recruiting, training, developing job descriptions, mediating labor laws, and employee relations, just to name a few activities.

Interestingly enough, the process of managing human resources does not stop at the human resources office door; it extends throughout the entire organization. The duties being performed by the human resources department need to be shared and competently practiced by the managers in every department. It is as critical for a restaurant manager to be knowledgeable in the field of human resources as it is for the HR professional. Therefore, the HR department has an obligation to train managers at all levels on issues such as the importance of asking legal questions during the interview process, avoiding discrimination, and developing and being a mentor for your employees. The success of the organization depends on everyone being familiar with these common HR practices.

Functions of a Hospitality Human Resources Manager

The HR department's functions are broad and varied. Human resources is multifaceted, with functions that are intertwined. One minute after mediating a disagreement between two employees, an HR manager may plan a strategy for the upcoming busy season' s hiring. The phone will ring, and someone will question the legality of pre-employment testing. Exhibit 10.1 presents a profile of the responsibilities of a human resources manager.

Exhibit 10.1 Human Resources Functions

Function	Description	Example
Enforcement of Laws	■ Upholding U.S., state, and local laws governing labor	■ The Civil Rights Act of 1964 ■ Americans with Disabilities Act (1990)
Job Analysis	■ Deciding what jobs are necessary ■ Determining required skills ■ Writing/updating job descriptions	■ "For Geneal Manager position: B.S. degree required from hotel management program; 10–15 years proven experience in large convention hotel."
Recruiting	■ Soliciting applicants for open positions	■ Attending job fairs, career fairs ■ Advertising jobs in newspapers ■ Offering walk-in application hours ■ Interviewing candidates
Training	■ Teaching new employees how the company operates ■ Updating current employees' knowledge	■ Developing manuals ■ Holding training sessions

Exhibit 10.1 *(Continued)*

Function	Description	Example
Evaluating/ Performance Management	■ Verifying each employee's level of productivity ■ Contributing to their growth/skills in their position	■ Completing evaluation forms in conjunction with department managers ■ Communicating results with employees ■ Establishing goals
Compensation	■ Determining salary for each position	■ Setting weekly or monthly pay cycles ■ Determining merit raises, cost of living increases
Benefits	■ Health Insurance ■ Pension/Retirement Planning ■ Profit Sharing ■ Life Insurance ■ Social Security ■ Unemployment ■ Workers' Compensation ■ Educational Programs (Tuition Remission) ■ Child & Dependent Care ■ Employee Assistance Programs	■ 2 weeks vacation per calendar year for new employees ■ Developing on-site day care facilities ■ Offering employee meals in company cafeteria ■ Reimbursement offered for college tuition
Unions/ Collective Bargaining	■ Working within the rules of the National Labor Relations Act ■ Negotiating contracts with employees ■ Negotiating grievance process	Bargaining contracts generally cover: ■ Wages ■ Work week ■ Salary ■ Overtime ■ Seniority ■ Work conditions ■ Drug testing
Safety	■ Upholding standards of OSHA—Occupational Safety and Health Act of 1970 ■ Providing a safe work environment	■ Investigating accidents ■ Maintaining accurate records ■ Posting signs reminding employees of hazards (i.e., grease fires in kitchens)
Turnover	■ Replacing personnel due to retirement, voluntary changes, or dismissal ■ Establishing appeals process and exit interview guidelines	■ Developing employee retention programs (e.g., tuition remission) ■ Reevaluating hiring practices

(Continued)

▬▬▬▬▬ *Exhibit 10.1* Human Resources Functions *(Continued)*

Function	Description	Example
Turnover *(Continued)*	• Labor planning	• Disciplining/firing poor performers • Analyzing staffing needs/ requirements
Ethics	• Social responsibility of organization • Attempting to enhance the interests of society	• Encouraging participation in volunteer activities • Charitable events
Employee Relations	• Organizing events for all employees • Communicating events companywide • Employee recognition/awards	• All employee meetings • Soccer leagues • Annual picnics/holiday parties • Company newsletter • Bulletin boards • Employee of the Month
Managing Diversity	• Providing equal opportunity • Accommodating all needs and capabilities	• Hiring minorities • Hiring people with disabilities • Changing job requirements/ tools to accommodate someone with a disability

What's in the In Box?

Imagine you are standing in the shoes of a director of human resources for a 1,200-room convention hotel in Hong Kong. You put your briefcase down and begin to tackle the issues on your desk. Here's what you might find:

1. The file on the talented employee who is interested in transferring to your property in the Philippines. You think the employee could use more training in his current position, but you don't want to risk losing him to the competition if he is not transferred.

2. A proposal you are considering from an international training company, titled "Are You Emphasizing the Internal Customer Enough?" You are concerned that the program will not be customized enough for your specific property.

3. The reservations manager is upset about an ongoing problem between his department and sales. His complaint involves a charge that the sales managers have been submitting incomplete contracts to reservations. Two days ago, the reservations manager charged that the sales department didn't inform the front desk of the increase in the number of guests in a group from Malaysia, and that, since the hotel was 100 percent occupied, the staff had to walk a dozen people from the group to a nearby competitor.

4. The director of sales and marketing at your hotel is one of the company's best employees, with a citywide reputation for his creativity. He is a dedicated leader with uncanny intuition. Last week you heard from one of the hotel's best sales managers (who reports directly

to the director) that the director has informed her that she was not being considered for a promotion because as a woman she won't be the right representative to sell to the top corporate accounts.

5. You have been tracking turnover in the housekeeping area, and have noticed a dramatic increase in the last three months. You need first to isolate the problem, then review with the department's managers the costs associated with turnover.

Measuring Success

The human resources manager is responsible for establishing and reviewing performance measures, keeping in mind that the purpose of these measures is to help achieve the greatest level of effectiveness possible. Different managers use different kinds of measurement tools, including: turnover and absenteeism, opinion surveys, exit interviews, employee and guest satisfaction questionnaires. For example, in one case, a manager has been experiencing high turnover and wants to determine exactly what percentage of the staff has turned over in the past year. He uses the following formula:

$$\text{Annual turnover rate} = \frac{\text{\# of terminations} \times 100\%}{\text{Average \# of employees}}$$

This hotel has had an average of 500 employees, and in the past year 612 employees have left. The formula is presented below.

$$\text{Annual turnover rate} = \frac{612}{500} \times 100\% \quad \text{Annual turnover rate} = 1.22 \times 100\% = 122\%$$

In this example, the hotel's staff is turning over approximately 1.2 times per year. The human resources manager then takes into consideration how much it costs to recruit, hire, and train a new employee, and then reminds himself to review the success tools for managing turnover! Exhibit 10.2 depicts the various kinds of measurements typically used in human resources.

Exhibit 10.2 Human Resources Measurement Tools

Productivity Measures	<ul><li>cost per hire</li><li>health care cost per hire</li><li># of employees</li><li>cost per trainee</li><li>Total Revenue/Total # of employees</li></ul>
Quality Measures	<ul><li># of qualified candidates/# of candidates interviewed</li><li>% of payroll</li><li># of descriptions redone</li><li># of description requests</li><li>% of correct paychecks</li></ul>
Timeliness Measures	<ul><li>time to fill jobs</li><li>time to process claims</li></ul>
Other Measures	<ul><li>% system downtime</li><li>accidents per 100 employees</li></ul>

Adapted from "Measuring and Improving HR Function," *Employment Relations Today,* Spring 1994

Creating Competitive Advantage

Human resources can be used as a powerful strategic tool to create a strong foundation of skills, culture, and talent, which can be translated into great service and profits, if properly managed. If organizations are to survive in a service-oriented economy and in a constantly changing, knowledge-based work environment, human resources must function as a strategic partner with management.[23] Projecting a competitive advantage in human resources involves hiring and supporting forward thinkers, investing in training and development, and offering competitive benefits and compensation.

Summary

In the end, the good news is that effective management of human resources will help those that apply the right tools move out of the pack into enviable leadership positions. These tools include:

- effective recruiting
- effective training and development
- encouraging diversity
- treating employees as internal customers
- constantly addressing motivation and morale
- empowering employees
- supplementing with part-time help
- implementing flextime
- implementing child care
- encouraging communication and participation
- employing internal guarantees
- investing in quality teams
- managing top down and bottom up
- understanding the impact of labor unions
- staying on top of workplace heath concerns

Current practices show wide variations in the range of responsibilities assigned to human resources executives in the hospitality industry. Hiring, training, payroll, and all of their corresponding forms are just a part of what a human resources department does. A human resources manager must be an integral part of the entire organization. He or she must understand the key features of human resources management and encourage human beings in the workplace to care more, know more, and do more.

Discussion Questions

1. Of all the functions performed in the management of human resources, which ones do you consider to be most important and which ones least important? Give your reasons.

2. What methods can a hospitality establishment use most effectively to locate and recruit employees who have the "right stuff"? Justify your answer.

3. What advantages and disadvantages do you see in the concept of participative management? Cite as many examples as you can from your own work experience, illustrating where and when such a concept could have worked and where and when it could not have worked. Explain why or why not.

4. To what degree do you believe that the HR manager is responsible for providing solutions to a company's overall problems?

5. What kinds of performance measures do human resources managers use?

6. What kinds of costs are created because of turnover?

7. How does an internal guarantee differ from a guarantee extended to customer? (See chapter 3 to review customers' guarantees.) How are they the same?

8. As the opening quotation suggests, changing human behavior requires measuring the difference between old behavior and new behavior, and rewarding the new behavior. Why are measurement and reward so important?

Assignments

1. Consider all of the items in the in box of the hospitality human resources manager. To which would you give the highest priority? The lowest priority? Why? How would you tackle each item? Assume the role of the human resources manager. Develop a work plan using the success tools in the chapter.

2. Pick a position in a hospitality organization that is of particular interest to you (it can be at any level). Create a list of 10 interview questions for that job. Why did you select the questions you did? What skill set are you looking for?

3. Provide an example of a hospitality company that has been particularly effective in handling a human resources issue. Clearly define the issues the company faced and the action steps it took to solve the problem.

4. Find an example of a hospitality company that features a particular employee in its advertisement. Is the advertisement only important to customers? Why might it be important to internal customers as well?

End Notes

1. Mark E. Nunnelly, Managing Director at Bain Capital, Boston, MA.

2. Bill Fromm and Len Schlesinger, *The Real Heros of Business* (New York: Currency Doubleday, 1994), 112.

3. Harold E. Lane, personal recollection of an actual event.

4. *Restaurants and Institutions* (7 August 1989): 44.

5. *Opportunity 2000: Create Affirmative Action Strategies for a Changing Workforce*, a study prepared for the Employment Standards Administration of the U.S. Department of Labor (Indianapolis: Hudson Institute, September 1988), 94–95.

6. Benjamin Schneider and David E. Bowen, *Winning the Service Game*, (Boston: Harvard Business School Press, 1995), 157.

7. Leonard L. Berry, *On Great Service—A Framework for Action* (The Free Press, 1995).

8. Janet H. Marler and Cathy A. Enz, "Child-Care Programs That Make Sense," *Cornell Hotel and Restaurant Administration Quarterly* (February 1993): 61.

9. *Lodging* (October 1988): 52. Author not identified, but list is from the Radisson Mark Plaza in Alexandria, Virginia.

10. Michael R. Neer, "The Recruitment Challenge," *Lodging* (June 1988): 66–69.

11. Ibid.

12. Sally Stephenson, "The Corporate Playroom," *Restaurants and Institutions* (28 October 1988): 80.

13. *Lodging Hospitality* (December 1987): 68.

    Note: In response to an inquiry in 1989 as to how well the People Circles program was working, Days Inn President Leven said that the only information he had about the program was what appeared in the magazine advertisement.

14. Christopher Orly, "Quality Circles in France: Accor's Experiment in Self-Management," *Cornell Hotel and Restaurant Administration Quarterly* (November 1988): 50–57.

15. Edward E. Lawler III, *The Ultimate Advantage* (San Francisco: Jossey-Bass, 1992), 123.

16. Christopher Hart, "The Power of Internal Guarantees," *Harvard Business Review* (January–February 1995): 64–73.

17. Robert H. Waterman Jr., Judith A. Waterman, and Betsy A. Collard, "Toward a Career-Resilient Workforce," *Harvard Business Review* (July–August 1994), 87–95.

18. "AIDS Toll," *USA Today*, 17 January 1992, D1.

19. John A. Fossum, ed., *Employee and Labor Relations* (Washington, DC: The Bureau of National Affairs, Inc., 1990), 103–105.

20. Robert H. Woods and Raphael R. Kavanaugh, "Here Comes the ADA—Are You Ready?" pt. 1, *Cornell Hotel and Restaurant Administration Quarterly* (February 1992): 29.

    For an exhaustive report on the anticipated impact of ADA on the hospitality industry, the reader is urged to read both the Woods and Kavanaugh article and the companion *Cornell Hotel and Restaurant Administration Quarterly* article by John P. Kohl and Paul S. Greenlaw, "The ADA, Part II: Implications for Managers."

21. Andrew N. Klebanow and Robert W. Eder, "Cost Effectiveness of Substance-Abuse Treatment in Casino Hotels" (*Cornell Hotel & Restaurant Administration Quarterly*) (February 1992): 56–67.

22. Ibid.

23. *HR Magazine* 39 (December 1994): 52–54.

Chapter Eleven

"Say, Tom, let me whitewash a little."

Tom considered, was about to consent; but he altered his mind: "No-no-I reckon it wouldn't hardly do, Ben. You see, Aunt Polly's awful particular about this fence—right here on the street, you know—but if it was the back fence I wouldn't mind and she wouldn't. Yes she's awful particular about this fence; it's got to be done very careful; I reckon there ain't one boy in a thousand, maybe two thousand that can do it the way it's got to be done."...

"Oh shucks, I'll be just as careful. Now lemme try. Say—I'll give you the core of my apple."

Mark Twain [1]

A Hospitality Marketer's Tool Box ↶

When you finish this chapter you should:

1. Understand the features of hospitality marketing and the success tools that can be employed in response to those features.

2. Understand why services marketing is different than product marketing.

3. Know what is meant by "tangibilizing the intangible."

4. Know how to think about manipulating supply and demand, and understand why it is easier to manipulate one than the other.

5. Understand the concept of yield management and know how it can be useful to a marketer.

6. Know what makes waiting lines for a service seem longer, and shorter.

7. Understand that services fall on a continuum from standardization to customization.

8. Explain the four elements of the hospitality marketing mix.

9. Identify the different types of communication vehicles used by marketers.

10. Define what elements comprise good positioning and be able to give an example of a positioning statement.

11. Be able to identify the kinds of issues that might be found in the box of a hospitality marketer.

Introduction

Though Tom Sawyer's salesmanship garnered him all the neighborhood's treasures while three coats of whitewash were added to Aunt Polly's fence in the 1870s, he would probably not have much success in the 1990s. Regis McKenna, a seasoned marketing consultant, notes in his article "Marketing Is Everything" that "we are witnessing the emergence of a new marketing paradigm—not a 'do more' marketing that simply turns up the volume on the sales spiels of the past but a knowledge- and experience-based marketing that represents the once-and-for-all death of the salesman."[2]

Establishing Effective Hospitality Marketing

So how and where do we begin in the hospitality business to establish good marketing?

Good **marketing**, above all else, requires vision. Keen perception of customers' needs and what motivates them, with an understanding of your own company and the competitive environment in which you operate, is the critical starting point for a marketer. In a classic article published decades ago but still applicable today, Theodore Levitt warns marketers of a blinding mistake, developing **"marketing myopia."**[3] This faulty perspective is one through which a firm fails to recognize changes in the environment, does not have a clear understanding of the nature of the business it is in, and therefore lets others take customers away from it.

At first blush, a theme restaurant like Benihana may think of itself as being in the restaurant business. It is true that it serves food like other Japanese restaurants, but because it also provides theater, this operation is really in the entertainment business as well. The chef cooking right at the table is definitely entertainment. This company should think about movie theaters and other evening entertainment concepts as competition. An airline that offers discounted fares, like the now defunct People's Express, should not think of itself as being in the airline business, but in the people moving business, as the name suggested. Other types of people transportation, such as buses, trains, and people driving themselves, should be considered as part of the competitive realm.

A company with "marketing myopia" is **product oriented**, not **customer oriented**. It assumes that the customer wants a better mousetrap, when what the customer really wants is dead mice. The focus is on selling rather than marketing.

There is more than a semantic difference between the words **marketing** and **selling**. The difference is in the focus. The focus of marketing is on what needs the buyer has, while the seller focuses on the needs of the seller. Marketing is devoted to satisfying the customer, while a seller is trying to convert a product into cash.[4] You may recall the *adult* customer in chapter 3 who wasn't able to order the peanut butter and jelly sandwich because it was on the *children's* menu. This is the nub of how a product orientation loses customers.

Distinguishing Features of Hospitality Marketing

Winning customers and retaining them involves a cluster of things, as Levitt mentions above. In his definition he speaks of products. In the hospitality industry, as with any service business, one must

Customizing Cuisine

"And which regional cuisine would you be interested in this evening—Northwestern, Southwestern, Southeastern, or Northeastern?"

think beyond simply products to products *and* services. A marketer in a service business can gain marketing advantage by understanding the nature of the differences between products and services. These differences have real and important implications for how a marketer should communicate with his customer.

In comparing services and products, the following characteristics emerge: Services are intangible dominant; services can't be inventoried; services are simultaneously produced and consume; and services are less uniform than products. These characteristics shape the success tools that a hospitality marketer can use to establish more effective marketing.

Feature: Services are Intangible Dominant

Shoes come in specific sizes. You can try them on, put them in a box, and take them home with you. They can be stored on a shelf until you are ready to wear them. When you put them on, they fit as they did in the store. If you wear them on Wednesday, they will look nearly the same as they did on Tuesday.

Vacations have unlimited outcomes. You can't sample the vacation before you go, though the use of CD ROM and virtual reality technology are moving the customers a step closer to sampling! You can't store up your vacation for later or take it home with you after it is over. You have a general impression about how much you enjoyed your trip; some things you liked, others you didn't. It was sunny on Tuesday. It rained on Wednesday.

These contrasting examples illustrate some of the differences between **products** and **services**. It is important to note that there are very few pure products or pure services, but in fact most entities are a combination of varying degrees of products and services. Services tend to be **intangible dominant**, and products tend to be **tangible dominant**. Figure 11.1 illustrates a continuum of products and services.

Success Tool: Tangibilize the Intangible Service marketers should look for ways to "tangibilize the intangible," to make services more easily grasped. Consider the following examples:

- Hotel Ducks
- Ronald McDonald
- Garfield the Cat

At precisely 11:00 A.M. every day, a fanfare is sounded, and four mallard ducks and their Duck Master parade across the red carpet in the lobby of the Peabody Hotel in Memphis, Tennessee. They take their places in the fountain for the afternoon. At 5:00 P.M., the procedure is reversed. The ducks leave the fountain for their evening accommodations. Crowds gather for the parade, and the Peabody is blessed with a longstanding and, perhaps more importantly, tangible symbol for the hotel. Ducks abound in the hotel's decorative scheme in everything, down to the embossed duck soaps. VIPs are given the privilege of escorting the ducks as Honorary Duck Masters, and the winged birds even go on the road to make sales calls.[5]

At first this approach may seem like quackery, but it illustrates an important tool that service marketers can employ to enhance their marketing efforts. Like Ronald McDonald, or finicky Garfield the Cat used by the Embassy Suites chain, the ducks create a tangible symbol for the predominantly intangible nature of hospitality services. These symbols also provide a means for creating **brand recognition**. The ducks communicate red carpet treatment, Garfield that even the most finicky client is satisfied, and Ronald, all the happiness and fun that a smiling clown stands for. Other types of services similarly attach a tangible symbol to help communicate with the customer—the "good hands" people at Allstate, Merrill Lynch's "bull," the Traveler's "umbrella," or a piece of the Prudential "rock."[6]

Success Tool: Clue Management The use of tangible elements need not be limited to corporate symbols. In fact, a hotel or restaurant can and should manage a collection of clues to create an overall impression or presentation in the customer's mind. Sanitation strips across toilet seats may change your guest's opinion about the cleanliness of a bathroom. Sending a maintenance person into a meeting room to "inspect" the thermostat (even if temperature is controlled centrally) may be important to an irate conventioneer who called to complain.

Clues can also dictate what a property is *not*. A lobby filled with priceless antiques and glass vases does not communicate "Children welcome here." Customers dressed in black tie attire do not communicate "cheap eats" to a student crowd. Note that customers themselves are important clues, which can be managed through rules such as dress codes.

What clues can be managed? In addition to price, which is perhaps the loudest clue of all, anything the customer can see, hear, touch, taste, or smell can be managed. An indoor restaurant that simulates outdoor space is a helpful illustration. The ceiling is high and dotted with stars, a gentle

Figure 11.1 Scale of Market Entities

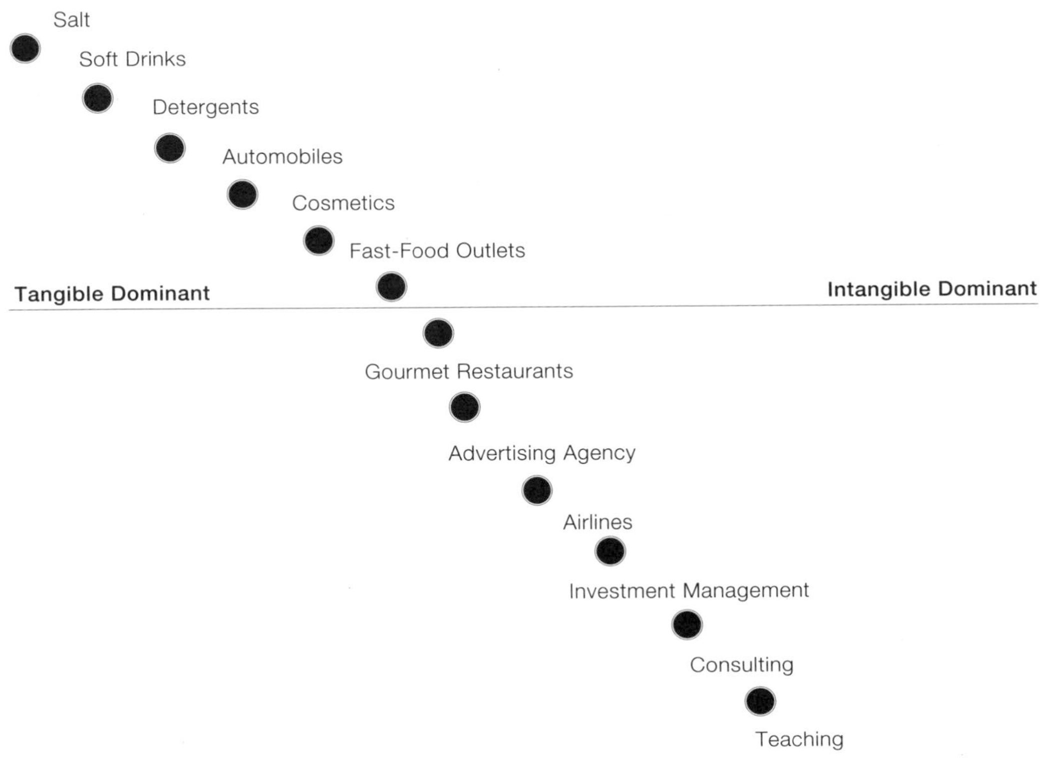

Salt

Soft Drinks

Detergents

Automobiles

Cosmetics

Fast-Food Outlets

Tangible Dominant

Gourmet Restaurants

Advertising Agency

Airlines

Investment Management

Consulting

Teaching

Intangible Dominant

Adapted from G. Lynn Shostack, " Breaking Free from Product Marketing ," *Journal of Marketing.*

breeze is fanned, tape recorded crickets pipe constantly, and the restaurant's furniture is what you'd expect to see on a front porch. In summary, understanding the intangible nature of services and consequently managing tangible clues is a useful marketing tool.

Feature: Services Can't Be Inventoried

Unlike products, which can be stored on a shelf, services can't be inventoried. When an airplane takes off, empty seats can never be recovered. Last night's vacant hotel room doesn't compensate for tonight's overbooking problem. Because services are time bound, they are more perishable than even the ripest fruit; at least the life of a strawberry can be extended as jam.

The implication for the marketer is to manipulate supply or demand, in the sense of managing skillfully, so that the largest number of customers can be served. Ideally, this means synchronizing the number of customers to match exactly the capacity available at all times, be it hotel rooms, restaurant seats, or lanes available in the health club's swimming pool.[7]

Success Tool: Manipulating Supply **Manipulating supply** to better match demand patterns in the hotel business can be difficult. There is a fixed number of rooms to sell in any given night. For a host city hotel to consider adding a new wing to accommodate Super Bowl weekend is hardly a workable option! A hotel may be able to provide better service, however, by increasing its part-time housekeeping staff to assure that all rooms are ready for sale at check-in time, even if the night before was sold out.

A hotel may also use **automation** to provide better service, particularly during peak times. Express check-out is a good example. A guest can call up her bill on the television screen in the room and sign off, or sign the express bill delivered to her room early in the morning. Some hotels are now also using express check-in. This allows the guest to check in with a credit card, bypassing the clerk at the front desk, and also the line of people waiting to see the clerk at the front desk.

A hotel or restaurant can use technology to provide the right amount of service. Sophisticated computer programs are now being used by chain organizations to project sales for each menu item, to project weekly and daily sales figures, and to schedule needed personnel according to hourly business forecasts. Similar software programs have been developed for hourly forecasting of rooms occupancy, rooms revenue, and the number of employees needed to service each hour of projected room sales.[8] Though the enhanced service that computer technology provides will be appreciated and will probably pay back in repeat business, a hotel is still limited by the unit it uses to count sales, the number of room nights.

A restaurant may squeeze in an extra table, offer a limited menu in the bar area, set up a take-out window, or hire extra part-time help to assist in busy times. The amount of capacity can be stretched but is still limited by physical space, and by the size and productivity of the kitchen. Another option to consider would be substituting equipment for labor. For example, a food processor could help the kitchen staff produce meals more quickly. Staff should be coached to perform only necessary functions during peak times and to reserve support activities for slack times. For example, a bartender should not be cutting lemons during the busy predinner cocktail hour.

Encouraging customer participation is another way to enhance capacity. Customers in some fast food restaurants now fill their own cups and clear their own trays. The advantage this approach provides is that the customers' needs are met at exactly the right time, presumably courteously and efficiently! (The disadvantage is that the customer may not be willing or able to participate.)

A cruise ship, like a hotel, has a limited number of accommodations. It also has some additional constraints. Guests don't **walk in** (a hotel term for a guest without a reservation). It is not surprising then that the cruise industry has become more flexible in letting people off and on board at every port, not just at the beginning and end of the cruise. There is a limited number of staff or service providers on a ship. It is helpful in this scenario to cross-train employees to perform different tasks so they can switch from one task to another as demand dictates.

When supply resources are expensive and underutilized, a service should consider sharing capacity with another business. Airlines, for example, may share gates or luggage carousels. A group of six hotels may agree to share the same set of vehicles to provide transportation to and from the local airport. This would allow each individual hotel to provide more frequent service for less cost. One disadvantage of such cost sharing, however, is that one hotel may "steal" customers from another hotel.

This series of examples demonstrates some of the ways that supply can be enhanced in the hospitality business:

- automate to provide better, more efficient service
- substitute equipment for labor
- use part-time employees at peak times
- cross-train so employees can perform multiple functions
- coach employees to use peak and slack times appropriately
- encourage customer participation
- share capacity.

Success Tool: Manipulating Demand **Manipulating demand** in the hospitality business, or any business in which adding incremental supply is costly and requires a long lead time, is generally easier than manipulating supply. In the hospitality business, too much demand or not enough demand occur in different time blocks, depending on the specific service. In the restaurant business, there are generally as many peak periods as there are meal periods (breakfast, lunch, and dinner) that the restaurant is open. Airlines tend to have peak demand at the beginning and at the end of the business day. Peaks and valleys for seasonal resorts occur in blocks of months.

Whatever the shape of the **demand curve, differential pricing** is the most commonly used tool to manipulate demand. Restaurants offer early-bird specials; airlines discount for Saturday night stayovers (which attract fliers who aren't planning their travel around a business meeting); hotels in urban business areas, where the Monday through Friday business is strong, offer attractive weekend packages. Off-season rates in resort areas drop considerably.

Many hotels have begun to use a **yield management** system, which hinges on differential pricing. Yield management attempts to match the right type of supply (the kinds of rooms available) with the right type of demand (the kinds of customers who want those rooms) at the right price to maximize revenue or yield.[9]

Yield management relies on information about customer booking patterns for the various market segments that the hotel services (for instance: How far in advance does each segment book?) It must also comprehend historical demand information (What room nights were sold in the past? to whom? for what purpose?), and finally, yield management requires an understanding of how changing price affects demand. Consider this example: If drop-in business (no advance reservation is made) or last-minute reservations on summer weekends are generally about 50 room nights for a particular hotel, should the sales manager turn down a convention that wants to book the same space three months in advance at a lower rate, or not? The dilemma occurs because the hotel is attempting to maximize both the occupancy percentage *and* the room rate.

Another tool is to establish a **reservations system**. This is critical for hotels, convention centers, or any service business where the customers' planning horizon is lengthy. Fine dining restaurants sometimes have a reservations system with time choice limited to two seatings. This allows the maximum number of persons to be served during the meal period.

A hospitality operation should also evaluate whether it has excess capacity due to an underutilized time period, and if so, it should attempt to generate new demand for that time period. McDonald's, for example, added breakfast to its menu to expand the use of buildings and equipment already in place. Some ski areas offer night skiing for the same reason: Widening the time window expands the potential for increased revenue with minimal increase in **fixed costs**.

Another alternative to manipulate demand is to encourage the customer to use a third party, like a travel agent. The timing is convenient to the customer, and the advance purchase can be very helpful to the service provider. It is significantly easier for a gate agent to load a full plane if all passengers are ticketed and have boarding passes prior to arriving at the airport.

Sometimes it is impossible to satisfy every customer immediately. In some businesses, customers will queue until capacity becomes available. Standby passengers will go on a "wait list" for the next available plane; restaurant patrons will wait for an available table. This is a wonderful problem for the service provider, and it also presents an opportunity to develop complementary services or techniques that change the nature of the wait.

In an article entitled "The Psychology of Waiting Lines," David H. Maister puts forth a series of propositions about waiting:

- Unoccupied time feels longer than occupied time.
- Pre-process waits feel longer than in-process waits.
- Anxiety makes waits seem longer.
- Uncertain waits are longer than known, finite waits.
- Unexplained waits are longer than explained waits.
- Unfair waits are longer than equitable waits.
- The more valuable the service, the longer the customer will wait.[10]

Some simple service steps can help change the perception of the length of the wait. Ski areas that use an extensive network of lift line corrals that are constantly moving give customers a sense that they are in process. They see signs of progress. This works better than funneling a mass of people into a short line.

Restaurants that take names and add them to a waiting list make customers rest easier than relying on a physical queue to hold their place. This takes some of the unfairness out of the wait. Providing musical entertainment or serving drinks while people are waiting helps occupy the time. Acknowledging customers immediately upon arrival gets them in process, and giving an accurate (or conservative, so the restaurant can overdeliver) estimate of the time for a table helps to explain the wait. Anyone who has ever waited at an airport gate with no explanation as to why the plane is late and no clear sense of when the plane will take off can attest to the frustration of uncertain and unexplained waits. Providing this information is important.

That a customer will wait longer the more valuable the service is clearly illustrated at a theme park like Disney World. You can understand which rides and shows the customers most value by observing the length of waiting lines! The lesson here is that enhancing the value of the service provided to a customer, in any business, means that your customer will wait longer. The longer the customer will wait patiently, the better the chances of maximizing revenue.

To recap, a hospitality service provider can alter demand by:

- varying price
- developing demand in a nonpeak time
- using a reservation system
- encouraging the customer to use a third party, or
- changing the apparent length of the wait.

Feature: Services are Simultaneously Produced and Consumed

It is important to recognize that goods are generally produced, then sold, then consumed. Services, on the other hand, are sold, then produced and consumed at the same time. The simultaneity of production and consumption means that the hospitality provider and the guest are integrally linked during the delivery or distribution of the service, and you only get *one* chance to deliver! With a product, a faulty item can be replaced with an identical one. With a service, there's no such substitute. The chance to deliver correctly is time bound. The best that a service provider can do after a mishap is to try to recover with a repeat performance at a later time, and/or to offer some additional sweetener. You can't fix the fact that a guest had a sleepless night in your hotel because of raucous guests next door, for example. Perhaps the best you can do is to not charge the tired guest, and to offer a complimentary return visit. (If the guest is willing to come back!)

Understanding this characteristic of **simultaneous production and consumption** is especially important to a hospitality marketer. In addition to the service's being delivered at the right time and in the right place, it must be delivered in the right way, a concern that is less critical in the delivery of a product.[11] In a hotel or restaurant, the right way hinges dramatically on the front desk clerk, the bellman, the hostess, the waiter, and all of the other service providers who come in contact with the customer, and the customer himself.

Success Tool: Empowering the Employee What tools can be employed to help assure that the service gets delivered in the right way? The first step to creating better service is to understand what is on the customer's "invisible report card" for evaluating the service. In other words, what does the customer care about? How a marketer begins to answer the question is quite simple, but often overlooked: Ask.

In an extensive study undertaken to create a better service system, British Airways found that the following four elements were important to the traveling customer.

- **Care and concern**. Does the service person genuinely care about helping the customer? Does he really want to solve the customers' problem?

- **Spontaneity**. Is the employee empowered to act on the spot? Does the employee have the right to think, not just shrug his shoulders because the problem is unusual, not in the rule book?

- **Problem-solving**. Is the employee armed with information and skilled enough to solve the problem?

- **Recovery**. If something goes wrong (as is inevitable in the service business), can the employee go out of his way to make amends? Is extra effort expended to right the wrong?

Each of these elements is not only broadly applicable, but critical to the hospitality business. *Hospitality*, by definition, demands that the service provider warmly attend to the customers' needs.[12]

Success Tool: Internal Marketing Good service must be continuous. Each encounter with an employee (sometimes referred to as a "moment of truth") matters.[13] For this reason, it is imperative that every employee have the ability and desire to make a difference. Ability is a piece that skills training can provide. Creating desire is more elusive.

Many companies try to create desire through **internal marketing**, treating employees as internal customers. Some of the same techniques used to attract and retain customers are used to attract and retain employees. These techniques can range from marketing research, which might uncover a need for more flextime in working hours, to advertising that highlights the problem-solving ability of a front desk clerk or a concierge. These ads effectively send the same message to two audiences, the customer and the internal customer.[14]

Another example of internal marketing was initiated by the Rainbow Room restaurant in New York. Those who worked in the Rainbow Room, along with spouses and guests, were invited to dine in the restaurant in grand style. The invitation was a full-page ad in the *New York Times* that listed every employee's name. The two regular bands played. The regular port was served. Moscow Circus characters and the Rockettes performed, as did some of the kitchen staff, in a burly ballet entitled *Rock Cornish Hen Lake*, and some of the staff imitated the restaurant's more noteworthy patrons.[15] This experience not only said "thank you" but allowed the internal customers *to be* customers in the truest sense of the word.

Success Tool: Seizing an Opportunity to Customize Because of the nature of services being produced and consumed at the same time, a marketer is presented with an opportunity to customize the service for each customer. **Customizing** may lend a competitive advantage. For example, Burger King allows customers to "hold the pickles and the lettuce" to provide an advantage to the customer over McDonald's, which offers only a standardized product.

Whether to customize or standardize is not an easy decision, however. Standardization creates a more consistent service and is cheaper to deliver. Customization meets the customer's needs to a greater degree and commands a higher price, but it is more expensive to deliver. A service provider can lean toward either customization or standardization (and, in fact, is better off on either extreme rather than somewhere in the middle) so long as the customer values the service for the price that is charged.

The lodging segment of the hospitality industry provides an appropriate comparison. The economy lodging room delivers very few frills. The product/service is a clean, comfortable room with limited amenities and limited services. A luxury hotel, on the other hand, delivers an array of amenities (like terry cloth bathrobes or fruit baskets) and services (like 24-hour roomservice or a concierge desk). The luxury hotel aims to customize as much as possible, tailoring service to the needs of the guest. A well-run property in either segment can be profitable, but the prices charged are very different.

What's in a Name?

Marketing is much more than just a name, but your name in the marketplace has critical implications. Names are changed for lots of reasons. Allegheny Airways decided to expand its routes beyond the Allegheny Mountains that surround Pittsburgh, its corporate headquarters. The company became USAir. Western International Hotels perhaps was sensitive to potential expansion into the eastern hemisphere when it changed its name to Westin several years ago. In good fun, though, its marketing campaign took advantage of this minor change by highlighting the company's inability to fit *Western* on its monogrammed towels. The campaign pictured a series of towels on a rack, each holding only a few letters.

Some name changes include a fresh new logo and an attempt to improve image. Howard Johnson's dropped the 's a number of years ago and changed the logo of the new Howard Johnson company. Best Western International, a referral organization, changed its trademark golden crown to a more modern-looking red one, in December 1994. Aramark, which emerged in 1995, formerly was ARA, best known as one of the world's largest institutional foodservice companies. Part of Aramark's motivation for the name change is to explain the breadth of the companies it services, such as the Shenandoah National Park, the BBC in London, and IBM in Germany. Richfield Hotel Management, one of the largest hotel management companies, has changed its name to Richfield Hospitality Services as it expands its growing services, particularly in the sales and marketing area. Boston Chicken, as it attempts to expand its variety, has changed its name to Boston Market—hoping to communicate that it offers more than chicken.

More and more companies continue to realize that to stay competitive in the hospitality industry, they have to "go global," and the name changes reflect their attempt to market in expanded geographical territory. Inter-Continental Hotels recently established Global Partner Hotels and Resorts. This Miami-based division of the company is seeking to establish strategic alliances with independent hotels and resorts worldwide. Another example involves the merger of Renaissance Hotels International and Stouffer Hotels. After 1996, all Stouffer Hotels in the USA will carry the Renaissance Hotels International name. This trend is not new. In the 1980s, Hotel Corporation of America became Sonesta, as the company expanded overseas. Similarly, Holiday Inn became Holiday Inn Worldwide.

In the spirit that there is an exception to every rule, we find one company that has changed its name to reflect a smaller geographic territory. Disneyland Paris is now the new marketing name for EuroDisney. As EuroDisney has been in financial distress since its opening in April 1992, it will be interesting to see how the new marketing strategy, which looks to identify more closely with its host city, evolves.

Feature: Services are Less Uniform

One final major difference between the nature of products and the nature of services is that services tend to be more heterogeneous or varied. This is caused by the extent to which human performance shapes the service, both in how the employee acts and how the customer reacts.

No matter how many manuals a company may have, it is impossible to govern exactly how each employee will handle a given situation. Even if every employee could deliver exactly the same service, what is acceptable to one customer may not be acceptable to another. There is a wide band of how customers measure quality. For example, presume a rental car agent who grew up in the area where he works gives detailed directions to every customer who rents from him; he is always armed with a yellow highlighter. Though one customer may be delighted by a rental car agent's detailed directions, another may simply want a map and the car keys.

The problem of variability is further compounded by how other customers act. One restaurant table may have an undesirable restaurant experience, even if the food and service were acceptable, because the noisy party of six nearby was distracting to an important business interview. Recognizing the heterogeneity of services, there are several tools a marketer can call forth to address this characteristic: take a production line approach to tasks that can be mechanized, don't make promises you can't keep, offer service guarantees, and finally, recognize that some things just plain can't be controlled.

Success Tool: Taking a Production Line Approach One of the approaches to taking some of the uncertainty out of a service experience is to substitute machines for people. Theodore Levitt termed this approach the "industrialization of service." The hotel industry, for example, has installed voice mail answering machines to take guests' messages. Because no operator is involved, voice mail assures that the message is delivered exactly as dictated with no time delay. McDonald's uses a timer and bell, a mechanized approach, to replace the human inconsistency of guessing when french fries are done. The result is high-quality french fries and employees who are free to wait on more customers.[16] Though these examples achieve greater consistency, the trade-off is less "personalization" or ability to customize.

Success Tool: Avoiding Promises You Can't Keep A key way to solve problems of inconsistency is to avoid promising the customer things that your service staff cannot deliver. These promises can be in two forms. The first is promising everything to everybody in generic terms. Telling a customer that he will experience the most wonderfully fantastic vacation ever is giving a promise waiting to be broken. What is wonderful for one customer may not be wonderful for another.

The second type of promise to avoid making is one that requires employees to jump hurdles they are unlikely to clear. For example, a sales manager who promises a tableside flaming dessert over ice cream for a banquet of 1,500 (because the group coordinator was lured by flair) has set the wait staff up for failure. The process is likely to melt down and to be more time consuming than the customer can bear.

Success Tool: Offering Service Guarantees Don't assume services can't be guaranteed. chapter 3 offers an explanation of how service guarantees can be employed. They can be employed effectively to enhance the uniformity of service delivery.

Success Tool: Recognize Some Things Can't Be Controlled Though taking a production line approach, offering service guarantees, or avoiding promises you can't keep may help to control some aspects of your service, trying to control everything is not a winning strategy. Murphy's Law will intervene.

Once those things that can't be controlled are appropriately identified, the employee should be empowered to make judgments in real time, as discussed in the previous section.

Success Tool: Consistently Meeting Expectations Successful marketers need to structure their service organizations always to meet customers' expectations, but not to exceed them sometimes and fail trying other times. Why not? Why shouldn't an organization go out of its way always to exceed expectations? The problem is this: If you exceed a customer's expectations, he may come to expect it as the norm. If you can't exceed his expectations, the next visit he will be disappointed. If you *can* consistently exceed expectations, then you *should* always deliver the service and be rewarded accordingly for the added service. Put your goalposts where you know you can reach them, not short of your capabilities, or you won't receive the maximum revenue. Similarly, don't place them beyond your capabilities, where you can only reach them some of the time and therefore deliver inconsistent service. Winning organizations, of course, should continually try to improve standards. In the course of that improvement, it works fine to under-promise and over-deliver in the short term, so long as you continually monitor your customers' expectations. When you think you can always exceed them, then it is time to move your goalposts. Consider a simplistic example to illustrate the point:

Take soap. In the chapter on the historical perspective, we learned that even a private bathroom within a hotel room, once upon a time, was an amenity, and so, therefore, was soap. But as we continually provided it, the customer came to expect it. Soap no longer exceeded expectations; it was expected. This thinking evolved, especially at the luxury end of the market, and there appeared facial soap at the sink and bath soap at the bath. The customer came to expect it. Then shampoo.

Say that a guest staying at a hotel last week had brought to his door a bottle of his favorite brand of shampoo, not what the hotel normally supplies, just by phoning. This week the guest is unable to get the same brand, because the clever employee who solved the problem last week has to report that the gift shop is all out. Or does he? Does the employee go outside the hotel to purchase some? The point here is not whether the employee goes searching for shampoo, or not, but rather that the hotel thinks about the ramifications of moving its goalposts, by delivering the special request the first time. Soap case closed.

Feature: Using Traditional Elements of Marketing

The features of marketing discussed thus far speak directly to the nature of services in comparison to products. This final feature turns attention to traditional elements used in marketing. These elements include managing the marketing mix, using communications vehicles, and market positioning. These elements help to create a framework for a marketer to design a successful marketing strategy.

Success Tool: Managing the Marketing Mix A **marketing mix** is that set of components that creates the overall offer of an establishment to its customers. The classic marketing mix, called the 4 "P's," was originally designed for the marketing of products.[17] The four elements of the mix are: product, price, place, and promotion. With some modification in thinking, these elements can be applied to services. Product should be thought of as products and services. Place, for services, should be thought of as how the product/service is distributed to the customer. Price is what the customer will be expected to pay. Promotion is all of the elements of communication that a marketer uses to tell the customer about the product/service.

Other marketing mix frameworks have been developed for service applications. For example, a mix designed specifically for the hospitality industry includes these four elements:[18]

- **the product/service mix**, which includes all of the elements of the offering, both products and services
- **the presentation mix**, which includes all of the elements used to increase the tangibility of the product/service mix
- **the communications mix**, which includes all communications between the firm and the customer, including elements that are tangible clues, that persuade the customer to purchase and that monitor customer expectations
- **the distribution mix**, which include all channels available for the customer to buy and use the service.

Whichever mix is used as the framework, a good marketer should be attentive to all of the elements. Many of the other success tools that a marketer may use are aimed at one or more elements in the marketing mix. For example, clue management is aimed at the presentation and communications mixes. Vehicles for communication, which follow, are aimed at the communications mix.

Success Tool: Using Communications Vehicles An important part of a marketer's job is to communicate with customers. To achieve this, there are several different types of vehicles that a marketer may use. These vehicles fall into the following general categories:

- **advertising**
  - various media
  - direct mail
- **public relations**
  - media publicity
- **personal selling**
  - direct contact
  - trade shows

Advertising includes all types of paid-for communications over which the marketer has direct control. (As we learned in chapter 7, this is distinguished from public relations, which is not paid for directly and is not in the direct control of the marketer.) Advertising may be through media such as television, newspapers, magazines, radio, billboards, or the Internet. Advertising may also be **direct mail** pieces sent by the marketing department to a specific target market, such as sales promotions or brochures.

Public relations, though not controlled by the company, can be managed. When the media thinks that an organization has done something newsworthy, they are apt to write about it. The organization can manage public relations by doing noteworthy things. McDonald's for example, sponsors Ronald McDonald homes for families with children in nearby hospitals.

Personal selling can take the form of phone calls, visits directly to clients, or customer interaction at trade shows. Personal selling relies on the ability of individuals to interact directly with one another. Employees can also be salespersons, whether they intend to be or not. A very friendly bellman can intentionally sell services in the hotel while escorting a guest to the room. A ski instructor may be unintentionally selling the host ski area as she interacts with guests in the base lodge lounge. Another constituency, customers themselves, can be salespersons. Word of mouth, both positive and negative, can have tremendous impact on service businesses. Getting satisfied customers to speak with potential new customers can have great rewards. For example, a sales representative can put a potential customer in touch with a convention coordinator who has already had a successful conference at the hotel.

Success Tool: Market Positioning Positioning is how the customer defines the attributes a company provides relative to the competition. Positioning should not be left to chance, but rather should be actively managed. In order to actively manage positioning, a marketer must understand its customers and its competition. For example, the director of marketing for a cruise line might determine that its cruises are selected because of superior activities for kids. It may discover that the competition is focusing on seniors, or married couples, or any number of target markets. This information begins to define the positioning that the company should take. The cruise line must also review its own attributes and be sure that it is providing the best activities possible for kids, and that it can do so consistently. Finally, the company must clearly communicate the benefits to the right customers. (In this case, it may be to kids, or parents of kids, or both, depending on who is influential in the purchase decision.)

Good positioning, in summary, should do the following things:

- Provide specific benefits to a specific market
- Be differentiated from the competition
- Be communicated clearly and consistently
- Be in synchronization with companies resources (financial, human, and marketing)

Many organizations choose to anchor their positioning with a **positioning statement**, or a succinct statement of what the company is all about. Some examples are: Hilton: America's Business Address; Au Bon Pain: Good Food Served Quickly; and Princess Cruises: It's more than a cruise, it's the Love Boat.

The Role of the Hospitality Marketer

Hospitality marketers are faced with numerous challenges. They must comprehend the nature of services fully. They must understand the potential application of traditional elements of marketing. They must be ready to apply the success tools that are responsive to those features. In day-to-day operations, a marketer may be doing such tasks as placing a cost effective piece of advertising, defining the right questions in pursuit of telling market research, or coaching sales staff to sell more effectively.

All of the day-to-day activities begin with the development of a **marketing strategy**. A marketing strategy takes a big-picture perspective and sets objectives after defining the market. Defining the market involves selecting that piece of the market, the **market segment**, that it will target. Next is the planning of a set of tactics to support the strategy. The **marketing plan**, a working document for implementing action against the objectives, results. A set of selected success tools is then used to execute the strategy. Finally, the strategy should be evaluated. The process of evaluation is what provides feedback for improvement. The continuous improvement and learning from the application of success tools is what leads a hospitality marketer to success.

What's in the In Box?

Imagine yourself standing in the shoes of the director of marketing for a major casino on Native American land. As you approach your in box, think about the various marketing success tools as you sit down to tackle the following items:

1. The casino has continued to meet with mixed reviews in the local community. Several factions remain opposed to gambling in their hometown area. You must devise a more extensive public relations effort.

2. The recently installed player tracking system, Casino Link, is working very well. The systems allow the casino to know how much each player at each slot machine is winning or losing as it is happening. It also lets you track the play of any given player for the day or for prior visits. You are challenged to find more ways to get people to join the slot clubs, so they can be tracked. (Players now insert their membership cards into slot machines

before playing so they can be eligible for extra prizes.) You are also challenged to find other marketing uses for the market research that is being gathered on players.

3. The casino manager is considering adapting an extension of the tracking system that applies to poker. Small computer chips are imbedded in the poker chips, which allows the casino to track the winnings or losings of its poker players. Your help is needed in evaluating if the new system is a good idea or not.

4. Yesterday one of the video poker machines was malfunctioning and displayed a payout of $10,000 instead of $1,000. A customer hit the jackpot and was not satisfied that his award should have been $1,000, even though all the machines on either side for an entire aisle were $1,000 machines. Today a lawyer for the customer arrived at the casino manager's office. You've been asked to watch for potential negative publicity and take any action you feel appropriate to avert it.

5. Business from 9:00 P.M. until midnight on Sunday is particularly slow relative to the casino's capacity. You need to devise some ways to manipulate demand to enhance the profitability of this time period.

Creating Competitive Advantage

Implementing success tools goes beyond Tom Sawyer's trading an apple for a chance to whitewash a fence. As the customer becomes increasingly more sophisticated and more demanding, the marketer is forced to open a dialogue that seeks to understand what the customer needs, to satisfy those needs, and to create and sustain a relationship between the customer and the hospitality provider. Adapted from a general explanation offered by McKenna in "Marketing Is Everything," for a hotel company the evolution of marketing has gone something like this: Decades ago, companies were sales driven—"You can have any kind of bed in your room you want, as long as it's a standard double." With increased competition, successful companies shifted their approach to "Tell us what kind of bed you want in your room." To survive in the 1990s, companies will have to go one step further, and ask, "Can we figure out together what room furniture and layout matters to you in the first place?" Marketers who start with the last question are on their way to creating competitive advantage.

Summary

By exploring the key criteria that help us to understand the nature of hospitality services—that these services are predominantly intangible, can't be inventoried, are simultaneously produced and consumed, and are not produced uniformly—a marketer can begin to formulate a series of tools that are useful in creating effective marketing. These tools include:

- tangibilizing the intangible
- clue management
- manipulating supply
- manipulating demand
- empowering the employees

- internal marketing
- seizing an opportunity to customize
- avoiding promises you can't keep
- consistently meeting expectations
- managing the marketing mix
- using communications vehicles
- market positioning

These success tools comprehend the unique nature of services marketing and the traditional elements used in marketing. A combination of these tools can be used effectively to develop, plan, execute, and evaluate a marketing strategy. A winning strategy is the end goal of a successful marketer.

Discussion Questions

1. What tools belong in the tool box of a successful hospitality service marketer? Structure your answer to include specific attributes of services.

2. What is the difference between marketing and selling? How does a product orientation lose customers?

3. Why is it hard to sample a service? What characteristics of services make it so?

4. What is it about the nature of services that makes Ronald McDonald important to McDonald's?

5. Why can't services be inventoried? What are the ramifications with respect to supply and demand in a service business?

6. How is price used to manipulate the timing of demand in a service business?

7. How can a service marketer make a waiting line appear shorter?

8. What special problems does simultaneity of production and consumption in services present for a hospitality service provider?

9. What can a hospitality marketer do to manage against the fact that services have many variables that cause lack of uniformity?

10. What success tools can be applied to each of the four elements of the hospitality marketing mix?

11. Give an example of a successful positioning statement and an example of an unsuccessful one (real or fictitious). Why did you categorize each as you did?

12. Why do hotels put sanitation strips across toilets after cleaning them?

13. Refer to the opening quotation. Do you think Tom Sawyer was a talented marketer? Was he a talented salesman?

Assignments

1. Consider all of the items in the in box of the hospitality marketing manager. To which would you give the highest priority? The lowest priority? Why? How would you tackle each item? Assume the role of the marketing manager. Develop a work plan, using the success tools in the chapter.

2. Visit a hotel or restaurant. Identify tangible clues that the service provider has created to "tangibilize the intangible." What can you learn about the target market of the hotel from these clues?

3. Obtain the Sunday travel section of a major newspaper. Look for an advertised weekend special for a hotel. Call the hotel directly and find out the room rate for the same hotel room during the week. Call the 800 phone number, if it is a chain, to obtain the rate. Are all the rates you have found the same? Why or why not?

4. Put yourself in a situation in which you have to wait in line for a service of any kind. How is the wait handled? Given what you've learned about the ways that waiting lines can be made to appear shorter, is it well managed?

End Notes

1. Mark Twain, *Tom Sawyer* (New York: Bantam Books, 1981), 14–15.

2. Regis McKenna, "Marketing is Everything," *Harvard Business Review* (January–February 1991): 65.

3. Theodore Levitt, "Marketing Myopia," *Harvard Business Review* (July–August 1960). Reprinted in Theodore Levitt, *The Marketing Imagination* (New York: The Free Press, 1986), 141–147.

4. Ibid., x.

5. *The Successful Hotel Marketer* (5 June 1989): 1, 6.

6. Leonard L. Berry, "Services Marketing Is Different," *Business* (May–June 1980). Reprinted in Christopher H. Lovelock, *Services Marketing* (Englewood Cliffs, New Jersey: Prentice-Hall, Inc., 1984), 29.

7. W. Earl Sassser, Jr., "Match Supply and Demand in Service Businesses," *Harvard Business Review* (November–December 1976).

8. Michael L. Kasavana and John J. Cahill, *Managing Computers in the Hospitality Industry* (East Lansing, Michigan: Educational Institute of the American Hotel and Motel Association, 1987), 329–330.

9. Sheryl E. Kimes, "The Basics of Yield Management," *Cornell Quarterly* (November 1989): 14–19.

10. David H. Maister, "The Psychology of Waiting Lines," in *The Service Encounter*, edited by John A. Czepiel, Michale R. Solomon, and Carol F. Suprenant (Lexington, Massachusetts: D.C. Heath and Co., 1985), 113–123.

11. Berry, 31.

12. Karl Albrecht and Ron Zemke, *Service America* (Homewood, Illinois: Dow Jones-Irwin, 1985), 33–34.

13. Albrecht and Zemke, 31.

14. Leonard L. Berry, "The Employee as Customer," *Journal of Retail Banking* 3 (1). Reprinted in Christopher H. Lovelock, *Services Marketing* (Englewood Cliffs, New Jersey: Prentice-Hall, Inc.), 272.

15. "Those Who Color the Rainbow Room Finally Sit Down," *New York Times*, 10 January 1990, B1.

16. W. Earl Sasser, Jr., Christopher W. L. Hart, and James L. Heskett, *Service Breakthroughs* (New York: The Free Press, 1990), 123.

17. E. Jerome McCarthy, *Basic Marketing: A Managerial Approach* (Homewood, Illinois: Richard D. Irwin, 1975), 75–80.

    Note: McCarthy adopted his four "P's" from Neil Borden, "The Concept of the Marketing Mix," *Journal of Advertising Research* (June 1964), 2–7.

18. Robert C. Lewis, Richard E. Chambers, and Harsha E. Chacko, *Marketing Leadership in Hospitality, Foundations and Practices* (New York: Van Nostrand Reinhold, 1995), 393–396.

Note: Lewis et al. adapted their hospitality marketing mix from a classic article by Leo M. Renaghan, "A New Marketing Mix for the Hospitality Industry," *Cornell Hotel and Restaurant Quarterly* (April 1981): 31–35.

Chapter Twelve

" *The electric light bulb, we all know, was invented by Thomas Edison. The telephone was the work of Alexander Graham Bell. And the computer. ... 'If you took a hundred people off the street and asked them who invented the computer, ninety-nine would have no idea. ...'* "

Steve Lohr [1]

A Management Information Systems Tool Box ❧

When you finish this chapter, you should:

1. Understand the features of hospitality management information systems, and the success tools that can be employed in response to those features.

2. Know how information technology affects and influences the hospitality industry.

3. Know what a management information system is.

4. Know the importance of selecting the right system, and utilizing the information appropriately.

5. Know what criteria a well-selected system should fulfill.

6. Know that technology changes rapidly, and the resulting importance for managers to be flexible.

7. Understand the various systems associated with a lodging property.

8. Understand the various systems associated with a foodservice operation.

9. Be able to identify the kinds of issues that might be found in the in box of a hospitality MIS manager.

Introduction

These are exciting times! Few areas of life remain untouched by developments in computer and communications technology. Though both can be costly to build and maintain, together they offer a variety of alluring opportunities for exploring the needs of customers, and for developing new services to meet those needs. There is no area of modern life that is untouched by computer technology; in fact, it's so pervasive we don't even notice how often it has an impact on daily life. Most likely the cash register in the local convenience store, or at the college student union, is tied into a companywide system, providing vital information to management on what's selling. But precisely because it does provide that information, like keeping tabs on inventory, you can be assured that every time you want to purchase a particular brand of soda, it will be in the case.

Establishing Effective Management Information Systems

Understanding and using the appropriate technology is critical to today's hospitality managers. At the minimum, travelers and guests expect accurate airline tickets, quality long distance phone service in hotels, rapid and accurate billing from all businesses, in-room entertainment on hotel televisions, and restaurant meals served in appropriate time at appropriate temperatures. Now it is becoming standard to have available fax machines, modem ports, additional phone lines, and automated message services in hotels, airports, conference centers, and even some restaurants. A traveler expects that either via an 800 reservations number or through a travel agent, it will take no more than one phone call to book a flight, hold a hotel room, schedule a rental car, and make dinner reservations. And the bill for each of these services, from different suppliers, should appear accurately on the monthly credit card statement. Miraculously, they usually do!

Effective hospitality management information systems consider both the guest and the business. Carefully selecting computer systems, thoroughly training staff, and utilizing the power of the information all allow hospitality managers to do what they do best: service the guest.

The Computer Basics

In simple English, a computer is a device that keeps track of information that the user considers vital—a college essay, an accounting spreadsheet, sales figures, or even graphics. In today's technology it can be defined as an electronic device capable of performing data processing and problem-solving functions. Until about 1970, all computers were called mainframe computers. At that time, they were too expensive to purchase, except for the largest companies. Eventually, smaller computers, or PCs, came on the market at prices that were more affordable by small businesses and individuals. Now, laptops weighing less than four pounds, and even handheld devices, are widespread.

Regardless of the type of computer hardware, every computer must possess the following hardware components:

- Input/Output Device—the keyboard, for instance, which allows you to put information into the computer system
- Central Processing Unit, or the "brain" of the entire computer system

- Screen for viewing information, and
- External Storage Device (a floppy or a CD ROM disk).

What is a Management Information System?

At this point, let us define what is meant by an **MIS**. The key word in the phrase is *information*. Companies and managers need information about their businesses in order to make decisions. Generally speaking, there is no universally accepted definition of a **management information system**. MIS has been described as a method, a function, a process, an organization, a system, and a subsystem. MIS is simply "a collection of interrelated and interdependent subsystems dependent on a data base that supports the managerial decision-making process, helps monitor and control operations, and is responsive to the dynamic needs of the firm."[2] A more graphic analogy describes a management information system as the heart of the organization. "Just as the rhythmic beat of the heart pumps blood and life-giving oxygen throughout the body, an MIS is constantly creating and disseminating information, the lifeblood of the organization."[3] An MIS helps a company store important information, share that information among different employees and departments, and manipulate the data to find out how the business is doing.

A management information system need not be extensive, or expensive. For a small restaurant, it could simply be a personal computer, installed with standard accounting and inventory software. As the restaurant grows, it could be linked to the cash register, or to a second store. But for large, international hospitality companies, the systems are highly complex, and generally custom designed and built to meet the needs of the business.

Distinguishing Features
of Hospitality MIS

The goal behind using technology in the hospitality industry is straightforward. Technology can help to maximize profits by increasing revenues and decreasing costs, a relatively basic business concept. How can technology help the hospitality industry increase revenues? For starters, providing critical information about the guest. The more a company knows about its customers, the greater service it can provide—and that translates into new customers, repeat customers, customers who purchase more, or potential customers. Information, therefore, can increase revenues. For example, a guest profile system can alert a front desk associate to a customer who prefers a room on a lower floor, or a guest who frequently requires use of the business center early in the morning. In the eyes of the guest, that extra service could be the factor that encourages him to return.

Second, technology can help to reduce costs, which also contributes favorably to the bottom line. Strategic use of technology can help reduce repetitive tasks, human error, or training costs, or it can eliminate unnecessary services. Think about housekeeping labor costs. A housekeeper might be waiting and repeatedly checking a set of rooms for the guests to leave, so that they can be cleaned. There is a lot of wasted time and effort returning to a floor just to see if a room is empty. Now let's say there is a system in place that alerts the housekeeping manager every time a room is empty. It's activated by sensing body heat. When the guest has left, the temperature in the room goes down. The manager can then inform the housekeeping staff which rooms are empty. Then they can be cleaned immediately. The system saves time, which saves costs, which maximizes profits.

The hospitality world is working 24 hours a day all year long, and is based upon providing or exceeding the quality of service a customer expects. Technology can be used in numerous ways to keep the guest happy at the lowest acceptable cost. Several features of hospitality technology are important to remember in pursuit of the highest-quality, most profitable service: timely information is critical, systems are plentiful, and technology is changing rapidly.

Feature: Timely Information is Critical

In today's hospitality businesses, up-to-the minute information is critical to survival. Information technology affects every transaction in a lodging or foodservice operation, from check-in, to room-service, to payment via a credit card. Think how lost a hotel is when the system goes down: All guest activity comes to a halt. Or a restaurant that utilizes a handheld computer that allows the server to input from the table directly to the kitchen what a party has ordered.

Systems do more than just help speed up guest requests; they provide essential history for a company. It is critical for a restaurant to track the number of specials it sold over a given period, to evaluate whether it should offer it again, or try something new. Tracking also provides information for purchasing, so a company can keep a lower inventory on hand and thus keep costs down. And

▬▬▬▬ Have Pager, Will Travel

Is there anything more frustrating than arriving at the restaurant of your choice, one that's right on the water, with a beautiful park on its doorstep—the same one that is so popular it doesn't take reservations, and you're told when you arrive there's at least an hour wait for a table? The waiting area is jammed with patrons who got there before you did. It's a beautiful evening for a walk, but you risk losing your place on the wait list if you wander down to the waterfront and don't hear your name called. Enter the magic of technology.

Being too popular can be a problem for restaurateurs—if it takes too long to serve your customers, you might not have any a few months from now. A potential solution? Many restaurants are now using hand-held pagers to keep those on the wait list happy. Good within a certain radius of the restaurant, guests can wander down to see the sights, or wander within a shopping mall. When the table is ready, the pager vibrates silently, letting the guest know it is time to return to be seated.

Taking the pager technology one step further, table top paging systems, developed by companies like Motorola and Service Alert, are making their way to restaurant tables. Simply press a button at the table, and your server's own pager vibrates. No more trying to flag down your server on a hectic night to refill water glasses or bring the check. If instant attention is what the customer wants, instant attention is what this technology can bring.

all of the back-of-the-house functions rely heavily on information technology, including items such as payroll and taxes.

Success Tool: Seamless Integration The key words in today's hospitality systems are **seamless integration**, keeping all the elements of a system working together precisely. As you will see when we talk about the different types of systems utilized by hospitality companies, there are many different groups within a company who all want information about a guest. And each department has particular needs, such as payroll and accounting, or food and beverage. It used to be that each department had its own separate system. Now it has become critical to link many of these systems together to create competitive advantage.

Competition in the gaming industry is leading the charge to integrate systems. Consider the hotels and casinos of Atlantic City or Las Vegas, all in close proximity to one another and in intense competition for guests. Which hotel is selected by a guest can come down to service. Imagine that a high-rolling guest has just lost $10,000 at blackjack, and then enters an on-premise restaurant for dinner. If the manager knew of the guest's poor fortune, the guest might find that the meal is **comped**, or free. Somehow, despite the guest's losses, the management wants that guest to leave happy (or as happy as possible!) and to come back. Going that extra step to provide a complimentary meal or room night just might convince the guest to return, and to tell their friends about the experience of being well treated.

Some large hotel companies have two room reservations systems—one right at the property, and one in a central location. The central reservations system handles inquiries on an 800 phone number, and provides room information on all the hotels in the chain, while the property-based system handles walk-ins and calls directly to that one hotel. Suppose the Hyatt in Cincinnati is fully booked for a Saturday night, and both the central and local reservations systems reflect that status. What if, late in the day, a reservation is canceled using the 800 number, but the two systems don't "talk" to one another in real time? It takes an hour for the local system to update. Within the hour, a walk-in guest tries to book a room for that Saturday night. The front desk associate looks, but to no avail—her system says the hotel is fully booked, and the guest is turned away. One hour later, when her system updates, she finds a room is now available, but the sale is lost.

Seamless integration of systems would solve this problem; immediate updates would prevent the loss of a reservation, and the resulting loss in revenue. As technology continues to evolve, and systems become faster and capable of handling more, the different applications will work together.

Success Tool: Planning for Various Hospitality Components to Work Together In addition to seamless integration of systems within a company, it is important for systems to comprehend various components within the hospitality industry. For example, travel agents work closely with airline and hotel reservations systems. Airline reservations agents have the ability to reserve cars for rental car companies. As the world of technology becomes more and more integrated, it will become important for the various components of the industry to talk to one another electronically. This will likely mean a continuous updating of hardware and software applications.

As noted above, a number of hotels have installed a computer based **property management system (PMS)**, with front office computer applications. In essence, a property management system provides an instantaneous two-way update. If a reservation is made at the central reservation office, a mirror image of the reservation is sent to the property within seconds, and inventories are properly updated. At the same time, if a reservation is made at the property, a mirror image of it is sent to the central reservations office with the inventory update. The central reservations office then becomes a complete reservation backup system to the hotels and resorts in case of catastrophic failure. In addition, the central reservations office is the repository for travel agency information. Using the list of travel agents certified by the International Air Transport Association Network (IATAN), SSMARTS (acronym for **S**touffer **S**ales, **M**arketing **A**nd **R**eservation **T**ransaction **S**ystem) can notify every property of travel agency information, flag potential fraudulent travel agencies, and track travel agency sales.

Perhaps as important as any feature of SSMARTS, room inventory and rate control are maintained at each property, not at the central reservations office. This keeps accountability at the property level. Hotel and resort managers can open and close room availability and rates as needed. However, the central reservation office reporting shows actual availability at all times.

Stouffer increased their computer capabilities by upgrading to an IBM ES9000 mainframe. While the older IBM 4381 was still meeting the needs of the company, Stouffer decided to assure future growth of the system as more and more needs were identified. The top priority is to connect SSMARTS to airline reservation systems, such as American Airlines SABRE, Covia Apollo, and Worldspan (a partnership of Delta, TWA, and Northwest). With this computer-to-computer connection completed in June 1993, travel agents can now use their airline reservation terminals to book Stouffer properties electronically. The entire confirmation process takes no more than seven seconds instead of the one to two hours it formerly took using manual processing. In addition, room and rate availability are considerably more accurate for travel agents. While Stouffer was not the first lodging company to create a computer-to-computer connection for reservations, it was among the first to provide a direct travel agent–property connection.

Feature: Systems are Plentiful

As the information age evolves, more and more kinds of systems, as well as software applications, are being offered. It can be difficult to assess which system is the best fit for a particular property. Later in the chapter, we will review the specific kinds and varieties of systems available to lodging and foodservice operations.

Success Tool: Choosing the Right System There are a few steps that any hospitality manager can take when choosing the most appropriate system. The right system should cover all of the following key points:

1. **Data collection**. A good system should be easy to use. Information about the guest should be input into the system quickly and with minimal effort.

2. **Data handling**. The proper system should help eliminate or reduce the number of unnecessary, often redundant, data transfer and recording procedures. This means: Gone are the forms that need to be filled out in triplicate, copied, and mailed to every manager in the company.

3. **Data processing**. The right system should enable management to better monitor and administer the guest cycle. All of the proper charges should be applied to a guest's account

during the night, so should the guest choose to leave at 6:00 A.M., there are no mistakes on the bill.

4. **Information output**. A comprehensive system should provide management with timely and accurate reports. A kitchen manager needs to know when the bakery chef is out of flour, long before it is scheduled to happen.

5. **Control**. An intelligent system should provide a high level of operational and internal control over company resources. Think about energy costs in a 2,000-room convention hotel. Knowing which areas need the most air-conditioning can help a manager determine whether remodeling is necessary.

6. **Effectiveness**. A well-designed system should enable management to make more intelligent and better decisions. If reports take too long to run, or are too confusing to interpret, they won't be used.

7. **Efficiency**. An accurate system should provide cost savings to the operation. Based upon the number of lobsters ordered on a Friday night, a restaurant manager should be able to determine how many to order for the following Saturday night.

8. **Proficiency**. The right system will enable the hospitality organization to provide improved and expanded guest services. If everything goes better than the guest expected, that guest will come back.[4]

Success Tool: Applying the System to Specific Needs Once a hospitality company has at its fingertips a system to access the latest information, what should be done with it? McDonald's restaurants, for example, early on assembled information on the American consumer's wishes for hamburgers and then proceeded to arrange a system of suppliers for each component (rolls, meat, onions, potatoes, pickles, condiments, and so on), thus assuring consistency and uniformity of its product at every McDonald's unit worldwide. Now every restaurant's performance is monitored via a computerized information system relating customer sales and vendor purchases, labor costs, and overall profitability.[5]

Other hospitality chains have similarly put technology to work. Boston Market, the former Boston Chicken, is using touch screen technology to get consumer reaction to service and food value. As customers exit, they indicate responses to a thermometer on the screen. Robotics have been applied to taco making at Taco Bell and are being researched for cleaning. For example, guest room robotic vacuuming is being tested by Marriott.

Other examples abound. For example, Pizza Hut has centralized and computerized its home delivery operations since 1986. Rather than having the separate tasks of order taking, baking, and delivery all in the same location, the company developed a system that works more effectively for both the company and its customers. Operators in a customer service center take requests for pizza. Working from a computerized database that shows past orders, trained operators take an average of 17 seconds to verify directions to a caller's home and enter his or her request. Operators then route the orders to the closest bake shops, which are strategically located throughout cities to ensure fast deliveries. Cooks in the satellite bake shops prepare pizzas on instructions sent to bake shop printers from order takers' computers. Drivers aim to complete their deliveries within half an hour of a customer's call and usually succeed.[6] American Airlines's renowned SABRE system handles nearly 2,000 messages *per second* during peak usage, and creates more than 500,000 passenger name records every day. In addition, its database contains 45 *million* fares, with 40 million changes being entered every month.[7]

Feature: Technology is Changing Rapidly

We are in the midst of an information explosion, the result of our having moved to an information society from an industrial one en route, inevitably, toward a global economy. From the beginning of this semester until the end of the next, what you are capable of doing with your personal computer will be staggering. And by the time you graduate? Just think about this: As recently as 1986, hospitality students were writing their papers on typewriters, electric ones if they were lucky! Already there are programs utilizing voice recognition; the user simply speaks, and the computer inputs. Imagine the applications of that technology to the hospitality industry!

Success Tool: Adaptability As a consequence of the technological explosion, since a major part of the typical hotel or foodservice manager's day is dedicated to information—receiving, communicating, and using it in a wide variety of executive tasks—systems have necessarily been developed to produce and manage it.

Plainly, the amount of information a hotel or foodservice business generates is vast, requiring, among other things, an ability to separate what information is *nice to know* from what is really *necessary to know*. The separation is important so that hotel and foodservice managers can employ information systems to maximize profits. This can be accomplished either by increasing revenues or decreasing expenses. A simple example of increasing revenue is keeping an accurate, accessible guest history that enables a hotel to offer more personalized service. The guest may visit more often as a result or may recommend the hotel to others. Both outcomes bring more revenue to the hotel. The use of an energy management system is a straightforward example of a way that technology helps to reduce costs. A computerized system can be programmed to turn down the heat in unoccupied rooms. That reduces real cost, which increases profit.

More spectacular, perhaps, are the current developments in telecommunications, leading to a single, worldwide information network in the global marketplace. Reportedly, by 1992, 16 million miles of fiber-optic telephone cables were in place, linking North America, Europe, Asia, and Australia. It has been asserted that "we are moving toward the capability to communicate anything to anyone, anywhere, by any form—voice, data, text, or image—at the speed of light."[8] In point of fact, global distribution systems linking travel agencies, airlines, hotel chains, and car rental companies were already in place by 1993. Now, technological packages such as Prodigy, CompuServe, and America Online are facilitating direct customer contacts with the hospitality industry worldwide. These on-line developments spell quite a challenge to the hospitality industry.

Success Tool: Training The profitable use of changing technology also requires an ongoing knowledge of the different capabilities of the hardware and software associated with computerized systems. In order to understand what is meant by such systems, we need to know what we really want, and then, how to get it. Then hospitality managers need to train their employees continually in the use of the system. The greatest, most expensive system created will be useless if employees and managers don't know how to operate it.

Training also includes understanding the reporting function, and guidelines for using and running reports appropriately. It also includes learning how to read the reports, or they could become just a mass of numbers printed daily. Many of the information technology companies working with the hospitality industry today hire former hotel and restaurant employees. Why? Because while these employees might not be computer programmers, they can become trainers. These technology companies send trainers out to hospitality companies to teach the employees how to use the systems. And since the trainers are familiar with the hospitality business, they are sensitive to what employees and managers want and need to know.

Lodging Systems

As we turn to the specific kinds of management information systems that are found in lodging properties and in foodservice establishments, the distinguishing features of hospitality systems and corresponding success tools for each can be readily applied. That timely information is critical; the fact that systems are plentiful and that technology is changing rapidly shape how MIS managers select and use computer technology in hospitality businesses. A lodging property has particular needs in computer systems. These needs can be broken down into two divisions with 12 categories. These are:

Front-of-the-House Lodging Systems

- Property Management System (PMS)
- Electronic Locking System (ELS)
- Point of Sale/Electronic Cash Registers (POS/ECR)
- Call Accounting
- Auxiliary Telephone Services
- In-Room Services

Back-of-the-House Lodging Systems

- Energy Management System
- Emergency/Security Systems
- Office Automation
- Back Office Accounting
- Time and Attendance
- Executive Information Systems

How a property is classified determines a great deal about its systems. A 3,000-room urban convention hotel that is part of an international chain will no doubt have a highly complex system for each of the above categories. A budget property most likely will not have all of these systems, and a bed-and-breakfast might not have any, or a simple set of hospitality-related software driven from a personal computer. One thing you'll notice throughout all of these systems is integration. No system stands alone.

Front-of-the-House Lodging Systems

The front-of-the-house contains the departments that have direct contact with guests. Systems in the front-of-the-house must always keep service needs in mind.

Property Management Systems The property management system revolves around the activities of the front desk. It is through this system that a hotel makes and confirms reservations, alerts housekeeping to the status of the room, and maintains guest accounts. There are three components to a PMS: **reservations, rooms management**, and **guest accounting**. When a guest calls a hotel or arrives at the property, the front desk associate simply inputs in the terminal at the desk the guest's last name, and a screen of information appears. This allows the associate to confirm departure date, room rate, and any special instructions. Changes can be made quickly and accurately. The front desk manager or the general manager use the PMS to check room availability. This is often referred to as **rooms control**. Instant access to current and projected occupancy figures helps determine staffing levels, and energy consumption, and can have an impact on room rates. For example, if the manager sees that the property is only 50 percent occupied during an upcoming convention, the sales manager could receive a memo instructing the sales force to offer a more competitive room rate. Finally, the PMS keeps track of the guest's account. Phone calls, room-service, in-room movies, dry-cleaning, and other fee-based services are automatically posted to each guest's account. Upon departure, the guest receives a computer printout detailing the charges and any applicable fees or taxes, and can settle the bill.

A property management system is usually integrated with electronic locking systems, point of sale systems, call accounting systems, and in-room service systems. All of these are utilized by the guest, and can appear as charges on the guest's account. Many hospitality companies are expanding their guest history or frequent guest systems, in an effort to track more carefully the travelers staying in their properties.

Electronic Locking Systems Nearly gone are the days of room keys. In a quest for the highest level of guest security, lodging properties are switching to the **key cards**, a credit card–size device that is unnumbered. A key card is programmed at the front desk, and will open a specific room only for those days reserved by the guest at check-in. If the guest chooses to extend his or her stay, the card must be reactivated by the front desk, or it will not open the door. Housekeepers are issued master key cards, to allow access for cleaning. Electronic locking systems have helped reduce costs in many ways. No longer do locks need to be changed if room keys are lost or stolen, an expensive and time-consuming process. The system also tracks entries to the room, and a guest can feel secure that if the card is lost, an unwanted guest will be unable to gain access to the room, for the hotel can simply deactivate the card and reissue a new one. Electronic locking systems are often tied to energy management systems. If the room is empty, energy can be reduced, and then increased when the guest returns.

Point of Sale Systems A **point of sale system** is an enhanced cash register, just like the one in the campus convenience store. They are found in any area of the property that produces revenue for the hotel, such as room service, restaurants, or gift shops. Point of sale systems are often tied to the guest accounting systems. This integration permits the guest to "charge it to the room." Any bills the guest incurs in an on-premise restaurant or facility can be added to the guest account. This allows the guest to pay for everything at check-out, removing the need to have cash or credit card on hand at all times.

Call Accounting It's a given that in every hotel room there's a phone, and a fairly sophisticated one. It allows the guest to make calls within the hotel, to a local number, or back home or to the office. The call accounting system offers the option of putting long distance phone charges on the guest's bill (a tie into the guest accounting system), and provides instruction for the guest who chooses to use a calling card or credit card. Any call from a guest room to a number outside the hotel sometimes incurs a service fee of between $.50 and $1.00 per call. These charges are automatically applied to the account, and appear on the guest's statement in the order that they were made.

Auxiliary Telephone Services Oh, the dreaded 6:00 A.M. wake-up call! It used to be made by the front desk clerk working the overnight shift; now it can be made by a computer. The front desk logs the time of the requested wake-up call and the room number, and the system automatically rings the phone at the appointed time, and continues to ring until the guest answers. This same system can put personalized messages on the television in the room. In addition, a voice mail system may be available for guests. This system functions just like a home answering machine; a flashing light or number on the phone indicates that a message has been left. The guest retrieves the message, and has the option of saving or deleting it. The voice mail system eliminates the need for the guest to call the front desk for messages, and permits the guest to call in to the hotel to obtain messages without physically returning to get them. These auxiliary telephone services are generally provided free to the guest.

In-Room Services This category of systems is constantly expanding. Beginning simply with a television set, it has quickly grown to include cable access, pay-per-view selections, touch screen check-out capabilities, computerized roomservice, and video games. Minibars can now be equipped with fiber-optic sensors, to record items as they are removed by the guest. The traditional business center in lodging properties is moving directly into the guest room, where modem and fax lines are now being installed.

Back-of-the-House Lodging Systems

In back-of-the-house systems, emphasis is placed on those departments that do not interact directly with the guest, but do have influence on the overall operation of the property. Functions of back-of-the-house systems are often tied to those in the front-of-the-house.

Energy Management Systems An **energy management system** is designed to control the equipment needed for a property's lighting, heating, ventilation, and air-conditioning systems automatically, in both guest rooms and function facilities. Just imagine what the electric bill might be for the MGM Grand Hotel in Las Vegas, with its neon lights and huge air-conditioned conference spaces. For a small bed-and-breakfast high in the Colorado Rockies, the winter fuel bill can eat into profits in no time. An energy management system is designed to help a property keep costs down. For example, the system can sense when a guest room is unoccupied, and from a central location the heat can be turned down. (Remember the electronic locking system, informing the hotel when a guest enters and leaves a room?) Large and small properties can partition space into zones, so late at night, there's no air-conditioning comforting empty banquet facilities. The high energy costs faced by all hoteliers have led to the development of sophisticated energy management systems.

Emergency and Security Systems Fire alarms, sprinkler systems, and emergency call boxes are systems all lodging properties need to have. Due to fire code regulations and other state and local requirements, emergency lights and automatic doors must be installed. Many emergency systems are connected directly to local fire and police departments, and a central location within the hotel is able to identify where on the property the problem is located.

Office Automation As with most businesses today, the hospitality industry utilizes the power of office computer systems. From financial spreadsheets to e-mail, the work of the hotel is done on computer. All back-of-the-house accounting systems are here, to maintain accurate records on accounts payable and accounts receivable. The flow of funds in and out of the property is kept in a master file called the general ledger, from which management reports can be produced. Timely and accurate information for payroll, the payment of vendors, and inventory are essential to the operation of the property.

Staffing Systems Many staff positions within a lodging property are paid by the hour. To track employee hours for payroll, taxes, overtime, vacation, and sick time accurately, electronic time clocks record when an employee begins and ends a shift. This data is sent directly to payroll to generate a paycheck.

Executive Information Systems A relatively new software application is emerging for management use. **Executive Information Systems (EIS)** attempt to integrate information from many different kinds of applications and present the most needed and most wanted information in summary form. As the kinds of applications become more prolific, and as the amount of information that can be and is stored expands, executives often find themselves overwhelmed with information that is nice to know, but not necessarily what they need to know. This type of system is evolving in response to that condition. This type of system is also applicable to foodservice systems.

Foodservice Systems

Foodservice systems include front-of-the-house restaurant systems, back-of-the-house restaurant systems, and function rooms and catering. These three divisions have various categories of applications. Summarized, they are as follows:

Front-of-the-House Foodservice Systems

- POS/ECR Systems
- Seating Charts
- Beverage Systems

Back-of-the-House Foodservice Systems

- Purchasing
- Inventory Management
- Recipe Management
- Menu Engineering
- Equipment
- Productivity Systems
- Accounting Systems
- Executive Information Systems

Function Rooms and Catering Systems

- Function and Banquet Room Sales
- Off-Premise Catering

Front-of-the-House Foodservice Systems

Front-of-the-house restaurant management systems offer ways to interact intelligently and effectively with customers. From order taking, to seating, to bill paying, a restaurant or foodservice operation can use technology to enhance service, save time, and increase profits if used effectively.

A restaurant system may comprehend one or more of the front-of-the-house *and* the back-of-the-house applications noted, and in fact, increasingly offers not only multiple functions but the ability to customize those functions to specific restaurant needs. As systems evolve, more and more functions are linked together, achieving seamless integration, as discussed earlier in the chapter.

POS/ECR Systems A computer based restaurant management system relies on the information collected through points of sale (POS) or electronic cash registers (ECR). There is a wide variety of **POS/ECR** hardware components as well as a wide selection of software packages. Combinations of the various kinds of hardware, such as keyboards, screens, and printers, and software packages, which manipulate different kinds of information, create many useful functions for a restaurant operation. For example, via a handheld keyboard device or a terminal at a station in the dining area, a member of the wait staff can send orders to a remote printer in the kitchen without leaving the front-of-the-house. **Touch screen technology** eliminates the need for a cashier to ring in prices. The cashier simply touches a button labeled with the food item, such as "hamburger." The price is automatically added. Touch screen technology is also being used in fast food restaurants for customers to place orders themselves without interacting with an order taker. The customer touches the word or a picture of the item he would like to order.

A POS/ECR system keeps track of important information that is useful to management. Information is logged for each item on the menu, such as a description and the price. It also keeps inventory of the various ingredients as each item is sold. When linked with back-of-the-house systems, inventory checks can also be done at the purchasing, receiving, and issuing stages. The system also keeps track of information about the servers who use it, such as the number of guests served by each waiter.

Such systems can produce useful management reports. A sales summary is a commonly used report. This kind of report gives the total sales of each item for a given time. It can also show the settlement method—that it was paid for by check, charge, or cash—or which server produced the sale.

Seating Charts A seating chart application allows a restaurant to keep an accurate track of each table in the dining area, the number of turns for each table, and the server assigned to each. This is especially useful for large operations. Some programs have a layout feature that allows for a graphic illustration of each chair and table in the dining room. The host or hostess can then keep track of occupancy of the various tables. Electronically lighted charts allow the status of each table to be readily viewed. For example, a red light might mean the table is occupied, a green light that the table is ready. The hours that tables are assigned can also be input into the seating chart.

Beverage Systems Beverage systems are an important control mechanism for any foodservice operation. Beverage systems automate the dispensing of drinks. For example, suppose a customer ordered a Bloody Mary. The system would automatically dispense the appropriate ounces of vodka according to the drink standards for that particular operation. Some systems also dispense the nonalcoholic mix such as the tomato juice and spices. The system is often linked directly to the cash register, so a drink is rung up as it is poured. Such systems keep track of the total sales of each kind of beverage and provide an excellent methodology for cross-checking quantities in inventory. The system also keeps track of who served a drink and from what location. The systems generally will not pour if a glass is not in place, as a savings feature. They can also alert the bartender when a particular bottle is empty.

Beverage systems may also be set up in the back-of-the-house. In this case, the system serves as an auxiliary bar where bartenders only come in contact with wait staff.

Back-of-the-House Foodservice Systems

Back-of-the-house foodservice applications include all of the functions involved in getting ready for service to customers. This includes purchasing items, keeping track of them in inventory, keeping track of them in recipe production, and designing the menu. Capital equipment purchases and maintenance, measuring productivity, and accounting functions are also important restaurant applications.

Purchasing A purchasing application helps a restaurant monitor what it purchases, from whom, when, and for how much, for every kind of item. Every order is assigned a **purchase order** number, which becomes an important element of tracking deliveries as they arrive at the loading zone. Records of deliveries are kept in a daily receiving log.

Monitoring costs and availability of product from competitive vendors, sometimes called **bid specifications**, allow a purchasing agent to make the most profitable purchases. These purchases are often placed directly with vendors via autodial modems. Some vendors provide on-line information so a restaurant can log on and check the price and availability of a particular item without interacting with a salesperson.

Inventory Management An inventory management system keeps track of the food and beverage and other materials (such as napkins, silverware, and so on) purchased and used by an operation. It gives management a control mechanism for monitoring what inventory is physically on hand versus what should be on hand. The difference or variance between the two should be very small. If it is not, management is alerted to another problem such as theft, waste, or shortages in deliveries.

Other information such as storeroom location, minimum stock levels, order lead time, and importantly the value of the inventory at any given time, can also be produced from this kind of application.

Recipe Management Recipe management software helps a restaurant operator to keep a listing of every ingredient purchased, including the cost of each ingredient, unit of measure, and how many units are used in each recipe. Each recipe is generally assigned a name, the recipe itself, portion sizes, and menu selling prices. With these building blocks, a restaurateur can monitor recipe costs and compare them to menu prices. This comparison yields **food cost percentage**, which is an important measure of a restaurant's profitability.

For monitoring inventory from start to finish, and to simplify the task of reordering, a restaurant would do well to link this application to its purchasing application and its POS/ECR system.

Menu Engineering The process of engineering a menu is discussed at length in chapter 9, "How Things Work: Foodservice Operations." One of the elements of menu engineering, the profitability/popularity matrix, is greatly assisted by computer application. The numerical information, such as the menu price, the food cost of the item, and the demand for each item determine where the item is on the matrix. The menu items can be monitored over time and by meal period and season to help reengineer the offerings.

Suppose, for example, a seasonal analysis reveals that a generally profitable and popular item, the fresh fruit salad, drops in popularity and increases in ingredient cost over the winter months. Management may substitute ingredients during this time frame or discontinue the item until spring.

Equipment Equipment applications take the guesswork out of properly maintaining kitchen equipment and therefore extending its useful life. Basic information is kept about each piece of equipment such as the purchase date, warranty information, vendor name, address, and phone, and service record details. When a piece of equipment should be serviced, in what way, and by whom is tied to a calendar function. Management is automatically reminded to schedule routine maintenance.

If a particular piece of equipment is troublesome, accurate service records can help management make capital purchase decisions. Suppose a pizza oven has repeatedly broken during peak hours of operation. With accurate records of service repair costs as well as a record of the time the equipment was out of operation, a manager can estimate the lost revenues and what it would cost to fix the oven. Whether or not to purchase a new oven becomes a more straightforward decision.

Productivity Systems Productivity systems take historic information and package it in a way that allows management to implement automated scheduling, forecasting, and productivity tracking. Consider a brand-new business. As the sales and revenues for each day are recorded over time, the management team can become more and more sophisticated in predicting future sales. When patterns emerge for a particular day or a particular meal period, management can order inventory and schedule staff more accurately. Productivity systems can automatically translate sales volume into staffing and inventory needs. Productivity measures, such as total guests served per staff member, can then also be monitored.

Accounting Systems As with many businesses, restaurants have need for accounting systems that keep track of accounts receivable, accounts payable, and cash flow. There is also a need for a payroll system and the ability to produce management reports for internal use and financial statements for external applications such as the filing of a tax return. The various elements of accounting will be discussed in the next chapter, "An Accounting Tool Box." A well-designed management information system makes the recording, classifying, and reporting functions of accounting significantly easier and more useful.

Function Rooms and Catering Systems

Though some of the systems used in foodservice management are readily applicable to catering, there are some specific characteristics of functions which cause need for separate software applications. Functions, which are typically booked well in advance, can involve complex arrangements for from a few to many people. The use of function software allows a hotel to keep orderly records and to assist customers more quickly. The programs can constantly update business forecasts and keep track of the contracts that have been signed and the proposals that are pending.

For chain properties, there is another application for future sales. Suppose a large association alternates its annual convention from the East Coast to the West Coast. A property in San Diego, California, could access the function records of its sister property in Hartford, Connecticut, to pitch the business for this year's West Coast event knowledgeably. The application of managing information extends to off-premise catering as well, where the needs of the customer may extend beyond food and beverage service.

Function and Banquet Room Sales For every function that is held by a hotel property, there is a specific set of information that must be recorded, including the type of function, seating arrangements, room location, time, including setup and breakdown requirements, rates, and food and beverage requirements. For banquets, the food and beverage requirements are obviously more complex than a coffee break for a meeting.

All pertinent information is recorded in a **function diary**, sometimes called the **bible**. Catering applications effectively create an electronic function book. The ability of a sales manager is greatly enhanced by computer aided searches. For example, dates can quickly be ascertained for a client interested in holding a meeting for 50 persons on a Saturday in July, with 25 persons needing to spend the evening in the hotel. Most function programs can be tied to hotel room inventory, allowing the sales manager to service the client fully with immediate information.

The electronic function book offers features such as quickly customizing menus, automatically recording changes to event orders, and maintaining a link to inventory that notes if an item is unavailable.

Off-Premise Catering The nature of off-premise catering may require the provision of service beyond a menu. Decorations, entertainment, chair and table rental, and valet parking may all need to be provided. The computer programs assist in cost analysis as well as keeping track of potential subcontractors who can provide these additional services.

Some programs can update production requirements due to changes. For example, suppose the coordinator of a charity event calls at the last minute to announce that 40 additional people will arrive late in the evening, after the cocktail hour but in time for dinner. The program can automatically increase the number of tables, chairs, dinner entrees, linens, and floral arrangements. The system recognizes, however, that a change in numbers does not affect items such as entertainment, and therefore does not adjust the original order for those items. But, in this case, since the late arrivals are coming after the cocktail hour, the coordinator will have to specify increases only to the dinner orders, and not to the number of hors d'oeuvres.

The Role of the Hospitality MIS Manager

With the advent of computer based systems and their astounding growth in business enterprises of all types, there is hardly anyone in the hospitality world today who is unaffected by such systems and the information they possess. Therefore, as a future manager of a hotel or a foodservice organization, it is important to ask these questions:

1. Will you be more successful tomorrow than you are today by gaining a better understanding of the uses of information systems?

2. How are decisions made in a lodging operation? Who makes them? How does any one department know what another department is doing? How are the financial transactions of the guest cycle controlled? How do the front and back offices of the hotel communicate?[9]

3. What characteristics of the foodservice business are generally regarded as unique when compared to other hospitality industry enterprises? What about the level of inventory turnover experienced; the number of points of sale maintained; the variable product mixes (breakfast, lunch, and dinner) and price modes (menu, coupon, happy hour, and entertainment specials); and the communications networks generated within a foodservice environment?[10]

Not all establishments have MIS managers, but nearly all establishments have managers who must tackle MIS issues. Regardless of who leads the charge, managers land square in the middle of this set of questions as they tackle their assignments. The problems faced can be very complex and may not be remedied with technology.

What's in the In Box?

Consider the in box of a MIS manager for the European division of a large American restaurant chain. The following items might surface for the restaurant chain MIS manager:

1. The current purchasing system application for the restaurant is out of date. The current vendor promises a new and improved version in six to nine months. You are debating whether to switch vendors immediately (to what appears to be a more sophisticated program) and incur the training and switching costs, or wait until the current vendor releases the update.

2. The director of marketing for the company has asked for help in designing a Web page for potential restaurant customers. The most critical task is deciding what questions the page should answer and what type of interactive pieces to provide. Differentiating the page from the competition will be critical as more and more restaurants go on-line.

3. Several unit managers have responded favorably to being test sites for collecting the marketing research database you have proposed. (The research method involves putting touch screen monitors into restaurants for customers to react to food, service, and so on, and to give demographic information.) What remains is designing the questionnaire more specifically, deciding what languages to use, and designing the kinds of reports you want the research to provide.

4. The shift managers at many of the units have found themselves overwhelmed with reports, particularly from non-European divisions. You need to assess the issue: Are the reports too complicated? Are the reports too numerous? Are general managers delegating too much? If there are issues, how can the shift managers assist in solving them?

5. One of your competitive chains wants to come and look at your computer systems. How should you handle the request?

Creating Competitive Advantage

An MIS manager must know every corner of the business well to be successful. In the course of a day, the manager must go out of his way to collect information that will help steer the uses of available technology. How is this information gathered? Listening to managers and line employees is a good start. Taking a good look at guest comment cards will often yield important data. Say, for instance, 90 percent of the comment cards over a given period noted the absence of video checkout, and the manager knows that all nearby competitors have recently installed that service; it could be time to invest.

A successful MIS manager will invest time in listening to the employees and the guests, but will also invest time in learning about what changes are going on in technology. Meeting the technology companies, attending industry seminars, and asking colleagues about new systems will all help a manager determine or anticipate the next step—which should lead to competitive advantage.

███████ **www.travel.com.**
_____

It's happened. Phone calls to individual hotels. Phone calls to central reservations systems. Brochures received in the mail. Trips to the local travel agency. Perusing the travel section of major newspapers. Videotapes. They all now have new competition. The hotel industry's first interactive travel catalogue is now on-line on the Internet. Logging in "www.travel.com" puts travelers on line to Travelweb. The interactive electronic travel catalogue allows a PC traveler to access color photographs, and get information on rates, local attractions, restaurants, and other amenities. By the end of 1995, users should be able to book reservations. In the immediate future, the reservation system will include properties from ITT Sheraton, Hyatt, Marriott, Hilton, Forte, and Best Western.

Airline reservations systems, such as the widely used SABRE system, are even further ahead of the game. A PC user can tap into the system via such links as America On Line, gather fare information about several fare classes, and book reservations worldwide.

The possibilities raise important questions about the distribution channels currently used by travelers and hoteliers. How will the network of travel agencies be affected? How might individual and chain organizations use the net as a source of direct marketing? Stay logged on. The best may be yet to come.

Summary

Today, as never before, management information systems are evolving faster than some organizations can monitor or control them. Nonetheless, as computer technology continuously improves and applications emerge to take advantage of new interfaces, the hospitality industry can scarcely ignore the opportunities afforded by such management advances. The tools that will help an MIS manager seize these opportunities include:

- seamless integration
- planning for various hospitality components to work together
- choosing the right system
- applying the system to specific needs
- adaptability
- training

Further, an MIS manager must be keenly aware of the kinds of systems available to lodging properties as well as foodservice establishments. These include numerous applications to both the front and back-of-the-house.

On the horizon are skyrocketing improvements in guest services, labor costs, and bottom line performance. It is critical to recognize the uses of information technology, and apply them across the industry. It is perhaps even more important to anticipate these improvement and changes, such as the Internet applications, to reap the competitive advantage of being first.

Discussion Questions

1. The computer has had far-reaching effects on our lives and on the hospitality industry. What elements of computer technology do you think will have far-reaching effects in the future?

2. Describe how what you did yesterday would change if you did not directly or indirectly use the capabilities of computers.

3. Think about the types of information a hotel manager needs in an urban convention hotel. Compare those reports to the owner of a bed-and-breakfast with a well-known gourmet restaurant.

4. How much does a manger need to know about a computer to operate one?

5. How do you think the use of the Internet and the World Wide Web affect travel agencies? Explain.

6. What types of lodging and foodservice applications work best when integrated with other types?

7. What is the difference between information that is nice to know, and that one needs to know? How can an MIS manager separate the former from the latter?

8. Why are room keys being replaced by key cards in many lodging properties?

9. What advantage does a beverage system provide to a restaurant operation?

10. What do you think it is about the evolution of the computer that it does not have a well-known inventor?

Assignments

1. Consider all of the items in the in box of the hospitality MIS manager. Which would you give the highest priority? The lowest priority? Why? How would you tackle each item? Assume the role of the MIS manager. Develop a work plan using the success tools in the chapter.

2. Consider the different computer systems available to hotels and restaurants. How can a hotel or restaurant maximize profits by increasing revenues or decreasing costs using each of these systems?

3. Collect information on several vendors of a particular type of computer system. How do they compare and contrast? Which one would you purchase? Why?

End Notes

[1] Steve Lohr, "The Face of Computer 50 Years and 18,000 Tubes Ago," *New York Times*, 19 February 1996. *Note:* Reference accessed via the internet.

NOTE: The mathematician and pioneer of game theory John von Neuman has been credited with early computer theory. Two later researchers, John Presper Eckhert and John W. Mauchly, of the University of Pennsylvania demonstrated their general purpose electronic computer, called ENIAC, on February 14, 1946.

[2] Michael L. Kasavana, *Hotel Information Systems* (Boston: CBI Publishing Co., 1978), 108.

[3] Larry Long, *Management Information Systems* (Englewood Cliffs, New Jersey: Prentice-Hall, 1989), xiii.

4. Michael L. Kasavana, *Effective Front Office Operations* (Boston: CBI Publishing Co., 1981), 97–98.

5. Kasavana, *Computer Systems for Foodservice Operations* (New York: Van Nostrand Reinhold Company, 1984), 3.

6. "Mr. Winchester Orders a Pizza," *Fortune* (14 November 1986): 134.

7. Max D. Hopper, "Rattling SABRE—New Ways to Compete on Information," *Harvard Business Review* (May–June 1990): 120.

8. John Naisbitt and Patricia Aburdene, *Megatrends 2000* (New York: William Morrow & Company, 1990), 23.

9. Kasavana, *Effective Front Office Operations*, 94.

10. Kasavana, *Computer Systems for Foodservice Operations* (New York: Van Nostrand Reinhold Company, 1984), 3.

Chapter Thirteen

Like any profession, the world of business has fostered the development of its own language. Words and phrases which are readily definable when they stand alone yet can be confusing when used in a business context. … Unfamiliarity with the technical words and idioms that have evolved can perplex the uninitiated and make seasoned executives appear out-of-date.

The Language of Business [1]

An Accounting
Tool Box ❧

When you finish this chapter, you should:

1. Understand the features of hospitality accounting and the success tools that can be employed in response to those features.

2. Understand the difference between financial and managerial accounting.

3. Be familiar with the format for a hospitality balance sheet, income statement, and statement of cash flow.

4. Understand the ways in which different users of financial statements are interested in them.

5. Know the relationship of the income statement to the balance sheet.

6. Explain the nature of the kinds of decisions made in managerial accounting.

7. Explain the purpose of ratio analysis.

8. Be familiar with the scope of ratios used in accounting and how they are classified.

9. Be able to identify the kinds of issues that might be found in the in box of a hospitality controller.

Introduction

The place is southwest Connecticut. The time, the late 1980s and early 1990s. The central character, a former senator from South Dakota, George McGovern. As for the plot, it's a familiar one—that of a harried traveler spending countless nights in hotels while on the campaign and lecture trail, telling himself, and later, his friends, "Some day I'd like to run a place the way it should be run."

As it turns out, the senator-cum-hotelier succumbs to the entrepreneurial bug, buys a 144-room Connecticut hotel—the Stratford Inn—and as a consequence soon finds himself in the same position as thousands of new business owners every year: broke!

Whatever may be the explanation for Stratford Inn's financial predicament, the senator's lament is scarcely one to be regarded with indifference. Did he not commission an in-depth analysis of the financial feasibility of acquiring the Stratford property—a task that major accounting firms in the hospitality industry are equipped to perform? Later, in ruefully commenting on the hotel's eventual bankruptcy, the senator admitted, "I wish I had known more about the hazards and difficulties of such a business, especially during a recession of the kind that hit New England just as I was acquiring the inn's 43-year leasehold."[2]

The lesson is plain. Whether a hospitality establishment is a small, owner-operated enterprise like the 144-room Stratford Inn or a major link in an international chain, an understanding of the language of business, a comfortable feel for the rigors of accounting basics, and an ability to interpret a company's financials and manage accordingly go a long way toward reducing the risk of financial disaster.

Can the Savoy Cut Costs and Still Be the Savoy?

A century ago, it advertised itself as "the perfection of luxury and comfort," with electric light everywhere, the finest river and garden views, and "no less than 67 bathrooms." Even today, at 105 years old, London's Savoy Hotel retains a special place in the hearts of the world's elite. Roomservice, valets, and maids are summoned not with a phone call but, as in a stately old home, by pushing buttons on a small bedside table labeled WAITER, MAID, and VALET. The Savoy ages its own meat, makes its own chutney, has its own florist, and makes its own beds. Literally. The Savoy makes the mattresses used in the guest rooms.

But some traditions may be toppled, because what is sorely lacking is profit. Though room rates start at £200 (about $315), last year the Savoy Group PLC eked out a mere £510,000 net profit on a revenue of £83.3 million.

Profits can be frustratingly elusive in the luxury trade, where standards must be maintained regardless of economic conditions and empty rooms. (Occupancy at the Savoy was 66 percent last year and will be about 77 percent this year, according to hotel sources.) And the costs of providing world-renowned service can be staggering. Each floor has its own waiter. Faxes can be folded to the guest's specification. And it takes four waiters and a carver to oversee the placement of roasts on a guest's dinner plate. All of this requires a lot of staff, three employees for every guest, about double the London average. And the Savoy is over 100 years old. In the past few years, the hotel has spent £3 million building a new health club, spent £5 million building a new kitchen for its head chef, and spent other funds to upgrade plumbing, heating, and electrical systems.

The Savoy recently hired a new general manager, in an attempt to bring costs down. How the hotel will manage to keep the customers happy and still turn a profit won't be known for some time.

Adapted from Janet Guyon, in *The Wall Street Journal*, 25 October 1994.

Distinguishing Features of Hospitality Accounting

What we seek to do in this chapter is to highlight the underpinnings of **financial** and **managerial** accounting without endeavoring to cover the in-depth mechanics of financial accounting or the extensive analysis managers may endeavor to pursue. The latter information is happily available in a number of contemporary accounting textbooks. Instead, we aim here to gain a better understanding of the major financial statements used in hospitality businesses, as well as a better understanding of ratios used by managers to evaluate those financial statements.

Feature: Financial Accounting

Financial accounting is that branch of accounting that follows a standardized format to record, classify, and summarize information. That information is summarized in the form of financial statements. Financial accounting does not interpret results or analyze performance.

Financial accounting follows the principles and standards developed by the American Institute of Certified Public Accountants. This format can be found in the **uniform systems of accounts** that have been developed by accountants and consultants from various segments of the hospitality industry. Standardization helps companies in many ways, from filing taxes to allowing for comparisons among competitors. Some examples of uniform systems of accounts are:

1. Uniform System of Accounts for Hotels

2. Uniform System of Accounts and Expense Dictionary for Small Hotels, Motels, and Motor Hotels

3. Uniform System of Accounts for Clubs

4. Uniform System of Accounts for Restaurants

Financial statements are used for a number of purposes, including:

- The provision of an internal reporting system showing the operating results of each revenue producing unit or department. The statements thereby provide a basis for analyzing and judging departmental performance. **Internal users**, or users affiliated with the company, can include the board of directors, managers, or other staff.

- The ability to compare results to those of other companies. Traditionally, statistics from compilations collected on a regional or national basis have reflected averages against which individual companies have compared their own results. However, it must be borne in mind that averages are *not* standards.

- The furnishing of timely, streamlined stockholder reports—albeit elaborately footnoted where required—to explain the workings of the company.

- The application of loans from creditors. Bankers and other financial institutions require financial statements in order to process loans.

- Government requirements. State and federal agencies, notably the Internal Revenue Service (IRS), require various kinds of information reported in accordance with standard accounting principles. The Securities and Exchange Commission (SEC) and public utility commissions may also request financial statements. Stockholders, bankers, the IRS, the SEC, and public utility commissions are examples of **external users**.

In order to understand the financial accounting information used by both internal and external users, we now turn to an understanding of the elements found on three major statements:

1. The Balance Sheet
2. The Income Statement
3. The Statement of Cash Flows

Success Tool: Understanding the Balance Sheet Not infrequently referred to as a snapshot of a company's financial condition at a given point in time, the **balance sheet** is of primary interest to owners and creditors as well as to managers, because it shows:

- How the company has used the funds entrusted to it: by paying its debts, offering dividends, and purchasing fixed assets; and

- What constitutes the company's **assets, liabilities, and owners' equity.**

A typical balance sheet is shown in Exhibit 13.1. This is a balance sheet of a small, international, independently owned hotel, with 100 rooms and approximately 18 employees.

Exhibit 13.1 International Hotel Balance Sheet

December 31, 1997

Assets		Liabilities and Owners' Equity	
Current Assets		**Current Liabilities**	
Cash	50,000	Notes Payable	25,000
Accounts Receivable	15,000	Accounts Payable	15,000
Supplies	25,500	Wages Payable	35,000
Total	**90,500**	Income Tax Payable	10,000
Property and Equipment		Total	**85,000**
Land	500,000		
Building	650,000	**Long-Term Liabilities**	
Equipment	250,000	Mortgage Payable	950,000
Furnishings	450,000	Total	**950,000**
Total	**1,850,000**	**Owners' Equity**	
Less Accumulated Depreciation	210,000	Stock	450,000
Net Property and Equipment	**1,640,000**	Retained Earnings	245,500
		Total	**695,500**
Total Assets	**1,730,500**	**Total Equity and Liabilities**	**1,730,500**

The first and most important numbers to look at on a balance sheet are the totals at the bottom. True to its name, a balance sheet must balance; total assets must equal total equity and liabilities. If they don't, it is an indication that something is very wrong in the accounting department!

Assets First, the left portion of the balance sheet shows International's **assets**—those things that the company owns. These assets are usually listed in decreasing order of **liquidity**; that is, the ones that can be turned into cash most quickly are listed nearest the top. You will notice that there are three categories of assets, as follows:

Current Assets: These include cash or items that can be converted into cash within one year or less. As seen here they are:

- **Cash** is the amount of cash on hand (or in a bank account) and in Exhibit 13.1 amounts to $50,000.

- **Accounts receivable** represents amounts charged to individuals or companies for which payment has not yet been received. As shown in Exhibit 13.1, this amounts to $15,000. An example of an item in accounts receivable would include room nights charged to credit cards, when payment has not yet been made. It is money owed to the hotel, and will eventually be collected.

- **Supplies** amount to $25,500 and include such items as alcoholic beverages, paper products, cleaning materials, and stationery.

Total Current Assets, or the sum of the above categories, are shown in Exhibit 13.1 as amounting to $90,500.

Property and Equipment is the second major category of assets. It amounts to $1,850,000 and includes land, buildings, furniture, and equipment, such as china, glassware, silver, linens, and uniforms. These items are recorded **at cost**, that is, the original amount that was paid for the item, regardless of what it may be worth today. For example, an Oriental rug in the lobby may have cost $1,000, but today is worth $10,000; $1,000 is the amount recorded.

Accumulated depreciation means that the cost of building, plus furniture and equipment— but not land—are reduced to reflect the decline in their value due to wear and tear, the passage of time, changed economic conditions, or other conditions. For example, if ware-washing equipment costing $10,000 is expected to have a useful life of 10 years—with an estimated trade-in value of $1,000 at the end of a 10-year life—the annual depreciation will be:

$$\frac{\text{value today} - \text{trade in value}}{\text{\# of years of useful life}} = \frac{\text{value to be depreciated}}{\text{\# of years of useful life}}$$

OR

$$\frac{\$10,000 - \$1,000}{10 \text{ years}} = \frac{\$9,000}{10 \text{ years}} = \$900 \text{ per year}$$

This is called the **straight-line method of depreciation**. It is a way for a hospitality company to reduce the value of an asset, over time, so that it will be economically feasible to replace the item at the end of its useful life. **Amortization** generally involves amortizing the cost, spreading the cost of certain intangible assets such as goodwill or franchises over the life of such assets. In the case of

International, calculating the depreciation for all items resulted in a total accumulated depreciation of $210,000. Subtracting $210,000 from $1,850,000 leaves **net property and equipment** of $1,640,000.

Total Assets totaled $1,730,000, the sum of current assets and net property and equipment. Liabilities and owners' equity must equal this amount.

Liabilities and Owners' Equity This half of the balance sheet simply shows where that $1,730,500 in assets came from. That is to say, it shows the *source* of the money put to the *uses* shown on the asset half of the balance sheet.

Current Liabilities, that is, those debts that must be paid, or are expected to be paid within a year are listed first:

- **Notes payable** refers to the current amount due, within the year, of the long-term debt. In this case, the mortgage is the only long-term debt the hotel has, although the hotel could borrow funds for other reasons. This figure is $25,000.

- **Accounts payable**, amounting to $15,000, is the money owed to suppliers of food, beverages, and other supplies purchased in the course of everyday operations. Most vendors or suppliers work on a 30-day billing cycle; that is, after delivery of goods, an invoice is sent, notifying the recipient that payment is due within 30 days.

- **Wages payable** simply refers to wage, salary, and employee benefit obligations as well as payroll taxes that have been incurred, but for which the corresponding payment has yet to be made. For this period of operation, it amounts to $35,000. For example, if some salaried employees are paid on December 15, and this balance sheet was constructed on December 31, wages payable reflects the amount that is owed to employees for work performed between December 16 and December 31, which will be paid on January 15, 1998.

- **Income Tax Payable** amounts to $10,000. This is the tax still owed to the government on the company's taxable profits.

Total Current Liabilities sum to $85,000.

Long-term liabilities are those debts due beyond one year. This category includes the mortgage on the hotel property.

- **Mortgage payable** is the amount outstanding owed on the mortgage, less the current amount due. In the case of International, the current amount due on the mortgage, found above under current liabilities, is $25,000. The total amount of the mortgage is then $975,000. On the balance sheet, the current and long-term portions are recorded separately, and thus, mortgage payable is $950,000.

Owners' Equity is the difference between total assets and total liabilities. It represents the equity, or interest, the owners have in the business. Owners' equity simply is the capital, the money invested in a company with the expectation that the owners will receive something in return from the company for allowing it to use their money.

In return for the capital an owner has supplied, he gets a **stock** certificate acknowledging his payment. This certificate is known as common stock. It represents his share of the company ownership, entitling him to a share of the company profits in the form of dividends. In this case, stock equals $450,000.

Retained Earnings represents the total of all the previous years' profits that have not been distributed as dividends to the shareholders, but kept instead within the company to finance operations and long-lived purchases. In this case, it is $245,500. Remember this figure; you will encounter it again when we examine the income statement.

Total Shareholders' Equity is $450,000, and then total liabilities and owners' equity equals $1,730,500. Total liabilities and owners' equity of $1,730,500 exactly equal total assets of $1,730,500. Thus, since assets and liabilities are in balance, this statement is called a balance sheet.

Success Tool: Understanding the Income Statement The **income statement** is variously called a **profit and loss statement**, a **P&L**, a **statement of earnings**, or a **statement of operations**. Official accounting terminology for what most people call "profit" is the phrase **net income**. By definition, the income statement reports the results of operations for a period of time such as a week, month, quarter, six months, or one year. It is generally regarded as one of the most important financial statements used by hotel and restaurant managers.

Relationship of Income Statement to the Balance Sheet The **income statement** covers the operating results over a period of time, whereas the **balance sheet** presents a picture of the financial condition of the business at a particular point in time. In other words, if company produces a balance sheet on December 31, and not again until the following December 31, the income statement tells management what went on during the 365 days in between. If a balance sheet is a snapshot at a point in time, an income statement is a movie of a time period.

What the income statement in general reflects is the **revenue** received by the company between the balance sheet dates, and the expenses that have been made to produce that revenue. When revenue exceeds expenses, the result is a **profit** or **net income**. When the reverse occurs, the result is a **loss**. Net income or loss is tied from the balance sheet to the income statement via **retained earnings**. Let's take a look at Exhibit 13.2, the income statement for International, a hotel with one dining room serving breakfast, lunch, and dinner, and a small gift shop.

As you can see in this example, income statements from two periods, in this case two years, are placed side by side, to allow for immediate comparison of numbers. Tracing the figures down the column, it is easy to see how an income statement is constructed. The first section is revenue—where the funds came from. In this case, the sales in rooms, food and beverage outlets, and the telephone provided the funds. The category "other" represents the sale of goods or services that don't fall into the larger areas. Some examples include gift shop revenues, charging guests for using a fax or copying machine, or revenues from transportation services to the airport. **Gross operating income**, or the total amount of funds flowing into the hotel, totals $3,031,900 for 1997.

The next section begins the series of deductions to that revenue. Income statements can be designed in a variety of ways, but salaries and benefits usually follow gross operating income. The amount allocated to employees is subtotaled, to reflect the entire amount spent on labor. Then follow all operating expenses. Operating expenses, wages, and benefits are totaled, and then subtracted from gross operating income, to leave **gross operating profit**. An important note: Operating expenses are considered to be **variable**. Variable costs are costs that change as the business changes. As sales volume goes up, variable costs rise, and the opposite is true. For example, as more customers choose to dine in the hotel dining room, food and beverage costs, utility costs, and labor

■■■■■■ **Exhibit 13.2** International Hotel Income Statement

	1997	1996
Sales		
Rooms	$ 1,910,000	$ 1,575,000
Food	697,500	575,000
Beverage	181,900	150,000
Telephone	91,000	75,000
Other	151,500	125,000
Gross operating income	**3,031,900**	**2,500,000**
Operating Costs and Expenses		
Salaries and Wages	879,000	725,000
Employee Benefits	151,500	125,000
Total Payroll and Related Expenses	**1,029,500**	**850,000**
Rooms	242,500	200,000
Food and Beverage	364,000	300,000
Maintenance	303,000	250,000
Advertising	90,500	75,000
Other	61,000	50,000
Subtotal	1,061,000	875,000
Total Operating Costs and Expenses	**2,090,500**	**1,725,00**
Gross Operating Profit	**941,400**	**775,000**
Real Estate Taxes, Insurance	303,000	250,000
Interest	90,900	75,000
Profit before depreciation	**547,500**	**325,000**
Depreciation	151,500	125,000
Profit before Income Tax	**396,000**	**200,000**
Income Tax	150,500	76,000
Net Income	$ **245,500**	$ **124,000**

costs will all rise proportionally. Note how operating expenses were lower in 1996, when the hotel did less business.

The next section itemizes **fixed costs**. Fixed costs are costs that remain constant in the short run, and are not affected by changes in sales volume. No matter how many meals are served, real estate taxes and interest on debt will remain the same. Over the long run, though, most figures will change somewhat. Deductions are noted here for rental of equipment, taxes, insurance, interest, depreciation, and income tax. Finally, we arrive at **net income**, the amount of money that, after all revenue is recorded and all expenses are deducted, can be considered **profit**.

Now, back to the balance sheet. All accounting statements are interrelated. On the balance sheet, retained earnings reflects the amount of net income on the income statement. Each time a balance sheet is produced, net income from the reporting period is added to the previous balance in the retained earnings category. You can see that the $245,500, the net income for 1997, appears as retained earnings on the balance sheet. Think of it like a checkbook. Retained earnings is your current balance, and net income is the amount you are depositing. In some cases, net income is negative, and the negative amount is seen on the income statement in parentheses. The business is operating at a loss. In these situations, net income is subtracted from retained earnings on the balance sheet.

Users of financial statements look to income statements for answers to such questions as:

1. How profitable was the operation? As you look at the income statement, how does the **bottom line** look?

   The bottom line is the net income line on the Income Statement. It is customarily used in reference to the net profit of a company.

2. What are the total sales? How much did sales increase or decrease over the prior year?

3. What were the operating expenses and how do they compare to operating expenses for the prior year?

4. How does net income compare to total sales?

To sum up, we see that the income statement, sometimes referred to as the profit and loss statement, shows money earned for the sale of various hospitality services, minus expenses incurred to earn that income for a specified period of time. Highlighting the more important financial aspects of a company's operations, the income statement is therefore seen as an indispensable tool with which the owners, managers, creditors, financial institutions, and government agencies evaluate the operational success (or failure) of any hospitality enterprise.

Success Tool: Understanding the Statement of Cash Flows A **cash flow statement** is of interest to owners, creditors, and managers for two basic reasons: (1) It shows where the company obtained its cash and how it spent its cash; and (2) it enables the company to look ahead to see whether its sources of cash are adequate to fund its uses of cash. Let's go back to your checkbook for an example. You as an individual could prepare your own cash flow statement by reviewing your checkbook records for the past year and determining where your cash deposits came from (sources) and for what purposes you wrote out checks (uses).

On the other hand, if you wish to predict what your checkbook balance will be at various points during the year, it will help you to identify those points where the uses are expected to exceed the sources, so you can arrange in advance to borrow funds to cover those shortfall periods, and to pay back those loans when cash inflows exceed outflows. Remember that net income or profit is *not* cash.

Let's look at Exhibit 13.3, a three-month cash flow statement for International Hotel. Some items remain constant, such as mortgage payable, while others vary from month to month.

To interpret the statement of cash flows for International Hotel, think again about a checkbook. Receipts are simply the total of cash that came into the hotel, or deposits. Receipts can be in the form of cash, or in the form of accounts receivable. An accounts receivable is a cash inflow when it is paid. For example, guests might charge their meals in the hotel restaurant. When the hotel receives payment from the credit card company, that income is recorded as a receipt.

Exhibit 13.3 Statement of Cash Flows January–March 1997

	March	February	January
Opening Bank Balance	**10,000**	**15,000**	**5,000**
Receipts			
Cash Sales	115,000	80,000	70,000
Accounts Receivable	5,000	8,000	5,000
Total	**130,000**	**103,000**	**80,000**
Disbursements			
Food and beverage costs	25,000	20,000	16,000
Accounts payable	15,000	25,000	15,000
Wages and related expenses	25,000	20,000	12,000
Supplies and related expenses	20,000	15,000	7,500
Utilities	2,500	5,000	7,500
Mortgage Payable	5,000	5,000	5,000
Other	2,500	3,000	2,000
Total	95,000	93,000	65,000
Closing Bank Balance	**35,000**	**10,000**	**15,000**

For disbursements, think of what bills need to be paid every month. The costs of purchasing food and supplies, paying wages, the electric bill, and the mortgage are all examples of categories for disbursements. It is cash that has flowed out of the hotel. Notice how when sales (receipts) go up, the variable costs related to sales also rise, but the mortgage payment stays the same.

The Hilton Example

A more complicated set of financial statements are shown in Exhibits 13.4 through 13.6. These are the balance sheet, income statement, and statement of cash flows for the Hilton Hotels Corporation, for the year ending December 31, 1995. As a company grows, its accounting needs grow along with it. In the case of Hilton, you'll notice that the figures recorded are in millions—for example, total assets for 1995 are $3,060.3 million, or over three billion dollars.

The "Consolidated Balance Sheets," Exhibit 13.4, for the Hilton Hotels Corporation shows all of the categories on the balance sheet for International Hotel, plus a few more. The additional categories reflect the complexities of a large, international hotel chain. On the asset side, for example, here are some of the additional categories:

- Cash and equivalents: The 1995 total of $338.0 represents Hilton's cash, and investments easily converted into cash, such as certificates of deposit and money market funds.

- Deferred income taxes are income taxes that have not yet been paid.

Exhibit 13.4 Hilton Hotels Corporation and Subsidiaries

Consolidated Balance Sheets

(In millions) Year Ended December 31,		1995	1994
Assets			
Current Assets	Cash and equivalents	$ 338.0	184.4
	Temporary investments	70.7	208.8
	Deferred income taxes	24.1	26.0
	Other current assets	284.5	254.5
	Total current assets	717.3	673.7
Investments, Property, and Other Assets	Investments in and notes from unconsolidated affiliates	576.2	518.0
	Other investments	19.1	18.7
	Property and equipment, net	1,695.9	1,664.8
	Other assets	51.8	50.7
	Total investments, property, and other assets	2,343.0	2,252.2
Total Assets		$3,060.3	2,925.9
Liabilities and StockHolders' Equity			
Liabilities	Current liabilities	$ 534.9	328.3
	Long-term debt	1,069.7	1,251.9
	Deferred income taxes	123.7	124.3
	Insurance reserves and other	78.3	93.6
	Total liabilities	1,806.6	1,798.1
Stockholders' Equity	Preferred stock, none outstanding	—	—
	Common stock, 48.3 million and 48.1 million shares outstanding, respectively	127.6	127.6
	Cumulative translation adjustment	(1.4)	(.7)
	Unrealized loss on marketable securities	(4.6)	(5.3)
	Retained earnings	1,274.6	1,160.7
		1,396.2	1,282.3
	Less treasury shares, at cost	142.5	154.5
	Total stockholders' equity	1,253.7	1,127.8
Total Liabilities and Stockholders' Equity		$ 3,060.3	2,925.9

Exhibit 13.5 Hilton Hotels Corporation and Subsidiaries

Consolidated Statements of Income
(In millions except per share amounts)

Year Ended December 31,		1995	1994	1993
Revenue	Rooms	$ 587.2	509.6	440.2
	Food and beverage	265.7	247.2	236.8
	Casino	511.0	480.6	502.1
	Management and franchise fees	100.5	94.5	85.1
	Other	125.4	124.2	93.8
	Operating income from unconsolidated affiliates	59.6	57.8	35.5
		1,649.4	1,513.9	1,393.5
Expenses	Rooms	186.4	171.8	152.5
	Food and beverage	229.4	216.4	202.4
	Casino	234.9	216.3	217.5
	Other costs and expenses	613.2	596.5	554.4
	Corporate expense	31.9	28.3	26.8
		1,295.8	1,229.3	1,153.6
Operating Income		353.6	284.6	239.9
	Interest dividend income	35.2	21.5	21.8
	Interest expense	(93.5)	(85.7)	(80.4)
	Interest expense, net, from unconsolidated affiliates	(16.5)	(12.2)	(14.6)
	Property transactions, net	1.5	1.1	(4.5)
	Foreign currency losses	—	(.7)	(1.3)
Income Before Income Taxes and Minority Interest		280.3	208.6	160.9
	Provision for income taxes	102.6	85.3	58.2
	Minority interest, net	4.9	1.6	—
Income Before Cumulative Effect of Accounting Changes		172.8	121.7	102.7
	Cumulative effect of accounting changes, net	—	—	3.4
Net Income		$ 172.8	121.7	106.1
Income Per Share	Before cumulative effect of accounting changes	$ 3.56	2.52	2.14
	Cumulative effect of accounting changes, net	—	—	.07
Net Income Per Share		$ 3.56	2.52	2.21

Exhibit 13.6 Hilton Hotels Corporation and Subsidiaries

Consolidated Statements of Cash Flows
(In millions)

	Year Ended December 31,	1995	1994	1993
Operating Activities	Net Income	$172.8	121.7	106.1
	Adjustments to reconcile net income to net cash provided by operating activities:			
	Depreciation and amortization	141.9	133.3	118.9
	Change in working capital components:			
	Inventories	(.7)	.7	.7
	Accounts receivable	(20.6)	(54.7)	(17.9)
	Other current assets	(7.2)	(5.5)	(19.9)
	Accounts payable and accrued expenses	24.1	35.9	(8.2)
	Income taxes payable	4.0	(1.2)	(9.2)
	Change in deferred income taxes	1.0	(20.8)	(6.6)
	Change in other liabilities	(13.7)	7.8	29.4
	Unconsolidated affiliates' distributions in excess of earnings	29.4	5.9	20.1
	(Gain) loss from property transactions	(1.5)	(1.1)	4.5
	Other	1.2	8.9	9.0
	Net cash provided by operating activities	330.7	230.9	226.9
Investing Activities	Capital expenditures	(187.1)	(254.4)	(156.8)
	Additional investments	(98.3)	(156.7)	(104.7)
	Decrease in long-term marketable securities	1.0	62.6	91.2
	Change in temporary investments	139.1	(118.8)	64.3
	Payments on notes and other	17.5	60.9	5.9
	Net cash used in investing activities	(127.8)	(406.4)	(100.1)
Financing Activities	Change in commercial paper borrowings and revolving loans	189.2	(112.9)	.8
	Long-term borrowings	1.0	170.0	1.0
	Reduction of long-term debt	(192.6)	(31.5)	(46.3)
	Issuance of common stock	11.0	11.5	6.9
	Cash dividends	(57.9)	(57.6)	(57.3)

(Continued)

■■■■■■■■ *Exhibit 13.6* Hilton Hotels Corporation and Subsidiaries *(Continued)*

Consolidated Statements of Cash Flows

(In millions) Year Ended December 31,	1995	1994	1993
Net cash used in financing activities	(49.3)	(20.5)	(94.9)
Increase (Decrease) in Cash and Equivalents	153.6	(196.0)	31.9
Cash and Equivalents at Beginning of Year	184.4	380.4	348.5
Cash and Equivalents at End of Year	$338.0	184.4	380.4

- Other current assets: These amount to $284.5. While the Hilton report does not detail the asset items included under this heading, the uniform system of accounts is instructive. The "other assets" it lists may include such items as:

    A. Security deposits, such as for telephone, gas, electricity, and water

    B. Preopening expenses, or those expenses incurred prior to the opening of a hotel or casino.

    C. Deferred charges, which cover costs relating to the issuance of bonds, mortgages, and other forms of debt. Such charges are customarily amortized over the life of the issue, and include such costs as accounting fees, underwriting, legal services, printing costs, advertising expenses, and registration fees.

On the liability side, you might notice additional categories such as:

- Deferred income taxes. This figure refers to federal, state, and foreign income taxes payable beyond the next 12 months after the balance sheet date. For 1995, such taxes total $123.7 million. Deferred income taxes may occur if assets are depreciated more quickly for tax purposes than they are for book purposes.

- Stockholder's equity is another name for owner's equity, and refers to the amount of stock held by Hilton's investors.

For Hilton, the income statement is titled "Consolidated Statements of Income," Exhibit 13.5. Additional revenue categories to note here include casino, management, and franchise fees. Hilton operates a number of casino complexes, and revenue from those facilities is listed separately on the income statement, since casino operations are not considered part of rooms or food and beverage. Hilton also manages lodging properties that the company does not own. In return for running the property, Hilton is paid a percentage of revenues from the owners of those hotels. The percentage is determined in the management contract signed by Hilton and the hotel owner. (We will learn more about management contracts in chapter 14, "So You Want to Own a Hotel?".) This income is listed on the cash flow statement as management and franchise fees.

You'll note under expenses that the category of casino appears again, reflecting the funds Hilton has paid to operate casino facilities. The category of corporate expense reflects the expenses of the corporation—its headquarters and all associated expenses.

Another expense to note is foreign currency losses in 1994 and 1993. This figure reflects the impact of exchange rates on a U.S.-based company doing business internationally. The parentheses indicate that this figure is a loss. Hilton enters into foreign currency contracts (similar to an insurance policy) guaranteeing specific exchange rates throughout the year. In some international locations, the economies are often volatile, and the value of the dollar in relation to the local currency can change often. This helps protect Hilton from the risk of exchange rates' fluctuating dramatically. Hilton's interest in foreign operations could be negatively affected if there is a severe adjustment in the value of the dollar in another country.

Finally, a look at "Consolidated Statements of Cash Flows," Exhibit 13.6, shows the complexity of Hilton's operations. What our example called "disbursements" Hilton's calls "Change in working capital components," a long way of describing cash that flowed out of Hilton's accounts. The categories here are more numerous than for International Hotel. Hilton adds, for example, two more categories, financing activities and investing activities. These segments reflect the complicated nature of the investing and financing activities of a major corporation.

In its investing activities (which are different from operations), Hilton could gain revenues, such as the $139.1 that it made in temporary investments. It could also spend money such as the $254.4 it used for capital expenditures such as building new hotels or casinos. Hilton's financing activities include borrowing $1.0 in long-term debt and issuing new stock for a gain of $11.0. These items are cash sources or cash inflows to Hilton. Paying cash dividends of $57.9, noted in parentheses, is an example of a financing activity that is a cash use or a cash outflow.

Feature: Managerial Accounting

The statements used in financial accounting—the balance sheet, the income statement, and the statement of cash flows—provide the reported facts about an establishment to a variety of users. For example, the balance sheet would reveal that International Hotel had $50,000 cash on hand, a straightforward fact.

The financial statements do not, however, provide managers with ways to interpret those facts and to steer the business accordingly. For example, will the business be able to meet its short-term debt obligations? Does it make sense to replace a piece of kitchen equipment or not? The interpretive answers fall into the realm of **managerial accounting**. Managerial accounting is that branch of accounting in which managers within an organization analyze financial information, and take action as a result of that analysis. This branch of accounting has more room for judgment and is more intuitive in nature than financial accounting. In addition to financial information, managerial accounting requires a manager to integrate nonquantitative information, such as customer behavior.

Some examples of the kinds of decisions made by managerial accounting include:

- Determining the fixed and variable costs associated with the business. Remember that fixed costs are those that do not change as volume of sales increases or decreases. Variable costs do change relative to sales. In a restaurant, the cost of food is variable, but property taxes are fixed. There are many decisions that relate to an understanding of fixed and variable costs. For example, evaluating costs could help a manager of a seasonal restaurant determine when to close. An analysis of costs also helps to determine what prices must be charged in order to **breakeven**, to have prices exactly match costs.

- Providing information to implement **internal controls**, methods that safeguard the firm's assets and check the accuracy of its financial reporting. Any organization must manage against loss and theft, but the hospitality industry is particularly vulnerable because of the large number of employees who handle cash transactions in hotels, restaurants, and casinos.

- Forecasting and budgeting. Management attempts to predict the revenue and expenses associated with future business, and then budgets accordingly. For example, accurate forecasting would allow a business to staff appropriately. Later, actual sales are often measured against the forecasts. Forcing an explanation of the variances between budget and actual is one way for the organization to maintain budgetary control.

- Managing cash. As is noted on the statement of cash flows, cash is sourced and is used in a number of ways. It is the job of management to manage cash in the most efficient and profitable way possible. For example, a manager needs to determine how much cash should be in the checking account rather than in short-term securities.

- Budgeting for capital expenditures. Management must be mindful of when, how often, and if fixed assets should be purchased. For example, should the old telephone system be replaced? And if so, when? Capital expenditure decisions must comprehend the **time value of money**, what something is worth today versus what it may be worth sometime in the future.

All of the above decisions can require an in-depth set of calculations and extensive analysis using a variety of tools. Here we offer a simplified introduction to principles of managerial accounting through just one kind of these management tools: ratios. Exploring the thinking associated with ratios is an indicator for how managerial accounting works.

Ratio analysis compares related figures that are found on financial statements. Ratios help managers to monitor their operations, to make judgments about changes in the operation, to set performance goals, and to evaluate their success. Ratios can be divided into five groups according to the purpose they serve:[3]

- liquidity ratios

- solvency ratios

- activity ratios

- profitability ratios

- operating ratios

Success Tool: Understanding Liquidity Ratios Liquidity ratios help managers to determine if they can meet short-term debt obligations. A business that is very liquid can comfortably meet its short-term obligations. The **current ratio** is a commonly used liquidity ratio. It is calculated as follows:

$$\text{current ratio} \quad = \quad \frac{\text{current assets}}{\text{current liabilities}}$$

The higher the ratio, the more liquid the operation. For example, suppose Restaurant Angola has current assets of $15,000 and current liabilities of $5,000, and Restaurant Brazil has current assets of $25,000 and the same current liabilities of $5,000. The more liquid of the two, Restaurant

Angola, has a current ratio of 3 (or $15,000/$5,000); Restaurant Brazil has a current ratio of .5 (or $2,500/5000).

$$\text{Restaurant Angola current ratio} = \frac{\$15,000}{\$5,000} = 3$$

$$\text{Restaurant Brazil current ratio} = \frac{\$2,500}{\$5,000} = .5$$

We learned earlier that many restaurants fail in the first year of operation. These restaurants are caught in a situation in which they cannot pay their short-term debts; they have insufficient liquidity, not unlike Restaurant Brazil. Creditors to business like to see a high ratio. Owners would rather have a low one, but not so low that they go out of business. Owners generally prefer to invest their money in more productive noncurrent assets. Creditors would like as much coverage as possible to assure that they will be paid. Creditors would be much happier with the current ratio of Restaurant Angola.

Success Tool: Understanding Solvency Ratios Solvency ratios help managers to determine if they can meet their long-term debt obligations. A company with strong solvency ratios is likely to be around for a while. Solvency ratios are predictors of how well a company can weather financial hardships. Any time a company's assets exceed its liabilities, it is said to be solvent. A common **solvency ratio** is calculated as follows:

$$\text{Solvency Ratio} = \frac{\text{Total Assets}}{\text{Total Liabilities}}$$

If the total assets divided by the total liabilities is greater than 1 for a given operation, then it is solvent. Suppose Hotel China had total assets of one million dollars and total liabilities of two million dollars. Because its solvency ratio is 1 million/2 million or .5, it would not be solvent.

$$\text{Hotel China solvency ratio} = \frac{\$1,000,000}{\$2,000,000} = .5$$

A company that uses **leverage**, that is, it uses relatively more debt rather than equity to finance its assets, would have a lower solvency ratio. For example, if Hotel Denmark borrowed $80,000 of the $100,000, or 80 percent of the cost of adding a new swimming pool, it would be more leveraged than Hotel Ethiopia, which borrowed 40 percent, or $40,000 of $100,000, of the cost. Creditors would rather see a higher solvency ratio and less leverage; they are more likely to be paid in this case. Owners would rather have a lower ratio and more leverage; they can spread the equity that they do have over more projects. For example, committing the same amount of equity capital, Hotel Denmark can build three pools to Hotel Ethiopia's one. This is because Hotel Denmark put in $20,000 of equity ($100,000 total minus $80,000 borrowed) to build a pool and Hotel Ethiopia put in $60,000 ($100,000 total −$40,000 borrowed). For the funds used just for the swimming pool, Denmark's and Ethiopia's solvency ratios would be:

$$\text{Hotel Denmark solvency ratio} = \frac{\$300,000}{\$240,000} = 1.25$$

$$\text{Hotel Ethiopia solvency ratio} = \frac{\$100{,}000}{\$40{,}000} = 2.5$$

Success Tool: Understanding Activity Ratios Activity ratios measure how effectively a manager uses the resources of the establishment. The resources include items in inventory such as food and beverage stocks, as well as fixed assets such as rooms and restaurant seats.

A common activity ratio to illustrate this category is inventory turnover. It can be used for any item that is held in inventory, such as beverages. This ratio determines how often inventory turns, how often it is used up and resupplied.

$$\text{beverage inventory turnover} = \frac{\text{cost of beverage used}}{\text{average beverage inventory}}$$

In general, a rapid turnover is better because it costs money to hold things in inventory. Inventory ties up money that could be used for something else and is costly to store and track. One caution is that inventory should not be turning over so quickly that stockouts occur. Being out of an item can disappoint customers. Consider the beverage inventory turnover of Cruise Line France and Cruise Line Greece. If last year, France had a cost of beverage used of $300,000 and an average beverage inventory value of $25,000, it turned over its supplies 12 times or $300,000/$25,000. If Greece had the same $300,000 of cost of beverage used, but an average inventory value of $50,000, it is turning over only half as often, or six times per year. Cruise Line Greece is incurring more costs to hold and track its inventory. Given that space on a cruise ship is so valuable, the problem is magnified.

$$\text{Cruise Line France Beverage Inventory Turnover} = \frac{\$300{,}000}{\$25{,}000} = 12$$

$$\text{Cruise Line Greece Beverage Inventory Turnover} = \frac{\$300{,}000}{\$50{,}000} = 6$$

In chapter 2, "The Big Picture," we learned about two of the other most commonly used activity ratios: **occupancy percentage** and **seat turnover**. Both of these ratios measure how often a resource is used. Because the nature of these assets contains a large service component, they are not really resupplied but are cleaned and made ready for the next customer. The higher the activity ratio, that is, the larger the occupancy percentage and the larger the seat turnover, the better for the company.

Success Tool: Understanding Profitability Ratios Profitability ratios measure how profitable a company is relative to such items as its sales, its assets, its owners' equity, or its stock price. Relative to sales, a profitability ratio shows how effective a company is in generating revenue and controlling expenses. For example, **profit margin**, which zeros in on the bottom line, is calculated as follows:

$$\text{Profit Margin} = \frac{\text{Net Income}}{\text{Total Revenue}}$$

The higher the profit margin the better. For example, consider Casino Hungary, which has a net income of $20,000 and a total revenue of $100,000 for a profit margin of 20 percent, versus

Casino India, which has a net income of $10,000 on $100,000 of revenues, for a profit margin of 10 percent. Casino India puts twice as much money in the pockets of its owners, revenue being the same for both.

$$\text{Casino Hungary Profit Margin} = \frac{\$20,000}{\$100,000} = .20 = 20\%$$

$$\text{Casino India Profit Margin} = \frac{\$10,000}{\$100,000} = .10 = 10\%$$

Profit, also measured relative to other things, such as assets or owners' equity, is concerned with the same notion, that is, how effective is a company in returning money to owners. Creditors, owners, and managers would all like to see higher profitability ratios. Owners make more money, creditors have a better likelihood of being paid, and managers can also profit, as profitability ratios are sometimes used to determine bonus compensation for managers or management companies.

Success Tool: Understanding Operating Ratios Operating ratios measure management's effectiveness in the operation of the business. Operating ratios often consider revenue relative to other things, such as per occupied room, per guest, per square foot, per full-time employee, or per available seat. One such ratio is calculated as follows:

$$\text{Food revenue per wait staff member} = \frac{\text{Food Revenue}}{\text{\# of full time wait staff}}$$

If last Saturday night, Restaurant Jamaica generated $5,000 of revenue with 10 wait staff, each staff member was responsible for generating $500 worth of revenue. This information can be compared to other nights. The actual figures for each wait staff member can also be compared to the average. Management can use this analysis for determining staffing and/or for evaluating individual performance.

$$\text{Restaurant Jamaica Food Revenue per wait staff member} = \frac{\$5,000}{10} = \$500.00$$

In chapter 2, "The Big Picture," we encountered another frequently used operating ratio for hotels, average rate or revenue per available room (also called REVPAR). This ratio compares total revenues to rooms available for sale. Calculating this ratio allows a manager to see how well the hotel operation is performing relative to the units for sale, rooms.

The Role of the Hospitality Controller

An accounting manager, often referred to as the **controller** or **comptroller**, faces a battery of questions in day-to-day operations and must be prepared to implement a variety of success tools in response to those questions. Finding the answers starts with accurate recording of information. The information must then be summarized in a useful way. The summary form includes not only the major financial statements but other kinds of reports specific to the audiences they serve. Hospitality accounting departments may be preparing reports for corporate headquarters, a general manager, other managers in various departments, owners, or government agencies. These reports can be the most formidable source of information for the business.

A successful accountant must know what stands behind the numbers and how certain actions can change the numbers to the desired direction. Sometimes the action will need to be immediate because of unanticipated scenarios, such as a sudden increase in food costs. Other times require a careful review of history and a methodical planning process, such as in budgeting for future sales or trying to reduce inventory stock.

Today technology has enabled management to generate computerized reports more easily and more swiftly. Because the amount of information can be overwhelming, a controller must be thoughtful in interacting with various managers to provide the right reports and the right level of interpretation.

What's in the In Box?

Imagine standing in the shoes of a controller or purser for a 70-ton, 2,100-passenger cruise ship based in Italy. As you approach your in box, you think about the various tools available to you from financial and managerial accounting. You sit down to tackle the following items:

1. One popular port used frequently by the cruise line was recently damaged by hurricane-force winds. Though the ship can be rerouted, up to 30 percent of the next voyage's business may be lost. You've been asked to determine if the ship can still sail at a profit, and if so, what cost-cutting measures should be implemented. Your first step is to outline the information you will need to collect.

2. Your cruise line has consistently provided excellent health care. Though no international maritime regulations require even that there be medical personnel aboard, Italy does have some regulations, which you exceed.[4] With the rising costs of health care, you are asked to assess the costs and benefits of cutting back to minimum standards.

3. The cruise line is thinking of a building a new ship on which a number of accommodations will have small outside balconies. You have been asked to evaluate what price the line can charge for the added feature and if that design element is worth considering.

4. The cruise line will need to take out a major loan if the new ship is built. You've been asked to make a short presentation about what financial information the banker may want as well as what ratios the banker may evaluate. You've also been asked to comment on how much leverage you think the company should try to use.

5. You have a phone message from an inquisitive management trainee. He wants to know two things about the company's financials: Where does net income show up on the balance sheet, and how come net income and cash were not the same on last year's annual report?

Creating Competitive Advantage

At the core of nearly every hospitality service establishment is the goal of maintaining a profitable business. Managing a profitable business is a complex task, which includes processing and summarizing information, making decisions based on the information, and executing those decisions. Competitive advantage occurs only when a controller is constantly searching for profit opportunities, implementing effective controls when or before problems occur, and intelligently interpreting financial data. A successful controller must go many steps beyond accurate financial statements to achieve competitive advantage.

A Night at the Plaza—For Only $5.00?

The management of a hotel involves the coordination of many departments, and the assumption that the department managers will all work together. On occasion, though, a great idea from one manager will have a greater impact than expected on the remaining departments.

Take, for example, a recent promotion at the world famous Plaza Hotel, in Manhattan. The marketing department put out advertising that said—if you celebrated your honeymoon at the Plaza, and kept your receipt, you can spend another night at the Plaza for the price you originally paid. Great idea, right? The idea stirs up thoughts of romance, for those who did spend their honeymoon there, and perhaps for those now considering doing the same.

Well, more couples than expected saved their receipts, which were needed as proof of the cost of the room night. Over 50 couples took the Plaza up on the offer, and one couple paid only $6.11, the cost of a room in 1944. Today, that room would normally sell for almost $300. By 1946, the room rate was up to $9.13, and in 1956, $26.25. The year 1970 brought rates of $46, with a view of Central Park.

Great publicity for the hotel, but imagine the impact on the revenues recorded by the accounting department! To book 50 rooms at $300 each yields $15,000. To book 50 rooms at an average rate of $25 is $1,250! And all the same work goes on, from housekeeping to front desk to room service. The utility bills, debt payments, and taxes all need to be accounted for.

It is also interesting to note how room rates have risen, in some cases dramatically, over the past five decades. Between 1944 and 1970, the room rate jumped 653 percent. From 1970 to 1996, it went from $46 to $300, or another 552 percent. These jumps reflect the high costs involved in running a luxury hotel in the heart of Manhattan, considering property value, the cost of goods, and the cost of labor. The hard part for the accounting department to calculate for this promotion is the revenue benefit from the public relations or potential future sales. Thus both financial and managerial accounting tools come into play, when selling rooms for $6.11 a night.

Adapted from Martha Irvine, "Some Take a Second Honeymoon at First Honeymoon Hotel Rates," *The Wall Street Journal*, 28 July 1994.

Summary

An accounting manager plays a very important role in providing information to the organization. The information can come from either of two branches of accounting, financial or managerial. A successful manager of the accounting function must have an understanding of the tools needed for both financial and managerial accounting. These tools must then be applied to provide facts and recommendations as needed by various internal and external users of financial information.

Financial accounting constitutes a process of measurement, the output of which is a series of financial statements that various internal and external users wish to understand. These statements are based on a set of ground rules common to business accounting whereby investors are told how the company is protecting and utilizing the resources entrusted to it. The primary vehicle performing this function is the corporate annual report, such as the Hilton Corporation report cited here. This report is sent to the shareholders of the firm and to others who may request it. It is also used by lenders (that is, banks and insurance companies), governmental agencies (that is, the Securities and Exchange Commission and public utility commissions, and the Internal Revenue Service). Annual reports are also useful in providing the framework for gathering and disseminating operating information that is vital to managers in the process of planning and controlling the company's activities.

Managerial accounting is more judgmental in nature than financial accounting and provides analysis of financial information for decision-making purposes. Managerial accounting is concerned with costs and pricing, forecasting and budgeting, managing cash, and providing internal controls and capital purchases. Ratio analysis provides one set of tools used for managerial accounting analysis. Ratios are classified according to the purpose they serve: liquidity, solvency, activity, profitability, and operating.

Discussion Questions

1. Why is a uniform system of accounts useful?

2. Identify and discuss in each of the following balance sheet categories at least two items usually included there:

   a. Current assets

   b. Current liabilities

   c. Long-term debts

3. For what purpose are financial statements used?

4. What is the bottom line? Is the bottom line the same as cash flow? Why or why not?

5. Define what is meant by retained earnings. Where is retained earnings found on the balance sheet? On the income statement? Explain.

6. If a balance sheet provides a "snapshot" of a company's financial condition, what does an income statement present?

7. What is decreasing order of liquidity? Why do you think balance sheets are organized in this fashion?

8. Why would a company implement internal controls?

9. Why would a creditor and an owner want different solvency ratios?

10. What kind of ratio is "average" check? (You may wish to review the calculations in chapter 2.)

11. Why is it important to understand the language that is used by a particular business? In other words, why is the understanding of key terms used by a particular industry necessary for "fluency" or success in management?

Assignments

1. Consider all of the items in the in box of the hospitality controller. Which would you give the highest priority? The lowest priority? Why? How would you tackle each item? Assume the role of the controller. Develop a work plan using the success tools in the chapter.

2. Try to create an inventory of every tangible thing that a hotel or restaurant might own. Consider how often they are replaced or how often the inventory turns. What patterns can you note about how often there is turnover? Why do you suppose inventory is valued at the lower cost or market? Consider a scenario where the price of something that is inventoried fluctuates, dramatically after it is purchased.

3. Compare the annual reports of two publicly held hospitality companies in the same business.

   - What elements of the three major financial statements discussed in the chapter are reported in the same way? What elements are different? What kinds of additional information is provided in the footnotes?

   - Calculate the current ratio and the solvency ratio for each company. Which is more liquid? More solvent?

End Notes

1. William McCaffrey, Roger Paradis, and Patrick Shea, *The Language of Business* (Cambridge: Cambridge Business Research, 1980), preface.

2. "A Politician's Dream—A Businessman's Nightmare," *Nation's Restaurant News* (21 September 1992): 60.

3. Raymond S. Schmidgall, *Hospitality Industry Managerial Accounting* (East Lansing, Michigan: The Educational Institute of the American Hotel and Motel Association, 1990), 151.

4. Betsy Wade, "Assessing Ships' Medical Care," *The New York Times*, 4 February 1996, 5: 4.

Part Five

Structural Elements of the Hospitality Industry

There are many different structural elements or building blocks that define how the hospitality business is organized. These elements involve a series of intertwining business relationships. In this section, these relationships are explained from the perspective of an owner.

In chapter 14, a hotel owner is faced with deciding what kinds of relationships will be established both in the course of building and in the course of running a hotel. From an owner's perspective, the puzzle of a hotel's development, financing, management, franchising and/or affiliation must be solved. This chapter shows the advantages and disadvantages of the key choices an owner faces. Such choices inevitably involve weighing the cost side as well as the benefit side of hotel development, all with an eye to carefully measuring the hotel's profit potential.

Chapter 15 gives an understanding of the structural elements of the restaurant business by putting you squarely in the shoes of a restaurant entrepreneur. A restaurateur, too, faces a series of decisions involving development, ownership, management, and franchising, as well as decisions involving strategic alliances. Only after careful consideration of all of the interrelated business relationships can an owner be confident in answering the question "So you want to own a hotel?" or "So you want to own a restaurant?"

Chapter Fourteen

" *The greatest gift is the power to estimate correctly the value of things.* "

François, duc de la Rochefoucauld [1]

So You Want to Own a Hotel? ✺

When you finish this chapter you should:

1. Know the difference between developing, owning, managing, franchising, and affiliating hotels.

2. Understand how and why hotel development has evolved since the 1980s.

3. Understand the strategies that hotel companies are employing in the 1990s to compete in a competitive marketplace.

4. Know the key expenditures involved in developing a new hotel, as well as the key elements in determining the revenue needed to make a hotel profitable.

5. Know how to measure a hotel's profit potential.

6. Understand what a management contract is, its key provisions and how it is used in the hospitality industry.

7. Offer a brief historical perspective on franchising and management contracts in the hospitality industry.

8. Know the advantages and disadvantages of franchising from the point of view of both the franchisee and the franchisor.

9. Be able to distinguish between franchising and chains.

10. Explain the sources and uses of the various kinds of fees charged by franchisors.

11. Analyze the difference between being a member of a franchise and a member of an affiliation.

Introduction

Many well-known hotel companies, such as Ramada or Holiday Inn, do not own any hotels! This may seem incongruous at first, but this scenario can be true if the company only manages hotels, or only lends its name to a hotel's owner through a franchise agreement. There are several management companies, such as Richfield or Interstate Hotels, that operate thousands of hotel rooms, but you've probably never heard of the names of the companies. For some hotels, such as Red Roof Inns, the units are all company owned, which means that they are a chain, but they have no franchisees.

All of these different relationships can be confusing. To sort the confusion, this chapter will put you square in the shoes of a hotel owner. From this perspective you can see the different kinds of relationships to which a hotel owner might be a party. An owner is faced with deciding what kinds of relationships will be established both in the course of building and in the course of running a hotel. From an owner's perspective, the puzzle of how a hotel is developed, financed, managed, franchised, and/or affiliated must be solved.

"Decoding" a Hotel Investment

Let's start with a simple premise. You own a piece of land and you want to build a hotel. The following questions can serve as a "decoder" or a way to understand which players are involved in developing a **to-be-built hotel**. Ideally, all the "decoding" questions for a new property should be answered in the planning stages. This is because one decision can influence another. Developing a to-be-built hotel should be distinguished from a transaction involving the sale, change in affiliation, or change in franchise for an **existing hotel**. Only when a hotel is to be built will its owner face the entire list of questions we evaluate in this chapter. Transactions for an existing hotel involve only a subset of the decoding questions. This is because if the hotel is already up and running, some decisions are already in place. For example, if a hotel owner is only considering a change in franchise affiliation, say from Sheraton to Holiday Inn, only the questions pertaining to franchising apply. The other questions do not. The set of questions below involve the key decisions that an owner will make in the process of getting from a piece of land to checking in the first guest:

1. **Who will develop the hotel?** Who will put together the land, the architectural plans, the necessary permits, the financing, and so on? Who will be the impetus behind getting the hotel built? In the world of hotels, the developer could be a real estate development company. It could be a major hotel company launching a new division, or it could be a local businessperson, such as yourself, who puts together a hotel project, perhaps with plans to become a franchisee of a major chain.

2. **Who will own the hotel?** In other words, who will have title to the hotel? This could be one person, such as yourself acting as an entrepreneur. It could be a group of partners who may or may not know anything about the hotel business. It could be a well-known hotel corporation, such as Hilton. The financing could be some combination of equity from an individual or a company, and debt from a bank, a pension fund, or an insurance company such as Equitable Life, which owns a number of hotels. The party that provides the debt (the loan) for the project is the "money partner." The person or people who provide the equity (a down payment) is the owner.

3. **Who will manage the hotel?** Who will be responsible for the day-to-day operations of the hotel once it is up and running? Who will see to it that the rooms are rented and that the restaurant meals are served? The management may or may not be the owner or the developer. When the management and the owner are two different parties, a management contract comes into play. The management could be an entrepreneur, or a professional management company, such as Interstate, that operates brand name or independent hotels, or a well-known hotel company that both manages and franchises hotels.

4. **Who, if anyone, will franchise the hotel?** Who grants the hotel the right to operate as a member of a specific chain, with specific privileges through a franchise agreement? The answer may be that the hotel is not franchised at all, in which case it is either an independent or a company-owned unit of a chain, which would not require a franchise agreement. If the hotel is franchised, that relationship would typically be between an individual owner or partnership, and a well-known company that provides brand name recognition and a reservations system, among other benefits.

5. **With whom, if anyone, will the hotel be affiliated or in consort?** With what group of hotels will a particular property be associated with on a referral basis? Affiliations typically occur between independent hotels that have something in common and would like to benefit from shared marketing efforts and a shared reservations system. A chain hotel can also have an affiliation. For example, a Four Seasons Hotel may also be a member of the Leading Hotels of the World. This typically happens at the luxury end of the market. Chain properties at the lower end of the market typically do not have affiliations.

Collectively, the above questions demonstrate the wide range of developer, owner, manager, franchisor, or affiliate players that can be involved with a hotel. There are many possible combinations (see Figure 14.1).

Hotel Development and Ownership

When hotels are initially started, the developer plays a key role. The **developer** is the party that puts all the pieces together. The developer may intend to sell the property to a new owner once it is developed, or to keep the property, in which case the developer and the owner are the same party.

A series of subcontractors may be hired in the development process. These could include site engineers, architects, environmental consultants, a general building contractor, or a food facilities engineer, who specializes in the layout and design of food facilities services.

The Stages of Design and Development

In our scenario, we assumed that a land site was in place. There may be cases when a developer decides to build in a particular area, but the site has not been chosen. This part of the process, known as **site selection**, can be a very sophisticated process. Site selection is the choosing of the physical location of the property. Elements such as access to transportation, surrounding geographic features and population, environmental hazards, and location of the competition are all considered. The next stage is **feasibility analysis**, which is a study of whether the hotel is likely to be successful or not. Given a particular site, will the hotel be successful? This phase creates a set of "what

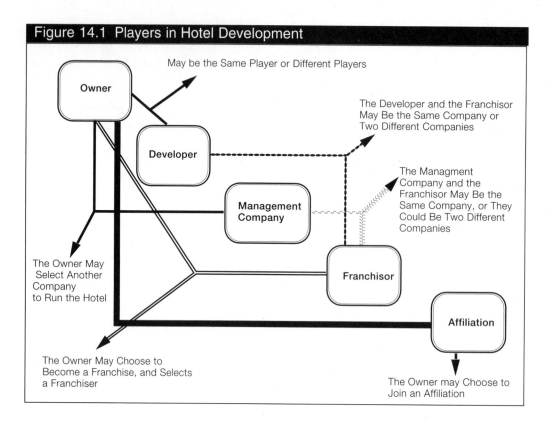

Figure 14.1 Players in Hotel Development

if" scenarios. For example, if the new hotel were able to charge an $80.00 average rate and attain a 68 percent occupancy, would it succeed? How well the competition is doing, how well the new hotel will do relative to them, the economic forecast of the area, and the expected growth or decline of various market segments are all factors in determining feasibility.

The feasibility analysis includes an analysis of both the costs and the benefits of the specific project. Before a project ever gets to the **construction phase**, which is when the hotel is actually built, it must demonstrate potential occupancies and room rates to cover the costs associated with operating and building the hotel. Without a feasibility analysis, it would be impossible to borrow funds from a lender to go forward with the project.

The Cost Side: What Does It Cost to Develop a Hotel? The unit for sale in the hotel business is a **room night**, so the most appropriate way to think about development costs is on a per room basis. (The more technical term used by hotel managers is **per available room**.) Remember that the number of available rooms may be less than total number of rooms; an adjustment such as removing a suite from inventory for the home of a resident manager would change the number of rooms actually available for sale.

Hotel development costs vary by the kind of hotel to be built. Exhibit 14.1 gives a breakdown of hotel development costs for three rate structures: luxury, standard, and economy. The categories of cost are divided into:

Exhibit 14.1 Hotel Development Costs

Hotel Development Costs (Dollars per Available Room)

	Improvements	Furniture & Equipment	Land	Preopening	Operating Capital	Total
1976						
Luxury	32,000–55,000	5,000–10,000	4,000–12,000	1,000–2,000	1,000–1,500	43,000–80,500
Standard	20,000–32,000	3,000–6,000	2,500–7,000	750–1,500	750–1,000	27,000–47,500
Economy	8,000–15,000	2,000–4,000	1,000–3,500	500–1,000	500–750	12,000–24,250
1986						
Luxury	62,000–120,000	13,700–30,600	11,500–27,800	3,100–5,200	2,200–3,100	92,500–186,700
Standard	39,000–60,000	9,700–16,800	5,800–15,400	2,000–3,800	1,500–2,500	58,000–98,500
Economy	21,000–37,000	5,100–9,000	3,500–10,000	1,000–1,800	1,000–1,500	31,600–59,300
1990						
Luxury	67,000–128,000	15,400–33,000	10,700–25,800	3,500–5,700	2,500–3,500	99,100–196,000
Standard	42,000–65,000	10,800–18,500	5,400–14,300	2,200–4,000	1,600–2,800	62,000–104,600
Economy	22,500–41,000	5,600–10,000	3,200–9,200	1,200–1,800	1,200–1,600	33,700–63,600
1991						
Luxury	65,000–122,000	14,500–31,500	10,200–24,000	3,700–5,900	2,600–3,600	96,000–187,000
Standard	40,000–63,000	10,000–17,800	5,100–13,500	2,300–4,200	1,700–2,900	59,100–101,400
Economy	21,000–39,000	5,000–9,500	3,000–8,600	1,300–2,000	1,300–1,700	31,600–60,800
1992						
Luxury	64,000–120,000	14,200–30,900	9,200–21,600	3,800–6,100	2,700–3,700	93,900–182,300
Standard	39,000–62,000	9,800–17,400	4,600–12,300	2,300–4,400	1,800–3,000	57,500–99,100
Economy	21,000–38,000	4,900–9,300	2,800–7,900	1,400–2,100	1,300–1,800	31,400–59,100

Continued

351

Exhibit 14.1 Hotel Development Costs (*Continued*)

Hotel Development Costs (Dollars per Available Room)

	Improvements	Furniture & Equipment	Land	Preopening	Operating Capital	Total
1993						
Luxury	63,000–119,000	14,000–30,500	8,700–20,500	3,900–8,200	2,800–3,800	92,400–180,000
Standard	39,000–61,000	9,700–17,200	4,400–11,800	2,300–4,500	1,800–3,000	57,200–97,500
Economy	21,000–38,000	4,900–9,200	2,700–7,700	1,400–2,100	1,300–1,800	31,300–58,800
1994						
Luxury	64,000–121,000	14,300–31,100	8,900–20,900	3,900–6,200	2,800–3,800	93,900–183,000
Standard	40,000–83,000	10,000–17,800	4,500–12,300	2,400–4,600	1,800–3,000	58,700–100,500
Economy	22,000–40,000	5,100–9,500	2,800–8,000	1,500–2,200	1,300–1,800	32,700–81,500
1995						
Luxury	85,000–124,000	14,800–32,300	9,200–21,700	4,100–6,400	2,900–4,000	96,000–188,400
Standard	41,000–65,000	10,400–18,300	4,700–12,800	2,500–4,800	1,900–3,100	60,500–104,000
Economy	23,000–42,000	5,400–9,900	3,000–8,400	1,600–2,300	1,300–1,800	34,300–64,000

Source: Hospitality Valuation Services, Inc.

- Improvements. This is the cost of the bricks, mortar, and all other construction materials necessary to build. It represents improvements made to the land.

- Furniture, fixtures, and equipment (FF&E). This includes the goods needed to furnish the hotel rooms, the hotel lobby, the kitchens, and so on. This includes "hard goods" like beds and dressers, as well as "soft goods" like carpet and drapes.

- Land. This is the cost of buying the land upon which the hotel will be built.

- Preopening. This includes the initial cost to get the hotel up and running. This would include marketing, training, salaries, and all the costs associated with maintaining the building before the first customer checks in.

- Operating capital. As with any business, a certain amount of cash is needed to actually operate the hotel.

The Benefit Side: What Does It Take to Make a Hotel Profitable? The economics of a successful hotel are such that there should be a relationship between the cost per room to build the hotel and the room rate charged to stay in the hotel. An old rule of thumb is that to break even a hotelier must charge $1 per room per night for every $1,000 invested in building. For example, building a luxury hotel in 1990 cost between $99K and $196K. Therefore, to break even, a hotel at the low end of the bracket would need to charge approximately $99.00 per room per night on average. But charging enough is only half of the equation. The other half is having enough customers to charge. This is measured in terms of occupancy. For most hotels the breakeven occupancy percentage is in the mid 60s. In summary, success on the benefit side is a function of making two things work: occupancy and average rate.

Measuring a Hotel's Full Profit Potential To a developer or an owner, as well as to others such as a manager or a lender, it is very useful to understand how well a hotel *is* doing relative to how well it *could* do in maximizing occupancy and average rate.

The best a hotel could do is to have every room occupied (100 percent occupancy), and have every customer paying the highest rate (100 percent of the **rack rate**, the published rate before discounting). Multiplied together, these two percentages yield the hotel's revenue generating efficiency, or what could be called the **full-house/full-rate percentage**. Assume, for example, a hotel was 70 percent occupied, and on average each guest paid 80 percent of the rack rate (that is, they received a 20 percent discount). This would happen if the rack rate were $100.00 and guests on average paid $80.00. In this case, the hotel's full-house/full-rate percentage is $(.70 \times .80) = 56$ percent. This hotel is therefore generating 56 percent of its total potential. The calculation, in summary, is:

Full-house full-rate % = (occupancy %) × (% of rack rate achieved)

$56\% = .56 = (.70) \times (.80)$

The full-house/full-rate percentage can be manipulated easily by changing the rack rate; lowering the rate would increase the occupancy, as these two factors are inversely related. In theory, one could assure a full house by keeping the rate low enough. So how can one estimate if a hotel is charging the right rate to maximize revenue potential? Hypothetically, a hotel could raise rates night after night until it dropped from 100 percent occupancy to having just one room left over. The hotel would then know that it did not turn away any customers, and it received the maximum rate from the customers that stayed. Unfortunately, many last-minute, uncontrollable variables like weather, guest change of plans, and canceled planes can influence occupancy, making it practically impossible to create a hypothetical test situation that works. So how *can* one estimate if a hotel is charging the right rate to maximize potential? A talented manager can only make a sophisticated, educated guess. As the quotation at the beginning of the chapter notes, that is the greatest gift.

Securing Financing One final, most critical step in the development project is for the owner to secure financing to start and complete the project successfully. The equity or ownership funds may come from individuals and partnerships, or from institutional sources such as pension funds or insurance companies. A **REIT**, or **real estate investment trust**, which raises money to invest in a portfolio of hotels, is another source. This is a kind of capital which has become increasingly popular in the mid-1990s. Debt financing could come from a bank or government loan. If a hotel project is determined to be viable and has secured an ownership structure, the project is on the way to **opening**. Hotels typically have a **soft opening**, in which a specified set of known guests are invited to stay overnight. This is a chance for the hotel to work out the final bugs in the operation prior to a public or **grand opening**.

How Hotel Development has Evolved

As witnessed by the above questions, potentially a large number of players can be involved in the development of just one hotel. It is possible to check into a hotel developed by one party, owned by a second, managed by a third, franchised with a fourth, and affiliated with a fifth. Finally, and all too commonly in the turbulent recent history of the hotel industry, the hotel could have been repossessed by an unlucky sixth who lent money to the second. Though most hotels will have some overlap of roles, reducing the number of parties involved, a scenario with all six parties is possible.

The unlucky sixth party who lent money to the second party, and now owns a troubled hotel, has surfaced with frequency in the early 1990s. Why this happened can be traced back to the previous decades. A fundamental realignment of the industry began in the 1970s and continued at an accelerated pace in the 1980s.

The Hotel Boom of the 1980s "Build, build, build!" was the motto of the 1980s. This frenzy of development was the consequence of a number of factors:

- Average annual nationwide occupancy was strong. Occupancy in the early- to mid-1980s was in the low 70 percent versus low to mid 60 percent in the late 1980s and early 1990s.[2]

- Average rates were strong and increasing.

- Future projections were based on extrapolations of current favorable growth rates, creating overly optimistic revenue projections.

- Tax incentives further enhanced the viability of hotel projects.

The demand for hotel rooms exceeded supply, creating strong occupancy figures. Strong occupancy meant that it was easy for hoteliers to raise rates. The combination of high occupancy and increasing rates meant better and better return on investment. As long as demand exceeded supply the trend could continue. The feasibility of future projects was based on the current growth picture. As long as the growth continued at the same pace, hoteliers could expect high returns on investment.

Tax incentives also created a favorable climate, which encouraged building. The incentives were such that a hotel received a 10 percent investment tax credit (ITC) on the purchase of furniture, fixtures, and equipment (FF&E) in the year the hotel was built. FF&E for a hotel, which typically accounts for a fourth or more of a new project's cost,[3] generally is a much more favorable percentage than that of an office or industrial building.[4] The options to use an accelerated depreciation schedule and a 19-year life for commercial real estate (relative to the subsequent straight line depreciation and 31.5 year life) were attractive. This meant that hotels could expense the project at a rate that was favorable. Tax incentives also helped hotels that wanted to refurbish. Existing hotels could claim a rehabilitation credit of up to 20 percent.[5]

Tax incentives created an environment where hotels could reduce breakeven occupancy by four to seven points.[6] In other words, if a hotel normally would break even at 68 percent, using the tax benefits, it could break even at 61 to 64 percent. Effectively, a hotel did not have to operate on its own economic merit to produce a return on investment. The tax structure lowered barriers to entry—people who did not know anything about the hotel business could enter. And they did. As long as the tax incentives remained in place, this trend could continue.

However, all of the conditions listed above didn't continue. Demand did not continue to outpace supply. Future growth did not track with current growth. The Tax Reform Act of 1986 changed the rules. Enter the 1990s.

What Will the 1990s Bring? By the early 1990s, after the hotel industry ambled down the yellow brick road of the 1980s, it found it wasn't in the same business anymore. The real estate market had collapsed. The overall economy softened, the stock market fell, and companies laid off employees. There was a glut of hotel rooms in the marketplace. Travel had declined. Occupancy rates had dropped. Many five- to seven-year bullet loans or mini-perms (loans that required interest only with a balloon, or very large, payment at the end) issued in the mid-1980s came due, with no hope of renewal or ability to pay. This meant that owners couldn't pay or renegotiate the interest on their overvalued properties. "Time was when the hotel industry mixed glamour and high finance in an intoxicating cocktail that attracted the most flamboyant entrepreneurs of the past century— Conrad Hilton, Richard D'Oyly Carte, César Ritz. But check in today at thousands of U.S. hotels, including Hiltons, Sheratons, and Marriotts, and your innkeeper will belong to far more somber groups: Citicorp, Wells Fargo Bank, Traveler's Insurance, and others."[7] Hotel owners were trying to reposition, or to get out of the business. Some continue to do so. As a result, a series of strategies to combat the decline in the hotel business have emerged in the 1990s: the facelift strategy, the consolidation strategy, the rework strategy, and the workout strategy.

The Facelift Strategy Several hotel companies tried to polish a lackluster image. This is particularly true of the older, larger chains, which had not seen renovations in years. Parent companies with deep pockets found themselves spending for improvements. For example, Bass PLC, the parent of Holiday Inns, announced a $1 billion expansion in 1990 to renovate existing properties and to grow the brand in Europe and Asia.[8] Sheraton began a multimillion-dollar stateside housecleaning in 1990 by renovating its New York properties, hoping to bring them up to the level of its international properties. It also defranchised its weaker sisters, to try to raise overall standards and attract guests (dropping more than 250 properties since 1986).[9]

The Consolidation Strategy There will likely be a continued consolidation of hotel ownership and of brand name, though not at the same frenetic pace as in the 1980s. Hoping that strength in numbers will be a winning strategy, large hotel companies may become part of even larger ones. For example, in the early 1990s, Hospitality Franchise Systems snatched Days Inns from the brink of bankruptcy and added it to their portfolio, which already contained Howard Johnson and Ramada franchise systems. Accor, the French hotel giant, purchased Motel 6, an already substantial American hotel chain, among others. (Review the table of mergers and acquisitions presented in chapter 2, "The Big Picture.")

The Rework Strategy The real estate slump, recession, and plunge in travel in the 1990s forced some companies to completely rethink the economics of their organizations—both on the balance sheet and on the income statement. The balance sheet equation has changed as organizations are selling assets, reducing long-term debt, refinancing, and looking for sources of credit. On the income statement, boosting revenues has been difficult, so all the burden has fallen on cutting expenses. Intercontinental Hotels (owned by the Japanese retailer Saison Group and Scandinavian Airlines System), for example, had to refinance its loans and face two waves of firings and several corporate reorganizations.[10] The Marriott Corporation, a star performer in the 1980s, began a major restructuring. It sold its restaurant operations, wrote down hotel properties, which meant it reduced the asset value of these properties on the balance sheet, and bailed out of troubled hotel partnerships.[11] The company found itself needing to sell $1.5 billion dollars' worth of hotel properties to reduce its interest payments. It suspended new hotel construction, eliminated 1,500 positions, consolidated the sales forces for various hotel brands,[12] and looked for other ways to cut costs.[13] Marriott asked its suppliers for credit, a move that triggered a switch from Coca-Cola to Pepsi, who offered Marriott a better deal.

The Workout Strategy If a hotel is unable to meet its expenses through reorganization, or is unable to find a way to restructure and stay current with loans, the bank is forced to take possession of the property. (This can be referred to as defaulting on a loan.) One newsweekly summed up the 1990s this way: "The banks are in hotel hell."[14] Some place to check into! More than 10,000 properties [were] expected in the hands of lenders by the middle of 1993![15]

What happens next? The money partners or lenders that find themselves with hotels will likely try to sell them, assuming in the transaction a major write down of assets. Other banks may look to independent hotel management companies who specialize in turning around troubled properties—a growing profession. The risk of this approach is that it requires additional expenditures that may or may not pay off. In rare cases, some properties may be converted to other uses like nursing homes or condominiums, although these generally are not very promising ways to realize value. Some hotels may simply be torn down.

New Hotel Development Though hotels were being torn down, and the market in the early 1990s was generally bleak, by about 1994, the life cycle for some shrewd investors began anew. The trough was realized, and hotels in the mid 1900s began again to reach their stride. Occupancies began to rise, rates stabilized, and overall performance again is approaching the strong performances of earlier decades.[16] Though the picture appears to be much brighter, hoteliers building in the mid- to late 1990s must still invest more carefully than ever, and consider both sides of the economic coin for new development: costs and benefits.

Hey, Wasn't This a Ramada?

In the complex, and competitive lodging marketplace, major hotel chains continue to try to carve out bigger sections of the market. Frequent travelers often find that their familiar Holiday Inn or Hyatt has changed names over the years, and changed names often. Some travelers like to stay at the same hotel, but when they call to make a reservation at, say, the Hilton in Los Angeles, they find it has become a Radisson. Some Holiday Inns and Ramada Inns become Days Inns. And in a particularly ironic switch, the Holiday Inn in Ithaca, New York became a Ramada. And the Ramada in Ithaca? It became a Holiday Inn.

Sometimes name changes are due to changes in ownership, and new owners wishing to become a franchise of a different hotel chain. Sometimes it is due to a bank's taking ownership and "reflagging" the property to attract new guests.

At times, the confusion can be blamed completely on the parent company. As the large chains aggressively target the market, a kind of "brand expansion" has developed. Over the past few years, take a look at the different names the major chains have launched: Hilton came out with Cresthil, and had big plans for a new chain. The name failed, and Cresthil became Hilton Garden Inn. There is also Hilton Suites. Sheraton recently launched Four Points Hotels, to replace Sheraton Inns, in an attempt to upgrade the midscale Sheraton Inn image. But don't forget Sheraton Suites; that's a different division. Then there's Doubletree, Doubletree Suites, and Doubletree Club; Holiday Inn, Holiday Inn Crown Plaza, Holiday Inn Express, and Holiday Inn Garden Court; Howard Johnson's and HoJo Inns. A traveler could be very confused, indeed.

Hotel Management

Once the development and ownership of a hotel project have been addressed, a hotel project becomes a tangible reality. Now the owner of a hotel must make a key decision about how it is to be managed. This is the third key question. If the owner himself or herself chooses to manage the property, it typically is called an **O and O**, which stands for **owned and operated**. Smaller properties are more typically O and Os than are larger properties. If the owner decides to hire an outside manager, a **management contract** is entered into. A management contract has two parties to the agreement, the **owner** of hotel and the **operator**. One of the leading experts on management contracts, James J. Eyster, defines the agreement this way:

A management contract is a written agreement between the owner and the operator of a hotel or motor inn by which the owner employs the operator as an agent to assume full responsibility for operating and managing the property. As an agent, the operator pays, in the name of the owner, all operating expenses from the cash flow generated from the property, retains management fees, and remits the remaining cash flow, if any, to the owner. The owner supplies the lodging property, including any land, building, furniture, fixtures, equipment, and working capital, and assumes full legal and financial responsibility for the property.[17]

Brief Historical Background

One of the first hotel management contracts to be signed was in Latin America, where Intercontinental Hotels, a wholly owned subsidiary of Pan American Airways (formed in 1946), signed a 10-year agreement with a local hotelier. The hotel owners did not want to lease the property, because they wanted more control than a standard lease agreement would provide. Consequently, the management agreement became, in the words of an Intercontinental executive, "the only way to keep the contract at a reasonable length (10 years) and give the hotel owners the feeling that we were working for them and they weren't turning over their whole property to us."[18] What Intercontinental, the operator, got from the owners in those days was a fixed fee, plus an incentive payment based on net cash profit. We will talk more about fee structure later in the chapter.

Following in the footsteps of Intercontinental, Hilton International was organized in 1949 and announced that its first property, the Caribe Hilton in San Juan, Puerto Rico, had been signed to a management contract. The terms of the contract stipulated that one third of the gross operating profit went to Hilton, and the remaining two thirds went to the owner.[19]

Growth in Number of Contracts By the late 1960s and early 1970s, the U.S. lodging industry had found the management contract concept so attractive that chain operating companies reported more than 200 properties being operated under management contracts. Among the reasons for this growth were such factors as:

1. Increasing costs of land. Because land was more expensive, hotel companies were moving more toward management and away from ownership.

2. The costs of building construction and mortgage interest. Ownership investment in large-size properties became more prohibitive to hotel companies.

3. Hotel companies could manage more properties much faster than they could own them. It was quicker to bring a hotel under management than to buy an existing hotel. Hotel companies widened their investment base by increasing the number of guest rooms managed through rapid penetration of new markets—and improving earnings per share of stock.[20]

Despite the economic recessions of the mid-1970s and the overbuilding of the 1980s, the lodging industry nevertheless continued to favor the management contract as its preferred form of operating agreement. This was especially true for new hotels/motels larger than 100 rooms, which were the more expensive properties to build. As a consequence, by the late 1980s, as many as 20 chain operating companies with nearly 700 properties were under management contracts, and more than 60 independent operating companies were managed with some 950 hotel and motor inn projects.[21] By the mid 1990s, the numbers grew even larger. The list of management companies and the number of rooms they have under management presented in chapter 2, "The Big Picture," illustrates this point.

When a Management Contract Makes Sense

If you are the owner of the hotel, you have to decide if you want a management contract in the first place. If you are a hotel owner with no management experience, particularly if it is a larger property, a management contract is a way to bring professional experience to your hotel. The advantages of hiring a management company include access to expertise and systems, and no hassles for the owner in terms of the day-to-day operations. If the owner is trying to secure financing from a lender, a management contract with a reputable company may greatly improve the chances of obtaining financing.

By contrast, an owner could hire a general manager and other key managers who do have expertise, but are not part of a management company. The relationship with each hire is that of an employer and an employee. This allows professionals to oversee the day-to-day operational decisions, but it is not the same kind of **turn-key** approach (where everything is taken care of), that a management company provides. In the employer/employee scenario, owners still have important operational decisions to make, must keep close tabs on the finances, and must manage the strategic direction of the property.

An owner may choose to manage as well as own. The biggest advantages are complete freedom in running the operation, which allows for a signature touch. The self-managed property also saves the cost of the management fees that otherwise would be paid to the management companies. Owners with hotel experience or desiring to be entrepreneurs are likely candidates for owner/managers. Owner/managers occur most often in smaller properties.

The "Typical" Management Contract

Because most management contracts reflect matters of concern to a specific property owner and a particular management company, it would be misleading to say that any one management contract is typical in the lodging and/or foodservice industry. Nonetheless, practice and custom established in the hospitality industry enable us to identify those provisions that are most likely to occur in contract management. Accordingly, at the risk of oversimplifying what is a complex process for both owners and management companies in the world of hospitality, we have undertaken to show in Exhibit 14.2 those key contract provisions with which we believe you should be familiar—and to explore briefly in the section that follows what these contract provisions usually mean.

Exhibit 14.2 Provisions Commonly Included in Management Contracts

1. Agreement and general purposes

2. Operator's duties and authority of the manager

3. Annual operating budget

4. Working capital, funding, and banking

5. Management fees

6. Accounting

(Continued)

▬▬▬▬▬ **Exhibit 14.2** Provisions Commonly Included in Management Contracts *(Continued)*

7. Term of agreement and termination fees

8. Cost of repairs, replacements, maintenance, and capital improvements

9. Insurance

10. Real and personal property taxes

11. Damage, destruction, or condemnation of the property

12. Default or termination rights

13. Indemnity

14. Transferability

15. Notices and miscellaneous

---

1. **Agreement and General Purposes**

   In this opening provision, owner and operator identify themselves as parties to the agreement and state concisely their respective goals and expectations. Note that the terms *operator*, *manager*, and *management company* can be used interchangeably.

2. **Operator's Duties and Authority of the Manager**

   This provision, sometimes referred to as the "owner's hands-off" provision, not only serves to prevent owner interference with the day-to-day management, but also specifies in detail the range of managerial discretion and authority to be exercised exclusively by the operator/manager as the sole agent of the owner.

3. **Annual Operating Budget**

   Customarily, a yearly budget is prepared by the operator, and submitted to the owner for his approval at least 60 days prior to the start of the fiscal year. A typical budget might include the following:

   a. An estimated profit and loss statement.

   b. Proposals for any expenditures for furnishings, revisions, rebuilding, replacements, or additions or improvements.

   c. Payroll and other operating expenses.

4. **Working Capital, Funding, and Banking**

   Working capital, the excess of current assets over current liabilities, is supplied by the owner. For example, the contract may state that the working capital amount may not be less than $15,000. In essence, working capital is what the manager needs for the operation and maintenance of the hotel. It includes cash, marketable securities, notes receivable, accounts receivable, inventory, and prepaid expenses. All of these may be used for revenue producing activities for acquiring fixed assets (such as new buildings) and for paying obligations (such as salaries and taxes).

5. Management Fees

A management fee is the cost to the owner of using a management company to operate the property. This is a very important provision of the contract, for it spells out how the operator will be paid for services provided. Fees can be paid monthly, quarterly, annually, or at some other set interval. Management fees can be calculated in many different ways. Some of these ways could be the following, or some combination of the following:

a. A fixed fee. This means that the management company will be paid the same fixed amount whether the hotel makes a profit or not.

b. A fixed fee plus a percentage of profit. In this fee structure, the management company is paid a set amount, plus a percentage of the profits as an incentive.

c. A fixed fee or a percentage of profit, whichever is greater. In this scenario, the percentage of profit amount would be what is paid to the operator if performance is strong, and the fixed fee is what is paid if performance is weak.

d. Pure profit and loss. In this fee structure, the fate of the management company is tied completely to profits. If no profits are made, no management fee is paid. This is not a common fee structure.

To offer a specific example, assume you decided to hire a management company, and pay a fee according to c. above. Your contract might read: "The owner agrees to pay the operator a base management fee equal to the greater of \$5,000 per month (this is the fixed fee) or 4% of gross operating profit (GOP)." Calculating for two sample months might yield the following for your hotel.

April GOP = \$75,000 × .04 = \$3,000   Base fee of \$5,000 is paid

May GOP = \$150,000 × .04 = \$6,000   Percentage of profits, or \$6,000 is paid

The kind of fee you selected is common. According to a survey of the 148 members of the International Council of Hotel-Motel Management Companies, a fee that offers some kind of incentive is used about half the time, and a flat fee basis is used the other half of the time.[22]

6. Accounting

According to this provision, the management will provide the owner with periodic accounting statements. These could be on a monthly, quarterly, or annual basis. These statements, as we learned in chapter 13, "An Accounting Tool Box," are necessary for the management team to maintain adequate operational control. In addition to the balance sheet, income statement, and statement of cash flows, specific management reports detailing ratios would be included.

7. Term of Agreement and Termination Fees

The length of the contract term and any termination fees are of prime concern to both the owner and the management company. This section of the contract spells out the length of notice that is required should either party decide to terminate the agreement, as well as any termination fees. Typically, an owner wants the contract length to be a short as mutually acceptable, and the operator wants it to be as long as mutually acceptable. A shorter contract gives an owner greater flexibility. A longer contract gives an operator more security.

8. **Cost of Repairs, Replacements, Maintenance, and Capital Improvements**

This provision requires the owner's prior approval for any expenditures that are not provided for in the annual budget and that are necessary to keep the property and equipment of the hotel in good operating condition. Most management contracts do identify what is included under the headings of repairs, maintenance, furniture, fixtures, and equipment. Capital improvements involve any revisions, alterations, or rebuilding of the hotel structure, the cost of which is not charged to normal repairs and maintenance. Such costs also require the prior approval of the owner.

9. **Insurance**

In most management contracts, either the owner provides, or the operator purchases, at the owner's expense, public and employer's liability, workmen's compensation, fire, property damage, and business interruption insurance, and other such customary insurance as needed for the protection of the interests of the owner and/or operator.

10. **Real and Personal Property Taxes**

Some contracts list the taxes that the management company must pay (that is, property taxes, sales taxes, Social Security taxes, and so on). Other contracts do not include a tax provision, in which case the owner, not the management company, would be responsible for paying the taxes.

11. **Damage, Destruction, or Condemnation of the Property**

This type of provision provides that if all or part of the hotel is damaged or destroyed by fire, casualty, or other cause, the owner will make repairs and/or replacements within a reasonable time period after the damage occurs. If the owner fails to do so, the manager may typically terminate the contract, and the owner will pay the termination fee. The contract may also speak to government action. For example, a contract may state that if all or part a hotel is condemned by government action and as a result can no longer be operated in accordance with the manager's standards, the contract may be terminated with payment of the termination fee to the manager. Remember that the management company often has an international reputation to uphold.

12. **Default or Termination Rights**

Many management contracts contain extensive provisions covering the variety of circumstances under which the owner and operator may terminate a contract.[23] These provisions typically speak to:

a. Default by the manager, and the consequent remedies available to the owner.

b. Default by the owner, and the consequent remedies available to the manager.

In either case, default means failure to abide by any material part of the agreement. The prescribed remedy is contract termination and payment of fees and other sums of money due to either party. This provision was noted by members of the International Council of Hotel-Motel Management Companies as one of the two most compelling ones. The second issue is management fees.[24] This is because when and how a contract might end is very important to both parties.

13. **Indemnity**

Most management contracts indemnify the respective parties for various losses and liabilities that are specifically enumerated. *Indemnify* is another way of stating that a party is insured against loss or damage. Thus the owner is said to "hold harmless" the manager from certain losses while the manager likewise is said to "hold harmless" the owner from certain losses.

14. **Transferability**

   This provision (customarily identified in most management contracts under the heading "successors and assigns"), refers to the owner's right to sell, transfer, lease, or sublease the hotel, subject to the manager's right of first refusal. The *right of first refusal* means that the owner cannot sell or lease the property without the prior written consent of the manager.

15. **Notices and Miscellaneous**

   This catchall provision covers not only communications between the parties to the contract, but also other matters such as the following:

   a. Manager's right to engage in competitive hotel operations elsewhere, provided such operations are not located within a certain distance, for example three miles, of the owner's hotel.

   b. If any provision of the existing management contract is determined to be legally invalid or unenforceable, the remainder of the contract shall continue in full force and effect.

   c. Agreement that nothing in the existing contract shall be construed as making the owner and manager joint venturers or partners in the hotel operation.

Comparative Analysis

In addition to reviewing the terms of a potential management contract, including the fee structure, an owner must evaluate the skill set of the management company itself. When comparing one management company to another, an owner should ask a set of questions that can lead to the best selection. Some of the key questions to ask in such an evaluation are:

1. Does the management company have a successful track record, and a reputation you can trust?

2. Does the company have experience with properties of similar type and size, and in the same market conditions?

3. If you are also a franchisee, does the management company have any other experience operating your type of franchise?

4. Does the company have proven ability to generate a profit?

5. Will the operating company be responsive to your goals and objectives?

6. Can the company deliver marketing and sales expertise to generate revenues?

7. Do you have confidence you will receive timely and meaningful reports from the management company?

8. Is the management company willing to be a small equity partner if you want it to be?[25]

As an owner, successfully asking and answering these questions can help narrow the field of potential operators to the one that will best suit your hotel.

Hotel Franchising

To recap thus far, the important issues facing an owner include defining who will be the developer, who will own, and who will manage. The fourth key question you would face as the owner is who, if anyone, will franchise the hotel. The franchising decision is independent from whether or not you agree to enter into a management contract. For example, suppose you have selected Richfield Management as your management company, and now you are considering a franchise, such as one with Hyatt Hotels. It is possible for the same parent company to extend to you, the owner, both the equivalent of a management contract *and* a franchise. For example, you may enter into a management contract with Marriott and a franchise with Marriott. These should still be thought of as two very different kinds of agreements, providing two very different kinds of services, even though the legal paperwork may be combined. You might find that both the management company and the franchisor have recognizable names. It is possible, and happens, for example, that Westin could manage a Hilton franchise. The owner entered into a management contract with Westin and a franchise agreement with Hilton.

If you did choose to enter into a franchise agreement, as the owner of the hotel, you would be the **franchisee**. The parent company from which you would obtain the rights of the franchise, such as Marriott or Hilton, is the **franchisor**. The agreement between the franchisee and the franchisor is known as a **franchise agreement**. Franchising is a business opportunity, in which a franchisor or a parent company grants the rights, trademarks, and service ideas to an owner, or the franchisee, for the local distribution or the hotel service. In return, the franchisor receives a payment or royalty.[26] Note that the franchise agreement does not provide the day-to-day management services that a management contract does. A separate management contract is necessary to ensure those provisions.

For example, suppose that as the owner of the hotel, you entered into a franchise agreement with Four Seasons Hotels. Four Seasons, as the franchisor, would grant you the right to become a hotel that bears the Four Seasons name, to use its logos and trademarks, to put up a Four Seasons sign, and to have your property listed in the Four Seasons reservations system. The entire business concept for Four Seasons, the marketing strategy, operating manuals and standards, quality controls and continued assistance and guidance would come to you in exchange for paying Four Seasons a franchise fee. Remember, it is possible that you could still enter into a separate management contract with a third party to run the day-to-day operations of your Four Seasons franchise, or you could enter into a management contract with Four Seasons.

▉▉▉▉▉ *Growth and Development of Budget Motels: United Kingdom*

Traditionally, inexpensive accommodations in the United Kingdom were provided by small, "mum-and-dad" guest houses, often with an uncertain range of services and amenities. As business gives way to changing leisure patterns, increased foreign travel, rising standards of living, and general customer demand for consistently reliable service quality—a new type of competitor has arrived. The emergence of budget chains in the United Kingdom, as well as throughout Europe, is an important phenomenon in the world of hospitality. Though these modern structures appear out of place amid the historic backdrop of centuries-old cities and towns, they are nonetheless reshaping the landscape.

The latter part of 1985 saw the emergence of budget chains in the United Kingdom with the opening of two budget-style properties: Little Chef Lodge (an affiliate of the London-based Trusthouse Forte group) at Barton-under-Needwood, and the Ibis Hotel (an affiliate of Accor S.A. in Paris) at Heathrow Airport. During the ensuing three years, some 80 budget lodging units were opened. By 1995, there could be as many as 500 budget properties with 25,000 rooms—presenting a formidable challenge to the more traditional suppliers of hotel accommodations in the United Kingdom.

Besides the French-based and U.S.-based companies now at various stages of buying land and building their first budget units in Britain, there is keen interest also in developing chains of budget/economy hotels throughout the United Kingdom by other companies such as the Rank Organization, the Granada Company, Whitbread, Arcade, and Tattinger Champagne.

Significantly, the pattern of budget hotel development in the UK closely follows that of the United States in terms of locating close to free-standing restaurants—some of which are hotel company owned but are operated independently of the hotel unit. Unlike the economy hotel sector in the United States, however, budget properties in the UK offer such slightly different core products, customer services, and tariff structures that consumers experience difficulty in perceiving differences among competitors. Thus, the distinctive competitive advantage of a memorable brand name has yet to emerge.

This new wave of American style budget properties in the UK and all over Europe could put independent "mum-and-dad" operations in financial trouble. If one or more of the budget chains does in fact begin to develop strong brand name recognition and loyal customers, then the independents may suffer the same ill fate that their counterparts in the USA have already experienced.

Distinguishing Between Franchising and Chains

You may see many hotels across the United States with the same name and logo. They may be franchises or chains. It is important in a discussion of franchising to understanding the distinction between franchising and chains. Although all franchises with more than one unit are part of a chain, not all chains with more than one unit are franchises. A **hotel chain** is two or more establishments at separate locations under common ownership or related through other legal ties such as franchising.[27] Therefore if you decided to start a two-unit hotel chain, called Student's Sleep Inn, and owned both properties, you would be a chain, but not a franchise. Say you decided to enter into a franchise agreement with an enterprising junior at your school. The third Student's Sleep Inn, owned by that junior, is a franchise. Your chain of three hotels would now include a franchise. The two properties you owned would be called **company owned units** and the one that you franchised would be a **franchised unit**. All three properties would be part of the chain. It would be very difficult for a guest at the hotel to distinguish between these two types of ownership.

As more and more chains are franchising in order to expand, and fewer and fewer continue to expand via company owned units, it is no wonder that the terms *franchising* and *chains* are constantly used together. The distinction between the two, however, remains. A franchise speaks to a legal agreement between two parties, and a chain is two or more units operating under the same name. The term *chain* is used in reference to multiple company owned units, franchises, or any mix of the two. The term *chain* can also be used to describe multiple units in a referral group, though the names of individual members are different. For example, Hotel San Felice and Hotel Filao Beach are both independent properties that operate as part of the Relaix and Châteaux referral group. Referral groups will be discussed later.

Brief Historical Background

Early on, the railroads, steamship lines, and airlines all became chain hotel owners and operators primarily to promote the development of desirable destination areas. Thus, for example, the Canadian Pacific Railroad, which originally sponsored the development of the Banff Springs Hotel in Alberta, today controls a chain of 26 hotels known as Canadian Pacific Hotels & Resorts. Similarly, the Matson steamship lines at one time owned and operated resort hotels in Honolulu. Moreover, with Pan American's establishment in the 1940s of its own overseas hotel chain, Intercontinental Hotels, it was not long before other competitors followed suit, with the result that by the mid-1980s more than two thirds of the world's airlines were involved in chain hotel operation.[28]

Along with these hotel developments, there were others such as Statler, Hilton, Sheraton—and, in the 1950s, Holiday Inns—that emerged with high visibility in the period following the end of World War II. At the same time, it was becoming increasingly apparent that chain operation affords economies of scale that are seldom enjoyed by nonchain hotels. Among the benefits most often cited by chain operators were instant name recognition through national advertising, computerized reservation services, a guest referral network to all units in the chain, volume purchasing with substantial trade discounts, improved productivity through centralized recruitment and training, and the relative ease of financing capital improvements.

Over the years since World War II, chain operations have become such a dominant force in the hospitality industry that today there are more than 800 chains listed by the American Hotel & Motel Association.[29]

Franchising, the most arresting development of recent years, provides attractive opportunities for hotel chains to make rapid penetration into the marketplace. In addition, it offers a potential franchisee such a full plate of alluring advantages that the American Hotel & Motel Association has publicized "an easy ten-step guide to picking the right franchise for you."[30] Wisdom suggests, however, that a rigorous analysis of both the advantages and the disadvantages—from the franchisee's *and* the franchisor's standpoint—be undertaken before one enters into any franchise agreement. Here are some of the more important ones to consider:

When a Franchise Makes Sense

If you choose to enter into a franchise agreement, you forgive a large amount of creative license in the operation of your hotel. Entering into a franchise agreement means meeting the specifications set forth by the franchisor, not your own. There are also costs associated with a franchise agreement that must be weighed against the benefits. Consider four perspectives, the advantages and disadvantages as seen by the franchisee and the advantages and disadvantages as seen by the franchisor.

Franchisee Advantages First consider the advantages that you, as the owner of a hotel and franchisee, would enjoy. These advantages speak to the benefits you would receive by being part of a larger organization, such as brand name recognition, purchasing economies, technical assistance, quality control, reduced financial risk, and a central reservations system.

1. The franchisee enjoys the benefit of an established product or service having consumer acceptance and is therefore free of worries about traditional startup costs, such as developing a market presence. In the case of such companies as Sheraton Hotels, Hilton Hotels, and Holiday Inns, franchisors spend a sizable portion of their advertising budget on national campaigns to keep the public aware of their hotel and restaurant services—for which the franchisee is customarily charged an advertising fee based on the gross revenues of a franchised unit. The **brand name recognition**, or the fact that customers have heard of the chain and have an image associated with it in mind, of the chain is a key advantage to the franchisee. Moreover, a franchisee saves all the time, effort, and expense that building a reputation would cost, if he were an individual entrepreneur—thus enabling his franchise unit to maintain its competitive edge.

2. A second advantage to the franchisee is the availability of managerial and technical assistance provided by the franchisor. Depending on the policy of a specific franchisor, the range of assistance available may, or may not, include managerial training, site selection, layout and design, furniture, fixtures and equipment purchasing, inventory control, and promotional plans for the grand opening.

3. Another advantage to the franchisee involves franchisor oversight of quality control standards. This is important not only to assure a consistent customer image but also to maintain employee pride in the workplace.

4. In many instances, franchisees benefit financially from the franchisor's advice and guidance on how much inventory to carry, thus avoiding waste and spoilage of perishables, and unprofitable storage of low demand items. Franchisees also benefit from **purchasing economies**, as the chain as a whole can negotiate better rates for things like soap and towels, as well as credit card fees and phone charges.

5. The carefully designed procedures of a franchised system minimize the financial risks for the franchisee and therefore tend to increase—but not to guarantee—the likelihood of generous franchise earnings.

6. Finally, substantial business is often referred to individual hotels via a **central reservations system** and chain directories, the cost of which is shared by all units in the chain. This makes the marketing dollars of individual units go much further.

Franchisee Disadvantages Next, consider the disadvantages that you as the owner or franchisee would face. You would give up the advantage as well as being constrained by the rules of the franchise organization.

1. Failure of the franchisee to read carefully the fine print in the franchise agreement, or failure to secure legal advice before signing such an agreement, may cause a prospective franchisee to succumb to false or misleading sales practices of franchise promoters. Like any other contract, the franchise contract spells out in detail precisely what the franchisor

will provide. Consulting with an attorney who understands the practical as well as the legal implications of a franchising agreement will enable a prospective franchisee to focus on those factors most likely to make his or her franchising relationship a successful one.

2. Since franchisors typically realize substantial revenues from franchise fees as well as continuing royalties from franchisees, it may come as a shock to prospective franchisees that the financial obligation up front, when the franchise agreement is signed, can be steep. The ongoing fees also cut into the profit one could make as an independent property.

3. Franchisees may be required to provide certain amenities and facilities such as swimming pools and/or 24-hour front desk service, in order to be part of the chain. These and other service costs to be borne by a franchisee may turn out to be higher than expected, and thus severely diminish the franchisee's expectations of a satisfactory return on the investment.

4. Territorial rights of the franchisor may overlap those of a franchisee, and thus limit the revenue that the franchisee might otherwise expect to realize. For example, many of the larger hotel chains, early on, granted franchises that prohibited the franchisor from making any other franchise agreements within a specified geographical area. This was designed to protect a franchisee from having the franchisor grant another franchisee the right to operate another unit in the immediate neighborhood (two Sheratons on the same corner). In recent years, however, segmentation of hotel markets has resulted in creation of different hotel brands with separate corporate identities. When such new brands have granted franchises, they have often disregarded the territorial restrictions agreed to by the parent company and its franchisees. Thus, such original franchisees are hurt by competition from another franchisee, in essence from the same company, being permitted to locate within territory originally designated exclusively for the parent company franchisee. For example, say you were granted a Holiday Inn franchise from Holiday Inn several years ago, and were given the exclusive rights to the city of Denver. Suppose, subsequently, Holiday Inn launched two brands, Holiday Inn Suites and Holiday Inn Select. It may be that the rights to those franchises are given to someone else, potentially hurting your sales.

5. With respect to a franchisee's desire to transfer or terminate the franchise, such occasions are generally covered by the language of the agreement. An uncooperative franchisor, however, may withhold approval of such a transaction if, for any reason, the franchisor believes the franchisee to have violated any provision of the franchise agreement.

Franchisor Advantages Next consider the advantages of franchising from the point of view of the franchisor. Franchising is the ticket to growth for a franchise organization, and its members have a vested ownership interest.

1. Franchisors regard business expansion through a franchising network as the most attractive means of achieving rapid growth without the necessity of having to inject large sums of their own money or of incurring substantial debt through borrowing from banks or insurance companies. Thus, the franchisee's investment in a particular franchise enables the franchisor to share the heavy burden of a rapidly growing hotel or restaurant empire, while at the same time allowing the franchisor valuable time for evaluating market opportunities in a wide variety of competitive environments.

2. Moreover, some franchisors suspect that a manager may be less enthusiastic about the operation of a **company owned** unit than is the franchisee-manager who is usually a resident of the local community. The personal investment of the franchisee-manager moti-

vates him to work hard in pursuit of financial success. Franchising creates motivated owner/managers.

Franchisor Disadvantages Finally, consider the disadvantages of franchising as seen by the franchisor. Multiple owners can mean lack of consistency and control, and finding qualified franchisees can be difficult.

1. The idea of using the franchisee's money to keep a franchisor's business expansion plan afloat is not without its drawbacks. In the first place, overseeing a quickly expanding chain of hotel franchisees is always a formidable challenge. If less desirable franchisees are allowed to enter the system, it reflects badly on the whole organization.

2. In addition, there can be no guarantee that a franchisee will not discover, sooner or later, that he/she would be able to do just as well—if not better—by operating the business without the franchisor. After the franchise agreement expires, the franshisee may not renew.

3. Furthermore, though the supply of prospective franchisee applicants may appear to be inexhaustible, some franchisors report a dearth of applicants whose experience, financial backing, and motivational drive are sufficiently persuasive to warrant taking a chance on their ability to become successful franchise operators.

The Typical Franchise Agreement

In summary form, the components of a franchise agreement are directly related to the kinds of fees that are typically charged. In exchange for each type of fee, the franchisor agrees to provide a certain set of benefits. There are several types of fees: initial costs, which are covered in a one-time fee, and a series of ongoing fees that are paid as long as the agreement is in place. These fees include a royalty fee, advertising or marketing fees, reservations fees, training fees, frequent traveler program fees, and other miscellaneous fees.[31]

Initial Costs The initial costs or initial fee is the only fee that occurs on a one-time basis. The balance of the fees are known as continuing or ongoing fees. The initial fee for a hotel franchise is typically a fixed amount plus an additional charge depending on the number of rooms within a hotel. The fee is submitted with the application for the franchise. In exchange for the fee, the franchisee receives review of the application, a site review, evaluation of the construction plans, and visits during construction. Initial costs may also be incurred for signage and computer software and hardware necessary to interface with the organization. If the hotel already exists and is changing from another name to a new franchise (say from Howard Johnson to Days Inn), the property is known as a **conversion**. If an application for a franchise is denied, the initial fee is returned in total; at times, 5 to 10 percent is withheld to cover costs of the review.

Royalty Fee A royalty fee is the fee paid as compensation for the chain's name, trademarks, logos, and goodwill. This fee is calculated to generate a profit for the franchisor. Royalty fees are generally calculated as a percentage of rooms revenue and range from approximately 3 percent to 6 percent.

Advertising or Marketing Fee The franchisor collects the marketing fees systemwide to use for various kinds of national or regional advertising that benefit multiple members. This fee includes the costs for publication and distribution of a chain directory. This fee is either calculated as a percentage of rooms revenue (ranging from approximately 1 to 3 percent), or a fixed dollar amount per available room. The income generated from this fee is used for specific purposes and does not generate a profit for the franchisor. In general, the same is true for the balance of the fees listed.

Reservations Fee The reservations fee is used to support the costs associated with the operation of the central reservation system. These include office expenses, telephone and computer expenses, and the salaries of reservations personnel. As with the marketing fees, the fees generated for reservations are designed to apply directly to the specified use and do not generate profits for the franchisor. The reservations fees may be calculated the same way as marketing fees (a fixed percentage of rooms revenue) or based on a fixed cost for each reservation sent through the central system. If the fee is calculated as a fixed cost, it would then typically be $4 to $6 per reservation.

Frequent Traveler Fees For those franchisors who maintain a frequent guest program, a fee is assessed to cover the costs of administering the program. This fee is based upon the benefit generated to a specific hotel by its frequent guests. It is calculated as a percentage of what each guest spends (ranging from approximately 5 to 7 percent), or as a fixed dollar amount per room occupied. On a fixed basis, the amount is typically $3 to $10 per guest room.

Other Miscellaneous Fees Sometimes a franchisor offers other specific services and products for a fee. These services could include training programs, assistance in purchasing, computer equipment rental, or assistance in opening a property. These fees are designed to cover the costs of the services provided and generally represent minimal, if any, profit.

Sleep Inns, a brand of Choice Hotels, demonstrates a real example of a franchise agreement. This franchise, which is an economy chain, charges five types of fees: initial costs, franchise royalty, reservations, marketing, and nominal other fees. Exhibit 14.3 offers a summary.

Exhibit 14.3 Sleep Inn Franchise Costs

Initial Fees

(One time only) $300 per room or $40,000 minimum payable upon application.

Royalty

A monthly assessment of 4% of gross room revenue.

Marketing

A monthly assessment of 1.3% of gross room revenue; plus $.28 per room, per day.

Reservations

A monthly assessment of 1.75 percent of gross room revenues. This includes software support and communications fees.

Other

A nominal fee for pre-opening materials and training services pacakge, billed 60–90 days prior to system entry. There are also support charges for signs and reservation send/receive terminals, which may be purchased or leased.

Comparative Analysis

The owner of a hotel is left with the question of whether to enter into a franchise agreement or not based on the advantages and disadvantages as well as the costs associated with the benefits. If, as the owner, you do decide to enter into a franchise agreement, you must first determine the kind of franchise that is appropriate. If you own a first-class hotel with extensive amenities and facilities it is inappropriate to join a budget chain. After the correct category is determined, a fee comparison between different franchisors in the appropriate category is a good next step. Exhibit 14.4 offers a comparison of fees for first-class or upscale hotels. Finally, an owner must also find compatibility with the operating philosophy of the franchisor. As a franchisor is being selected, an owner would be wise to consider the following important steps in franchising.

Exhibit 14.4 Summary of Chain Franchise Fees—First-Class Hotels

Chain	Total Royalty Cost	Total Other Cost*	1994 Total 10-Year Cost	1994 Total Cost as a % of Total Room Revenue
Clarion	$2,866,409	$2,736,661	$5,603,073	5.8
Doubletree	2,880,814	3,390,949	6,271,763	6.5
Doubletree Club	2,880,814	3,450,949	6,331,763	6.6
Doubletree Suites	2,880,814	3,390,949	6,271,763	6.5
Embassy Suites	3,814,085	3,630,983	7,472,068	7.8
Guest Quarters Suites	2,880,814	3,390,949	6,271,763	6.5
Hawthorne Suites	3,841,085	2,520,678	6,361,763	6.6
Hilton Garden Inn	4,801,356	3,520,103	8,321,459	8.7
Hilton Inn	4,801,356	3,559,832	7,361,188	7.7
Hilton Suites	4,801,356	3,520,103	8,321,459	8.7
Holiday Inn Crowne Plaza	4,801,356	3,741,174	8,542,530	8.9
Homewood Suites	3,841,085	3,984,785	7,825,870	8.1
Marriott	7,487,115	2,024,553	9,511,667	9.9
Omni	2,880,814	3,410,949	6,291,763	6.6
Preferred Hotels**	390,000	1,040,235	1,430,235	1.5
Radisson	3,841,085	4,754,852	8,595,937	9.0
Residence Inn	4,622,359	2,997,377	7,619,736	7.9
Sheraton Inn	4,801,356	2,890,258	7,691,614	8.0
Sheraton Suites	5,761,627	2,792,599	8,554,226	8.9
Westin	4,801,356	3,644,306	8,445,662	8.8

* Total Other Cost includes initial costs, and costs for reservations, marketing, frequent traveler programs, and miscellaneous.

** Preferred Hotels is an affiliation. Note dramatic difference relative to chains.

Assumptions:

Number of Rooms:	300 Rooms
Average Room Rate—Year One	$95.00

Continued

■■■■■ **Exhibit 14.4** Summary of Chain Franchise Fees—First-Class Hotels *(Continued)*

Assumptions: *(Continued)*

Room Rate Growth	5% per year
Occupancy:	
Year 1	60%
Year 2	70%
Year 3–10	75%
Projection Period:	10 years
Total Room Nights	799,350
Total Rooms Revenue During 10-Year Projection Period:	$96,027,117
Total Food and Beverage Revenue During 10-Year Projection Period:	$57,616,270
Number of Reservations from Franchisor:	15% of occupied rooms
Percent of Rooms Occupied by Frequent Travelers	8% of occupied rooms
Percent of Rooms Occupied by Third Party Reservation Travelers	5% of occupied rooms
Average Length of Stay	Two nights

Source: HVS International, Inc., Mineola, New York *Hotel Franchise Fee Analysis Guide*, Third Edition

Important Steps in Franchising

1. Since risk is inevitably involved in any form of investment, a potential franchisee needs to evaluate not only the franchisor's performance record but also his/her own personal experience, business skills, and aptitude for successful franchise operation. In other words, a thorough self-evaluation is important before undertaking the risk of investing in a franchise.

2. Undertake comparison shopping of other franchisees in the same or related line of business to obtain their comments on the downside as well as the upside of their franchise experience.

3. Study very carefully the initial package of information that you have received from the prospective franchisor and compare its terms with those of other franchisors whom you have met.

4. Before signing a franchise agreement, you need to protect yourself by obtaining competent legal advice as to:

   a. what you are legally bound to do or not do under the franchise contract;

   b. what requirements of federal, state, or local laws you must observe;

   c. what personal liabilities—financial, tax, or license liabilities—you are obligated to meet.

Hotel Affiliations ─────────────────────

The final decision for you, as the owner, is whether you would want to enter into an **affiliation**, which is also known as a **referral group** or a **consortium**. This type of affiliation offers many of the same advantages as a franchise, but typically is less expensive and less restrictive. Because of reduced cost, reduced restrictions, and ease to terminate an affiliation, the agreements are much less complex in nature than franchise agreements or management contracts. An affiliation is a marketing alliance with other lodging properties of the same kind, as we learned in chapter 2.

The key distinction between a member of an affiliation and a member of a franchise is in how the lodging property is named. All members of a chain of hotels with franchised units will go by the same name, such as Radisson Hotels or Four Seasons Hotels. On the other hand, all members of Best Western hotels, which is the largest and best-known referral group, will go by an independent name, such as Kvikne's Hotel in Balestrand, Norway, or Pacific Inn and Conference Center in White Rock, British Columbia, which are members of the Best Western group. The Best Western logo will be displayed prominently along with the hotel's name.

Referral groups typically group together properties that share a common set of attributes and have met a minimum set of criteria. For example, Relais and Châteaux, whose properties are primarily in Europe, is a group of relatively small properties (less than 100 rooms). These hotels typically come with old-world charm, often formerly having been castles, convents, and other historic sites. The group also requires exceptional restaurant offerings for guests in order to be a member. (A listing of referral groups is offered in chapter 2, "The Big Picture.")

Unlike franchises, referral groups are structured as non-profit or not-for-profit associations. They aim to match the fee income to the expenses incurred in providing benefits for members. The governance of the referral group rests primarily in the hands of its members, although it employs full-time employees in a central office.

The term of obligation for a referral group is much shorter than that for a franchise agreement. Typically the relationship is extended for one year and is renewed on an annual basis. Furthermore, there are typically no penalty fees if you decide to leave the group.

When an Affiliation Makes Sense

Affiliations are appropriate for owners who are interested in maintaining their own name and more independence in management style than a franchise provides. Such owners would be attracted by the advantages that an affiliation offers, such as a central reservations system, nationwide or international advertising coverage, and purchasing economies. Affiliate members do not want to pay the fees associated with a franchise, nor do they want a long-term commitment. In general, the benefits provided by an affiliation are not nearly as extensive as those provided by a franchise.

Members of franchise organizations, particularly in the midprice and budget end of the market, typically do not enter into a relationship with an affiliation. There is not a lot of incremental advantage to doing so, as the franchise has already provided all of the benefits that an affiliation could provide. At the luxury and upscale end of the market, most franchised properties do not affiliate either. However, some more prestigious affiliations, such as Preferred Hotels and Leading Hotels of the World, attract some properties that already have a chain affiliation. An example is the Bristol Hotel Kempinski in Berlin, Germany, which is a member of the Kempinski chain and Leading Hotels of the World affiliation.

A Typical Affiliation Agreement

An affiliation agreement, not unlike a franchise agreement, carries with it a set of rules and regulations by which members must abide. For Best Western, for example, there are rules regulating: the governance of the organization, signs and advertising, the use of the reservations system, the length of memberships and the fees associated with belonging, the appearance of the lobby and front office, guest rooms and bathrooms, the maintenance of buildings grounds and public areas, the use of logo items, violations and sanctions if a member does not perform, and procedures for canceling a membership. Though the properties in an affiliation may look physically very different, all member hotels within a particular country or set of countries are held to the same standards.

So that all of the properties in an affiliation have the same minimum quality standards, the rules can be quite detailed. Minimum scores are obtained by meeting a minimum number of governing regulations. For example, Best Western regulations specify that guest bedrooms provide individually controlled thermostats and one current local telephone directory. All properties must use the logo soap and a least three other logo items, such as guest towels, menu covers, matches, or pencils, to be selected from an extensive list.[32]

Joining an affiliation requires the payment of different kinds of one time and ongoing fees. Best Western, for example, charges the following types of fees:[33]

- *ENTRANCE FEES* (effective December 1, 1994)

   (One time fee to accompany application)

   A. AFFILIATION FEE. Minimum $20,000 (20 rooms or less), plus $100 for each additional room, plus

   B. EVALUATION FEE. $4,000 nonrefundable.

- *ANNUAL DUES*

   Base fee of $1,163 for 20 rooms plus: $39.10 per room for 21 to 50 rooms, reducing to $15.20 per room for 51 to 400 rooms.

- *MEMBERSHIP FEE*

   $0.72 per room per day for first 25 rooms plus: $0.67 per room per day for 26 to 50 rooms, reducing to $0.60 per room per day for 51 to 100 rooms.

- *RESERVATION FEE*

   For the first 12 months of activation, a new property will be charged $0.33 per room per day.

   After 12 months, the reservation fee is based on the number of rooms booked through the reservations system.

- ■ *SPECIAL ASSESSMENT*

   A special assessment to fund a specific project. For example, in 1994 a special assessment was charged to fund a new reservation system. To put fees in perspective, a 99-room hotel would be charged the following amounts:

	Entrance Fee	Annual Dues	Membership Fee	Reservation Fee	Total Annual Cost
99-Room Hotel	$31,900.00	3,081.00	23,415.00	11,925.00	38,421.00

Summary

This chapter tackles the tough task of unraveling all of the ways that the different players in the hotel business are intertwined. A series of examples demonstrates some of the combinations of relationships between developers, owners, managers, franchisors, and affiliates of hotels. The decoding framework we have presented here offers a way to understand the players involved in any given transaction, and can be readily applied to current events. How the hotel business evolved to include these various players is traced through a historical perspective.

From an owner's perspective, this chapter reveals the advantages and disadvantages of the key decisions that an owner faces in getting a hotel up and running. From a development perspective, the owner must consider the cost side and benefit side of hotel development, with an eye toward measuring a hotel's profit potential. For management contracts, franchise agreements, and affiliations, an owner must weigh the appropriateness of each agreement and then systematically evaluate the best course of action.

For management of the hotel, an owner must decide if a management contract makes sense, then must comprehend the key provisions found in a management contract, ranging from term length to fees. In choosing to franchise or not to franchise, an owner must weigh the advantages and disadvantages of being part of a larger organization. Benefits like brand name recognition and a reservations system must be weighed against the fees to be paid and lack of freedom in running the hotel.

For affiliations, an owner must again consider personal preferences and the advantages of an affiliation in light of the characteristics of the lodging property and whether or not it already has a franchise agreement.

Careful consideration of all the different relationships involved in hotel development will help a potential owner confidently answer this question: So you want to own a hotel?

Discussion Questions

1. Explain the different players involved in hotel ownership and operation. What roles does each play?

2. Of the decisions that an owner must make, which can be the most costly if the owner makes a bad decision? Why?

3. Explain the relationship between a hotel's occupancy and average rate. Why are they so closely linked? How is each important in determining a hotel's profit potential?

4. What are the key categories of costs involved in building a new hotel?

5. Explain the key reasons the hotel industry went through a boom period in the 1980s.

6. How are troubled hotel companies coping in the 1990s?

7. How is it that a franchised unit is always part of chain, but a chain unit is not always franchised?

8. What are some of the advantages and disadvantages of franchising to franchisors? To franchisees?

9. What are the most important provisions of a management contract?

10. The carpet in the lobby of a hotel is badly worn. The management company that operates the hotel insists that it be replaced. The owners do not want to put any funds toward replacing the carpet. Should this issue have been addressed in the management contract? If so, how?

11. If a hotel wants to be relatively independent, but sees the advantages of a reservations system, what could you recommend? Why?

12. According to the opening quotations, what is the greatest gift that one could have to operate a hotel successfully? Why?

Assignments

1. Choose a current event from a recent periodical or newspaper that describes a transaction involving a hotel company. (The transaction can involve the change of a hotel's name, franchisor, management company, owner, and so on.) Apply the framework presented here to identify all of the players that were involved. What type of transaction is involved? Which players are unknown, based on the information that you have?

2. Review any hospitality trade publication for advertisements by various franchisors to potential franchisees. What benefits are noted most aggressively? Compare the ads of various organizations. How are they similar? How are they different?

End Notes

1. Francois, duc de la Rochefoucauld, from *Maximes,* published in 1664. The quotation is from *Money Talks,* edited by Robert W. Kent (New York: Simon and Schuster, 1985), 37.

2. "Hotel Restaurants—Help Your Guests Comply with the Tax Reform Act," *Hotel Motel Insider* (5 January 1987): 1.

3. From a lecture delivered by Alan Ostroff, March 31, 1992, at Boston University.

4. "Hotel Restaurants."

5. "Tax Revision Will Slow Construction, Predicts L&H," *Lodging Hospitality* (July 1986): 13.

6. Ibid.

7. Bernard Baumohl, "The Banks Are in Hotel Hell," *Time* (27 May 1991): 44.

8. Susan Carey, "Breathing New Life Into Holiday Inn," *The Wall Street Journal,* 29 October 1990, B1.

9. Brian Bremner, "America's Innkeepers Brace for the '90's," *Business Week,* 13 August 1990, 106.

10. Susan Carey, "Hope Persists at Inter-Continental Hotels," *The Wall Street Journal,* 23 May 1991, A-10.

11. Dean Foust and Mark Maremont, "The Baggage Weighing Marriott Down," *Business Week,* (29 January 1990): 64.

12. Dean Foust, "Marriott is Smoothing Out the Lumps in Its Bed," *Business Week* (1 April 1991): 74.

13. Eben Shipiro, "'80's Building Binge Slows Marriott," *New York Times,* 22 March 1991, D-1.

14. Baumohl, 44.

15. Ibid.

16. Sean Hennessey, "Hotel Investment Outlook," *Landauer Hospitality Services* 4 (1) (January 1995): 1–4.

17. James J. Eyster, *The Negotiation and Administration of Hotel and Restaurant Management Contracts*, 3d ed. (Ithaca: School of Hotel Administration, Cornell University, 1988), 4.

18. Robert Kiener, "The Management Contract," *Hospitality* (April 1975): 43. Quotation here is from James E. Potter, Intercontinental Hotels vice president.

19. Ibid.

20. Michael M. Coltman, *Financial Management for the Hospitality Industry* (New York: Van Nostrand Reinhold Co., 1979), 208–209.

21. Eyster, 1. It should also be noted that some 206 hotel management companies are shown for the year 1990 by Stephen Rushmore in *Hotel Investments, A Guide for Lenders and Owners* (Boston: Warren, Gorham & Lamont, 1990), 61–83.

22. 1989 survey results. International Council of Hotel-Motel Management Companies, a subsidiary of the American Hotel & Motel Association.

23. Eyster, 178–180.

24. 1989 survey results. International Council of Hotel-Motel Management Companies, item #47.

25. Adapted from Peter Yu, president of Richfield Management Company, "Selection of Management is Key to Successful Hotel Investment," *Transactions* (Kansas City, MO: Hotel and Motel Brokers of America, 1993): 24–26.

26. Robert Justis and Richard Judd, *Franchising* (Cincinnati: South-Western Publishing Co., 1989), 6.

27. D. Daryl Wyckoff and W. Earl Sasser, *The U.S. Lodging Industry* (Lexington, Massachusetts: Lexington Books, D. C. Heath & Co., 1981), 251.

28. Harold E. Lane, "Innkeeping: A New Role for the Airlines," *Columbia Journal of World Business* (July–August 1971). See also this author's "Marriages of Necessity: Airline Hotel Liaisons," *Cornell Hotel & Restaurant Quarterly* (May 1986).

29. American Hotel & Motel Association, *1994 Directory of Hotel & Motel Systems*.

30. Michael Cahill, "Rally Around the Flag," *Lodging* (October 1991): 35–41.

31. Discussion of fees is adapted from Michelle S. Russo, "Hotel Franchise Fees Analysis Guide," (Mineola, New York: Hospitality Valuation Services, April 1994), 1–5.

32. Selected from "Rules and Regulations," Best Western International's 1995 Membership Information.

33. Selected from "Membership Fees" Best Western International's 1995 Membership Information.

Chapter Fifteen

Commenting on the smarts and success of restauranteurs as a large percentage of the total franchising economy,

> *"...generally speaking, the world is divided into two types of entrepreneurs: those who wear paper hats, and those who don't. ... [and] it's what's under that paper hat that counts."*

Jay Finegan, Inc. Magazine [1]

So You Want to Own a Restaurant? ✍

When you finish this chapter you should:

1. Know the difference between developing, owning, managing, franchising, and strategically aligning of restaurants.

2. Understand the difference between owning and leasing in the restaurant business.

3. Know the key expenditures involved in developing a new restaurant.

4. Know how to weigh the costs and benefits of a restaurant to determine whether it will be profitable.

5. Offer a brief historical perspective on restaurant franchising.

6. Explain why the decision to franchise or not to franchise is critical for a restaurant owner.

7. Explain the various kinds of fees charged by restaurant franchisors.

8. Offer guidelines to assist an owner in choosing the right franchise.

9. Explain the various constituencies with whom a restaurant might strategically align.

10. Explain the advantages of the various kinds of strategic alignments.

Introduction

The restaurant business holds great appeal to entrepreneurs around the world. And it's no wonder. It is a business that is highly fragmented, that is, there are many people who can capture a very small share of the total business. It has low barrier to entry. One can begin a restaurant with a small amount of capital, relative to many other businesses. It is a business that allows an owner also to be a hands-on operator, satisfying a need to be right in the thick of things.

In entering this exciting and dynamic business, an entrepreneur must be mindful to address a series of questions about how the restaurant will be developed, owned, and managed, and if it will be franchised or strategically aligned. The answers shape the kind of establishment that will result.

"Decoding" a Restaurant Investment

This chapter puts you square in the shoes of a restaurant owner. From this perspective, you will see the set of questions a restaurant owner answers, from taking an idea for a restaurant to turning it into an establishment serving its first customer. Most of these decisions are not unlike those encountered in the previous chapter, "So You Want to Own a Hotel?"

When starting a new restaurant, all of the questions that follow should be answered in the planning stages. This is because one decision can strongly influence the other decisions. For example, a decision to become a restaurant franchise structures how the restaurant will be developed, owned, and managed.

1. **Who will develop the restaurant?** Who will put together the menu concept, the layout of the food facilities, the necessary permits, the financing, and the restaurant space itself? Who will be the impetus behind getting the restaurant in operation?

It is very common in the restaurant business for an individual owner to be the developer. An entrepreneur interested in a restaurant that has a distinct signature is interested in controlling the development process. If the owner chooses to become a franchise, then assistance for much of the development function is provided by the franchisor. The restaurant's physical design and layout, the format for the restaurant's operation, and expertise for selecting a site may all be provided. For example, the McDonald's chain would provide these kinds of services to its franchisees.

Restaurants can also be developed by major corporations, both public and private. For example, Starbuck's Coffee is a public corporation that has rapidly developed many outlets. All of these outlets are developed and owned by the company; they are not franchised. Thus, all outlets are company developed and company owned.

2. **Who will own the restaurant?** In other words, who will have title to the restaurant? This could be one person, such as yourself, acting as an entrepreneur. It could be a partnership, such as with a classmate or family member. It could be a restaurant corporation such as the Wolfgang Puck Food Company.

The ownership of a restaurant may not involve owning land or a building. This is because a restaurant's space may be purchased or **leased**. If it is purchased, the restaurant owner has title to the land, the building and the furniture, fixtures, and equipment (FF&E) where the restaurant is housed. If the restaurant space is leased, which is a common arrangement in the restaurant business, then the restaurant owner has the right to use the land and building space for some period of time according to the **lease agreement**. The land and building are owned by the **lessor** of the space. Rent is paid by the restaurant owner, who is the **lessee**, in exchange for the right to operate the restaurant within the space. FF&E is occasionally leased as well, particularly if the space was previously another restaurant. The FF&E may also be purchased by the restaurant owner, which is the more typical scenario. Whether the restaurant space is owned or leased, financing for a restaurant can come from various kinds of sources, such as equity from a partnership or debt from a bank.

3. **Who will manage the restaurant?** Who will be responsible for the day-to-day operations of the restaurant once it is up and running? Who will see to it that the kitchen is preparing meals and that the meals are served? Typically the owner of a restaurant is very involved in managing the operation. The owner/manager may be actively working in the front or back of the house. Ownership partnerships can involve persons with different skill sets applicable to running a restaurant. For example, one partner who may be skilled in the culinary arts would oversee the kitchen, while another, with business expertise, would handle the finances.

The use of management companies in commercial restaurants is rare, though management companies are widely used in institutional foodservice settings such as schools and health care facilities. Commercial restaurant owners are likely either to actively manage themselves or to hire individuals to run the operation for them.

4. **Who, if anyone, will franchise the restaurant?** Who will grant the restaurant the right to operate as a member of a specific chain with a specific restaurant concept? If the restaurant is franchised, that relationship would typically be between an individual owner or partnership, and a well-known company. A franchise offers an owner the advantage of large chain affiliation while leaving ownership and management control in the owner's hands.

Whether or not to franchise is a critical decision for a restaurateur owner. It shapes how much influence a restaurateur can have in the implementation of a restaurant concept. A franchise arrangement dictates a very specific set of standards and management practices. A restaurant owner must assess what pieces of owning and managing a restaurant are important in weighing this decision.

5. **With whom, if anyone, will the restaurant be strategically aligned?** In this definition, we consider **strategic alignment** in the broadest possible terms. A strategic alignment involves an agreement, formal or informal, between the restaurant and any other party, where the relationship brings mutual benefit. These relationships are sometimes referred to as **VMRs—value managed relationships**. The relationship could be between a restaurant and economy lodging property with no foodservice. It could be a relationship with another type of retail outlet, such as a gas station or a 24-hour store, or with potential sources of customer referrals such as taxi drivers or hotel concierges. It could be with suppliers of food and beverage, frequent guests, or the local community.

The nature of the restaurant business is such that word of mouth is very important. Furthermore, a restaurant can be an important social center for a community. Thus, establishing the various kinds of relationships, though not by any means mandatory, can make good business sense.

Restaurant Development and Ownership ___

This first two questions an owner faces involve who will develop and who will own the restaurant. The development of a restaurant concept may be an owner original or follow the proscribed formula for a franchise unit. If the concept is to be a one-of-a-kind entrepreneurship, the development process may take years of planning and thought. In this case, the owner functions as the developer.

If the restaurant is to be a franchise, then the systems and management of the restaurant are a replication of the other units in the chain, and are therefore immediately available. Thus, with a franchise operation, the site selection and building of the restaurant space is the only time-consuming part of the development process. In this case, the owner is still the developer, but the development process is greatly governed by the dictates of the restaurant franchisor. This is because of the restaurant chain's desire to have a consistent food and service delivery system in each of its individual units.

Key Issues in Design and Development

Regardless of the kind of restaurant, those startup elements noted in chapter 9, "How Things Work: Foodservice Operations," are applicable to the development process. To review, it is critical to engineer a menu that works, including meeting customers' needs, and being attentive to nutritional values and availability of ingredients. The development process also involves comprehending service style, matching culinary skill and kitchen equipment to the menu, and offering profitable and popular items. The process should also be set up such that a restaurant opens smartly and not too soon, tests the revenues and costs associated with the concept, and avoids physical design pitfalls. Last, and far from least, it is critical to be very thoughtful in choosing a location.

All of these elements should be considered throughout the various stages of the design and development process, from menu concept to site selection to construction to opening.

Profile: One Restaurant Owner's Story

Viewing the evolution of Rialto, a stand-alone restaurant in Boston, gives insight to the kinds of decisions that an owner faces in the development of a unique restaurant concept. Michela Larson, an experienced restaurateur, and her partners, Jody Adams, a chef, and Chris Myers, a restaurant manager, began the process of developing the restaurant in 1990. The development process would take some five years before the birth of Rialto.

The goal of the partnership was to establish the best restaurant in the city and to focus on food and customers. There were a lot of conversations and brainstorming sessions throughout the first stage of the process, with each partner lending his or her specific expertise. Issues such as style, uniforms, food, partners' roles, and decor are a sampling of the different topics of the brainstorming sessions. In terms of cuisine, the partners decided they wanted to mix the foods of Spain, France, and Italy in the menu development.

During the early stages, the partners cut out pictures from magazines from all over the world to use for idea generation. They clipped pictures of furniture, design, bars, chairs, walls, and so on. As the discussion progressed, they focused on the American era from the 1920s to the 1940s. Next the team hired a graphic designer to help them design the image of the restaurant and to find a name. They liked a dance image as part of the restaurant theme. At this same time, Judy started work on the menu.

The partners found a prospective site, which was located within the Charles Hotel in the Boston area. (The Charles is an independent hotel that uses a management company.) The partnership would have a lease arrangement with the hotel, whereby the partnership would pay rent in exchange for the use of the space. The partnership would be responsible for the costs associated with design and the purchase of furniture, fixtures, and equipment. Once the prospective site was identified, the partnership hired an architect, a year and a half after beginning. As a key criterion, they wanted someone with experience in designing high volume restaurant space.

Michela, via her financial and business expertise, forced the structure to the process. She wrote a business plan for the new restaurant. This enabled the partners to come to decisions involving the menu development, culinary choices, and personal preferences of the partners. The plan also gave the partners a road map during the construction and opening process. During the entire process, the partnership was attentive to the costs and benefits involved, with an eye on profitability.

The Cost Side: What Does It Cost to Develop a Restaurant?

The range of costs to develop a restaurant can vary widely depending on the type of restaurant, the size of the restaurant, the service style, and how the restaurant is financed, and whether or not it is franchised. For example, a restaurant with drive-through only service would require much less space, no seating, and more limited equipment than a gourmet restaurant, and would therefore be less expensive. All other things being equal, a restaurant with more seats requires more capital than a restaurant with less seats. A restaurant that uses a lease arrangement requires less up-front capital than one that purchases land and develops a building. A franchised restaurant must pay an incremental set of fees to the franchisor that an independent restaurant does not pay.

The following two examples offer an estimate of the kinds of costs involved in owning and developing two different restaurant franchises, a sit-down restaurant with a specialized menu and a full bar, TGI Friday's, and a McDonald's fast food outlet. You will see that restaurant costs include items such as initial franchise fees and opening inventory. The examples provided here offer a minimum, a maximum, and an average cost estimate. The McDonald's example (Exhibit 15.1) is a lease arrangement, whereby the franchisee pays rent for the real estate and the building.[2] In the TGI Friday's example (Exhibit 15.2), the franchisee must purchase the land and building for the restaurant.[3] You will see that the land and building purchase is a large portion of the cost.

■■■■■■■ **Exhibit 15.1** Cost of a McDonald's Franchise

	Minimum	Maximum	Average
Initial Franchise Fee	$45,000	$45,000	$45,000
Signs, seating, equipment, and decor	320,000	430,000	375,000
Travel and living expenses while training	2,800	8,500	5,650
Additional funds	10,000	25,000	17,500
Security deposit	15,000	15,000	15,000
Miscellaneous opening costs	15,000	30,000	22,500
Opening Inventory	10,000	20,000	15,000
Total Excluding Real Estate	**$417,800**	**$573,500**	**$495,650**
Real Estate and building—three months' rent	4,800	77,850	41,325
Total for Leased Real Estate	**$422,600**	**$651,350**	**$536,975**

■■■■■■■ **Exhibit 15.2** Cost of a TGI Friday's Franchise

	Minimum	Maximum	Average
Initial Franchise Fee	$75,000	$75,000	$75,000
Hiring expenses, training	135,000	190,000	162,500
Working capital	20,000	50,000	35,000
Liquor licenses (varies greatly)	2,000	450,000	226,000
Insurance	90,000	150,000	120,000
Miscellaneous costs	10,000	100,000	55,000
Opening inventory	30,000	50,000	40,000
Building construction	845,000	1,545,000	1,195,000
Furniture, decor, equipment, and antiques	555,000	650,000	602,500
Developmental costs	90,000	165,000	127,500
Total Excluding Real Estate	**1,852,000**	**3,425,000**	**2,638,500**
Land (cannot be estimated)	0	0	0
Total for Leased Real Estate	**1,852,000**	**3,425,000**	**2,638,500**

Source: Frandata, 1995. Reprinted with Permission.

A third example (Exhibit 15.3) offers the profile of an independent restaurant that would be competitive with TGI Friday's.[4] Though many of the cost categories are the same, there are several differences between the independent and the franchise operation. Because an independent owner has so much more discretion in the execution of the restaurant, one would expect to find a wider range of costs than with a franchise. The independent may turn out to be much more or much less expensive as a result. The more a restaurant owner is capable of doing, the less outside expertise that needs to be hired. Development costs will tend to be higher as the owner does not have the benefit of a predetermined package. Finally, there are no franchise fees to be paid by the owner.

Exhibit 15.3 Cost of a Sample Independent

	Minimum	Maximum	Average
Initial Franchise Fee	0	0	0
Hiring expenses, training	100,000	260,000	150,000
Working capital	20,000	50,000	35,000
Liquor licenses (varies greatly)	2,000	450,000	226,000
Insurance	50,000	150,000	100,000
Miscellaneous costs	10,000	150,000	50,000
Opening inventory	20,000	70,000	30,000
Building construction	600,000	2,000,000	1,300,000
Furniture, decor, equipment, and antiques	350,000	600,000	450,000
Developmental costs	150,000	250,000	200,000
Total Excluding Real Estate	1,302,000	3,980,000	2,541,000
Land (very difficult to estimate)	50,000	2,500,000	1,250,000
Total for Developed Real Estate	1,352,000	6,480,000	3,791,000

The Benefit Side: What Does It Take to Make a Restaurant Profitable?

In addition to following all of the rules of successfully opening and running a restaurant, there is a rule of thumb that governs whether a restaurant will be profitable or not. A restaurant should try to have, as a minimum, a one-to-one sales-to-investment ratio.[5] That is, for every dollar that is invested to develop the restaurant, the restaurateur needs to generate a minimum of one dollar in sales each year. For example, if the total investment in a restaurant is $1 million, annual sales should be a minimum of $1 million. Many successful restaurants will offer a 2:1 or a 3:1 return.

The amount of analysis an owner will do to determine profit potential varies widely. Some restaurateurs will use gut instinct to determine if it will be successful. Others do various kinds of market research, such as interviewing potential customers. Some such as McDonald's consider certain mathematical formulas. For example, McDonald's uses the following formula to determine how many units it can build in a particular country. The formula considers the population and per capita income of each country relative to the United States.

$$\frac{\text{Population of Country X}}{\text{No. of People per McDonald's in U.S.}} \times \frac{\text{Per Capita Income of Country X}}{\text{Per Capita Income of U.S.}} = \begin{array}{c}\text{Potential Penetration of McDonald's in Country X}\end{array}$$

$$\quad\quad (25,000) \quad\quad\quad\quad\quad\quad ($23,120)$$

This formula reveals a worldwide potential of 42,000 units, including 6,100 in Japan and 190 in South Africa.[6]

However formulaic the analysis of the costs and benefits of a restaurant, an owner is wise to plan extensively, to use outside expertise when the owner is unfamiliar with various aspects, and to err to being conservative when estimating costs. The better planned a restaurant project is, the more likely it is to be able to secure financing from outside sources.

Securing Financing

How an owner actually secures financing to start the restaurant can be from a variety of sources. Owners may fund all or part of the project themselves or with the help of family or friends. Sometimes a partner with operating experience will team up with a partner who is not looking to be an operator, but only to be an investor or money partner. Traditional lending institutions such as a local bank may provide a loan to the partnership.

If the owner has chosen to open a franchise operation, then financing may be available from the franchisor. For example, TGI Friday's offers financing for up to 100 percent of the restaurant goods and supplies, and 85 percent of building and improvements, for up to seven years.

If the entrepreneur is successful enough to get an operation up and running and wishes to open a second, third, or even a chain of additional units, then a more extensive type of financing is needed. Once such type is **venture capital**, which is capital provided to new or growing businesses. Venture capital funds are managed by firms that put together pools of capital to invest in new ventures. The entrepreneur gives up some percentage of ownership in exchange for the funds. Chains such as Bertucci's, Boston Market, and Java City have been funded by venture capital.

Restaurant Franchising

Perhaps the most critical question that the restaurant owner will face is whether or not to franchise. The decision involves determining when franchising makes sense, investing in the right franchise, and understanding the terms of a franchise agreement. Because of the importance of franchising in the restaurant business today, we begin with a brief history.

Brief Historical Background

Though historians have traced the origins of franchising back through mercantile practices and common law to the Middle Ages, it was not until the 1850s that a franchise-oriented system of distribution appeared in the United States. It involved the Singer Sewing Machine Company, which needed to educate the potential consumer about the benefits of using a machine for sewing. Accordingly, agents who worked on a commission basis were chosen to demonstrate, sell, and repair its line of sewing machines.

By the turn of the century, General Motors had granted its first dealer franchise to William E. Metzger of Detroit to sell its automobiles, then powered solely by steam. Soon thereafter, other auto manufacturers, including Henry Ford, began to follow suit. Not surprisingly, as the success of the franchise approach in the auto industry became apparent, other sectors of the business world discovered that the franchise idea was soundly applicable to their pursuits. Thus did the Rexall drugstores in 1902 and Western Auto, an auto parts company, in 1909, give birth to their respective franchise systems.[7] Franchising in the restaurant business was not far behind.

The year 1925 witnessed the beginning of the Howard Johnson ice cream enterprise in his Wollaston, Massachusetts, drugstore, a venture that later became the prized franchised possession of a number of East Coast restaurateurs. By 1954, the first Howard Johnson Motor Lodge had opened for business, laying the foundation for what ultimately became a franchised chain of some 500 motor lodges.

Franchising literally exploded on the American landscape during the years 1950 to 1980. Ray Kroc acquired McDonald's in 1955. At the same time, Colonel Harlan Sanders was creating his niche in the fast food industry with Kentucky Fried Chicken. By 1959, the International House of Pancakes was equally visible to countless millions now accustomed to fast food for breakfast.

Now in the 1990s, the ubiquitous franchise has moved toward a heyday worldwide. Fast food establishments are so popular that McDonald's golden arches are spread from Aruba to Moscow, to Istanbul, Munich, Buenos Aires, Taipei, Belgrade, Budapest, Sao Paulo … you name it. Whatever the country, you can order a Big Mac. (See "Kentucky Fried Chicken, Szechuan Style" below.)

Kentucky Fried Chicken, Szechuan Style

China, the third largest economy in the world behind the United States and Japan, has emerged as the new hot spot for global hospitality industries. A growing domestic economy and a rapid increase in foreign tourism have fueled this interest. In 1992, over four million visitors, including some 350,000 Americans, chose China as a destination.

The hospitality industry has responded to this growth. In just the past few years, fast food restaurants and hotel chains have moved aggressively into China, and many have ambitious plans for expansion. McDonald's plans to have 300 retail units operating in China by the year 2000. KFC, with 23 units in 1994, anticipates 300 outlets over the next 10 years. Pizza Hut hopes to grow from six stores in 1994, to 100 by the end of the decade. In April 1994, the Hard Rock Cafe opened in Beijing, complete with rock memorabilia and an opening night performance by B. B. King. The company has plans for two more restaurants in Shanghai and Shenzhen. There seems to be no limit for restaurant franchise expansion in Asia's newest market.

When Franchising Makes Sense

As noted above, in the United States today, and increasingly in the world, restaurant franchising is pervasive. John Naisbitt, in *Megatrends*, a widely read best seller, commented that almost every community in the United States had at least one franchised restaurant along its main street.

Unquestionably, the world of restaurants is user-friendly when it comes to franchising. Seasoned observers of today's restaurant scene who are supportive of franchising believe that it is difficult, if not impossible, for an individual to be well informed about all aspects of the food business. For example, the advantages of bulk purchasing, corporate financing to fund expansion at a rapid pace, and reliance upon national advertising to build an attractive business image are seldom affordable by an individual entrepreneur. Franchisors, therefore, with their specialized expertise in these areas, have not only proven to be singularly adept in their efforts to fill this void, but have been responsible for the steady growth of franchised restaurant chains.

On the other hand, if an entrepreneur is interested in independence in operations and individuality in the execution of the restaurant concept, then a franchise does not make sense. An owner of an independent restaurant also saves the cost of franchise fees. Other advantages and disadvantages to franchising can be found in the preceding chapter. Though it is spelled out for hotel franchising, the reasoning is applicable to restaurants as well.

If an owner elects to enter into a franchise, a **franchise agreement** is signed between the **franchisee**, the owner of the individual unit, and the **franchisor**, the parent company. The agreement works just as it does for a hotel franchise, in that fees are paid by the franchisee in exchange for the right to be a member of the chain. The operations procedures for a restaurant franchise are very specific. A restaurant chain is extremely concerned that all units are alike and that quality, taste, and service delivery expectations are consistently met.

Rules for Investing in the Right Franchise

Once an owner is convinced that owning a franchise operation is an advantageous choice, the next step is to invest in the right one. The following set of rules offered by *Success Magazine* gives a framework for making an intelligent selection.[8]

1. Know Who You Are

Not everyone is cut out manage a franchise. While potential for success exists in a fast food franchise, an owner could find that the policies are too strict, that there is not enough room for self-expression, while others would rally to the consistency of format.

2. Research Your Opportunities

There are many foodservice franchise possibilities. Get to know them, and what each one offers.

3. Calculate Your Commitment

Commitment means up-front cash contributions. How much are you willing to invest? At what price point is a franchise out of your reach? When do you anticipate making profit?

4. Watch the Clock

Commitment also means time. How many hours a week do you want to work? An early morning doughnut shop requires a different commitment than a restaurant open only for lunch and dinner.

5. Ask the Tough Questions

Don't be afraid to ask about results of other franchisees. Ascertain the level of commitment of the franchisor. Will the parent company continue to do national and regional advertising? What is its long-term marketing plan? Does it have a strategic plan? Be wary of a franchisor unwilling to share information.

6. Seek Professional Counsel

Get an attorney and an accountant, and review the fine print. Don't get caught short because you misunderstood a passage in the franchise agreement.

7. Look to the Future

Can you expand within this franchise, or are their limits to how many outlets one franchisee may own? What are the termination rules? Can you get out if the agreement is ever violated?

8. Size Up the Competition

What is the market share of your major competitors? Can you compete? Look to see if your franchise has a stable management team, or one that has handled leadership transition well.

9. Get the Inside Scoop

Talk to as many people in the know as possible—current owners, old franchisees, potential owners. Would they do it again? This could be the best question of all.

The Typical Franchise Agreement

After a specific franchise is selected, entering into an agreement with a franchisor involves an initial application process. That process gives the franchisor a chance to evaluate the quality of the applicant and the franchisee a chance to evaluate the costs and benefits associated with that particular franchisor via an offering document.

Entering into a franchise agreement involves signing a series of legal documents. For a Boston Chicken franchise, for example, there are up to 15 different agreements that may be required, such as: a Catering Agreement, a Computer and Communications System Agreement, a Franchise Agreement, a Lease Agreement, and an Accounting Services Agreement. Each of these documents covers a different aspect of the relationship. For example, Boston Chicken franchisees may elect to include a catering operation in addition to the restaurant itself. The systems, procedures, and knowhow for the catering aspect of the business would become part of the overall agreement via a specific legal document.

Key Aspects of a Franchise Agreement A restaurant owner should pay particular attention to several important aspects of a franchise agreement. The following questions identify the key concerns of the owner when evaluating a particular franchise company. An owner should do a comparative analysis of the answers to these questions for each franchise under consideration:

- How are initial fees calculated?
- How are royalties and other ongoing fees calculated?
- What is the term of the agreement?
- What financing does the franchisor provide?

- What services are provided for each fee?
- Can the franchise agreement be transferred?

Because many owners consider the long term and are interested in operating multiple units of a franchise, two additional questions surface:

- Are exclusive territories outlined? How are they determined?
- Are initial fees reduced for multiple unit ownership?

In answer to the above questions, consider a real life situation. Exhibit 15.4 gives a very brief synopsis of the key terms of a McDonald's franchise. As the owner of the restaurant, you would be keen to know this information if you were considering opening your own golden arches.

Exhibit 15.4 Snapshot of McDonald's Agreement

	Definition	**McDonald's Agreement**
Initial Fee	The flat fee charged per franchise. Initial fees are usually collected by the franchisor upon signing of the franchise agreement. These fees are payment for the right to license the franchisor's system, and as compensation to the franchisor for its costs of training and helping open the franchise.	$45,000
Development Fees	Development fees are collected by the franchisor when the franchisee wishes to "develop" a geographic area. These fees allow the franchisee to reserve the rights to an area: no other franchisee can open an outlet in that territory.	None. McDonald's does not offer any development programs.
Advertising Fees	These are periodic payments to the franchisor to be used for national or regional advertising and marketing programs.	Total advertising spending is 4% of gross sales/ revenues.
Royalties	Periodic payments from the franchisee to the franchisor. These fees are usually calculated as a percentage of gross revenues.	4% of gross sales/revenues.
Initial Term/ Renewal	The length of time of the initial agreement. It may or may not contain language pertaining to renewal.	The term of the initial franchise agreement is 20 years. The agreement does not contain a provision for automatic renewal by the franchise.
Financing Offered	This refers to any financing programs offered by the franchisor to assist a franchisee with the purchase of property, or other capital needs.	The McDonald's agreement includes provisions for financing. Should a franchise seek

▬▬▬▬▬ *Exhibit 15.4* (Continued)

	Definition	McDonald's Agreement
		assistance from McDonald's to purchase an existing location, there is a program in place to accomplish that goal.
Reduction for Multiple Units	In some franchisee agreements, if the franchisee owns multiple units, there may be a reduction in certain fees such as advertising.	There is no reduction in initial fees for multiple franchise purchases.
Exclusive Territory	Similar to development fees, these are the fees paid to guarantee an exclusive territory for operation.	McDonald's does not grant an exclusive territory to its franchisees.
Transfer	This clause refers to the ability of a franchisee to transfer a unit to a third party.	Upon the approval of McDonald's, the franchise agreement may be transferred to a third party, without a fee.

Evaluating the Franchisor In addition to evaluating the agreements themselves, an owner must evaluate other aspects of the franchisor. From the owner's perspective:

- How successful is a franchised unit?
- What are the total sales of a typical unit?
- How strong are the relationships between the corporation and its franchisees? its suppliers?
- Do restaurant owners typically own or lease the restaurant space?

Exhibit 15.5 offers a brief summary of the answers to these questions for McDonald's.

▬▬▬▬▬ *Exhibit 15.5* Evaluating The McDonald's Franchise

Success of a Single Unit

Franchisees of restaurants typically look for approximately a 15% return on their investments after all royalties and fees are paid.[1] Though success for individual units varies by owner, it is safe to assume, given McDonald's track record, that its franchisees do well relative to expectations.

Relationships with Franchisees and Suppliers

McDonald's prides itself on extraordinary relationships with both franchisees and suppliers. On the international front, McDonald's has gone so far as to set up bun factories, potato farms, and meat processing plants. For its franchisees, McDonald's invests heavily in training, both at Hamburger University, located at corporate headquarters, and in the field.

(Continued)

▬▬▬▬ **Exhibit 15.5** Evaluating The McDonald's Franchise *(Continued)*

Total sales

In 1995 McDonald's domestic sales totaled over $25 billion in approximately 15,000 restaurants. That makes average annual sales approximately $1.6 million per unit.

Owned vs. leased restaurants

McDonald's owns about 60%, or 9,000 of its 14,000 locations, and leases this 36 million square feet of space to franchisors. Franchisors own therefore, 40% of the restaurants' locations. [2]

---

[1] Laura M. Litvan, "To Franchise, or not...," *Nation's Business*, V83 8 (1 August 1995) 62.

[2] Andrew E. Serwer, "McDonald Conquers the World," *Fortune* (17 October, 1994): 112.

Restaurant Management

Once a restaurant is up and running, the day-to-day management begins. A restaurant owner is then faced with the question of who will manage the operation. In a commercial operation, the owner will almost always be either directly or indirectly involved in management. Direct involvement will find the owner on site, actively managing some aspect of the business. If only indirect involvement is desired, an owner will hire a full-time manager or managers. If more than one partner is involved, none, some, or all may be actively involved in some aspect of management.

Keys to Successful Management

Regardless of whether owners choose to manage by themselves or to hire managers, the same management tools can be applied. The key elements for successfully managing a restaurant include, in short: finding and keeping focus, continually training and inspiring employees, remembering that raw ingredients matter, preparing for constant revision, knowing where costs and profits are, listening to customers, and remembering that there is no annuity in the restaurant business. A successful restaurant must have attentive management every day. (A complete explanation of each of these elements can be found in chapter 9.)

Profile: One Restaurant Owner's Story, Continued

After the successful opening of the Rialto restaurant, the partners turned their attention to the day-to-day management of the business. The menu, by design, reflects the seasons, so menu items are constantly changing. The profitability and popularity of each item is continually evaluated.

The partners watch for every penny, as the restaurant business demands. Food cost control, inventory control, and damage prevention are all addressed. The partners conduct financial and

■■■■■■■ **One Kind of Restaurant Ownership**

"I understand it's family-owned and run."

operations meetings every week. Marketing and promotion efforts are targeted to encourage customer feedback, to participate in special events, and to keep in contact with peers, the press, and the community. The partners continually monitor the environment: the atmosphere, the wait staff, and the customers. In response to demand, the partners decide to incorporate a private dining room into the restaurant.

Staff training is taken seriously. Every new wait staff person goes through a seven-day training session covering hosting, the kitchen, the dining room floor, and the bar. Each new person is tested on the training manual at the end of the week. Staff go out with the management to dine at the competition in order to evaluate certain situations.

Critical issues for success, including monitoring food costs, labor costs, customer preferences, and employee morale are all attended to today, and the next day, and the next…. The partnership recognizes that there is no annuity in the restaurant business.

Learning from the Masters

In managing a new restaurant, there is much to be learned from skilled restaurateurs, such as the partners in Rialto, and from others who have successfully launched one or more restaurant concepts. Exhibit 15.6 presents some management tactics from various restaurateurs.

◼◼◼◼ *Exhibit 15.6* A Restaurant Owner's Tip Box

From:

Marian Ilitch, secretary-treasurer of Little Caesars:

Do your books by hand the first year. You don't learn as much with the computer.[1]

Jeff Fields, an executive with Italian Oven:

Think about a food fad as you do a glacier. It moves in and takes over a lot of space. It's slowly moving out as soon as it arrives—though you may not detect the motion. And when it moves out, it leaves a lot of space behind.[2]

Debbie Fields, founder of Mrs. Field's cookies:

Read every comment sent in by customers yourself.

(Even if it's several hundred a month—which she receives.)[3]

Stephen Reinemund, senior vice president of operations for Pizza Hut:

Look for eagles willing to fly in formation (as his boss at parent company Pepsico suggests)—*people with a point of view but willing to work with others.*[4]

Richard Melman, owner, Lettuce Entertain You Enterprises Inc.

Focus on a single aspect of a restaurant's performance and use it to measure how the rest is doing. When you have a lot of restaurants, you put small areas under a microscope and look carefully."[5]

Louis Kane, cochairman, Au Bon Pain:

Share all financial information from all outlets with all managers and assistant managers. It helps them run their stores better.[6]

Martin Kupferman, president of Pasqua:

You can't stay competitive if you do silly real estate deals. You can't have rents that are 15 percent of your gross sales.[7]

[1.] Adam Bryant, "He's Marketing, She's Finance: A $2 Billion Mom-and-Pop Shop," *New York Times*, (6 December 1992) 8F.

[2.] From an interview with Jeff Fields, February 1993.

[3.] Katherine Weisman, "Succeeding by Failing," *Forbes* (25 June 1990): 160.

[4.] Paul Frumkin, "Reinemund: Balancing Strategy and Details," *Nations Restaurant News* (18 November 1991): 74.

[5.] Joshua Hyatt, "The Odyssey of an Excellent Man," *Inc. Magazine* (February 1989): 77.

[6.] From a lecture delivered by Louis Kane at Boston University, March 12, 1992.

[7.] Martin Kupferman, " Hot Concepts! Pasqua," *Nation's Restaurant News* (22 May 1995): 133.

Restaurant Strategic Alliances

In addition to decisions involving development, ownership, management, and franchising, an owner of a restaurant can elect to enter into any number of strategic alliances with different constituencies. These alliances, be they with suppliers of food and beverage, referral sources, frequent customers, a lodging operation, or the local community, can help a restaurant in a number of ways. The various kinds of alliances may help a restaurant to save costs, generate new customers, increase repeat visits from current customers, find a new point of distribution, or generate favorable public relations.

Because of the benefits to be gained, strategic alliances, not just in the restaurant industry, but across varied facets of hospitality, are increasing in kind, number, and importance. We will see this subject again as we turn to the twenty-first century in the final section of the book.

Suppliers of Food and Beverages

As the quality of the raw ingredients is critical to the successful execution of a recipe, every restaurant is helped by consistent delivery of quality food supplies. Thus, an individual restaurant or an international chain can both be helped by establishing a relationship with suppliers of food and beverage. The relationship may not only assure consistent quality, but also creates cost savings. For an individual restaurant, the relationship may be with a local farm or produce market. For McDonald's, it may be with a consortium of Idaho potato farmers for a billion-pound order. These relationships, like all strategic alliances, provide mutual benefit for both parties. The suppliers are helped by a steady order from a good customer.

Referral Sources

Taxi drivers, front-of-the-house hotel workers, a travelers' aid information center, or other members of a local community who encounter travelers can all be helpful in referring potential customers to a restaurant. Though relying on reputation can generate referrals, some restaurants actively manage a flow of information to these audiences. For example, a restaurant could offer discounted meals to taxi drivers or sponsor a free lunch for the front office staff of the local hotel. These relationships tend to be informal but can be very effective in generating new customers.

Frequent Customers

Not unlike frequent flyer or frequent hotel guest programs, some restaurants have established a relationship with frequent diners. Some restaurants offer a punch card that can be redeemed for free food or drink after a certain number of purchases are made. For example, after 12 coffee purchases, the 13th cup is free. Some restaurants allow frequent customers charge privileges and send a bill at the end of the month. This service is useful for businesses that have frequent luncheon meetings. Given all of the benefits that repeat guests provide (see chapter 3 to review the benefits), it is no wonder that this kind of strategic alliance is a worthwhile endeavor.

Dining and Credit Cards

Some restaurants elect to accept various kinds of credit cards for purchases. There are occasions when a credit card company will send promotional information on a group of restaurants in a particular area to its credit card customers. For example, American Express may send a coupon to its customers in Dallas who use their cards to charge meals in the downtown area. The promotion will likely offer a discount when that specific card is used at the featured restaurants.

A restaurant may also elect to accept cards from a dining club. These clubs solicit both memberships from customers and participation from restaurants. Members pay a fee for the card and in exchange receive discounted meals, free dessert, or some other offer from the participating restaurants. The clubs may encourage customers who otherwise might not have tried the restaurant. For example, Transmedia, In Good Taste, and Entertainment Publications are the largest national dining clubs, offering 20 to 30 percent discounts at specified restaurants which have agreed in advance to participate.

Lodging Operations

Increasingly restaurants are entering into strategic alliances with lodging properties. This relationship can take several forms. A restaurant, particularly a franchised restaurant, may agree to build next to or near to a unit of an economy lodging chain that has no foodservice. For example, Bonanza steakhouses have paired up with Comfort Inns. A restaurant may open within a lodging property. The Palm, a gourmet restaurant with a handful of locations in the United States, opened in the Westin Hotel in Boston. Finally, a restaurant that has take-out service may agree to deliver to hotel guests. In 1996, Pizza Hut entered into a strategic alliance with nearly 7,000 hotels, including all members of the Hospitality Franchise and Choice Hotel systems. These kinds of relationships allow both parties to focus on what they do best.

Retail Outlets

Restaurants may find benefit in a strategic alliance with other kinds of retail establishments, such as a department store, a gas station, or a 24-hour store. McDonald's has opened more than 700 units in Wal-Mart department stores; Taco Bell and Dunkin' Donut outlets can be found in 24-hour stores. Picking up french fries and a quart of oil in the same location is becoming commonplace. Though franchised restaurants tend to be the most likely candidates for this kind of alliance, local entrepreneurs can employ the same strategy. For example, Peter Christian's restaurant, in the town of Hanover, New Hampshire, supplies fresh sandwiches for the deli case of the local 24-hour store.

The Local Community

Restaurants, particularly those that serve as a social gathering place, may elect to contribute in visible ways to their communities. Gestures of goodwill tend to generate positive public relations, loyal local patrons, and positive word of mouth. For example, the local franchisee of four Wendy's restaurants in Chicago donates to block clubs and civic groups. He also willingly offers his parking lots to a local radio station for an annual summer broadcast. Other restaurants in urban areas have teamed up with charities to distribute unsold food.

All of the above strategic alliances are optional. A restaurant owner does not have to elect to enter into any of them. However, it is increasingly clear that such alliances can create competitive advantage. Given all of the hard work that opening and operating a restaurant entails, these kinds of initiatives will likely appeal to a restaurateur in pursuit of success.

Summary

There is much excitement for an entrepreneur in the development and ownership of a restaurant. It is important for the entrepreneur to be sensitive to a number of key issues, which are critical to the success of the operation, from the start. Through a decoding process, the owner, developer, and manager are decided. It is also determined whether the restaurant will be a member of a franchise, and with whom it may be strategically aligned.

Costs can vary greatly in the development of a restaurant, depending on size, service style, the type of financing secured, and whether or not it is a franchise. Fees are a critical aspect to address before becoming a franchise, for fees are costs an independent restaurant does not face. Profitability is often determined by a one-to-one sales-to-investment ratio analysis; that is, for every dollar invested in the development of a restaurant, a dollar in sales must be recorded in order for a restaurant to be successful. Owners will also invest in market research, and even complicated mathematical analysis, to determine profitability.

Whether or not to franchise is perhaps the most critical question a restaurant owner faces. Franchises have been part of the U.S. economy for over 100 years, and in the restaurant business they are particularly successful. Franchising in the restaurant industry has many advantages, among them menu concepts that are known to work, bulk purchasing options, and national brand awareness. The key questions to consider about franchising involve knowing who you are as an owner and knowing what type of business you want to operate. It is important, too, to do your homework about the franchisor. You should know the important elements in the franchise agreement, including fees and the length of the agreement.

An entrepreneur must continually address the day-to-day management of the restaurant. The day-to-day operations may involve interaction with important strategic alliances. These strategic alliances provide many benefits, including lower supply costs and complimentary advertising. Referral sources, frequent customers, and suppliers are also constituents an owner must interact with regularly. Credit card agreements and relationships with local hotels, retail outlets, and civic groups can also help make a restaurant work. Careful consideration of all the different relationships involved in restaurant development and operations will help a potential owner confidently answer this question: So you want to own a restaurant?

Discussion Questions

1. What are the key questions a potential restaurant owner should address before a restaurant opens?

2. What are the key elements in restaurant design and development? How is leasing different from owning?

3. What ownership structure is in place at the Rialto restaurant? How did the partnership make decisions about the restaurant?

4. Why do development costs vary? Give examples.

5. Why is it more expensive, on average, to open a TGI Friday's franchise than a McDonald's franchise?

6. What is a one-to-one sales-to-investment ratio? Why is it important?

7. When does a franchise make sense for an owner?

8. What are some helpful rules for investing in a franchise?

9. What kinds of fees are charged by franchisors? What are they used for?

10. What are the key aspects of a franchise agreement? How would an owner evaluate a franchise agreement?

11. Why are strategic alliances critical to a successful restaurant operation? suppliers? referral sources? good customers? credit card agreements? What other relationships are important? Why? Which do you think are most important?

12. Compared to many other businesses, why is the concept of franchising so widely used for restaurants? In what kinds of businesses is franchising readily applied?

13. The opening quotation speaks of chain restaurant entrepreneurs. Do you agree that successful chain restaurant managers need entrepreneurial skills just as independent restaurant managers need them?

Assignments

1. Describe a recent visit you may have made to a franchised restaurant, and explain why you selected that particular establishment. Price? Menu specialty? Location? Fast service? Reputation?

2. Interview a manager or owner of a franchised establishment to find out if:

   a. the franchisee has realized the savings promised by the franchisor when purchases were made through the franchisor's central purchasing facility;

b. the franchisee has found that using a brand name in advertising actually attracts customers;

c. the franchise fees are fair.

3. Interview a manager or owner of an independent establishment to find out:

a. why the owner did not elect to enter into a franchise agreement

b. what advantages the owner sees to being an independent restaurant

c. what the owner thinks are the key ingredients to success. Phrase your answer in the form of a tip, as in the owner's tip box in this chapter.

End Notes

1. Jay Finegan, "The Smartest Franchisees in America," *Inc. Magazine* (November 1995): 48.

2. Information is from McDonald's offering documents, interpreted by Frandata.

3. Information is from TGI Friday's offering documents, interpreted by Frandata.

4. Cost estimates are the authors interpretation relative to a TGI Friday's unit. All costs can have a wider range than those shown as a realistic expected case. This is especially true of land costs.

5. "30th Annual Report on Franchising," *Restaurant Business* 94 (16) (1 November 1995): 35–48.

6. Serwer, Andrew E. "McDonald Conquers the World," *Fortune* (17 October 1994): 114.

7. Robert Justis and Richard Judd, *Franchising* (Cincinnati: South-Western Publishing Co., 1989), 12–13.

8. Carol Steinberg, "Become an Expert," *Success Magazine* (November 1995): 110–113.

Part Six

Issues and Trends

All managers must face the future. In this section we look at the prospective aspects of planning and thinking, underscoring the importance of doing so with business savvy and a keen sense of integrity.

Chapter 16 explores business ethics, offering several definitions along with an explanation of why precision in those definitions can be difficult. The chapter is intended to provoke a discussion of the ways people can connect principle and purpose to their professional lives, and to take a fresh look at how managers should be in touch with common sense standards of integrity. The specific kinds of ethical dilemmas that occur in the context of the hospitality workplace are communicated here.

Building on what has already been learned in the text, chapter 17 surveys the landscape of the twenty-first century. In a scan of the environment, clues and patterns emerge that, to a sophisticated interpreter, become the building blocks for future strategy. Topics such as branding, diversity, ecotourism, outsourcing, strategic alliances, and technological applications are scrutinized. The exploration of these topics is intended to give the reader a framework for developing a personal vision of what might be the hospitality world of tomorrow.

Chapter Sixteen

Above all, not knowingly to do harm.

Hippocratic Oath

Business Ethics ⤴

When you finish this chapter you should:

1. Know what the term *ethical behavior* means.

2. Explain why defining ethical behavior precisely can be difficult.

3. Give examples of the kinds of unethical behavior that might occur in hospitality establishments.

4. Know why Laura Nash asserts that even though unsolicited "freebies" are common practice and legal in the travel industry, they are not ethical.

5. Know what kind of codes of ethics have been adopted by trade associations.

6. Know to what extent some colleges and universities are now engaged in bringing ethics into the classroom, and to what extent corporations are bringing ethics into the workplace.

7. Know what is meant by the Rose Bowl Test in evaluating ethical dilemmas.

8. Explain how certain characteristics of the hospitality industry can affect ethical choices made by hospitality professionals.

Introduction _____

If it isn't one thing it's another in today's front page tales of corporate misconduct. What could have driven erstwhile Wall Street firms with spectacular track records for financial accomplishment in the 1980s to make bad ethical choices in the marketing of junk bonds? Why is it that our newspapers are littered with the stories of misbehavior of not just a few clever crooks but a host of apparently respectable business people, deviously acting in ways that are callous, dishonest, and illegal? Why should we care—especially since the hospitality industry takes pride in encouraging the actions needed to map the high road to ethical performance?[1] For one thing, we care because the hospitality industry, like others, is scarcely immune to the unethical and often illegal behavior that persists elsewhere in society.

Holding out the promise of future business, vendors may agree to make expensive "gifts" of TV sets or to furnish cash-filled envelopes monthly to the hotel management.[2] When situations such as this occur, that's extortion, pure and simple! Another example of unethical behavior is when a menu featuring an item called "fresh Colorado mountain trout" turns out to be frozen, not from Colorado, and not mountain trout.[3] That's a **truth-in-menu** violation! Other situations that occur include undercover fees paid to health and fire inspectors to avoid large capital expenditures for refrigeration or for installation of fire escapes. That's plain bribery. How about purveyor kickbacks to purchasing agents in the form of cash, gratuities, weekend outings to country clubs and resort hotels, choice season tickets to sports events, and lavish Christmas gifts? More bribery! Ever hear of fraudulent billing to help customers pad their company expense accounts? What about money laundering to conceal drug transactions? These are all examples of unethical conduct.

What is Ethical Behavior? _____

Applied to management decision-making, **ethical behavior** or more specifically, good **business ethics** may involve choices about the law; choices about the economic and social issues that are beyond the law's domain (the so-called "gray areas"); and choices about the relevance of one's self-interest versus the interest of the company or one's fellow employees. Ethics derives its meaning from the Greek word ethos, which embraces the dual meaning of "character" and "community sentiment." In today's business climate, it has come to mean rules, standards, codes, or guidelines for right behavior on the part of individuals and/or companies.

Ethics involves judgment. Thus, even in defining ethical behavior, one will encounter different viewpoints from different individuals. In this chapter, we will offer several perspectives on ethics from consultants to business leaders to scholars to professors. We will also look at the hospitality industry specifically, and at the kinds of ethical decisions that hospitality managers might face. We begin with several views on ethics.

To Peter Drucker, renowned management consultant, the ethics of an individual manager are best expressed in the physicians' 2,000-year-old Hippocratic oath: "Above all, not knowingly to do harm." The managers' job, writes Drucker, is to "scrutinize their deeds, words, and behavior to make sure that they do not knowingly do harm.... As the physicians found out long ago, it is not an easy rule to live up to. Its very modesty and self-constraint make it the right rule for the ethics [that] managers need, the ethics of responsibility."[4]

Sir Adrian Cadbury, chairman of Cadbury Schweppes PLC, who won the *Harvard Business Review*'s 1986 Ethics in Business prize for the best original article on the ethical problems business executives face, suggested that we judge companies and managers by their actions, not by their pious statements of intent. He feels that ethics are some of the guidelines or rules of conduct that we aim to live by. Business decisions almost always involve some degree of ethical judgment. Few decisions are made solely on the basis of arithmetic.[5]

The Rose Bowl Test

For the president and chief executive officer of Pizza Hut, Inc., Steven S. Reinemund, "defining the ethical challenge" means applying the "Rose Bowl test." In other words, "How would this marketing strategy be viewed not in the comfort of our internal meetings, but on the fifty-yard line of the Rose Bowl before 100,000 people?... Every time we work with openness and honesty we strike a blow for ethical values in business."[6] Broadly speaking, the Pizza Hut CEO's vision of ethics is rooted in strength of character, which he believes has four important attributes:

1. **Internal allegiance to excellence.** What really matters, says Reinemund, is the act of doing something really well. It is the quality that separates the merely good from the truly great.

2. **A fundamental openness and honesty with co-workers and the world in general.** For example, if you are told that you get six months of probation in return for getting an illegal business deal worth $10 million in profits to you, would you make the deal? A research firm asked this question of over 1,000 people. Six out of 10 admitted that they would probably take six months' probation for an illegal $10 million.

3. **A commitment to teamwork and selflessness.** The Japanese are right when they say, "One step by 100 persons goes further than 100 steps by one person."

4. **The ability to take a balanced perspective.** Here's where the Rose Bowl test is applied.[7]

These attributes, if applied in the workplace, create an environment of sound ethical behavior. That is, every member of the work community strives for excellence, cares about co-workers and all others that the company interacts with, and behaves in a way that any reasonable person would judge the behavior to be honest.

██████████ If You Really Need a Hotel Room, Don't Ever Ask for an Ashtray

David Daut and his family were traveling by car from their home in Kansas to a family wedding in Chicago. Along the way they developed car trouble in Bethany, Missouri, at the unlucky hour of 3:30 A.M. And in the middle of nowhere, or so the family thought. But luck was on their side; a service station was close by, and even better, they broke down in front of a Best Western. The lucky streak continued when Mr. Daut was told by the front desk clerk that there was one vacancy.

The clerk began asking Mr. Daut some questions for the registration form, and here the Dauts' luck once again began to go sour. Mr. Daut asked if smoking was allowed in the room. The clerk in turn asked if Mr. Daut was a smoker, and he replied that yes, he indeed was a smoker. And the registration form went up in smoke. As the last remaining room was designated a "nonsmoking" room, the clerk determined that Mr. Daut could not have that room, and voided the registration before his very eyes. Mr. Daut was dumbfounded.

Panicked at the thought of losing the room, Mr. Daut pleaded with the clerk, promising not to smoke in the room, and even offering to leave his cigarettes at the desk as proof of his commitment to respect the rules. No deal—the clerk still said no. Mr. Daut then offered to sleep in the car, if his wife (a nonsmoker) and their children could have the room. Still no deal. Even after a consultation with the manager, the rule was upheld. The Daut family was not getting that room. They slept in the car.

While the policy of setting aside certain rooms as "nonsmoking" has been applauded by many travelers, the ethical issue here involves the obligation of a lodging establishment to provide accommodations to a guest. In light of the situation, should the rule have been upheld? Should the hotel be allowed to ask if someone is a smoker, and then refuse to sell a room? Would this story encourage other guests simply to lie? A hotel would only find out if a guest was smoking after the guest departed the room—or should the hotel patrol the rooms, sniffing out smokers?

Adapted from *The Wall Street Journal*, 8 December 1994

Tough Choices

To Barbara Ley Toffler, a former assistant professor of business administration at the Harvard Business School, ethical situations at work have to do with "a general conception of right and wrong in the attitudes and actions of individuals and the communities (institutions) of which they are a part."[8] However, in *Tough Choices*, her study of 33 managers' ethical situations at work, the right thing is not always easy to discern. In fact, it can be so difficult that one viewpoint suggests that defining business ethics is like nailing Jell-O to a wall.[9] Everyone, it seems, wants to do what is right, given a clear choice between doing right and doing wrong. But good intentions frequently get lost amid conflicts of interest, office love affairs, pressures to meet bottom-line goals, and the compromises managers feel compelled to make with their superiors. In short, Toffler's message is that managing means more than just taking charge and more than simply settling for "the way we do things around here." Above all, it depends on what Toffler calls the ability to create "an environment in which all employees have the capacity to act (unfailingly) with integrity." The example that follows illustrates how one company's executive struck a blow for integrity in business when he refused to engage in what he perceived to be bribery of a labor union official.

One day, not so many years ago, the newly appointed human resources director of a growing hotel chain reported to his CEO a labor union demand for huge increases in the wages and working conditions at the company's downtown 800-room hotel. Becoming alarmed at the prospect of a strike that the union had threatened if its demands were not met, the company president made a novel suggestion. In a one-on-one meeting, he asked the human resources director:

Why don't you do what our director of government relations does whenever he has a problem like this? For a rather substantial legal fee, he gets a politically influential law firm here in town to sidetrack any potentially adverse governmental proceeding ... like, for example, the recent threatened increase in our hotel real estate assessments. That strategy saved the company tax bill thousands of dollars. I happen to think that the union that is holding a gun to our heads with its threat of a strike might be interested if you gave some thought to how our government affairs man operates.... I'm sorry I don't have any more time to discuss this with you now. I've got to attend a stockholders' meeting. Let me know how you make out with our union friends.[10]

Shaken by the discovery that the president had, in effect, recommended bribery to end the union's strike threat, the human resources director was not about to embark on the slippery slope of unethical as well as illegal business practices. The next day he tendered his resignation, telling the president bluntly that bribery under any guise was contrary to his own sense of business ethics—and contrary as well to the clear provisions of national labor relations law. The day following this resignation witnessed a lengthy meeting of the president and the general counsel, resulting in their joint announcement of a two-day home-office seminar for all corporate executives to discuss guidelines for resolving ethical business problems.

Dilemmas Faced by Hospitality Managers

There are a number of issues that managers confront daily, which can raise ethical dilemmas. Not everyone agrees as to what is ethical behavior in response to those dilemmas. Because of the disagreement, defining ethical behavior precisely is difficult, as noted before. Consider these examples and responses from the hospitality industry:

Believing that many critical issues facing the lodging industry today are ethical issues and that they call for tough choices, Raymond S. Schmidgall, Hilton Professor at the Michigan State University Hotel School, asked hundreds of hotel managers in a survey how they felt about ethical problems.[11] The survey entailed sending a questionnaire to 1,000 hotel managers asking whether they agreed or disagreed with the managers' decisions reached in 15 hypothetical scenarios. The five examples that follow are typical of the ethical problem scenarios calling for a lodging manager's response.[12] These scenarios are instructive in that they raise the kinds of dilemmas that hospitality managers might face.

1. **Educational Materials.** You belong to an organization that, with apparently noble intentions, asks your cooperation in distributing educational materials to your hotel guests. You, wanting to help the organization, provide a copy of the hotel's influential guests, including names, addresses, and telephone numbers.

2. **Bumped Reservations.** You have just been approached by a very influential guest regarding a surprise birthday party he would like held at the hotel two months hence. Unfortunately, the hotel is totally booked. The guest, after discussing the bookings for the targeted date with you for 30 minutes, suggests bumping a less influential party who reserved the desired room yesterday. The influential guest suggests you tell the other party "the salesperson made a major mistake in booking a room that had previously been reserved." You concur.

3. **Fringe Benefits.** The board of directors of your hotel recently provided full-time employees with free health insurance. In an attempt to maintain the hotel's profitability and your bonus, you have decided to reduce six full-time workers to three-quarters time and hire two additional three-quarters-time workers. Three of the workers are single parents. The bottom-line result is considerable savings in the cost of the hotel's fringe benefits.

4. **Spotter's Spies.** You have just contracted with Spotters, Inc., to provide spotters to "spy" on your bartenders to determine if they are preparing drinks according to the standard recipe and if they are properly charging guests for all drinks served.

5. **Free Wine.** You recently purchased 20 cases of wine for the hotel from a new beverage purveyor. Without your advance knowledge, the purveyor delivers one free case of wine to your residence. You decided to keep the free case for your personal use since it did not influence the purchase of the 20 cases for the hotel.

Overall managerial responses to these scenarios are shown below in Table 16.1.[13]

Table 16.1 Your Action was Ethical

Number	Reference	Strongly Agree	Moderately Agree	Unsure	Moderately Disagree	Strongly Disagree
1.	Education Materials	1.3	3.3	3.5	11.4	80.5
2.	Bumped Reservation	1.3	5.1	4.6	13.7	75.3
3.	Fringe Benefits	6.1	12.2	8.9	26.6	46.2
4.	Spotter's Spies	61.2	26.1	3.3	4.1	5.3
5.	Free Wine	7.4	16.5	17.5	17.5	48.0

Despite wide variations in some hotel managers' responses to ethical dilemmas, Schmidgall found that such differences were not associated with levels of education, years of managerial experience, size of hotels managed, or professional certification. Finally, there was little in the Schmidgall study to recommend creating a so-called code of ethics for the lodging industry. Instead, it appeared that the ethical consciousness of hoteliers might best be elevated by a continuing discussion of ethical issues in the literature of the hospitality industry.[14]

Student Perceptions of Ethical Issues

There are other examples of ethical dilemmas that can be found in the field of hospitality. Seeking to determine the extent to which students in six different hospitality and tourism programs do in fact perceive ethical issues confronting the hospitality industry today, researchers Enghagen and Hott collected data from a survey of 349 students.[15] The results revealed that students perceived the following ethical issues to be of primary importance:

Solid waste disposal	Vendor honesty
Race discrimination	Conditions of employment
Sex discrimination	Employment theft
Sexual harassment	False advertising
Sanitation violations	AIDS discrimination
AIDS in foodservice	

These issues could raise questions such as: Is it okay for a hotel to advertise rates that it offers under such strict conditions that no one can take advantage of them? Or to transfer an employee with AIDS to a non-food-handling position? Can employees help themselves to a buffet lunch if the guests won't notice the missing food? What about an employee on the receiving dock that accepts inferior produce in exchange for personal kickbacks?

Perceptions About the Ethical Behavior of Others

As much of the work in the hospitality field involves teamwork, it is important to realize that the behavior of one person can affect that of another. The industrial psychologist and author Ronald Morgan wrote a report on four surveys of managerial populations, which is a fascinating and instructive look at managerial beliefs about the ethical behavior of their superiors. Morgan found that "the ethical behavior of others, especially superiors, affects their own attentiveness to the ethical aspects of decisions and action."[16] Superiors who typically assert "I don't want to know how results are obtained, as long as you achieve the desired outcome" leave little doubt in the minds of their subordinates that where valued outcomes are concerned, ethical issues are of secondary importance. Ethical behavior plays a key role in the enhancement of a manager's stature as a credible leader.[17]

Unsolicited Freebies Shape Purchase Decisions

Because of the nature of the business, hospitality managers may find themselves faced with ethical decisions involving freebies. For example, in a book titled *Good Intentions Aside: A Manager's Guide to Resolving Ethical Problems*, Laura Nash draws attention to the standard practice of the travel industry of offering incentives to high volume purchasers of travel services.[18] Such incentives may include "gifts" of free airline travel, complimentary Caribbean cruises, or other inducements to do business with a particular travel company. Not only are such practices legal, but are indeed regarded as common marketing tactics in the highly competitive travel industry. So, even if this approach is legal, does it necessarily follow that such incentives are ethical? In Nash's view, they are not ethical. Why? Because access to a travel company's unsolicited freebies has so colored the purchaser's judgment, that he fails to perceive his involvement in a conflict-of-interest situation. Nonetheless, Nash admits that, as a practical matter, whenever the gifts-versus-bribes discussion arises, the upshot in any given case is to "go along with industry practice."[19]

As the evidence began to mount in the 1980s that an "anything-goes-if-you're-not-caught" philosophy was much more attractive than a firm commitment to ethical standards, educators began to take notice. This translated into greater awareness and discussion of ethics in the academic arena.

Bringing Ethics into the Classroom

In a decade of changing American values that has been described as reflecting "a finely balanced mix of cosmetic refinement and moral coarseness," the 1980s sparked a resurgence in academe of profound concern for ethics. At a roundtable discussion of "The Challenge of Business Ethics," on the occasion of Harvard Business School's (HBS) 25th reunion of the class of 1962, the focus was on the tough choices faced by management intent on right behavior rather than on avoidance of wrongdoing. What seemed to come through for the most part was the realization that ethical codes of conduct do change. What was seen as ethical in one era might in another era be seen as unethical. Nonetheless, the roundtable perceived "a core of ethical principles that constitute a kind of highway code of society that everyone has to abide by." Learning these core principles, it was felt, is best achieved when students wrestle with ethical dilemmas in each course of instruction rather than in one specific course on ethics.[20]

Ethics in Applications and Coursework

By the spring of 1992, the focus on ethics at Harvard Business School had been widened to embrace admissions requirements as well as new courses. The plan that was implemented:

a. Asks applicants to write an essay on how they managed and resolved an ethical dilemma.

b. Requires all MBAs to take a nongraded, nine-session course on ethics. This course is titled "Decision Making and Ethical Values" and is taught by a number of Harvard's most experienced faculty.

c. Works with faculty to integrate ethics into the core courses in such subjects as accounting, marketing, and operations.

d. Encourages mainstream faculty to do case studies on ethical questions.

e. Offers three ethics electives.[21] (Of the 806 members of the class of 1992, approximately 30 percent were enrolled in one of these electives.)

An in-depth, 1991–1992 20-page report on "Ethics in the MBA Curriculum" gave the program high marks.[22] Its conclusion was that Dean McArthur and Professor Thomas Piper had "set the stage for a project that would challenge the minds and hearts of HBS faculty and students for many years to come." Whether or not these developments will enable students to behave more ethically in the future has yet to be tested. In then-President Bok's opinion, "we may never know. But surely the experiment is worth trying, for the goal has never been more important to the quality of society in which we live."[23]

Elsewhere, associate professors Herman and Cullen of the Cornell School of Hotel Administration were reporting that whether a student is enrolled in marketing, finance, human resources management, or food science courses, he or she can still learn ethical precepts.[24] Clearly, as tomorrow's managers, today's students will be required "to face the very problems they are now studying, problems involving allegations of price-fixing, bribery, and cultural exploitation; adherence to equal-employment and affirmative-action laws; and meeting truth-in-menu and fair-advertising regulations."[25] Therefore, it is argued that hospitality educators can do no less than to design their course curricula and syllabi so as to lead the way in bringing ethics into the classroom. "In so doing, perhaps we can help halt the erosion of ethical behavior in our society."[26]

Ethics Training in the Workplace

In addition to discussion in the classroom, training in ethics is also happening in the workplace. Statistics compiled by the Center for Business Ethics at Bentley College in Waltham,

Massachusetts, show that 44.4 percent of 223 companies surveyed had ethics training programs for employees, generally conducted in a workshop or seminar format. Besides the ultimate goal of developing employee awareness of ethics in business decision-making, the Bentley survey indicated that another objective of corporate training is to draw attention to crucial ethical issues to which employees may be exposed—such issues, for example, as the reporting of unethical behavior and compliance with local, state, and federal regulations.

Not all companies have or want a formal training program. As one hotel chain CEO observed anonymously, "We don't make hypocrites out of our employees by setting up some high-minded code of ethics for their guidance. That's nonsense. Everybody knows we are a decent hotel organization whose people always act with best of intentions." Nonetheless, as Laura Nash has observed, good intentions do not necessarily provide automatic immunity from wrongdoing. Decent instincts are not always strong enough to hold up under the adverse and complex conditions that managers inevitably encounter.[27]

Factors Affecting Business Ethics in the Hospitality Industry

The very nature of the hospitality business, the kinds of service it provides, the nature of the interactions, and where and how business is transacted shape the ethical dilemmas that hospitality managers must face. The dilemmas presented earlier in the chapter, such as bumping reservations or spying by spotters, result from specific characteristics of the business. Further, the characteristics of the business determine the codes of conduct by which the industry abides. Formal codes of conduct are represented here by those of industry associations.

Industry Characteristics Shape Ethical Dilemmas

In *Principles and Practices of Management in the Hospitality Industry*, the author James R. Keiser identifies by example four specific characteristics of the hospitality business that can have an impact on the ethical choices hospitality professionals make—and that they cannot afford to overlook. They are the following:

1. **Travelers are often far from home.** If travelers are tired, are on the road, and need accommodations, they are vulnerable to price gouging or other pressures.

2. **Hospitality is a service, not a product.** If a product is unsatisfactory, consumers can take it back for a refund or an exchange. They cannot easily do this with an intangible service. Also, a hotel can raise rates or impose minimum stays during periods of peak demand, responses that can raise ethical considerations.

3. **The hospitality workforce can be vulnerable.** Much of the hospitality workforce comes from the lower economic or other disadvantaged groups, which can tempt unscrupulous managers to push them around or withhold appropriate rights and benefits.

4. **Alcoholic beverages often accompany the profession.** Many hospitality establishments serve alcoholic beverages, which can present opportunities to take advantage of inebriated customers or to serve customers who should be shut off. This problem has been

ameliorated to some degree by increased alcohol awareness and the encouragement of programs such as those for designated drivers.

Codes of Ethics

The desire to protect the industry image from specific vulnerabilities is evident in trade associations' written codes of ethical conduct. Two associations, the National Restaurant Association and the American Hotel & Motel Association, have in their past history adopted codes of conduct for its members.

NRA Truth in Menu As far back as 1923 the National Restaurant Association first adopted standards of business practice designed to foster truth in menu representation. Subsequent legislation, fueled by consumer demand, particularly in the 1990s, has put strict laws around what constitutes truth in menu. In its standards of business practice, members were advised that:

a. The foodservice operator shall be accurate in his printed or oral words, whether they be in a menu, part of a sales talk, or general conversation with patrons or others.

b. The foodservice operator shall not misname food articles on the bill-of-fare, as regards to the materials of which they are composed, their quality, their method or place of manufacture or origin.

c. The foodservice operator shall not use advertisements which are false, or which have a tendency to mislead, or which do not convey the whole truth, or which do not conform to business integrity.[28]

Restaurateurs' widespread failure to follow these standards during the half century following their adoption led the Los Angeles County Department of Health Services in 1976 to identify the following five categories of violation:

1. Quality or grade of products misrepresented.

2. Point of origin of food products not as advertised.

3. Size, weight, or portion of food not as advertised.

4. Products advertised as fresh which have been frozen, canned, or preserved.

5. Merchandising terms used to describe food not accurate.[29]

Subsequent threats of corrective legislation in several states led the National Restaurant Association to encourage its members' adherence to stringent ethical standards as shown in Exhibit 16.1.

AH&MA Code of Conduct Equally significant in the 1970s was the American Hotel & Motel Association's adoption of a similar code of conduct for its members. In the words of President George Johnson, adoption of such a code was desirable because "in today's world of consumerism, it has behooved us to take a positive approach as to what will be presented to the public, rather than a defensive attitude every time the innkeeping industry was charged with negligence and poor service."[30] Within a year following board approval by the AH&MA, 22 state lodging associations had adopted the code, indicating the hotel industry's growing acceptance of its social responsibilities

◼◼◼◼◼◼ *Exhibit 16.1* Truth in Menu

Accuracy in Menu Offerings: A Position Statement of the National Restaurant Association (Adopted February 1977)

The foodservice industry has long recognized the importance of accuracy in describing its products ... on menus, and through visual or oral representation, both on ethical grounds and from the standpoint of customer satisfaction. The National Restaurant Association incorporated standards of accuracy in all representations to the public in its Standards of Business Practice, originally adopted by the Association in 1923. We re-affirm and strongly support the principles therein expressed.

"Truth in dining" or "truth in menu" laws and ordinances have been proposed in some government jurisdictions, and in a few cases adopted in the belief that representations on restaurant menus present a unique problem in consumer protection. The National Restaurant Association believes that such legislation is unnecessary as Federal, state, and many local governments have laws and regulations prohibiting false advertising and misrepresentations of products, and providing protection from fraud. In an industry such as ours, where economic survival depends upon customer satisfaction, misrepresentation is most effectively regulated by the severe sanction of customer dissatisfaction, and loss of patronage.

To be equitable, the complexity of such legislation would be staggering. It is conceivable that standardized recipes for each menu listing would be required if regulatory refinement followed its logical course. The problems of enforcement, and proof, if due process is observed, would be monumental, if not impossible.

The "truth in dining" movement is not confined to the proposition that restaurant menus be absolutely accurate in their representations. Legislation and ordinances have been proposed that would require the identification of a specific means of preservation, method of preparation or statement of food origin. Such requirements could unjustly imply that certain foods, processes or places of origin are unwholesome or inferior.

Government action must be confined to problems where its intervention can be effective and at a cost commensurate with the benefits to be gained.

---

toward its customers. Alas, acting on advice of its legal counsel five years later, the AH&MA announced that it would no longer encourage its remaining state associations to adopt the code because of the risk of violating antitrust laws.[31]

Notwithstanding trade association efforts to codify ethical standards for the hospitality industry, rarely do such dry documents contain within themselves what one authority has called "the final emotional power of commitment."[32] Instead, such commitment comes about only as a consequence of organizational achievement. Thus, it's only through a concerted effort on the part of an organization that high standards are part of the day-to-day culture.

Ethical Issues in the 1990s

According to the *New York Times*, the trend toward formal corporate ethics programs is likely to be accelerated as a consequence of the new federal sentencing guidelines that became effective on November 1, 1991. Since that time, judges have been encouraged to hand out more lenient punishment for legal and regulatory violations to companies that can demonstrate that they have committed substantial resources to programs that encourage ethical behavior.[33] Several companies outside the hospitality industry are grappling with the high cost of corporate misconduct by establishing ethics offices.

But is the creation of ethics offices and the work they do enough? Some are not so optimistic, as reported in *Fortune*, a respected business magazine. Driven by the continuing economic slowdown, many companies reportedly were "putting the heat on subordinates." Gary Edwards, president of the Ethics Resource Center in Washington, D.C., was quoted as saying, "The message out there is: Reaching objectives is what matters and how you get there isn't that important." Despite the proliferation of ethics workshops, appointments of ethics officers in more than 200 major corporations, installation of hot lines through which any employee may register a complaint about wrongdoing, a prominent consultant, Michael Josephson, is quoted as predicting, "We are going to see a phenomenal number of business scandals during the 1990s. We are swimming in enough lies to keep the lawyers busy for the next ten years."[34]

Optimists have a different perspective. Taking an active stance, by placing ethical behavior into school curricula and into corporate culture, training by sound example, and setting standards that parallel the intent of the Hippocratic Oath, can in fact create environments that encourage exemplary behavior.

▓▓▓▓ *Too Much of a Good Thing?*

Consider the country of Malaysia. Of all the economic growth taking place in Asia, Malaysia is the fastest growing country of them all. Over the last decades, Malaysia has transformed itself from a commodity based economy to a manufacturing one. In the decade of the 1990s, in order to diversify its economic base, it has made a bid to increase the service piece of its economy in the form of tourism. In the early 1970s, 80 percent of its exports were commodities like tin, lumber, rubber, and oil. By 1994, manufactured goods were 65 percent of exports.[1]

The tourism story is a successful one. Malaysia has experienced nearly 10 percent growth annually in each year of the 1990s. It has very low unemployment, and hotel companies are coming in droves. The lineup of foreign investment that will be represented by 1997 will include Minneapolis-based Carlson Hospitality Group's Colony Hotel and Inn division and its Radisson division, which will both open hotels in Kuala Lumpur. France's Accor will have opened a Sofitel in Johir Bahru, and Westin Hotels and Resorts will have opened a resort on Langkawi Island, off Malaysia's northwest coast. Properties will also be developed by New World Hotels International, Hilton International, Hyatt International, ITT Sheraton, Nikko Hotels International, Marriott, Mandarin Oriental, Pan Pacific, Singapore Mandarin International, Royal Hotels, and Shangri-La International![2]

The Malaysian government is a strong supporter of the development. It created a new Ministry of Culture and Tourism in 1987. It launched and celebrated Visit Malaysia Year in 1990 and again in 1994, supported by millions of advertising dollars. The country is sensitive to the lack of international airline service, but is encouraging more charter service and scheduled foreign service.

The extensive development, though providing a strong economic plus, raises other issues. Fear of inflation (running at approximately 6 percent in the mid-1990s) is present. Are the developments sensitive to the preservation of the environment and to the culture of the local residents? Will the infrastructure be overtaxed? Though all financial indicators show promise in the short run, are their long term costs yet to be paid? Is all the development promising or too much of a good thing?

[1.] Somerset R. Waters, *Travel Industry World Yearbook: The Big Picture 1993–94* (Rye, New York: Child and Waters, 1994), 118.

[2.] *Hotels* (February 1994): 6.

Summary

Defining ethical behavior precisely is difficult. Because of the judgment involved, it has been likened to nailing Jell-O to a wall. This difficult task has nonetheless been attempted by various scholars and industry leaders, among them Barbara Ley Toffler, Laura L. Nash, Peter Drucker, Sir Adrian Cadbury, and Steven S. Reinemund. Their observations have given great momentum to the current state of the art in meeting the ethical challenges of the hospitality industry as well as those of other industries.

Because each industry has different characteristics, each faces its own set of ethical dilemmas. Those dilemmas faced by hospitality managers are reflected in both the formal and informal codes of conduct of the business. Written codes are those defined by law or written as standards of business practice by associations. Informal codes are reflected by the behavior of company employees and standard practices. Whether standard practices are ethical is a different question, as is noted in Laura Nash's discussion of the practice of accepting unsolicited freebies.

Front-page tales of corporate misconduct turned attention to the need for bringing business ethics into the classroom and into the workplace. Accordingly, the Harvard Business School has undertaken courses of study designed to heighten ethical sensitivities on the part of their students. Other hospitality schools have followed suit. Increasingly ethics is being integrated into coursework; the inclusion of this chapter in this book is a case in point.

Corporations concerned about ethical behavior are implementing ethics programs and are also looking to prevent and detect violations in day-to-day operations, to create an environment that encourages exemplary behavior, and to institute systems and leadership that facilitate integrity. Whether the increased attention to ethics in the classroom or in corporations will have positive benefits is difficult to judge. Fortunately, however, many corporations and schools feel that investing time, effort, and training to raise ethical standards is a worthwhile endeavor.

Discussion Questions

1. Do so-called truth-in-menu laws or regulations work to the customer's advantage, or not? Explain.

2. Under what circumstance, if any, is bribery justifiable? Do "freebies" given as a favor to a valued customer constitute a bribe? Discuss your answer.

3. Professor Ackoff of the University of Pennsylvania's Wharton School writes, "Although corruption is widely believed to be evil it is widely tolerated."[35] Do you agree? Why or why not? Cite specific examples to support your view.

4. In your opinion, is it ethical for an employer to hire "spotters" to check on bartenders' honesty in ringing up the correct amount for drinks served? Give reasons for your answer.

5. Review the other four ethical dilemmas faced by hospitality managers noted earlier in the chapter. Do you think the actions were ethical?

6. Define ethical behavior in your own words. Which of the viewpoints expressed in the chapter most closely aligns with your own?

7. How should the values presented by the quotation from the Hippocratic Oath be applied to hospitality and other industries?

Assignment

Consider an ethical dilemma that a hospitality manager might face, given the characteristics noted in the chapter, followed by a question. Share your ethical dilemma with others and ask them to answer the question. Does everyone answer the same way? If possible, ask persons of different nationalities. Are the answers the same? How much does culture and heritage influence what is considered ethical?

End Notes

1. Some inkling of the industry's earlier need for such a road map may be gleaned from Harnett T. Kane's fascinating book, *Louisiana Hayride* (New York: William Morrow & Co., 1941). The author's history of the 1928–1940 heyday of Huey Long's "American Rehearsal for Dictatorship" records the sordid political entanglements of Seymour Weiss, a prominent New Orleans hotelman, who, together with other cronies of the Long regime, ultimately served time in Atlanta Penitentiary for his misdeeds. Many years later, Weiss was elected to the presidency of the American Hotel & Motel Association for a designated period of *one day only*!

2. Richard Hammer, *The Helmsleys: The Rise and Fall of Harry and Leona* (New York: New American Library, 1990), 204–205.

3. John J. Bilon, "Taking Another Look at Accuracy in Menus," *Cornell Hotel and Restaurant Administration Quarterly* (November 1979): 11.

4. Peter F. Drucker, *Management: Tasks, Responsibilities, Practices* (New York: Harper & Row, 1974), 368, 375.

5. Sir Adrian Cadbury, "Ethical Managers Make Their Own Rules," *Harvard Business Review* (September –October 1987): 70.

6. Steven S. Reinemund, "Defining the Ethical Challenge—A View from Above," *Corporate Ethics: Developing New Standards of Accountability*, Report No. 980 (New York: The Conference Board, 1991), 10.

7. Ibid., 9–10.

8. Barbara Ley Toffler, *Tough Choices* (New York: John Wiley & Sons, 1986), 10.

9. Philip V. Lewis, "Defining Business Ethics, Like Nailing Jell-O to a Wall," *Journal of Business Ethics* 4 (1985): 337–383.

10. Anonymous.

11. Raymond S. Schmidgall, "Hotel Managers' Responses to Ethical Problems," *FIU Hospitality Review* 10 (2) (Spring 1992): 11–18.

12. Ibid., 16–18.

13. Ibid., 12.

14. Ibid., 16.

15. Linda K. Enghagen and David D. Hott, "Students' Perceptions of Ethical Issues in the Hospitality and Tourism Industry," *Hospitality and Research Journal* 15 (2) (1992).

16. Ronald B. Morgan, "Self- and Co-Worker Perceptions of Ethics and Their Relationships to Leadership and Salary," *Academy of Management Journal* 36 (1) (February 1993): 200–214.

17. Ibid., 210.

18. Laura L. Nash, *Good Intentions Aside: A Manager's Guide to Resolving Ethical Problems* (Boston: Harvard Business School Press, 1990).

19. Ibid., 194.

20. Proceedings of a roundtable discussion by eight academic members of the Class of 1961 at Harvard Business School on the occasion of their 25th reunion, *Harvard Business School Bulletin*, October 1986.

21. "Can Ethics Be Taught? Harvard Gives It the Old College Try," *Business Week* (6 April 1992): 34.

22. "Ethics in the MBA Curriculum," *Harvard Business School Bulletin*, December 1991 and February 1992. Author's identity is not disclosed.

23. "Ethics in the MBA Curriculum," 10.

24. Francine M. Herman and Thomas P. Cullen, "Still Needed: Ethics in Business Instruction," *The Cornell Hotel and Restaurant Administration Quarterly* 27 (2) (August 1986): 51.

25. Herman and Cullen, 52.

26. Ibid.

27. Nash, x–xi.

28. "Standards of Business Practice" (Chicago: National Restaurant Association, 1923).

29. John J. Bilon, "Taking Another Look at Accuracy in Menus," *Cornell Hotel and Restaurant Administration Quarterly* (November 1979): 9.

30. AH&MA Board of Directors' Meeting, December 5–6, 1972.

31. Harold E. Lane, "The Corporate Conscience and the Role of Business in Society," *Cornell Hotel and Restaurant Administration Quarterly* 23 (3) (November 1982): 14.

32. Kenneth R. Andrews, "Ethics in Practice," *Harvard Business Review* (September–October 1989): 102.

33. "Helping Corporate America Hew to the Straight and Narrow," *New York Times*, 3 November 1991, 5f.

34. Kenneth Labich, "The New Crisis in Business in Business Ethics," *Fortune* (20 April 1992): 167–176.

35. Russell L. Ackoff, *Management in Small Doses* (New York: John Wiley & Sons, 1986), 61.

Chapter Seventeen

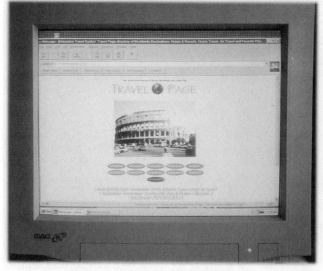

" Cheshire puss, " she [Alice] began… " Would you please tell me which way I ought to go from here? "

" That depends on where you want to go, " said the cat.

Lewis Carroll [1]

Strategic Thinking: Looking Toward the Twenty-First Century ✍

When you finish this chapter you should:

1. Know what is meant by the word *strategy*.

2. Know what is the difference between strategic planning and strategic thinking.

3. Understand how environmental scanning unearths the clues that can lead to new strategies.

4. Explain the advantages of embracing diversity.

5. Be able to explain how environmental concerns affect strategy.

6. Know how the concept of branding evolved, and why it is important to the hospitality business.

7. Be able to explain outsourcing, and how it can help control costs.

8. Explain what a strategic alliance is and how one can create competitive advantage.

9. Explain how technology can have an impact on strategy and can help create competitive advantage.

10. Know how the hospitality industry responds to customers with special needs, and identifies market niches.

Introduction _____

Ask almost anyone these days what *strategy* is, and they will define it as some kind of a plan or guide to *future* behavior. Then ask them what strategy they themselves or their companions have actually pursued. They will describe a pattern of *past* behavior—regardless of whether it was a deliberate, planned process or whether it just simply emerged, as one event led to another. Regardless of how a strategy evolves, a company that wishes to create competitive advantage must constantly be looking for winning strategies and must be implementing them in meaningful ways.

In this chapter we focus our attention on what a strategy is, including the important elements of strategic planning and strategic thinking. Then we turn to the future of the hospitality business itself. By examining the clues and patterns emerging in the hospitality environment, we potentially can uncover either insights, or questions that lead to insights that in turn can set a strategy in motion. For it is through the successful implementation of a strategic vision that a company can compete in the future.

What is a Strategy?

Actually, the word *strategy* derives from the Greek word *strategia*, meaning "the science and art of military command." Thus arose the concept early on of business management as a war, with the CEO as the general being backed up by well-drilled ranks of corporate soldiers, all motivated by the message "We're in this to win." Today, with rare exceptions, the military concept of management strategy is obsolete. Instead, the term *strategy* now simply connotes "a plan for getting something done."[2] Implementing a strategy involves two important tasks, strategic thinking and strategic planning.

What is Strategic Thinking?

Strategic thinking is about synthesis. It involves intuition, creation, and vision. In the words of Michael Porter, a Harvard Business School professor who has written extensively on strategy, strategic thinking is the glue that holds the many systems and initiatives within a company together. In his view, strategic thinking occurs rarely, and therefore formal planning is the disciplinary tool needed in order to inform a company's strategic thinking. Moreover, as others have noted, **strategic vision**, or **strategic insight**, important synonyms for strategic thinking, require the ability to scan the environment, capturing a broad range of data from both formal and informal sources, and to look for patterns, relationships, and linkages. Strategic thinking does not produce plans. It creates clearly articulated and easily understandable visions and strategies that describe a business, technology, or corporate culture in terms of the direction it should pursue over the long term.[3] **Strategic thinking** means synthesizing learning into a vision.

What is Strategic Planning?

Strategic planning is different from strategic thinking. Strategic planning is about analysis—about breaking a goal (derived from strategic thinking) into steps and formalizing those steps into a series of anticipated results. In effect, strategic planning articulates strategies or visions that already exist. Strategic planning is especially important as organizations grow and become more complex. **Strategic planning** is a step-by-step approach to setting a strategy.[4]

Strategic planning is highly useful for three reasons: first, it breaks a goal down into a series of steps; second, it formalizes those steps so they can be implemented almost automatically; and third, it articulates the expected consequences of each step.[5] Strategic planning is the road map that gets you from point A to point B. Planning does not show you where point B is. That is the domain of strategic thinking.

How Strategies Evolve

Successful strategies may often begin as intuitive rather than precisely articulated ideas. Thus franchising, for example, had its origin in the Middle Ages when local governments intuitively moved to offer important persons, such as church officials, a license to maintain law and order and to collect taxes. And in return, the licensee paid the government a specified sum for the privilege of receiving military protection. This early chance happening may have been where the strategic insight to capture the power of franchising began.

As the twentieth century dawned and the economic benefit of franchise organizations became clear, the franchise contagion spread to many product and service industries, among them hotels and restaurants. At this junction, franchising became a deliberate strategy. For example, in the 1920s, restaurant franchising slowed with the evolution of A&W "walk-up" root beer stands and Howard Johnson ice cream emporiums. By the 1990s, chain organizations, such as Boston Market and Starbuck's Coffee, systematically and intentionally opened hundreds of outlets in less than half a decade.

Another example of the evolution of a strategic insight involves the motel. We learned in chapter 1, whether by chance or intent, an innovative Californian had created the first highway motel in 1924. It displayed an electric sign showing the letters "…….OTEL." The first letter on the sign flashed "H" and "M" alternately, becoming the first use of the word MOTEL in the U.S. lodging industry. As the interstate highway system expanded from the 1950s on, the number of motels or motor hotels exploded. By this time, the concept of a motel chain was a deliberate, planned strategy. But when did the strategic insight occur? In 1924? Perhaps the true insight came from a much earlier time. For example, the development of resorts by railway companies at destinations at the end of rail lines may have been the true forerunner of motels at the end of the driving day.

Could other successful strategies be traced to intuitive insights from earlier times? Could sixteenth-century courtyards, where carriages entered and entertainment flourished, have influenced the design of the atrium hotel, most often attributed to John Portman? Did the family crests and foliage, such as a vine leaf, used in medieval society offer the first insight into branding as an important element of marketing a hotel? Do successful concepts happen by chance or by intent? Did the first pairing of a lodging concept without foodservice and a unit of a restaurant chain happen by chance, or were they planned together? Was the first all-suite hotel, as we know it today, designed as such, or was it a residential building converted from another use?

Turning Insight into Success

When a strategic insight first begins is not necessarily clear. The important point is that companies that are able to identify a strategic insight and to formulate that insight into a strategic plan are those that transform businesses. These are the companies that profoundly change the nature of their business and that control the competitive landscape. In the hospitality field, historically, such vision came from the minds of leaders such as Ray Kroc, who founded the McDonald's chain, and Kemmons Wilson, who founded Holiday Inn.

Native Branding in Russia

In Moscow, the age of the American fast-food monopoly might just be coming to an end. Well, maybe not an end anytime soon, but Russian competition is on the way. If local restaurateurs have their way, the on-the-go Muscovite will be passing up the Big Macs, fries and shakes for rasstegai (meat pie), pirozhki (little dumplings), and a good bottle of brailovsky, described as a sour-tasting milk product, rumored to be good for hangovers. All this and more is available at the Russkoye Bistro, in Pushkin Square.

That a home-grown fast-food joint should spring up in Moscow should come as no surprise. The French word "bistro" comes from the Russian word for "quick," a cultural exchange courtesy of the Napoleonic wars. Also not to be ignored is the prohibitively high prices at the Moscow McDonald's, far out of reach for the average working Russian citizen. The average price for a Russian meal is about one-fifth the price of a Big Mac. And it's comfort food for the Russian people. Just as Boston Market and other restaurants have responded to a market niche in the United States, so has the Russkoye Bistro. Oh, and one more advantage to the Russian product—the management is contemplating adding vodka to the menu. And there are plans for 200 more outlets in Russia alone. Look out Paris, they might be heading your way, too.

Source: David Filipov, "Russian Fast Food Goes Native" *Boston Globe*, 4 August 1995

Finding a Strategic Vision for the Future

Hindsight allows us to identify historic strategic success stories. Finding a strategic vision for the future is not so easy. Current literature suggests that while much is known about strategy-making, less is known about strategic vision itself, "because it is locked in the head of the individual."[6] To the visionary, distinction arises not from luck but from a profound ability to articulate in words and action a sense of immediacy and vitality. A visionary must translate what the future holds into a plan.

Creating such a plan comes only from an ability to scan the environment carefully and to integrate the resulting findings into a vision of what an organization should be. Environmental scanning looks at the political, economical, ecological, sociocultural, and technological areas. Changes found in these areas dictate changes in strategies. As we look to what the twenty-first century holds for hospitality companies, we undertake an investigation to find these potential sources of vision.

Looking Toward the Twenty-First Century

If we were to scan the hospitality environment for clues, patterns, and linkages, what could we find that would help to define the future visions of hospitality companies? What forces will shape the competitive landscape and how will successful players in the marketplace react? What new ideas and companies will emerge? How should companies think? What strategies should they plan to map a competitive position in the next century? What insights lay waiting for the taking? What should successful companies be doing?

Several areas emerge that may provide the answers to the above questions. Those areas that are experiencing much change include: responding to increased concern for the environment, global branding, saving costs through outsourcing, forming strategic alliances to create competitive advantage, adopting technology to increase revenue and decrease costs, responding to special populations, identifying new market niches, and embracing diversity.

Responding to Increased Concern for the Environment

So many travelers and hospitality companies have turned their attention to saving the environment that a whole new vocabulary has emerged. Hotel, restaurant, and travel companies that are doing their part are **green**. Tourism that demonstrates sensitivity to ecological issues is **ecotourism**. Many tourism-related businesses are responding to the call on behalf of the environment. Here are some examples:

Going Green McDonald's is one company that responded to environmental concerns raised by consumers. It abandoned Styrofoam packaging in favor of recycled paper even though the heat retention properties were inferior. The Inter-Continental hotel chain published a 200-page guide for its properties worldwide outlining environmental goals for hotel operations and a checklist of required action steps. Bonuses of general managers are tied to how well the hotels comply.[7] Canadian Pacific Hotels and Resorts returns all refundable cans and sends nonrefundables to a recycling plant. The World Travel and Tourism Council (WTTC) has launched the Green Globe Program, whose purpose is to establish an environmental standard of excellence for travel and tourism, making it, in effect, an environmental code of ethics not unlike those we saw in the chapter on business ethics. The Green Globe Program is converting its code into practical action. Immediate agreement from dozens of members makes WTTC confident that over 250 companies will commit to its international guidelines.[8]

The Ritz-Carlton and Hyatt hotel companies have begun companywide recycling programs. The Hard Rock Cafe has been vocal about its concern for the environment and has implemented multiple efforts to recycle within its restaurants. Disney World manages its own 28,000-square-foot recycling center handling an impressive 30 tons of trash a day. It also reclaims and treats four million gallons of waste water a day, put to horticultural use on its golf courses and lawns. Jiminy Cricket now appears throughout Disney as an environmental logo, proclaiming "I've got

Environmentality!"[9] Many hotels and restaurants are giving leftover food, soap, and worn linens to homeless shelters. Others are recycling glass, cans, plastic containers, kitchen grease, cardboard, and paper. Why?

First, because it's the right thing to do. Customers are seeking out companies that look out for the environment, which is good for public relations and good for business. A 1995 study by the Travel Industry Association of America showed that people will pay 6.2 percent more for travel goods if the supplier is environmentally responsible. Hotels with extensive green programs like the Boston Park Plaza have noted "a dramatic increase in business from individuals and groups who want to align with a company committed to the environment."[10]

Saving Natural Resources Means Saving Money Saving energy also saves money. This has been accomplished by recycling and by reducing waste. "Retrievable" goods like silverware are pulled from the garbage. Recycling paper, cardboard, and cans reduces garbage hauling costs.

In many cases, guests are asked to help. In various operations signs are posted asking guests to separate recyclables, turn out lights upon exiting, conserve water when brushing their teeth, and indicate towels that are dirty so clean ones aren't replaced. More efficient heating and cooling systems have also been installed. For example, "smart room systems" detect if a guest is in a room and then adjust the temperature accordingly. For the hospitality company, conserving and recycling can mean saving money and natural resources, and ultimately adding to profits and positive marketing.

As consumers are likely to become more environmentally demanding, and as laws and regulations are likely to become more abundant, responding to increased concern for the environment presents opportunities for insightful companies. What new products and services that cost-effectively recycle materials and reduce waste will emerge? Will an environmental seal of approval be granted to green hotels and restaurants and emerge as a new type of affiliation? Will that seal have clout and attract the growing number of ecotourists? In predicting the answers to these questions and in monitoring the responses to concerns for the environment, a hospitality company with its eye on the future may find the underpinning of a strategy imbedded in the information that is collected. Future strategic ideas may also be uncovered in an exploration of global branding, the next topic.

Global Branding

In chapter 2 we learned about the changes in how hotels were owned and managed in the 1980s verses the early 1990s. Among those changes were increased segmentation of brands or creating different tiers of products, according to price. These changes continue to be instructive in understanding future trends, particularly with respect to increased segmentation of brands. Today and into the future there are likely to be important strategic marketing implications associated with increased segmentation of brands, especially internationally. Thus **global branding**, creating brand name recognition in multiple countries, is worth investigating.

Hotels The fundamental worth of a franchise system is created by establishing and maintaining a strong brand name. The proliferation of brands continues to unfold at a staggering pace. In the mid- to late 1990s alone, we will find on the drawing boards three new brands for Holiday Inn: Holiday Inn Select, Holiday Inn Hotels and Suites, and Holiday Inn Garden Court; a new entry called Amerihost, targeting small towns in America with no modern hotels; and Four Point Hotels, a new launch by Sheraton in the midscale price range. Hampton Inns and Suites will be added to Promus Companies' three other brands. These are additions to an already extensive set of franchising choices offered by major players in franchising. The major franchisors will also continue to buy up brands to expand their network and will continue to grow overseas. This trend emphasizes the critical importance of brand name recognition and of scale in successful franchise systems. Will all of the brands survive? Unlikely. People don't spend more nights in hotel rooms because they have more choices of brands to accommodate them. Which brands will be able to create competitive advantage, and why? Which will be able to maintain a global presence and be able to cater to guests of varying cultural backgrounds? Which companies will smartly allocate resources to winning brands and act quickly to redirect brands that are losing?

Casinos What of segmentation and branding in other areas of hospitality such as restaurants and casinos? In the casino market, branding is a newer phenomenon. Given the explosive growth of the casino market, with more and more geographic locations allowing casino gaming, will segmentation and branding become more important? Will national casino chains emerge and offer different casino "flags" or brands to potential franchisees? Will gaming complexes begin to narrow their customer segments as competition becomes fiercer? Will there be an increased number of casino management companies?

Commercial Foodservice Restaurants will continue to see an increasingly large number of meals being consumed outside the home, and a larger and larger portion of those meals will be served by chain operations. Thus, chain organizations will capture a larger portion of **share of stomach**, the total food consumed. As has happened historically, the pockets of growth in restaurant chains will occur relative to changing tastes. The so-called comfort food segment, for example, has emerged in the mid-nineties. These chains, such as Boston Market, offer home-style menu choices with fast food–style delivery. Coffee, as a focal point of restaurant operations, has also received increased attention. Coffee specialty chains have seen extensive growth. What will be the coffee and comfort food of the twenty-first century?

Institutional Foodservice Institutional foodservice has also increasingly gravitated toward branding in its offerings within institutions. Chain brands such as Pizza Hut and McDonald's have been found within institutions such as army bases and hospitals for some time. There is increasing use of brands in other areas, however, such as high schools and college campuses, where fast food outlets have found their way to school cafeterias. On campus, meal cards are accepted. In repeated examples, food sales have increased as a result of the branded offerings. Missouri State, for example, quadrupled its pizza sales once Pizza Hut came to campus.[11] Other untapped **points of distribution (PODs)** are likely to emerge. Some fast food chains, for example, have begun home delivery. None other than McDonald's is testing home delivery in the New York City market. What other PODs remain undiscovered?

Airline Catering Airline feeding has also seen the emergence of its own form of branding. Several airlines have revamped menus to include food products with recognizable names. United Airlines, for example, has launched a campaign to promote the serving of Starbuck's Coffee. From entrees to desserts, foodservice has veered from what some would unkindly call "airline food." Will there be other major shifts in airline foodservice?

Saving Costs through Outsourcing

Successful companies focus on what they do best and on what generates the most profit. In order to do this, companies are increasingly **outsourcing** some functions, hiring outside services to complete certain tasks. Outsourcing is not new for certain functions. For some time, hospitality companies have outsourced functions like processing payroll checks and laundering linens and uniforms. These outside companies can provide services more economically than hospitality companies do themselves. For example, a laundry company, which has scale economies because it processes a large volume of laundry for numerous customers, can offer a lower rate.

Outsourced Functions With increasing competitive pressures and attention to cutting costs, more functions traditionally done in-house are being outsourced to save money. One California hotel and conference center, Northwoods Resort, outsourced its preopening sales and marketing effort, rather than assigning it to an in-house team. Parking garages for hotels and valet parking for restaurants are additional candidates for outsourcing. Parking cars is not part of the core business for hotels and restaurants, and not something they are necessarily good at doing. Night cleaning services are also being outsourced. This reduces the complexity of scheduling cleaning crews on a 24-hour basis. Hotels using outside night cleaning services find it cost effective. Some conference hotels are using outsiders to provide audiovisual services. This off-loads the responsibility of keeping up with the latest technology, servicing equipment and enhancing the chances that backup equipment is available when a machine goes down.

With the increasing capability and complexity of databases, hotel companies that maintain a frequent guest program often outsource the maintenance and administration of the database to an outsider. Again, the logic is for hotels to stay focused on their core business and to give outsiders functions in which greater expertise can be hired more cost effectively. Outside vendors are also available for establishing follow-through guest satisfaction programs. These services contact guests to assess the quality of their stay. Callers may play the role of a concierge of the hotel, but are in fact outsiders whose task it is to bring objective evaluation of performance to the hotel's management.

In what may come as a surprise, hotels are increasingly outsourcing a traditional department, food and beverage operations! Unlike European hotels, which are often known for having the best restaurant in town, American hotel restaurants are often faced with the stigma that the food will be sub par, and guests choose to go outside the hotel, particularly for the dinner meal. Hotels are, therefore, bringing brand name restaurants within the hotel, seeking to maintain the separate identity. Wherever physically possible, a separate outside entrance for the restaurant is incorporated.

Sometimes the restaurants are national chains, like a TGI Friday's within a Radisson hotel, or a Pizza Hut within a Marriott. In other cases, a hotel will team up with a well-known local restaurateur who has already demonstrated success in the marketplace. For example, to great success, a well-known chef with several Davio's Restaurants in the Boston area opened up an additional Davio's in the Sonesta Hotel. Hotels may not outsource all of the food and beverage functions. The banquet and catering function may continue to be serviced in-house while the restaurant space is leased to an outsider, for example. Likely candidates for outsourcing of various food and beverage functions are those hotels that consider food and beverage a necessary evil.

Faux Outsourcing An unusual hybrid of turning over pieces of the operation to outsiders is **faux outsourcing**. In this effort, the establishment tries to create a scenario in which the guest believes that the service is independent. Pizza delivery is a classic case. Some hotels noticed that instead of ordering from the roomservice menu, guests were just as happy to dial the local pizza delivery. In an effort to recapture the business, some hotels went so far as to establish an outside number and have pizzas delivered from the hotel kitchen by a delivery person, suitably clad in a delivery uniform with warming box!

Other hotels are seeking to capture take-out business with the establishment of what appear to be stand-alone operations in hotel lobbies. Hyatt has launched an in-house concept called Sarah's Pantry, and Hilton has introduced Intermezzo. Both concepts are designed to have an identity separate from the hotel and to service guests on the run and local traffic looking for quick service.

Foodservice companies are also jumping on the in-house branding bandwagon. Companies like Aramark have introduced their own set of brands. These are typically interspersed with franchised units in food court settings. The idea of outsourcing leaves rich opportunity for entrepreneurial thinking. What other functions are likely to be outsourced? What innovative vendor services could add bottom-line profits to hospitality companies?

An ITT Sheraton Strategy Story

Big strategies can grow from small, unplanned beginnings. In its early days of property diversification, ITT Sheraton bought its first residential hotel inadvertently. Temporarily stranded in the doorway of a downtown real estate broker's office, during a thunderstorm, Sheraton's cofounder chanced upon an auction in progress. Upon hearing the auctioneer describe the property as a "steal" for anyone experienced in the development of commercial real estate, ITT Sheraton's cofounder, in an unguarded moment, bid a low figure "just to pass the time of day during the rainstorm." Alas, there were no other bids. Sheraton's bid prevailed, and the buyer was astonished to discover that what he had purchased was not an office building, as he had assumed, but was instead a residential hotel! Thereafter, during the decades of the 1950s and 1960s, top management at ITT Sheraton Corporation let it be known that company growth was being driven not by shopping for bargains at real estate auctions but rather by an overall corporate strategy—the formulation of which remained the private province of the company founder/president. ITT Sheraton's strategy continues to unfold in the 1990s.

Sheraton has turned its strategic focus to gaming, expanding internationally, strengthening its brands, and restructuring management. To establish a place in the fast growing North American gaming segment, it has purchased several gaming operations including casino hotels and riverboats in the United States and Canada. To strengthen its position overseas, it has purchased controlling interest of a European-based chain of luxury hotels, CIGA SpA, and plans extensive expansion in Asia. In its franchise division, ITT Sheraton "deflagged," that is, it took away the franchise rights from many hotels that did not fit the new quality standards. In July 1995, it introduced a new midscale brand of hotels called Four Points Hotels. Sheraton's newest management structure will center around individual business units, where different departments within a hotel will function as individual businesses. By using this structure, the company hopes to eliminate layers of supervision and to be able to measure the performance of its employees.

A major strategic decision on the part of ITT Sheraton's parent corporation, ITT Corporation, profoundly changed the future of Sheraton. Beginning in 1995, ITT Corporation spun off its businesses and created three separately owned public companies. ITT Lodging, Entertainment and Gaming is one of the three new corporations. It includes ITT Sheraton, Caesar's World, CIGA, and ITT's interest in Madison Square Garden. The new name itself suggests the strategic plan for the future.

Forming Strategic Alliances to Create Competitive Advantage

The concept of a strategic alliance or value managed relationship is about synergy. Two partners get together, and both are theoretically better off as a result of the alliance. History has demonstrated numerous alliances among hospitality businesses, not all of them successful. The story of Allegis is one of the greatest failures. At one time, Westin Hotels, Hertz Rent-A-Car, and United Airlines were part of the same company, Allegis. Though it seemed logical at first that a traveler could be helped by one-stop shopping, the three companies were in fundamentally different businesses and didn't bring together the expected synergistic benefits. Other alliances have a proven track record, such as independent hotels aligning together in a referral groups to create marketing advantage.

Some new relationships, such as marketing alliances, hotel-restaurant teams, frequent guest, referral, and goodwill alliances, have recently emerged. Some are entirely new; others have shades of history imbedded in them. Which will be successful remains to be seen, but it is clear that a wave of alliances is part of doing business in the nineties.

Marketing Alliances In an effort to lure large groups to a particular city, some hotels, that are in fact direct competitors to one another are joining together in marketing alliances to sell their entire city. The idea behind this is to make a joint effort to capture large conventions that need thousands of rooms. For example, all of the hotels in downtown Cleveland may get together and target a large technology convention that could only be accommodated by multiple hotels' rooms.

Another kind of marketing alliance is captured in InterContinental's launch of Global Partners Hotels and Resorts. InterContinental is seeking to add affiliate hotels with properties in markets where it does not have hotels. Members receive the kinds of benefits traditionally associated with referral groups, such as media buying power and an 800 number reservations line. It effectively allows an independent hotel to be marketed with the hotels that are members of the chain. InterContinental benefits because it expands the number of places where its customers can be served.

Hotel-Restaurant Teams Though hotels and restaurants have been located next to each other historically, especially in the economy lodging segment of the market, more formalized relationships are occurring and in additional market segments. Holiday Inn, for example, has formed an alliance with Perkins Family Restaurants. The restaurants are located next to and sometimes within the Holiday Inns. In the more upscale market, California Pizza Kitchens will be debuting in Westin Hotels. Other examples abound. Chain restaurants such as Bob Evans Farms, Bonanza, Ponderosa, and Bennigan's have also formed alliances with various hotel companies.

Frequent Guest–Frequent Flyer Programs The idea of rewarding frequent customers with benefits began with the introduction of frequent flyer programs in the airline industry. The concept spread to hotel chains in the form of frequent guest programs. In these programs, guests are awarded points for dollars spent during their hotel stays. As more and more companies create these programs, the competitive advantage of having one declines. Thus keeping the points or miles to be more valuable currency has meant creating more flexibility for guests to use them. Different options for point redemption have emerged, among them travel packages, in which currency is redeemed for air travel, hotel stays, and rental cars. Thus partnerships across these industries are desirable. Many alliances have been formed, and more are continuing to form. For example, Marriott recently announced an alignment with United. It joins Westin, Sheraton, Hilton, and Hyatt, which are already partners.

Retail Alliances Restaurants have recently found new opportunities by aligning with other retail establishments. Restaurants have long been found near where people shop, ranging from food courts in shopping malls to outdoor stalls at country arts and crafts fairs. Some new alliances are taking hold. Among them is a relationship between convenience stores and fast food. Taco Bell, Subway, Blimpie, Wendy's, McDonald's, and Burger King are among the fast food chains that have opened or are opening in hundreds of locations in convenience stores across the country. The convenience stores are happy to have well-established systems for delivering food to customers. Fast food outlets are happy to have prime locations. As there are nearly 100,000 convenience stores across the country, this new point of distribution has expansion potential.[12]

Another restaurant-retail alliance with national potential is a take-out food concept called Harry's In a Hurry. The Atlanta-based food retailer is being tested in Wal-Mart department stores. Though department stores have had food outlets in the past, the magnitude of this venture speaks to the power of chain organizations in many different industries besides hospitality. Are there other nonhospitality chains that are ripe for inclusion of a restaurant concept? Which alliances will be synergistic? What potential new alliances might be available to hospitality companies?

Goodwill Alliances There are companies that in the course of doing business don't lose sight of making a contribution to the communities in which they live. Many companies and organizations are seeking to make a difference in helping the less fortunate. The National Service Act, a federal bill that has given momentum to many service organizations in the 1990s, is representative of a renewed call for action.

The hospitality business, by virtue of what it does, are aptly suited to assist in efforts to feed and house the homeless. Numerous restaurants across the country donate leftover food to organizations like Project Bread. In numerous cities like Providence and Boston, restaurateurs band together for fund-raising events. Local chefs provide food and talent for preparing it in gala festivities to raise money for charity.

Marriott's Fairfield Inns division has announced a national affiliation with Habitat for Humanity. This organization works with the private sector to help provide homes for families in need. With the opening of its 200th hotel in Austin, Texas, Fairfield announced it will work with Habitat in all markets where Fairfields are developed. In Austin, employees of the hotel and corporate representatives will participate in the building of homes.

Adopting Technology to Increase Revenue and Decrease Costs

Technology's rapid advancement has had and will continue to have a profound influence on the hospitality business. It has influenced the package of services and products that are offered, allowing for new amenities for guests. It has reshaped the way hotels and restaurants are operated, and it has created a whole new set of communication vehicles. These changes, when effectively applied, can increase revenues or decrease costs, creating competitive advantage for those companies that keep the pace.

The Net Just as the evolution of new types of transportation has had powerful influence on the hospitality industry, so too will the evolution of the information superhighway, the Net. Though it doesn't physically move people, it gives them the capability to go places. Consider, for example, 3D technology. The concept of a 3D restaurant visit via the Internet is under development by the Sony corporation and restaurateur Barry Wine.[13] The imaginary web site metropolis, called Restaurant City, will allow a browser to choose a city, choose a restaurant, then tour the dining room and even the kitchen. Menus, restaurant reviews, and recipes will also be available. Chat rooms for restaurateurs, culinary stores, and information on food will also be part of the City.

Travelers can make a quantum leap in the kinds of information they can gather without using a third party. The Internet links customers directly to hospitality service providers. Graphics, photos, audio, and visual brochures for hotels are now available. Imagine being able to walk through a lobby and hotel rooms and feel the atmosphere visually. The Internet allows customers to book worldwide travel on airlines and increasingly to book hotel rooms. Currently 100 percent of air travel is booked electronically, compared to 25 percent of hotel rooms, which are typically booked through the airline systems.[14] You can access train schedules abroad, reserve a rental car, view a restaurant menu, or even order a pizza from Pizza Hut without ever leaving your desk chair.

How popular are on-line booking services verses traditional approaches? In one 1994 study by the US Travel Data Center, about 70 percent of adults were found to have used a travel agent to make trip arrangements and about 8 percent had used on-line services. In the 18-to-24 age group, though, the gap had tightened considerably. About 50 percent had used a travel agent, and 17 percent had used on-line services.[15]

In the not too distant future, will most hotels have the capability to receive Internet reservations? Will restaurants have the same service for dinner reservations? Will the nature of travel agencies as we know them today be dramatically different?

While there are many advantages to these on-line services, there is cause for caution. Making reservations on the Internet signals that the traveler will be away from home. Transmitting credit card numbers also raises security issues. What if computer hackers can inappropriately access the system and cancel reservations? The high-tech approach also removes the high-touch component of hospitality. Will some find electronic communication too impersonal a way to plan a family vacation?

Job seekers will find that the Internet provides an efficient clearinghouse for job opportunities. More and more companies are listing jobs. Will it be that students graduating from hotel and restaurant management schools will surf the Net as their first career stop?

Technology Means New Amenities As technology increasingly facilitates consumers' daily lives, both at home and at work, they look for the same advantages while traveling. Some hotel rooms now offer fax machines, two-line telephones, voice mail, laptop computers, and in-room computer games as in-room amenities. Besides offering the latest Nintendo games, so-called **smart TVs** allow guests to access "Places to Eat" and "Things to See and Do," and even print maps of the local area via compact disc interactive software such as Info Travel Video Guide.

Business centers within hotels are also offering increasing services as technological applications become more cost effective. Videoconferencing is one such service. Though the idea is not new, the ease of implementation, cost, and quality have all improved, making some hotels take a closer look. Some hotel chains like Hyatt are using the technology to bring famous speakers to their hotels for seminars. Will there be a market for room-to-room private videoconferencing via computers and TV screens?

The restaurant business has also found a new service to offer its patrons: computer terminals. Cyberia, for example, a coffee shop off London's Tottenham Court Road, is serving up coffee and chips. Patrons can check their electronic mail while munching. Two and a half English pounds (about four U.S. dollars) buys 30 minutes of on-line time. The owners, one of whom serves as the technical director, has plans to launch 27 franchises across the globe. Will we begin to think of terminals in restaurants and hotel lobbies as being commonplace as telephones? Airlines, too, have added technology-driven amenities. For example, Virgin Airways offers a TV screen with multiple channels at every seat. In-seat video poker and other gaming choices are also in the wave of the future.

Technology in Operations Though technology in and of itself is a very impersonal thing, it has allowed hotels and restaurants to do some things in a more personal way in their operations. There has been increasing sophistication in managing databases: identifying and selling to potential customers, and tracking and satisfying frequent guests. The ability to keep accurate, user-friendly guest profiles that can be accessed by any hotel in a chain allows a front desk clerk in Seattle to know that the guest he is checking in requested an extra pillow last week in Minneapolis. Will profiles of all guests become standard fare for competitive hotel chains?

Advertising and marketing approaches are also using new vehicles: interactive kiosks, the Internet, and on-line services provided by the hospitality company. Hotel directories and brochures may be supplemented or replaced by **Web pages**, that part of the Internet that allows customers to download and print information. Travel Web, whose address is www.travelweb.com., is one such service.

For convention hotels, meeting planners may no longer receive the traditional meeting planning packet. Computer software programs are now available that allow them to access layouts, seating capacity, and sizes of meeting rooms and prefunction areas. The near future is also likely to add virtual setups of meeting rooms. That is, a meeting room can be set up on screen and viewed in three dimensions, with the click of a button. Cruises, charter yachts, casinos, and a whole host of other hospitality providers may find themselves giving virtual reality tours as part of their marketing approach.

Hoteliers can also access information via on-line **electronic bulletin board systems (BBS)**. HotelNet, for example, offers a way for hotel operators to exchange information, access **share ware**, which is software that the user pays for on an honor system basis, or sample spreadsheet templates related to the business. It's also a site to post a résumé or a job opening, or to have a conversation with an operator in another part of the world.

For managing the inventory of rooms, yield management takes on new meaning, given the capabilities that technology can provide. Central reservations systems can have two-way real time interaction with individual property management systems and with a global distribution system—anyone on-line can access the reservation system.

Technology has not only changed the service part of hospitality, but the product part as well. Not unlike the earlier impact of canning or of frozen food, vacuum sealing is changing the way food is prepared and stored. The "sous vide" technology yields shelf-stable portions of even complicated recipes, which can be prepared quickly with only a microwave. Could this technology create a kitchenless, chefless restaurant?

In food preparation, advances in robotics have stepped well beyond what a Cuisenart can do. Taco Bell, for example, has pioneered taco-making robots, which never call in sick, make fewer mistakes, and work much faster than their human counterparts. Hotel companies have experimented with robotic housekeepers, which handle a vacuum cleaner quite nicely. What's next?

Responding to Special Populations

The nature of the purest form of hospitality extends itself to all guests, especially those with special needs. Responding in a thoughtful and responsible manner makes good business sense. Not responding can be illegal, and can cause great harm to individuals and to organizations.

Americans with Disabilities Act (ADA) With the passage of the American's With Disabilities Act in 1990, a wide-ranging list of populations with disabilities became protected. This affected several facets of business operations in the United States. For hospitality businesses, laws were established that affect both employees and guests. To accommodate disabled guests, the law affects physical access and dictates the way guests are treated. The act also gives disabled guests legal grounds for suing hotels that don't comply. Noncompliers are losing lawsuits in greater numbers. Failure to make appropriate accommodations is an increasingly riskier business.

Making disabled guests feel welcome goes beyond the required physical elements, which include facilities such as handicap parking, accessible restaurants, and mobility in and around guest rooms, bathrooms, and entrances. The hospitality service must also be hospitable, not just accessible. To this end, training front line employees to interact with disabled guests, who might have, for example, vision, mobility, or hearing impairments, is critical. Some hotel chains effectively use role playing to dispel myths and create sensitivity. For example, it is important to understand when a guest does and doesn't need extra help. Achieving a hospitable welcome, for example, means creating an environment that doesn't shout out the differences provided for special needs guests. There is opportunity for ideas that cost effectively comply with ADA requirements but don't compromise design. Getting physical features to blend in is important for all guests. In a guest room, for example, features need to benefit the disabled guest but not make the regular guest feel he is in a special-class room.[16]

Acquired Immune Deficiency Syndrome (AIDS) Working with and serving people with AIDS is one of the most difficult issues facing hospitality companies today, particularly in the food-service sector. Many people are troubled that food handlers with AIDS could transmit the disease, despite the fact that scientific research overwhelmingly dictates otherwise. The law supports the scientific evidence. Persons with AIDS applying for food handling positions cannot be discriminated against because they have AIDS. This population is covered by the ADA.

AIDS is a widespread problem. The Atlanta Center for Disease Control estimates that 10 percent of all small companies and 75 percent of large companies employ at least one person with AIDS.[17] One major foodservice company, Daka, found in interviewing its employees that AIDS was the biggest concern in terms of people's welfare.[18] Despite the concern and the growing numbers of persons with AIDS, most companies are not addressing the problem proactively, but rather are reacting on a case-by-case basis.

There are, however, some models of proactivity that have been launched. Marriott, for example, introduced "Breaking Down Barriers" in 1991 to dispel myths about AIDS and to teach managers how to make accommodations for workers with AIDS. In companies where the issue is addressed, employees have been found to be more secure in their jobs and better performers. Further, the likelihood of discrimination lawsuits is reduced. Though it will not eliminate the disease more quickly, courageous dialogue about the subject can create a more effective workplace.

Identifying New Market Niches

By scanning the environment to identify new services and new markets, a company can be on its way to defining a strategy. At the heart of breakthrough performance in the service business, researchers have found that such breakthroughs for the most part are attributable to finding a strategic service vision, and identifying a target market or market niche that highly values the service.[19]

Chief executive officers of 15 major service firms, including Marriott and McDonald's, demonstrated a spectacular accord on what it takes to differentiate breakthrough service firms from their competitors. Along with overriding concern for results, distinctive benchmarks of their strategic service vision show that breakthrough companies:

   a. target market segments by focusing on how customers think and behave, instead of demographics.

   b. instead of a service delivery system's being viewed as a facility where the service is produced and sold, it is seen primarily as an opportunity to enhance the quality of the service.

If consumer thought and behavior is in fact a keystone to identifying new market niches, successful companies will note changes in consumers' attitude toward their health, toward how they use their work and leisure time, what they care about, and how their lifestyles have changed what they demand. Here is a limited sampling of potential evolving market niches:

The Nonsmoker Fewer people in the United States are smoking, and more are becoming uncomfortable about being in smoking environments. In some communities smoking has been banned in public places. Many hotels and restaurants have responded, either by law or by choice. Many hotel companies offer nonsmoking rooms, restaurants have a segregated (if at all available!) section for smokers, and car rental companies offer no-smoking cars. One hotel chain (though it has only two properties, it is technically a chain), La Suite, includes the international no-smoking symbol on its logo and claims to be the first nonsmoking chain.

The Health Conscious Consumer Nonsmoking is only the beginning for so called "green roomers." This new health conscious audience has found the availability of rooms equipped with water and air filtration systems, biodegradable soaps, 100 percent recycled paper goods, and organic cotton sheets and towels. Customers are willing to pay a premium for the services. Health conscious customers are also becoming more demanding in terms of the nutritional content they find acceptable in restaurant offerings. Many restaurants, hotels, and airlines have responded to customer demand for special dietary requests, alternatives to alcoholic drinks, and lighter menus.

Twenty-Somethings That group of consumers born after the baby boom generation, currently in their 20s, have been characterized as self-reliant, cynical, leisure oriented, and technologically savvy. As they come of age and become an increasingly important market for the hospitality industry, it is likely that reaching them will require different approaches than were needed for their parents. In particular, they will likely respond to technology based distribution methods.[20]

Dual Career Couples—and Their Kids The phenomenon of increasing numbers of women working has given rise to dual career couples and their children as an important target market. Dual career couples tend to have higher disposable incomes and to travel more with their children. Look no further than Camp Hyatt, an extensive children's program offered at many Hyatt properties, and other programs like it that are very much integrated into hotel operations, and not just at resorts. As dual career couples increasingly combine business and leisure trips or take short getaways to a greater variety of destinations, kids are part of their travel plans.

The Aging Population The over-55 population is growing larger and controlling more disposable income. They have more time and more money to travel. Aging travelers are also more sophisticated and more demanding. As this audience gets larger, there will emerge subtargets within it. A niche strategy that focuses on one or more subsets presents opportunities for hospitality providers. There is also opportunity in crossing over to the health care sector, as companies like Marriott and Hyatt have already done, in establishing health care/senior living facilities.

The list of potential target markets is hardly exhaustive. By definition, as customer service becomes more niche oriented, the number of categories of customers will grow. The important learning is that companies will have to become increasingly focused and sophisticated in identifying customer niches and in serving them well. Companies will have to create a position that offers perceived benefits to customers and that distinguishes them from the competition.

Embracing Diversity

An important segment of the U.S. population, 25 percent, is now composed of minorities. That percentage is expected to more than double by the year 2050.[21] Designating the United States as a melting pot of cultures has never been truer. This presents opportunities for multicultural employment in the workplace and for catering to diversity among consumer populations.

Diversity in the Workplace Managing diversity in the workplace begins with designing jobs and training programs to assimilate persons from many backgrounds. If this is done properly, an organization can create value and access a broader pool of candidates to fill job openings. Diversity in its broadest definition can be said to encompass differences in age, tenure in an organization, educational background, sexual orientation or preference, physical abilities or qualities, social status, economic status, lifestyle, religion, ethnicity, and gender, among many other characteristics.[22]

As diversity is increasing on both sides of the front desk or host stand, those companies that are embracing diverse populations in their hiring practices can reap competitive advantage. A recent experience of the Sheraton Hotel and Towers in Chicago illustrates the point. The hotel played host to the international audience attracted by the World Cup soccer tournament. The hotel staff was qualified, in total, to speak 60 languages! Not only did Sheraton place value on its employees' differences, the hotel also thoughtfully assessed the English language skills needed for each job. One of its first steps in empowering employees to better serve guests and to improve job performance was language training. Today, several hotel operators around the country have launched English as a second language programs.

Incorporating diversity is not always easy and may create culture clashes within the organization. This necessitates ongoing training and sometimes sacrifice. One Indian woman who owns a Comfort Inn and a Howard Johnson in Columbus, Ohio, noted that she stopped greeting guests at her hotel in her traditional dress. She adopted Western-style clothing after realizing some Americans didn't like encountering a foreign appearance.[23] Other hotels have been able to capitalize on their diverse employees by attracting guests who were supportive of their approach.

Multiculturalism A new wave of tourism programs focuses on encouraging one ethnic group to learn about another (cross-culturalism) and to promote visits to attractions that have historical or cultural significance to African Americans, Asian Americans, Hispanic Americans, and Native Americans. Local tourism boards are pitching in, and the US Travel and Tourism Association is looking to bring both domestic and international tourists to previously undermarketed points of interest.

Such marketing efforts include bringing Arab travelers to Detroit (which has more Arab residents than any other city besides Baghdad) and convincing European and Japanese travelers to visit Harlem and Chinatown in New York City, in addition to more traditional attractions. Atlanta and Philadelphia are targeting African American travelers to visit attractions that were important in African American history.[24] What kinds of attractions are likely to succeed in selling diversity? What other multicultural opportunities to expand tourism will unfold?

Summary

It's a tough job, predicting the future. Understanding the difference between strategic planning, the act of articulating a current business plan, and strategic thinking—the act of combining intuition, creativity, and vision—is critical to success. Those that can think strategically can have the power to change an industry. As you look back at the history of the hospitality industry, how often do you marvel "How did they think of that?" As we scan the environment, we see responding to increased concern for the environment, global branding, outsourcing, strategic alliances, increased use of technology, responding to special populations, identifying new market niches, and embracing diversity as just some of the areas where changes are occurring.

Some of these areas have uncovered ideas that are older, undergoing new evolutions; others are newer ideas. Understanding how each is changing can lead to the development of a strategy for success. These changes include innovations that have changed the hospitality landscape, and will affect how we move forward to the next century.

The nature of predicting future trends raises more questions than it answers. Raising these questions, as we have done here in this chapter, however, as well as reviewing past history and monitoring current happenings, can identify the strategic directions in which companies are heading. Some patterns have already launched new companies, new services, and new ways of doing business. There are insights, however, that are showing themselves today only as glimmering "what-can-be"s. As you prepare to enter into the world of hospitality, be on the lookout for what can be. Go. Scan. Create vision.

Discussion Questions

1. What is the difference between strategic planning and strategic thinking?

2. Why is strategic planning necessary and useful?

3. How has concern for the environment affected the future of hospitality companies? Give examples of your own experiences in hotels and restaurants.

4. Why are hospitality companies concerned with branding? How can brands create competitive advantage?

5. If you were CEO of a major hotel company, would you choose to expand into casino gaming in the United States? Internationally? Why or why not?

6. Can you predict the comfort food of the twenty-first century? Explain your answer.

7. Define *outsourcing*, in your own terms. What do we mean by *faux outsourcing*? Why did it develop? How are databases essential to outsourcing?

8. What is a strategic alliance? What elements need to be present in order for one to work? Look in a recent trade journal for examples of strategic alliances. Why do you think they were formed?

9. How do special customers affect the way hospitality companies do business? Why is it important to recognize these populations?

10. What is strategic service vision? How can it be identified? The chapter mentions several market niches. What others do you think will be important in the twenty-first century, and why?

11. In your own words, define diversity in the workplace and in the hospitality industry. Why is it important to recognize diversity in hospitality?

12. As noted by the Cheshire puss from Alice in Wonderland in the opening quotation, why is knowing where you want to go the most important part of developing a strategy?

Assignments

1. Go to your college student union or main cafeteria. What kind of food and beverage outlets are located there? Are your fellow students content with the offerings? How can you pay for your meals? Can you use your meal plan to purchase food in off-campus outlets? Would you like to? How about your friends at other schools? How do their options compare with yours? Why do you think there are differences?

    If you could design the college cafeteria of the twenty-first century, what would you include and why?

2. Log into the Internet, and find www.travelweb.com. What do you find? Is it helpful? What would you like to see included? Find another Web page from a hospitality company, and explain what it listed. Why do you think the company is using the Internet? Do you think it is creating competitive advantage? Why or why not?

End Notes

1. Lewis Carroll, *Alice in Wonderland* (Cutchogua, New York: Buccaneer Books, 1988), p. 102.

2. *Field Guide to Strategy* (Boston: Harvard Business School Press/The Economist Book Ltd., 1994), 3.

3. Gregory G. Dess and Alex Miller, *Strategic Management* (New York: McGraw-Hill, 1993), 321.

4. Michael Porter, "The Strategic Thinking," *Economist* (23 May 1987): 17.

5. Henry Mintzberg, "The Fall and Rise of Strategic Planning" [sic] *Harvard Business Review* (January–February 1994): 108.

6. Henry Mintzberg, *Mintzberg on Management* (New York: The Free Press, 1989), 121.

7. "How Green is Your Hotel," *In Business* (the magazine for environmental entrepreneuring) (December 1992): 38–39.

8. Susan Eardley, "WTTC Initiates Green Globe Program," *Hotel and Motel Management* (5 July 1995): 39.

9. Philip Hayward, "Disney Does the Environment," *Lodging* (March 1994): 46–58.

10. Ted Saunders, Environmental Program Director for the Boston Park Plaza, as quoted in "How Green is Your Hotel."

11. Suzanne Alexander, "Hungry Fast-Food Companies Invade College Eateries as Nutritionists Groan," *The Wall Street Journal*, 27 November 1990, B1.

12. Louise Kramer, "A Marriage of convenience: C-Stores Hitch Their Future to Fast Feeders," *Nations Restaurant News* (26 June 1995): 33.

13. Bryan Miller, "After the Quilted Giraffe, There's Sony and Cyberspace," *New York Times*, 24 May 1995, C3.

14. Tony Dela Cruz, "Fast Change Coming for Reservations Systems, PMS and Marketing," *Hotel Business* (7–20 July 1995): 13. Quotation is from John Biggs, chief operating officer of Regency Systems Solutions, the MIS unit for Hyatt Hotels.

15. "The Numbers News," March 1994, American Demographics, Inc.

16. Shannon McMullen, "ADA Upgrades: Hoteliers Rethink Approach," *Hotel Business* (21 March–6 April, 1995): 12.

17. Suzanne Kapner, "Cutting-edge Companies Taking Proactive Steps," *Nation's Restaurant News* 29 (14) (3 April 1995): 1.

18. Ibid.

19. James I. Heskett, W. Earl Sasser, Jr., and Christopher W. L. Hart, *Service Breakthroughs* (New York: The Free Press, 1990), 19.

20. Paula Francese, "Rising Stars in the Consumer Constellation: A Peer Personality Profile of the Post Baby Boom Generation," *Hospitality Research Journal* 17 (1) (1993).

21. Kathy Seal, "Clinton Officials Push Muticultural Tourism," *Hotel and Motel Management* (5 July 1994): 3.

22. Robert H. Woods and Michael P. Sciarini, "Diversity Programs in Chain Restaurants," *Cornell Quarterly* (June 1995): 19.

23. Richard Bruns, "Diversity: From Top Management to the Front Line, " *Lodging* (November 1994): 77.

24. Michael L. Pina, "Selling Diversity," *Lodging* (October 1994): 55–60.

Part Seven

For Students Only

This section of the book is composed of two different tools designed specifically for students entering the hospitality field. The first piece, chapter 18, is sequenced to facilitate a career search within the field of hospitality. Beginning with a self-assessment and proceeding to creating, evaluating, and executing an action plan, the chapter provides a road map for developing and excelling along a chosen career path. The chapter takes a hands-on approach, offering tactics and resources for corresponding, interviewing, and résumé writing.

The second element of the section is a master case, which explores the world of Disney. The case is a capstone to the book, challenging students to apply what they have learned from the entire text in tackling the case questions. In keeping with the theme of the book, the case is international in scope.

Chapter Eighteen

"Don't wait until March of your senior year and expect to get your dream job."

Eileen Grabowski [1]

Taking Your Place
in the World of
Hospitality ❧

Introduction:
The Hospitality Job Market

The hospitality job market is a promising one with a bright future. According to the Department of Labor, through the year 2005 the demand for hospitality managers will exceed the supply. The industry will also continue to be highly diversified and segmented. Each segment in the hospitality industry—lodging, foodservice, entertainment, travel distribution channels, and transportation—has numerous subsegments. For example, career opportunities in the lodging segment can be found in urban hotels, destination resorts, suburban motels, and many other classifications of lodging properties. There are opportunities to satisfy a diverse set of interests and abilities. (See Exhibit 18.1.)

Exhibit 18.1 Sample Hospitality Careers

Lodging	Foodservice	Travel Distribution Channels	Transportation	Entertainment
Conference/ Meeting Planner	Maître D'	Tourism Planner	Inflight Caterer	Club Manager
Multitask Guest Services Agent	Chef	Internet Web Site Writer	Tour Guide	Cruise Ship Activities Coordinator
Reservations Manager	Director of Restaurants	Travel Agent	Marketing Coordinator	Casino Manager

Each segment offers a variety of career choices ranging from sommelier and hotel manager to service consultant and tour operator. Each career path can lead to a promotion and advancement in the same subsegment or in related areas. Exhibit 18.1 provides a glimpse of the possibilities in each of the segments, followed by Table 18.1, which offers some representative salaries in the hospitality industry.

The hospitality industry strives to have professional and educated employees who can manage the multitude of challenges in the 1990s and the next era. Each career, as well as each property or company, will face its own challenges in reaction to the trends that will unfold. Your career could be affected by technological adaptation, diversity in the workplace, environmental issues, compliance with the Americans with Disabilities Act, increasingly sophisticated customers and owners, increased competition, and globalization, just to name a few concerns.

With the steady challenge to keep on top of the changes in the world you will rarely hear a hospitality professional claim to be bored. Who has time to be bored when an immediate need might involve developing training programs to address the volatile issue of sexual harassment? Or when a sales manager's current task is to guarantee that the block of rooms with an ocean view will be ready as promised to the meeting planner? For the front office manager, the entire front-of-the-house operation depends on timely check-ins. These are just some of the day-to-day issues hospitality managers will continue to face as we look toward the twenty-first century.

Table 18.1 Sample Hospitality Salaries (in 000s/thousands)

Hotels—Corporate	Low	Medium	High	Foodservice	Low	Medium	High
CFO	75	95	136	Regional Manager	41	49	61
Corporate Controller	44	58	74	District Manager	36	45	54
VP Operations	56	74	109	Foodservice Director	30	36	45
VP Sales & Marketing	53	74	103	Cafeteria Manager	25	31	43
Corp. F&B Director	46	64	91	Production Analyst	29	35	40
Corporate Chef	45	62	85	Unit Manager	24	33	45
Dir. of Development	48	60	76	Assistant Manager	20	25	30
Dir. of Construction	44	60	77				
Dir. of Human Resources	36	51	67	**Restaurant/Fast Food**			
Dir. of Purchasing	32	43	61	**Corporate**			
Regional Manager	42	55	71				
				Chief Operating Office	70	94	128
Hotels—Operations				Division Manager	60	76	97
				Regional Manager/VP	54	69	84
General Manager	40	57	81	Marketing Director (Chain)	42	55	80
Assistant Manager	28	40	50	Controller	40	47	55
Controller	32	42	52	Human Resources Director	34	43	56
Mgr. Human Resources	27	35	43	Training Director	31	37	44
Rooms Div. Manager	27	37	47	Purchasing Director	34	44	56
Front Office Manager	22	30	36	Real Estate Manager	39	49	63
Food & Beverage Director	31	44	61				
Restaurant Manager	23	31	38	**Operations**			
Maître d'	23	30	38				
Beverage Manager	26	30	36	Operations Director (Chain)	48	60	72
Banquet Manager	26	33	40	District Manager (Multiunit)	36	46	59

(Continued)

447

Table 18.1 Sample Hospitality Salaries (in 000s/thousand) (*Continued*)

Hotels—Operations	Low	Medium	High	Operations	Low	Medium	High
Director of Catering	25	34	48	General Manager (Fast Food)	26	32	39
Catering Sales	25	31	37	Assistant GM (Fast Food)	20	24	29
Executive Chef	30	45	58	General Manager (Nonliquor)	26	33	47
Sous-Chef	24	32	38	Assistant Manager (Nonliquor)	21	24	30
Pastry Chef	21	27	37	General Manager (w/Liquor)	30	36	54
Banquet Chef	20	26	31	Assistant Manager (w/ Liquor)	24	28	35
Director Sales & Marketing	29	36	51	Chef	27	33	43
Sales Manager	24	31	37	Sous-Chef	23	29	35
Conference Manager	26	29	34	Kitchen Manager	24	29	35
Executive Housekeeper	24	32	40	Pastry Chef	22	27	33
Assistant Housekeeper	15	23	31	Banquet Manager	23	28	34
Chief Engineer	22	30	40				
Guest Services Manager	23	31	36				
Motel Manager	24	30	37				
Motel Manager (Couples)	27	33	44				

Country Clubs (Golf)

	Low	Medium	High
Manager (500+ Members)	42	54	70
Manager (> 500 Members)	34	43	51
Clubhouse Manager	30	37	45
Athletic/City Club Manager	36	52	69

All salaries shown have been rounded to the nearest $1000
Source: Roth Young Recruiters

What's Ahead: Looking to the Twenty-First Century

We learned in chapter 5 that in 1994, the travel and tourism industry generated direct and indirect employment for more than 200 million people, or one of every nine workers worldwide. By the year 2005, the industry is projected to support almost 350 million jobs.[2] That's big business and good news for hospitality program graduates.

The worldwide growth in travel and tourism has been generated by two main factors. First, the leisure time and disposable income of many workers worldwide have increased since the beginning of the 1990s. Second, the progress of peace in the world has enabled tourists to travel in regions that were once considered dangerous. The peace progress in the Middle East, the new South Africa, the ongoing dialogue in Northern Ireland, and the opening of the People's Republic of China are only a few examples of areas and countries that have enjoyed increased numbers of tourists recently. As a growth industry, the hospitality industry will be able to offer a vast variety of career paths. The demand for professional and educated employees, associates, and managers will continue to increase across many segments, making available many exciting opportunities as you launch your career.

Finding the Right Job Ingredients for Success

Your job search begins here! To help you with the search process, this section will provide you with an organized approach to career exploration and research. It is designed as a guide to help you locate potential job resources. You will find, in detail, people, places, and materials available to you that will be useful in your search. This section also provides ways for you to assess your skills, investigate potential career opportunities, and prepare for your job search. You don't have to do this alone! There are many resources available to help you ultimately realize your career goals.

Defining Your Goals and Interests—A Self-Assessment

Considering the vast size of the hospitality industry and the bountiful opportunities it offers, perhaps the most challenging task at hand is determining which segment of the industry to choose, and then determining the best type of job that will match your skills and personality. The challenge lies in the process of narrowing the possibilities to those which maximize your personal potential and best suit you as a career. While this sounds simple, it can involve a significant amount of soul-searching and learning how to realistically evaluate your skill set.

Where Am I Heading? The stages involved in finding the right path depend on your interests and your abilities, both of which are important. For example, it is unrealistic to enter the casino segment of the industry if you are morally opposed to legalized gambling. Likewise, it would be unproductive and dissatisfying to enter into accounting if working with numbers is not your forte. The career matrix in Exhibit 18.2 will help you evaluate these two dimensions of your career.

███████ *Exhibit 18.2* Career Matrix

	High Interest in Job	Low Interest in Job
Strong ability to perform job	A great career fit.	Potential stepping stone to job with more interest. Evaluate what you can change in the work environment.
Weak ability to perform job	Potential to learn job skill set. Evaluate training needed.	Not a good fit.

To undertake an analysis of your interests and abilities, ask yourself many questions: "What kind of organization suits me? Large or small? Stable or changing?" "What do I want in a job? Security? The fast track? Achievement? Power? To be part of a team?" "Would I prefer a front-of-the-house or back-of-the-house position?" "What segment(s) interest me?"

Once you identify what interests you most, you will find it easier to narrow down the wealth of opportunities. Be realistic in your timetable. If your goal is to be the general manager of a hotel, consider for now the best first step. Perhaps this would be a job at the front desk, in housekeeping, or at the concierge desk, to learn the ropes.

Consider your first job in the industry as practice and not as a career-defining position. A career is constantly evolving, and experience along the way will help you to evaluate your interests and abilities continually. Work during the summer or part-time during school to explore as many areas as possible. Try alternating departments in a hotel. Work at the front desk to experience what it is like when a guest's room is not ready. Work in housekeeping to learn the importance of turning over a room so a guest can check in quickly. Try your hand at managing the flow of the restaurant and experiencing the challenge of accommodating a party of 10 in a fully booked dining room. Experience the feeling of a banquet hall overflowing with guests at an event you helped to plan. Pore over a guests' group folio to answer questions about a specific charge. Work in engineering when the electricity fails and the hotel is 100 percent occupied. It is important to remember that the hospitality industry, just like other industries, has glamorous and nonglamorous moments.

Who Am I—And What Do I Have to Offer? Each person's skill set is different. Some people are great at solving problems, while others prefer executing solutions. A payroll manager thrives at the desk all day knee-deep in paperwork, while a restaurant manager is constantly interacting with guests on a regular basis. Reservations agents interact with guests over the telephone and need to be particularly adept at perceiving guests' needs according to their voices, while front desk agents must be conscious of personal appearance. A marketer flourishes when under pressure to create a new campaign, while a salesperson is more capable of selling the idea than creating it.

When searching for the job that is right for you, think about that extra "umph" that you would bring to a job that no one else would bring. Do you have an innate knack for solving computer problems quickly and efficiently? Are you particularly effective at figuring out statistical information? Do you find that you are good at solving other people's problems? Are you a natural leader? Are you effective working in a team? Are you organized? Do you thrive on chaos? Some additional questions to ask yourself include:

- What do I enjoy? What inspires me or motivates me?
- What are my strengths and weaknesses? Why do I want this work?
- What do other people think of me? Am I a leader?
- How would I describe myself? Tolerant? Energetic? Direct? Honest?
- Do I lose confidence when I make a mistake? Am I objective?
- Do I compromise my values and integrity, or do I stand up for what I believe?
- What have I accomplished? How do these accomplishments relate to my career goals?

Once you think about and answer these questions, you can move into the next step; creating a career plan.

Creating, Evaluating, and Executing Your Action Plan

Your answers to the above questions will help you draw a picture of your future, which is a very helpful tool. Not only does it help you put your search into perspective, it will also make the whole process seem less daunting. The sooner you start your action plan, the better your chances are of finding something that is right for you.

Creating an Action Plan An action plan is a strategic plan, a way of getting from point A to point B. There is no better time to start your job search than right now. Exploring the chart in Exhibit 18.3 will help you organize your career search while you are still in school. It is meant as a general guideline to activities, and each student's progression will be different.

Your career search begins early on in your freshman year. Keep in mind that recruiters will interested in many things about you, not just your grades or your work experiences. College and community activities are an important part of your career development, for they show that you have outside interests and goals. Joining industry associations while you are in college will also help you make connections to the hospitality industry. Check out the activities at your school, and see what interests you.

Informational Interviewing One way to learn about careers in the hospitality industry is by reading some of volumes of books and periodicals on possible careers. This is one productive way to narrow down your choices. However, a more productive and interactive way to stay up to date on what's hot in different areas of the hospitality industry is to speak with professionals themselves. The best people to provide you with the pulse of the field you are interested in are those who are currently there. By speaking to people in the field, you will develop a network of people who can provide information and possibly a job opportunity. It is essential to make contacts and maintain them throughout your college career and beyond.

Informational interviewing is a useful networking tool for two very important reasons. It is perhaps the most productive way to gain contacts for future employment and to learn about specific jobs. There is no commitment of employment involved in an informational interview. It is simply an

Exhibit 18.3 Sample Timeline of Career Activities

Freshman Year Fall	Sophomore Year Fall	Junior Year Fall	Senior Year Fall
Investigate career services at your school.	Meet with your faculty advisor about career paths and update your résumé.	Update your résumé, adding most recent positions.	See your career services counselor and your faculty advisor for critique of your updated résumé.
Join student activities, to enhance your college experiences as well as your résumé.	See your career services counselor for help with your updated résumé.	See your career services counselor and your faculty advisor for critique of your updated résumé.	Identify companies you want to work for; compile names, titles, and addresses of potential contacts.
Start thinking about a job for next summer.	Ask your faculty advisor to critique your résumé.	Start identifying industry professionals for informational interviews.	Do company research, and write to contact list requesting advice and informational interviews.
Start your résumé over winter break.	If you are thinking of studying abroad, start investigating your options.		Start to set up interviews, both on and off campus.

Freshman Year Spring	Sophomore Year Spring	Junior Year Spring	Senior Year Spring
Work on your résumé with college career counselor.	Attend as many career fairs as you can, to see how they run.	Set up informational interviews. Remember to write thank-you letters.	Continue to set up interviews; remember thank-you letters.
Apply for summer positions.	Apply for summer positions.	Attend career fairs, and set up summer position	Identify career fairs you want to attend.
			Keep on interviewing.

(Continued)

Exhibit 18.3 (*Continued*)

Freshman Year Summer	Sophomore Year Summer	Junior Year Summer	Senior Year Summer
Complete work experience. Remember to keep in contact with those you meet at work.	Complete work experience. Remember to keep in contact with those you meet at work.	Complete work experience. Contact previous managers, to let them know you'll be graduating this year.	Enjoy commencement and your new job!

opportunity to gather information on the life of a front office manager, controller, corporate trainer, service consultant, or any other career of interest. Whatever job interests you, there is most likely someone out there who already does it and is willing to share their experience.

There is homework involved in informational interviewing. You need to be able to ask educated questions so that you can learn about the major responsibilities of various positions. Think of an informational interview as a springboard to jump over four major hurdles:

Hurdle No. 1. **To gather information about certain positions**.
You will meet with people who will share with you the kind of work they do and the challenges they face.

Hurdle No. 2. **To determine exactly where you want to work**.
By visiting a number of environments in the industry, you will find some that are more comfortable than others. By ruling out those that are not comfortable, you'll come closer to discovering the right environment for you.

Hurdle No. 3. **To become more comfortable with the interview process**.
It will help you become adept at interviewing techniques when you are applying for a specific job.

Hurdle No. 4. **To distinguish yourself from others in this market**.
You will walk away from your informational interviews with a competitive advantage over other people who have not learned some of the ins and outs of the company. The preparation that you do in advance will allow you to ask insightful questions.

Most anyone can be a source of information: friends, family, faculty, current and former employers, alumni, professional association members, and so on. The whole purpose of an informational interview is to ask questions and get answers. Here are some suggested questions to ask:

- How did you get involved in this field?
- How does your job fit into the big picture of the organization?
- What are your major responsibilities?
- What kinds of challenges/critical issues do you face?
- What do find most satisfying in your job? Most frustrating?
- How did you prepare yourself for the work you do?
- How is performance evaluated in this field?
- How much interaction with other people is involved?
- What social or other obligations, outside of business hours, go along with this job?
- What do you do in a typical day?
- What kinds of problems do you face?
- What skills or abilities do you find important in your work?
- How much flexibility does a person have regarding self-expression, or decision-making?
- How much work-related travel is required?
- What are the chances of relocation?
- How many hours per week do you work, on average?
- Is there seasonal pressure?

- What sort of changes are occurring in your field?

- What is the employment outlook in your area?

- What attributes do you seek in employees?

- How would you advise a person like me to prepare for a career in this field?

- What type of education is required? Training? Experience?

- Is there a definite career path in your field/organization? Can you describe it?

- Do you belong to any professional organizations?

- Can you suggest anyone else for me to contact for additional information?

Let's assume that some of what you learned while gathering this information interested you. You now have a contact in that company, and if you left a strong positive impression (which, since you did your homework, you certainly did), you have increased your chances of getting an interview with the company if the right position becomes available. This could eventually lead to a job with that company. Now that you know the advantages of the informational interview, there is no doubt that you are eager to start! There are many methods to begin the process.

Resources: Where to Go for Information

You have to invest time in collecting information for your job search. The collection process can vary, but know that there are many places to go for help.

Your First Stop: On Campus Resources Every college in the country has at least some, if not all, of these resources available to students. Your task is to make use of them.

- **Campus Career Center**. Visit your school's career center, where you will find information on everything ranging from what companies are out there to how to prepare for an interview. Make an appointment with a career counselor to guide you through the process and to show you what is available.

- **Job Postings**. Companies will typically contact colleges and universities in their area and beyond to post positions on a regular basis. Check the listing every week for positions that interest you.

- **Career Seminars**. Look for seminars and workshops on interviewing, résumé writing, and other topics available to students.

- **Library**. You will soon find that the library will become a valuable resource. This is where you will find business directories and reference books for job placement. You will also find books on résumé writing, interviewing, and other job skills. Ask the library staff for information on a specific company in which you are interested. Your library should have information on the companies that come to recruit on your campus. You will be able to obtain information from the periodicals, newspapers, and employment newsletters to which your library most likely subscribes.

- **Faculty Members and Alumni**. The faculty at your school has a direct link to the industry and is a valuable resource in your job search. Perhaps one of your professors has experience or contacts at a company in which you are interested. Also, use an alumni listing to contact alumni for summer or permanent job information.

- **Other Students**. Many students, particularly in the upper classes, have already gained worthwhile experiences that they will readily share. You may also want to join student organizations that give you exposure to other students as well as industry professionals.

Your Second Stop: Books and Directories   Read and take notes. The following list of books has been recommended. Don't wait until your senior year to try to read all of them; they should be used as a source of information about careers throughout college.

What Color Is Your Parachute? by Richard Nelson Bolles
This is an extremely helpful guide to job hunting, self-assessment, and career planning. Bolles's other books include *The Three Boxes of Life, Where Do I Go from Here with My Life?,* and *The New Quick Job-Hunting Map.*

Bernard Haldane Associate's Job and Career Building by R. German and P. Arnold
Coming Alive From 9–5 by Betty Neville Michelozzi
Blue Chip Graduate by Osher and Campbell
The Resume Catalog: 200 Damn Good Examples by Yana Parker
The Resume Handbook by David Hizer and Arthur Rosenberg
The Overnight Resume by Donald Asher
Does Your Resume Wear Bluejeans? by C. Edward Good
The American Almanac of Jobs and Salaries
Directory of New England Manufacturers
Employment Opportunities Directory
Encyclopedia of Associations
Standard and Poors' Register of Corporations
Bond's Source Book of Franchise Opportunities
The Food Service Operator's Guide
The Hotel and Motel Red Book
The White Book of Ski Resorts
The Restaurant Operator's Report by the National Restaurant Association
The National Directory of Addresses and Telephone Numbers
The National Trade and Professional Associations Directory (lists professional associations and contains a subject index as well as an alphabetical list of organizations)
Directory of American Firms Operating in Foreign Countries
Ernst & Young Resource Guide to Global Markets
International Jobs—Where They Are and How to Get Them by Eric Kochner
Dun's Career Guide
Dun's Employment Opportunities Directory
Dun's Million Dollar Directory (basic information on over 160,000 companies)
Your Job—Where to Find It, How to Get It by Leonard Cowen
The Job Bank Series (detailed information of employers in specific regions; includes Atlanta, Dallas, Phoenix, Metro New York, San Francisco, Seattle, Boston)

Your Third Stop: Resources Off Campus   Don't limit your search to on-campus facilities. Learn to broaden your horizons in your search for information. Here are some suggestions:

- **Local Libraries and Bookstores**. Contact the local library to find information on businesses and companies near your hometown or in the region in which you are interested.

- **Other Colleges and Universities**. See what other area programs have to offer. They may have career fairs available to students from nearby campuses. They may also let you look at their job postings and use their resource library. You should also check campuses in your hometown. You can never have enough information, and other colleges are usually pretty good about sharing with all students.

- **Job Hotlines**. Many companies use this great tool to publicize their positions to the public. The hotline is a prerecorded message detailing current open positions and application procedures. It can be easily accessed by calling the human resources department of the company and asking for the free hotline number.

Your Fourth Stop: The Information Superhighway Spend some time surfing! There's more information on the Internet than you'll ever be able to use. The main attraction of the Internet is that it offers exposure to companies and current positions available nationwide and worldwide. You simply need to turn on your computer, hop on-line, and surf the information highway. Thousands of professionals post their electronic resumes on-line, using the Internet as their primary tool for finding a job and networking. Opportunities abound on the Internet for every profession. Exhibit 18.4 is an example of a posting on the Internet.

▬▬▬ ***Exhibit 18.4*** Job Postings on the Internet

Job Alert Bulletin

Entry Level Positions:

A&W Restaurants, Inc.-IL. Assistant Manager for Chicago area.
Send resume: Attn. Human Resources, 1791 N. Laurel Park, Livonia, MI 48152
Applebee's International, Inc. Southern, MI. Managers. Send resume to Recruiter, 4551 W.
107th St., Suite 100, Overland Park, KS 66207
Ritz-Carlton Hotels, Chicago, IL. F&B Management positions available. Send or fax resume to:
HR Manager, 160 E. Pearson, Chicago, IL. 60611

Your Fifth Stop: At Your Workplace If you are lucky enough to already have a part-time job or internship, you will find a number of resources readily accessible. Ask around!

- **Your Colleagues**. Find someone who is established in the industry and has made contacts already. Pool your resources. Share your experiences and ask your co-workers to share their own experiences and contacts.

- **Your Superiors**. Your manager and other superiors have made contacts in their career. Remember to tap into these resources as a way to increase your contact base.

- **Company Manuals**. Most companies publish a manual that is packed with information related not only to their company. Read your company's manual and look for relationships with other related companies.

Your Sixth Stop: People on the Inside The hospitality business has many organizations that are designed to help professionals learn about new technology, make some friends, and basically expand their knowledge to better serve their customers. They often have specific events targeted at college students. It's worth your while to investigate the ones appropriate to your interests.

- **Conferences, Seminars, and Trade Shows**. The old adage, "Birds of a feather flock together" rings true here. You will find involved professionals at local and national conferences, seminars, and trade shows. These professionals attend these gatherings to learn from their peers, all who have a mutual interest. Perhaps the largest exhibition in the United States is the annual International Hotel, Motel & Restaurant Association trade show, held in November in New York City. One day of the show is devoted to career information, and interviewing. If possible, check it out!

- **Associations**. This industry does not suffer from a lack of associations to bring people with the same interests and professions together. In Exhibit 18.5 you will find an association for virtually all interests ranging from dude ranching to a pizza and pasta association.

Exhibit 18.5 Associations

Lodging Associations

American Bed & Breakfast Association (ABBA)	600 members
10800 Midlothian Turnpike., Richmond, VA 23235	804-379-2222
American Hotel & Motel Association (AHMA)	12,000 members
1201 New York Avenue NW, Suite 600, Washington, DC 20005	202-289-3100
American Travel Inns (ATI)	30 members
349 South 200 East Suite 170, Salt Lake City, UT 84111	807-521-0732
Dude Ranchers' Association (DRA)	103 members
Box 471, Laporte, CO 80535	303-223-8440
Hotel-Motel Greeters International (HMGI)	550 members
Independent Innkeepers Associations (IIA)	250 members
P.O. Box 150, Marshall, MI 49068	616-789-0393
International Society of Hotel Association Executives (ISHAE)	804-276-8614
9415 Hull Street, Suite B, Richmond, VA 23236	
Hospitality Sales & Marketing Association International (HSMAI)	6,000 members
1300 L Street NW, Suite 800, Washington, DC 20005	202-789-0089
Les Clefs D'or USA (hotel concierges)	250 members
c/o John Neary, The Carlyle Hotel, 35 E. 76th Street, New York, NY 10021	212-744-1600

Restaurant and Foodservice Associations

American Culinary Foundation (ACF)	18,000 members
P.O. Box 3466, St. Augustine, FL 32084	904-824-4468
American Dietetic Association (ADA)	59,000 members
216 W. Jackson Blvd., Suite 800, Chicago, IL 60606	800-877-1600
American Institute of Food Distribution	
28-12 Broadway, Fairlawn, NJ 07410	201-791-5570
American Institute of Wine & Food (AIWF)	800-274-2493
Association of Food Industries	
5 Ravine Drive, P.O. Box 776, Matawan, NJ 07747	908-583-8188
International Food Service Executives Association (IFSEA)	5,000 members
1100 State Road 7, Suite 103, Margate, FL 33068	305-977-0767

■■■■■■ **Exhibit 18.5** *(Continued)*

Restaurant and Foodservice Associations *(Continued)*

International Foodservice Manufacturers Association (IFMA)	
321 North Clark Street, Suite 2900, Chicago, IL 60610	312-644-8989
Mobile Industrial Caterers' Association (MICA)	200 members
7300 Artesia Blvd., Buena Park, CA 90621	714-521-6000
National Association of Catering Executives (NACE)	2,700 members
304W Liberty Street, Suite 201, Louisville, KY 40202	502-583-3783
National Association of Pizza Operators (NAPO)	4,500 members
P.O. Box 1347, New Albany, IN 47151	812-949-0909
National Association of Restaurant Managers (NARM)	350 members
National Bed & Breakfast Association (NB&BA)	2,000 members
P.O. Box 332, Norwalk, CT 06852	203-847-6196
National Pizza & Pasta Association (NPPA)	1,535 members
P.O. Box 100, Holland, IN 47541	800-844-5049
National Restaurant Association (NRA)	20,000 members
1200 17th Street NW, Washington, DC 20036	800-522-7578
National Soft Serve & Fast Food Association (NSSFFA)	350 members
9614 Tomstown Road, Waynesboro, PA 17268	800-535-7748

Institutional Foodservice Associations

American Correctional Food Service Association (ACFSA)	1,000 members
McCann-Cannard & Associates, 20-40 Chestnut Street, Harrisburg, PA 17104	717-233-2301
American School Food Service Association (ASFSA)	65,000 members
1600 Duke Street, Alexandria, VA 22314	800-877-8822
National Society for Healthcare Food Service Management (HFM)	533 members
204 E. Street NE, Washington, DC 20002	202-546-7236
Inflight Food Service Association (IFSA)	1,200 members
304 West Liberty Street, Suite 301, Louisville, KY 40202	502-583-3783
National Association of College & University Food Services (NACUFS)	
7 Olds Hall, Michigan State University, East Lansing, MI 48824	

Entertainment and Recreation Associations

Club Managers Association of America (CMAA)	4,000 members
7615 Winterberry Place, Bethesda, MD 20817	301-229-3600
National Association of RV Parks & Campgrounds	3,000 members
8605 Westwood Center Drive, Vienna, VA 22122	703-734-3000
Society of Recreation Executives (SRE)	1,375 members
P.O. Drawer 17148 Pensacola, FL 32522	904-477-7992
Resort & Commercial Recreation Association (RCRA)	1,500 members
P.O. Box 1208. New Port Richey, FL 34656	813-845-7373

(Continued)

▇▇▇▇▇▇▇▇ *Exhibit 18.5* Associations *(Continued)*

Travel Distribution Channels Associations

American Society of Travel Agents (ASTA)	23,000 members
1101 King Street, Alexandria, VA 22314	703-739-2782
Association of Corporate Travel Executives (ACTE)	700 members
570 Springfield Avenue, Summit, NJ 07901	908-273-3336
Association of Retail Travel Agents (ARTA)	3,000 members
1745 Jefferson Davis Hwy., Suite 300, Arlington, VA 22202	703-413-2222
Association of Travel Marketing Executives (ATME)	400 members
P.O. Box 43563, Washington, DC 20010	202-232-7107
Cruise Lines International Association (CLIA)	
500 5th Avenue, Suite 1407, New York, NY 10110	212-921-0066
Independent Travel Agencies of America Association (ITAA)	
1945 E. Ridge Road, Suite 24, Rochester, NY 14622	716-436-4700
Institute of Certified Travel Agents (ICTA)	16,000 members
148 Linden Street, P.O. Box 812059, Wellesley, MA 02181	800-542-4282
International Association of Tour Managers-North America (IATM-NAR)	1,300 members
65 Chaners Drive, East Haven, CT 06513	203-466-0425
National Association of Business Travel Agents (NABTA)	1,600 members
3255 Wilshire Blvd., Suite 1514, Los Angeles, CA 90010	213-382-3335
National Association of Cruise Only Agencies	800 members
3191 Coral Way, Suite 630, Miami, FL 33145	305-446-7732
National Business Travel Association (NBTA)	1,475 members
1650 King Street, No. 301, Alexandria, VA 22314	703-684-0836
National Tour Association (NTA)	3,800 members
546 E. Main Street, P.O. Box 3071, Lexington, KY 40596	606-253-1036
Professional Guides Association of America (PGAA)	800 members
2416 S. Eads Street, Arlington, VA 22202	703-892-5757
Society of Incentive Travel Executives (SITE)	2,100 members
21 W. 38th Street , New York, NY 10018	212-575-0910
Travel Industry Association of America (TIA)	1,900 members
2 Lafayette Center, 1133 21st Street NW, Suite 800, Washington, DC 20036	202-293-1433
Travel & Tourism Research Association (TTRA)	750 members
10200 W. 44th Avenue, Suite 304, Wheat Ridge, CO 80033	303-940-6557
United States Tour Operators Association (USTOA)	470 members
211 E. 51st Street, Suite 128, New York, NY 10022	212-750-7371

Convention and Meeting Planners Associations

Association for Convention Operators Management (ACOM)	650 members
c/o William H. Just & Associates, Inc.,	404-351-3220
1819 Peachtree Street N.E., Atlanta, GA 30309	

■■■■■■■■ *Exhibit 18.5* (*Continued*)

Convention and Meeting Planners Associations (*Continued*)

International Association of Convention & Visitors Bureaus (IACVB)	
P.O. Box 6690, Champaign, IL 61826	217-359-8881
International Association for Exposition Management (NAME)	3,200 members
8910 Purdue Road, Suite 630, Indianapolis, IN 46268	317-871-7272
International Institute of Convention Management	800 members
9200 Bayard Place, Fairfax, VA 22032	703-978-6287
Meeting Planners International (MPI)	12,000 members
1950 Stemmons Fwy., Infomart Bldg.,	
Suite 5018, Dallas, TX 75207	214-712-7702
Professional Convention Management Association (PCMA)	3,200 members
100 Vestavia Office Park, Suite 220, Birmingham, AL 35216	205-823-7262

Related Associations

International Association of Hospitality Accountants (IAHA)	
P.O. Box 27649, Austin, TX 78755	
National Association of Black Hospitality Professionals (NABHP)	450 members
P.O. Box 5443, Plainfield, NJ 07060	908-354-5117

Educational Associations

Council of Hotel & Restaurant Trainers (CHART)	240 members
c/o Richard's Restaurants, RR 1, Box 180-B, Bryant, IN 47326	219-997-6823
Council on Hotel, Restaurant and Institutional Education (CHRIE)	2,200 members
1200 17th Street NW, Washington, DC 20036	202-331-5990
Educational Foundation of the National Restaurant Association (EFNRA)	
250 S. Wacker Drive No. 1400, Chicago, IL 60606	312-715-1010
Eta Sigma Delta (ESD)—Honor Society for Hospitality Students	
c/o Donna Muge, CHRIE,	
1200 17th Street NW, Washington, DC 20036	202-331-5990

Your Seventh Stop: The Magazine Stand Use current periodicals to keep up to date on what's new in your field of interest, or a company you have your eye on, and to remain informed about other aspects of the hospitality industry. Below you will find a list of many reputable periodicals to choose from, to guarantee that you'll never lack information. You can find these periodicals in the library, some larger newsstands, bookstores, or direct from the publisher. (See Exhibit 18.6.) Those directories published for members only can usually be found on the shelf of a faculty member; remember to check with your professors.

▓▓▓▓▓▓ *Exhibit 18.6* Periodicals

U.S. Periodicals—Hospitality Industry

- *American Hotel & Motel Association Source Book*—Directory for members only.
- *California Inntouch*—Published by the California Hotel & Motel Association. Features industry news, legislative updates, and advice for hospitality businesses on improvements, innovations, and other developments (916-444-5780).
- The *Cornell Hotel & Restaurant Administration Quarterly*—Covers management trends and principles relevant to the hospitality and foodservice industries. Academic publication (212-989-5800).
- *Culinary Trends*—Serves the culinary industry with emphasis toward executives, chefs, food & beverage directors, proprietors and general managers of hotels, resorts, private clubs, high-end catering establishments, and fine restaurants (310-496-2558).
- *Directory of Hotel and Motel Companies*—Published by the AHMA (202-289-3100).
- *FIU Hospitality Review*—Academic publication (305-948-4500).
- *Florida Hotel & Motel Journal*—Provides management advice to hotel owners and managers (904-224-2888).
- *Food Arts*—Deals with national and international trends in the restaurant industry (212-684-4224).
- *The Food Paper*—Contains articles on food and wine (415-552-4664).
- *Foodservice East*—Covers the restaurant business on the East Coast of the USA (617-695-9080).
- *Foodservice Product News*—Covers manufacturers' services and new products and literature for the foodservice market.
- *Hospitality Law*—Helps lodging managers understand the legal environment and reduce their risk of going to court. Covers legal issues and key cases (608-246-3580).
- *Hospitality Management*—A general hospitality magazine. Published monthly (612-457-2289).
- *Hospitality Manager*—A hospitality publication with management emphasis (515-296-2400).
- *Hospitality Research Journal*—Published by CHRIE. Contains articles related to hospitality tourism education and research (202-331-5990).
- *Hotel & Motel Management*—Covers marketing hotel and hotel services: lodging, food, beverages, and meeting facilities. News about new products, business management, security, and investor outlooks (216-826-2839).
- *Hotel & Motel Management*—International Edition [Europe, Africa and the Middle East; Caribbean and Latin America; Asia]—Reports current news and analyzes business trends affecting the industry throughout the world (216-243-8100).
- *Hotel & Motel Red Book*—Published by the AHMA—an extensive directory.
- *Hotel & Resort Industry*—Covers primarily the lodging aspect of hospitality (212-888-1500).
- *Hotel & Travel Index*—The worldwide hotel directory (201-902-1600).

▬▬▬▬▬ **Exhibit 18.6** *(Continued)*

U.S. Periodicals—Hospitality Industry *(Continued)*

- *Hotel & Travel Index—ABC International Edition* (201-902-1600).

- *Hotel Business*—Focuses on industry related issues such as legislation, analysis of statistics, and finance (516-979-7878).

- *Hotel Update Newsletter*—Provides information on attractive industry offerings for lodging, dining, leisure activities, and travel (313-637-8432).

- *Hotels*—For hotel, foodservice, resort, and tourism industries. Provides information in marketing, new business development, investment, interior design, hospitality, and foodservice (708-635-8800).

- *The Inn Guide*—Lists approximately 700 California bed-and-breakfasts, inns, and small hotels (707-542-4667).

- *Inn Marketing Newsletter*—Presents news of people, places, and events of the inn and bed-and-breakfast businesses (815-939-3509).

- *Innside Government*—Published by the AHMA for members only. Covers congressional and executive branch activities affecting the hotel, motel, travel, and tourism industry.

- *Journal of Hospitality & Leisure Marketing*—Examines marketing issues in the hospitality and leisure industries. Aims to improve the understanding of relationships between hospitality and leisure organizations and their customers, and to improve the management of those relationships (800-342-9678).

- *Journal of Restaurant & Food Service Marketing*—Presents new developments in the field and provides state-of-the-art knowledge on restaurant and foodservice marketing (800-342-9678).

- *Lodging*—A general hospitality publication offering current events with emphasis on lodging operations (202-289-3164).

- *Lodging Hospitality*—Focuses on site selection, design and decor, financing, building, personnel, maintenance, sanitation, computerization, merchandising, and renovation (216-696-7000).

- *Marketshare*—Measures the market shares of hotel chains and management companies; extensive statistics information (512-734-3434).

- *Midsouthwest Restaurant*—Focus is on this specific geographic region; offers current events in restaurants (405-942-8181).

- *Midwest Food Service*—Serves the restaurant business and its suppliers (614-235-1022).

- *Motel News*—Emphasis is on the motel or economy roadside segments (415-349-1234).

- *National Directory of Budget Motels* (516-422-2225).

- *Nation's Restaurant News*—A current events publication. Though a magazine, is like a newspaper in reporting style (212-756-5000).

- *Night Club & Bar Magazine*—Focus on the beverage aspect of the business (601-236-5510).

- *Official Hotel Guide*—A directory of hotels (212-902-2000).

(Continued)

■■■■■■■ **Exhibit 18.6** Periodicals *(Continued)*

U.S. Periodicals—Hospitality Industry *(Continued)*

- *Restaurant Briefing*—Highlights the advertising, promotional, customer service, managerial, and legislative aspects of the restaurant industry (212-921-4314).
- *Restaurant Business*—Information on food equipment, supplies, services, and personnel for restaurant and foodservice executives (212-592-6200).
- *Restaurant Digest*—Provides news, interviews and marketing information for the Mid-Atlantic states (202-328-3811).
- *Restaurant Exchange News*—A general restaurant-focused publication (914-638-1108).
- *Restaurant-Food Review*—Contains restaurant reviews, personality features, food stories, and general restaurant news (718-996-5406).
- *Restaurant Hospitality*—All phases of management in commercial foodservice operations (216-696-7000).
- *Restaurant Journal*—Covers legislative and business news affecting the restaurant industry (717-232-4433).
- *Restaurant Management Insider*—For owners, managers, and marketing executives in the restaurant, foodservice, and hospitality industries (718-583-8060).
- *Restaurant Review* (718-996-5406).
- *Restaurant Row Magazine*—Covers Los Angeles and Orange County markets with articles on restaurant dining, food, wines and spirits, hotels and resorts (213-438-6565).
- *Restaurant Wine*—Guide to wine service, sales, and marketing for the hospitality industry focusing on trends, innovations, staff training ideas, wine marketing, and inventory control (707-224-4777).
- *Restaurants & Institutions*—For the foodservice and lodging industries. Features food trends, new products, menu concepts, recipes, and merchandising ideas (708-635-8800).
- *Restaurants & Institutions Marketplace*—Contains new product reviews, recipe cards, and ideas for the foodservice industry (708-635-8800).
- *Restaurants, Resorts and Hotels*—A general information publication with a wide range of offerings (203-378-1223).
- Restaurants USA—Covers foodservice industry developments and trends. Includes feature stories and new columns (202-331-5900).
- *Restaurateur*—Designed to enhance the knowledge of the foodservice professional by discussing area of professional concern (703-356-1315).
- *Trends in the Hotel Industry*—Focus is on financial trends in hospitality (212-867-8000).
- *Travel & Hospitality Career Directory*—Emphasis is on careers in the business (313-961-2242).
- *Who's Who in the Lodging Industry*—Short biographies of people important to the hospitality business. Directory (202-289-3100).

Job Correspondence: Writing Résumés, Cover Letters, and Thank-You Letters _____

You have only one opportunity to create a first impression. That first impression can make the difference between being noticed and not being noticed. When searching for employment, the most widely used method of informing potential employers that you are available is by sending a résumé and cover letter. This section will show you what ingredients are needed for a competitive and attention-getting résumé and cover letter. Also, if you ever wondered about the importance of sending a thank-you letter, you'll soon be convinced about the benefits.

Résumés—The Hardest Part

Did you know that if you laid out end to end all of the résumés currently circulating out there, they would circle the world 15 times? Where does yours fit in? The fact is, your résumé needs to stand out from all the others. Here are some alternatives to just sending an ordinary résumé:

- Research the company you are interested in and identify the person who is responsible for the hiring. Tailor your letter to the job for which you're applying and incorporate your qualifications and accomplishments. Without having to send a résumé you have communicated your interests and your skills. Make sure to follow up with a phone call to determine the status of your request.

- Walk right in! That's right. Spend a day going into the companies of interest to see if you can meet with a representative from the company. Make a phone call prior to your visit to identify the person who can be the most helpful. Since you are asking people spontaneously for their help, be sure to keep the meeting brief. And, always remember to follow up by sending a thank-you letter to any person who assisted you.

The Purpose of a Résumé A résumé presents your experience, skills, and accomplishments in a manner and sequence that best connect your background with the requirements of the positions in which you are interested. Since most managers spend less than 15 seconds on each résumé, it is important that yours makes a lasting impression. Spend quality time compiling your information and developing the résumé. Make sure the résumé is free of mistakes. One spelling mistake could make the difference between getting the call for the interview or the rejection postcard. Remember that your résumé is your marketing tool; it is the main determinant of whether or not you'll be granted an interview. (See Exhibit 18.7.)

The most important thing to remember when developing your résumé is to be concise. Selectively describe your background in a comprehensive manner and limit it to one page. If there is an aspect you want to elaborate on, do so in your cover letter. Focus your job descriptions on those skills essential to the position for which you are applying. If a volunteer activity or personal interest does not enhance what you are offering, leave it out. Keep in mind that the purpose of the resume is to *get* the interview, *not* replace it.[3] Here are some good reference books to help you get started:

- *The Resume Catalog: 200 Damn Good Examples* by Yana Parker
- *The Resume Handbook* by David Hizer and Arthur Rosenberg

███████ *Exhibit 18.7* Sample Résumé

Julie Lee
400 Maple Street
Bloomington, VA 10000
(201) 555-1234   jlee@univ.edu

EDUCATION

State University of Virginia, School of Hospitality Administration, College Park, Virginia
Bachelor of Science degree candidate, May 1999
GPA: 3.7/4.0 Dean's List
University of Switzerland
Study Abroad Program, Spring 1997

WORK EXPERIENCE

Hotel Geneve, Geneva, Switzerland   May-August 1997

Summer Intern
Selected as one of 2 students to work in Switzerland following study abroad program. Rotated through all departments of this 200 room, 5 star hotel, with special emphasis on rooms control. Special projects included creation of English-language guide to local restaurants and attractions.

State University of Virginia Campus Dining Service   January-December 1996

Kitchen Manager
Managed 1 shift per day in main campus dining facility, accommodating over 500 students. Scheduled 15 part-time student employees in 3 stations. Maintained proper sanitary conditions. Responsible for ordering supplies and inventory as needed. Promoted from Kitchen Assistant.

Kitchen Assistant   September-December 1995
Responsibilities included preparation of hot and cold sandwiches during dinner hour. Mastered operation of all kitchen equipment.

The Mountain Top Inn, Riverside, Vermont   May-August 1995

Summer Intern
Served as front desk associate for a 30 room inn with dining room. Responsibilities included timely processing of guests' registration and check out. Duties included reception and phones; provided information on accommodations to callers and walk-in guests. Assisted with meal preparation and clean up.

ACTIVITIES

School of Hospitality Administration Student Government

Class Representative   August 1995-present
Elected as representative to serve on School Government Board. Also represent School on University committees.

The Pine Street Inn, College Park, Virginia

Volunteer   August 1995-present
Volunteer 2 Sundays per month, preparing meals for homeless guests.

Women's Field Hockey Team, State University of Virginia

Team Member   August 1995-present
Walk-on member of nationally-ranked women's college field hockey team.

AWARDS

Selected as recipient of Dean's Scholarship, an annual award of 1/2 tuition for 4 years.
National Merit Scholar.

LANGUAGES

Fluent in German and proficient in French.

SKILLS

Computer software knowledge includes Microsoft Word, Word for Windows, Excel, Lotus 123, and various Internet applications.

- *The Overnight Resume* by Donald Asher
- *Does Your Resume Wear Bluejeans?* by C. Edward Good
- *The Perfect Resume* by Tom Jackson

Types of Résumés There is no universally accepted format for preparing a résumé; in fact, there are various formats that meet individual needs. There are some basic rules, though, to keep in mind. The choice of font size and type is entirely personal, but it should be neat and easy to read. Your résumé should be brief and businesslike, and accurately reflect in terms of style and content the type of job you are seeking. Probably the most common format is the chronological résumé, which describes each job in reverse chronological order.

Contents of a Résumé Below are some suggestions to help you structure the individual categories within your résumé. When you first start, don't be concerned with style and format or getting it all on one page! Aim first for the content; then you can edit and rearrange for style.

Identification

- Your full name
- Address (present/permanent)
- Phone number (present/permanent)
- E-mail address, if applicable

Career Objective A career objective should clearly and accurately describe the kind of position that reflects your abilities, interests, and temperament, as well as your work and academic experience. It should consist of:

- the job for which you are applying
- your greatest strengths
- results you expect to produce

There are different opinions on the value of including a career objective statement. Should you choose to include it, make sure it is well written. A vague objective is not going to enhance your resume, and is better omitted.

Education Emphasize the positive aspects of your academic career and extracurricular activities. Describe any academic honors or scholarships you have received as well as any positions of leadership you have assumed. If your GPA is above average, you may include that as well. Items that may be included under this section of your résumé include:

- institution/degree/concentration
- relevant courses/class projects
- academic performance
- honors/special certificates
- extracurricular activities
- professional organizations

Work Experience Use action words to describe the skills and responsibilities that best relate to the position you are seeking. Try to avoid words or phrases like *assisted* or *responsible for*—they don't sell. Emphasize your accomplishments and quantify them wherever possible. For example, there's a big difference between saying "Scheduled employees" and "Created employee schedule for 15 kitchen assistants that reduced overtime costs by 50%."

Remember that it's okay if your skills seem relatively minor as compared to the "real world." Indicate progressive increases in responsibility. Include volunteer work, leadership positions, and so on. Be specific and avoid generalities. Include all relevant experiences, summer or otherwise. This includes all paid and unpaid positions. Remember to include:

- name of employer
- location
- dates
- title
- brief job description
- level of responsibility

Skills This section can include computer skills, or other special skills not mentioned in the descriptions of your work experiences.

Languages If you are fluent or proficient in more than one language, this should be indicated in a separate section.

Activities and Affiliations This section can be used to list any memberships or affiliations you may have. Where applicable, indicate any offices held and achievements related to these activities. Volunteer experiences can enhance your résumé, and should definitely be included.

Interests We caution against using interests, if they only include such generalization as reading, music, and sports. However, if you cycle every year in the Pan Mass Challenge for Muscular Dystrophy, or have completed three New York marathons, or sing with the Tanglewood Festival Chorus—those are definitely worthy of mention.

A Few Final Guidelines No book will tell you everything you need to know about writing your résumé. Make an appointment with a counselor in your school's career office for individual help with yours, and ask your faculty advisor, current employer, and co-workers for their opinions.

Resume language should be:
- specific, not general
- action oriented, not passive
- written to express, not impress
- articulate, not flowery
- fact based

Do:
- be consistent in format and content
- make it easy to read and follow
- use spacing, underlining, italics, bold, and capitalization for emphasis
- list categories in order of importance
- use 8 1/2 X 11-inch bond paper, in white or ivory

Don't:	▪ use personal pronouns	▪ abbreviate	

Don't:
- ▪ use personal pronouns
- ▪ use a narrative style
- ▪ use slang or colloquialisms
- ▪ include age or sex

- ▪ abbreviate
- ▪ number or letter categories
- ▪ use a picture
- ▪ list references on résumé (put these on a separate page)

Cover Letters and Thank-You Letters

The purpose of a cover letter is either to obtain an interview, or to follow up an interview. There are three types of letters:

- ▪ Application—requesting an interview for a specific position
- ▪ Inquiry—requesting an interview or a meeting, either for a position or for information
- ▪ Thank you—expressing gratitude for an interview or meeting

While each one is different, the following set of guidelines will help you write a powerful letter, no matter the type.

The Letter Writing Rules

- ▪ Each letter should be an original, and addressed to a specific person.
- ▪ Double check the spelling of the person's name, title, and address.
- ▪ Use simple and correct grammar.
- ▪ Include your mailing address and the date.
- ▪ Use the standard business format.
- ▪ Spell check each letter.
- ▪ Limit sentences that begin with "I."
- ▪ Use same paper stock as your résumé.
- ▪ Limit each letter to one typewritten page.
- ▪ Sign your name, preferably in black ink.
- ▪ Keep a copy for your files.

Thank-You Letters After any type of interview or meeting, be sure to send a thank-you note promptly. You might even consider preparing the envelope for the thank-you note before you go to the interview. There are many reasons why thank-you letters are important. First of all, someone took the time to provide you with valuable information that will help you make a decision. It is proper to thank them for their time. Secondly, when the person contemplating the candidates receives a thank-you letter, that leaves a strong impression on their mind. Plus, it places your name in front of them again. Sometimes a thank-you letter is used as a tie-breaker in a tough decision. If there are two candidates being considered for a position and only one sends a thank-you note, some recruiters use that as an indication of character, and of someone they would like to see working in their company. It also shows follow-through and expresses a real interest in the position.

Interviewing _____

Congratulations! The hard work you put into your résumé and cover letter has paid off. You received your first request for an interview. This is an exciting and nerve-wracking time. The time has come to meet face-to-face the person you impressed with your résumé. Think of the interview as the "moment of truth"; a one-time opportunity to market and sell yourself. With such limited opportunity, you should make sure you are prepared for your meeting.

Research is Critical

If you aspire to earn top grades, chances are you work hard to earn them. You study for hours, days, even weeks to prepare for an exam. Thrifty consumers take valuable time to research important purchases. When they buy a car, they do not go directly to the dealership, point to a car, and take it home. There is some research involved, important details they need to know before they even go to the dealership. Depending on their priorities, they may first research which cars fall into their price category. Next, they may research which cars have a reputation for being the safest, and so on.

Researching a company with which you are interviewing is similar. This section will focus on the important aspect of conducting in-depth research into the company with which you have received an opportunity to interview.

Prior to your interview, you'll need to call the company and ask for any information it has. Hotels offer sales kits that are packed with information about the property. Public companies publish an annual report that contains not only key numbers detailing their success, but also the phi-

---

General Outline of Cover Letter

Today's Date
Name of Person
Title
Organization
Street Address
City, State Zip

Dear _____:

Opening paragraph: Your reason for writing. Name the specific position, or type of work, or information for which you are applying.

Body of letter: Explain why you are interested, and why you are qualified. Don't just reiterate your résumé—elaborate on one or two items that are relevant.

Closing paragraph: This should pave the way for an interview or meeting. Indicate your interest and desire to interview.

Sincerely,

(Your signature)

Your name typed
Enclosure

February 1, 1996   **Letter of Application**

Mr. Paul Brown
General Manager
Four Seasons Hotel Boston
15 Arlington Street
Boston, MA 02146

Dear Mr. Brown:

I am aware that the position of Assistant Manager, Room Service, is available at the Four Seasons Hotel Boston. I am very interested in pursuing this position, and feel I am a qualified candidate. For your reference, I have enclosed a copy of my résumé.

As my résumé indicates, I will graduate magna cum laude from the School of Hospitality Administration at Name University in May 1997. Having worked extensively in food and beverage for over five years, I would like to remain in the field. My internships have been in hotels, which have enabled me to develop the necessary skills for this position. During the summer of 1996, I was fortunate enough to obtain a position in Room Service at the Four Seasons Tokyo, an experience that would facilitate a transition to the Four Seasons Boston.

The combination of my work experiences and education matches the demands of this position. I would welcome the opportunity to meet with you to discuss my application.

Sincerely,
Julie Candidate

Enclosure

---

losophy of the company. In the annual report you'll usually find a letter from the president or CEO, along with articles highlighting certain areas of the company. Read periodicals and newspapers for current events about the company. Also be sure to familiarize yourself with the requirements of the job. This is valuable information for you to use during your interview.

Based on your research, develop a list of questions to ask your interviewer. If you don't write them down, nervousness may cause you to forget the questions. Writing questions down also shows that you are a responsible person with foresight. If you show up prepared for the interview, and with intelligent questions, you will impress the interviewer by showing your initiative, enthusiasm, and knowledge of the company.

The Day of the Interview

The day of the interview has finally arrived! Gather all of the items you need to bring with you to the interview. These include directions to the company, fresh copies of your résumé (you might meet with more than one person), a list of references, the list of questions you prepared, and a pen and notepad. It is recommended that you gather everything you need the night before, to eliminate the possibility of accidentally leaving something important behind.

Before the Interview

- Dress professionally. Don't be eliminated in the first few seconds because your appearance is inconsistent with the "culture" of the organization. Being conservative is the safest bet.

February 1, 1996   **Personal Referral**

Mr. Paul Brown
General Manager
Four Seasons Hotel Boston
15 Arlington Street
Boston, MA 02146

Dear Mr. Brown:

Mr. Thomas Smith, General Manager of the Four Seasons Tokyo, suggested I contact you concerning the position of Assistant Manager, Room Service, currently available at the Four Seasons Hotel Boston. I am very interested in pursuing this position, and feel I am a qualified candidate.

As my résumé indicates, I will graduate magna cum laude from the School of Hospitality Administration at Name University in May 1997. Having worked extensively in food and beverage for over five years, I would like to remain in the field. My internships have been in hotels, which have enabled me to develop the necessary skills for this position. During the summer of 1996, I was fortunate enough to obtain a position in Room Service at the Four Seasons Tokyo, an experience that would facilitate a transition to the Four Seasons Boston.

The combination of my work experiences and education matches the demands of this position. I would welcome the opportunity to meet with you to discuss my application.

Sincerely,

Julie Candidate

Enclosure

February 27, 1996   **Letter of Inquiry**

Mr. Paul Brown
General Manager
Four Seasons Hotel Boston
15 Arlington Street
Boston, MA 02146

Dear Mr. Brown:

I am currently a Junior in the School of Hospitality Administration at Name University, expecting to graduate in May 1998.

At this time, I am exploring career possibilities, and was hoping you might be able to meet with me. I have worked extensively in the industry for over five years, but I am unsure how to direct my search. My internships have been in hotels, both in food and beverage and the rooms division.

Enclosed is a copy of my résumé for you to review. I will call you early next week, to see if we can arrange a brief meeting. I appreciate your time, and look forward to meeting with you.

Sincerely,

Julie Candidate

Enclosure

March 12, 1996   **Thank-You Letter**

Mr. Paul Brown
General Manager
Four Seasons Hotel Boston
15 Arlington Street
Boston, MA 02146

Dear Mr. Brown:

I would like to thank you and your staff for your time and consideration during my interview on Friday.

The Four Seasons Hotel Boston is an impressive hotel, with a staff dedicated to the ultimate in customer service. Based upon our conversation, I believe I could make an immediate contribution to the hotel, as my background and interests are compatible with the position of Assistant Manager, Room Service.

Again, thank you for the informative interview and your consideration. If I can provide you with any additional information as you make your decision, please do not hesitate to contact me at 555-1234.

Sincerely,

Julie Candidate

- Arrive early and allow a generous amount of travel time. Use the extra 15 to 20 minutes once you arrive to relax and collect your thoughts and observe what is going on around you. Get a feel for the work environment. If you are unsure about the meeting place, go a day or two ahead of time; see how long it takes you to get there, and make sure you know where the office is located.

- Take extra résumés to the interview. You may unexpectedly be asked to meet with additional interviewers. A clean copy of your résumé on bond paper is more impressive than the xeroxed copy your interviewer might pass along.

- Bring a typed list of the names and phone numbers of your references.

- Take a pen and notepad along for any notes you may wish to make immediately after the interview. Use the notes to write your thank-you letter.

You have arrived at the company, and you have butterflies in your stomach. Don't worry! It is very natural and normal to be nervous in this situation. Use the nervousness to your advantage. Believe in yourself. Use the nervous energy to think about the interview's resulting in a positive outcome. Picture the upcoming interview in a positive light. Imagine yourself answering all the questions smoothly and flawlessly, and the interviewer listening intently. This should give you a certain amount of confidence to help you through the interview.

You spent a long time putting together the materials, so you can proceed with the interviewing process; now it is time for you to sell yourself and your personality. You are now in the role of salesperson, and the product you are selling is yourself: your skills, talents, and character. Your résumé got you in the door; now it is your job to get a permanent invitation back.

During the Interview Here are some tips to help you during the interview process:

- Interviewers have different styles of interviewing. Let the interviewer set the pace for the interview.

- Provide answers that are honest and to the point. Do not elaborate too much on one thing.

- Remain positive about your experiences and your relationships with peers.

- If you don't know the answer to a question, don't be afraid to say you are not sure. That is a more appropriate response than lying, or making something up just to answer the question.

- If there is an aspect of your skills that you feel was not covered during the interview, and the interview is wrapping up, close the interview by mentioning the skill that you think is valuable.

- Be calm. Most interviewers expect applicants to be slightly nervous, so try not to worry about it. Employers use different interviewing styles, and some may be inexperienced at interviewing. It's possible the interviewer is as nervous as you are!

- Be friendly and enthusiastic. Establishing rapport is as much your responsibility as the employer's.

- Be aware of body language. Maintain good eye contact, but don't stare. Control distracting and/or nervous habits, and don't slouch. Practicing your interview techniques beforehand will help you spot and reduce any distracting mannerisms.

- Don't wait for the "right" questions in order to talk about your skills and experience and how they qualify you. If the employer fails to ask the questions you want to answer, attempt to steer the conversation tactfully, using the employer's questions as a springboard. Any question or line of conversation should be an opportunity for you to get across points you have on your agenda.

- Be direct and don't ramble: introduce a point, develop it, give an illustration, and close.

- Speak through your experiences at every opportunity. Concrete examples that "show" are much more compelling than broad generalizations that simply "tell."

- Listen. Good communication skills mean listening as well as speaking.

- Leave the interview on a positive note, even if you do not feel that the interview went well. You can huff and puff to no end once you leave the interview, but don't risk ruining something good even if you feel negative.

Stages of the Interview Most interviews will include the following phases:

1. The Ice Breaker

   This is the "How's the weather" polite conversation. Relax, participate, and enjoy it. You are showing a basic social skill that is important in virtually any job.

2. The Heart of the Interview

   The interviewer will want to talk to you about your experiences so that she can evaluate you according to the organization's criteria. The goal of the interviewer is to find out as much information as possible in a short amount of time. The interviewer will ask you many questions to determine your likes and interests, your skills, talents, weaknesses, attitudes, ambition, and so on. Just a few examples of questions that you may be asked are:

- What are your long-range and short-range goals and objectives?
- What do you see yourself doing five years from now?
- How do you plan to achieve your career goals?
- Why did you choose the career for which you are preparing?
- Why should I hire you?
- What are your strengths? weaknesses?
- Describe your most rewarding college experience.
- What qualities do you think are important for this position?
- What academic subjects do you like best? least?
- What kind of work environment do you think you would enjoy the most?
- How well do you work under pressure?
- What do you know about our company?
- Are you willing to relocate?
- What have you learned from your mistakes?

You will often be asked if you have any questions about the organization, program, or job during this phase. Think of something you would like to know and ask it—don't ask a question just because you think you have to. Also, don't ask questions that could have been answered in your research. Here are some questions you may want to ask:

- What specific tasks does the position require?
- Where does this job fit into the organizational structure?
- How will the work be evaluated?
- What kind of supervision will there be?
- Whom would I be working for and with?
- Where is the organization going?
- What opportunities for advancement exist?
- What kind of orientation and training are available to new employees?
- Are there any long-range plans for the office or department?

3. The Closing

The interviewer will likely be watching the time and will give overt cues that the interview is approaching the end. She will often tell you what will happen next and when. If she doesn't, you should ask. Be sure to thank the interviewer for her time and restate your interest in the job.

After the Interview Phew! The interview is over, and you have made your first impression. Right after your interview, take a few minutes, whether while you are traveling home on the train or after you leave the building, to jot down the important highlights from your meeting. Then:

- Write the interviewer a brief thank-you note. In this note, you may refer to specific issues that were discussed, express your thanks, and restate your interest in the position. Also provide whatever credentials, references, or employment applications the employer may have requested.

- Think about the interview and make some notes on what you learned about the job, organization, or career field. These will be helpful if you are invited for a second round of interviews.

- If an interview doesn't go well, learn from your mistakes (another reason to plan practice interviews).

Excelling and Developing Your Career Path: First Steps to Success

Just as the success of the President of the United States is judged by the first 100 days in office, so it will be with you as you launch your career. Success or failure depends, in most cases, on the individual. Thus, it is crucial to be prepared for the first steps. To be motivated and passionate about your work is very personal, and takes effort and dedication; no one else can do it for you. Motivated professionals who regularly find something new and exciting about their jobs don't view their ride home as the best part of their day. The following steps may help you build a strong foundation on which to build a satisfying and fulfilling career. Refer to the list as a reminder of ways to renew your motivation and passion for your work continually.

- Go out of your way to learn. Don't settle for knowing only how your department runs. Visit other departments and show an interest in how they operate. Stay after your "normal" working hours to learn about other areas.

- Seek feedback early. Feedback from your manager and co-workers can be helpful throughout your career to gauge your contribution to the team and to develop a powerful management style.

- Be prompt, if not early, for work. Being on time exhibits strong initiative and a sense of respect and responsibility for your job. Your boss may quietly notice that you are always ready for the early morning meeting and will be sure to consider that factor when it is time for a promotion.

- Volunteer for extra tasks and do those tasks with 100 percent effort. See each job through to completion. If a different department has a large, timely project, try your hand at something new. Show your abilities at all times, for you never know when a superior is looking for a talented person to fill a new position.

- Look for and adopt a mentor. Most people are willing to share their experiences with others. Remember, they all had a first job at some point in their lives, too! A mentor can be helpful in charting out a career path or providing advice on an important project.

- Stay aware of other opportunities within the company. If you are interested in working in another department, offer to observe an employee for a couple of hours a week. Then, when a position becomes available, you might be the first one to be considered for it.

- Monitor your own passion, dedication, and motivation. Keep yourself fresh by constantly challenging yourself. Every day, ask yourself if you learned something new, make sure you put forth your best effort and give yourself credit for a job well done.

- Continue to network. Networking can not only help you get a job, it can keep moving your career to the next level.

What is Networking?

Networking is the science and art of developing and maintaining contacts on a professional and social level. This is an essential part of your job search, and your professional life. Every person you meet, whether it is by accident or on purpose, has the potential to help you find a job. Conversely, you have the potential to assist them. The key to successful networking is meeting as many people as possible and publicizing your availability as a candidate. But it is not enough just to declare that you are looking for a job. It is necessary to explain to your networking contacts the job that you are looking for in order to make it easier for them to help.

Networking is essential not only when you are looking for a new job but also during your entire career. Developing and maintaining contacts should be done on a regular basis for current and future purposes. The following are the top five advantages of networking:

1. Networking might lead you to your next big job opportunity.

2. Networking can prepare you for future job opportunities at your company.

3. Networking can help you keep updated about competitors, industry trends, innovations, and developments in your subsegment or the whole industry.

4. Networking contacts can help you with questions or problems regarding your job or project.

5. Networking will help you expand your social network.

Where Do I Network?

You can network basically anywhere. The following are some suggestions for networking places:

1. Your workplace.

2. Association meetings.

3. Trade shows, conferences, and seminars.

4. On-line (Internet).

5. On the commuter train, bus, or in a carpool.

6. On the airplane.

7. Through your high school and college alumni associations.

8. Informational phone calls and meetings with colleagues in the industry.

9. Wherever there are people!

Networking is much easier than you may think. Just as you made friends when you arrived at school, in your dorm and in your classes, you can make professional friends when you enter the workforce. Be yourself, be open to new ideas, and be friendly. Treat your co-workers and managers as you would like to be treated, and you will be well on your way to networking.

International Opportunities

Due to the increase in tourism worldwide, the global nature of the hospitality industry, and the international growth of hospitality companies, the employment opportunities for hospitality professionals abroad are extensive. Many leading companies in the hospitality industry have properties or outlets worldwide. Holiday Inn, Accor, McDonald's, Four Seasons, and TGI Friday's are only a few examples. By taking a job or internship abroad, you can expand your experience beyond the borders of your native country. However, finding a job abroad is not necessarily easy. We'll discuss how to get a job overseas later in this section.

The World is Your Oyster

"Why, then the world's mine oyster...."[4] is how we started chapter 4, the international chapter. And the world is yours, if you are interested in exploring it. An international career has many unique advantages. It presents challenges unlike anything you might face at home. It enables you to explore new cultures and regions. It offers an opportunity to "hurdle the hurdles" of international management that we discovered in chapter 4. International experience can also contribute significant value to your professional portfolio.

The Hospitality Business is a Global Business Though there are many differences to encounter abroad, there are also many similarities, making the hospitality education you receive applicable worldwide. The physical nature of a guest room in a five-star hotel in Tokyo is not different from one in a five-star hotel in Mexico City. Though the words may be different, the language of service is universal. The basic needs and desires of a tourist from Belgium are similar to the ones of a tourist from Kenya. Each wants to enjoy good service and relaxation on his or her vacation, or efficient, thoughtful support to make a business trip successful. To succeed in translating good service to various guests, fluency in more than one language is an enormous asset to a potential candidate for an international career.

Study Abroad So you're determined to land a job in Europe or Asia after graduation. What can you do to make sure that happens? Start to plan early, very early. Study a foreign language throughout all your college years. Ask the faculty in your department if they've ever worked or lived abroad. See if you can meet with local hospitality companies that have international concerns, and ask what advice they might have for you. One of the best ways to determine if you'd be happy working overseas is to spend a summer or semester abroad. Early in your freshmen year, check with your school's study abroad advisor, to see what your options are.

If you can, study abroad for a semester or a year. It'll give you a great chance to perfect your knowledge of a second (or third!) language—a terrific skill to have on your résumé. While you are abroad, set up some informational interviews with local hoteliers and other hospitality professionals.

Check with the U.S. consulate and see if there are any Americans working nearby, and set up meetings with them as well. Through these interactions you can gain valuable information and advice, making it that much easier to get there after graduation.

How to Start the Process

Just as you would research domestic opportunities, searching for an international experience begins with research. Develop a strategy that includes the countries of interest, the main advantages of such an experience, and why your skill set is particularly adaptable to that experience. Define what your goals are and how you can achieve them in a specific country. After mapping your goals, you can begin the research process.

The process of pursuing an international career is not easy, and it will take dedication and a lot of time to research. You will be at a powerful advantage if you already work for an international company. As a current employee, it is easier to conduct research about internal, international career opportunities. For a head start on your research, contact the human resources department, the international franchise, or the operations department to find out where the opportunities lie.

If you are not already working for an international company, meet with your international advisor. Most campuses have a work abroad department, where you can collect information about the process. If your college does not have a international office, ask a college guidance counselor for a list of universities that do offer international experience. Next, meet with your professors. They will likely have some tips about a destination, a specific type of job, and how it will help develop your career. Also consider contacting a U.S.-based property or outlet of an international company. They may be able to put you in touch with a professional who has worked abroad but is now in the United States.

How to Find International Opportunities

Working in an international company provides you with an opportunity to explore international openings and to meet peers who have international experience. Consider taking a job with an international company as a step toward an assignment abroad. You can also apply directly to international hospitality companies. Read trade magazines and attend events with international presence, such as events of international tourism management. Various associations have events that are international in scope. In addition, the career office at your school or your professors can be helpful in finding contacts.

Basic Steps

Finding a job overseas, even when done properly, can be a time-consuming process. Though individual circumstances vary, there are some basic steps that apply to nearly everyone:

Passports Your passport is your ticket to entering a country legally. Most countries won't even allow entry without it. You can apply for your passport at many U.S. postal offices. You can also apply at any federal or state court, or at passport agencies in Boston, Chicago, Honolulu,

Houston, Los Angeles, Miami, New Orleans, New York, Philadelphia, San Francisco, Seattle, Stamford, and Washington, D.C. If you are not a U.S. citizen, contact the embassy of your country. You must apply for your passport in person, unless you are renewing an expired passport. You will need the following:

1. Proof of U.S. citizenship.

    You can provide a copy of your birth certificate, a naturalization certificate or, if you were born abroad, a consular report of birth of a U.S. citizen.

2. Two recent identical photographs, measuring 2" by 2".

    These may be in color or in black and white, and your head should measure 1 3/8" from top to chin. Many photocopy and photograph shops will print acceptable passport photos while you wait.

3. Proof of identity.

    If you don't have a valid driver's license, you can use an expired U.S. passport, a birth certificate, a certificate of naturalization or citizenship, or recent government identification card.

4. A completed form DSP-11, "Passport application," is available wherever you apply for your passport.

5. Payment of processing fees.

    Call in advance to find out the fees and what form of payment is accepted.[5]

You can contact a government office that will provide you with a brochure, "Your Trip Abroad," by sending a written request and $1 to Superintendent of Documents, U.S. Government Printing Office, P.O. Box 371954, Pittsburgh, PA 15250, or by calling 202-512-1800.

Visas and Entry Permits Some countries require a visa to enter, which is official permission to enter granted by the country you plan to visit. Visa requirements and fees vary from country to country, and differ depending on how long you plan to stay. The consulate of the country you are planning to visit will be able to provide you with detailed visa information. Copies of foreign visa requirements are available from the U.S. government by writing to The Consumer Information Center, Department 354A, Pueblo, CO 81009.

Work Permits To work legally in another country, U.S. citizens must receive formal permission from the government of the country they are entering. As a student, you have access to organizations whose main purpose is to help students obtain permits for work overseas. Contact the Council on International Educational Exchange (CIEE), 205 East 42nd Street, New York, NY, 10017. The CIEE sponsors reciprocal programs with government approval and is therefore able to obtain overseas work authorization for U.S. students and recent graduates.

Français? Español? The best scenario heading abroad is being bilingual, but that's not always possible. Don't worry if you are only at the beginning stages of the language—you'll be forced to pick it up quickly! You will also be able to communicate using body language, and by having lots of patience and a sense of humor. Don't forget a dictionary! If you are seriously considering working abroad, studying a language while you are in school is essential.

Good Luck and Bon Voyage! _____

There is no doubt that the hospitality industry is demanding. Depending on the nature of your job, it is not unusual for hospitality employees to have long, erratic hours. A restaurant manager's hours, for example, can well exceed the standard 40-hour work week common to other industries. A front office manager can often work on weeknights as well as on weekends. A cruise ship employee never really leaves his work, literally, for days at a time, and faces tight living quarters. It is a great challenge to give wonderful service during the final hours of a long shift or when you are faced with particularly trying circumstances.

The very challenge of the work, however, is why many people consider the hospitality industry to be so exciting. Those not involved in the industry are often puzzled by those who are attracted and dedicated to the dynamics of service. It is a labor of love if you derive significant pleasure in meeting and exceeding guests' expectations. Very few professions provide so many opportunities to satisfy others' needs in unique and creative ways. Though at times it may not seem to pass quickly, graduation day is not as far off as you might think. By the time that long-awaited day comes, you will have dedicated years to studying for exams, forging lasting friendships and determining a structure for your future. You will have gained work experience in your field of interest, met and networked with professionals, and, like many others before you, wondered: Where do I go from here? When you sum it up, everything you do on a daily basis that helps you reach your goals is part of a learning process. You continuously replace old information with new, and improve the way in which you do things by practice. This entire learning experience will escort you into your future. Good luck!

End Notes

1. Quotation is from Eileen Grabowski, who in large part authored this chapter. Eileen has worked extensively with hospitality students in their career searches at Boston University's School of Hospitality Administration. She is currently the Recruiting Manager in the Office of Career Services at Harvard Business School.

2. Bob Gatty, *World's No. 1 Employer*, Hotel & Motel Management (1 November 1993).

3. Ruth Friedman, "Interviewing" *Technique Magazine* (November 1995) p. 47.

4. William Shakespeare, *The Merry Wives of Windsor*, 1600–1601, act 2, scene 2.

5. Council for Educational Exchange, *Student Travels Magazine* (Spring–Summer 1995).

Walt Disney World, Orlando

The Walt Disney World destination resort is located on approximately 30,000 acres of land, owned by the company, 15 miles southwest of Orlando, Florida. Walt Disney World consists of three parks: The Magic Kingdom, Epcot Center, and the Disney–MGM Studios. Walt Disney World also contains numerous hotels, shopping centers, entertainment complexes, campgrounds, water parks, golf courses, and other attractions to promote long-term visits. Roughly twice as many people visit Walt Disney World as visit Disneyland each year, and it is estimated that approximately 5 percent are European.[3]

Attractions in the Park

Encouraged by the success of Disneyland, the Walt Disney World complex is actually three separate and distinct parks. The idea here was to be bigger and better, and to allow room for expansion.

The Magic Kingdom The Magic Kingdom opened in 1971, and has seven major areas: Main Street, Liberty Square, Frontierland, Tomorrowland, Fantasyland, Adventureland, and Mickey's Starland. In these areas are rides, including the world famous Space Mountain, and shops and restaurants.

Epcot Center Epcot opened in 1982, and has two major areas: Future World and World Showcase. Future World displays many high-tech products of the future, and it highlights the changes here on earth through Spaceship Earth. World Showcase is a community of nations focusing on cultures and traditions from around the world. More than 10 countries are featured here, such as France, Norway, Mexico, and China. Costumes, entertainment, food and beverage, signage, and architecture are all presented as they would be in the native lands. Both Future World and World Showcase have themed rides, restaurants, and shops.

Disney–MGM The Disney–MGM Studios park was opened in 1989. It is a theme park and working production facility for making full-length feature movies. The theme park features the Hollywood of the thirties and forties along with a backlot tour, restaurants, and shops.

Resort Facilities As of 1994, Disney owned and operated 10 resort hotels and a complex of villas and suites at the park in Orlando, for a total of nearly 12,500 rooms. In addition, the Fort Wilderness campsite accommodates 1,200 sites and cabins. Several of the hotels provide conference facilities.

There is also a variety of recreational activities available, including golf courses, tennis, sailing, horseback riding, and two water parks, River Country and Typhoon Lagoon.

The Disney Village Marketplace is a shopping facility and entertainment complex, with restaurants and nightclubs. On Pleasure Island within the Village Marketplace, the largest Planet Hollywood Restaurant in the world opened in 1993. There are seven independently operated hotels in the Village, all of which lease space from Disney. Rooms total 3,700. The Swan and Dolphin hotels near Epcot, with 2,300 rooms total, are owned by Disney but are operated as units of third-party hotel chains.

Disney Vacation Club In 1994, Disney Vacation Development, a wholly owned subsidiary of Disney, built a 531-unit Vacation Club. Designed as rental property, it is operated as a time-share resort. To participate in the time-share, potential owners must purchase points, which are redeemed for night stays. The minimum purchase is 210 points, at $61.50 per point as of November 1994. (Historically, point cost has increased $1.50 per point every six months.) Time-share owners also pay annual dues of $2.6986 per point. Plans are under way for additional vacation clubs in Vero Beach, Florida; Hilton Head Island in South Carolina; and Newport Beach, California.

A Brief History of Walt Disney World

When construction for Walt Disney World began in 1968, it was the largest private construction project ever undertaken in the United States. Some 8,000 workers were involved, and some 8 million cubic yards of earth were moved. Swamps were drained, and canals and lakes were built.

In October 1971, Walt Disney World opened the gates to the Magic Kingdom with 5,500 cast members on staff. The staffing needs grew quickly. By the summer of 1972, more than 10,000 cast members were needed to operate the park. Today there are over 37,000 cast members employed at Walt Disney World, a testimony to the growth of the facilities over time.

Eleven years after the opening of Walt Disney World, in October 1982, Epcot Center, the Experimental Prototype Community of Tomorrow, opened as a showcase of technology and the world. Seven years following that, on May 1, 1989, the Disney–MGM Studios park opened so that guests could experience movies in a whole new way.

In the spring of 1998, Disney plans to open a fourth theme park: Disney's Wild Animal Kingdom, a park filled with the natural drama of animal life in the wild. The park will be the largest of all Disney parks in the world, some 500 acres, five times the size of the Magic Kingdom. The center feature of the park will be a giant Tree of Life, which will be 14 stories tall. The park will be divided into three major areas: the real, the mythical, and the extinct.[4] See Exhibit B for Disney World ticket information.

Disneyland Paris

Disneyland Paris is the newest of the Disney parks to be built. It is a 5,000-acre park located 32 kilometers from Paris. Disneyland Paris has its own Metro station, just at the park entrance. It can be accessed quite easily by high speed train from the city center. An elaborate network of roads and a section of the l'auto route provides express access for those traveling by car.

The park's official languages are French and English. All signs are multilingual. Cast members wear flags to indicate the languages they speak fluently. The reception desks at the hotel can also assist guests in German, Spanish, and Italian. Restaurant menus are always offered in at least French and English. German, Italian, Dutch, and Spanish can also be found. Of the some 15,000 employees in the park, one third are American, one third are French, and one third are from other European nations.

Attractions in the Park

Disney focused on the success of the layout of the U.S. and Japanese parks when designing Disneyland Paris.

Exhibit B Walt Disney World Ticket Information

Type	Ages 10+	Ages 3–9
1 Day 1 Park	$38.50	$31.00
4 Day Value (1park per day)	129.00	103.00
4 Day Park-Hopper Pass	144.00	115.00
5 Day World-Hopper Pass	196.00	157.00
Annual Pass (new)	236.00	205.00
Annual Pass (renewal)	215.00	184.00
1 Day River Country	14.75	11.50
1 Day Typhoon Lagoon	23.95	17.95
1 Night Pleasure Island	16.95	16.95
Pleasure Island Annual Pass	40.95	—
Magic Kingdom Club Members		
1 Day 1 Park	$36.50	$29.00
4 Day Value (1park per day)	123.00	98.88
4 Day Park-Hopper Pass	138.24	110.40
5 Day World-Hopper Pass	186.20	149.15
Annual Pass (new)	220.00	195.00
Annual Pass (renewal)	200.00	174.00
1 Day River Country	14.75	11.50
1 Day Typhoon Lagoon	21.50	16.25
1 Night Pleasure Island	14.40	14.40
Pleasure Island Annual Pass	36.85	—

Source: Walt Disney World Web Page (Internet)

Main Street USA Main Street USA is the place to go for daily parades, the Liberty Arcade, and the Disneyland Band. It is center of the park, and all attractions spread out from it. The Railroad has three real steam trains, and carries you through the Grand Canyon diorama and the Pirates of Penzance.

Frontierland Based upon the Wild West of American history, Frontierland boasts the River Rogue Keelboats, the Lucky Nugget Saloon Revue, and Chaparral Stage for live entertainment. There's nothing French or European about the food offerings here—from the Silver Spur Steakhouse to the Lucky Nugget Saloon to the Cowboy Cookout Barbeque, this is the American West only Disney could re-create.

Adventureland Here in Adventureland you'll find Pirates of the Caribbean, La Cabane des Robinsons, Indiana Jones et le Temple de Péril, and Le Passage Enchanté d'Aladdin, a walk-through of scenes from the movie *Aladdin*. Les Pirouettes du Vieux Moulin is a small Ferris wheel. Hungry guests in Adventureland can try the Blue Lagoon restaurant, or the waterside Café de la Brousse.

Fantasyland Fantasyland boasts Le Château de la Belle au Bois Dormant (Sleeping Beauty's castle), Les Voyages de Pinocchio (a ride based upon the story of Pinocchio), Le Carrousel de Lancelot (a carousel) and Le Petit Train du Cirque (a mini roller coaster). You'll also find Au Chalet de la Marionnette (Pinocchio's restaurant) and Auberge de Cendrillon (Cinderella's coach), also a dining spot. Looking for a little ice cream? Try Fantasia Gelati.

Discoveryland You can walk through the Nautilus submarine at Les Mystères du Nautilus, go on a time travel trip at Le Visionarium (a 360-degree theater) or ride the grand prix raceway at Autopia. The popular Star Tours from the U.S. parks is here too, as well as Space Mountain.

The EuroDisney Resort The EuroDisney Resort has its own manmade Lake Buena Vista, and six hotels with over 5,000 rooms. Shops and restaurants are part of the Disneyland Hotel, the Hotel New York, the Newport Bay Club, and the Sequoia Lodge. The Hotel Cheyenne and the Hotel Santa Fe are more moderately priced lodging properties. Camp Davy Crockett offers simulated log cabins—complete with all the comforts of home, including microwaves and dishwashers.

A Brief History of Disneyland Paris

Construction began on EuroDisney in August 1988, and by December 1990, Espace EuroDisney, the information center, opened to the public. In September 1991, the Casting Centre opened, in anticipation of the grand opening scheduled for 1992.

EuroDisney opened on April 12, 1992, on a beautiful, spring day. It had been expected that 500,000 guests would enter on the first day, but only about 50,000 people came. By April, the first phase of development was complete, with the theme park, the hotel complex, and the golf course constructed at a cost of 22 billion French francs.

From its opening, the park was plagued with problems. The European recession was a troubling backdrop. Hotel occupancies were much lower than expected, 55 percent in its first year of operation versus a forecast of 68 percent.[5] With over 5,000 rooms to fill, occupancy rates were dismal. The number of attendees was at the very low end of estimations, but importantly people spent much less than expected.[6]

By May 1992, it was reported, 3,000 employees had quit over pay and working conditions, although Disney management contended that the number was closer to 1,000. Attendance continued to be below expectations, with only 20,000 to 30,000 guests over a weekend instead of the anticipated 60,000. Importantly, only three out of 10 visitors were French. The low attendance had a financial implication, and stock in EuroDisney fell from FFr 165 ($30.50) to FFr 123 ($20.70). By August 1992, revised attendance estimates for the year were down from 11 million to 9.6 million.

Cultural differences undermined the success of the park. In the local lexicon and in the national press, the park became known as a "cultural Chernobyl." Staff and training issues surfaced almost immediately. The French employees bristled at the thought of a dress code in writing, much less one that stipulated such items as appropriate undergarments. Because of a housing shortage, Disney had to provide some 3,000 employees with housing. After less than a year of operation, nearly 1,000 staff positions, mostly in management, were cut to save costs.

Disneyland Paris Passport

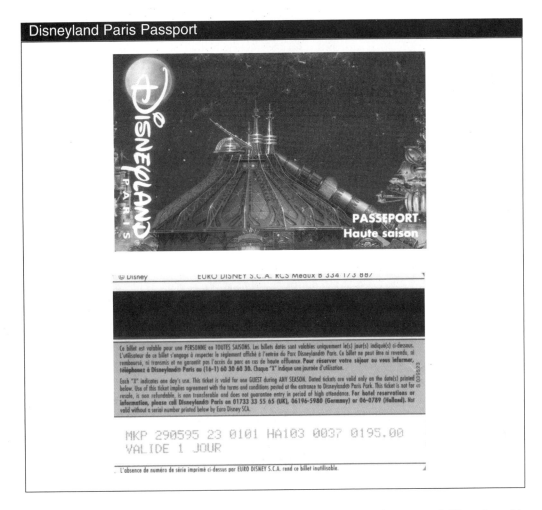

Lunch was served without wine, an important French tradition, in keeping with Disney's world-wide policy against alcoholic beverages. (Disney later changed that policy in response to customer demand.) Furthermore, waiting in lines for attractions and food was not well received.

The park got into disputes with neighboring villages and with the Ministry of Equipment over who should maintain the lawns on the highway leading to the resort. Disney was concerned that the road signs were inadequate.

Things continued to get worse as 1992 pressed on. Some of the key issues faced by EuroDisney through 1992 were:

- The continuing European recession, which forced citizens to cut back on entertainment spending.
- High interest payments on debt. Disney had borrowed heavily to finance the park, confident that high attendance rates would bring sufficient revenues. Without sales, the company was having trouble meeting its current debt obligations.

- The value of the U.S. dollar. The value of the dollar compared to European currencies was poor. It was actually less expensive to fly to Orlando and visit Walt Disney World than to travel within Europe to EuroDisney.

- Overcapacity in EuroDisney hotels. The park, it could be argued, is really only a one-day visit, so there was no need for guests to reserve hotel rooms.

- Food and gift prices were considered too high by European standards.

In April 1993, an American, Robert Fitzpatrick, who oversaw the theme park in its development phase and first year of operations, was replaced by a Frenchman by the name of Philippe Bourguignon. When Bourguignon first took his new post, his key aim was to boost attendance, particularly among the French, who represented only 29 percent of the park's total visitors between April and September 1992. One of Bourguignon's first decisions was to slash prices for local residents.[7]

Bourguignon was able to stem the tide of some of the problems faced by EuroDisney, but not all. By 1994, EuroDisney was in a financial crisis, and there was considerable talk among management and the many banks involved in the development about closing the park.

In June 1994, a financial deal was worked out among Disney, the 63 banks involved in the lending process, and Prince Alwaleed Bin Talal Bin Abdulaziz Al Saud, the Saudi prince who invested a massive amount of cash ($500 million) to save the park from bankruptcy. Prince Alwaleed bought over 74 million shares of Euro Disney stock. The restructuring helped put Disneyland Paris back on track.

The Walt Disney Company now owns approximately a 39 percent share of the EuroDisney park, down from the original 49 percent and Prince Alwaleed owns a 24.6 percent stake in EuroDisney. The terms of the new agreement include a change in the payment of royalties back to Disney. Beginning in 1999, the parent company of the Disneyland Paris, EuroDisney, will pay the Walt Disney Company royalties of 5 percent of park admissions and 2.5 percent of food, beverage, and merchandise sales, until 2004. They must also pay the Walt Disney Company management fees starting at 1 percent in 1999 and gradually rising to 6 percent by 2008.[8]

After the financial dealings were worked out, things started to look up. In August 1994, all hotels had strong bookings, and attendance was high, although food and merchandise were still considered expensive. That optimism did not last long, however. On August 31, 1994, EuroDisney stock fell to $1.40, and trading stopped for 15 minutes on the Paris exchange. Disney attributed the stock crash to the continuing European recession, a fall in real estate prices, and poor spending by tourists.

In an attempt to break the downward spiral, October 1994 saw a name change. The official new name of the park is Disneyland Paris. It was hoped that dropping *Euro*, which had developed a negative image throughout the continent, would help market the park. The use of *Paris* is also hoped to be an advantage, capitalizing on the image of one of the world's most famous cities.

By November 1994, financial losses were cut from $650 million to $200 million, but the number of visitors was still a concern. Only 8.8 million visitors had made the trip to Disneyland Paris in 1994, far below the anticipated, and necessary, numbers.

More changes were on the way. By the spring of 1995, attendance was up, due in part to a "kids go free" promotion to attract more guests.[9] Entrance fees were lowered by about 20 percent, and attendance continued to rise slightly. An added attraction brought more guests by June, with the grand opening of Space Mountain, touted as the best roller coaster ever built. EuroDisney finally turned the profit corner in fiscal year 1995, with a profit of 114 million French francs, or $22.8 million. Much of the profit was due to the financial restructuring. Before the addition of exceptional items, as this was, profit was only 2 million French francs. The stock price continued to slide, despite the profit, because investors apparently felt that the recovery was only temporary.[10] See Exhibit C for Disneyland Paris ticket information.

Tokyo Disneyland

Tokyo Disneyland is located approximately 10 kilometers from Tokyo, in Urayasu City, Chiba Prefecture, Japan. There is access to the park by train, on the JR Keiyo Line to Maihame Station. There are also direct buses from Narita and Haneda Airports and from various train stations around Japan. The owner of Tokyo Disneyland is Oriental Land Company. The Disney company earns royalties on revenues generated by the theme park (10 percent of admissions and 5 percent of food and souvenirs). Disney designed the park and licensed the use of its characters and trademarks. The park has numerous corporate sponsors, including Matsushita Electric, Fuji Film, and Kirin Beer.

Attractions in the Park

There are six themed lands in the park, along with attractions, shops, restaurants, and live entertainment. The six lands include:

Exhibit C Disneyland Paris Ticket Information (Prices in French Francs and British Pounds)

	Adult FFr	Child FFr	Adult UKP (£)	Child UKP (£)
High Season (Summer & Christmas)				
One Day	195	150	23	18
One Day, after 5:00 P.M.	150	100		
Two Days	370	285	45	34
Three Days	505	390	61	47
Low Season (Winter, excluding Christmas)				
One Day	150	120	18	15
Two Days	285	230	34	28
Three Days	390	310	47	37
Annual Passport				
Standard Annual	695	495		
Annual Plus	995	695		

World Bazaar This land reflects early 20th century America in the form of a small American town. The Victorian-style buildings include a bank, a cinema, restaurants, and shops. A gallery of original Disney art is displayed in the town.

Adventureland This land of adventure includes rides such as the Jungle Cruise, a boat trip through the depths of the jungle, and Pirates of the Caribbean, a thrilling adventure in which pirates and their treasures are encountered. Exotic regions of Asia, Africa, and South America are featured.

America's Wild West frontier during pioneering days can also be found in this land. Big Thunder Mountain, a wild ride through an abandoned gold mine, and the Diamond Horseshoe Revue, a show about the Old West, are two of the attractions found here.

Critter Country This is a land of critters, including some from the American Southern tradition: Brer Rabbit, Brer Fox, and Brer Bear. Splash Mountain, a hollow log boat ride that journeys through backwoods and bayous, is perhaps the most famous ride in this land.

Fantasyland The land of dreams and Disney characters is brought to life in this land. Mickey Mouse, Pinocchio, and others greet guests here. Disney villains can also be found at Cinderella's Castle Mystery Tour. Guests can become fairy-tale heroes and save the castle from the powers of darkness.

Tomorrowland The world of the future, a race through outer space called Star Tours, and futuristic restaurants can all be found here. This land reflects Walt Disney's passion for looking toward tomorrow's adventures.

There are also many special events and days in the park, including Mickey Mania, a entertainment program and fun-filled parade starring Mickey Mouse. Pecos Goofy's Wild, Wild West is a special event presented in Critter Country that features canoe races. Mother's Day is celebrated in commemoration of the day, as is the New Year. A Japanese-style New Year with traditional pine decorations and Mickey and Minnie in traditional kimonos are part of the celebration. Though New Year is traditionally a serious time in Japan, tens of thousands of visitors typically visit the park for a festive party. Disney's Dance Party is held to mark the Respect for the Aged Day holiday and includes a dance party for senior citizens.

A Brief History of Tokyo Disneyland

Tokyo Disneyland was the first Disney theme park to be constructed outside the United States. In the early 1980s, Oriental Land Company was a struggling developer trying to figure out what to do with the 204-acre tract of landfill it owned outside Tokyo. Oriental Land, a privately held company, was formed by the Mitsui Real Estate Development Company and the Keisei Electric Railway Company. Disney took a cautious course in this development, passing on an opportunity to buy an interest in the park, instead opting to collect royalties.

The park was considered a success from the time that it opened in 1983. The 1980s was a decade of prosperity in Japan. Coupled with a trend toward leisure in Japan, as well as a strong affinity for American-style entertainment, the park was off to a great start. By 1994, with some 16 million visitors, each spending an average of $85, attendance at Tokyo Disneyland surpassed the Disney theme parks in the United States. The Oriental Land Company, as a result, enjoyed a pretax profit of $202 million dollars in the year that ended on March 31, 1994.[11]

Visitors to this park seem to have adapted to the other Americanized aspects of the park. Of the 30 restaurants in the park, one serves Japanese food and one serves Chinese food. The retail establishments note brisk sales of Disney souvenirs. The Japanese are happy to have quick food and quick service for their meals and so have adapted well the American concept of fast food.

Almost all signs in the park are in English, with occasional Japanese ones and, more recently, signs also in Chinese. Though cast members speak primarily in Japanese, shows and attractions are conducted in English. Many repeat visitors keep coming back to the park; an estimated 80 percent of visitors return. This percentage is much higher than that of the U.S.-based parks.[12] Increasingly it is drawing affluent young visitors from all over Asia.

The staff of the park seems to have adapted well to the Disney's approach to human resources training. (See chapter 3 for more information on Disney's approach.) From the start, the staff seemed to respond well to Disney's clean-cut image. They seemed comfortable wearing uniforms and being part of a team. The park has more than 15,000 employees, 2,600 full-time and 12,400 part-time. Staff are offered free use of the park after closing, as well as special in-park appreciation holidays.

To cope with the frequent rainy weather in Japan, many buildings have extended overhangs. The entire World Bazaar section of the park is under a roof. To market the park, several large ad agencies based in Japan are used. This is unlike the American parks, where in-house marketers are used.

The success of the park is also reflected by continued expansion into the 1990s. When it completed the All Star Music Resort in the spring of 1995 (in combination with the hotel projects finished in 1994), it added more rooms in this two-year time period than it the first 10 years that the park was opened. Also in 1995, on a private island in the Seven Seas Lagoon (a part of the park), Disney Development Corporation (the development branch of Disney that manages the construction projects within the park) opened the Fairy Tale Wedding Palace to host wedding parties of up to 250 people. A neighboring attraction, Toontown (a replication of its counterpart at Disneyland, USA) opened in 1996. Disney's Boardwalk, a distinctly upscale resort reflective of turn-of-the-century Atlantic City, NJ, also opened in 1996. ESPN Enterprises collaborated with Disney to open a multimedia entertainment center restaurant featuring 50 television monitors to broadcast every sports event imaginable.[13] See Exhibit D for Tokyo Disneyland ticket information.

Exhibits E–G illustrate many of the financial and accounting aspects of The Walt Disney Company.

Exhibit D Tokyo Disneyland Ticket Information (Prices in Japanese Yen)

	Adults (ages 18 and up)	Juniors (12–17)	Children (4–11)
Tokyo Disneyland Passport (good for admission & all attractions)	4,800	4,400	3,300
Senior Passport (adults 60 & up)	4,100		
Starlight Passport (certain evenings only)	3,800	3,500	2,600
General Admission (good for admission & all free shows)	3,400	3,100	2,300

Source: Tokyo Disneyland Frequently Asked Questions (Internet Web Page), 1995

▉▉▉▉▉ **Exhibit E** The Walt Disney Company—Condensed Consolidated Statement of Income

(in millions)	Nine months ended June 30		Three months ended June 30	
	1995	**1994**	**1995**	**1994**
Revenues				
Filmed Entertainment	$4,482.1	$3,534.7	$1,156.8	$1,003.7
Theme Parks & Resorts	2,877.2	2,513.6	1,132.1	942.2
Consumer Products	1,629.2	1,308.4	475.1	407.7
	8,988.5	7,356.7	2,764.0	2,353.6
Costs & Expenses				
Filmed Entertainment	3,573.6	2,867.0	1,003.5	836.3
Theme Parks & Resorts	2,225.4	1,984.8	829.6	703.9
Consumer Products	1,229.8	977.8	368.6	320.8
	7,028.8	5,829.6	2,201.7	1,861.0
Operating Income				
Filmed Entertainment	$ 908.5	$ 667.7	$153.3	$167.4
Theme Parks & Resorts	651.8	528.8	302.5	238.3
Consumer Products	399.4	330.6	106.5	86.9
	1,959.7	1,527.1	562.3	492.6
Corporate Activity				
General & administrative expenses	126.8	120.6	38.7	39.6
Net investment & interest expense (income)	101.3	(17.7)	21.1	(5.1)
	228.1	102.9	59.8	34.5
Loss from investment in EuroDisney	(19.6)	(52.8)	(14.4)	(52.8)
Income before income taxes	1,712.0	1,371.4	488.1	405.3
Income taxes	595.9	486.9	169.9	137.8
Net Income	1,116.1	884.5	318.2	267.5
Earnings per share	2.11	1.62	0.60	0.49
Average number of common & common equivalent shares outstanding	530.2	546.3	531.7	546.1

Source: The Walt Disney Company

Exhibit F The Walt Disney Company—Condensed Consolidated Balance Sheet

(in millions)	June 30, 1995	September 30, 1994
Assets		
Cash & cash equivalents	956.7	186.9
Investments	1,457.3	1,323.2
Receivables	1,449.9	1,670.5
Merchandise inventories	727.9	668.3
Film & television costs	1,974.9	1,596.2
Theme parks, resorts, other property, net of accumulated depreciation of $2,943.7 & $2,627.1	6,131.9	5,814.5
Investment in EuroDisney	559.9	629.9
Other assets	1,122.8	946.8
Total	14,381.3	12,826.3
Liabilities and Stockholders' Equity		
Accounts and taxes payable & other accrued liabilities	3,170.3	2,742.2
Borrowings	3,362.2	2,936.9
Unearned royalty & other advances	687.6	699.9
Deferred income taxes	787.1	939.0
Stockholders' equity		
Common stock	1165.2	945.3
Retained earnings	6,773.7	5,790.3
Cumulative translation & other adjustments	38.4	59.1
	7,977.3	6,794.7
Less treasury shares, at cost	7,977.3	6,794.7
Total	14,381.3	12,826.3

Source: The Walt Disney Company

■■■■■■ **Exhibit G** The Walt Disney Company—Condensed Consolidated Statement of Cash Flows

(in millions)	Nine Months Ended June 30	
	1995	**1994**
Cash Provided by Operations before Income Taxes	3,057.1	2,329.8
Income taxes paid	(311.3)	(313.7)
	2,745.8	2,016.1
Investing Activities		
Film and television costs	(1,373.1)	(1,074.0)
Investments in theme parks, resorts, & other property	(694.6)	(784.7)
Purchases of investments	(893.1)	(675.1)
Proceeds from sales of investments	830.6	791.4
Investment in EuroDisney	144.8	
Other	(65.9)	21.7
	(2,051.3)	(1,720.7)
Financing Activities		
Borrowings	1,185.7	1337.6
Reduction of borrowings	(760.4)	(1,172.5)
Repurchases of common stock	(348.7)	(58.4)
Dividends	(132.7)	(114.0)
Other	131.4	55.9
	7.3	75.3
Increase in Cash and Cash Equivalents	769.8	344.0
Cash and Cash Equivalents, Beginning of Period	186.9	363.0
Cash and Cash Equivalents, End of Period	956.7	707.0

Source: The Walt Disney Company.

Exhibits H–J illustrate facts regarding weather and visitor statistics for the Disney Theme parks in the U.S. and abroad.

■■■■■■ **Exhibit H** Weather Around the Disney World (Average High & Low)

	Jan.	Feb.	Mar.	Apr.	May	June	July	Aug.	Sept.	Oct.	Nov.	Dec.
Disneyland	44	46	52	58	63	70	73	77	75	60	50	47
Paris	27	35	39	43	45	55	58	60	55	48	41	37
Tokyo	46	48	54	62	72	75	82	86	79	70	60	51
Disneyland	29	31	35	46	54	63	70	72	66	55	42	33

███████ **Exhibit I** Most Visited Theme Parks in the World (1993)

Location	Park	Attendance
Urayasu, Japan	Tokyo Disneyland	15,815,000
Lake Buena Vista, Florida, USA	Magic Kingdom at Walt Disney World	12,000,000
Lake Buena Vista, Florida, USA	Epcot Center at Walt Disney World	12,000,000
Anaheim, California, USA	Disneyland	11,400,000
Marne-la-Vallée, France	Euro Disneyland	10,000,000
Jakarta, Indonesia	Jaya Ancol Dreamland	9,500,000
Lake Buena Vista, Florida, USA	MGM Studios at Walt Disney World	8,000,000
Orlando, Florida, USA	Universal Studios Florida	7,400,000
Blackpool, England	Blackpool Pleasure Beach	6,800,000
Seoul, South Korea	Lotte World	5,000,000

Source: "Tokyo's Magic Kingdom Is a Winner," *New York Times*, Monday, March 7, 1994

███████ **Exhibit J** Visitors to EuroDisney by Nationality

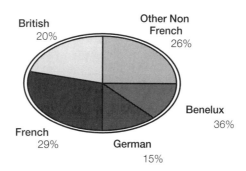

Source: EuroDisney, as quoted in *The Wall Street Journal,* November 20, 1992

Questions to Answer After You Have Read the Case

1. What are the key steps involved in the successful development of a theme park? What can cause failure? Explain.

2. What are the critical elements involved in operating a theme park successfully on an ongoing basis? What can cause failure? Explain.

3. In what ways are theme parks constantly evolving?

4. Compare the four parks: Disneyland, Walt Disney World, Tokyo Disneyland, and Disneyland Paris. What do they all have in common? How are they different?

Questions to Answer After You Have Read the Case and Section I: Overview

1. Compare entrance prices from all four parks. Do some sample currency conversions using today's exchange rates. Is it more expensive to visit one park rather than another? Why? Which is the least expensive? The most expensive? Why?

2. Chapter 2 includes a chart of the components of the hospitality business. Where does Walt Disney Attractions appear on that chart? Why?

3. What is the key to the Disney "magic"?

4. What makes Disney a successful service company? What pieces of service did not go well in Paris? Why?

5. Given the hurdles introduced in chapter 4, what obstacles do you suppose Disney encountered in opening Tokyo and Paris?

6. Upon opening, Tokyo Disneyland was considered very successful, but EuroDisney was considered a failure. What was different about the cultures and situations of the two locations that may have contributed to the dramatically different outcomes?

7. Compare Tokyo Disneyland and Disneyland Paris to their American counterparts. How are the attractions and special events alike from one park to another? How are they different?

8. Why do you think Disney teamed up with the Oriental Land Company in Japan?

Questions to Answer After You Have Read the Case and Section II: Places to Stay

1. What do theme parks and casinos have in common as tourist attractions? To what extent are they different? Why do you think Disney has not become involved in the casino business in any of its theme parks?

2. Disneyland only owns and operates one hotel, whereas Disney World and Disneyland Paris both have a number of company-owned lodging properties. Why do you think Disney decided to expand its involvement in the lodging business?

3. Disney refers to employees as "cast members." Do you think this applies to those employees working in the back-of-the-house?

Questions to Answer After You Have Read the Case and Section III: Places to Eat

1. There's a Planet Hollywood at Walt Disney World. Why do you think Disney entered into an agreement with an outside restaurant chain? Why do you think Planet Hollywood agreed to the arrangement?

2. Is Disney a commercial foodservice provider? An institutional foodservice provider? Does it operate stand-alone restaurants?

3. Consider the food and beverage options at the two international parks. What obstacles do you think Disney encounters in these outlets?

Questions to Answer After You Have Read the Case and Section IV: Management Tools

1. From a management perspective, why was it that Tokyo Disneyland was such an immediate success, while Disneyland Paris was not?

2. Consider the vast number of "cast members" employed by Disney. What tactics do you think Disney employs to assure successful recruiting?

3. Compare the historical staffing patterns of Paris and Orlando. What problems do you think Disney encountered when it was forced to cut staff in Paris? How does this compare to the issues Disney was likely to have encountered in Orlando?

4. What public relations benefit do you think Disneyland Paris enjoyed when it appointed a French president in 1993?

5. How important do you think the impact of word-of-mouth marketing is in the United States? In Tokyo? In Paris?

6. In what areas of operations do you think technological applications are used in the theme parks? Consider the different kinds of systems available to hospitality companies in formulating your answer.

7. Compare the operating profits (revenues minus expenses) of Disney's three major divisions: theme parks, filmed entertainment, and consumer products. How important are theme park revenues, compared to revenues from the other two divisions?

7. How much would it cost today for a minimum point time-share purchase at Disney's Orlando Vacation Club?

8. Consider each of the four management topics presented in this section: management information systems, marketing, accounting, and human resource operations. How would you apply the tools presented here to helping Disney solve its problems in Paris?

Questions to Answer After You Have Read the Case and Section V: Structural Elements of the Hospitality Industry

1. In Florida, Disney chose to own but not operate two of its hotels, the Swan and the Dolphin. Explain how this could be possible. Try to obtain reservations information at these two properties. What did you learn about the identity of these properties?

2. Chapter 15 introduced the concept of a formula used by McDonald's in determining where and how many McDonalds restaurants it could build. What kind of formula might Disney consider for potential expansion to future nations? Where do you think Disney should build its next park?

3. Do you think the fact that Disney did not elect to take an equity interest in Tokyo influenced its decision in Paris?

4. Location has repeatedly been stressed as an important decision for a hospitality operation. What criteria do you think Disney considered in locating its four theme parks? What role do you think weather played in the decision?

Questions to Answer After You Have Read the Case and Section VI: Issues and Trends

1. Where do you think Disney should expand or build next? Why? What strategic questions should be asked?

2. Does Disney have competition in the theme park business? Research other parks, both in the United States and abroad. What do they offer that Disney might not?

3. Does Disney face any ethical issues in its U.S. parks? In its international parks? Why or why not?

4. Disney has teamed up with other companies (such as Planet Hollywood and the Oriental Land Company). Why? Research one of the partnerships. Is it successful?

5. Disney was planning to open a new theme park in Virginia, to celebrate America's history. Designated to sit near the site of a historic Civil War battlefield, the project was finally canceled due to local opposition. Research this project. How was it different from other Disney theme parks? Why did the project fail?

Question to Answer After You Have Read the Case and Section VII: For Students Only

1. Would you want to work at Disneyland Paris? Tokyo Disneyland? What steps would you need to take to work at either park?

End Notes

[1] The Walt Disney Company 1994 Annual Report, p. 17.

[2] Ibid., pp. 9, 14, 16.

[3] Joe Flower, *Prince of the Magic Kingdom: Michael Eisner and the Re-Making of Disney* (New York: John Wiley and Sons, 1991), 56.

[4] Disney press release, Lake Buena Vista, Florida, June 20, 1995.

[5] Roger Cohen, "When You Wish Upon a Deficit," *New York Times*, July 18, 1993, p. 1.

[6] Ibid., "Euro Disney Trying to Warm Up Winer," *New York Times*, December 12, 1993, p. 27.

7. David J. Jefferson and Brian Coleman, "American Quits Chairman Post at Euro Disney," *The Wall Street Journal*, January 18, 1993, p. B1.

8. Christine Tierney, Reuter News Service from Marne La Vallée, France. Internet news release, March 12, 1996.

9. Andre Willey, *Frequently Asked Questions and General Information List, Disneyland Paris*, January 4, 1995 (Internet Web Page: http://www.nsu.nsk.su/faq/f-disney-disneyland-paris/qo-1.html.)

10. Thomas Kamm, "EuroDisney Post First Annual Profit, Stock Slides 14%," *The Wall Street Journal*, November 16, 1995, p. A15.

11. James Sterngold, "Tokyo's Magic Kingdom Outshines Its Role Model," *New York Times*, March 7, 1994, p. D1.

12. Peter O. Keegan, "Japan's Love Affair With Disney Is Still Going Strong," *Nation's Restaurant News*, November 23, 1992, p. 82.

13. Disney 1994 Report, p. 16.

Case One

Riding an "E-Ticket" ✒

The Walt Disney Company opened its Florida DisneyWorld Resort in 1972 with great fanfare. When the park opened, Disney set up its admissions such that everyone would pay a fixed price for a book of tickets. These ticket books contained a series of coupons labeled *A* through *E*. An *A* ticket was assigned for what were anticipated to be the least crowded attractions, and an *E* ticket was assigned to the big hits in the park. *B*s, *C*s, and *D*s were similarly assigned. A particular person who ran out of any letter ticket could get another. Additional tickets could be purchased at kiosks inside the park. The tickets would be collected at the individual rides, which would allow Disney to keep accurate track of the attendance of each attraction.

The system was abandoned some months into use. Instead, a one-price admission that gave guests unlimited access to all attractions was installed.

Discussion Questions

1. Why was the admission system changed?

2. Where was Disney using extra labor in the park under the first system that was eliminated with the unlimited-use ticket?

3. How do you think customers perceived the price/value relationship of what they had purchased in each of these two systems?

4. How do you suppose customers with two leftover *B* tickets and one *C* ticket would feel as they left the park?

5. Which system do you suppose the company controller preferred? How about the ride attendants? The maintenance crew?

6. Which system do you suppose is more profitable for Disney on any one given day? In the long run?

Case Two

Ruby Tuesday's "Other List"[1] ↜

In many ways, Paula Doricchi seems too good to be true. She's a waitress who is so good that customers wait in line for up to an hour to eat at one of her tables, passing up empty tables elsewhere in the restaurant so they can be served by her. Recounting his first weekend as the manager in Greenville, a former manager has written, "I was a bit perplexed when I walked to the hostess stand and saw two separate waiting lists being taken at the front door. I quizzed the hostess, thinking this might be a new system they were using. 'No,' she replied, 'This is the list of people waiting for the regular tables. The other list has people waiting for Paula's section.'" This, said the former manager, was his introduction to Paula Doricchi, who waits tables six nights a week at a typical Ruby Tuesday—one of 175 Ruby Tuesday restaurants in the Morrison chain, in a typical American shopping mall in Greenville, South Carolina. "As we discovered, Paula's whole style revolves around trying to know the people she serves. She is doing what the best service performers do: establishing a relationship of trust with her customers. And she is doing it in a most unlikely setting, a chain restaurant, a place where you would expect not to find personalized service." Thirty-five years old, with luxuriant black hair and flashing green eyes, Paula is a woman around whom a certain folklore has grown up. She remembers favorite drinks, favorite dishes, even the names of the customers' dogs. If she's not working when customers show up, they eat somewhere else. Although Ruby Tuesday #24 has the same menu and same decor as every other Ruby Tuesday, Paula has transformed her place into what is almost a neighborhood tavern, a place of warmth and amiability that manages to be comfortable for regulars and welcoming to those who just wander in.

Early on, researchers Fromm and Schlesinger concentrated on finding frontline service workers who deliver great service every day. Their countrywide search uncovered the stories of 14 outstanding service people whom the researchers describe as the real heroes of business. Paula Doricchi was one of them.

Even so, the formula for Paula's unique customer service is not to be found in any Ruby Tuesday training manual. What Paula does is more than turning customers into regulars. She turns the regulars into friends. When regulars stay away for a few weeks, she calls them at home to see if everything is OK. Moreover, Paula doesn't function simply as a waitress who takes orders and

504

delivers food. She a menu consultant to her friends. She sells more food and drinks than anyone else in the restaurant.

The bottom line is this: Do customers of Ruby Tuesday do business at that restaurant because of the services it provides, or because of the people who perform those services? Research indicates that of all the types of frontline service jobs in the world, there are relatively few that require skills that can't be easily taught. The personality of the employee is something that management finds it difficult, if not impossible, to change, however. In a word, when you get past a person's personality, there isn't much else that's important to consider when you're hiring a server for a Ruby Tuesday. Not to be overlooked, however, is what Paula Doricchi is really worth to that restaurant. Based on the management's estimate of the business that Paula would take with her if she left to work for a competitor, Paula is doubtless worth $37,500 per year to Ruby Tuesday. Consequently, the question arises: What steps can be taken to recruit service performers of Paula's caliber?

Discussoin Questions

1. How can service establishments recruit performers like Paula?

2. What does Paula's style say about the importance of the entertainment component of the restaurant business?

3. Consider the worth of a repeat customer. What value is Paula creating by generating repeat customers?

4. Can other staff members learn from Paula? How could management assist in that effort?

5. Can what is happening here be translated to other units in chain? Why or why not?

End Note

1. Adapted from Bill Fromm and Len Schlesinger, *The Real Heroes of Business, and Not a CEO Among Them* (New York: Currency/Doubleday, 1994). Used with permission.

Case Three

Southwest has No Reservations ✌

Most airlines rely heavily on travel agents, the intermediaries who bring customers and airlines together, to funnel business to them. Travel agents have access to a reservations computer system to make their bookings for customers. On average, about 85 percent of airline reservations are booked through travel agents, a substantial portion of bookings.[1]

Three of the largest reservations systems used by travel agents are Apollo, System One, and World Span. In 1994, the three systems decided to "delist," to take off the reservations system all airlines that would not agree to pay a booking fee, or a percentage of the fare, to the reservations system. (The fee would typically be about $2.50 for a round-trip ticket.) Southwest Airlines decided it would not agree to pay.

Southwest, based in Dallas, Texas, considers itself a low-fare, no frills airline. Their fares never go on sale. They pride themselves on keeping rates low every day for every flight and on keeping the fare structure simple. In response to the booking fee problem, Southwest considered the three potential outcomes, as it saw them. First, Southwest would become a subscriber, pay the fee, and be forced to increase fares. Given its positioning in the marketplace, even a small increase mattered greatly to the airline. Second, it could choose not to subscribe and, as a result, to lose an enormous amount of business as a result. The company estimated that up to half of its bookings came from this set of systems. Third, it could choose not to subscribe and somehow do just fine. Southwest chose the third option.

The impact of Southwest's decision was immediate. Some agencies advised clients to take their business elsewhere. Other agents found that hard to do when Southwest had the best fare, and so called the airline directly. These agents, though, were grumpy about the extra steps. Southwest responded by installing computer terminals at agencies that book many tickets, with direct access to the internal Southwest system.

Fortunately, the lure of low fares kept most customers coming. Many called directly. Business appeared to have found alternative pipelines, but Southwest still faced obstacles. It was forced to figure out a way to service many more customers directly, or through the American Airlines Sabre

System, the largest reservations system, with which it continued to be affiliated. (Southwest reluctantly agreed to join the Sabre System in 1984, as part of a package plan, when it purchased its own internal reservations system.) It had to scramble to get tickets out. Employee volunteers found themselves stuffing envelopes.

Discussion Questions

1. Which of the options that Southwest thought about would you consider to be the most risky? Why?

2. How did Southwest's fare structure and its positioning in the marketplace work to its advantage in making the decision that it did? What kind of airline would be more heavily dependent on the services of travel agents?

3. As time evolved, Southwest responded to its problem by implementing a ticketless reservations system. Customers could exchange a reservations number for a boarding pass once they reached their gate. What advantages and disadvantages do you see for this innovation? Can you think of any other unconventional moves that might further help Southwest?

4. Do you think Southwest will be able to train its customers over time to buy its tickets in new ways? Why or why not?

5. In 1996 Southwest created a way, via the Internet, @ www.iflyswa.com, whereby customers could make reservations directly with the company. Assume that more and more customers will make their own reservations via the Internet as opposed to doing it through travel agencies. How will Southwest be affected? How will other airlines that are currently paying the subscriber fees be affected? How will travel agencies be affected?

End Note

[1.] Bridget O'Brian, "Southwest Airlines Fares Well Minus Some Reservations," *The Wall Street Journal*, August 3, 1994, p. B4.

Case Four

Big Mac with Mozart 🎵

At the McDonald's at 160 Broadway, in the financial district of New York City, you are greeted by a uniformed doorman and seated by a hostess, and you can watch the stock quotes on a digital ticker tape board. Upon entering the restaurant, patrons find a leatherbound guest book, along with comment cards.

You can order espresso and international pastries that are served on silver trays, or you can stick with a traditional Quarter Pounder, french fries, and chocolate shake. Fresh flowers decorate each table, and a pianist at a grand piano serenades customers from the balcony. There are marble walls and floor-to-ceiling mirrors, since the owner told the architect to "build me the Taj Mahal."

This McDonald's, which opened in December 1988, is trying a new service concept. The prices are a little higher than usual, although not substantially. A Big Mac costs about a dime more than at the McDonald's in nearby Times Square. This service seems to be a big hit with the customers. A sampling of the comment cards reveals from "cleanest restrooms in New York City" to "a smashing place." It seems to fit in with McDonald's corporate philosophy—Provide good food quickly in a clean environment—but it also shows some entrepreneurial spirit.

Like all other McDonald's operators, this franchisee has some freedom with respect to creating an unusual atmosphere. However, he is still required to adhere to rigid operating rules that ensure consistency in the production of burgers and fries.

Discussion Questions

1. Though this is not your typical McDonald's, is it a good idea?

2. What can you infer about the customers who come to this McDonald's, assuming that the restaurant is responding to customer needs?

3. If you were the owner of the McDonald's in Times Square, how would you react to this concept?

4. If you were the owner of a McDonald's in Tokyo, how would you react to this concept?

5. How should a restaurant think about charging for "elegance"?

6. What service problems might occur in this unit?

7. What about this concept might confuse the customer?

Case Five

Keeping Score ✍

Addressing the 1990 U.S. Economy/Limited-Service Conference in Chicago, Todd Clist, executive vice president and general manager of Fairfield Inn by Marriott, described that company's Scorecard system for measuring guest satisfaction. Each Fairfield Inn front desk is equipped with a computer monitor (labeled Fairfield Inn Scorecard) enabling the guest service representative (i.e., the front desk clerk) used to ask each guest to rate the quality of his or her stay, and the service received by entering the appropriate answers on the Scorecard monitor keypad—a process designed to take the guest no more than 30 seconds while checking out.

Among the six Scorecard items that guests are asked to rate are: room cleanliness, staff hospitality and efficiency, the value of their stay for the price paid, and their overall rating of Fairfield Inn. The result of this rating system is a performance scorecard for each property and for every employee who regularly came in contact with the guest. This is accomplished by assigning each guest service representative and each guest room attendant (maid-housekeeper) a special employee code number. The Scorecard software automatically matches each guest's rating for every question to the appropriate Inn employee. Employee scores are posted monthly at each Inn and form the basis for a quarterly bonus, not to exceed 10 percent of regular salary. Half of the bonus is for individual performance, and the remaining half is based on the entire staff performance.[1]

Clist explained that the typical Fairfield Inn is a two- or three-story building, of 80 to 135 rooms, with a small meeting room, a swimming pool, complimentary coffee and tea each morning in the lobby, free local phone calls, a fax machine, vending machines, and smoking and non-smoking rooms. Room amenities generally include a work desk with an upholstered chair, a king-size bed or two double beds, an individually operated heating and cooling system, remote control television with free cable television, a long-cord telephone, a separate vanity outside the bathroom, and large thick towels.

By January 1, 1991, Marriott had reported a total of 76 Fairfield Inns open, an occupancy range of 70 to 75 percent, and an average daily rate of $35 to $40. Projections for the future envisioned approximately 300 Fairfield Inns to be in operation by the mid-1990s. In addition, beginning in June 1991, a new 63-room prototype Fairfield Inn emerged in a joint venture with a North Dakota franchise partner, Tharaldson Enterprises.[2] The long-term strategy involved in this particular develop-

510

ment is to permit the Marriott-Tharaldson partners to enter smaller markets where financing for 60- to 70-room properties is more easily obtainable.

Fairfield Inn's Scorecard system's response rate is notable relative to other methods. Even Marriott's own hotel room questionnaire, *Will You Let Me, Bill Marriott, Know?* draws only a 5 percent guest response, whereas the Fairfield Scorecard daily feedback rate typically yields a 50 percent response, thus enabling management to maintain a continuous check on meeting or exceeding customer needs and expectations.[3] Clearly, such ongoing market research is a major foundation stone of Marriott's early success in the budget hotel business. As Fairfield's marketing vice president has stated, "'Scorecard' is the single most unique thing we are doing. It is not a typical hotel amenity, but it may be our most powerful amenity."[4]

Not to be underestimated, however, is the fact that the Scorecard incentive pay system and Fairfield's focus on customer hospitality are inextricably related to recruitment and training of good staff people. Typically, each Inn has a payroll of about 21 people, composed of a manager, assistant manager, and 19 hourly paid employees (including four guest service representatives, 11 guest room attendants, one guest room supervisor, one maintenance chief, one custodial attendant, and one guest linen attendant). Besides taking great care in its selection of staff people based on a specially designed personality skills profile test (one Fairfield Inn reported having interviewed more than 500 people to fill 19 positions), Fairfield undertakes an employee-management team building exercise in which the group generates a list of what each one of them would want (a) as a guest, (b) as an employee interacting with a fellow employee, and (c) as an employee interacting with the boss.

Furthermore, an attendance bonus program provides an extra two weeks' vacation to any Fairfield employee with perfect attendance for one year—in addition to the standard one week of vacation to which each employee is entitled after one year of service.[5]

Inn managers can earn a bonus of up to 40 percent of their compensation. Fifty percent of the bonus is determined by Scorecard ratings, and the remaining 50 percent is determined on the basis of occupancy and other quarterly operating objectives.[6] In the end, service management scholars at Harvard Business School, who spent five years of exhaustive research in 14 service industries, judged the lesson of Fairfield Inns to be most instructive for the hospitality industry. "We'll leave it up to you to decide whether this is a breakthrough concept or not, but it is unlike any other we've seen in the innkeeping business. And it appears to be eliciting strongly positive responses from the 'right' customers, the 'right' managers, and the 'right' personnel."[7]

Discussion Questions

1. Why would the Scorecard system be considered a powerful amenity?

2. Why is the response rate achieved by the system important?

3. What pieces of the Fairfield Inn operations are affected by the results of the Scorecard System?

4. What measures are used by Fairfield Inns to recruit and train good staff persons? Do you think that the measures are fair?

5. What questions would you include if you were designing the Scorecard System?

6. Do you think the bonus vacation weeks for perfect attendance are a cost effective benefit? Why or why not?

End Notes

[1] W. Earl Sasser, Jr., Christopher W. L. Hart, and James L. Heskett, *The Service Management Course*, (New York: The Free Press, 1990) 631.

[2] "Marriott's Fairfield Inn Unveils 63-Room Prototype," *Lodging* (June 1991): 8.

[3] James L. Heskett, W. Earl Sasser, Jr., and Christopher W. L. Hart, *Service Breakthroughs* (New York: The Free Press, 1990), 196.

[4] Sasser, et al., *The Service Management Course*.

[5] Ibid., 633, 635.

[6] Heskett, et ll., *Service Breakthroughs*, 196.

[7] Ibid., 196–197.

Case Six

Mc Sleep

Inns ⁌

Imagine that you are an experienced hotel chain with a number of well-established brand names. You decide to launch a new brand of economy lodging.

The chain is intended to be positioned as a low-price economy property. Each room will be designed to have upgraded furnishings and high tech amenities but in a downsized guest room, about 30 percent smaller than a more typical room. The reduced square footage in each room will allow developers to build more economically and therefore to charge lower rates to guests. The layout and design are intended to be easily replicated for maximum efficiency in building.

Guest room doors will feature credit card–activated locks, an innovative bathroom design, and a bay window designed to create the illusion of space. Every room will have a queen-size bed, a stereo TV, VCR, and remote control. The properties will be designed to operate with a minimum of personnel, the equivalent of 11 full-time workers. Reservations can be made through a central system with a toll-free number.

As you search for a name for the new division, you settle on McSleep Inns. The tie to the restaurant company with golden arches is intentional. You feel that the name alone conveys a dramatic amount of information to the customer. The above scenario was actually launched in 1987 by Quality International (now Choice Hotels).[1]

Discussion Questions

1. What do you think the name McSleep Inns would convey to potential customers about the service and product of the inns?

2. How would you describe the Inns if you just heard the name and knew nothing about them? You may wish to pose the question to others who have not read the case. How do they describe a property called McSleep?

3. How important do you think the name of a hotel is?

4. How do you think the McDonald's restaurant chain (which is not affiliated in any way with the inns) might react to this new product offering?

End Note

1. Michael Deluca, "Quality's Newest Entry: McSleep," *Hotel and Motel Management* 202 (14) (September 28, 1987) p. 63.

Case Seven

A World Series of Yield Management

You are the front office manager of a 500-room commercial hotel in an urban location. Your facility caters mostly to traveling businesspeople during the week and to families and tourists on the weekends. The property has three food and beverage outlets on site, including a coffee shop for fast-service breakfast and lunch, an informal dining room serving Italian cuisine, and a very popular sports bar. The sports bar and restaurant has a large screen TV and frequently hosts sports celebrities as guests. The room seats approximately 200 people and is decorated with signed posters, photos, and sports gear. The menu includes an assortment of finger foods, hot and cold sandwiches, and a variety of alcoholic and nonalcoholic beverages.

The hotel is a franchise of a well-known hotel chain and is managed by a management company. Most of the ownership of the hotel is held by institutional investors, including a large insurance company. The property is 10 years old and has had an excellent financial track record.

The fall season is particularly strong for this hotel, as it services many business meetings and transient business guests during the week. Weekends have lower occupancies and lower average rates than do Monday through Thursday, but business is still solid. It is now part way through September, and the fall of 1997 has promise to be stronger season than any of the previous five. A summary of occupancy and average rate for the month of October for the last five years is presented in the following table:

	Oct. 92	Oct. 93	Oct. 94	Oct. 95	Oct. 96
Occupancy	77%	74%	83%	86%	85%
Avg. Rate	$85	$81	$88	$88	$92

As the front office manager, you are now reviewing the projected occupancy for October of 1997. You are faced with an unusual dilemma; you must decide which guests to accommodate. The city's baseball team will almost certainly be a contender in the World Series. If it is, games 1 and

2 will be played at home on Sunday, October 19, and Monday, October 20. If needed, game 5 will be played on Saturday, October 25. The hotel rooms in the city would most certainly sell out at top rates on those dates. As of September 15, 400 of the hotel's 500 rooms in your hotel have already been sold at an average rate of $90.

The sales and marketing department has requested a block of 100 rooms to accommodate a very loyal business group from the night of October 20 through the night of October 25, a six-night stay. This group would expect to pay their corporate rate of $75 per room. Three evening banquets and various meeting rooms will be needed during the course of their stay. The group would like to book immediately.

Reviewing historical booking patterns, you note that the hotel would typically sell 75 to 95 rooms to repeat, transient guests on Monday, October 20, Tuesday, October 21, Wednesday, October 22, and Thursday, October 23. Friday night is typically slower; an estimated 50 to 60 rooms would likely be booked by transient guests. These transient guests generally book rooms three to seven days in advance. The average rate for these sales would be expected to be $98.

If the World Series games are in fact played in the city, you would easily expect to be able to charge the full rack rate of $125 on all remaining rooms, however you would not anticipate those bookings to be made until the last minute. As you review the roster of guests already booked in that October week, you note a large concentration are from one city: the fans of the likely opponents in the series. If both teams are not the finalists, or if the series is over in four games, you anticipate a large number of cancellations. The hotel has a 24-hour cancellation policy.

Discussion Questions

1. What guests should you try to accommodate? Compare the average rates and booking patterns of each of the three potential types of guests in evaluating your answer.

2. What are the anticipated average rates, occupancy percentages, and total room revenues under each of these three scenarios for the nights of the three World Series games? How certain are the revenues under each scenario?

3. What other factors besides total room revenue should you consider in evaluating this decision? Would the nature of the hotel's ownership influence the decision?

4. What is the least risky decision you can make? What is the most risky? Do the rewards, in terms of revenue, match the risk?

5. Explain why this dilemma presents a case of yield management for you as the front office manager.

Case Eight

A Flair for First Impressions [1] ↝

People say that Phil Adelman, the doorman at the Cambridge, Massachusetts, Marriott, doesn't just do his job. He revels in it; he's proud of it. No question about, pride is his prime requirement for outstanding service performance. Yet, when one comes to think of it, there was little in Phil's background to recommend him as a likely candidate for a hotel doorman's job.

In the first place, when Marriott hired him, he was 59 years old and unemployed. He was a high school graduate who had been laid off after 23 years at Lechmere, a New England department store. He had neither hotel experience nor, in fact, any experience in the hospitality industry. At the time of his initial interview, he had been unemployed for three and a half years. Nonetheless, with brochures from the Marriott Essex House, New York, in hand, he went to that interview enthusiastically suggesting that Marriott Cambridge should have an "escape weekend, and a seafood restaurant." Despite these unsolicited recommendations for running the hotel, Phil got the job. He celebrated the occasion by driving with his wife all over Cambridge and Boston to make notes of the step-by-step directions from the Cambridge Marriott to places that hotel guests were most likely to go, so he would know how to direct them.

On a typical day, Phil arrives ready for a tornado of red carpet activity: commuters passing through the lobby on their way to the subway, guests checking out, businesspeople heading off to meetings, as well as others arriving to meet at the hotel. There is Phil, grabbing doors, stowing baggage, maneuvering his brass-colored luggage cart with the skill and style of a drum major with his baton. So far as Phil is concerned, no one's needs are allowed to go unmet. This is the first key element of great first impression service.

Phil treats his workplace like a theater stage. His uniform is his costume. His work is his performance. The talent and charm of his performance is that he does these small favors for people without the slightest suggestion that they are favors, with a graciousness and assurance that leave the hotel's customers with a feeling of well-being and confidence, and that is the second key element of great first impression service.

First impressions are lasting impressions. In the opinion of Marriott management, Phil Adelman meets the three requirements of the art of first impression:

1. He properly identifies himself as the first Marriott person to interact with the customer.

2. His personality and style are consistent with the message of hospitality that the hotel wants him to convey.

3. He understands how critical he is to the success of the Cambridge Marriott, and especially realizes that what he does will have major impact on whether or not Marriott gets a chance to make another impression. Eccentricities aside, Phil Adelman is a winner.

What is Phil Adelman worth? Management's arithmetic in estimating Phil's value reflects some interesting calculations. For one thing, his grace and style as an outstanding doorman performer are so impressive that management estimates he attracts at least one percent of the hotel's guests. With an average room rate of $100 per night, corollary spending of $30, a 55 percent margin, 200 rooms, and a 70 percent occupancy rate, Marriott's estimate of how much one percent is worth adds up as follows:

$130 per day
× 7 days per week
× 52 weeks
× 200 rooms
× 70% occupancy
× 55% margin
× 1%
= $36,436 per year, Phil's worth to the hotel.

Management figures that a bad doorman might cause potential guests to select a different hotel, thereby driving off $36,000 in hotel business. If this is added to the $36,000 that a great doorman like Phil delivers, than his potential worth to the hotel is $72,000.

Discussion Questions

1. What do you think Phil Adelman is worth? In what way do you think worth can be calculated?

2. How can your worth calculations be used to incent employees?

3. What can service companies do to attract and retain more Phil Adelmans?

4. How could the marketing department make use of successful stories like this one?

5. If you were the controller of a company and were asked to book Phil Adelman on the corporate balance sheet, where would you put him? What other unconventional assets and liabilities related to its human resources could a company assess?

End Note

1. Adapted from Bill Fromm and Len Schlesinger, *The Real Heroes of Business, and Not a CEO Among Them* (New York: Currency/Doubleday, 1994). Used with permission.

Case Nine

AIDS in the Workplace ❧

David Norton has had a very successful five-year career with Medium Size Restaurant Company. The restaurant company has two chain concepts and has 23 units. David began his career as a waiter, successfully completed the company's management training program, and was promoted to manager over a year ago. David is the manager of one of the most successful units in the company. He is considered by many to be a nominee to head the smaller of the two chains in a couple of years. He would be the youngest regional manager in company history, potentially overseeing 10 units.

In the last several months, sales in David's restaurant have dropped steadily, while other units met or surpassed sales targets. The company president, clearly concerned by the reports, dropped by to investigate. In conversations with several employees, the president learned that the chef has AIDS. Much of the staff seemed to be aware of it, and some suggested that regular customers had found out and were no longer coming to the restaurant.

The president called David in to his office and told him to fire the chef. As the chef had been with the company for four and a half years, was an outstanding employee, always received superb performance evaluations, and had never missed a day of work, David refused. The president then told David that if the chef was not gone by the end of the week, David himself would be fired.

Discussion Questions

1. What should David do?

2. What ethical issues are raised by the case?

3. What options do you think the company has?

Case Ten

"Decoding" a Hotel Investment ✍

Recall that the following questions can serve as a "decoder" to understand what players are involved in developing a to-be-built hotel, or in a transaction involving the sale, change in affiliation, or change in franchise for an existing hotel. (See chapter 14, "So You Want to Own a Hotel?" for a complete explanation.)

1. Who developed the hotel?
2. Who owns the hotel?
3. Who manages the hotel?
4. Who franchises the hotel?
5. With whom is the hotel affiliated or in consort?

Applying the Questions to Real Events

The following set of newsclips of real events illustrates the usefulness of these questions. Some of the examples are more complicated than others. Collectively they demonstrate the wide range of developer, owner, manager, franchisor, or affiliate players that can be involved with a hotel.

Example of a New Hotel Development This newsclip involves a corporate hotel company with different divisions, each of which is a chain. Because the expansion plan involved new properties, these are to-be-built hotels.

> *1988, BETHESDA, MD—"Marriott announced expansion plans involving more than $500 million in development over the next five years for Fairfield Inn, its new national economy chain."[1]*

In this case, Marriott launched the Fairfield concept, so Marriott itself was the developer, at least at the onset. (Over time others, like the franchisees themselves, could become the developers of individual units.) It is not known who will be the owner of the hotels. It would be wrong to assume that Marriott will own them. It may, but it could just as easily own a small percentage or none of each of the hotels. It is possible that Marriott will manage the hotels, but it is not a certainty. Having the Fairfield name on the door only assures that it is a Marriott franchise. It is very unlikely, because it is intended to be a large chain and is at the budget end of the market, that it will have an affiliation with Marriott.

Marriott's Fairfield Inns

DEVELOPER:	Marriott
OWNER:	unknown
MANAGER:	unknown
FRANCHISOR:	Fairfield Inn
AFFILIATION:	probably none

Examples of Change in Status of Existing Hotel Properties Consider these news headlines involving various kinds of changes in status for existing hotels:

> *1988, MONTREAL, CANADA—"The Canadian National Hotels, Inc. has agreed to sell the company's four owned and operated properties and five management contracts to Canadian Pacific Hotels Corp."*[2]

In this case, two different types of transactions occurred. Four actual hotels, the properties themselves, were sold. For these properties, the ownership and the management changed hands. For the second piece of the transaction, involving five hotels, only the management changed hands; the owners remained the same. Who developed the hotel in this case is unknown. It is possible that it was Canadian National, but it may have worked with another developer or it may have purchased these hotels from someone else, or some combination of both. As the developer would not have played a part in this transaction (the hotels already existed), this question is less applicable. If there exists a franchise agreement, it is also unknown from this newsclip. That information could be determined by looking at the names of the individual hotels. If, for example, a particular hotel was called L'Hotel (which is not a national chain), then that particular property is not a franchise. Again, a review of the individual hotels may show that some or all of them may be a part of an affiliation, like Preferred Hotels. Any individual hotel could be a franchise and could have an affiliation. A summary of the two parts of this transaction are shown on the following page.

> *1990, CHARLOTTE, NC—"The signing of an agreement of sale between Image Realty, Inc., the parent of Econolodges, and Silver Spring, Maryland–based Manor Care, Inc., the parent of Choice Hotels International, occurred on August 14."*[3]

This newsclip does not say what Choice Hotels purchased! As it happened, Econolodges was composed of 100 percent franchised hotels. Therefore, the owners are individual franchisees who have the right to manage their own hotels as long as they follow the standards set by the franchise agreement. What Choice purchased was the right to collect franchise fees and to add more Econolodges to the chain. At the time of purchase, Choice had a collection of other franchise names (Clarion, Quality, Comfort, Sleep Inn), so its intention may be to convert some Econolodges to other

Canadian National–Canadian Pacific Transaction
First Four Properties

	Before Transaction	After Transaction
DEVELOPER:	unknown	unknown
OWNER:	Canadian National	Canadian Pacific
MANAGER:	Canadian National	Canadian Pacific
FRANCHISOR:	unknown	unknown
AFFILIATION:	unknown	unknown

Canadian National–Canadian Pacific Transaction
Next Five Properties

	Before Transaction	After Transaction
DEVELOPER:	unknown	unknown
OWNER:	third party—not CN	Canadian Pacific
MANAGER:	Canadian National	Canadian Pacific
FRANCHISOR:	unknown	unknown
AFFILIATION:	unknown	unknown

names. It may also be that the Econolodge franchise could remain intact. It is unlikely that a large chain at the budget end of the market would seek any kind of other affiliation.

Sale of Econolodge Franchise System

	Before Transaction	After Transaction
DEVELOPER:	unknown	unknown
OWNER:	franchisees	franchisees
MANAGER:	franchisees	franchisees
FRANCHISOR:	Econolodge	Econolodge/Choice
AFFILIATION:	none	none
PARENT OF FRANCHISOR:	Image Realty	Manor Care

Case Assignment

Analyze the following additional newsclips. Use the preceding newsclips as examples and the decoding questions box, which follows, as a framework. First fill in the box; then offer written explanation where necessary. You may not always have complete information. Use your best judgment, if necessary, to speculate about the answer.

Framework for Analysis

	Before Transaction	After Transaction
DEVELOPER:		
OWNER:		
MANAGER:		
FRANCHISOR:		
AFFILIATION:		
OTHER:		

1. 1986, WEST COAST—"In what appears to be a growing trend in the hotel industry, four West Coast chains with a total of 10,000 rooms have banded together in a marketing alliance in order to optimize each other's sales efforts. Vagabond Inns, Sandman Hotels & Inns, Nendels Motor Inns, and Sheffield Hotels comprise the four members of the 'First Choice' alliance."[4]

2. 1990, DALLAS, TX—"Motel 6, the budget motel company, agreed today to be acquired by the French-based hotel giant Accor S.A. for $1.3 billion in cash, the two companies announced."[5]

3. 1986, BETHESDA, MD—"Marriott Corp. recently strengthened its presence in the United Kingdom with the signing of at least 18 new hotels. ... The franchise agreement was reached with Scott's Hotel Ltd. Toronto, which has been developing and operating hotels in the United Kingdom since 1970."[6]

4. 1992, NEW YORK—"The latest acquisition also serves to establish an ITT Sheraton presence in Paris through the five star [Marriott] Prince de Galles. ... Some reports speculated that Sheraton is paying about $41 million for the operating rights to the hotel."[7]

5. In this case, trace the hotel in 1985 in Boston through its initial development and three subsequent changes.

   a. 1985, BOSTON, MA—The Beacon Companies opened the Embassy Suites, Boston. Beacon developed the property and owns and manages it.

   b. 1988, BOSTON, MA—"Beacon has now acquired Guest Quarters—an 11 property all-suite chain. According to a spokesperson, the agreement gives Beacon the sole right, title, and interest in the Guest Quarters name ... as well as all future rights to the development and operation of Guest Quarters properties."[8] The Embassy Suite Boston property became a Guest Quarters.

c. 1988, BOSTON, MA—"The Beacon Cos. said yesterday it sold its interest in Guest Quarters Hotels Limited Partnership, the nation's 10th largest hotel management company. Under the terms of the sale to GE Investments, Beacon retained the ownership of six Guest Quarters hotels plus six other hotel properties operating under other franchise affiliates. The properties still owned by Beacon include the Guest Quarters in Boston. … GE said it does not plan many changes for the Guest Quarters management operation which includes the 28 member Guest Quarters chain plus eight other hotels."[9]

d. 1995, BOSTON, MA—Guest Quarters announces a change in all properties. All Guest Quarter properties will bear a new logo and be renamed Doubletree Suites. The move is as a result of the merger of Guest Quarters and Doubletree.

End Notes

[1]. "Marriott Earmarks $500 Million for Fairfield," *Hotel and Motel Management* 112 (2) (May 30, 1988): 28.

[2]. Michelle Fisher, "Canadian National Sells Hotel Interests," *Hotel and Motel Management* 106 (2) (March 28, 1988): 2.

[3]. "Addition of Economy Lodging's Leading Franchisor Strengthens World's Largest Franchise Hotel Company," Econolodge News Release, Econolodges of America Inc., Charlotte, NC, August 15, 1990.

[4]. "Four West Coast Chains Form Alliance," *Lodging Hospitality*, May 1986, p.13.

[5]. Thomas C. Hayes, "1.3 Billion Buyout Set for Motel," *New York Times*, July 13, 1990, p. D1.

[6]. "Marriott OKs U.K. Agreement," *Hotel and Motel Management* 207 (3) (February 24, 1992): 1.

[7]. Kevin Pritchett, "ITT Sheraton Pays $160 Million for Marriott Hotels," *The Wall Street Journal*, February 21, 1992.

[8]. "All-Suites No Longer Just a Niche?" *Motel/Hotel Insider* (38) 9 (November 10, 1986).

[9]. Marie Gendron, "Beacon Cos. Sells Guest Quarters," *Boston Herald*, January 22, 1992.

Case Eleven

The Day of a General Manager ∽

Place yourself in the shoes of a general manager. Consider the following issues that have emerged this week.

A Matter of Priority

A new preemployment drug testing policy in the hotel has been in effect for one month. All the employees were informed of the new policy, and the managers were trained in the proper procedure, since the new test affected and slowed down the hiring process. The memo you sent out clearly stated that no new employees were to be hired until their drug test results were relayed to the hiring manager. Yesterday, your recruiting manager, Pierre, informed you that the food and beverage director gave a start date to a prospective candidate, but without having the results from the drug test. The candidate now expects to begin work in two days, the day before the expected results of the drug test.

Crashing Systems

As part of a chainwide program, the reservations system has been upgraded to a new model. The old system had been place for nearly five years. Although it was a bit slow, it was easy to use, and new employees were quickly trained to use the applications. The new system was designed to eliminate the time delay and to provide more accurate information to guests. It was expensive to install, but you thought the investment was worthwhile. Now all you hear is grumbling: The new system is not user friendly, and the MIS manager insists he's too busy to help out constantly. Why? Because he's busy bringing it back up throughout the day—it keeps crashing.

The Numbers Just Don't Add Up

Late one Friday afternoon, you finally get around to reading the financial and managerial accounting reports you've asked the controller to put together. Occupancy rates have been higher than had been predicted, and you want to see how the increase in fuel, supplies, labor, and other costs are affecting net profit. You've asked the controller to make the reports clear and to run the numbers for you, but what you find in the folder are simply the statement of cash flows for the quarter, the income statement for the quarter, and last year's balance sheet. Frustrated, you realize that you've got to figure it out, and you start to think of what to do first.

Discussion Questions

1. After reviewing the current issues in the general manager's in box, what is your analysis of each situation? Write a step-by-step potential solution for each issue. What tools from the marketing, accounting, human resources, or management information systems management tool box can help you design a solution?

2. What other kinds of problems do you think a general manager might face? Explain in detail.

Index

H

haciendas, 120–121

health care, for hotel guests, 103

health care affiliated lodging, 171, 182–183

health concerns, in workplace, 266, 437, 520

high-tech/high touch, 69, 99–100

hiring, 257, 268

history, 3–29, 161, 176, 366, 388
time line chart of "firsts," 4–11

hospitality industry
components of, 32–37
distinguishing features of, 37–40
history of, 3–29, 161, 176, 366, 388
major players, 41–57, 58, 59, 60–67
size of, 40–41, 42
structure of, 37–40

hospitals, 171, 182–183, 222–223, 228

hostels, 169, 174

hotel casinos, 8, 11, 143, 169, 176–177

Hotel Employees & Restaurant Employees
International Union, 265

hotels
banquets in, 215–216, 225, 314
branding for, 50, 367, 428–429, 513–514
career information, 446, 447–448
consumer spending statistics, 41
current trends summarized, 59, 68–69
development of, 122–123, 348, 349–357
distinguishing features, 37–40
entertainment in, 4, 18, 25, 165, 175–181
foodservice in, 193–194, 215–217,
225–226, 398, 430, 432–433
franchising, 68, 349, 364–372, 522
history of, 4–18, 20–25
information systems for, 303–304, 307–310
international, 110–113, 115–125, 126, 192,
364–365
major operators, 42, 45–48, 50, 57, 60–67
managers for, 50, 55–56, 68, 349, 357–363
opening, 351–352, 353, 354
operations, 116–120, 187–203, 510–512,
515–519, 526–527
operator's role defined, 50
referral groups (affiliations) for, 57, 58, 349,
373–375
strategic thinking about, 428–429

types in overview, 33–34, 35, 166–171
See also chain hotels; lodging; ownership,
hotel; *specific types*

housekeeping department, 191

human resources management, 69, 193,
255–275
empowerment of employees, 91, 99,
241–242, 260, 285–286
entertainment concept and, 25, 100–102
ethical issues, 270, 408–409, 410
for foodservice, 130, 241–242, 248–249
issues summarized, 256
legal concerns, 265–267, 268
for lodging, 118–120, 123, 193, 526
measuring success of, 271
role of human resources manager, 193,
267–272

I

ice cream parlors, 214, 225

income statements, 327–329, 332, 334–335,
494

income tax payable, 326

independent hotels, defined, 42

independent motels, 172, 173

independent restaurants, defined, 210

information directory, 455–464

information systems. *See* MIS (management
information systems)

ingredients, for menu items, 130, 234, 242,
312, 397, 410

in-room services systems, 309

institutional foodservice
associations directory, 459
defined, 210–211
development of, 232–233
major operators, 50, 53–54
opening/operations, 210, 245–250, 429
types of, 34, 50, 221–223, 227

intangible dominance, 280, 281

internal controls, financial information for, 336

internal customers, 259

internal marketing, 286

internal user financial information, 323–324

international guests, defined, 113

international operations, 68, 109–134

physical plant
  foodservice, 239–240, 247
  hotel, 120–121, 165, 196, 349, 350,
    355–356
    configuration, 165, 168–169, 173–174
    history of, 5, 6, 7, 10, 18, 20, 21
point of sale systems, 309
points of distribution (PODs), future trends,
  429
positioning, market, 291–292
POS (point of sale) systems, 311–312
posting houses, 4, 14
pre-Christian era, 4, 11–16, 18
preopening expenses, 236, 351–352, 353
presentation mix, 290
price, 165, 167–168, 171–173, 209, 283
private clubs, 169, 174, 219, 227
production line approach, 288
productivity systems, 313
product oriented marketing, 278
product/service mix, 290
products vs. services, 280
profit (net income), 237–238, 322–323, 327,
  339, 353–354, 387–388. *See also* revenue
profit margin, 339
pro forma analysis, 237
property and equipment, as asset, 325
property management system (PMS), 303–304,
  308
property size, 165
proposal, institutional foodservice, 245
public relations, 192, 291
purchasing, 234, 242, 312, 367, 397, 410

Q

quality circles, 263
quality management, 96–100, 244, 249,
  510–512
quality of work life (QWL), 263
quality teams, 264
quick service restaurants. *See* fast food
  restaurants

R

rack rate, 353
rail companies, 19–21, 23, 152–153, 154

ranches, 171, 181–182
rating services, 57
ratio analysis, 336–339
ratio of arrivals to rooms, 113
ratio of population to rooms, 115
receipts, from tourism, 139
reception, 188
recipe management systems, 313
recreation, outdoor, 142, 145, 171, 181–182,
  459
recruitment, of employees, 257, 268
referral groups (affiliations), 57, 58, 349,
  373–375
referral sources, for restaurants, 397
registration, 188
REIT (real estate investment trust), 354
Renaissance, 4–5, 16–18
rental cars, 152, 154
reservations and reservation systems, 10, 69,
  189, 304, 308, 434–435, 506–507, 526
  consumer direct access to, 146, 148, 150,
    316–317, 434–435
  ethical issues, 409
  fees for, 370, 374
  franchising and, 367, 370
  for manipulating demand, 284
residential hotels, 168, 174
resort hotels, 6, 10, 21–22, 24, 169–170,
  177–178
restaurants (commercial foodservice)
  associations directory, 458–459
  career information, 446, 447–448
  community relations, 398–399
  consumer spending statistics, 41
  development of, 129, 131, 232, 237,
    382–388
  entertainment in, 101–102, 221, 227
  evaluation by customers, 243, 244, 286
  history of, 4–11, 14, 15, 18–20
  industry size, 50
  information systems for, 310–314
  international, 125, 127–131, 247
  for lodging properties, 193–194, 215–217,
    225–226, 398, 430, 432–433
  major operators, 42, 49, 50, 51–52
  opening of, 233–240

taxi service, 153, 154

technology, 243, 249, 306–307, 434–436. *See also* computer technology; MIS (management information systems)

teleconferencing services, 190

telephone service, 190, 309

theme park hotels, 170, 178–179

theme parks, 9–11, 24–25, 100–101, 141, 483–503

theme restaurants, 212–213, 224

thermopoliums, 4, 14

time intensiveness, 261–262

time sharing, 10, 178

time value of money, 336

tips, reporting as income, 241

to-be-built vs. existing hotel, 348

touch screen technology, 311

tourism, 137–160

case studies, 156–159, 416–417

consumer spending statistics, 41

defined, 35, 138–140

entertainment and, 140–146

international, 113–115, 116, 139, 154–155, 416–417

multiculturalism and, 439

perspectives on, 138, 154–156, 159

See also transportation services; travel distribution channels

tourism export, 154. *See also* tourism

tourism offices, 148–149, 151

tour operators/wholesalers, 147, 150

training and development, staff, 257–258, 259, 268, 306–307, 411–413

transportation services, 33, 35, 37, 151–154, 157, 158, 446

history of, 5, 7, 10, 11, 13–14, 16, 19–21, 23–24, 38

travel agencies, 6, 9, 57, 59, 146–147, 150, 158

travel distribution channels, 33, 37, 138, 146–151, 158, 446, 460. *See also specific channels*

travel plazas, 220, 227

travel services, defined, 35. *See also* travel agencies; travel distribution channels

truth-in-menu, 235, 406, 414, 415

turn-key approach, 359

turnover, employee, 91, 241, 259–261, 269–270

turnover, seat, 40, 237, 338

U

uniformed services, 190, 191

uniform systems of accounts, 194, 323

unions, 265–266, 269, 408–409

V

value added tax (VAT), 155

value managed relationships (VMRs, strategic alignment), 234, 383, 397, 398

vending machines, 216, 225

videoconferencing, 435

virtual reality, 10, 179

visible kitchen, 221, 227

voluntary chains, 57. *See also* referral groups

W

wages payable, 326

waiting lines/lists, 284–285, 302

walking, of guest, 189

walk-in guests, 189, 283

water transportation, 10, 153, 154

Web pages, 435

work orders, 196

Y

yield management, 283–284, 515–516